316822316

TIONIS NAVTICÆ

terrarum orbis ambitum circumnavigans, unica tantum navi, ingenti cum gloria ,
DDITA est etiam viva delineatio navigationis Thomæ Caundish nobilis
no & temporis spacio : vigesimo-primo enim Iulij 1586 navem conscendit, & decimo
ij & cum omnium admiratione reversus est.   Iudocus Hondius.

Drake

Drake

The Life and Legend of an Elizabethan Hero

Stephen Coote

THOMAS DUNNE BOOKS
St. Martin's Press ♒ New York

THOMAS DUNNE BOOKS.
An imprint of St. Martin's Press.

Map of Drake's Caribbean and the Voyage of 1585–1586 © John Gilkes, 2003. Endpaper illustration: 'Vera Totius Expeditions Nautica' by Jodocus Hondius, 1595, courtesy of the Library of Congress, Washington DC.

PICTURE CREDITS
1, 9, 12, 19, 20, 21: Bridgeman Art Library
2, 3, 5, 6, 7, 10, 11, 23: National Portrait Gallery
4, 8, 13, 15, 16, 17, 22, 24: National Maritime Museum
14, 18, 25, 26: Hulton Getty

www.stmartins.com

Library of Congress Cataloging-in-Publication Data available upon request

ISBN 0-312-34165-2
EAN 978-0312-34165-7

First published in Great Britain by Simon & Schuster UK Ltd., 2003
A Viacom company

First U.S. Edition

10 9 8 7 6 5 4 3 2 1

for Toni

Acknowledgements

In the preparation of this book I have drawn on the work of many scholars. In addition to those Victorian and twentieth-century editors who so scrupulously prepared the greater part of the contemporary documents for publication, I would like to acknowledge my debt to Drake's leading contemporary academic biographer Harry Kelsey. I have also greatly profited from the researches of Kenneth R. Andrews into the broader context of Drake's activities. The scholarship of Geoffrey Parker has marvellously illuminated the Spanish background. In many cases I have drawn on their translations from the Spanish. All of these works have been made readily available to me through the unfailing courtesy and efficiency of the staffs of the Bodleian and London Libraries. I would also like to thank my friend Steve Hope for translating the lines from Castellanos quoted on p. 214.

Contents

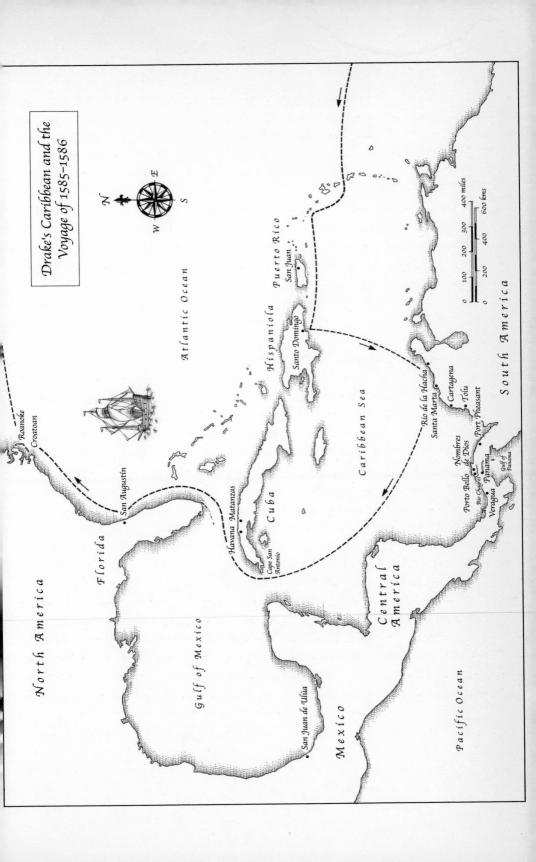

Drake's Caribbean and the
Voyage of 1585–1586

Prologue

1567

The ships were being readied for the expedition and there was much for the short, stout, bull-strong young officer with his reddish-blond hair and beard to do. Stores had to be laded. Barrels of fresh water needed to be stowed. Casks of salt beef and pork, carefully pickled during the winter months, required to be counted as they were rolled up the bowing planks and on to the deck. Beer, pease, cheese and butter followed, along with supplies of biscuit and salt fish. Then there was the matter of the General of the Fleet's silver plate and, because he must at all times appear as a gentleman of culture and learning, his musicians and their instruments to attend to as well. The woollen cloths to be traded had to be taken on board while, much to the concern of the ever observant Spanish Ambassador, quantities of guns had been transported to the quayside from the armouries in the Tower of London.[1]

As the men went about their work, the quays along the Medway and the Thames rang loud with rumours of how the English were sailing to West Africa where, it was said, they had been told by two renegade Portuguese Catholics about a gold mine of fabulous wealth. There were great risks to be faced if the mine was to be captured since the Guinea trade was notoriously dangerous. For all that the King of Portugal declared himself lord of the region, his grip on it was weak and this encouraged interlopers. Adventurous English sailors, narrow-eyed with greed, had for years ensured that robbery, slaughter and reprisal were the order of the day. Sharking their paths through barely known waters they sacked Portuguese forts, captured Portuguese ships, and made and broke brief alliances with the native peoples so that, with any luck, their battered ships could eventually return along the mild, familiar Thames laden with bloodstained ivory and gold.

The young Queen Elizabeth, constantly pressed for money, did little to stop the trade. Quite the reverse. Complaints from the Portuguese were treated with evasion and, hoping for a profit herself, Elizabeth lent her ships to the syndicates of merchants who funded such expeditions and then let it be known that her Protestant subjects could trade where they would. Necessity compelled her. The vicious tangle of international politics threatened the country's traditional wool trade with Antwerp and, along with it, the Queen's tax revenues. New possibilities needed urgently to be explored. It was a matter of business. If enterprise brought in its wake well-equipped ships, ambitious merchants, and restless seamen like Francis Drake, then that was all to the good. Such men could assist the country's defence in times of peril while also profiting hugely from their own initiatives, as Drake himself well knew.

Now aged about twenty-six or twenty-seven, Drake had invested much of his modest capital in the current venture. If it were successful then it would bring him a handsome return. And money would buy him what he wanted. It would allow a man such as he – a man of no particular distinction of birth or ancestry – to fashion a name for himself. He could acquire social position in a country deeply conscious of such considerations. Money won by whatever means from the perils of the sea could purchase a man an estate ashore, fund a good marriage, and perhaps lead to such coveted things as a coat-of-arms, the title of gentleman, and even a knighthood. In these ways Drake could join the country's elite and enjoy some measure of power and influence. In the words of the motto Drake would one day take as his own: from small beginnings great things may come. It was an exhilarating prospect for the young man as he toiled with the other seamen amid the smell of tar and alongside the gently rocking hulls and tall masts of the waiting ships.

When everything was as ready as it could be, Drake's older kinsman, the famous John Hawkins – a seasoned sailor with slow, intelligent, deep-set eyes under sharply pointed brows – was piped aboard his flagship, the *Jesus of Lubeck*, which had been lent to him by the Queen. To the watching landlubbers the *Jesus* was a brave sight: a floating four-masted wooden fortress of 700 tons, carrying great guns low on its broadside and stern and further guns above and in its beak head. To make it seem more fearsome still, its poop and forecastle rose like twin turrets and were unassailable to even the foolhardiest of enemies who, if they dared to board the vessel by the waist, would be slaughtered instantly in the cross-fire of swivel-mounted guns firing at point blank range. But to more experienced men like Drake and Hawkins the *Jesus of Lubeck* was not as invincible as it appeared. The ship had not been built for the hazards of the deep Atlantic it was soon to face. The *Jesus* was a ship for summer campaigns fought in home waters where, should the need arise, it could turn quickly about and head for port. Besides, like much of the English Navy, it was in an exhausted condition. Years of neglect had left the vessel so decrepit that, at the start of Elizabeth's reign, it had been condemned as unworthy of repair. The *Jesus* had nonetheless been kept in service and worked hard all that time.

For the moment, and whatever their misgivings, Drake and his fellow officers busied themselves in an atmosphere of expectation. As pennons streamed from the mastheads and the Queen's ensign waved from the flagship's stern, they watched while a proud Hawkins commanded his men to weigh anchor. He then ordered his pilot to navigate the huge, unwieldy *Jesus* and its fellow ship the *Minion* down the Channel. With the help of his rutter, that little book of creased and greasy pages which recorded each landmark along the way, the pilot did so with the expertise for which the English were well known and eventually brought the vessels safely into Plymouth. There the four other ships Hawkins and his family had assembled were waiting for them. Compared to the *Jesus* and the *Minion* they were tiny. The largest was the *William and John* which, at 150 tons, cannot have been more than seventy feet from stem to stern. Then there was the 100-ton *Swallow*, the 50-ton *Judith* (which Drake himself was later to command), and lastly the little *Angel* which was a mere cockleshell of thirty tons. Such was the flotilla from which Drake, Hawkins, and the rest of the crew were soon to raid the legendary wealth of a savage and barely known continent.

In the meantime there was much to do. During the two months spent in Plymouth, Drake watched Hawkins carefully and learned from his example. There were the final details of supplying and victualling to settle. There was a combined force of 400 men (including the band of Negroes brought along to serve as interpreters) for Drake to keep out of the town's easy taverns and frowsty beds. Finally, he had regularly to assemble the crew in St Andrew's Church for divine and strictly Protestant devotion. This last was far more than lip service. In an age when churchgoing was compulsory, Drake himself and many of the people of the West Country were keenly committed to the new Protestant dogmas enforced on the country by the Crown, and to the new powers and opportunities these seemed to open up. Gone were the once familiar Catholic ways, and the teachings now fiercely promoted by the Protestant elite insisted that the doctrines of the Old Church were wholly unnecessary to salvation. Indeed, they stood in its way, and were the mummeries of Antichrist. All a man or woman needed for redemption was an absolute inner conviction that God's Word, transmitted through the scriptures, was meant for him or her. The whole superstitious edifice of the Catholic Church – its false sacraments, its confessions and saints, its purgatory and excommunication, its relics, its indulgences, monks and supposedly celibate priests – could be, and was, violently swept away.

It had all happened a generation earlier. Wiseacres among the Plymouth townsfolk could still remember how, thirty years before, Henry VIII's representatives had come to the nearby Abbey of the Blessed Virgin Mary and Saint Rumon where they briskly required the monks to surrender all their wealth, rights and privileges. The defeated, grim-faced brothers had agreed with barely a murmur and their wealth passed rapidly into grasping Protestant hands. To many this seemed right, virtuous and normal. Opposition was mercilessly crushed and the Reformation proceeded apace. Amid much grumbling the number of Catholic holy days was reduced. The lamps and candles that once burned before the kindly images of the saints were snuffed out. There would be no more prayers to the

Virgin, no more imploring the help of Saint Rumon. It was ordered that their statues should be destroyed and, after three years of vandalism, such images disappeared from across the length and breadth of the land. Other Catholic rituals were soon abolished too, and the might of the law was evoked to enforce the new Protestant liturgy and the reading of the new Book of Common Prayer.

Divine service was no longer conducted in the obscure Latin of priests but in the splendid, resonant English of Tyndale and Coverdale, a language which Drake himself pronounced in his broad West Country accent. An English Bible was also needed (the people must have their faith delivered in their own tongue) and the printing of the first English New Testament in 1525 marked for many a turning point in history, an exultation of light after centuries of darkness. God now spoke directly in their own language to all sorts and conditions of men, and the printing press made sure that everyone could have access to a copy of the Scriptures. The English were becoming, willy-nilly, the people of the Book and the Word. They were a Protestant nation living under a Protestant Queen.

But, as every Protestant knew, there were dangers all around. Relations between England and mighty Catholic Spain had long been deteriorating. Great harm had been done to popular feeling when Mary Tudor, the Queen's late Catholic sister, married Philip II of Spain and then horribly stoked the fires of anti-Catholic feeling by her judicial murder of righteous Protestants. Lurid stories of their final hours were told in Foxe's *Book of Martyrs*, the great best-seller of the age. It is hardly possible to overestimate the importance of this grim and monumental work. For a hundred years it gave the English their sense of being a Protestant people chosen by God for His special favour. By recounting the history of their persecution by Catholics from the earliest times to the present day it gave their new beliefs a past, the sense of a righteous tradition created in suffering. They could believe they made up what the book of Exodus called 'an holy nation'. Foxe's work offered a sense of destiny, a sense of the guiding hand of Providence, and a sense of virtuous commitment to a benign and Protestant crown. An ideal of Protestant nationhood was forming around Drake and his contemporaries and, if Foxe's book was not enough, political events deepened the loathing of what seemed the ever-present Catholic menace.

It was clear to everyone that the vast might of Philip II and the Spanish Empire was still the greatest danger.[2] Philip was the absolute ruler of possessions which, as his supporters enthusiastically declared, stretched from Sicily to Cuzco and covered a quarter of the known surface of the globe. A mighty bureaucracy was necessary to administer such an accumulation of Catholic power and, spider-like at its centre, sat the rigid, black-suited King as an unending series of documents passed before his wary, and often weary eyes. Philip might lament that, 'The burden of business weighs on me in such a way that I do not know what I am saying or doing,' but his unresting capacity for administrative grind was as extraordinary as it was dangerous. At its worst it encouraged his belief that his power might indeed be omnicompetent and could put into effect his unwavering belief that he had been charged by God to uphold the Catholic faith whenever and wherever he could. This duty extended to England. For all that Philip had lost his title to the English throne with his wife's death, it genuinely grieved him to see the country relapse into detested heresy. As he wrote in his voluminous correspondence, he greatly desired to take the steps to stop it, but years of expensive wars against France and the Turks had exhausted his treasury and now required his presence at home, from where he planned to interfere in the affairs of England and that other Protestant bugbear, the nearby and troubled Spanish Netherlands.

Revolt in the Netherlands had broken out in 1566, and those who now watched Drake and his fellow officers preparing their expedition knew that, across the narrow sea, Philip had arranged with the Pope to increase the powers of the Catholic bishops and the Inquisition there. Violent protests and a wave of iconoclasm were directed against the newly augmented Catholic authorities and, as a consequence, 10,000 Spanish troops under the terrible Duke of Alba had recently entered Brussels virtually unopposed. Secret tribunals were at once set up to punish the offenders horribly, and in such ways as these the might of Spain and the Catholic Church was revealed at its most dreadful. Here was Antichrist in arms, tyrannical and pitiless. As the English learned of the sufferings inflicted on their co-religionists and realised that the same fate awaited them if ever the Spaniards were to invade their shores, deep ethnic sentiments were stirred and enhanced the sense of nationhood. Then, suddenly, amid all the preparations for Drake and Hawkins's voyage, the Spanish appeared off the Devon coast.

Their ships, commanded by Baron de Wachan, had supposedly been sailing from the Netherlands to meet Philip II when a storm drove them into Plymouth. Whether from hostility or ignorance, the Baron steered his fleet straight for the narrow Cattewater where Hawkins's newly provisioned vessels rode at anchor. Their fluttering ensigns made it perfectly clear that the English ships were a flotilla under the patronage of the Queen, and de Wachan added insult to injury by deliberately refraining from making the customary salute by dipping his flags and lowering his topsails. Since this was conventional seagoing courtesy, the failure could only be interpreted as a hostile gesture, an act of intimidation designed to suggest to the English the dangers they faced if ever they interfered in the affairs of the Netherlands. Such action called for a rebuff, and Drake watched as a furious Hawkins, observing the insult from the decks of the *Jesus,* acted with characteristic decisiveness. The *Jesus* and the *Minion* were ordered to open fire and to continue firing – not merely warning shots across the Spanish bows but direct shots aimed at the Spanish hulls. A flustered de Wachan at once changed course and anchored his beleaguered vessels north of what is today called Drake's Island. From there he wrote an indignant letter to the Mayor of Plymouth roundly declaring his innocence and outrage. The Mayor, feeling out of his depth in what was clearly becoming an international incident, referred the matter to Hawkins.

Hawkins prepared to meet the enemy envoy with all the dignity becoming to a Protestant gentleman. Dressed in the finest clothes – velvet doublet, beaver hat and a great weight of large-linked gold chains extending down the length of his chest – he ordered an armed guard to attend him on the hushed deck of his flagship. Thus prepared, he stared at de Wachan's emissary with the look of a man who would brook no impudence. It was an example to the young Drake of how things were done. The civil Flemish messenger too

7

was suitably impressed and made his excuses as best he could. The fleet with which he had sailed, he explained, was the innocent victim of foul weather. His Commander had naturally expected refuge and was surprised by the hostility with which he had been received. The man was careful to point out the diplomatic implications of Hawkins's actions. The King of Spain, he suggested, would be grievously upset by what had happened. Hawkins's answer was direct and to the point. The Commander of the Spanish Fleet, he declared, 'should consider that though there is great friendship between them and us, the haven which he entered was the Queen's, the ships that rid therein hers also'. That put the matter fairly and squarely and now, knowing that diplomacy could sometimes be the better part of conflict, Hawkins sent the departing de Wachan a present of some chickens and a barrel of London beer. The incident had been patched up, but the underlying facts were obvious. The Spaniards were the enemy and, as Hawkins later confessed, 'I know they hate me.'

In response to the diplomatic protests that inevitably arose from the incident, the Queen sent Hawkins a public rebuke, but both knew that this was not the end of the affair. Things had gone too far. For all that Elizabeth was cautious by nature and necessity, the Spanish invasion of the Netherlands put considerable pressures on her both as a politician and as a Protestant. She was bound to react, but her reaction could not be obvious. Her principal aims were always defensive for she was Queen of but half an island surrounded by enemies. An outright challenge to the Spanish would have been reckless, and her wisest policy was to pursue a typically conservative aim by whatever indirect means were available. She would try to persuade Philip to restore to the Netherlanders something of the rights and privileges they had enjoyed before the Duke of Alba's invasion while, at the same time, aiming to secure for her co-religionists a measure of toleration. She would not openly declare hostility. The wisdom of such a course would exasperate her sea-dogs, Drake included, but Elizabeth's moderate ways were the measure of the woman and she would show extraordinary adroitness in pursuing them. She would also make use of every circumstance that came to hand.

Such a circumstance presented itself now. No sooner had de Wachan and his ships sailed ignominiously away than the two mysterious Portuguese, con men both, who had originally talked up the idea of a marvellous African gold mine, appeared in Plymouth. Clearly overawed by the extent of Hawkins's initiative and realising that it would inevitably expose their fraudulent claims, they disappeared as suddenly as they had come. They had been entertained well while in England and there had been some slight pickings for them from the merchants who provisioned the flotilla. That, they decided, was enough, and made as speedily as they could for France.

Hawkins wrote a skilfully worded letter to the Queen. It now seemed that, without his guides, his expedition would collapse before it set sail. Even small investors like Drake might well lose their money. Hawkins was at pains to point out to his royal mistress that he was in a potentially embarrassing situation. A fully equipped flotilla had been raised at great expense and he would be undone if he were forced to disband it. Her Majesty would surely not wish so loyal and enterprising a servant to be humiliated in such a way. And it was precisely Hawkins's loyalty and enterprise that would save the interests and line the pockets of the entire consortium, the Queen's especially. Hawkins promised Elizabeth that if he were allowed to sail then he would 'bring home (with God's help) forty thousand marks gained without the offence of the least of any of Your Highness's allies or friends'. The offer was very attractive to the frugal, hard-pressed Queen, and Hawkins carefully unfolded further details of his plan. He and his crew would indeed sail to Africa, but not in pursuit of an illusory gold mine. Instead they would sail to get black slaves by whatever means they could. These they would then ship to the West Indies where, for all there was an embargo on English traders, the Spaniards provided a ready market for human misery. All Hawkins needed was royal permission to sail.

Hawkins's letter was in all ways pleasing to the Queen for he had asked to do of his own initiative what Elizabeth could never command him to do in her own person. His plan was certainly what they both wanted and might even have been what was intended from the start: the Portuguese con men's tales of a gold mine being something they had always seen through and used merely as a cover for their true intentions. Elizabeth fully appreciated that Hawkins's expedition might indeed return her a handsome profit and, by letting it sail, she was relieved of the considerable cost of maintaining two large warships while they rode unemployed in port. But beyond all this, if the expedition did indeed find success in the Spanish Caribbean, it would show Philip that her sea power was stronger than he might have reasonably supposed. This was a veiled threat, the merest hint of the possibility of terrorism that might, for the moment at least, cause Spain to think twice about invading English shores. It was a risk worth taking and, on 2 October 1567, Hawkins and his crew set sail.

But luck was not with them. Four days out they ran into a storm of biblical fury. The mountainous waves, black and racing with hysterical foam, reached for the sky and the once orderly expedition was shaken across the sea. A storm like this was something even the most seasoned sailors feared.[3] They might have been able to predict its onset from such natural phenomena as porpoises 'passing through the ocean in herds', but unless they could make rapidly for port they faced grave dangers, dangers often made worse by the bad state of their ships and their own careless practices. Obvious precautions could be swiftly taken. Amid increasing terror, hatches could be battened down and lifelines rigged. Excess goods stored on the decks could be moved below not only to preserve them but also to lower the ship's centre of gravity and reduce the problems of tophamper. Over-tall masts, 'working' in the furious winds as the saturated hempen ropes that supposedly held them taut began to stretch, might be lowered. Excessive quantities of sail (which all too easily swung to windward) might be lowered as well, but other poorly designed and badly built equipment was rarely of help and was often a hindrance. Rudders could be torn away. Masts could split and, as heaving vessels began to lose any possibility of being controlled, it was all too often found that their pumps were unable to cope with the sudden deluges of water that poured in through the badly caulked hulls.

Experienced mariners such as Drake and Hawkins knew perfectly well that a ship like the *Jesus of Lubeck* was wholly unsuited to such conditions, and what now began to happen proved the vessel's weakness. The floating fortress was thrown about like matchwood. As the ship plunged and rolled, Drake watched the high towers on its poop and forecastle tumbling to the sea and then righting again in helpless abandon, placing an intolerable strain on the main body of the vessel. Planks and timbers began to work apart and, as they did so, the caulking that was supposed to keep the *Jesus* watertight worked loose, especially about the stern where water entered with torrential abandon. It was a moment of desperation which called for the coolest nerve. Even though the fine cloths aboard had been meant as items of profitable trade, Hawkins realised that only by stuffing them into the gaping holes might there be any hope of preserving the Queen's ship and his crew. Young officers like Drake were ordered to do the only thing that could be done, but it was difficult and onerous work. Even violent leaks were difficult to find with swaying lanterns that cast a feeble light on the mass of ribs, timbers, ballast and filth in the bilges. Nonetheless, in one place no less than fifteen bolts of cloth were thrust between the gaping planks. Perhaps, even as he shouted his orders and strove alongside the other drenched and frightened men, Drake knew that such desperate measures might be insufficient. Hawkins certainly did, but he apparently would not allow so much as a twitch of fear to show in his face as he realised that it was now as hopeless to turn back as it was to sail on. A display of leadership was essential.

Believing all human effort was in vain, Hawkins very publicly put his trust in his Protestant God. Had not the fathers of the English Reformation declared that Christ's elect would surely know how to 'spy out their Lord, and trace out the paths of His feet, and follow; yea, though He go upon the plain and liquid water, which will receive no step?' Now was the time to search that doctrine out. Hawkins summoned the crew together on the heaving deck of the *Jesus*. As the chaotic waters pounded in their fury, Drake heard him explain in measured if shouted words how the position was beyond remedy and that prayer was the only resort. The impression Hawkins made was profound. 'He desired them to pray unto almighty God that He would take us into His mercy.' Hawkins's strong, intelligent face remained resolute, 'But his words pierced the hearts of all his company, and it seemed unto them that death had summoned them when they heard him recite the aforesaid words, for they knew such words could not issue out from so invincible a mind without great cause.' The emotion among the crew was intense. 'There was not one that could refrain his eyes from tears, the which when our general saw he began to enter in prayer and besought them to pray with him, the while indeed he letted not with great travail to search the ship fore and aft for her leaks.'

Eventually, as if in answer to their prayers, the storm blew itself out, but Hawkins's reaction to the crisis made a profound impression on Drake. Now, as the *Angel* alone of all the scattered flotilla rejoined them, he was deepening his understanding of the nature of authority and was coming to understand how, in times of utmost peril, the man who could fashion himself as the master of the moment was master indeed. Others would naturally follow him. It was a lesson profoundly learned and one that Drake would apply at critical moments throughout the rest of his career — a career that even now, as he went slaving with the connivance of the Queen of England, was becoming set in its pattern of piracy, plunder and Protestant nationalism. It was out of such elements as these, constantly shaped and reshaped by himself and others, that the legend of Sir Francis Drake would eventually be made.

1

On the Margins

1540–1569

Slaving and the Africa trade had fascinated Drake and Hawkins since their earliest youth when the riches of Guinea were the common talk of the Hawkins household, where Drake himself spent his formative years. The records are scanty but it seems likely that Drake was born in about 1540, the son of a moderately prosperous farmer named Edmund Drake who hailed from Crowndale near Tavistock.[1] In addition to farming, Edmund Drake supplemented his family income in two ways: he was a skilled clothworker and a part-time priest whose marriage to a woman of uncertain name was probably of dubious legality. He was by temperament a hot-blooded man – a trait he passed on to his son – and it was as the result of an affray, along with the theft of a horse and some money that, in 1548, he was obliged to leave the Tavistock area and flee to Upchurch in Kent, a small parish on the Medway where a little port gave shelter to a dozen tiny boats. There, having received a pardon for his misdemeanours, Edmund Drake acted as curate, saying the Communion service and teaching the beliefs enshrined in the *Book of Common Prayer*.

Although not perhaps utterly disgraceful, none of this makes a particularly inspiring tale, and those who wanted a more telling background for Francis Drake (including Drake himself) gradually improved on it. Drawing on anecdote and a measure of wishful thinking, an image of Drake's father began to emerge which presented him as a zealous Protestant who was obliged to flee Devon

not because he was a petty criminal but because Catholic funda-
mentalists, rebelling against the word of God and the law of the
land, rose up and drove the good preacher from his home, forcing
him to faraway Kent. There, on the banks of the Medway, Drake
senior supposedly read prayers and scripture to the sailors, inspiring
them and his son with his own fervent Protestantism while his
suffering little family (Francis in particular) found such shelter as
they could in what Drake himself later claimed was the hulk of an
abandoned ship. This is the stuff of legend with everything to
recommend it except the truth. The Catholic uprising in Devon that
supposedly drove out Edmund Drake actually took place in 1549, a
year after his somewhat ignominious flight, while his religious
beliefs seem to have been comparatively mild and orthodox. The
legend made the better story, however, and the Victorians especially
loved it. Drake, the devoutly religious sailor, could become an image
for them of how and why imperial and Protestant Britannia ruled
the waves and would continue to do so come what may. Such
posthumous and largely fictional lives of Francis Drake tell us a
great deal about the wants and fears of those who fashioned them
and are quite as fascinating (and in some ways quite as important) as
the altogether more probable facts.

These facts suggest that around the time of his father's hasty
departure from Devon, young Francis Drake joined his 'cousin-
bretheren', the Hawkinses, at their home in Plymouth. What
opened up to him there was not a Victorian empire but a thrilling
world of Tudor enterprise and extraordinary imaginative daring.
William Hawkins senior, the patriarch of the family, was by any
standards a remarkable man whose tough-minded, ambitious ways
could hardly fail to inspire a vigorous little boy like Drake. Hawkins
was at once the local political boss and a successful merchant whose
business interests, stretching far beyond the narrow range of most of
his contemporaries, brought him the wealth that allowed him to live
comfortably in Plymouth's prosperous Kinterbury Street. It was
there that Francis, growing up with his patron's sons John and
William the younger, became literate although, as he later avowed,
'my bringing up hath not been in learning'. What he did learn about,
of course, was everything to do with ships – their handling,

navigation and manning – and to view the oceans of the known world as vast expanses to be crossed and recrossed by vessels filled with fabulous cargoes of gold, spices, and elephants' teeth culled from the remote shores of Guinea and Brazil.

These new horizons had been opened up by the Portuguese and the Spanish when, during the 1490s, they at last learned how the winds and currents of the Atlantic could be used to carry them far beyond the medieval limits of Latin Christendom. Columbus's second voyage of 1493 established that there were indeed natural routes back and forth across the central Atlantic.[2] Cabot's voyage to Newfoundland three years later showed how the spring easterlies could bear a ship to North America while, in the following year, the voyage of Vasco da Gama revealed how the southern Atlantic trade winds could carry Europeans to Africa, to much of South America and thence to the fabled wealth of India. These voyages were nothing less than revolutionary. Initial success encouraged further enterprise and, as early as the 1520s, word picked up around the ports of France, Spain and Portugal suggested to the older Hawkins how far England lagged behind in this vast and lucrative expansion of world trade by the acquisitive, aggressive drive of a newly energised merchant class in search of luxury goods such as silks, satins, spices, medicines and precious metals. Determined to win his share of this bounty, Hawkins senior had, by 1530, fitted out a ship to sail to the River Sestos in Upper Guinea. There, he laded malaguette pepper and ivory before heading across the Atlantic to Brazil, that fabulous land named after the dye wood which was so valuable to clothmakers that they were prepared to pay up to £10 a ton for it. Other voyages followed, and in a shrewd bid to gain royal attention, Hawkins returned from one of his expeditions accompanied by a Brazilian prince, with bone-pierced cheeks and a jewel in his lip, who he introduced to Henry VIII.

It is likely that Hawkins continued his business throughout the 1530s, but it was King Henry – who had been so beguiled by his royal Brazilian 'brother' – who probably brought it to a close when he became embroiled in a war with France. This necessitated all English sea power being harboured at home in order to foil the threat of an invasion. Ever the man to pursue his own advantage,

William Hawkins turned pirate, profiting greatly from the age-old tradition of robbing French ships in the Channel. Drake no doubt served his apprenticeship as a pirate during this time, perhaps sailing aboard the little *Tiger*, a vessel of 50 tons which was one of William Hawkins's few ships from this period whose name is known. The tough but ageing operator himself was dead by 1554 but his two sons, John Hawkins especially, vigorously followed his example.

The Guinea trade had been ineffectively prohibited during the brief, unhappy reign of Queen Mary, but when Elizabeth gave it as her opinion that the people of her country should be allowed to do business with whom they pleased, memories of what his father had achieved stirred John Hawkins's ambition. Contacts made during regular trading visits to the Canary Islands showed what might be done, and done in a new and profitable way. The Canaries were at this time legally a part of Spain but a treaty had opened them up to English traders and, carefully ingratiating himself with the local Catholics, Hawkins began to gather information and formulate his plans. He learned that black slaves were urgently needed by ruthless Spanish settlers in the Caribbean and, having been assured by his Spanish friends that 'that store of Negroes might easily be had upon the coast of Guinea', he resolved to try his hand at the business – a hand that was, like those of his contemporaries, wholly unrestrained by any qualms of conscience. Instead, it was extended in friendship to powerful and influential friends in the City of London whom he persuaded to back him. These men included his father-in-law Benjamin Gonson, who occupied the lucrative post of Treasurer of the Navy, and his colleague William Winter who was both the Navy's Surveyor and Master of Ordnance. By October 1562 a hundred sailors had been recruited, among whom Francis Drake was most likely one.

It was on expeditions such as these that Drake learned about the life of ordinary English seamen the hard way – by being one of them.[3] He would have been familiar since boyhood with the rough, tanned appearance of these men with their plain leather jerkins worn over dirty shirts, their breeches of yellowish-red and white wool, and their heads covered by a shaggy felt hat. They were far from easy to discipline and disorderliness ashore prior to sailing was commonplace. The seasoned Captain of an expedition and his would-be young officers such as Drake knew perfectly well that they would have to roam round a port like Plymouth with the local Justices of the Peace searching lodgings, taverns and ale houses where they would pry the drunk and lachrymose from the arms of their women, carry the stupefied on board ship, listen to the lies of those who claimed they had suddenly fallen sick, bail out those who had pawned necessary possessions for drink, and try to find those who had taken their money and run. Such desperate self-indulgence was understandable in view of the fact that, once aboard, the ordinary seaman would have to endure what one described as 'cold and salty meat, broken sleeps, mouldy bread, dead beer, wet clothes, want of fire'. Life aboard an Elizabethan ship was hard indeed, as Drake knew.

The food and drink were not only poor and monotonous but often also unpalatable. A pound of biscuit, a pound of meat, and a gallon of beer was allowed to every man four days a week, with cheese and dried fish making up the remainder. Disease, and scurvy in particular, was consequently rampant, and enlightened efforts to improve matters were not helped by the obstinacy of the sailors themselves who were 'so besotted on their beef and pork as they had rather adventure on all the calentures and scorbots [delirious fevers and scurvy] in the world than to be weaned from their customary diet'. Illness was made the more prevalent by overcrowded conditions and a lack of ventilation which made the holds so disgusting that many men preferred to sleep on deck. On his own expeditions Drake would be active in ensuring the health of his men as best he could and the doctor was always a respected member of his officer corps. The unruly and frequently disgruntled men were also subject to the severest discipline. In an age when the Protestant gentry were ever more assured that it was their business to be godly magistrates and keep the lower classes in line, orders were frequently issued to see that there was no gambling on board – 'neither carding, dicing, tabling nor other devilish games' – along with a rigorous embargo on bad language which tried to ensure that there should be 'no blaspheming of God, or detestable swearing . . . nor communication of ribaldry, filthy tales, or ungodly talk'. Such pious hopes were reinforced by medieval punishments: swearing and blasphemy, for example, were punished by sticking a marlin spike in the offender's mouth, tying it behind his head with excessive tightness, and making him stand a whole hour while the blood ran copiously down his chin. This, it was reckoned, was an excellent cure for swearers. Perhaps so, but Drake himself always regarded sailors as the most envious and unruly people in the world and was constantly aware of the perils of mutiny.

It was under such conditions as these that Elizabethan ships set sail. The navigation of the first part of a long voyage such as Hawkins now intended would have been within the competence of an experienced English pilot and Drake became one of the most famously adept of these, a man whose navigational skill was rivalled only by his fearsome reputation as a pirate.[4] A basic knowledge of how to pilot a ship through known waters and their tides was learned from experienced ships' masters, men who could teach an aspiring sailor like Drake how to use a rutter, memorise the appearance of familiar coasts under all the varying conditions of light from fair weather to foul, how to use the sun, moon and stars, and how to employ the secrets of various basic navigational instruments.

Chief among these last, of course, was the compass. A small number still survive from Tudor times and show that sixteenth-century compasses were mounted on gimbals in wooden boxes or sometimes ivory bowls. The card itself was graduated into thirty-two points, the north being indicated by a conspicuous device such as a *fleur de lys*. The compass needle or 'wire' was just that – a length of soft steel wire. This was bent double into a loop and pinched at each end so it exactly corresponded to the diameter of the compass card to whose underside it was then attached, aligned due north-south. The wire and card were then placed on a brass cone or 'capital' which allowed them to pivot freely. It was essential to preserve the magnetism of the 'wire' and this was done by stroking it with a lodestone, a naturally magnetic oxide of iron which can transfer its powers to other metals. By means of his compass a pilot could plot his ship's position and progress on a sheepskin chart covered with directional lines. He would first have estimated his speed by the use of a half-hour sandglass, and a logline regularly divided by knots which gave rise to the term used to express speed at sea. In addition to his skill with the compass, chart and logline, an aspiring pilot like Drake would also have learned how to sound the seabed up to a depth of 100 fathoms with a lead and line and then to read the deposit raised in order to estimate his position. An arcane but essential expertise was developed whereby the experienced pilot knew exactly what was implied about his position when he raised peppery black sand at sixty-five fathoms off the Scillies, or fragments of shell and sharks' teeth ten leagues south-west of the islands.

It was with his ships managed in such ways as these that Hawkins's flotilla of 1562 arrived at the Canary Islands. There, having traded the woollens he had brought from Devon, Hawkins took on board that figure of fundamental importance to any long oceanic voyage: a skilled navigator – in this case a Spaniard from Cadiz named Juan Martinez. This was a practice Drake himself would invariably follow in his later career, and a voyage down to the Guinea coast would have proved to him how indispensable were the skills of such men. To navigate the ocean and perform such necessary operations as measuring the height of the sun and stars in order to determine latitude required skills and equipment altogether more advanced than those familiar to many an ordinary pilot. Oceanic navigation was the cutting-edge of sixteenth-century science and something that the English – and Drake in particular – were to become immensely proficient at after a very slow start. Ironically, they received their earliest lessons from the Spaniards. In 1548 the Privy Council had managed to lure no less a figure than Sebastian Cabot from Spain to England, where he trained a select handful of men in the art of navigation; and, when Philip II married Mary Tudor, international relations were furthered by sending Stephen Borough to Seville where he observed how the Spanish trained their navigators. Book learning far deeper than the knowledge possessed by coastal pilots was essential to this, and initial interest in ocean sailing eventually resulted in Richard Eden's translation of a Spanish work on the subject which he issued in 1561 as *The Art of Navigation*.

Drake knew Eden's book well and appreciated its invaluable advice on the use of those two essential instruments of navigation, the astrolabe and the cross-staff. The astrolabe had been developed by the Portuguese, the pioneer navigators of the Iberian peninsula, and was a disc used to measure the altitude of the sun. Efforts were constantly made to improve its accuracy but, even so, the astrolabe was gradually being replaced by the cross-staff. This instrument was already of considerable antiquity, having probably been invented as early as 1342 by Levi ben Gerson. It too was used to take the altitude of the sun, or of a star above the horizon to determine latitude. The cross-staff itself was a four-sided wooden rod about 80 centimetres long, engraved with scales of degrees from 0 to 90, and fitted with one or sometimes two crosspieces. The mariner would hold it to his eye and then move the crosspiece up and down the shaft until its lower end was aligned with the horizon. The upper edge was meanwhile aligned with the bottom of the celestial body being observed. If this was the sun then the operation was a dangerous one, and the idea of mariners commonly being blind in one eye was not wholly a fabrication. Complicated calculations and the use of tables then helped to establish the ship's latitude, and it was an appreciation of matters such as these that marked out intelligent and forward-looking sailors like Drake from the great mass of traditionalists who derided 'mathematical seamen' and, happy enough to grope their way round familiar waters, belonged quite literally to the old world.

Certainly, it was the skills of Juan Martinez that brought Hawkins's expedition safely past Cape Verde and its islands and on down the Guinea coast to where Drake had what was probably his first encounter with Sierra Leone.[5] The great bay of the estuary was, and remains, a place of extraordinary beauty, with summer thunder roaring on the great peaked hills to the south and golden palm-fringed beaches to the north. The estuary runs from the Atlantic eastwards through a score of little islands, their edges lined with mangrove swamps. In European terms, the Portuguese had laid claim to the area and jealously guarded the rich profits it could produce. A significant number of Portuguese were settled there and, protected by a handful of small coastal forts, exported cloth, dyes, hides, livestock and, above all, Negro slaves to Europe and the Americas.

Slaves were what Hawkins was after and, as a mere first-time interloper, he proceeded to capture those he wanted with a brutal naivety the Portuguese themselves had long since left behind. Some he simply stole from their European owners, while others he obtained by raiding native villages. The stolen slaves had come to their original masters in a number of different ways. On rare occasions individuals might have surrendered themselves or been sold by their families during times of famine. They might also have been criminals (or supposed criminals) sold by the native chiefs as punishment. Others were prisoners of war, while many were persons brutally kidnapped by native gangs of Africans who so willingly colluded with the Europeans that slave-raiding became a profession with a number of individuals dedicating themselves entirely to it.

If stealing slaves was a guaranteed method of infuriating the Portuguese, raids on native villages were a sure way of disturbing the indigenous population. Certainly, at this stage in their careers, neither Hawkins nor Drake showed the least concern for the subtleties of the social and political complexities of native peoples, although Drake himself was to acquire a deep respect for Negro warriors and eventually put their abilities close to the very heart of his strategy. But, for the moment, he and Hawkins failed particularly to recognise the full importance of the kings and chiefs living in their whitewashed brick and adobe houses which were decorated with fine mats and three-legged stools. These houses were enhanced by the presence of porches where the cotton-shirted aristocrats relaxed and gave orders to the ordinary people about them, reinforcing their commands by ceremoniously knocking the iron rings on their thumbs against the jingles they carried in their palms. Time would teach Hawkins and Drake that co-operation with such people was altogether more profitable than aggression, but for now the English were satisfied merely with raiding to fill the holds of their ships, and one stolen Portuguese vessel, with their prey. Then, with the work in Africa done, Hawkins sailed with some of his own ships and the stolen one to the West Indies, there to sell his human cargo cheaply but profitably to eager Spanish buyers. The remaining English vessel, probably with Francis Drake aboard, sailed back to England with the other goods the expedition had so far obtained.

What happened when Hawkins reached the Caribbean suggests the long-term plans he, and later Drake himself, had in mind. Hawkins was perfectly well aware that by venturing into the Spanish South American Empire he was breaking the three cardinal rules of Spanish overseas trade.[6] He had sailed without a licence, he had failed to clear his cargoes with the authorities in Seville, and now he was about to do business without the necessary permission. It was a blatant try-on, and it was wholly successful: the slave-hungry Spaniards, after a token show of resistance, eagerly bought his 'goods'. The reality of an English trading presence in the Caribbean was thus established and now, probably in the hope that the Spaniards would accept the point, Hawkins sent part of his newly acquired goods back to Seville for clearance, despatching some in a chartered Spanish vessel and the rest in the captured Portuguese one. The message to Spain was obvious. The English in the Caribbean would behave honourably (or fairly honourably) if the Spaniards recognised their right to be there.

The Spaniards would do no such thing. The cargo in the chartered vessel was impounded on arrival in Seville, while that in the Portuguese ship found its way, inevitably, to Lisbon. An angry Hawkins claimed he had thereby lost £20,000 and went to London to demand royal support against Spain and its outrages. Nonetheless, when the accountants had done their work, it was clear that the venture had made a substantial profit. It had probably cost less than £2,000 to fit out while, with slaves fetching an average price of £22 a head, a favourable balance in the region of £4,000 was not inconceivable. Certainly, this was a sufficient return to attract great merchants, aristocratic speculators like the Earl of Leicester, and even the Queen herself. It was known to everyone that Spanish trade in the Caribbean was officially closed to foreigners but it was obvious that there was money to be made by prising it open – by force if necessary. In such ways as these, the possibilities of getting rich quickly in Drake's world were becoming clear and he himself took them to heart.

Determined to profit from Hawkins's enterprise, Elizabeth lent him a ship for his second slaving expedition of 1564. The Queen was joined in her interest by the Earls of Pembroke and Leicester and Lord Admiral Clinton, along with that very small minority of City merchants who dared to venture their capital outside of Europe. The aims of the expedition were in many respects a repetition of the first and it is probable that Drake himself was again part of the crew. If so, this gave him the opportunity to see at first hand not only the Spanish Caribbean but to experience the mounting hostility of Spain towards the English. A number of recent incidents had fomented this. The activities of the Duke of Alba in the Spanish Netherlands ensured that trade between England and Antwerp was temporarily suspended, with painful economic results, especially on the tax revenues of the Crown. The crisis was aggravated by the embargoing of English ships in northern Spanish ports and the fact that other English vessels had been arrested in Gibraltar and their crews sent to the galleys. Revenge was called for and attacks on Spanish ships multiplied as a consequence. This wary atmosphere of savagery was made all the fiercer by English indignation at how their sailors were treated by the Inquisition once they had been captured, an indignation which in turn encouraged a greater vehemence of religious and nationalist belief among many English Protestants. They increasingly saw themselves as the chosen children of God pitted against the Devil and all his Catholic works. In such a situation as this, with trading rivalry and religious hatred becoming ever more viciously intertwined, it was all too easy for men like Francis Drake to begin characterising Spain as the evil empire.

The European centre of that empire was Seville where the *Casa de la contratacion de las Indias*, founded by royal decree in 1503, and the *Consulado* or Guild of Merchants, exercised a comprehensive monopoly over every aspect of Spanish trade with the New World. The port of Seville itself was sited forty miles up the winding Guadalquivir. It was from there that the heavily protected *flota* or treasure fleet sailed in April or May for Vera Cruz, the returning and richly loaded *galeones* leaving for Nombre de Dios on the Panama isthmus in August. All other sailings to the Indies were also required to clear Seville, as were all flotillas returning richly fraught from the Caribbean. It was the Caribbean that was the hub of Spanish trade in the New World, a source at one and the same time of fabulous wealth and appalling human suffering. Silver was the principal treasure. It was mined in vast quantities, particularly at Potosi in Upper Peru where convenient deposits of mercury proved invaluable for extracting the silver from its surrounding ore before it was cast into ingots. These ingots were then carried on an agonising journey along the roads of the Panama isthmus to Nombre de Dios before being sent by sea to Cartegena and thence to Havana. At Havana, the treasure ships reconnoitred with others come down from the Gulf of Mexico, before jointly sailing north through the Florida Strait, thence east to the Azores and finally to Seville. This traffic, fabulously valuable and obtained with immense effort and cost in human life, would soon prove an irresistible temptation to Drake. Meanwhile, Spaniards in such places as Hispaniola needed slaves.

Among the major islands of the Caribbean, beautiful and fertile Hispaniola was the first, and for many years the only, Spanish base in the region. Driven by an insatiable thirst for precious metal, fertile land and slave labour, the conquistadors had found Hispaniola adequately provided with all three. A gold rush triggered the first American boom which exhausted itself even as the native Arawak population was decimated in the process. Native couples were torn apart, the men being sent to work for eight or ten months at a time in the gruelling conditions of the mines while their women were condemned to backbreaking work in the fields. When the couples were eventually reunited they were usually too exhausted, wasted and weak to make love, and such feeble babies as were born died of starvation as they vainly sucked at their mothers' withered breasts. After such hideous exploitation, only the natural fertility of the ground remained and, by the early years of the sixteenth century, it was discovered that this ground was particularly suited to growing sugar. Labour was naturally needed to work the cane fields and sugar mills and, with the native population all but wiped out, it became evident that the small number of African slaves shipped to the island during the last stages of gold fever could be usefully increased for the benefit of the new trade.

In such an atmosphere as this an arrangement was readily reached between Spain and the Portuguese slavers on the Guinea coast whereby Negroes could be shipped to the Caribbean under licence, providing always that they had first been cleared in Seville. The Portuguese soon found this last condition irksome and the altogether more convenient practice grew up of smuggling slaves across the Atlantic in considerable numbers. There was, for the moment, very little the Spanish authorities could do to prevent this, and in the absence of effective policing, other illicit traders slipped in. Among these was Hawkins. He knew he would face difficulties, and hostility was at once apparent. Having arrived at La Margarita, the Governor refused Hawkins a licence to trade, evacuated the town, and sent a message of warning to the authorities in Santo Domingo. Shrugging his shoulders, Hawkins moved on to Burburata where a sequence of events that was to become typical now took place. The Spaniards desperately wanted to trade, but they wanted to do so under proper licence and asked for ten days' grace to obtain the necessary permission. Hawkins agreed but the Spaniards, looking across at the mighty guns of the Englishman's ship, realised that his patience was likely to be short-lived. Hoping to keep the peace, they soon agreed to buy some thirty, rather sickly, slaves. This was a start, but Hawkins thought they were trying to beat the price down by keeping him waiting. Knowing that the Spaniards needed his slaves as much as he wanted to sell them, he threatened to depart and the Spaniards, keen to keep him friendly, bought some more.

When the Governor himself finally arrived, Hawkins protested loudly and disingenuously that he was only anchored off Burburata because of bad weather. He explained that he urgently needed to trade his slaves and protested that he was, of course, a loyal and 'great servitor' to King Philip. This was mere smooth talking and Hawkins lent an edge to his words by roundly declaring that if the Spaniards did not comply with his wishes then his guns would speak for him. The threatened Spaniards reluctantly complied, bought some of his cargo, and then insisted on payment of customs duties of seven and a half per cent plus an additional thirty ducats a head per slave. That was too much and a lesson for Drake in Spanish duplicity. Hawkins and a hundred of his men, well armed with bows, arrows, arquebuses and pikes, marched towards the town. Talk of thirty ducats a head was suddenly dropped and nearly £4,000 worth of business was quickly transacted, establishing a mode of trading that saw the same formula repeated at Rio de la Hacha: talk of bad weather, hopes of friendship, threats of violence. Again it worked. A licence was produced by the authorities, favourable terms were agreed after a display of English force, and something close to £6,000 worth of business was done, giving a total return on the voyage of about £10,000 or a rate of profit of 59 per cent, which some of the greedier investors would later think insufficient. Cracks in the slaving enterprise were already beginning to appear.

There was one final task to be undertaken before returning home. The English were not the only interlopers in the Caribbean. French Protestants, or Huguenots (with whom Drake was soon to work closely), were also determined to seize what profits they could and had, much to the concern of the Spaniards, established a Protestant colony on the Florida peninsula from which they could observe the passage of the Spanish treasure fleets. The colony, difficult to establish and even more difficult to maintain, had not been a success. Its founder at one point came to England where, with royal encouragement, a plan had been hatched for an Anglo-French settlement in America. This came to nothing, but the Queen retained an interest in French initiatives and Hawkins was charged with the responsibility of visiting the colony to see that all was well. It was not. Fort Caroline was on the verge of collapse, menaced by hostile Indians, furious Spaniards, hunger and mutiny. The Huguenot commander, René de Laudonnière, was more than ready to quit his post but was altogether too wary to accept Hawkins's promise of transport home. Instead, he gratefully took the offer of a little ship, victuals, and shoes for his men. Having done what he could, Hawkins himself sailed for home, unwittingly leaving the French to the Spaniards' terrible revenge.

By now, Spanish annoyance at what Hawkins's effrontery had so far achieved was such that it was considered altogether more diplomatic to have another man command the third Caribbean voyage, on which Drake himself certainly sailed. Captain John Lovell was a Protestant of the most ardent kind, and the tone of the expedition he led reflected the fact.' Something altogether more extreme than hitherto was creeping into English maritime life and Lovell personified this new strain of religious fundamentalism. He made no secret of his intense loathing of all things Catholic and was loud in his vulgar boast that he would like to burn an image of the Virgin Mary and roast a goat in the coals that were left. His ships became little floating seminaries of Protestant enthusiasm. There were, as always, daily prayers, readings and sermons. The Spanish authorities learned how the crews 'recited psalms in every ship, along with the other things that are specified in . . . the books the Protestants use in England'. Indeed, even while the Negroes in the holds below suffered in the most agonising and insanitary conditions, issues of the Protestant faith were taught and discussed every day between the zealous believers on the decks above.

Among the most vigorous of these proselytisers was Francis Drake who, according to the testimony of one Morgan Tillert, was personally responsible for his own conversion to the new faith.[8] This was no gentle process of persuasion. Drake was, Tillert said, 'a firm English Protestant' who was clearly convinced of his missionary role. This suggests that Drake's beliefs were far more than conventional lip-service. They were part of the wellspring of his being and of that outstanding energy which, in this instance, during the cramped and monotonous conditions of a long sea voyage, spilled over constantly in an effusion so powerful that other, lesser men were subdued to his will. Drake's treatment of Tillert was, as much as anything else, an exercise in power, the behaviour of an apparatchik, even a bully. Drake's was a resolute if theologically unsophisticated Protestantism, the Protestantism of a man of action and driving ambition who saw England and her Queen as existing by the special favour of divine Providence. This belief lay at the core of all that Drake was to do, all that he was to achieve. He had his ideology and, using it with increasing dexterity, would never flinch from it.

Meanwhile his commander proved altogether more feeble. If Lovell could inspire his men's religious fervour he was considerably less successful when it came to matters of slave trading. He followed Hawkins's example in Guinea and stole Negroes from the

Portuguese along with valuable shipping, but he proved singularly incompetent when it came to selling his slaves in the Caribbean. Liaising with the French off Burburata, Lovell and his little ships followed their fleet to Margarita where, for all that some of the citizens were seized, the demand for a trading licence was refused and a mere twenty-six slaves were exchanged. At Rio de la Hacha Lovell was again unsuccessful. He was dismissed by the Governor, having landed ninety-six slaves who were old and weak and on the point of dying, and returned to his ships, sailing ignominiously away. Outgunned, outmanoeuvred and outclassed, Lovell had attempted to follow Hawkins's aggressive tactics without either his means or inherent qualities of leadership. Hawkins himself was to blame the expedition's lack of success on the 'simpleness' of his deputy who 'knew not how to handle these matters'. This was true and, to Francis Drake, Lovell's expedition was a lesson in failure and Spanish untrustworthiness.

Drake returned from the voyage to be greeted with the news that his father had died some months earlier. Edmund Drake's sad little will makes no mention of his most famous son, nor of Drake's oldest brothers, John and Joseph, probably because the dying man thought they were sufficiently well provided for by their own efforts. Most of what Edmund Drake had to leave – a bed, pillows, five shirts, an inkwell and so on – was bequeathed to his youngest son Thomas who was still underage. Clearly it was not from this meagre resource that the newly returned Drake found the money to invest in Hawkins's next slaving voyage which was even then being readied. Nor did he obtain it by the means related in an often repeated but unlikely story, first told by the historian William Camden. According to this account, Drake's father early apprenticed him to a skipper on the Medway who, finding in young Francis the son he never had, bequeathed him his boat. Drake's early experiences of the Medway almost certainly revolved around the vessels John Hawkins had there and used for privateering, and this was the probable means by which Drake began to build up his capital. Certainly, his funds were sufficient for him to invest in Hawkins's fourth great slaving expedition of 1567 on which, as we have seen, he sailed as a junior officer.

*

The sheer scale of the 1567 expedition was impressive, and was meant to be, for it was in part a political gesture. The Queen was perfectly well aware that Philip II would understand it as a veiled threat and a demonstration at one and the same time of her country's naval power and his relative weakness in the Caribbean. But aggressive gestures in a diplomatic war were only one reason for the mighty tonnage that was put to sea. The other reason was, or appeared to be, more immediately practical. Trade of the sort Hawkins and Elizabeth intended was becoming increasingly dangerous. The Portuguese in West Africa were resisting inter-lopers with mounting force and with heavily armed galleys and galleons. Piratical attacks on these vessels, along with shore raids on African villages to seize slaves, required a degree of armed superiority which, in its turn, led to an escalation of hostilities. Nor was it only African considerations that were responsible for the commissioning of the huge *Jesus of Lubeck* and the flotilla's large number of guns. The sheer presence of a vessel like the *Jesus* in the waters of the Caribbean spoke directly of the aggressive capabilities of the English and the threat of force which was Hawkins's chosen means of stimulating trade.

Hawkins also made it abundantly clear that this was a Protestant expedition. Displays of religious conviction increased with com-mercial hostility. Although he carried no chaplain aboard his ships a daily religious routine was sternly enforced. 'During the voyage of the said fleet,' recalled one of its crewmen, 'when night fell and the new watch began to come on deck and the hourglass was turned, everyone on board the ship would assemble around the mainmast, kneeling and bareheaded, and the quartermaster would begin praying, and everyone would recite the Psalms of David, Our Father, and the Creed, in the English language.' Such apparent devotion was guaranteed by the usual punishments. Attendance was not voluntary and the boatswain applied the unplaited end of a rope to the backs of those who thought they could shirk the occasion. Many wished they could, 'half of the men on the flagship' saying when called to prayers, 'Body of God, what an amount of singing, praying and preaching: may the Devil fly away with the preacher!'

Their devotions had no doubt been more heartfelt when the great storm descended on them, but for piety to be put to practical use it was necessary for Hawkins's scattered flotilla to regroup. The rendezvous point was supposed to be Tenerife where, accompanied now by the *Judith* in addition to the *Angel*, Hawkins sailed. The Canary Islands were thoroughly familiar to him and he intended, in his usual way, to take on supplies and fresh water from the friends he had there. He was to find conditions changed. There was exasperation over the activities of the English at the highest level of Spain's bureaucracy and the Spanish were determined that the provision made by the papacy in its Bull *Inter Caetera* – a ruling which stated that no foreigner had any right to trade in Spanish territories west of the line drawn midway between the Azores and the West Indies – should be sternly enforced. Pointed letters had already been sent from Madrid demanding that Hawkins be treated with circumspection and, as he hoved into view, the local Canarian militia was put on alert.

Hawkins replied in kind, confident that he was breaking no law for he believed, like the Queen's great advisor Mr Secretary Cecil and all good Protestants, that 'the Pope had no right to partition the world and to give and take kingdoms to whomever he pleased'. Having taken adequate precautions Hawkins, with that raw and bigoted humour that came so easily to English Protestants, joked that he had a special dispensation from the Pope himself to eat meat on a Friday and invited those of his old friends who would to come aboard to feast with him off his silver plate. As they did so his musicians played their exquisite tunes, but such pleasantries did not blind Hawkins to the fact that, just at nightfall, the Spanish ships in the road lying between the *Jesus* and the castle guns of Santa Cruz, quietly shifted their position. He made sure that his own vessels were moved out of their range, and such violence as did erupt was of a domestic rather than an international nature.

Two hot-headed English gentlemen aboard the *Jesus of Lubeck*, Edward Dudley and George Fitzwilliam – the sort of figures Drake was often to have trouble with – began arguing with sudden and violent Elizabethan anger. They believed the argument could only be ended by a duel. It was clearly unwise for them to fight aboard their General's flagship, and Dudley had already set off for land when an exasperated Hawkins ordered Fitzwilliam to remain on board. A furious Dudley was recalled and, when Hawkins gave him a well deserved dressing-down, he replied with rude anger. Hawkins struck him with his fist, Dudley drew his knife, Hawkins drew his. Blood flowed before a panting Hawkins directed Dudley to be placed in irons and brought before him to hear his sentence. Determined to make it seem that personal choler was not clouding his judgement, Hawkins told Dudley that while the insult to himself might be forgiven, that to the Queen in whose ship they were sailing could not. Treason was treason and Hawkins, seizing a loaded arquebus, pointed it at Dudley, ordering him to say his prayers and prepare for death. The prisoner, suddenly cowed, begged for mercy. The bystanders backed his plea and, before the watching eyes of Francis Drake, Hawkins tempered his absolute authority with sufficient mercy to let the hot-headed Dudley live.

It was necessary now to reconnoitre with the rest of the English flotilla which, Hawkins discovered, was waiting for him off Gomera. He fired what was intended as a passing salute as he left Santa Cruz but, whether by accident or design, the cannonball reached the town and badly damaged one of its houses. There were those who said that Hawkins had really wanted to hit a nearby church and there were others who added that, when Hawkins and his men reached Gomera, they made up for their disappointment by burning the images of the saints they found there. This was strenuously denied but now, with his freshly watered ships reunited once again, Hawkins could make his way to the western coast of Africa.

Just as the Spaniards had shown their hostility to Hawkins's expedition so, once he arrived off the African coast, he found the Portuguese similarly intransigent in their attitude.[9] It was well known that an English ship had been sunk in the area during the previous season and another captured. The King of Portugal stood shoulder to shoulder with the King of Spain on English illegalities, and Hawkins was determined to go about what he regarded as his legitimate business with reasonable care. It was hardly to be expected, however, that such an expedition assembled for such a purpose would invariably proceed with scrupulous niceness. For

31

example, Robert Barrett, master of the *Jesus,* led a river-borne expedition up to where the Portuguese had a permanent and long-standing commercial settlement. His intentions were clearly hostile and, when the Portuguese refused to trade with him, Barrett and his men burned the town, captured their rivals' ships, and fought a pitched battle against the combined army of Europeans and Africans who inhabited the place. Four of Barrett's own men died. The English believed that such a resort to force was necessary because there was no prospect of bargaining for Negroes in the wake of a French fleet which had recently traded in the same area, but it was not only the Portuguese settlers whom the English attacked.

At one point Hawkins mounted a strongly armed night expedition to besiege and set fire to an inland native village, 'meaning to take the Negroes sleeping'. This was a mistake. Altogether more experienced than the English at interpreting the nocturnal sounds of the region, the Africans avoided the snare laid for them. Even the Englishmen's few successes were paltry affairs, an attack on another village yielding only a dozen Negroes of whom four had to be set at liberty as they were thin and old. The remaining eight slaves were then taken to the English ships but only at the cost of an African counter-attack in which ten or eleven of Hawkins's own men died. Things were going badly. Areas that had once proved fruitful in slaves were now depopulated, and even when the local tribespeople were lured out of their fastnesses with the promise of bartering for artificial pearls, 'our men thinking to set upon them to take them, they doubted and fled'. It was all very frustrating.

Amid such activities, the piety of the English crews was to be kept honour-bright and strenuous efforts were made to ensure that this was so. By the time slaving had begun in earnest, the boats that were sent up the rivers in search of Negroes were carefully provided with rush baskets filled with hymn books. This was observed by a bemused Portuguese sailor named Miguel Ribeiro. He noticed how these books were distributed to, all the crew who then sat down in two rows and began to sing the Psalms 'for half an hour or so, and when they finished they shut up the books, and the English pilot would shout something which I did not understand, and the others would respond just as when we respond "Amen"'. But Drake and the unlikely little choir singing their Psalms beside the mangrove swamps hardly needed to be reminded that they were traversing the valley of death. Mortality in its most awful and suprising guises stalked them constantly. Horrified survivors remembered that fevers were sudden and lethal. 'Look ye, sir, when we were off the Guinea coast picking up blacks, we would go on shore of a morning to do that which was needful, and more than once some Englishman after walking a distance would fall down dead without a word'. There were those who decided that the men who were lost when their boat capsized were eaten by the hippopotamus that tipped it over, but laughter at the little pinprick arrows fired at them by the natives turned to horror a couple of days later when the poison on their tips caused the wounded to fall dead or dying to the ground, their mouths clamped tight in a terrible paralysis.

It is possible but far from certain that Drake himself was given the captaincy of one of the expedition's vessels at this time, but it was already abundantly clear to him and Hawkins that they were picking up far too few slaves. The mere 150 or so Negroes gathered so far were hardly worth the effort of crossing the Atlantic for and something had to be done. The officers were debating as to whether they should proceed down to the Gold Coast when help came in the unexpected form of an emissary from the King of Sierra Leone who, along with another chief, was jointly besieging the nearby settlement at Conga. The warriors clearly thought that the gunpowder-bearing white men might be a useful adjunct to their struggle and suggested that success would be rewarded with a gift of slaves. Hawkins, Drake and the others, nothing averse, proceeded to play their part.

This was no little tribal war in which they were about to fight.[10] For almost two decades now the local Sapi people had been harassed by waves of armies surging towards them out of present-day Liberia. These Mani warriors were terrifying men who carried small but immensely practical bows and arrows, and protected themselves from the assaults of their enemies by means of huge shields made of reeds. Each man carried two knives, one of which was strapped to his left arm and, while their bodies were covered with loose cotton shirts that reached down to their knees to become shorts, their warlike appearance was enhanced by the abundance of feathers waving from the bands on their red caps. The Mani had recently been pushed back towards the Sierra Leone estuary and perhaps 8–10,000 of them and their camp followers were now occupying a fortified town on the island of Conga. It was this vast, timber-rimmed stockade that the local kings were besieging when they asked for Hawkins's help.

Some ninety Englishmen were at first despatched but, twenty of them having been wounded or killed in the first two days and no obvious progress made, Hawkins himself determined to join the siege with reinforcements. It was arranged that the Sapi warriors should attack from the land side and the English from the river. This position allowed the English – and Drake in particular – to witness the extraordinary valour of the black warriors. 'To see the stoutness of these people,' one of them recorded. 'As our men were putting off one of the boats, a certain Negro leapt into the water and perforce plucked an oar out of our men's hands, and though one of our men shot him so into the body that the arrow went clean through him, he carried the oar and ran with it about forty paces and then fell down dead.' But guns inevitably carried the day and Hawkins's munitions finally made a breach in the fortress's great timber surround. The houses inside were then set on fire with burning arrows and the English charged through the breach, driving the enemy across the blazing town and into the arms of the Sapi kings who had now burst through on the other side.

A massacre followed, with 7,000 men, women and children driven into the sea to drown while an altogether more ghastly fate was reserved for those whom the victors decided to take prisoner. The horrified English chronicler described the fate of a typical captive with all the objectivity he could muster. 'They bind him to a stake and make a fire hard by and round about it,' he wrote, 'and the miserable creature while alive they will with their knives cut off his tender places and eat it, eating his own flesh by portions before his eyes, a terrible kind of death.' The chronicler was a man sufficiently intelligent to require some form of explanation and he added that 'this eating one another, it is said, is because they should be without pity and fear, as well as putting in their mind that they do not only spoil their enemies but give themselves sustenance'.

The majority of the English in the meantime were altogether more concerned about getting live prisoners as slaves. They had themselves seized about 250 captives, but the victorious Sapi had taken some 600 and were unable and unwilling to eat them all. Hawkins and his men hoped that they might have the choice of the best of them, but in this they were disappointed for reasons they were too unsophisticated to appreciate. The son of one of the victorious Sapi kings had been killed in the battle and the mourning father left the conquered town to return home, bidding his allies visit his homestead on the Scarcies River at a later date to collect their prizes. Hawkins, misunderstanding what was going on, interpreted it all as a flagrant breach of contract and lamented that the Negroes were a people among whom 'is seldom or never found truth'. He decided it was time to go and, on 3 February, he set sail, the holds of his ships crammed with Negroes who, having been saved from the horrific practices of the cannibals, were now to be handed over to the altogether more protracted cruelties of the Spaniards.

By the end of March the lookouts in the English crow's-nests sighted the island of Dominica where the flotilla stopped briefly to take on water before sailing to Margarita. There the port town of Cubagua was still recovering from an attack by French pirates some six months earlier and Hawkins sent the Governor a letter telling him that he merely wanted to trade for victuals and intended to stay for no more than five or six days. The Governor supplied him with what he needed, and so agreeable was the stay that it was nine days before the English sailed on to Burburata. This was the centre of the Spanish pearl industry and its attendant cruelties. Here Negro slaves were kept under lock and key in a large dormitory, ostensibly to prevent them from having sex and thus enabling them, so it was believed, to dive deeply under the water for long periods of time. Those who disappointed their masters by finding insufficient quantities of pearls were punished for their shortcomings by being kept in the dormitory and cruelly flogged. Much to the inconvenience of the Spaniards, the lives so led by their pearl fishers tended to be short, while the slaves also had the exasperating habit of using the canoes from which they dived as a means of escape whenever they could. Surely, fresh supplies of slaves would be wanted in such a place.

Hawkins wrote the Governor a letter explaining that, while he knew perfectly well how trading with foreigners was strictly forbidden, the Governor would surely have no objection to purchasing a mere sixty slaves, the money from the sale of which would cover 'the payment of the soldiers I have in my ships'. This suave combination of promise and implied threat availed Hawkins nothing. A fortnight's delay, an appeal to the local bishop, and an armed march on the town of Valencia provided the English with little more than the few light refreshments the bishop left for them in his palace before evacuating the town. Eventually, a small amount of trading was done with the returning residents, while the little *Angel* and the *Judith* – the latter now commanded by Francis Drake – were sent off to explore what proved to be the meagre possibilities offered by nearby Coro and Curacao.

Having returned empty-handed from there, Drake was sent ahead of the rest of the flotilla as it quitted Burburata for Rio de la Hacha, where he was personally determined to have revenge on the Governor for the humiliation and losses inflicted on Lovell's expedition the year before. A loathing of what he refused to see as anything other than Spanish duplicity was growing in him and the combination of vengeance and violence that ensued – the reckless hot-headedness, courage and sheer greed – were the very essence of the school that was shaping Drake's lifelong attitudes. For all that the Governor had recently placed elaborate defensive fieldworks along the shore and round the port, Drake moved in close and, when his request to take on water was answered with gunfire, he aimed two shots through his enemy's house and then anchored out of range. There he waited for five days, diverting himself by chasing a caravel from Santo Domingo. The terrified Captain made for the Spanish port where Drake pursued and disabled him under the fire of 200 Spanish arquebusiers. Such unprovoked and reckless bravado was hardly the way to encourage trade with the mortified Spaniards, but their need for slaves was altogether stronger than their affronted honour and Hawkins, arriving on the scene, hazarded that they could yet be persuaded to trade by fair means or foul.

Foul means proved the more effective. When a letter comparable to that sent to the Governor of Margarita was returned with insults by the Governor of Rio de la Hacha, Hawkins responded by landing 200 of his men. Training the guns of his flotilla on the walls and disregarding the ineffective fire of ninety Spanish arquebusiers, he raced into the all but deserted town where, under the cover of night and guided by a Negro who now chose to desert to his side, he loaded the contents of the treasury on to some stolen carts. The townspeople, altogether more angered and upset by the potential loss of their wealth than by the insult done to their King, demanded that the Governor negotiate with Hawkins before the treasure found its way on to the English ships. The furious Governor gave way defeated, muttering that the townsfolk did not realise that Hawkins was a man whose personality and powers of speech were such that he could subdue anybody to his will. Certainly the Governor himself was subdued, for he acceded to all Hawkins's demands. Gold from the King's chest bought sixty of Hawkins's Negroes, gold from the Governor's own twenty more. After this the Spanish planters and pearl traders were given the opportunity to buy the slaves they so badly needed and quickly purchased 150 of them.

Eventually it was time to move on and, as the Governor of Rio de la Hacha wrote a supine letter to his King explaining how he had been the victim of English aggression, Hawkins arrived at Santa Marta. There, the by now familiar ploy of a formal English request for trade, a Spanish denial and subsequent skirmishing, ensured that business was eventually conducted. Cartagena proved less amenable, but it was by now growing late in the year and Hawkins decided to make for home since the hurricane season was well advanced. But he was already too late. As he pointed his ships towards the Yucatan Channel they were surprised by a furious storm which split up the fleet and wrenched the planks of the *Jesus* so far apart that fish swam in and out over the ballast. For four days the storm threw the *Jesus* and the remaining vessels about the seas until they were eventually left hundreds of miles north off the coast of Florida. Two further weeks of anxious searching failed to show a natural harbour where the ships might be repaired, and it was only when Hawkins had captured and interrogated the pilot of a Spanish ship that he realised his sole hope lay in sailing south towards Mexico and the port town of San Juan de Ulúa.

While his grievously battered ships sailed down the coast the captured Spanish pilot, Francisco Maldonado, whether willingly or not, provided Hawkins with a great deal of essential information. San Juan del Ulúa itself, the Spaniard told him, was a wretched and dangerous place, a port made, as Hawkins himself was later to write, from the shelter afforded 'by a little island of stones not three feet above the water in the highest place, and but a bow-shot of length any way'. The island was thus about 240 yards long and lay some 500 yards from the shore. Miserable though it may have been, the place was nonetheless of the utmost strategic importance for Hawkins to get possession of, or else he would lie at the mercy of the Spaniards who currently controlled the anchorage on the mainland. But such strategic considerations were not Hawkins's only worry. San Juan de Ulúa was a regular port of the Spanish treasure fleet, the *flota*, whose arrival was even now imminent. Hawkins had no wish whatsoever to risk a confrontation with the ships that represented the might and wealth of imperial Spain, but the state of his own flotilla was desperate and his only possible recourse was to gamble on making the necessary repairs in the ten or twelve days which he believed were left before the Spaniards might be expected to appear.

As his ships approached the port in line Hawkins did what he could to disguise and camouflage them. He ordered that all the crosses of St George be struck and the royal standard flown only from the height of the main topmast of the *Jesus* and the fore topmast of the *Minion*. The condition of these flags was so exhausted through foul weather that the Spaniards who came out of the port to greet the new arrivals, believing that they were the *flota* prematurely arrived, 'never perceived the lions and the flower de luces' until it was too late. The wretched defenders of the island were similarly duped, fired a salute and then, realising their mistake, tumbled pell-mell into their little boats and rowed hard for the mainland. The brilliance of Hawkins's ruse and the slovenliness of the enemy allowed him to gain the all-important island without loss or difficulty.

But the following morning made clear that their luck had been foiled by forces altogether beyond their control. The eleven large merchantmen and two escorting ships of war that made up the *flota* had made an unexpectedly swift passage from Spain and now hoved into view. Drake had his first glimpse of the might of Spanish sea power while, as he was soon to discover, aboard the Spanish flagship was no less a figure than Don Martin Enriquez de Almansa, the incoming Viceroy of New Spain. The position for Hawkins could hardly have been worse. He was the commander of some dreadfully battered ships which were rapidly coming within range of the enemy guns. If he sued for peace he would be at the Spaniards' mercy; if he refused their ships entrance to the port he would condemn the pride of Spain to the random and terrible violence of the north winds which, at this season in particular, blew across the region with destructive fury. Hawkins resolved that the only thing he could do was to allow the *flota* entrance to the harbour and then negotiate whatever terms he could.

The indignant Viceroy was obliged to parlay in order that he might gain his own port.[11] It was an insult beyond bearing, and Don Martin Enriquez was a man quickly moved to indignation – the very image of the poor, proud Catholic *hidalgo* whose sensitivities easily provoked conflict. Even the Inquisitor-General of Mexico, a man with whom he would soon be at daggers drawn, came to loathe him for what he called his exaggerated self-esteem, his hoarding of money and his 'exacting adoration' in the pettiest ways. How inevitable it was then that Hawkins, a mere heretic and a pirate, should be seen by the arrogant Don as an intolerable threat to all the divinely sanctioned power of Spain that he himself embodied. After all, had not the Spanish dreamed up an image of their ambitions which was known across the whole of Europe and their American territories, an image in which the Pillars of Hercules entwined with the motto *Plus Oultre* suggested how their empire would stretch further than that of Ancient Rome? And was this not God's wish? Providence, after all, had so arranged matters that vast stretches of Europe and the New World were in the Hapsburgs' hands. The wealth of conquered Mexico and Peru promised that it was only a matter of time before Spain and Catholicism would seize control of the whole world and the Spanish monarch would indeed be *dominus mundi* or, as the dictionaries phrased it, 'absolute lord and sole prince, who acknowledges no other'. Every other nation would be beholden to him.

But not, so it appeared, this pathetic little fleet of battered English ships manned by heretics who were now blocking Don Martin's way. It was galling in the extreme: an affront to God's evident will, to national pride, and to the invincible purity of Spanish blood, that *limpieza de sangre* which coursed through Don Martin's veins. But honour, it appeared, could only be salvaged by deceit. Don Martin was obliged to negotiate terms. He agreed with Hawkins that the English should indeed carry out the necessary work to their ships unmolested and even occupy the island while they did so, but, as he signed a letter agreeing to this, Don Martin resolved to break his word at the first opportunity. This act of Spanish treachery was to affect the rest of Drake's career – to convince him that Catholicism and deceit were alike of the devil's making – and so contribute with disproportionate importance to the mounting bitterness of the hostilities between England and Spain.

Having eventually anchored his fleet, the details of the treacherous plan were elaborated in Don Martin's cabin. It was agreed that at the earliest opportunity Spanish sailors would board the *Jesus* and the *Minion* from one of their merchantmen moored close by, while Spanish soldiers were to leap down from the ships in which they were stationed and take the island by surprise. The English would be overwhelmed. It was a desperate stratagem, and the necessary preparations and busy movement of their men revealed the Spaniards' deceit. Hawkins resolved to attack and a long, unequal battle raged from ten in the morning until four in the afternoon. The Spaniards' early attempts to capture the *Jesus* and the *Minion* were foiled, but the soldiers who now poured from the Spanish ships outnumbered the English on the island and easily overpowered them. This at once made it evident that the English would have to evacuate San Juan as soon as possible and Hawkins, hoping that he might steal away by night, concentrated the furious fire of the *Jesus* and the *Minion* on the two warships that had accompanied the *flota* in the hope of immobilising them. He was remarkably successful but he had no hope of regaining the all-important guns on the island that were now aimed at him. For all their power these failed to wreak extensive damage on either the *Jesus* or the *Minion*, but Hawkins's little ships fared far worse and only Drake's *Judith* got clear, dropping anchor at a safe distance and waiting to be called on as required.

With Drake anchored out of harm's way, Hawkins laboured valiantly to transfer essential victuals and valuables from the increasingly immobilised *Jesus*. He would save what he could. Encouraging his men with a toast of beer drunk from a silver cup, Hawkins put the goblet down only to see it immediately shot away. 'Fear nothing, for God, Who hath preserved me from this shot, will also deliver us from these traitors and villains,' he allegedly declared. But even now a Spanish fire ship was bearing down on him. This was the end. The desperate men on the doomed *Jesus* struggled to board the fleeing *Minion*, which eventually managed to sail out to safety and anchor in the neighbourhood of Drake and the *Judith*. These ships were the only survivors of the battle and their crews watched in awe and despair as the mighty *Jesus of Lubeck* flamed ever more desperately until the fire reached her powder store and she blew apart in a final agony of destruction. Her charred timbers sank and the silence of night fell on the desolation. Under the cloak of its secrecy desperate men made desperate plans. It was *sauve qui peut* and, as the dawn rose with merciless clarity, it became obvious to the company that Drake, forsaking his companions in their 'great misery', had gone, leaving Hawkins and his men to make for England as best they could.

2

The Caribbean Pirate

1570–1573

That Francis Drake abandoned John Hawkins at San Juan de Ulúa was a measure of the man. The act was clear, practical, realistic – and ruthless. Hawkins's ship was barely seaworthy and was, besides, under-victualled and overmanned. To sail back across the Atlantic in convoy would not have been to share the burden but to double it. Events would soon prove that the *Minion* was indeed a liability. A while after setting sail for England, conditions on board became so intolerable that Hawkins was obliged to make for the Mexican coast and there land roughly half of his crew before making for home. Some of these stranded men died, while others, falling into the hands of the Inquisition, were examined under hideous conditions of torture and then condemned either to the flames or the galleys, their only memorials being the written accounts of their confessions preserved by the Catholic authorities in their archives of pain. Many of those fortunate enough to escape so ghastly a fate died on the journey home and, in all, Hawkins's expedition lost about 300 men out of an original company of 400.

Many of those who did survive were men who sailed with Drake, and they owed their lives to a decision that was as wholly lacking in sentimentality as the sea itself. But if Drake's decision to sail alone was coldly practical, what did burn within him – and would continue to burn with undimmed ferocity for the rest of his life – was a loathing of Spain and what he was now convinced was irremediable Spanish duplicity. This hatred was deep and genuine and Drake would skilfully exploit it for his own fame and fortune. If the Spaniards were to pay for their treachery he would profit from it. In such ways as these Drake would grow enormously rich while, at the same time, consciously fashioning an image of himself as a Protestant national hero. He was at last coming into his own.

Drake's enemies were to make sure that his desertion of Hawkins at San Juan de Ulúa returned to haunt him during his periods of disfavour, but for the moment his priority was to get his men and his ship safely back to England. Having arrived, he faced the melancholy duty of telling William Hawkins of the desperate end of the enterprise and was at once despatched to London to inform the Queen and the rest of the investors about the shameless behaviour of the Spanish and what appeared to be the expedition's substantial losses. William Hawkins reckoned that these could be as much as £2,000 and drastic measures were taken to make them good. Early in December 1568 a Spanish fleet, sailing for the Netherlands and carrying all the wealth of the Crown payroll, was driven by storms into the English ports where the government at once confiscated the heavily filled chests of gold and silver. These were loaded on to packhorses and sent to London under the command of the newly returned John Hawkins who hoped to reimburse his failure from their contents. Hawkins put it about that he had lost £25,000 on his last expedition but, despite this, the Spanish Ambassador believed he had managed to salvage £7,000 worth of gold as well as secreting a small chest of pearls on the *Minion*.

How strained relations between Drake and Hawkins were at this time is unclear but, while it is probable that Drake too had suffered 'in the loss of his goods of some value', it is highly unlikely that these losses were offset by what the Spaniards many years later claimed was his theft of the gold that had been entrusted to him just before his flight from San Juan de Ulúa. Enemy propaganda was to play a great part in magnifying and distorting the legend of Francis Drake, and the Spaniards would eventually claim that Queen Elizabeth had thrown him in prison for his alleged crimes and only set him free when she came at last to believe the unlikely story that he had given the gold away to his sailors. What is altogether more certain is that, despite his losses, Drake now had sufficient funds to think about taking a wife since, on 4 July 1569, he married a certain Mary Newman in St Budeaux Parish Church near Plymouth.[1] It is just possible that her family originally came from London and that she might even have been the sister of one Harry Newman who had sailed with Drake on earlier expeditions. More than that is not known and the marriage was to prove childless, with Drake himself out of the country for much of its duration. This almost total lack of detail about Drake's private life is characteristic of his entire career, and such lacunae oblige us to concentrate almost exclusively on the public image he was now beginning assiduously to cultivate. Indeed, less than five months after his wedding, Drake was already sailing back to the West Indies on a reconnaissance trip largely funded by piracy and which he hoped would allow him 'to gain such intelligences as might further him to get some amends for his loss'. Drake's grievance against the Spanish was now apparently a personal one for it concerned his pocket. He was also determined that it should be given wide publicity. He was as adept as his enemies when it came to enhancing his image and was now deliberately fashioning himself as the wronged Protestant, the vengeful and patriotic enemy of Spain: an innocent, honest Englishman of great heart who would take on a mighty and evil enemy to nationwide acclaim.

But slaving in the manner practised by Hawkins was no longer the obvious way for Drake to make his fortune. A number of matters were becoming clear to those who had been stung by the failure of the last expedition. These included the Queen herself whose great flagship had been lost, an expense which, according to the terms of the original agreement, she herself would have to bear. But it was not only royal disappointment that put an end to slave trading. Hawkins's chosen methods of doing business in the Caribbean became that business's undoing. With the enthusiastic support of the Queen, who was fully aware of the advantages to be gained from showing the Spaniards the might of her naval power, Hawkins had mounted increasingly elaborate expeditions, the setting-up and operational costs of which had risen astronomically. His first rather modest but successful venture had probably cost no more than £2,000 and produced an entirely satisfactory rate of return. The initial outlay of £7,000 for the second expedition returned a profit in the region of 59 per cent, but the involvement of royal shipping and heavy armament was a considerable drain. For all the evidence that small, lightly armed expeditions were quite as successful as great displays of national intent, the failure of Lovell's voyage suggested to Hawkins at least that a huge armed presence was essential to cower the Spaniards into commercial submission and the result had been the financial failure of his last expedition. It is likely that this had cost over £10,000 to fit out and that the return was more or less the same. The great investors at court and in the City now believed there was no future in the slaving business, and English trade to the Caribbean fell into abeyance for the better part of three decades.

Drake, however, was neither so pessimistic nor so lacking in imagination and enterprise as to abandon all attempts to seize the riches of the West Indies. He had sailed to the Caribbean and seen something of the Spanish wealth that was there. He had suffered the loss of money and friends at Spanish hands and he was fired with a deep and increasingly nationalistic hatred of all things Spanish and Catholic.[2] This last was now endemic in the country at large and Drake could advance his reputation by drawing on the nation's deep wellspring of fear and loathing. It had become a commonplace in England that the Spaniards were motivated purely by bigotry, hypocrisy and vice, covering these with what was merely a thin veil of piety. They were, in fact, that most abhorred of people: atheists who used religion solely to set up the miseries of tyranny, exploitation and slavery. No single institution more flagrantly illustrated their evil designs than the Inquisition, and sensational stories blackened its reputation utterly. Foxe, as might be expected, led the way and the gloating anger of the *Book of Martyrs* dwells in detail on 'the distresses and horrors of the prison, the injuries, threats, whippings and scourgings, irons, tortures and racks' which the victims of the Inquisition endured. Their lives in jail were presented as a living death as they were 'detained there, some many years, and murdered by long torments, and whole days together treated more cruelly out of all comparison, than if they were in the hangman's hands to be slain all at once'. Indignation burned with particular fury when the victims were English sailors, and Drake was closely aware of the efforts a furious Hawkins was now making to free those members of his crew who had fallen into the hands of the Inquisition in Mexico and Spain. The result of these efforts was an extraordinary episode in the history of Anglo-Spanish mutual deceit.

In February 1570, Secretary Cecil received a letter from George Fitzwilliam, one of Hawkins's captured men, pleading for the government's help to get him and his companions released from a Spanish prison. Hawkins himself had several meetings with the Spanish Ambassador, Don Guereau de Spes, and Fitzwilliam was eventually freed. Fortuitously, the man's arrival in England was a moment of the utmost importance in the game of international espionage, for Cecil and Hawkins were well aware that Spain was even at that moment backing the Ridolfi plot which proposed, among other plans, an invasion of the country from the Netherlands by the dreaded Alba, the murder of Elizabeth, and the subsequent enthronement of Mary, Queen of Scots, who was to marry the Duke of Norfolk and then restore Catholicism to the country at large. Philip II, with that messianic imperialism that was all too often his substitute for policy, was wholeheartedly in support of the wildly impractical plan for regime change: 'I am so keen to achieve the consummation of this exercise,' he wrote to Alba, 'I am so attached to it in my heart, and I am so convinced that God our Saviour must embrace it as His own cause, that I cannot be dissuaded.' It was a time of real peril.[3]

The newly freed Fitzwilliam was sent back to Madrid as a double agent to liaise with Philip II about the possibility of an invasion. Hawkins himself meanwhile, drawing on his deep reserves of guile and knowledge of the Spaniards in order to trick them, began convincing de Spes that he was really a devout and even ardent Catholic who wanted nothing more than to have England ruled by a Catholic queen. To ensure that this would indeed happen he promised that his and his family's sixteen ships and crews would desert to Spain the moment Alba set sail. Those who needed to be gulled fell completely for the plan. De Spes certainly was hood-winked and his correspondence with his King was such that Philip sent Hawkins a patent of Spanish nobility, a pardon for his recent activities off San Juan de Ulúa, and even a promise of money for the maintenance of his ships. More than this, Hawkins was made privy to the invasion plans, which he passed straight to Cecil. That was enough. The conspirators confessed, Norfolk was executed, and de Spes went home in disgrace.

It was all very neat and satisfactory, but men like Drake knew perfectly well what they and the country were still up against. The Spanish and Catholic threat was everywhere: in the dungeons of the Inquisition where Drake's colleagues were suffering, in the houses of the great Catholic nobles of England where more plots were being hatched and, most frighteningly of all, across the Channel in the Netherlands where Alba and his menacing army had subdued a Protestant people with such ruthless and efficient severity that their behaviour had become a byword for Catholic atrocities. The result was an important shift in politics. England's traditional and long-standing Spanish connections were all but completely severed and a militantly pro-Protestant group emerged in the Privy Council to which Drake himself would eventually become attached. In the meantime, as English policy began to look favourably at the activities of Protestants in France, Drake understood that the Queen and Secretary Cecil were sufficiently convinced of the need to take offensive action against Catholic Europe that they were prepared, stretched as their resources were, to provide money and arms to the Protestant French pirates operating out of La Rochelle. When the Spaniards responded to such actions by seizing English property in the Netherlands, an unofficial war of reprisal broke out and English pirates led the English attack.

Drake's time, it seemed, had come. He was himself an experienced pirate, albeit a pirate who had mostly learned his trade with the Hawkinses around the coastal waters of northern Europe. Perhaps now, in the Caribbean, little ships such as he was familiar with could succeed in harassing the Spaniards where the great ones had failed. One or two small instruments of war could strike terror into the heart of a great empire's world trade. The Queen would almost certainly turn a blind eye to activities she could not officially condone, and perhaps, too, a little man could make himself rich by acts of outright plunder and theft. National pride and rampant self-interest began to meld in Drake's mind and, as we have seen, by the closing months of 1569 he was ready to test the Caribbean waters once again. For all that war between England and Spain had not been officially declared, there is no question that armed robbery by land and sea was Drake's principal intention and evidence is wholly lacking to suggest that he felt any qualms of conscience about this. After all, piracy had long been part of his adopted family's business and there was, as he would always assert, the outrage at San Juan de Ulúa to avenge. This notion that Drake was acting very largely from righteous indignation when he went raiding in the Caribbean became deeply embedded in the image he presented of himself and, in its turn, conditioned the way his contemporaries and immediate successors viewed his achievements. The image nonetheless presented a problem to those who wished to portray Drake not only as a great man of action but also as a devoutly Protestant hero. Piracy and piety are, after all, uneasy companions but there were those who sought to reconcile them.

Intellectuals such as Thomas Fuller, writing their books after Drake's death and in the effort to shape national consciousness, were not above a certain moral sleight of hand when they addressed such issues.[4] The events at San Juan de Ulúa were legitimately useful to them; Drake's genuine desire to avenge an affront could be read as the praiseworthy action of a gentleman (or would-be gentleman) restoring his honour along with that of his country and his kin. But a wash of pious approval was also desirable, and with no more authority than his own say-so Fuller declared that, during what was presumably the homeward journey of the *Judith*, 'Drake was persuaded by the minister of his ship that he might lawfully recover in value of the King of Spain, and repair his losses on him anywhere else.' Under certain circumstances robbery with violence was acceptable to the Church, and ecclesiastical support for such acts had obvious advantages. Nonetheless, when Fuller tried to explain the reasoning behind his approval he was obliged to be witty rather than morally rigorous. 'The case,' he declared, 'was clear in sea-divinity, and few are such infidels, as not to believe doctrines which make for their own profit.'

It seemed that Drake the 'poor private man' could (if he had any qualms about the matter in the first place) legitimately revenge himself on the King of Spain and make himself wealthy in the process. If this was not quite a rags-to-riches story it nonetheless had all the allure of the tale of a man magnificently self-made, and this was the image of himself that Drake was constantly to promote with an unblushing lack of modesty. His ego expanded in proportion to his success, but there was more to it than this. If Drake was the shamelessly parvenu hero of his own drama, he was also the little guy who took on the giant and won. Drake against Philip II was, in the popular imagination, David against Goliath, and just as the stripling shepherd saved the Chosen People from Philistine tyranny, so the English pirate saved a Protestant people from the clutches of rapacious Catholic evil and a monarch who, in Fuller's words, 'not content that the sun riseth and setteth in his dominions, may seem to desire to make all his own where he shineth'. Drake's success against such overwhelming odds could be seen by some at least as nothing less than miraculous – quite literally so since Fuller and his con-temporaries, devout and intelligent people as they unquestionably were, chose to find the workings of the hand of God in Drake's achievements. His fame and wealth were to be understood as the blessings showered on an individual and a nation alike when a stout-hearted Protestant, 'standing on the mount of God's providence', put his trust in the Lord of Hosts. In such ways plunder and piety could indeed be reconciled and the pirate and terrorist could become an almost saintly figure in the drama of the nation's salvation.

In the meantime, and whether saint or sinner, Drake had to make the necessary preparations for the first of the expeditions to the Caribbean that he himself was to captain. Not a great deal is known about this initial voyage but it seems that Drake sailed in a flotilla of three ships owned by William Hawkins. He went first to Guinea for slaves before John Hawkins, who had accompanied him thus far, returned to England and he himself headed for the Caribbean. It is probable that Drake's slaves were sold once he arrived, but what is altogether more certain is that his quick intelligence appreciated the changes that were occurring in the region and that he saw how these might be exploited to his advantage. He noted in particular that his

French rivals had developed a highly effective technique whereby small rowing boats, launched quickly and quietly from a mother ship, could make devastatingly effective raids on the Spaniards and then return whence they had come while the Spanish sought them out in vain. This was a threatening development, and the Spaniards themselves were beginning to feel that their once easy grip on the region's wealth was being seriously weakened, if not actually wrenched from their grasp.

Drake's second expedition, launched the following year, showed him precisely what he could achieve by small-scale piratical attacks in the French manner.[5] He sailed out to the West Indies in a little 25-ton pinnace called the *Swan* which was probably part of a larger flotilla organised by a group of West Country entrepreneurs that included William Hawkins. It appears that, in addition to the *Swan*, they provided a mother ship which was anchored off Cape Cativa. This was a useful point from which joint expeditions of English and French pirates could reconnoitre and launch raids around that part of the Isthmus of Panama – an area which included the settlements of Nombre de Dios, Puerto Bello and Panama itself, as well as the Chagres River along whose banks the citizens of Panama had set up two trading posts. These were relatively substantial operations where goods were stored during the dry season when the Chagres itself was too low for navigation by large vessels. At that time of the year the only practical way of reaching either outpost was by small rowed galleys, whose use in piracy the French had perfected. Drake now joined the French on a daring raid. Guided by an escaped Negro, or *cimarrone*, called Pedro Mandinga, thirty-two oars rowed the armed men towards their prey.

For all he was to prove untrustworthy, the presence of Mandinga is interesting for it suggests exactly how threatened the Spanish really were. While pirates from England and France were sailing openly to the Caribbean to harass their trade, escaped Negroes and Indian slaves proved an equally dangerous and uncontainable threat. The anxious citizens of Panama had already sent letters to Madrid which told how these *cimarrones* were inflicting heavy damage in robbery and death on an almost daily basis. Many of these people (who numbered over 3,000 in all) were living either in a large settlement far to the east of Panama or in hideouts concealed in the inhospitable mountains. From there, they could launch raids (often in combination with French pirates) on the road between Nombre de Dios and Panama, or on the traffic that plied the Chagres River. A force of 150 Spanish soldiers was supposed to keep this enemy in check but the task proved expensive and unavailing. The authorities began to fear the worst. They believed it was entirely possible that the *cimarrones* might indeed join forces with both the English and the French, and there were ominous, frightened mutterings about an unwinnable war and about conquest and the loss of Peru. These were possibilities that Drake himself was even now considering.

In the meantime, he was to prove to his own satisfaction that there were rich pickings to be had and much damage easily to be done, albeit on a smaller scale. A little Spanish vessel was seized and its contents looted, thereby allowing the pirates to return to their mother ship with a considerable prize. They did so in complete safety since Drake and his colleagues took the precaution of stoving in the bottoms of Spanish boats moored in the vicinity which might have followed or reported them. It was all so easy – too easy in fact – for it was at this point that Mandinga chose to desert the English and French and retreat to Panama where the Captain General of the Indies fleet very soon learned about what was going on. He resolved to attack, pursued the pirates' vessels, and obliged their crews to abandon three of their captured frigates along with a considerable quantity of valuable goods.

Nothing daunted, Drake resolved to continue his activities, savagely attacking a poorly defended Spanish frigate whose terrified passengers and crew eventually cut its moorings and allowed it to drift towards the swampy shore. There it was abandoned to the enemy who seized its goods as soon as they had tackled a second Spanish frigate which even then came into view. Not content with merely stealing such prizes as these, the English were determined to add insult to injury and left behind a defiant note which has all the characteristics of Drake's own bravado. The note outrageously accused the Spanish of being responsible for their own misfortunes since they refused to negotiate honourably and courteously with those whose sole business was, in fact, to wreck their trade. The note made it perfectly clear that the English attitude was one of open and undaunted defiance from men who claimed to be 'well disposed, if there be no cause to the contrary'. Were the Spanish to persist in defending themselves however, 'we will be devils rather than men'.

And such indeed Drake and his crew now strove to be. A successful raid was launched against the nearer of the two Spanish warehouses on the Chagres and considerable quantities of clothing and merchandise were stolen. Little Spanish ships, that had hurriedly weighed anchor in the hope of reporting the outrage to the authorities, were seized and their bottoms were again stoved in so that no alarm could be given. Able now to operate in comparative safety, Drake and his men easily picked off the numerous richly loaded river boats innocently sailing to the raided warehouse. They came by so much booty thereby that they were obliged to use captured vessels to transport their sudden wealth. All the Spaniards could do was wring their hands and lament how the English, 'Did rob divers barks that were transporting of merchandise of forty thousand ducats and velvets and taffetas, besides other merchandise with gold and silver.' It seemed that there was nothing they could do to protect themselves, and an exhilarated Drake realised that he had found a highly effective way of greatly enriching himself while causing distress to his country's enemies. Having established a base, which he called Port Pheasant, for his future use, an exultant Drake sailed back to England with prizes worth in the region of £100,000.

All of this wealth had been seized with a blatant disregard for legality but, if the law could be flouted in the Indies, matters might yet be more delicate in England. Arrived at Plymouth, Drake waited offshore while a messenger was sent to London to inform the authorities of what he had achieved and to establish whether Her Majesty would indeed turn the expected blind eye to it. After all, he had sailed without her authority. No letters of reprisal had been issued to Drake or to anyone else. England and Spain were not official enemies, but to condone Drake's actions even tacitly was to admit that the atmosphere of mutual hostility was growing ever more tense. To Drake's delight no objections were forthcoming from the Crown and the international atmosphere began to darken towards a storm. By the time Drake was ready to launch his next expedition that storm was ready to rage with unparalleled fury across the North Sea and southward to the Canaries, the Azores, over the Atlantic to the Caribbean and into those seas where Drake himself was determined to be master.

Drake's third expedition to the West Indies set sail on 24 May 1572, with Drake himself as Captain of the *Pascoe* and his brother John in charge of the little *Swan*.[6] The crew, with the exception of a man of fifty, were all aged under thirty: vigorous, strong, and ardent enough easily to shoulder the strains and dangers of whatever they might face. Drake himself had been careful to provision the voyage as thoroughly as he could, providing not only victuals and clothing for a whole year but also 'all manner of munition, artillery, artificers, stuff and tools that were requisite'. Having become thoroughly familiar with the skills of the French pirates, he also had three pinnaces made — small, two-masted, shallow draught vessels with auxiliary oars. These were stowed aboard in pieces so that they could be reassembled when called for. Clearly Drake meant business and his plan was on a scale with his ambition. He knew that the goods stored in the easily raided warehouses along the Chagres were destined for Nombre de Dios. He also knew that it was from this port that the greater part of Spain's South American bullion was shipped after its onerous overland passage from Panama. His plan was nothing less than to sack Nombre de Dios and steal its immense store of treasure. This silver was the lifeblood of the Spanish war effort and to cut off its flow would be to threaten the very heart of the enemy's enterprise. The idea would become an obsession and Drake would return constantly to it throughout his career. If he were to succeed, then he would hugely enrich himself while savagely attacking the Spaniards in their pocket, their pride and their power.

Landing on a rocky island off Dominica, Drake ordered his ships to remain there for three days while his men had a necessary rest and collected fresh mountain water in barrels. That done, the expedition was ready to sail on towards the mainland. Skirting Santa Marta, where he knew he would not be welcome, Drake made for the base he had established the year before and named Port Pheasant after the abundance of game to be caught there. The ships arrived within six days of setting out but found that the natural fertility of the soil had resulted in the base becoming so overgrown as to be barely recognisable. Drake was determined to land all the same and gave orders to his brother as to what to do should Spaniards from nearby Tolu or Nombre de Dios appear while he was away. As Drake was rowed to the shore, however, it became increasingly clear that all was not well. Not only was the fort overgrown but he could see smoke rising from the woods. Alerted to potential danger, he ordered armed men from a second boat to accompany him in case the Spanish were lurking nearby. Exactly what had happened was only too obvious when the landing party came upon an enormous tree to which a plate of lead was nailed. The Spanish had indeed been at Port Pheasant, and the inscription scratched on the plate by a passing English sailor informed Drake that they had stolen everything he had left there and advised him to 'make haste away'.

That was not Drake's style. He had determined to reassemble his prefabricated pinnaces at Port Pheasant and was not minded to change his plans. The pinnaces were duly brought ashore and the carpenters were ordered to busy themselves with them while Drake and the rest of his men set about building new fortifications. The entire company began 'felling ... great trees and bowsings and haling them together with great pulleys and hawsers' until, in a week, they had built a strong pentagonal stockade some thirty feet high. This was an impressive achievement and, to make assurance double sure, Drake constructed a single gate on the seaboard side 'which every night (that we might sleep in more safety and security) was shut up, with a great tree drawn athwart it'. Drake and his crew were now ready for action and had by this time been joined by an English bark out of the Isle of Wight. It was captained by James Raunce, who had sailed both on Lovell's expedition and on Hawkins's third voyage. Raunce had recently captured a Spanish caravel bound for Nombre de Dios along with another, lesser boat and, meeting up, the two pirates joined forces once they had agreed terms. Port Pheasant had been made defensible, Drake had increased the size of his flotilla and, prepared for the plundering that was his real purpose, he now set sail to reconnoitre Nombre de Dios, agreeing with Raunce to divide the spoils between them.

So far everything had proceeded satisfactorily and it seemed that the expedition's luck was still in when they arrived at the Isle of Pines to find two frigates being loaded with timber by a band of Negro slaves. Fully aware that the men loathed their masters as deeply as Drake himself did, he made the slaves his prisoners and questioned them closely. As suspicious of their new captors as they were of their old, the Negroes told Drake they believed that Nombre de Dios was undefended, adding that there was nonetheless an artillery battery on a hill to the east. They also said they had heard a report of soldiers having recently been despatched by the Governor of Panama to defend the town against the threat of the *cimarrones* who, a mere six weeks before, had attacked it. What the Negroes did not tell Drake was that the treasure fleet which annually anchored at Nombre de Dios and which was his real prize had already departed and that the immense treasure stored in the town was on its way to Spain.

Drake returned to Port Pheasant to prepare his raid, unaware that his principal prize was beyond his reach. Fifty-three of his own men and twenty more of Captain Raunce's were readied, and it was agreed that Raunce himself would stay behind to secure the rear while Drake moved on to the town. Further preparations had to be made, however. Arrived at the island of Cativas, Drake ordered his men to disembark, divided them into two companies, and set about drilling and training them in the use of the armaments with which they were going to sack Nombre de Dios. In addition, he ordered his two drummers and two trumpeters to practise on the instruments which, it was hoped, would instill fear into the townspeople even while exciting the valour of Drake's own men who, he now decided, needed a pep talk. 'Exhorting them after his manner, he declared the greatness of the hope of good things that was there, the weakness of the town, being unwalled, and the hope he had of prevailing to recompense his wrongs, especially now that he should come with such a crew, who were like-minded with himself.'

With excitement mounting high, Drake pointed his little raiding party towards Nombre de Dios, hugging the shore so that he would not be seen by the Spaniards.[7] Then, under the cover of darkness, he ordered his men to row as hard and as quietly as possible to the outlying point of the harbour. Once there, and under orders to preserve utter silence, the men rested themselves for the purposed attempt on the town the following dawn. But the little force was uneasy at the prospect before them and the silence that had been imposed was ever more loudly broken by their murmurings about the size of the town and how strong the enemy inside might be. Realising that action was the only cure for such uncertainty Drake, with that decisive improvisation which was the hallmark of his genius, took advantage of the rising moon and began the assault straight away. It was three in the morning. Moving between a Spanish ship and the town itself so that the enemy aboard the Spanish vessel could give no easy warning to the sleeping townsfolk, Drake and his men gained the port and dismounted the defensive guns while the gunner manning them fled. But the town, barely recovered from its recent assault at the hands of a Negro army, was almost immediately aware of the English presence and the great bell of the church rang out maniacally as warning Spanish drums thundered up and down the streets.

The cacophony of terror continued while Drake marched up the hill east of the town where, finding that contrary to the report of the Negroes, there were no artillery emplacements, he regrouped his men and marched them back to the central plaza. Meanwhile, the forces under the command of his brother John circled about and approached the plaza from an easterly direction. They hoped the town square would be their killing field. The terrified population of some forty people – men and women, black and white – were by now assembled on the southern side of the plaza and pathetically ordered two or three of their arquebusiers to march up and down as if they were expecting reinforcements. The men were chased away as Drake ordered the guns on his pinnaces to fire at the plaza while he himself concentrated on its southern side and the fearful citizens gathered there. Frightened, surprised, and dragged from their beds, they nonetheless managed to kill one of Drake's trumpeters and even to wound Drake himself at the very moment when his brother appeared to help him drive the enemy out of the town and along the road to Panama. The musket ball that hit Drake was to remain lodged in his leg for the rest of his life, a part of his legend altogether more real than the published account of the events that now supposedly took place in Nombre de Dios.

This marvellous fabrication (or downright lie) tells how, once his men had returned to the marketplace, Drake ordered two captured Spaniards to take them all to the Governor's house where the immense wealth of the New World was customarily unloaded before everything except the silver was removed to the treasury. When the men got to their destination (Drake's wound by this time bleeding profusely) the great door of the Governor's house stood open and a candle was flickering at the top of the stairs. Its frail, wavering light revealed riches beyond belief: a pile of silver bars seventy feet long, ten feet wide and twelve feet high, each bar weighing at least thirty-five pounds. It was an Elizabethan dream come true but the agonised Drake, with exemplary and uncharacteristic self-restraint, supposedly ordered his men not to touch the treasure, bidding them remember instead there were armed enemies all about and adding that there was more gold in the as yet unraided treasury than their four pinnaces could easily carry away. They would seize the silver when the time was right. But that time, of course, never came. Apparently Drake received a message which told how the men in his pinnaces were being menaced by soldiers. A band of Englishmen was sent off to investigate as a sudden and torrential rainstorm burst over Nombre de Dios, ruining bowstrings and gunpowder alike. There were mutterings of retreat among the English, but Drake would have none of it. He had, he said, 'brought them to the mouth of the treasure of the world'. They should bide their time.

The chronicle tells how they waited for half an hour while the storm abated its fury, after which a party was duly despatched to the treasury. As Drake prepared to set off, however, he fainted through loss of blood. At the very moment of his supposed triumph he was suddenly speechless and enfeebled. It was an appalling situation. His wound was now bleeding so copiously that his blood 'filled the very prints that our footsteps made' – a marvellous detail. His men wondered how he had survived at all and gathered loyally around him. They begged him to let them carry him back to his vessel where his wound could be dressed. He demurred, they protested, and finally got their way. Heedless of the wealth of Croesus, the chronicle says that Drake's loyal men carried their leader to the safety of his boat, confident that he and he alone could lead them to other riches and knowing that without him they were lost.

This is a compelling story – the very essence of Elizabethan derring-do – and, as we have seen, is wholly or very largely untrue. It seems that Drake himself invented it near the end of his life when he was in disgrace with the Queen and desperate to regain her favour. It was a blatant effort to exploit his legendary prowess and exalt his own myth, but Elizabeth, if she read the manuscript (which is extremely unlikely) was not a woman to be bamboozled. Subsequent generations were more credulous. With the publication of *Sir Francis Drake Revived* in 1626, the supposed incident at Nombre de Dios entered the national memory. The publisher's hype guaranteed the work's authenticity,[8] and there was no reason to question it. After all, as the title page boldly claimed, the book had been prepared for the press by Drake's nephew 'now living'. The reports of two members of the expedition itself had been taken down by a preacher and used in its compilation. Above all, the text had been 'reviewed' by Drake himself 'and much holpen and enlarged, by divers notes, with his own hand here and there inserted'.

What could be better? The story had never been told before and was, besides, just the sort of publication the times seemed to call for. Charles I had recently ascended the throne and might be persuaded to become another Elizabeth to encourage the nation's explorers. Something was needed to encourage them. The title page of *Sir Francis Drake Revived* suggested the 1620s were 'a dull or effeminate age'. They required all the pep they could get. Peace had long ago been concluded with the Spaniards and, for all the slow but significant advances made in the setting up of an English trading empire, there had been some dispiriting reverses. Three years before, the massacre of English merchants in Amboyna had outraged everyone and seemed to many the reason why the English had decided to withdraw from the profitable Moluccas trade. A year after this the Virginia Company had collapsed, spoiling business with North America. In such an atmosphere, Drake's supposedly heroic deeds at Nombre de Dios might well inspire men to great things again.

As so often, the Drake myth was thought of as useful to the nation: a rallying call to fearless courage, heroic deeds and self-justifying aggressive virility. The story was relished for generations, and it was only in the early part of the twentieth century that a search through a less glamorous treasury – the Spanish archives – found that the incident at Nombre de Dios was largely a fantasy. The documents, unread for generations, made clear the chillingly unromantic fact that the Spanish treasure fleet had sailed some while before Drake's arrival and, as a result, when he got to Nombre de Dios he found it was bare. The silver ingots glimmered in imagination only. Far from being a glorious episode from a heroic age, the incident exposed embarrassingly poor preparation and, for all that Drake and his fleeing company tried to make up for it by stealing the wine they found aboard a ship in the harbour, it turned out that the wine was worth so little that its owner offered a derisory reward for its return.

The citizens of Nombre de Dios fired a parting shot as Drake and his men retreated to the nearby island of Bastimentos. Under other circumstances the two days spent there would have been a time of idyllic rest amid the flourishing gardens and the plump, delicious poultry with which the place abounded, but Drake himself was in an unenviable position. He was the wounded commander of a failed expedition which was surrounded by enemies and now had no clear objectives. It was difficult to know what to do. After a while the Governor of Nombre de Dios arrived to parlay and a sort of peace was patched up, but deep anxieties denied Drake any real relaxation or, more importantly, any clear and decisive planning. The position was worrying indeed. Drake had equipped an expedition which he had hoped would return to England rich with spoils. He had achieved no such thing. Instead, several of his crewmen had been wounded and one killed in an assault that had not only been humiliatingly inglorious but, as it now appeared, badly planned. It would be difficult to keep up the morale of his men in such circumstances and difficult as well to maintain his own.

Various possibilities offered themselves but none could be firmly resolved upon. A captured Negro called Diego who was with them suggested to Drake that they would be able to plunder huge quantities of silver and gold if they enlisted the help of his fellow *cimarrones*. But there was a problem with this. Diego confessed he was despised by his own people since he had too often been obliged to betray them to his Spanish masters. Indeed, they would kill him if they ever captured him alive. Nonetheless, he urged, if Drake protected him all might yet be well because he knew that the commander's name was highly honoured among the Negro warriors. It was a possibility and the plan was discussed, but there seemed to be much against it. To be sure, Drake knew with what ferocity the *cimarrones* could fight, but if their courage was not in question their reliability was. The information they had given about the condition of Nombre de Dios had been partial and inaccurate, and the Negro who had guided Drake and his allies down the Chagres the previous year had deserted them to their cost. Diego might well do the same.

Raids along the Chagres itself nonetheless remained a possibility. They had proved eminently profitable before and Drake sent a party off to investigate. Then, still unresolved, he gave orders that the rest of his men should quit Bastimentos and make for their ships still moored off Port Pheasant and the Island of Pines. When they got there Drake's conversation with Captain Raunce was dispiriting. Raunce raised objections to lingering any longer on so perilous a coast, but this was almost certainly a mere excuse. Drake had returned a failure. His competence was not all it seemed to be and there was, besides, a dangerous suggestion of bad luck about him. When the crew sent to explore the possibilities of raiding along the Chagres returned without encouraging news, Drake and Raunce parted company. Drake and his men were now alone on a hostile shore and something needed to be done. But what? It was impossible for them merely to stay where they were and sit idle and depressed. They must go somewhere, and Drake eventually gave orders that they should set sail for Cartagena. There might yet be good raiding to be had there.

There was not. Drake left his ships moored off the little island at the entrance to the harbour and went forward with his pinnaces. A frigate was riding at anchor and the one old man who was aboard told the English that the rest of the crew had gone ashore to fight about a mistress. More usefully, the old man said that a large merchant ship out of Seville was to be found round the next point, where she was unloading prior to setting sail for Santo Domingo the following morning. The old man was forcibly taken aboard Drake's pinnace and rowed to where he said the Spanish ship might be found. She was indeed where he had said she was, but when the crew aboard asked where Drake and his men had come from and were told that they had rowed out from Nombre de Dios, they were not believed. The English nonetheless ranged their pinnaces for boarding: one on the Spaniards' starboard bow, another on the starboard quarter, and Drake's own vessel in the midship on the larboard side. High though the Spanish vessel was, it was eventually boarded and the crew retreated to the hold with all their weapons. Drake and his men nimbly set about cutting the mooring cables and then, securing the ship to their pinnaces, proceeded to tow the prize out of the harbour. But their courage was foiled. The watch at Cartagena had seen what was happening and raised the alarm, ringing church bells, shooting off great guns and sending men on horse and foot to discharge their calivers at the English pirates who now cut their ropes and retreated to the outer anchorage with all possible speed. From there, the following day, they had the meagre satisfaction of capturing some Spanish despatch boats and tossing their mails into the sea before burning the vessels themselves.

The position was now growing desperate and called for desperate measures. Leadership had to be shown and Drake found the idea that he might ally himself with the *cimarrones* increasingly appealing. He had also convinced himself that his expedition needed to be leaner and meaner. Two ships were one too many and the little *Swan* would have to go.[9] He knew that such a decision would be hugely unpopular with the crew who, as was the wont of sailors, had grown fond of the ship and vested their loyalty in it. If Drake were to get his way then he would have to do so by deceit. He sent for Thomas Moone, the carpenter on the *Swan*, and took him into his cabin where he gave him his orders. In the middle of the second night watch Moone was to creep secretly down into the well of the *Swan* and bore three large holes near her keel; he would then cover them over so that the rising water would be neither seen nor heard as it began dragging the hapless vessel down to the ocean bed. Moone was appalled. What Drake was asking him to do was commit an act of gratuitous vandalism to a fine and erstwhile lucky ship. If the *Swan*'s crew found out what Moone had done they would kill him. Drake knew it was absolutely necessary for him to override the man and win, if not his confidence, then at least his obedience. He turned the full force of his personality on him, gave Moone his reasons for what he was doing, told him that no one would find out until the time was right, and so got his way.

For deceit to be effective it had to be cloaked in jollity. The next morning Drake declared he would go fishing and had himself rowed over to the *Swan* to collect the Captain – his brother John. Would John like to go fishing with him? A request from Drake was invariably in the nature of a command and, as the two men were rowed off with their rods and lines, Drake asked his brother why his ship was riding so low in the water. A messenger was quickly despatched to find out. The steward of the ship, wet to his waist, cried out that the vessel was full of water. It was extraordinary. The crew had barely needed to pump it out twice in the last six weeks but now the water was man-high in the hold. John Drake asked his brother's permission to leave the fishing expedition and deal with the crisis.

He was given this and, when Drake returned with the fish they were to eat for supper, he found to his secret satisfaction that the desperate labours of the crew at the *Swan*'s pumps had achieved nothing more than merely keeping the ship afloat. The maximum amount of water the pumps could discharge was a mere eighteen inches and, with most of the crew so occupied, there was no conceivable hope of finding where the damage lay and repairing it. Drake disingenuously asked the men what they thought should be done and, as he had gambled, received a vote of confidence in reply. The men would do as he thought best. It was now time for a display of apparently magnanimous and decisive leadership. Drake proposed that his brother should be made Captain of the surviving ship, the *Pascoe*, while he himself would sail in one of the pinnaces until they had captured a frigate which Drake could use as his own

62

vessel. As for the *Swan*, she was obviously in a hopeless state and the best thing to do was to salvage her valuables and then burn her so that she would not fall into Spanish hands. The bewildered company agreed and the *Swan* was fired that night.

The following day the *Pascoe* made for the Gulf of Darien. There the crew were able to moor in relative safety and build a fort, after which Drake and two of the pinnaces explored the Rio Grande while the third, commanded by his brother John and with the African Diego aboard, sought out the *cimarrones*. But still things were against them. Drake's expedition up the Rio Grande was physically exhausting and largely fruitless. The current was flowing in the wrong direction and when his exhausted men disembarked to rest for the night they were drenched by a violent storm. Once this had passed, clouds of mosquitos rose up and bit the men so badly that they were deprived of sleep. The following morning they nonetheless took to their oars and eventually spied some houses on the farther bank of the river which turned out to belong to a lone Spaniard. Believing the Englishmen to be his compatriots the man signalled for them to come over. Then, realising his mistake, he took to his heels and allowed Drake and his crew to steal his supply of bacon, sweetmeats, jams and delicious cheese which had been intended as luxury goods for the Spanish market. With their pinnaces loaded with dainties, Drake and his men turned round and drifted back to their base.

Arrived there, a little piracy produced a further supply of victuals. These were stored in huts built with the help of the African Diego, who had now returned with John Drake from his expedition to liaise with the *cimarrones*. Diego had been as good as his word and had been able to persuade his fellow Negroes that it was to their advantage to join in with Drake and his assaults on the mutually detested Spaniards. This, as we have seen, was precisely what the Spaniards themselves most feared. The Municipal Council in Panama wrote at once to Madrid in the most urgent terms declaring 'this league between the English and the Negroes is very detrimental to this kingdom, because, being so thoroughly acquainted with the region and so expert in the bush, the Negroes will show them methods and means to accomplish any evil design they may wish to carry out'. This was precisely what was to happen. The Spaniards' worst fears were being realised. Now, as two 'very sensible' *cimarrones* came back with John Drake to confirm their chief's decision to join with the English, Drake began to reformulate his plans. After a careful and circumspect conversation, he decided that he, his brother and the two Negroes should set out that very evening for the warriors' settlement where the rest of the crew and their ship would follow them. From now on the idea of an alliance with the *cimarrones* would be central to Drake's strategic thinking.[10]

When all was ready Drake entertained his African allies aboard the *Pascoe*. The occasion was satisfying to both parties, the *cimarrones* 'rejoicing that they should have some fit opportunity to wreak their wrongs on the Spaniards, we hoping that now our voyage should be bettered'. It would have been bettered very quickly if the *cimarrones* had been able to show Drake how he could lay his hands on some gold and silver. This, the *cimarrones* said, they could have done at any time but the present. Not living by a cash economy, they stole treasure from the Spanish merely to spite them and then hid it in the rivers. These, however, were now in full spate because of the rainy season and it was quite impossible to retrieve any of the booty concealed under the surging waters. The rainy season was also responsible for the fact that the Spaniards did not transport any of their treasure by land at this time of the year and so shore-based raiding parties on the treasure trains were out of the question. Five months of relative inactivity had been imposed on the English and the *cimarrones* alike, and the next two weeks were spent building a great triangular fort which was left in John Drake's care while Francis took the pinnaces off to Cartagena in search of prizes.

He was hardly any luckier than he had been before and he was, besides, badly prepared. A second journey up the Rio Grande yielded nothing, while the inhabitants of Santa Marta, alerted to his coming, fired a warning shot that sent Drake and his pinnaces hurrying for the open sea. Discipline, if not at breaking point, was by now severely strained. The men were moving about aimlessly in cold, wet weather on leaky boats and, with provisions running low, were restlessly and ravenously hungry. On one of the pinnaces eighteen men were reduced to surviving on a gammon and thirty pounds of biscuit. The others were hardly better provided. This was the sort of crisis which, as Drake himself was aware, could only be surmounted by the force of his own personality and perhaps a resort to the Divine. This is what he had seen Hawkins do years before. He now chided his dismayed and disgruntled men by telling them that if he could put up with such a situation so could they, and that they should, besides, 'depend upon God's almighty Providence, which never faileth them that trusteth in Him'.

God and Drake combined were sufficient to silence the grumbling, and the hungry men set off for Curacao where, it seemed, Drake's prayers were almost immediately rewarded. A Spanish sail was spied to westward. For all her firing her guns across the storm-swollen seas, the exhausted and hungry men in the pinnaces pursued her for two hours until the storm abated and allowed them to board. They found the vessel 'laden with victual well powdered and dried, which at that present we received as sent us of God's great mercy'. It was, perhaps, a case of God helping those who help themselves, but even now the joy and the relief were short-lived, for death was stalking the expedition in several guises. The famished and wearied men aboard the pinnaces began to fall ready victims to disease and Charles Glub, one of the quartermasters, died of a malady his suffering mates could not identify but blamed on the cold and hunger they were all enduring. Then, when the expedition finally returned to base, Drake learned that his brother John had been killed in a reckless attack on a Spanish ship. Nothing suggests that Drake experienced the death as a personal tragedy (family loyalty and family sentiment were emotions which, in his hardness, he had long ago learned to distance at will) but it would later become clear that he was determined to get his hands on the greater part of his brother's estate, despite the fact that John left a young widow behind him.

For the moment, however, Drake's ruthless pursuit of personal wealth was threatened by the sickness of his crew. They were being attacked by an epidemic of what was probably yellow fever, some ten men falling ill at the turn of the New Year. Most of them died within a couple of days. As more and more men fell sick, Drake found himself the commander of a weakened expedition marooned in an unfavourable season on a remote and hostile coast. After a second of his brothers, Joseph, had died in his arms, Drake ordered the expedition's surgeon to cut open his body in order that the cause of the fatal illness 'might be better discerned and consequently remedied to the relief of others'. The corpse was duly given an autopsy but the surgeon, even as he reported that Joseph's liver was swollen and his heart 'sodden', contracted the disease he was supposed to diagnose and fell down dead four days later. Fatalities were mounting alarmingly, and it seemed that only Drake's huge and pitiless reserves of willpower would see him and his surviving men through.

It was clearly essential that the men be got away from the multiplying horrors of what they now called 'Slaughter Island'. Harassed by death, weakness and misfortune though they were, captain and crew had sailed from England with the sole purpose of winning booty from the Spaniards by piracy, and nothing would weaken Drake's resolve to do so. His crew had recently captured a Spanish provision frigate whose presence confirmed the *cimarrones'* reports that the treasure fleet had now arrived in Nombre de Dios. Drake determined to intercept the Spanish treasure train as it lumbered its painful away along the Nombre de Dios road. He knew perfectly well he could achieve nothing without the help of the *cimarrones*, however, and having taken their advice about what weapons, victuals and clothing they should supply themselves with, Drake and an ardent and desperate little band of eighteen English-men and thirty Africans set off on the long and arduous march towards their prize.

The expedition was to show Drake much about the qualities of the *cimarrones* and to break down in part at least the barriers of race. Strong and fearless men, the Negroes were not only able effortlessly to carry the greater part of the supplies that were needed but to defend themselves and live off the land with great skill. Here their bows and arrows were of the utmost importance. Arrows tipped with metal, wood or fish bones were lethal against any enemy, while a range of other arrows with iron heads weighing anything up to a pound and a half served to bring down large mammals and all manner of birds. The iron heads rarely broke and could be frequently reused before blunting. As a result, the *cimarrones* held iron 'in far greater account than gold: and no man among them is of greater estimation than he that can most perfectly give this temper unto it'. Drake was to appreciate this, as he was also to recognise how skilful these men were in quickly preparing shelters made of palm trees. These shelters were not only waterproof but were carefully adjusted to the climate so that they were adequately airy in humid, low-lying areas; and they could also be warmed with cleverly ventilated fires when built in the piercingly cold highlands. But the *cimarrones* were not merely hunter-gatherers. They had their own large and well-defended settlements, sometimes numbering over sixty households, 'which were so clean and sweet that not only the houses, but the very streets, were very pleasant to behold'. A constant watch was maintained against the threat posed by the Spanish who, without a qualm of conscience, the *cimarrones* would kill like beasts. There was relative safety in these settlements but, for all the *cimarrones'* generous invitations to Drake that he and his men should stay with them for a few days, ambition pushed him on and the overland march continued.

The men rose at dawn and marched until ten when they rested by the river for a couple of hours, after which they continued until four in the afternoon. The *cimarrones* were clearly in charge both of path finding and the necessary discipline. Drake, for once, had to follow. Four Negro warriors who were most familiar with the route took the lead, marching about a mile in front of the others, breaking boughs to indicate the path, and enjoining absolute silence on all those bringing up the rear. What little muttered conversation there was concerned one of the great natural features of the area: a steeply rising, tree-crowned hill from which it was supposedly possible to look in both directions across the isthmus of Panama and glimpse the Atlantic on one side and the Pacific on the other. This was a place much treasured by the *cimarrones*, who clearly appreciated something of its geographical significance and natural wonder. Certainly they had themselves cut a flight of steps to the top of the hill and constructed a sheltered viewing platform there.

This was not a wonder to be passed by and the *cimarrones* escorted Drake up to the top of the hill where, for the first time, he saw two of the great oceans of the world spreading out to the far horizon with limitless possibility.[11] He felt amazement, surely, but his known response was altogether more precisely that of an Elizabethan adventurer bound by his faith, his nationalism and his ambition. Drake was aware too of being a public man, a figure whose self-consciously fashioned gestures, recorded as they would be by the chroniclers, were an important part of his image both then and to posterity. Now, as he and John Oxenham – one of his crew who was to have his own impressive but tragic career as an adventurer – stared at the cloudless panorama of the Pacific Ocean, Drake himself 'besought Almighty God of His goodness to give him life and leave to sail once in an English ship in that sea'. The devout tone was no doubt sincere and the exhilaration profound but, underlying them both, was the ambition of a Protestant sailor loyal to a Protestant Queen who saw how he might advance his career by pursuing, harassing and plundering the Catholic and Spanish enemy in every ocean of the known world.

With his moment of exaltation over Drake descended the hill and the long march continued. It was now possible to see the town of Panama five or six times a day in the breaks between the mountains. Strategy took over from ambitious dreams, or at least gave them substance. The Spanish treasure ships were anchored in the road off Nombre de Dios and were waiting for the bullion travelling along the treacherous mountainous highway that led to the port. In absolute silence and secrecy, the English and the *cimarrones* made their way to a wood where they resolved to plant their ambush. A *cimarrone* spy was sent down to reconnoitre and find out as nearly as he could when the King of Spain's heavily laden carriers would be passing. Theirs was a journey they would almost certainly make at night to avoid the heat. The spy returned with the glad news that the Treasurer of Lima and his family were due to appear in the next few hours along with fourteen mules, half of which were laden with gold and jewels. A hundred more mules were following, some of them bearing silver.

The English and the *cimarrones* moved silently out of the wood, their white shirts worn over their other clothes so that they could recognise each other in the dark and none would be taken for a

Spaniard. Two of the Negroes were then sent ahead and soon detected a sleeping Spanish guard from the smell of the burning match of his arquebus. They fell on him, gagged him, put out his match, bound his arms and brought him back well-nigh strangled to the main party. What did he know? The man confirmed what Drake's spy had already told him and then, in abject fear, begged Drake to save him from a terrible death at the hands of the *cimarrones*. Then he realised that to escape the hatred of the African warriors was only to expose himself to the vengeance of the Spaniards he had been forced to betray. The wretched captive implored Drake to give him such gold and silver from the treasure train as would allow him and his mistress to live in safety. Drake's response is not recorded, but he and his allies now divided themselves across the Nombre de Dios road and lay in waiting for an hour or so as the deep-toned bells of the burdened mules could gradually be heard coming nearer and nearer.

Complete silence from the waiting ambush party was absolutely necessary. The tension was mounting and, for one man, it proved too much to suppress. Robert Pike, drunk on *aqua vitae*, blearily resolved on derring-do and persuaded one of the Africans to slip away with him and be the first to attack the mule-train. The couple lay in wait and heard hooves coming closer. Pike rose up to look. The sober *cimarrone* pulled him sharply to the ground and lay on him. But it was too late. A Spanish officer had seen the flicker of Pike's white shirt and, fiercely spurring his horse, rode off to give the alarm. The sound of the galloping mount alerted Drake to the fact he might have been betrayed but he remained where he was as hurried, Spanish whispers of English pirates on the loose persuaded the Treasurer of Lima and the greater part of his train to turn back. The other mules continued on their way but, as Drake and his men fell on them, they found they carried little of any worth and realised that they themselves had best be quickly on their way if they were to avoid the bands of angry Spaniards who were sure to be sent out after them.

This was yet another reverse, and an exasperated Drake knew that action was once again essential if heightened expectations were not to sink into morale-destroying disillusion. A brief talk with the chief of the *cimarrones* convinced him that his best plan now was to make for the storehouses along the Chagres and sack them. There at last he might get something for his pains. The expedition made its way to the trading stations, some of the men mounted on mules they had stolen from the Spaniards. Arrived at their goal they surprised a band of Spanish soldiers who were escorting some Dominican friars to Panama. A fight broke out in which the English and the *cimarrones* each lost a man while several Spanish soldiers and one of the friars also lost their lives. The Spaniards admitted defeat and the victors entered the settlement where the Africans looted it of the things they wanted. These, being of little use to Drake, he allowed them to take before ordering a swift return to his base camp.

What followed was, at Drake's insistence, a hard, forced march during which his men were often hungry and complained constantly of torn and bleeding feet. The Africans yet again proved themselves indispensable and 'many times when some of our company feinted with sickness or weariness, two *cimarrones* would carry him with ease between them, two miles together'. In such ways the party returned safe but haggard and bitterly disappointed at their failure to secure any booty. Drake's assurance that he would try again seems to have revived their spirits and he realised, as always, that he must act on this. Morale in such circumstances was vulnerable and Drake characteristically recognised that he could not afford 'to suffer this edge of forwardness . . . to be dulled or rebated, by lying still idly unemployed, as knowing right well by continual experiences that no sickness was more noisome to impeach any enterprise than delay and idleness'. Consequently, he ordered one party under John Oxenham to take a pinnace in the direction of Tolu and search for victuals while he himself set off west for what he had heard were the great riches of Veragua. Since, after so many deaths, there was now only crew sufficient to man two of his pinnaces, the third was sunk.

But for all the talk of great wealth stored at Veragua – riches stored in great chests two feet deep, three feet broad and four feet long – the attempt to seize them proved no more successful than any of the others the expedition had so far mounted. Cannon fire across the harbour warned Drake and his men that they had been sighted and they were obliged to retreat, comforting themselves with the desperate belief 'that it was not God's will that we should enter at that time, the rather for that the wind, which had all this time been easterly, came up to the westward and invited us to return again to our ship'. There was really nothing else they could have done but, meeting with Oxenham on Maundy Thursday, Drake was happy to discover that he at least had captured an excellent little 20-ton frigate fully stored with maize, hogs and hens. These were welcome, as was the frigate itself which was new, strong and well designed. Drake ordered that it be tallowed and then planned a last and desperate attack on the Spanish ships sailing up the Chagres.

Chance now played its all-important part. On their way to the Chagres, and while moored off Cape Cativas, Drake fell in with a French pirate whose situation was as wretched as his own.[12] The meeting was to be the salvation of the expedition. Guillaume le Testu was a Huguenot privateer and distinguished hydrographer in desperate need. His ship had run out of water and his sickly crew had been forced to survive as best they could on an unwholesome mixture of vinegary cider and wine. Le Testu had heard rumours that Drake was in the vicinity and now looked urgently to him for help. Drake responded by sending a small quantity of water. Further presents were then exchanged, le Testu offering Drake a gift of pistols and a magnificent scimitar that had once belonged to Henri II, the late King of France. The Englishman responded by presenting his fellow Protestant with a gold chain. Some measure of mutual trust had now been established, and le Testu hoped to strengthen the bond by sharing with Drake his outrage at the recent horrors of the St Bartholomew's Day Massacre when, on the orders of the French Catholic Regent Catharine de Medici, almost the entire Protestant population of Paris and beyond had been slaughtered by the soldiery and the mob. In all, some 70,000 died. The Catholic authorities of Europe – the Pope and the King of Spain especially – welcomed the news of the bloodbath but, as France plunged once again into the horrors of civil war, Protestant opinion in England and elsewhere was ever more deeply outraged at papist atrocities.

Despite this sympathy, Drake was understandably wary of le Testu, for all the man's making clear how keen he was to fall in with the English plans to try once again to raid the treasure train. The French pirate commanded over twice the number of Drake's own surviving crew, while his 80-ton ship, dwarfing the English vessel and the captured frigate, was both a threat and a liability that could play no possible role in the forthcoming expedition. Reinforcements were useful nonetheless and, in the end, Drake agreed to allow le Testu and some twenty of his men to join him, a number that boosted Drake's own capability without threatening his safety or a reasonable division of the spoils which the two men agreed to halve. With these matters settled, a joint party of French, English and *cimarrones* set out for the Rio Francisco, where they found the river running shallow. Drake decided to anchor his frigate in deeper water, leaving strict instructions that it was to indulge in no piracy until his return in the pinnaces that now took him and his allies to the shore. There, as Drake and le Testu disembarked, the crews of the pinnaces were ordered to return in four days' time. By then, it was hoped, the pirate alliance would have captured vast quantities of bullion from the Spanish treasure trains.

To the amazement of the French, the party moved in their now familiar silence across the countryside until they came to rest for the night in a place where they could hear the distant, busy hammers of the Spanish carpenters working to refit the treasure ships. When dawn rose, the incessant noise was overlaid by the altogether more welcome sound of deep-toned mule bells. The delighted *cimarrones* promised that soon their European friends would have more gold and silver than they could possibly carry away. Three large mule trains then ambled into view, a combined weight of thirty tons of silver rocking on their backs. The allies pounced, seizing the heads of the leading mules and those bringing up the rear. The other mules came to a stop and lay down on the ground as they had been trained to do. Forty-five surprised Spanish soldiers offered what resistance they could but, for all they wounded le Testu, they thought it best to run for help. In their absence the mules were rapidly relieved of their burdens and the thieves made off with as much plunder as they could carry, having hurriedly buried the rest in land crab burrows, under fallen trees, or – as the *cimarrones* were wont to do – in the gravel bed of the shallow river nearby. An immediate retreat was now essential, and as the sounds of Spanish reinforcements grew louder the party headed for the woods. Only a single drunken Frenchman failed to keep up with them and fell a prisoner to the Spanish.

Spanish forces had also been sent out in pinnaces and were even now scouting the coast for their enemy. Understandably, the Spaniards felt that the insult done to them was intolerable. While they searched up and down the coast, agonised and importunate letters were sent to Madrid telling King Philip how his people in the Caribbean were victims of forces they were unable to resist and how, as loyal subjects, they were grieved to see with their own eyes the ruin of the realm unless His Majesty remedied the situation promptly. Exaggeration underlined the urgency, and it was from such reports as these that Drake's reputation was to be magnified until he came, in Spanish eyes, to resemble a monster – the 'dragon' his transliterated name so easily suggested. Certainly, there was reason for the Spanish to fear him, as events now showed.

When Drake and his men returned to their original landing place at the mouth of the Rio Francisco they saw the Spanish pinnaces hovering off the coast and, realising that their own boats were not there as they should have been, were concerned that the Spanish might have taken or sunk them. Drake was particularly worried lest their crews had been taken prisoner and the men tortured in order to make them confess the whereabouts of the rest of his party. The thought was as distressing as the knowledge that he and his men now appeared marooned once again on a hostile coast and were, after so many disappointments, burdened with a store of booty that was apparently useless to them. It was once again time for Drake to set an example. He turned to his men and addressed them with that practical, forceful eloquence of which he was capable in times such as these:

'If the enemy have prevailed against our pinnaces, which God forbid, yet they must have time to search them, time to examine the mariners, time to execute their resolution after it is determined. Before all these times be taken, we may get to our ships if ye will, though not possibly by land, because of the hills, thickets and rivers, yet by water. Let us therefore make a raft with the trees that are here in readiness as offering themselves, being brought down the river, happily this last storm, and put ourselves to sea! I will be one. Who will be the other?'[13]

One Englishman, two Frenchmen and all the *cimarrones* immediately volunteered. The tree trunks were hurriedly assembled and roped together to make a raft, the sail of which was a sack used for storing biscuits. A young tree was then rapidly shaped into an oar to help steer the raft and, as Drake and his three volunteers put to sea, he promised that once he was safely aboard his frigate then he would, God willing, come to rescue his comrades 'despite of all the Spaniards in the Indies'. Drake and his little crew sailed some three leagues out to sea, waist-high in water, while the mounting waves rose to their armpits. For six desperate and exhausting hours the parching sun beat down on their skins while the salt water rubbed them sore. At length the crew could just make out the two English pinnaces heading in their direction. The night before, the pinnaces had been held back by a storm and now, wholly unaware that their captain was desperately seeking them on his crazy craft, they rowed for cover from the night winds behind the point of a nearby island. Drake made straight for them. To test their mettle he ran towards them as if he and his companions were being chased by the Spanish. The crews of the pinnaces thought that this was indeed the case but, as Drake approached, they saw that they were safe and quickly took him and his companions aboard. They earnestly asked how things had gone. 'Well!' Drake declared coldly. The men doubted his word, and it was only when he pulled a gold bar out of his jacket that their confidence returned.

It was in this mood, their spirits heightened and encouraged by the sort of dramatic gesture which Drake knew so well how to make, that the party in the pinnaces rowed back to pick up the rest of the crew and salvage the remaining booty. Once arrived at their destination they learned that le Testu was dead and that the drunken Frenchman taken by the Spaniards had confessed under torture to where the stolen booty lay hidden. The Spaniards and some 2,000 slaves had at once sought it out and reclaimed it. Drake's party was nonetheless determined to see if any had been missed and eventually uncovered thirteen bars of silver and some few bars of gold. They returned with these to their ships, where the prize was equally divided between the English and the French before each side went their separate ways, it being in Drake's opinion 'high time to think of homewards'.

Flushed with success at last, the English sailed in defiant style 'with a flag of Saint George in the main top of our frigate, with silk streamers and ancients down to the water'. Another little Spanish frigate was captured close to the mouth of the Rio Grande and it was found that the plentiful supplies of honey it carried were a helpful medicine to many of the sick men aboard. Once they had arrived at Cape Cativas, Drake decided to careen the vessels – that is to lay them over first on one side and then the other to clean and repair their bottoms – after which they were tallowed in preparation for the long homeward voyage. The necessary repairs took about a week and were concluded by the payment of one final debt of honour.

The *cimarrones* who had rendered Drake such admirable and devoted service cared little or nothing for the gold and silver which had been the whole reason for Drake's hazardous enterprise. They cared much more for iron, which they could fashion into arrowheads and Drake, having ordered that he no longer needed pinnaces to be broken up and burned, presented the men with all the ironwork they contained. He wondered if there was anything else the *cimarrones* wanted and asked four of their headmen to see what they might like for themselves, as well as offering them silks and linens for their wives. One of their leaders took a fancy to the scimitar that le Testu had given Drake. He did not dare to ask for it in person and begged a member of Drake's crew to do so for him. Drake willingly complied and the delighted *cimarrone*, who knew that his King would make him a great man as soon as he presented him with the weapon, pressed four pieces of gold on Drake 'as a token of his thankfulness to him and a pawn for his faithfulness during life'.

Drake apparently donated the gold to the common store that all his men would share when they finally gained Plymouth. This they did on Sunday, 9 August 1573, at sermon time. The news of Drake's arrival at once reached the church and the congregation melted away before the preacher's eyes as they ran down to the quay to praise 'the evidence of God's love and blessing towards our Gracious Queen and country, by the fruit of our captain's labour and success'.[14] That success had not been inconsiderable, for all it had been won at a heavy price and by a combination of courage and luck rather than planning. Drake had returned with at least £20,000 in booty. Nonetheless, if he nurtured dreams of further Caribbean expeditions those dreams could not be immediately realised. The intricate galliard of international politics for the moment required his Queen to move closer to Spain, and such a *rapprochement* would be seriously damaged by Elizabeth openly countenancing piracy. Drake would have to look for opportunities elsewhere if he were to continue in his role as a Protestant and national hero.

3

The Circumnavigation of the Globe

One: Preparations

1575–1577

There were a number of matters for Drake to attend to before committing himself to another large project. It is possible that he used some of his new wealth to buy a house in Plymouth's Notte Street and he certainly took on his ten-year-old cousin to serve as his page. There was also the question of his brother John's estate.[1] Drake himself claimed it was John's dying wish that he should act as his executor and a brief will bearing the names of two witnesses was produced. This gave Drake authority over all John's possessions save the £300 he had invested in the last venture, along with its expected profits. These John apparently desired Drake to administer on behalf of his young widow Alice. Alice herself soon remarried and brought a suit questioning the authenticity of the will. Drake in his turn raised objections, but judgement was given against him and in terms which suggest that the judge took a dim view of Drake's behaviour in the matter. Apparently undeterred, Drake continued to profit from his recent voyage, selling the ships he had captured from the Spanish and looking for ways profitably to use his remaining vessels. Legitimate, peaceful trade may have been one option, but by early 1575 an altogether more attractive prospect had presented itself. The Earl of Essex was proposing to subdue unruly Ulster and had his eye on Drake's ships as the means by which he might transport his soldiers. The Earl would pay some of the expenses but Drake's profits would come in the usual way: from theft and the forced seizure of the enemy's goods.

Ireland was an old problem and the story of the Elizabethans' involvement with it was one of unmitigated ghastliness; many leading figures of the age receiving a training there in the bloody cruelty of which they were so easily capable. Drake was no exception.[2] To him, as to the greater number of his contemporaries, Ireland was a little known country half covered with undrained bogs and forests. Effective English authority from Dublin could rarely be exercised beyond the protective semicircle of the Pale. The remainder of the country was either in the hands of feudal landlords of Norman descent who professed a dubious loyalty to the Crown or, like the larger part of Ulster, was governed by the leaders of Gaelic clans who usually recognised no other law than their own. Meanwhile, the million or so peasants who made up the rest of the population were not only among the wildest peoples of Europe but were also defiantly and dangerously Catholic. It was believed that something had to be done. The English authorities regarded the situation as a threat, the ambitious saw the land as a place of opportunity, and there were those like Essex who, combining both attitudes, believed that strong-minded private individuals could subdue the Irish at a minimum cost to the Crown and great profit to themselves. The Queen was ready to concur.

She had watched over Essex's rise, benefited from his virulent anti-Catholicism, and given him his earldom. But Essex did not possess the vast estates enjoyed by many of Elizabeth's other grandees and he was determined to have Ulster as his domain. Two years before his involvement with Drake, he came to an arrangement with the Queen whereby he would share with her the cost of raising an army of 1,200 men, his half of the expense to be met by a £10,000 mortgage granted to him by Elizabeth on his English lands. Essex, in his turn, was given rights over large parts of what is now County Antrim, always provided, of course, that he could get his hands on them. But the Earl's venture was doomed from the start.

He was barely out of port when his ships were scattered by a storm and, once landed in Ireland, the small size of his army soon required him to sue for a humiliating truce. A year of inactivity at Carrickfergus saw his men dying daily by the score and, in spring 1574, he was obliged to limp off to Dublin with the mere 200 soldiers that remained to him. Trickery was now Essex's only resort. He invited his chief Irish enemy to a conference in Dublin and, while feasting him and his retainers, had the greater number of them murdered where they sat before executing the leaders themselves a little while later. Essex believed that the ravished Irish would now submit and the Queen, creating him Earl Marshal, appeared to encourage further acts of violence. For these he required Drake's assistance.

Essex had decided that his purpose would be furthered if he seized the relatively prosperous and strategically important island of Rathlin which lay about five miles off the northern coast of Antrim and immediately opposite Ballycastle. The island itself was at this time owned by Sorly Boy, the self-appointed chief of the Irish-Scots or *galloglaighs*, who had for generations been main players in Ireland's interminable local wars. Sorly Boy was well aware of Rathlin's advantages and considered it so safe that he had placed there, as Essex knew, 'most of his plate, most of his children, and the children of the most part of his gentlemen . . . and their wives'. An expeditionary force of some 1,200 horse and foot was required for what Essex deemed the necessary slaughter, and he realised that Drake's ships would be invaluable to him as his transport since 'they will brook the sea well and yet . . . draw so little water as they may pass into any river island or creek'. What had served along the isthmus of Panama would be equally useful in Ireland, for Rathlin was an exceptionally difficult place on which to land. The island was a mere four miles long and three miles wide, its shores surrounded by shoals. Violently conflicting tides known locally as the *slogh-namorra* added to the problems but, while the west end of the island was mountainous and devoid of a harbour, the eastern end was more level and fertile, and offered a number of landing places. Here Drake could anchor once he had set sail from Carrickfergus.

He and Captain John Norris set out early on the morning of 20

July 1575, and at once ran into a storm which delayed them for more than two days. Nonetheless, once the storm had blown itself out, Drake and his companions 'so well guided themselves' in Essex's words, 'that they met at the landing place . . . at one instant'. This landing place was almost certainly Church Bay and the islanders were drawn up there ready to defend themselves. Their ensuing action was as pitiful as it was brave. The islanders were determined to contest every foot of land but the sheer numbers of English pouring from the ships were overwhelming. At length defeated, the wretched inhabitants were forced to retreat to Bruce, 'a castle which they had of very great strength'. Alas, it was not strong enough to withstand the bombardment it received from Norris's guns which eventually breached the walls. By 26 July the defeated Constable of Rathlin was obliged to sue for a virtually unconditional surrender. He and his wife and child would be spared but all of those under him were, in a chilling phrase, to 'stand on the courtesy' of the victors.

The atrocious massacre that ensued was made more offensive by the note of righteous indignation with which Essex (who by this time had retreated to Dublin and so did not witness the action) chose to describe events. The English soldiers, he declared, 'being moved and much stirred with the loss of their fellows which were slain, and desirous of revenge, made request, or rather pressed to have the killing of them [i.e. the islanders], which they did all, saving the persons to whom life was promised'. But even the slaughter of 200 innocents was not enough for Drake and the English. As news of the massacre was brought to Sorly Boy's camp and the great warrior ran wild with grief, some 300 more terrified people sheltering by the island's caves and cliffs were dragged out and butchered. The resulting profits, some of which undoubtedly went to Drake, were only moderately satisfactory and it is possible that Drake's share of this booty did not entirely compensate him for the expense the expedition had involved him in. Nevertheless, if he was out of pocket, he had gained a new and important colleague who had access to some of the mightiest figures in England. Drake was about to move closer to the centre of power and influence, a position which he would rarely and only ever temporarily leave.

*

Thomas Doughty was a gentleman adventurer with much of the allure and many of the shortcomings of the breed.[3] He was part of that collection of minor aristocrats and younger sons who had followed Essex to Ireland in the hope of wealth and action. Over-conscious of his social status (perhaps because he was insecure about it) and invariably on the look-out for the main chance, Doughty was drawn to Drake's altogether stronger personality. He found that if the tough and widely experienced mariner could not match his own gloss of breeding he could at least open up seemingly limitless horizons. These were badly needed since this was not a favourable time for men of Doughty's stamp. In the early years of Elizabeth's reign there was too little opportunity for adventure and there were those who lamented that 'martial men presently bear no price'.

Drake's ambitions and known achievements seemed to fill the void, and Doughty's conversations with him turned to the riches that might be gained from raids on Spain's South American possessions – the glittering silver mountains of Potosi especially – and from the establishment of a definite English presence in the vast and largely unknown region that stretched south from the River Plate and round the Strait of Magellan to the continent's Pacific seaboard. Such things would surely be more profitable than Essex's doomed and ghastly venture in Ireland which was even now reaching its sorry end. Harassed, defeated and broke, Essex himself returned to Ireland after mortgaging the remains of his English estates and was almost immediately laid low by a fatal attack of dysentery. Doughty, skilled at intrigue and double-dealing as he supposed himself to be, realised the way things were going and probably worked to discredit the ruined Essex even as he ingratiated himself with Leicester, the Queen's favourite, and with the new rising star at court, Sir Christopher Hatton, the man who was to become the Queen's mouthpiece in the House of Commons.

Doughty became Hatton's secretary and, so a friend later claimed, used his position 'like a true subject' to bring himself, Drake, and their plans to the attention of the Queen's spy-master general and Secretary of State, the virulently anti-Catholic Walsingham, and thus to the Queen herself. Drake would have none of this story. It made him appear all too dependent on other men's initiatives. In time, he came to loathe Doughty with a murderous hatred and it was in his interest to discredit the man utterly. This Drake did with his customary aplomb and a characteristic disregard for factual niceties when his own reputation was at stake.[4] It was not Doughty who was responsible for propelling him towards royal circles and royal favour, Drake claimed, but his own merit – a merit that was, he declared, self-evident to the greatest men in the land. Had not the Earl of Essex himself recognised it when they were both in Ireland? And had not Essex written 'in my commendations unto Secretary Walsingham more than I deserved?' The alleged letter made it clear that Essex thought Drake 'to be a fit man to serve against the Spaniards, for my practice and experience that I had in that trade'.

The letter apparently had the desired effect for, a little while later, Walsingham supposedly paid Drake a visit. He was the ideal man to encourage him to 'annoy' the King of Spain. Dark, passionate and severe, gifted and internationally educated, Walsingham was a Puritan inflexible in his belief that the nation's safety depended on the annihilation of Spanish influence. This was a policy he pursued with an outspoken fearlessness that often exasperated his altogether more pragmatic Queen who, nonetheless, recognised Walsingham's unswerving loyalty and the exceptional efficiency of his secret service which he funded from his own increasingly threadbare pocket. Walsingham had a taste, too, for the long odds and the huge potential profits promised by the schemes of such Elizabethan sea-dogs as the Hawkinses, Grenville, Gilbert and Frobisher. Drake's expedition to the isthmus of Panama was proof of his abilities in such matters and Walsingham, realising that by means of Drake's enterprise he might himself serve both God and Mammon, eagerly supported his cause.

He allegedly told Drake that the Queen, having suffered 'divers injuries' at the hands of the King of Spain, wished to take her revenge, and Drake was the man to carry it out. According to Drake, Walsingham then unfolded a map on the table in front of them and asked the eager pirate to mark out the places where he thought the Spaniards might be 'most annoyed'. Drake, with that gift for circumstantial detail which always made his stories so convincing, replied that he was reluctant to do so since, if the Queen were to die, a Catholic sympathiser might succeed her and have evidence of the plans he was even now being asked to formulate. Walsingham allegedly saw the sense in this but, supposedly at the request of the Queen, sent for Drake sometime later in order that she might meet him. Drake said he received the message late at night and, rather surprisingly, postponed the meeting to the following day.

When he finally came into Elizabeth's presence he said that she turned to him and declared: 'Drake, so it is that I would gladly be revenged on the King of Spain for divers injuries that I have received.' They then apparently discussed their plans and the Queen concluded the meeting by swearing Drake to secrecy and informing him that anyone who told Philip of Spain about what they had discussed would lose their head. Drake told this story at a moment of dire crisis and, since it was absolutely necessary for him to convince his hearers that he was a man known in the highest places and familiar with the secret intricacies of foreign policy, his words should be taken with a large pinch of salt. It was not Elizabeth's style to initiate plans, especially in a *tête à tête* with a notorious pirate, but it is nonetheless true that she gave Drake and his backers permission to sail on the voyage that eventually became the circumnavigation of the globe, a voyage which inevitably involved considerable harassment of Spanish possessions. Why did she do so?

For all their fragile and face-saving efforts to patch up a peace, the exposure of the Ridolfi plot ensured that Elizabeth never fully trusted Philip again. She had good reason not to. Financially and militarily harassed though he was, Philip was still determined to make his best endeavours to return England to the Catholic fold, to encourage regime change wherever he could and suppress the heretical beliefs of the Protestant axis of evil. However, his Mediterranean war against the Turks absorbed vast amounts of money, sums that were so prodigiously increased by his conflict in the Netherlands that, by the time Don John of Austria arrived there at the close of 1576, the entire Spanish army had either mutinied or deserted and Philip, for all his apparently vast resources, lacked the wherewithal to take on any additional major enterprise. Left to himself he might have seen the wisdom of passivity, but he was being hounded by the new Pope Gregory XIII actively to pursue what came to be known as 'the Enterprise of England'.

Philip was an exasperated man under great pressure. 'Nobody desires more than I that the matter should be put in hand,' he wrote of the Pope's plans for England, 'but when and how depend on the way things go in Flanders, and on many other considerations.' The chivying from his Catholic peers nonetheless continued and it became an accepted truth in the Spanish court that 'His Majesty will never be at peace until England is conquered'. Numerous reconnoitrings were made and plans drawn up for the possible invasion of the country. Letters concerning this last were eventually intercepted and deciphered. Elizabeth was apprised of the situation and, as the Spanish Ambassador to Rome lamented, the Queen felt the same indignation as if the enterprise had actually taken place. Elizabeth had already signed an alliance with the French promising them her assistance if they should be attacked by a foreign power such as Spain, and she was now prepared to lend support to the Netherlanders too. She also welcomed into the country those who were known to be in open rebellion against Philip. In addition, she began to spend large sums of money she could barely afford on the defence of the realm and turned a blind eye to the eleven major English pirate expeditions that sailed to the Caribbean between 1572 and 1577 to wreak what damage they could. Drake's expedition was thus sailing on an ever-swelling and popular tide of anti-Spanish feeling.

The Spanish made strenuous efforts to contain the threat to their Caribbean possessions. They were, for example, all too painfully aware of the dangers posed by an alliance between the English and the *cimarrones* and were determined to bring the latter to heel. A well armed body of volunteers was sent out from Panama to invade the Negroes' settlements and spent six months scouring the countryside and burning the warriors' villages and crops. By 1579 the campaign had been completed, the Blacks having agreed to settle in a large *pueblo* where they enjoyed a measure of self-determination under Spanish rule. This effectively put an end to English hopes of a land alliance with escaped slaves, while the increased vigour of the Spaniards also ensured that a number of English sea-based expeditions came seriously to grief. For example, when John Noble and his twenty-eight men arrived off the coast of Nombre de Dios and succeeded in pillaging various ships, Noble was successfully pursued and captured. His entire expedition was then condemned to death except for two boys who were sent to the galleys for life, a victory which, according to the reports sent back to Spain, occasioned great joy.

A similar fate to Noble's attended the expedition of John Oxenham, the man who on Drake's earlier voyage had accompanied his leader to the top of the hill from where both men had had their exhilarating view of the Atlantic and Pacific oceans. Oxenham personified the very best and worst features of the type of man he was. He was exceptionally brave, ambitious and determined. His crossing of the isthmus of Panama and capture of two treasure vessels set the Spanish colonial community by the ears, while his vainglorious boasting terrified them. 'He expects to be greatly rewarded by his Queen,' worried officials wrote back to Spain, 'and promises that next year he will . . . settle with 2000 men and make himself master of all this realm, the strength of which is very little to resist such an onslaught as he announces.' Urgent and heartfelt requests were forwarded to King Philip begging him to send reinforcements sufficient to withstand such a force.

But it was the very qualities which ensured Oxenham's short-term success that undermined his expedition and brought it to its horrible end. While he was as ruthless as Drake, he was altogether more abrasive and lacked those real qualities of leadership – the setting of a personal example and a sure intuition in the handling of ordinary men – which Drake possessed in abundance. He squabbled with his subordinates, his subordinates squabbled among themselves, and all of them squabbled with the *cimarrones* to such a degree that the party was easily tracked down and captured. The greater part were summarily executed, but Oxenham and two of his colleagues were spared in order that they might be taken to Lima and closely examined by the Inquisition. Even as, unbeknown to them, Drake was sailing on the early stages of what became his circumnavigation of the world, so the Spanish authorities, applying the wrack and the thumbscrew to their captives' ever more agonised bodies, managed to force from them vital information about the true nature of Drake's ambitions.

These were on an altogether astonishing scale for, as it emerged, they consisted of nothing less than sailing down the eastern coast of South America, rounding the Strait of Magellan, and then exploring the coast of Chile to look for places where English outposts might be established.[5] What the English, and Drake in particular, clearly had in mind was nothing less than establishing the nation as a colonial power south of the Tropic of Capricorn. This idea – the ambition of bringing under English influence that vast tract of land which comprised southern Brazil, the River Plate, the Strait of Magellan, Patagonia and Chile – was a long-treasured dream. A contemporary explained its allure. By 'maintaining in the bays of the Straights [of Magellan] a good navy, there is no doubt but that we shall make subject to England all the gold mines of Peru and all the coast and tract of that firm of America', wrote Richard Hakluyt, the great propagandist of Elizabethan exploration. The Strait of Magellan could also be seen as 'the gate of entry into the treasure of both the East and the West Indies'. It was thus the strategic core of dreams of fabulous wealth and the wherewithal to challenge the might of Spain. To establish an English colony in this inhospitable region, a colony manned by English pirates and 'hundreds or thousands' of *cimarrones* brought down from Panama, would make Elizabeth and her nation major players in the new game of global politics that was now being played out by the leading countries of the western Atlantic seaboard.

The dream proved to be as insubstantial as such things often are, but to Drake and his generation there was much that seemed to give it substance. The wealth of Brazil, widely advertised by Cabot and his supporters, could still be recalled by men who had sailed on the Hawkins family's earliest expeditions, and there were London merchants who were well aware of how successful the Portuguese Brazilian sugar trade was. The French knew even more and when, in 1568, the information they had gathered appeared in English translation, Drake and his contemporaries learned that the Portuguese had found mines of silver there. The estuary of the River Plate was fabled as a treasure trove while 'the rest of the country hath not been frequented by Christians' and therefore lay open to that ruthless exploitation and ecological rape which the Europeans had established as their preferred means of business. By early 1570 the Spanish Ambassador was aware that a Portuguese merchant was trying to persuade the Privy Council 'to occupy and colonise one or two parts in the kingdom of Magellan in order to have in their hands the commerce of the southern sea'. All of these factors fed the ambitions of men such as Drake, who had almost certainly gained some personal insight into the matter from his conversations with le Testu in Panama.

Le Testu's mapping of the region in his *Cosmographie Universelle* of 1536 was not particularly distinguished even by contemporary standards, and knowledge of the Peruvian coast especially remained sketchy and fanciful. Maps either left the region blank or tried to cover over ignorance with various largely imaginary coastlines. The great efforts of Mercator and Ortelius popularised these erroneous ideas and were among the principal sources of Drake's mis-information. Meanwhile, knowledge of European involvement in the area was only slightly more certain. The Portuguese grip on Brazil was known to be tenuous, especially below the River Plate, while Spanish influence over the Pacific coast south of Peru was rightly believed to be incomplete. Elizabeth herself was fully aware that beyond the Strait of Magellan there were settlements made by Spaniards, these probably being the somewhat frail centres estab-lished between 36 and 41 degrees south. The Spanish frontier zone could not, however, be exactly determined, and it seemed perfectly reasonable for English explorers to rationalise their ambitions by an appeal to the divine and celebrate: 'the aptness and as it were a fatal convenience that since the Portugal hath attained one part of the new found world to the East, the Spaniard another to the West, the French the third to the North: now the fourth to the South is by God's providence left for England'.

This apparently uncontentious assertion was made by those who were urging the Queen to support the plan for a South American involvement first put forward in 1574 by one of the greatest Elizabethan seamen, Sir Richard Grenville. The proposal for this is somewhat generalised in content but its purpose can be very precisely detailed by the confession extracted under torture by the Spanish Inquisition from John Oxenham who had resolved to sail on it. Grenville's aim was, he said, to found a settlement on the River Plate and then pass to the Strait of Magellan and establish settlements wherever suitable country for such could be found. All of those involved made much of the fact that their intentions (in public at least) were peaceful. They did not want to 'annoy the King of Spain'. Elizabeth briefly concurred and granted Grenville's expedition a licence to sail, but then revoked it. On reflection, she saw perfectly well that Philip would not tolerate such acts of international trespass and, in 1574, it seemed inadvisable to upset him. By 1577, however, things were different, as the torturers in Lima were well aware. They were also aware of Drake and had reason to fear his prowess. Would Drake now put Grenville's plan into action if the Queen gave him permission? Oxenham confessed that no English sailor was better able to do so. He also added that if Elizabeth were to grant him a licence then Drake would pass through the Strait of Magellan and found settlements there. But, the anxious torturers enquired, *would* Elizabeth give him a licence? Oxenham thought not.

In this he was wrong, for Drake, who had £1,000 of his own money invested in the scheme, had already set sail with the connivance of the Queen. If Elizabeth had been reluctant to 'annoy' Philip in 1574 now, in 1577, the deteriorating situation in the Netherlands and the fact that Philip was extricating himself from his Mediterranean war against the Turks and so would have men, and even money, with which to resume his war against the Dutch, was deeply troubling.[6] The Queen suddenly had every reason to lend her ear to those strongly anti-Spanish members of her court and their followers – Leicester, Walsingham, Hatton, the Wynters, Hawkins and Drake himself, who were the expedition's backers – and agree to a voyage by which she could lose very little and perhaps gain a great deal. Of the great and the good only Secretary Cecil, created Lord Burghley in 1571, was not, it seems, officially privy to the expedition, a fact that was later to help provoke a major crisis. Burghley had played a leading part in organising Hawkins's expeditions to the Caribbean but, great and scrupulously careful politician that he was, he would certainly have disapproved of this venture being launched at this time as something unnecessarily provocative. It is inconceivable, however, that he did not come to hear about his mistress's involvement.

Details of what Elizabeth agreed to are preserved in a badly charred document in the British Library. Partially reconstructed by modern scholars (their words are printed here in italics) the plan required that Drake *'shall enter the Straight of Magellanas lying in 52 degrees of* the Pole and *having passed therefrom into* the South Sea then *he is to sail* so far to the northwards as *xxx degrees seeking* along the said coast a*forenamed . . .* to find out p*laces meet* to have traffic for the ven*ting of commodities* of these her Majesty's realms'.[7] Imports from these regions were expected to be extremely profitable, there being 'great hope of *gold, silver*, spices, drugs, cochineal, and *divers other* special commodities, such as may *enrich her* Highness' dominions and also *put* shipping a-work greatly'. With these possibilities explored, Drake was then to head for home 'by the same way . . . as he went out'. The whole expedition was expected to take thirteen months, five of which were to be spent in 'tarrying upon the coasts, to get knowledge of the princes and countries there'. What all of this makes clear is that Drake's orders required him to reconnoitre the eastern seaboard of South America, navigate the Strait of Magellan, explore the coast of Chile up to the latitude that marked the uncertain limit of Spanish influence, then double back on himself and make for home. These aims are specific, limited and clear.

But the document is quite as interesting for what it does not say as for what it does. There is no mention, for example, of colonisation. It is probable that even in a climate favourable to the enterprise, those who were urging the expedition considered the idea too tendentious to make it explicit. Besides, reconnoitring suitable locations was an objective that could be achieved without the Queen's attention being too obviously drawn to it. Not only this. If Elizabeth guessed that the adventurers about her had such an idea in mind (as she surely did if only because the plan so closely resembled Grenville's) she would have objected – and not only on political grounds. Elizabeth was surrounded by men forever promising her paper empires, but she was rarely if ever beguiled by them for long.

She might, from time to time, allow these pioneers to have their head but she would never open her modest purse for them. She could not be an imperialist even if she wished to be. Elizabeth was obliged to be a realist. As such, she knew she was very nearly at war with the already existing empire of Spain and needed all her finite resources to defend her half an island against it. An empire of her own was, quite simply, beyond her reach. Hence the lack of co-ordination and state support – the piecemeal and often tragic nature – of the Elizabethans' efforts to establish colonies overseas.

Elizabeth was however, as we have seen, more than happy to profit from the illicit trading and downright piracy of her would-be empire builders, a subject which again the plan of Drake's expedition could hardly make explicit, even though all of those involved knew that piracy had at the very least to cover their investment. Finally, and most interestingly of all, the document makes no mention of a plan to circumnavigate the globe. Quite the reverse. Since Drake was to come back the way he had set out, there was at this stage no such plan. It was unforeseen circumstances that were to turn an ambitious plan for a reconnaissance expedition into something altogether more heroic which was, in its turn, to have its effect on the Queen's subsequent foreign policy. In the meantime, with her risks reduced to a bare minimum, Elizabeth gave her consent to the expedition and lent the adventurers a ship for a voyage which, Drake and his colleagues let it be known, was intended as nothing more than an unremarkable little trading expedition to Alexandria, Tripoli and Constantinople.

This last was so much flummery, as even those who were supposed to be duped by it realised. The Spanish Ambassador was informed by one of his agents that 'Francis Drake is going to the Antilles, although they are spreading the rumour that they are going to Tripoli. Even so, there is no doubt they are going where I say, and they will do much harm if your mercy does not take measures to keep them from going'.[8] As the Ambassador began to build up his file on the matter so it became apparent to him that Drake's expedition was an enterprise of much importance to Spain. Notwithstanding that he was uncertain about the Englishmen's precise destination, the Ambassador had a sure insight into the part that piracy was expected to play in it and who the chief backers were. These were proceedings that promised to bring in a great deal of treasure, the Ambassador wrote earnestly to his master, adding that the Queen was also involved and others from the Council, because they hoped to gain much from the business. It was important for Spain to know the location in order to send the expedition to the bottom of the sea.

While the Spanish Ambassador collected what information he could, Drake set about his preparations for the voyage. These were both intellectual and practical. He assembled a useful collection of charts and rutters that included not only Ortelius' great map, but also hand-written Portuguese manuals which detailed oceanic routes and provided navigational details about the coasts of Brazil, Chile and Peru. He also studied such printed books as might be useful to him. In particular, he was familiar with the *Decades* of Peter Martyr, which had been translated into English by Richard Eden and was the standard reference work on westward navigation. Drake also had a copy of Pigafetta's report of Magellan's voyage, a vivid eyewitness account which, for all its bias towards hero worship and its sketchy appreciation of the problems of navigation, nonetheless alerted Drake to the potential dangers he faced from scurvy, the horrors of the Patagonian seas, and the very real risk of mutiny among disenchanted and exhausted men when they found themselves thousands of miles from home in tiny ships tossed by hostile and barely charted oceans.

Drake also needed to assemble a complement of sailors and ships. Ninety-six of the 170 or so men and boys who sailed with him are known by name. Most of these are the gentlemen volunteers whose presence was to cause their commander such serious difficulty, for all that he tried to acknowledge their status by ensuring that they formed part of the council which he called together for even the most trivial matter – even if he did not listen to them. Chief among these figures was Thomas Doughty, who brought along with him his younger brother John. Another gentleman, John Winter, although only in his late twenties, was the son of the Surveyor of the Queen's Ships. Already a seasoned sailor, Winter was put in command of the *Elizabeth*, a new ship of some 80 tons which had been built by his father and uncle from timber allegedly acquired from the Queen's private naval stores. Drake himself was accompanied by his younger brother Thomas, a foolish, hot-headed youth of twenty-two who served as an ordinary sailor 'like any one of the crew'. Drake also took his young cousin John, a talented youth and 'a great painter' who would while away the long hours of the voyage in his uncle's cabin where, with the help of Drake himself, he drew the passing coastlines and flora and fauna which enriched the now lost rutter-journal that was the official record of the voyage.

At the start of the expedition, these three leading men – Drake, Winter and Doughty – were reckoned to be 'equal companions and friendly gentlemen' in the enterprise, but the enormous strains under which they were placed, the conflicts of their fiery egos, the bitter squabbles over pecking-order politics, and something at once vindictive and pitiless in Drake's own personality, would rupture their association and lead to desertion, death and Drake's final triumphant fashioning of himself as the supreme and unquestioned master of the expedition – the Protestant hero who alone of all of them was capable of mastering the oceans of the world. Such clarity of purpose would destroy Doughty utterly and it is possible (indeed probable) that the rivalry and jealousy that Drake inspired in him were expressed in characteristically petty and underhand ways before the expedition even set sail.

Doughty treasured visions of a great future.[9] If the English were indeed going to found a South American empire to rival those of Portugal and Spain then Thomas Doughty, gentleman, wanted a lion's share of the credit and the glory, the wealth and the power. He believed that these were nothing less than his deserts. His birth, his education and his contacts all suggested no less. His was a society where extraordinary care was taken to emphasise differences of social status and where a rubicon flowed between those who were members of the gentry and those who were not. It was a rubicon that could be crossed (as Drake was to do) but Doughty believed that he himself was already on the sunnier bank of the great divide. 'For whosoever studieth the laws of the realm, who studieth in the universities, who professeth liberal sciences, and to be short, who can live idly and without manual labour, and will bear the port, charge and countenance of a gentleman, he shall be called master'. Drake's expedition would test this universally accepted idea to breaking point but Doughty, convinced of his superior status, would not play second fiddle to a mere pirate and a parvenu like Francis Drake.

Nonetheless, wholly lacking Drake's personal stature and force of personality – indeed, already resentful of them – Doughty knew he could mount no direct challenge and contented himself with using the only means of trouble-making at his disposal: gossip, rumour-spreading and what eventually emerged as below-deck intrigue. It was all as pitiful as it was dangerous, and a conversation allegedly started in a Captain's garden in Plymouth before the expedition set sail suggests Doughty's way of operating through a poisonous farrago of truth, half truth, fabrication and innuendo. He suggested that the expedition would never have gone forward at all if he himself had not recommended Drake to the Earl of Essex at a time when, he alleged, Drake was in bad odour with the Privy Council because of his Indies voyages. It was true, he alleged, that Drake and he had indeed discussed the possibility of such a voyage as they were now entered on while they were together in Ireland, but it was Doughty's scrupulous loyalty and respect for the social order that made him realise that mere private individuals such as themselves should not dare to initiate such a plan. It was he who had dutifully gone to the great and the good – to Walsingham and Hatton – to broach the matter in the hope that they would mention it to the Queen. It was thus Doughty who was responsible for bringing Drake to Elizabeth's personal attention and so, indirectly, for her issuing an order that 'our captain was not to do anything without the assent of the said T[homas] D[oughty]'. It followed from this, Doughty further alleged, that he could exercise considerable patronage and that wealth would be showered upon those who were loyal to him. It was all very dangerous, divisive and, as it would prove, ultimately lethal.

Rather less is known about the other gentlemen on the voyage. These included John Hawkins's nephew William; George Carey, a nephew of the Queen's cousin Lord Hunsdon; Leonard Vicary, a lawyer from the Inner Temple who may have been a kinsman of the late royal surgeon; George Fortesque, the son of the Keeper of the Royal Wardrobe, and John Chester, who commanded the 50-ton

Swan (the expedition's victualling ship) and whose father had been Lord Mayor of London. Of the other important figures on the voyage, John Thomas was Captain of the 30-ton *Marigold*, while the little *Christopher* or *Bark Benedict* was captained by Thomas Moone, who had earlier sailed with Drake as a ship's carpenter on his Nombre de Dios expedition.

Unfortunately, very little is known about Francis Fletcher, the expedition's puritanical and God-fearing preacher, who may have been sent by Walsingham and whose account of the early part of the voyage is so valuable a source of information. Like other more or less contemporary accounts of the circumnavigation, the original of this manuscript has been lost – it is likely that Drake, acutely sensitive to his reputation, impounded them all on his return and retained them for his own use – but an incomplete copy made in the seventeenth century survives. This document provides partial evidence of the principal source of *The World Encompassed by Sir Francis Drake*, a highly selective and exculpatory account of the circumnavigation published, like *Sir Francis Drake Revived*, in 1628, and a volume almost certainly edited under Drake's own supervision before 1595 and during the period of his disgrace. It was this period in the wilderness that was also responsible for the difficulties Richard Hakluyt faced in issuing his account of what he called 'The Famous Voyage' in his monumental *Principal Navigations, Voyages, Traffics and Discoveries of the English Nation*. Hakluyt's patron Walsingham forbade him to publish the original narrative of the circum-navigation which he possessed. Realising, however, that Hakluyt's project would be absurd if it omitted all account of Drake's achievement, Walsingham probably allowed the great editor or his assistant access to some of his own records which, along with the Fletcher manuscript as it had been modified for *The World Encompassed*, became the outstanding short, if uncontroversial, narrative of the circumnavigation. As this rather complex situation suggests, the sources for the history of Drake's circumnavigation are fairly plentiful but none are first hand.

Drake himself made the greater part of the circumnavigation aboard the *Pelican*, a ship later to achieve immortality as the *Golden Hind*.[10]

The vessel's original name derived from one of the Queen's favourite emblems: a pelican plucking at its breast to feed her young from her own blood, which Elizabeth saw as an apt representation of the loving self-sacrifice she made for her people. The *Pelican* itself was reckoned at about 150 tons which meant that her beam was in the region of nineteen feet, her keel somewhere between forty-seven and fifty-nine feet, while her overall length did not exceed eighty-one feet. She was thus hardly bigger than a modern London bus. The Portuguese pilot Drake captured during the voyage described the *Pelican* as being 'in a great measure stout and strong' and the vessel was, he declared, 'fit for warfare and . . . well fitted out and finished with very good masts, tackle and double sails'.

Drake made sure that the ship was also heavily armed, with eighteen pieces of bronze and cast-iron artillery poking out from her ports and ready to fire nine-pound balls which could wreck the superstructure and timber work of any aggressor. In addition to this, he also saw to it that his flagship was adequately supplied with arquebuses, calivers, pistols, pikes, fire-bombs, fire-pikes, bows and arrows. The *Pelican* was thus a small, swift floating fortress and carried seventy to eighty men. Stored in the nine-foot-deep hold were many of the necessaries they would require on a long voyage: iron and seasoned timber for repairs, pitch-sealed kegs of gunpowder, meat, fish, and precious drinking water. There was, besides, a smith's forge and the necessary coal to fire it, along with pickaxes, spades, shovels, and other tools which would prove themselves to be of the greatest use when the men landed on strange shores from the four pinnaces that were stowed aboard ready for assembly at need.

In this age before the widespread use of hammocks the ordinary sailors had their own sleeping places between the guns or on the deck, while the gentlemen adventurers declared their superior status by being assigned two cabins situated below the poop deck. Some may have slept there, while others spent the night on truckle beds in the great cabin where Drake held his meetings and dined in considerable pomp off silver plates with gold borders and to the music of viols. His officers dined with him less in a spirit of conviviality than in respectful and even cowed deference, none of them being allowed to sit or wear their hats in Drake's presence without his explicit permission. Further to enhance the isolation and splendour that was a necessary part of his position as commander or 'General' of the expedition, Drake had his own small, comfortably appointed cabin. In such ways he made sure he appeared self-fashioned as the very image of the Elizabethan gentleman commander, a role he would now play to the hilt and often in the most dangerous circumstances.

4

The Circumnavigation of the Globe

Two: The Voyage Out

December 1577 – June 1578

Everything that could be done to ensure the discipline, order and success of Drake's still secret mission had been done, but now it was suddenly made clear how the best efforts of men could all too easily become the playthings of nature. The expedition set sail on 15 November 1577, but Drake had barely given his order to weigh anchor when a violent storm whipped the Channel into a pounding fury. As the desperate flotilla made for Falmouth, the *Marigold* was driven against rocks and the main mast of the *Pelican* had to be cut away to prevent the ship from running aground. It was about a fortnight later before the battered vessels could limp back to Plymouth for the necessary repairs. An expedition bound for the limits of the known world had been unable even to leave its home waters. This was hardly an auspicious start.

Drake's storm-tossed flotilla eventually set sail from Plymouth on 13 December 1577. The crew, still in ignorance about the expedition's true aims and destination, were given a slight if confusing clue as to their purpose when Drake informed them that their first point of rendezvous was to be the island of Mogador lying a mile off the North African coast.[1] There was nothing particularly unusual about this. For more than a quarter of a century English sailors had supplied the famously sweet Elizabethan tooth with such luxuries as the sugar, dates and almonds which the region provided in abundance. There were even men among Drake's crew who had made the journey so often that they could brag of talking a little Arabic. The Barbary trade was nonetheless not without its dangers. The Portuguese, the first Europeans to establish themselves in Africa, were resentful of what they considered the English invasion of their monopoly. Threats and diplomatic scuffles were commonplace, but with the rise of the native Saadian dynasty under the vigorous leadership of Muhammad al-Shaikh the position changed. The Portuguese were driven back to the coast and the greater risk now lay in native conflicts altogether more intricate than trading disputes. But, for the moment there was peace – or, at least, the appearance of it. Holding their way on a prosperous wind, Drake's crew crossed the Bay of Portugal with no more mishap than the loss of a boy overboard. Drake spied the bleached and baking sands of the Moroccan coast on Christmas Day and dropped anchor between Mogador and the mainland. His men found the uninhabited island to be a haven where they could rest up, fish, and watch the goshawks chasing the multitudinous doves before they set about assembling one of the four pinnaces they had brought with them.

Naturally enough, the English presence came to the attention of the local authorities who were immediately suspicious. For all his recently established power, the local King did not sit unchallenged on his divan, and his armies were even now drawn up against those of a rebellious uncle. It was only the expectation of Portuguese reinforcements that kept the warring parties from an engagement, and it was now a question as to whether those European contingents had finally arrived. Were Drake's men the advance guard? Perhaps so, perhaps not. It was well for the Arabs to be wary since a throne was at stake. They made signals from the mainland suggesting that they wished to parlay and Drake, nothing averse, raised a white flag of friendship and sent out a pinnace with one of his Arab speakers aboard.

A halting conversation in a half-understood language was not sufficient to clarify the facts or allay suspicions. Still unsure as to whether the new arrivals were friend or foe, the Arabs offered conventional gestures of courtesy, 'casting up their eyes to heaven, and after looking down upon the ground, as though they had sworn by heaven and earth, promising peace'. Such exchanges resulted in the sailor who spoke for the English being left on the mainland as a pledge for the two Arabs who now came aboard Drake's ship. There, with spirits raised by generous quantities of forbidden alcohol, the visitors were presented with shoes, linen and a spear. Returning delighted to their shore, the Arabs promised that they would come back the next day with supplies of fresh meat. As a token of good will, they sent back the man they had earlier taken hostage.

A little bartering such as this was insufficient proof of friendship. Neither Drake nor the Arabs were unaware of the possibilities of treachery. The Englishman was naturally cautious and the Arabs were still unwilling to trust him. Both sides took precautions. When darkness fell, a number of Turkish infantrymen, or janisseries, were concealed about the mainland coast and waited there through the following day as a party of Arab merchants appeared with a train of laden camels. Drake had already given orders that a pinnace should be despatched when these men were sighted and added that none of his crew should step on the mainland unaccompanied. Discipline being ever secondary to conspicuous display among Elizabethan sailors, the command was ignored and one of the men, named John Fry, stepped out of the boat and ran ashore. He was seized at once. A dagger was held to his throat and, as he was thrown over a horse and taken off for interrogation, the concealed janisseries rose from their hiding places and sent the remaining Englishmen scurrying away. The captured Fry was duly questioned. Having satisfied the local King that he was a member of Drake's crew and knew nothing whatsoever about a Portuguese army, he was duly freed but, unable to find Drake who had in fact set out to look for him, Fry was eventually sent back home on a visiting English merchantman.

Drake now set sail for Cape Blanco, his crew convinced that they had been worsted by 'crafty slaves' and 'known enemies to Christ', even as they themselves, like true pirates, kept a predatory eye open for potential Spanish and Portuguese prizes.[2] They were not long disappointed. Having borne with a contrary wind, the flotilla was able to set a course south-south-west with 'every sail at command . . . as if Neptune had been present'. As they approached Agadir, three little Spanish fishing smacks appeared and were easily captured. These prizes were soon followed by two Portuguese vessels and now, as Drake's flotilla began to approach the Tropic of Cancer, the Southern Cross rose conspicuously in the night sky and helped them steer their way to Cape Blanco. There, a third Portuguese ship was seized. Having pillaged the vessel, Drake eventually set his prizes and their crews free, keeping back only one of the Spanish fishing smacks, along with a Portuguese pilot who was familiar with this stretch of the African coast.

Cape Blanco proved a suitable anchorage and Drake determined to stay for a few days to gather fresh supplies. The victualling of a long expedition such as this was always a major concern to its commander. Preserved foodstuffs obtained in England would only keep for three or four months at the most and the means of supplying them was neither wholly reliable nor efficient. In addition, ships such as Drake's, with their fine underwater lines designed to facilitate speed and ease of handling, were limited as to the weight they could carry especially when, as on this occasion, the vessels were heavily armed. In the long term these problems meant that the establishment of far-flung colonies such as Drake and his backers had in mind were severely hampered. Luck and enterprise might allow some ships – even many – to make voyages of exceptional duration, but regular victualling could not be taken for granted and the search for food and water on strange and often hostile coasts could involve long delays and loss of men.

But it was not only such practical matters that concerned some of the crew. Difficulties aside, both the geography and the people they encountered were viewed with all of the curiosity and much of the Protestant bias of alert Elizabethan eyes.[3] On their way down from Mogador for example, Fletcher, the expedition's chaplain, had been intrigued by the sight of the Atlas Mountains and their permanent cap of snow which 'seemeth never to be dissolved, because it reacheth so high into the cold or frozen region that the reflection of the sun can never come to it from the face of the earth'. This was dubious if conventional science, but Fletcher knew that this – to him – unfamiliar phenomenon had its practical uses. He wrote, with an approval rarely found in his descriptions of non-Protestant peoples, how the Arabs made regular trips to the snow line and 'from thence . . . ever continually fetch snow and bring it into the city and other places to sell in the markets, which they use for many things, but chiefly to mix with wines and other drinks, which otherwise would (for the extreme heat of the country) be unnatural and contagious to their bodies'.

Cape Blanco afforded no such comfort. It was a place of such cruel dryness that the natives were willing to sell anything (even their women) so that they could fill their leather water bags. To the Elizabethan mind such suffering could only be seen as a heavy judgement of God on the region but Drake, for all that the desperate natives offered him ambergris and valuable gums, would apparently take nothing and preferred instead freely to offer water and victuals from his own valuable store. Such untypical generosity (which might have been intended to woo the people from the Portuguese, who provided the natives with water in return for gold and slaves) nonetheless had one unexpected and rebarbative consequence. As they watched the locals devouring the supplies they had been given, their manner of eating and drinking proved to be so loathsome that even the strong Elizabethan stomach churned in revulsion.

For some at least, this was proof that such alien people could barely lay a claim to true humanity, to living in a mannerly and reasonable way which, as the educated knew from Aristotle, was the distinguishing feature of mankind rightly conceived. Man, Aristotle had declared, was a creature of civil community. For the Reverend Fletcher, waxing eloquent with vindictive righteousness, man was also the creature of a Protestant God. For him the misery of the Cape Blancians marked not only their hardly suprising lack of classical excellence, but also their altogether more woeful ignorance of the true church. His scathing sentences are the very stuff of late sixteenth-century English bigotry and racial hatred. Look at these people, he says. They are lazy. They never get up before midday and, when they do, they worship the sun and bow down before sticks and stones in the pathetic and unenlightened hope of appeasing some higher power. Thus the life without Christian revelation. But even some of those who profess to know the true God abuse the knowledge vouchsafed to them. Roman Catholics – 'I mean the Pope and his malignant synagogues of Satan' – similarly worship graven images, wooden saints and all the trash the Reformation had swept away. Such people were, in the view of Fletcher and the larger part of his congregation, lower than pagans like the Cape Blancians they so wilfully abused. It was best to be shot of both and, on 21 January, having greased and trimmed their ships, 'We addressed ourselves with all expedition on shipboard, with detestation of their religion and manners, praising our good God that He had called us unto so gracious a state, and had not left us in their miserable condition of ignorance and infidelity, almost degenerate from the course of natural men.'

While Fletcher was relieved to be quitting the spiritual wastes of Cape Blanco, Drake was worried by altogether more practical concerns. If he and Thomas Doughty had indeed left Plymouth with the appearance of being 'equal companions and friendly gentlemen', that friendship was under increasing strain. The deep and irrational antipathy which can force itself between the hairline cracks of even the warmest friendship, widening them until they leave a gulf down which one or other of those involved must fall, was already at work. Malicious gossip played its part in this. Doughty was not for long able to conceal the competitive and envious feelings he nurtured towards Drake, and the crews became aware of the nature of his grudges. Doughty needed to make clear to them that he was the more influential gentleman, the one with the contacts, and he began to boast about these. He let it be known that it was he who had broached the whole matter of the expedition to Hatton and Walsingham and that it was they who had mentioned it to the Queen. In such ways as these, Drake was beginning to be cast as a low-class and dishonest adventurer out for his own gain rather than a patriotic subject like Doughty. Obviously, Doughty went on, the initiatives he himself had taken were appreciated in the highest circles, and both the Queen and her Council had commended him for his conduct in Ireland and, as a result, given him joint command with Drake on the current voyage. Doughty was not even above bribing allies to his side, promising one of the crewmen (and perhaps others) that he would make him the wealthiest man in his family in return for his support. Vague hints were also dropped about how there was disapproval of Drake's Caribbean voyages in royal circles but, above all, there was the constant suggestion that Doughty was the man of real initiative without whom the voyage would never have happened.

With such rumours as these creeping about, Drake certainly could all too easily find cause for concern – a concern which, for the moment, he would do his best to ignore. Nonetheless, Doughty's talk was difficult to forget and there were, besides, other causes to be suspicious of him. For example, during the days they had spent on the Cape, Doughty had legitimately (indeed properly) begun exercising the men and reinstilling in them elements of military discipline which could all too easily slacken with potentially disastrous results. Doughty was, wrote Thomas Cooke in his account of the voyage, 'always careful in that respect and took great pains in that behalf', being zealous to 'train his men in warlike order that they might not be unskilful in time of need'. This makes clear that Doughty the gentleman officer was dedicated to his duty but, in that very dedication, lay danger. To train men in such ways as he was doing was to exercise authority over them and command their loyalty if not necessarily their hearts. The men Doughty marched up and down, practised in the use of the arquebus and accustomed to his voice were, all too plainly, *his* men, his favourites, the willing listeners to his gossip, and a group with a common bond outside Drake's immediate control. In the confined and easily mutinous conditions of a long voyage, all of this could be both rankling and a threat – dangers which, feeding on the poisonous envy of class difference, and distorted and magnified by the cramped and often dull days spent at sea – could turn all too easily into something very unpleasant indeed.

Deliberately to try and suppress such worries perhaps exacerbated them, but at least along coastal waters action could be a palliative. Besides, provisions were running low again and something needed urgently to be done. With favourable winds behind him, Drake

headed his flotilla south-west past the island of Bonavista and on to
Mayo where he anchored on 28 January. The captured Portuguese
pilot told him that plentiful supplies of dried goat meat were to be
had there, but the locals who made a business of preparing this
unappetising necessity for the Portuguese refused to trade illegally
with the English. Drake was obliged to land some seventy of his men
with orders to search for much-needed victuals. Perhaps to
emphasise his authority, he put Winter and Doughty in charge of the
party, the latter being a man who, in the words of his apologist,
'always showed himself not unskilful in such affairs'.

The party set off before daybreak in order to benefit from the cool
of the early morning. Dawn showed them that the island was largely
deserted, the locals having been forced to flee to the hills to hide from
the numerous other pirates who found the place a useful anchorage
and had already beguiled their time by looting the local church.
Nature was nonetheless plentiful even if people were not. Doughty
and his men were delighted by the abundant fertility of tropical
Mayo and intrigued by its produce: grapes, figs, bananas and, above
all, its sweet fleshy coconuts full of 'comfortable and cordial' milk.
The numerous goats were, by and large, too wild to capture easily
but, supplied with healthy fruit, the expedition returned to the ships
and the flotilla weighed anchor once more, sailing this time in the
direction of the island of Santiago which lay some ten leagues
distant.

In an area notoriously infested with pirates Drake was
determined to show himself the equal of any. The shipping lanes off
Santiago gave him his opportunity. He spied two Portuguese
merchantmen bound for Brazil and, under the guns of the local
fortress, dispatched a pinnace to command them to repair to his fleet.
As the little English vessel approached the *Santa Maria* – the more
distant of the enemy prizes – the soldiers in the fort fired their
cannon in the hope of providing cover for their fellow countrymen.
If they also hoped to warn Drake's men off their prey their action
was to no avail. The need for victuals, plus their native greed, gave
the crew the courage to fall on the *Santa Maria* and bring her away.
Such efforts were amply rewarded. The captured vessel was 'laden
with singular wines, sacks, and canaries, with woollens and linen

cloths, silks and velvets, and many other good commodities which stood us in that stead, that she was the life of our voyage, the neck whereof otherwise had been broken for the shortness of our provisions'. Supplies such as these were essential and, perhaps to mollify him, Drake put the zealous if difficult Doughty in charge of the captured ship, newly renamed the *Mary*, and ordered him to keep a keen eye on the cargo. Anyone, absolutely anyone who dared tamper with it, was to be reported to Drake at once and without exception.

An order so peremptory was nonetheless not easily obeyed. Both the chastened captives and the exultant English crew made difficult demands on Doughty's integrity. For their part the terrified Portuguese sailors tried in whatever ways they could to win his sympathy in the hope of being leniently treated. One of them even opened his private chest and, in full view of friends and foes alike, offered some all but worthless gifts: gloves, a little ring and some few pieces of money in a strange coin. This was a pathetic if apparently harmless gesture and Doughty was sufficiently mean-minded to accept it. He was not, however, able to prevent some of his own crew from helping themselves to overgenerous rations of the 'good store of drink' aboard the *Mary*, and a few of them clearly got drunk with what were soon to prove disastrous results.

Welcome as the goods aboard the *Mary* were, it contained another and altogether more valuable prize: a pilot deeply versed in the trade routes between Portugal and Brazil who might readily be intimidated into sharing his knowledge with Drake. The man's name was Nuño da Silva.[4] He was an intelligent and literate figure approaching his sixties, whose greying hair, long beard and quietly dignified black clothes gave his obvious experience an enhanced air of authority. In addition to Portuguese, da Silva spoke a little Spanish and, as guest at Drake's table, later acquired a smattering of English too. His altogether invidious position aboard an enemy ship made him a wary if gimlet-eyed observer of everything around him and of Drake especially. Much later, when giving evidence under oath to the Spanish authorities, da Silva tersely but accurately described his captor as being 'about thirty-eight years old, two years more or less, short, thickset, and robust'. He added that Drake had 'a red beard and a ruddy complexion . . . and in a leg he has a ball from an arquebus which he received in the Indies'. Da Silva also described the voraciousness with which Drake seized on the most valuable things the Portuguese could offer. He took from him, da Silva bitterly recalled, 'my astrolabe, my navigation chart which embraced however only the Atlantic ocean as far as the Rio de la Plata on the West and Cape of Good Hope on the East, and my book of instructions'. This last was da Silva's rutter and thus an invaluable item. Drake himself was scrupulous in keeping careful navigational records, and da Silva made clear to his Spanish interrogators how the Englishman carried 'a book in which he writes his log and paints birds, trees and seals'. His nephew, young John Drake, was as we have seen, a skilled and valuable helper in this task, and da Silva told how, shut up in Drake's cabin, they were always painting.

These records made by Drake and his boy have been lost, but the logbook would certainly have recorded the day of the month, the distance covered from noon to noon, and all noteworthy events. The navigational notebook that survives from a later voyage of Drake's suggests what other material might have been recorded too. Beautifully neat and precise, the paragraphs of strong italic script describe in more detail what the illustrations above them show, usually from the vantage point of a well-drawn miniature of a galleon under full sail. The pages describe the varying coastal elevations, harbours and tidal streams encountered, along with records of the depths of water and the nature of the material from the seabed brought up on the end of the mariner's leaded line. The accuracy of this work was remarkable and was attested to by a Spaniard, later captured by Drake, who lamented how grieved he was to see Drake's rutter 'for each thing is so naturally depicted that no one who guides himself according to these paintings can possibly go astray'. Today only a faint shadow of what Drake and his boy achieved can be gained by examining the rather crude drawings copied in the late seventeenth century from those that once adorned Fletcher's now lost manuscript account of the voyage. This is information at third hand.

It is nonetheless possible to think of Drake's own rutter-journal as an example of scrupulous early scientific method, a suggestion of the rigour and profound discipline that helped to make Drake himself one of the great navigators of his day. His flamboyance, hot-headedness and sheer courage were as recognised in his own time as in ours, but it was his carefully acquired knowledge and expertise in navigation that won the appreciation of his peers. Nor, as we have seen, was he above stealing their research when it suited his purposes, and then making good use of it. Da Silva records how Drake took the charts of his master and boatswain and divided them among his officers, as well as insisting that da Silva himself translate for him details of a map of the coast of Brazil which Drake kept on verifying when finally he arrived there. In such careful, if not altogether reputable, ways Drake assembled the information for the great chart of his journey. Though now lost, it was seen around 1618 by the Jacobean historian of English voyages, Samuel Purchas, hanging in the King's gallery at Whitehall, near the Privy Chamber. This was an honoured place for a map of the utmost importance to national strategy and it was, characteristically, an elaborate and lovely thing that had Elizabeth's name 'expressed in gold letters, with a golden crown, Garter and arms affixed'.

But disciplined navigational practices were not always easily to be followed aboard an Elizabethan pirate ship. In addition to his portrait of his captor and his captor's activities, da Silva also mentioned the presence on the expedition of Drake's younger brother Thomas, whom he described as being 'twenty-two years old with a scanty reddish beard, a white complexion, short and broad shouldered'. Da Silva described him as 'a good seaman'. The latter may have been true up to a point but da Silva did not see fit to add that Thomas was a hot-headed, ill-disciplined youth who was no brighter than he should have been and was capable of causing a great deal of trouble. Now that da Silva's ship had been captured and the crew had broken open his supplies of alcohol this soon became apparent. It is possible – even probable – that Thomas Drake was one of those seamen aboard the *Mary* who had all too thoroughly helped themselves to the liquor it was carrying. His actions certainly suggest over-excited energies for, in flat contradiction of his brother's express command, Thomas went to the captured Portuguese treasure chests and broke one open.[5]

Doughty was appalled. It was perfectly obvious that he would have to obey orders and report the matter to the youth's brother, and it was altogether likely that there would be hell to pay as a result. What could Doughty do? Quickly deciding that reason might yet instil repentance, he gravely lectured the young man on his stupidity. Thomas, as readily supine as he was hot-headed, cringed before his accuser. He confessed, he whinged, he cast round desperately for some way to patch things up. Master Doughty could keep a secret, couldn't he? There was no need to tell 'the General', was there? Doughty looked at the pathetic youth and realised the impossible position the foolish Thomas had put him in. There was no possibility of hushing the matter up. Gossip spread as wildly as fire aboard a cramped Elizabethan ship and was just as dangerous. Drake would have to be told but Doughty would, he said, put as good a colour on the incident as he could.

It was probably at this point that certain members of the crew, aware of the increasingly difficult relationship between Doughty and Drake, and realising that their loyalty lay with the 'General' and his family, decided to discredit the abrasive Doughty. John Brewer, the expedition's trumpeter, Edward Bright, 'and some others of their friends went to Drake and declared that Doughty had purloined to his proper use to deceive the voyage some things of great value, and therefore was not to be put in trust any longer, lest he might rob the voyage and deprive the company of their hope, and Her Majesty and other adventurers of their benefit, to enrich himself, to make himself the greater to the overthrow of all others'. Drake, realising that the matter, if true, was a deeply serious one, immediately went aboard the *Mary*. It was apparent to him at once that the accusations against Doughty were fatuous (he had only taken a few trivial items from a captured sailor) but Doughty himself was under orders to report to Drake just such behaviour as he himself had been accused of. Perhaps it was now, with his zeal redoubled by his difficulties, that he told Drake of young Thomas's foolishness.

With his family honour at stake, Drake turned not on his brother but on Doughty, exploding in an outbreak of apoplectic fury. Oaths of Elizabethan virulence ricocheted across the *Mary* as Drake, cunning even in his anger and borne on tides of long pent-up irrational hatred, demanded 'what Thomas Doughty should mean to touch his brother, and did as it were assure himself that he had some further meaning in this and that he meant to shoot at his credit, and he would not, nor could not (by God's life as he sware it) suffer it'. It was appalling, a sudden storm whose terrible violence could well wreck the whole expedition. Drake in the very ecstasy of his anger, knew that he must prevent this. Some sort of face-saving compromise had to be patched up and, far more importantly, the invaluable supplies on the *Mary* had to be secured. There appeared to be only one solution. Doughty would have to be sent aboard the *Pelican* as its Captain while Drake himself would stay on the *Mary*, which would now be nominally in charge of his exasperating brother. Doughty's honour, Thomas Drake's reputation, and the well-being of the flotilla might just be secured in such a way.

Doughty, however, the whole thrust of his malicious gossip and desire for pre-eminence having received so sudden and public a reverse, was grievously and bitterly angry. It was very likely in this tense situation, hot-headed with wounded pride, that he blurted out once again that he alone had initiated the voyage, adding how he could have done it himself well enough. His very public humiliation and his burning need to feel that he had the ability to be the master of any situation, led him to speak badly not just of Drake but of all those people in high places who had backed the voyage. Members of the Privy Council like Walsingham were the merest sharks, two-faced people who could be bribed and bought. 'Yea, the Queen's majesty herself' was no better. They were all corrupt, money-grabbing and worthless. This was the anger of a peeved and foolish man, but the whole incident marked an early crisis in the voyage and it was now clear to Drake that morale could only be fully restored by a challenge. There could be no more island cruising. It was time to breast the rigours of the Atlantic.

Such decisiveness was, for Dr Johnson, a principal key to Drake's genius as a leader. 'Eager of action, and acquainted with men's nature, he never suffered idleness to infect his followers with cowardice, but kept them from sinking under any disappointment, by diverting their attention to some new enterprise'.[6] Johnson's *Life of Sir Francis Drake* is an eighteenth-century version of the heroic, and the hero Johnson created and moralised on is rooted in a firm and practical grip on reality. Not for him an indulgence of 'chimerical schemes', those flights of the imagination which, falling to earth, illustrate Johnson's great theme: the vanity of human wishes. But Johnson's Drake is no mere oafish man of action. His moral qualities are real and the author highlights them to inspire his readers. Drake had 'that ardent spirit that prompted him to adventures, and that indefatigable patience that enabled him to surmount difficulties'. One may, perhaps, question Drake's possession of the last quality, but Johnson rightly saw that he had 'an intrepidity never to be shaken, and a judgement never to be perplexed'. The *Life* suggests that such qualities belong to a man by virtue of his nature and, for Johnson at least, prove that 'no obscurity of birth, or meanness of fortune, is insurmountable to bravery and diligence'.

It is interesting in the light of future developments – and future portraits of Drake – that Johnson saw nothing inherently British in Drake's virtues. They are the qualities of a representative heroic figure, independent of race. The idea of a distinctly British national character was, however, in the process of formation even as Johnson was writing, and images of Drake would soon play a part in fashioning it. A contemporary of Johnson's wrote of his fellow countrymen that 'there is a haughty courage, an elevation of thought, a greatness of taste, a love of liberty, a simplicity and honesty among us, which we inherit from our ancestors'. Such a relatively new sense of national character and national identity needed to create a past for itself, and Drake would in time come to be seen as a useful figure in this. The versions of his exploits written but unpublished during his lifetime were collected together and appeared in lightly edited form as *The English Hero*, a work first issued in 1681 and many times reprinted.

Drake was needed in this form – a form which, by his editing of the text, he had done much to fashion. His hatred of the Catholic menace was famous, and *The English Hero* was first issued when that Catholic threat reached its last and most hysterical crisis with the Popish Plot and the desperate manoeuvring to exclude Charles II's Catholic brother from the English throne. The Glorious Revolution seven years later ensured a Protestant monarchy under the control of Parliament, while a Toleration Act allowed freedom of worship to Catholics at the cost of heavy penalties and permanent debarment from public office. Drake the heroic Protestant could be seen as an early warrior in this struggle while, with the extraordinarily rapid commercial revolution that was now taking place – the founding of the Bank of England, the Stock Exchange and the National Debt – his exploits could be seen as having prefigured the nation's hugely expanding network of maritime trade. He could be praised as a founding father of 'the naval domination of Britain and the extent of her commerce and navigation'. By the 1760s, the country had annexed most of India, North America and the wealth of the West Indies. Britannia ruled the waves and, if she did so 'at heaven's command', men like Drake were the Almighty's instruments. Just as Drake and his contemporaries looked back to the figures in Foxe's *Book of Martyrs* for a reassuring sense of continuity with an elect Protestant nation specially chosen by God, so new generations could begin looking back on Drake as a heroic and near mythical creator of what, by 1812, was beginning to be called an empire and which, with 'skill and courage true', would forever remain 'unchanged, unshaken, unsubdued'.

The Elizabethan pirate was on his way to becoming an imperial icon but, to do so effectively while currently facing one of the great crises of the circumnavigation, he needed to act with that decisiveness Johnson praised and unencumber himself of any extraneous liabilities before braving the Atlantic. He did so with characteristically pitiless logic. He put his Portuguese prisoners on to a little pinnace and set them adrift with no more necessities than some wine, food, and the clothes they stood up in. Only then, on 2 February 1578, did he feel able to order his remaining ships to sail out across the Atlantic and 'travel in the new discovered parts of the world'.

Despite the swelling undertow of acrimony, there were those among the crew who were exhilarated by the new vistas opening up to them. As the ships approached the equator after three weeks of being becalmed, cramped horizons dropped away and the warnings of the ancient philosophers who taught that men would fry to death in these regions were shown to be old wives' tales. A delighted Fletcher spoke for this new knowledge when he declared that experience showed how the equatorial belt, far from being a place of catastrophe, was really the earthly Paradise, adding that 'nothing can be more pleasant to the life of man than to live and to abide therein'.[7] This was a pardonable exaggeration, but there was considerable discomfort. As John Winter recalled, once they had passed the equator, 'they sustained such heat, with often thunder and lightnings, that we did sweat for the most part continually, as though we had been in a stove, or hothouse'. In such an atmosphere as this, damp piles of clothes quickly rotted in the rains that descended on them. There nonetheless remained a resolute determination to view everything in this new world as a sign of the benevolence and glory of God. For example, the intense and oppressive heat killed off the lice with which the men had been plagued since leaving England, while the violent rainstorms ensured that there was little need to worry about that constant peril of long voyages, namely the drinking water running dry.

Quite as welcome was the abundance of wildlife. For all that this was a long passage on the vast ocean where nothing but sea beneath and air above was to be glimpsed, God, it appeared, had taken care to provision Drake and his men with princely munificence. Fresh dolphins, giant mackerel and flying fish were all wholesome nourishment. Fletcher found the flying fish particularly delectable, and so unlikely that he felt compelled to write a delightful paragraph about them to convince 'green-headed carpers' at home that there really were fish which escaped their predators by taking to the air. This was not always to their advantage, however, for the flying fish often crashed into the sails and masts of the ships and the sailors would quickly cut up prey so easily caught to use as bait with which they hoped to catch dolphins.

Fletcher's observations of natural life are as fresh and vivid as a studious child's, but he was not above being taken in by a tall story. He saw that the numerous pelicans were partial to flying fish, and da Silva spun him a good yarn to the effect that pelicans loathed getting their feet wet and therefore relished capturing prey that rose clear out of the water. Nor was this all. 'When they slept they mounted up into the air, and casting their wings abroad, descended without waking, fast on sleep, till they came near to the water, which nature abhorring, they presently awake, and flying up again to fetch out the rest of their sleep as before'. It seemed that the pelicans were equally averse to dry land. Hence they had very curious mating habits. 'They engender in the air,' Fletcher reported, 'and never come at land but only in the time of laying their eggs, which is as it were but a moment, for with all speed the female drops her eggs in the sands, and, covering them, presently departeth, never repairing any more to them, but leaveth them to the heat of the sun and the nature of the sands in the providence of God to bring them forth living creatures, like to them in their kind, without showing any spark of natural affection towards them.'

Fletcher does not record if he ate pelican, but other birds were to be had in abundance. He noted with delighted amazement how the fowls he had seen on the coasts could be found 500 leagues out to sea, adding that it was the crews' daily exercise to trap them. There was no difficulty in doing this, and Fletcher accounted for the fact by saying that the birds confused the ships with rocks and, innocently landing on them, 'they suffered themselves to be strucken dead with cudgels one by one, to be snared with lines put about their necks with poles, and to be taken with hands without motion or removing away'. It was as if God Himself had commanded them to such acts of unwitting altruism, and there is in these passages a sense of Fletcher's faithful trust, and his gratitude for a God Who had seemingly 'commanded and enjoined the most profitable and glorious works of His hands to wait upon us, not alone for the relief of our necessities, but also to give us delight in the contemplation of His excellence in beholding the variety and order of His providence, with a particular taste of His fatherly care over us all the while'.

Such benevolence did not extend into the human world. Here, during long periods of being alternately becalmed and drenched, 'grudges did seem to grow . . . from day to day'. Doughty did his best to feed them. Severe cracks began to appear in morale and there were even whispers of mutiny and plots to set one ship against another and to hijack the *Pelican*. There were those who asked

Doughty to summon up what remained of his influence with Drake and tell him what was being whispered but Doughty naturally refused, saying that Drake hated him so much he would certainly cast him as the chief conspirator. When Fletcher said he would go to Drake, Doughty earnestly begged him not to 'for, said he, I shall be suspected'. Relations between these two leaders of the expedition had sunk to this rancorous low – a mutual, bitter suspicion – for the removal of Doughty to the *Pelican* had done nothing to draw the venom that was festering in Drake's mind. This now began slowly to poison all his thoughts. The fragile peace that had been brokered between the two men was, on Drake's part, merely an outward show, and circumstances now conspired to expose it as such.

The equatorial climate did not help. There were long, monotonous periods when the ships were becalmed in sullen and enervating heat. The sails hung from the great yard arms limp, hopeless and still. The caulking, turning to liquid, started to spread and suppurate across the hot planking of the decks. There was not breeze enough to stir the dust, leading to a loss of appetite, and the consequent failure of the men to ingest sufficient protein all too easily made everyone edgy and so magnified the ever-present sense of conflict. Boredom, too, was a real threat and was made all the worse by the unending, hysteria-inducing view of flat seas and unshadowed skies. There was no escape, no privacy, nothing new to see, no one new to meet. The tiny ships enforced on every man a stifling sense of constriction. As day after day dragged on, too many men with nothing to do were constantly obliged to eat, drink, sleep and amuse themselves in cheek-by-jowl closeness. The irksome habits of some could be magnified to exasperation in the minds of others. Resentment became endemic while, for the greater part of the crew at least, sexual frustration was swollen into ill-concealed aggression and ebbed back again into bitterness, resentment and depression.

The situation was most difficult of all for Drake. A measure of distance, of isolation even, was essential if he were to maintain command, but his enforced separateness served greatly to heighten his anxieties and distort his view of Doughty. Anything and everything can feed suspicion, and few emotions are more bitter than a sense of trust betrayed, the thought that 'equal companions' are such no more. Feelings like these can cut to the core of a man's identity and encourage him to gather or manufacture, with perverse rapaciousness, evidence against those he has come to hate, as Drake himself was now to do. Old doubts and new rumours fed his bitter hunger and were legion. Had there really been difficulties between the two men right at the start? Had there perhaps been a serious argument back in a garden at Plymouth? And what was Doughty's real purpose now? Why had there been 'great fallings out and quarrels' aboard the ships? Doughty, equally rancorous, put these last down to the perils of divided command. 'Every of you have been uncertain whom to obey', he told the men aboard the *Pelican*. There was much truth in this, but there were still those among them who chafed at Doughty's command and thought that he was too peremptory and exceeded his authority. Word of this came to Drake himself and deepened his hostility. He now began actively looking for an opportunity to 'disgrade' Doughty.

That opportunity, whether by chance or design, now presented itself. John Brewer, the expedition's trumpeter, made a visit to the *Pelican*.[8] What followed was meant as horseplay but was to have dire consequences. Brewer was given a 'cobby' or jovial beating by the crew. Doughty joined in, saying, 'Fellow John, you shall have in my hand, although it be that light amongst the rest.' Brewer was livid. The ritual humiliation ceased to be a joke and the trumpeter swore violently at the company, telling them that he knew perfectly well that they were not all loyal to Drake. He then turned on Doughty himself and made his suspicions clear: 'God's wounds, Doughty, what dost thou mean to use this familiarity with me considering thou art not the General's friend?' Doughty tried to laugh it off. 'What, fellow John, what moves you to this and to use these words to me, that am as sure and good a friend to my good General as any in this fleet, and I defy his that shall say the contrary.'

Brewer would have none of it and went straight back to Drake and the *Mary*. There was a hurried conversation, and the boat in which Brewer had returned was at once despatched back to the *Pelican* with orders to fetch Doughty. He arrived to find himself the victim of a masterly piece of Elizabethan theatre. Drake was leading his crew in prayer. No untoward behaviour could possibly disturb this central rite of Elizabethan maritime life: a crew brought together by their Captain to commune with the Almighty, Whose true church Providence had placed in the hands of the nation's Queen and her delegated representative – as Drake claimed to be. The very sound of Doughty's boat drawing alongside was a gross intrusion and, when Drake eventually turned to the new arrival, his terse words carried absolute authority: 'Stay there, Thomas Doughty, for I must send you to another place.' That place was the little *Swan*, the expedition's fly boat. It was, Drake said, an altogether fitter place for him than the *Pelican*. Drake would not listen to a word the protesting Doughty tried to say; he had resolved to re-establish his authority by means of Doughty's very public humiliation. This was all too painfully obvious, and Doughty's hatred at being refused a hearing boiled over the minute he was aboard the *Swan*. He had been sent there as a prisoner and a traitor to the General, he said. But he would have his revenge. 'He would purge himself in England afore their betters that did accuse him, if law would serve him.'

By the end of February the increasingly divided and bitter expedition was nearing the coast of Brazil and the Bay of Todos los Santos. After so long and demanding a journey, Drake wanted to put in there in order to water and refresh his men, but da Silva warned against this since it was all too likely that they would encounter Portuguese vessels that were usually anchored there. It was altogether safer to turn south, navigating the distantly visible coast by means of da Silva's purloined papers and the information provided by soundings. Even so, the first indication that this would be far from an easy stretch of the expedition came on 28 March when the *Mary*, her precious provisions and twenty-eight men, were temporarily lost. It was, throughout, one of Drake's principal aims 'to keep our whole fleet (as near as possible we could) together', and the brief disappearance of the vessel caused much sorrow in the whole company since its loss might well result in the overthrow of the whole voyage. For all that the *Mary* reappeared the following day, her brief loss was an augury of greater troubles to come.

1. Drake's home at Buckland Abbey.

2. Drake as circumnavigator and gentleman.

3. The 'Armada' portrait of Elizabeth I.

4. Drake's inveterate enemy, Philip II of Spain.

5. Sir Francis Walsingham.

6. Sir Christopher Hatton, a patron of the *Golden Hind*.

7. Lord Burleigh.

8. A triple portrait of Cavendish, Drake and Hawkins.

9. Drake painted by Hilliard.

10. Sir Walter Raleigh, also by Hilliard.

11. Lord Howard of Effingham, English Admiral at the Armada.

12. Lady Drake.

13. Drake in his maturity.

These were apparent almost at once. Having reached 22 degrees south, the expedition turned south-south-west in order to skirt the abrupt change of the coastline. The regular, dutiful work of piloting continued and soundings began to bring up soft ooze, indicating they were in thirty-two fathoms of water and then in twenty-eight. They were nearing land and eventually espied a low coast rising sharply to distant mountain peaks. A sure sense of relief buoyed up the whole company, only to be turned to sudden panic. Drake's simple shipboard instruments and careful use of charts were no defence against the forces of nature they minutely measured. A dense fog – the sudden and notorious Argentine *pampero* – engulfed the fleet with a blinding thickness so impenetrable that no one ship could see another.[9] And, in the fog, was hidden a storm of such terrible ferocity 'as heaven and earth had gone together, and the roots of the rocks and the bottom of the sea should have been discovered'. This violent anarchy of the elements threatened to drive the vessels to their ruin on the shoals of a lee shore, and da Silva cried out desperately that the only hope was to turn back or else drown. One of the ships had already touched the shoals and divine Providence alone, Fletcher declared, saved it from destruction and cast it out to the wider and mutinous seas where the scattered vessels made what separate ways they could.

How had this appalling experience come about? What was its cause? Drake realised it was essential to find out; such perils threatened not just the immediate fate of his expedition (a matter serious enough) but its whole purpose and future plans. Was the Atlantic coast of South America, which men in their desk-bound studies could dream of as a region of limitless wealth, destined forever to preserve its promise with fire and brimstone? Drake turned to anxiously to da Silva and, what science could neither describe nor explain, superstition, hand in hand with bigotry, leaped in to account for. The old Portuguese pilot, exasperated that he was still a captive and ever quick to make use of maritime lore garnered over a lifetime, voiced his opinion.

There was little comfort to be drawn from what he said. His fellow countrymen, da Silva declared, had so harassed the local inhabitants that, in desperation and despair, they had turned to devil

117

worship, summoning up evil spirits and diabolic winds in ceremonies brought to a ghastly climax by tossing great heaps of blinding sand into the roaring and satanic gales. Elizabethan minds, all too easily trapped in a lurid confusion of religion and magic – a confusion which made the witch and the cunning man apparently familiar figures on every village green – could easily believe that such forces were indeed at work at the edge of the world. And how obvious it was that the barbarity of a Catholic race like the Portuguese – people who believed that priestly incantations could horribly turn bread and wine into the body and blood of Christ – should be responsible for such abominations. A virtuous Protestant shudder ran down Fletcher's spine as he recorded his belief that good Anglican Englishmen such as he, could at least find eventual safety in the loving hands of the Divine. Drake may well have agreed in part but, with the loathed and dangerous Doughty still rancorous against him and now aboard a missing ship somewhere off the South American coast, he was not altogether minded to think that devil worship was the preserve of primitive tribesmen alone. Something sinister had worked its way into the expedition, polluting its atmosphere, and Drake was not averse to using it for his own ends. Doughty might very well be capable of witchcraft and raising storms.

Meanwhile, as the *pampero* blew itself out, the altogether more sober work of reconnoitring an alien coast went on. The ships, slowly regrouping, made their way down the shore, keeping 'sometime to the seaward, and sometimes towards the shore, but always southward'. Eventually they reached the mouth of the River Plate where Drake anchored off what he named Cape Joy because the errant *Swan* rejoined them there along with another of the lost vessels. Once landed after so long a time at sea the crew found, much to their relief, that the region was temperate, fertile, and flowing with much needed fresh water. Having replenished their supplies, the ships then made their way up the estuary towards the Bay of Montevideo where a large colony of seals was found basking on a rocky island. Both their pelts and their oil were useful but the animals were not easy to catch. 'The only way to kill them speedily,' Fletcher wrote, 'is to strike them upon the nose with a cudgel, for no other place can hurt them; and they be of great strength and cast stones and gravel mightily with their hinder feet at them which pursue them in their flying.'

Meat so obtained was welcome, but their real purpose of reconnoitring the western shore of South America to find safe anchorages and safe access to the interior – was proving something of a disappointment. The River Plate was shallow, full of shoals and troubled by dangerous winds, making it advisable to turn seawards again. After a fortnight's exploration of the estuary, the ships did so, only to run once again into a dreadful storm, a *pampero* which for a second time separated Doughty and the *Swan* from the main contingent. If the situation was at once terrifying and exhausting, it was also useful to Drake for, as the battered ships were engulfed once more 'with a palpable darkness of Egypt', so Drake believed he could turn the feelings it engendered in the crew against Doughty and thus to his own advantage. If he were to destroy the loathed Doughty (and it is clear that his thoughts were already tending in that direction) then it was essential to win as many of his divided crew to his own side as possible. He would deliberately manufacture a crisis of confidence in the most scurrilous and ruthless way. He let it be known that it was obvious that such terrible and unnatural storms as they had all endured were the devil's work and, in Doughty's absence, Drake never ceased to inveigh against him 'terming him a conjuror and witch, and, at any time when we had any foul weather, he would say that Thomas Doughty was the occasion thereof, and would say that it came out of Tom Doughty's capcase, and would avouch the same with great oaths; which he at no time scanted, they cost him so little.'

Exhausted and ill-educated men, in peril, far from home and with readily superstitious minds, could be won over by such poisonous talk as this, the more so since the divisions that had opened up among the officer corps were obvious and threatening to them all. Besides, the men were largely minded to trust Drake for, in the last resort, he was one of them as Doughty was not. He was their own West Country man who, driven by the immense energies that gave him his charisma, had risen through the ranks to become their commander and feast off silver plates. He knew them, knew their ways. He had done manual work like them. He knew the hardship, monotony and sudden dangers of the seaman's life. He knew the techniques of their trade with a sure and practical knowledge that had nothing to hide. Besides, his reputation and his wealth spoke with obvious authority and were a surer path to riches than that which Doughty might lead them along. They might fear Drake, at times even loathe him, but he could still speak to them in their own language, and by coming among them he suggested that he would take care of their interests and prove that they were all, quite literally, in the same boat.

Such men were stubborn but they were not stupid. Their loyalty was not something lightly secured and Drake, with a genius for leadership rooted deep in his own experience, knew that actions spoke louder than words, however bitter those words might be. As the *Pelican* neared Cape Tres Puntas, he realised his men needed rest but, refusing to anchor off so rocky a place 'without good and perfect discovery beforehand made', went himself to investigate the place. It was the sort of decision that commanded instant and lasting respect. Few could deny such a man, but as Drake was being rowed across to the mainland yet a third *pampero* descended with terrifying speed and fury. The fog thickened so horribly that Drake disappeared from the onlookers' view and it was only through the bravery of one of his Captains, acting upon 'the abundance of his love and service to his General', that the leader was saved from the storm. Meanwhile, the other ships in the company, forced to put off from the shore for their own safety, fared badly. In particular the *Mary*, with da Silva aboard, was so tossed by the gale as to be driven out of sight. Drake had lost both a ship and his pilot while, in addition, Doughty and the *Swan* were still nowhere to be seen. No doubt, in this anxious state, the execrations heaped on Doughty's head by Drake had a venom and a force which surely convinced many among the men that Doughty was indeed a sorcerer, a familiar of demons raising tempests that would destroy them all.

In fact, the embittered object of their animosity was hastening his own destruction by altogether more prosaic means. The atmosphere aboard the *Swan* was by now thoroughly poisonous. There was a strained alliance between Doughty and John Chester, the ship's erstwhile Captain whom Doughty had replaced, while both men were at loggerheads with the *Swan's* master who was, it seems, the strongest character aboard as well as one of Drake's supporters.[10] Meanwhile, the murmuring against Drake himself grew louder and more insistent. There was a smear campaign about 'certain secrets' which Doughty said he knew and his exposure of them would do Drake no good. There were more mutterings about Doughty's influential contacts and Drake's supposedly corrupt dealing in Ireland and elsewhere. There were more assertions, too, that Doughty's much-vaunted gentility was such that Drake 'could not cast him off from being equal with him'. Worse, there were whisperings of mutiny. During an after-dinner talk about what should happen to those who might turn against Drake and his efforts, one man gave it out as his opinion that such traitors should be hanged. After all, Magellan had seen fit to take such action when faced with a similar challenge off this very shore. Doughty put a quick stop to these ideas and determined to show that Drake had no such power as Magellan enjoyed: 'Nay, soft, his authority is none such as Magellan's was . . . and for hanging, it is for dogs and not for men.'

Meanwhile, the master of the *Swan*, placed in an invidious position, conducted his own campaign. His little ship was alone on a hostile sea, he had a bitter and hot-headed gentleman aboard, and his supplies were running low. Like Drake himself, he sought to confirm his alliance with his ordinary seamen and sat with them to ensure that they were all amply fed while Doughty and his friends were kept on short rations. The situation inevitably provoked an incident. Doughty began whispering to Chester, saying, 'I marvel, Master Chester, that you will take it at his hands to be thus used.' He then turned to the master and told him that he did 'use too much partiality, considering the extremity that for want of victuals they were like to fall into, and it was against reason that he and his mates should be so plentifully fed and others to be at point to starve'. Surrounded by his loyal men and with his authority challenged, the master began to lose his temper, telling Doughty that 'rascals' such as he should be grateful for being allowed to chew the rollocks on the ship's boat when he would let them.

No gentleman could tolerate being called a rascal and Doughty tried to pull rank, saying that at the very least he should be treated like the rest of the crew since he had money tied up in the venture. The master replied he would be hanged if he cared about that. The two men came to blows, the master adding that Doughty could lick the turds out of his arse and would indeed have to unless they met up with Drake again soon. This was too much. Doughty turned to Chester: 'Master Chester, let us not be thus used at these knaves' hands, lose nothing of that authority that the General hath committed unto you, if you will we will put the sword again into your hands and you shall have the government.' There were those who later added that Doughty told Chester that if he complied with his wishes then Doughty himself 'would make the company to be ready one to cut another's throat'. This was simply, stupidly, hot-headedly an incitement to mutiny. It could hardly be long concealed from Drake when, on 17 May, he finally caught up with the Swan and escorted her to Port Desire.

Here, hard decisions had to be made. It was by now perfectly obvious to Drake that the dangers of the South American Atlantic coast – the sudden storms and frequently scattered ships – were such that he would have to reduce the size of his flotilla if he were to keep it together. He could not go on careering off the ocean in pursuit of stragglers, especially when those stragglers were men he could no longer trust. Seasoned sailors were well aware that reducing the number of ships was an eminently sensible move since 'fewer ships might the better keep company, and that they might also be the better appointed with new and fresh supplies of provision and men'. Doughty's vindictiveness blinded him to such common sense. He had been humiliated beyond endurance by a man of lower social standing who was determined to crush him and against whose force he stood no chance.

Doughty had progressively compromised any of the respect his loudly trumpeted gentility might have entitled him to and, with every assertion of his worth, had proved himself a liability. The antagonism was now approaching its crisis. Aboard the *Pelican*, Doughty turned on Drake and, with a fury as vehement as it was fatuous, told him that while they were supposed to be equal partners and comrades in arms, such things were impossible when Drake was a man as worthless as his word. There was an instant response. 'The General did not only strike him, but commanded him to be bound to the mast, for the accomplishment of which the master of the fly boat, his old heavy friend, took a little pain with him.' Doughty was then relegated to the *Christopher* and the company of his growing number of enemies, while Drake ordered the *Swan* to be stripped, broken up and burned before the humiliated Doughty's eyes.

While the timbers of the *Swan* disintegrated into ashes a band of some thirty of the local inhabitants, attracted by the strange goings-on, came down to within a hundred yards of the shore.[11] Having gingerly accepted some proffered gifts and ascertained that the English might be friendly, they began to make themselves very pleasant. They were not, for all Fletcher's assertion, the Patagonian giants of legend, but somewhat simple people who, for all their bows, arrows, painted faces and evident martial discipline, soon proved themselves to be 'much given to mirth and jollity, and are very sly, and ready to steal anything that comes within their reach'. One of them in high spirits even snatched Drake's scarlet sailing cap with its band of gold off his head, something which caused no offence since Drake was determined not to make enemies of these people. But the laughing, dancing and the delight with which the natives responded to the sound of the trumpet and viols had eventually to come to an end. The altogether more serious business of barrelling up water and slaughtering the plentiful seals was attended to before the expedition set off once again, only to lose the *Christopher* and, with it, Doughty. When the vessel was eventually found Drake's actions were again swift and peremptory. The *Christopher* was stripped and abandoned.

Meanwhile, Drake had prepared carefully for the humiliations Doughty and his brother were to endure. He had himself gone aboard the vessel to which they were to be confined and, summoning the company together, told them he was handing over to them 'a very bad couple of men'. Both, he said, were witches and conjurers, adept with poisons and ever stirring up mutiny. They were the devil's brood and no one should talk to them. If any one did then

Drake would 'hold them as his enemies' who wanted to destroy the entire expedition. Nor was this imposition of silence all. Doughty and his brother were to live, sleep and eat with the lowest hands on the ship and were to be denied pen, ink and books. Socially humiliated and deprived of any vestige of physical comfort, their busy, vengeful minds were not to be occupied by recording their woes or casting spells and raising storms. Theirs was to be as total an isolation as could be achieved aboard a crowded Elizabethan ship, a wholesale stripping away of human contact. Doughty and his brother were now untouchables, to be reduced to the very barest existence while those loyal to Drake, even the meanest boy aboard, would soon be rewarded with wealth beyond their dreams and 'have gold come as plentiful as this wood unto the ships'. This was a blatant and crude appeal for loyalty, and even now there were those who were not entirely won over. The Doughtys prevailed on the bosun to provide them with a cabin, an offence for which the man lost his office and suffered Drake's continuing and heavy displeasure. It was in such a hostile, volatile state as this, with morale collapsing, suspicion endemic and the season turning foul, that Drake pointed his remaining flotilla south and, on 20 June, reached Port Saint Julian. Here, having finally caught up with the *Mary*, he would spend the winter and finally resolve on Doughty's death.

5

The Circumnavigation of the Globe

Three: The Middle Passage

June 1578–March 1579

Port Saint Julian was a suitable backdrop for the tragic and ghastly events that were soon to be played out there. The harbour was a windswept, treeless place, with inadequate food and poor and brackish water contaminated by a salt marsh festering at the far end of the bay.[1] The season being winter, Port Saint Julian was also bitterly cold – colder, some of the men thought, than the depths of an English winter. Far from being a haven where Drake could 'refresh his wearied men, and cherish them which had . . . tasted such bitterness of discomfort', Port Saint Julian was a place where fatigue and despondency could easily bite deep into morale already corroded by deep hostilities. This atmosphere was made worse by the sense of fatality that hung over the place. Here, as many of the sailors knew, a desperate Magellan nearly sixty years earlier had executed the ringleaders of his mutinous crew. Was this an omen? The discovery of a gibbet with human bones littered beneath served as a reminder of the grim episode until Drake's cooper, in an act of gallows humour, tried to laugh it off by hacking the structure down and making tankards out of the fragments for such of the company as would drink from them.

Contact with the primitive Tehuelche natives further tested tried nerves. With conspicuous readiness to ease the lot of his crew and brave personally all he expected them to endure, Drake himself led the party that now went ashore in search of victuals. Their efforts were watched by two of the local people who were at first intrigued by the strangers and, from a safe distance, vied with Oliver the master gunner to see who could shoot an arrow furthest. It all seemed friendly enough, surprisingly so since Magellan and his chronicler had spread rumours about the men being giants of legendary strength. This was clearly untrue but, if the Tehuelche were no taller than a large Englishman, there were those among them who were equally easily moved to suspicion and worse.

A third native soon appeared and angrily bade the others to withdraw while a certain Robert White was drawing his bow. The string snapped and, as Drake and his men turned back to their boat, a shower of arrows suddenly rained down on them from a posse of hidden warriors. White was hit in the shoulders and then in the lungs but staggered on as Oliver, levelling his gun to fire in revenge, was felled while vainly seeking to ignite the damp powder he had loaded. Drake, shouting at his men to shift from place to place rather than remain as standing targets, snatched up the apparently useless gun and, aiming a successful shot at the warrior who had slain Oliver, 'tore out his belly and guts with great torment'. The terrified tribesmen fled as the anguished White was carried back to the ship. He died two days later after which, under the cover of darkness, Drake returned to the shore to collect Oliver's body and then ordered that both corpses be buried side by side in 'earthen tabernacles . . . with such commendable ceremonies as belong unto soldiers of worth in time of war'.

Such public honours were in sharp and no doubt deliberate contrast to the way in which Drake now resolved to settle once and for all the festering problem of Thomas Doughty.[2] Long nurtured hatred, so deep and so bitter as to suggest that it touched painfully Drake's insecurities, combined with the ruthless decision-making necessary in a great commander. Drake resolved on a public trial – or the appearance of a trial – the inevitable verdict of which would result in the guilty Doughty's public execution. Such barbaric rites lay at the core of the Elizabethan concern to reinforce social discipline through what they considered to be an edifying act of horror. The crowds who gathered to watch such events were spectators in a theatre of cruelty and Drake conspicuously stage-managed this show so that he could finally appear to his men self-created in the role he wished to play: that of the Queen's loyal and heroic commander whose words were law. What he had in mind was a show trial that would give every appearance of being in accordance with the deepest beliefs of the majority of those who observed it while, at the same time, drawing them into a situation where Drake, and Drake alone, was the obvious and absolute master. If this involved ruses and deceptions, blatant bullying, emotional appeals, and the outward semblance of judicial process then so be it. Drake had at all costs to preserve and unite his expedition and clearly establish himself as the focus of legitimate authority. Only in this way, he believed, could he prevent his crew from disintegrating into self-destructive chaos on an alien and distant shore. Pitiless necessity drove him to an appearance of justice that was wholly untempered by mercy.

It is clear that he made careful preparations for, when he summoned his men to the shore on the last day of June, he made sure that John Thomas brought with him a bundle of affidavits in which members of the crew had sworn to having heard various statements Doughty had allegedly made. Among the allegations were whispered suggestions of mutiny, promises of large sums of money to those Doughty thought he could win to his side, allegations that Drake himself had been involved in shady doings whose exposure would damage him, and repeated suggestions that Drake's social status had given him neither the friends nor the influence to command an expedition that was really Doughty's initiative in the first place. Worse matters would be exposed later.

When the papers had been unrolled and the accusations read out, Drake turned to Doughty, saying: 'Thomas Doughty, you have here sought by divers means, in as much as you may, to discredit me to the great hindrance and overthrow of this voyage, besides other great matters wherewith I have to charge you withal the which if you can clear yourself of, you and I shall be very good friends, whereto the contrary you have deserved death.' Doughty told Drake that the accusations could never be proved. Drake waved this aside (the niceties of the law meant nothing to him in such a situation) and asked Doughty who he would choose to be tried by. Doughty answered: 'Why, good General . . . let me live to come into my country, and I will be there tried by Her Majesty's laws.' This entirely reasonable statement was denied even as it was uttered. 'Nay, Thomas Doughty . . . I will here empanel a jury on you to enquire further of these matters that I have to charge you withal.'

Doughty, pitifully hoping that he might yet be subject to due process, challenged Drake's authority by saying, 'I hope you will see your commission be good.' Drake tersely replied that it was good enough. Doughty asked to see the commission, declaring that, 'It is necessary that it should be here showed.' Drake would have none of this. Challenged to produce a document he almost certainly did not possess, his only option was a show of force and a skilfully contrived appeal to the shocked and horrified sailors gathered on the Patagonian shore. Drake would be both judge and prosecuting counsel in this kangaroo court-martial. Saying that he knew Doughty threatened his very life, he peremptorily ordered the wretched man to be bound with his arms behind his back and gave vent to 'divers furious words'. He then transported his audience in imagination back to Ireland where he and Doughty had first met. So Doughty had claimed that it was he who first introduced Drake to the Lord Essex, did he? This was arrant nonsense. Drake was, he declared, 'daily with my Lord' and only saw Doughty in that exalted circle once. Essex, everybody knew, had come to a pitiful and painful end in Ireland, and Drake gratuitously charged Doughty with poisoning him. So much then for Doughty's loyalties and his friends in high places. Sensing that he now had the upper hand, Drake immediately ordered the empanelling of a jury and, having appointed John Winter foreman, required John Thomas to read out the list of accusations levelled against Doughty. This was to be done once and once only so that no one present was in danger of memorising the counts accurately and recalling them at a later date.

The hapless accused made little effort to contradict the charges levelled against him until Drake produced his star prosecution witness: that Edward Bright who was one of those who had earlier shopped him to Drake about the gifts he had received from a captured Portuguese sailor. Relishing his moment of glory, Bright declared that he had things to say about Thomas Doughty that would 'bite you at the quick'. Doughty looked across at the man with nervous defiance. 'I pray thee, Ned Bright, charge me with nothing but truth and spare me not.' Bright then levelled his accusation. He declared that, back in England, Doughty had said to him in Drake's own garden that all the Privy Council and the Queen herself 'would be corrupted' by stolen gold. Such words were treason and a triumphant Bright, his venom discharged, pointed an accusing finger at Doughty, declaring, 'How like you this gear, sirrah?' An appalled Doughty fell back on what stumbling defence he could. How could Bright say such things? The two men had never enjoyed the sort of close familiarity to speak thus and Doughty strenuously denied that he ever said such things. It was possible, he added – just possible – that 'I said if we brought home gold we should be the better welcome, but yet that is more than I do remember.'

Such unsubstantiated accusations of treason were not enough. As the ghastly farce of the trial continued, Doughty – flustered, defensive and hopelessly cornered – began to tangle himself ever more fatally in the snares set by his accuser. He blurted out that Burghley, the one man on the Privy Council who was thought to be opposed to the whole expedition and was therefore kept in ignorance of it, in fact knew perfectly well what was going on. He had been given 'a plot' of the voyage. Cross-questioned by a genuinely horrified Drake, who feared the consequences of such a leak, he asked how Burleigh had come by it. 'He had it from me,' Doughty said. Drake was suffused with a sudden triumphant vindictiveness. Beyond his wildest hopes Doughty had accused himself of disloyalty out of his own mouth. This was surely, Drake said quickly, the Lord's doing. 'Lo, my masters, what this fellow hath done, God will have his treachery all known, for Her Majesty gave me special commandment that of all men my Lord Treasurer should not know it.'

Such a confession was enough to ensure Doughty's certain death and Drake 'greatly . . . seemed to rejoice at this advantage'. A horrified Doughty, realising what he had done, desperately declared that he would here and now agree to anything that he was accused of, provided only that Drake would allow him to live and answer his accusers in a properly convened court of law once they had returned to England. Realising that such an appeal for mercy was dangerous to him, Drake acted with that quick-witted and malicious cunning of which he was so easily capable. It would be disastrous if he pandered to any sentiments of mercy that might have been treasured by his watching crew and so, rather than expose himself in such a way, he ordered the jury to set about their deliberations at once, saying that he might give further consideration to a trial in England after the men had reached their verdict.

Only one juryman dared break the tense silence. Leonard Vicary, Doughty's friend and a lawyer of the Inner Temple, roundly told Drake that 'this is not law, nor agreeable to justice that you offer'. Drake's quick reply was a combination of popular sarcasm and unmitigated bullying. 'I have not . . . to do with you crafty lawyers, neither care I for the law, but I know what I will do.' Vicary was not so easily overawed. He protested that he did not wish to have the matter of Doughty's life or death placed in his hands under such circumstances. Again, Drake was quick to reply. 'Well, Master Vicary . . . you shall not have to do with his life, let me alone with that, you are but to see whether he be guilty in these articles that here is objected against him or no.' Vicary was relieved. 'Then there is, I trust,' he said, 'no matter of death.' Drake looked him straight in the face and lied. 'No, no, Master Vicary,' he said.

The awe-struck jurymen set about their deliberations with befitting earnestness and rigour. They knew the seriousness of their business perfectly well and did not want innocent blood on their hands. The evidence of Edward Bright troubled them particularly. Surely they could give it no credence. It was the merest hearsay and what Bright had alleged was in a high degree treason. It was inconceivable that a truly honest man would conceal such a matter until obliged to appear in a kangaroo court. They said as much to Drake himself (who very soon afterwards punished Bright for his failure to be convincing) but then declared that they believed the other accusations levelled against Doughty were indeed proven.

Drake had got what he wanted, but it was not enough that he should triumph in a terrible parody of justice. Such a victory might in time be held against him and it was essential now that he step down from the judicial bench he had so arbitrarily erected and mingle among the men he had persuaded to condemn Doughty. He would present himself as the very model of wronged virtue.

Drake summoned all the crew, save Doughty and his brother, to the beach. Here, confessing to having absentmindedly forgotten to bring with him the supposed royal commission that empowered him to hold Doughty's trial, he produced a bundle of letters which he said had been sent to him by the great and the good. These appeared to attest to a familiarity with people equal to Doughty's connections. Having displayed what purported to be his credentials, Drake turned to his men and addressed them directly. The speech as reported by John Cooke is a skilful blend of threat, promise and hurt feelings, all of which were designed to portray him in a sympathetic light and to persuade his listeners that his masterful presence was absolutely essential to the success of the expedition. Above all, having contrived matters so that the jury had declared the loathed Doughty guilty of the most serious misdemeanours, it was now Drake's intention that they rather than he alone should urge the man's execution.

Precisely what Doughty's deceit entailed was made clear to them. The villain had intended nothing less than the destruction of the entire voyage and of Drake himself. First he had sought to sully Drake's good name and discredit him before taking his life. This wish was heinous enough in itself but, if carried out, would surely have resulted in acrimonious division among the crew who, in a bitterly mutinous state, would then have been 'fain one to drink another's blood'. And how would men so divided against each other ever have been able to find their way home? Drake was one of the supreme navigators of his age. Without him the disintegrating expedition would have been either marooned on an alien coast or condemned to wander remote and unknown seas. Rather than face these terrible prospects, surely it was better for the men loyally to follow Drake whose proven abilities as a pirate would ensure their safety and success?

'The worst in this fleet shall become a gentleman,' he promised, 'and if this voyage go not forward, which I cannot see how possible it should if this man live, what a reproach it will be, not only unto our country but especially unto us.' All Doughty could promise was division, dishonour and likely death. 'Therefore, my masters, they that think this man worthy to die let them with me hold up their hands, and they that think him not worthy to die hold down their hands.' The chastened and bewildered men, cowed by so persuasive a performance and unwilling to cause further divisions, lifted up their hands, although in some cases this was against the wishes of their hearts. As Drake had gambled, they followed his superior initiative and took on the responsibility for the judicial murder of the man he wished to destroy. An exultant Drake returned to his judgement seat where he pronounced Doughty 'the child of death'.

The whole ghastly business was shrewdly managed, and perhaps in the last resort necessary, but the events that followed had a sadistic refinement which suggests that Drake's revenge was not a dish he chose to eat cold. He toyed with the possibilities of mercy as a cat toys with a mortally wounded mouse. Having pronounced sentence of execution, he asked any member of his crew to come and talk to him if they could think of a way between now and tomorrow morning of saving Doughty's life. The desperate Doughty himself, his mind fearfully concentrated by the prospect before him, begged to be taken to Peru and left there. Drake's answer was a firm no. 'Master Doughty, I cannot answer it to Her Majesty if I should do so.' Nonetheless, if any of the captains would undertake to keep Doughty a prisoner and guarantee that he would not make an attempt on Drake's life then 'sure you shall see what I will say unto you'.

Doughty turned desperately to John Winter, the nominal third leader of the expedition, and begged him to do this for him. Winter agreed. Drake was for a moment silent before delivering his last and meanest challenge of all. Was this really what the men wanted? Did they really want to keep Doughty alive? 'Lo then, my masters, we must thus do, we must nail him close under the hatches and return home again without making any voyage, and if you will do so say your minds.' There would be no glory in such an action and, above all, there would be no prize-money, no rich pickings from captured ships. By saving Doughty, the men would be voluntarily closing themselves off from the limitless and golden horizons Drake had so recently promised them. He pandered to the lowest instincts of greed and got his way. Poor and desperate men, who had suffered so much and for so long only in the hope of winning wealth to match their dreams were not prepared to let the life of one man stand between them and an overflowing purse. Greed made them loyal to the man who could so skilfully lead them in whatever way he chose and Drake, sanctimonious in his victory, told Doughty to prepare for death, saying that he would give him a day 'to set all things in order', a day during which Drake himself would pray that God would show His victim mercy.

Nothing in Doughty's life became him like the leaving of it. He spent that night, the succeeding day and the following night in prayer, interrupting his devotions only to distribute such worldly possessions as he had among his friends. He then asked to be allowed to receive Communion. This was granted him and Drake, who was now determined to be the spiritual as well as the physical leader of the expedition, knelt beside him at the Communion table, the very image of the devout Protestant gentleman. Gentility, indeed, remained an issue. Drake asked Doughty which way he would choose to die, saying that if he would consent to Drake's shooting him then he should at least 'die of the hands of a gentleman'. This was the repulsive suggestion of a man determined to stand before the world clothed in the social prestige he so urgently longed for.

Doughty, staid and firm, declined the nauseating offer and said that, as a gentleman born, he chose to be beheaded. He too was determined to fashion a virtuous image of himself by which he might be remembered. The proper ways of leaving the world were a known and practised art among the Elizabethans, a public act to which they considered it proper they should bring all their skill and fortitude. Doughty was in this at least no exception. His career so far as it may be known had been largely filled with bitterness, backbiting, and futile plotting for a prestige that he did not have the stature to carry, but in death he would display a dignity he had rarely if ever revealed in life. Having dined with Drake and told his destroyer that he was now ready for his fate, he was surrounded by armed men and marched to the place of execution. Here, he knelt and prayed aloud. He prayed for the Queen, for the good success of the expedition, and for his friends. He asked the company in general to forgive him and for Drake in particular to pardon those who were believed to be associated with him. Drake did so, and allowed Doughty to embrace him as the condemned man bade his Captain farewell and placed his neck on the block. The axe fell. The bleeding head was displayed to the whole assembled company to whom Drake turned triumphantly, declaring, 'Lo, this is the end of traitors.'

But even a severed head was not enough. As Drake was well aware, there was a feeling among a number of the crew that something morally and spiritually polluting had occurred. This was never entirely to leave those who recognised it and it made its presence felt in their later written accounts of the voyage. John Cooke, for example, regarded Doughty's death as 'most tyrannical blood spilling' and roundly declared that Drake had murdered him. To such men, Drake's actions were an abominable abuse of the friendship that had once existed between them. A more or less silent groundswell of horrified bitterness was running under the whole expedition, occasionally breaking into murmured resentment and, with a crew suffering from the winter cold, a shortage of victuals and consequent sickness, Drake realised that he had to seize the moral and spiritual initiative as the necessary means of fully establishing his authority. There would be universal love and brotherhood, and Drake would enforce them.

Every member of the crew was ordered to make his confession to Fletcher the chaplain and then to receive Communion the following Sunday. Drake had decided that he would 'have all old quarrels whatsoever between any man to be forgiven, and that whatsoever he were that from that time forth should abrade any man with anything past, he would lay such and so heavy a punishment on him as should be a terrible example to the whole fleet'. Charity was to be enforced by the harshest discipline but, when Fletcher offered to preach a sermon at the meeting of the crew convened on shore on 11 August, Drake, standing in a tent with Winter on one side of him and

Thomas on the other, declared that he would give the sermon himself, 'although I have small skill in preaching'. It is probable that Drake had already drafted out what he was going to say, writing his words down in the great paper book that a servant now opened in front of him. Before starting, he told his congregation that those who chose to write his words down as a permanent record (a common practice among the literate in church) could do so, but the sermon itself was like nothing they had ever heard before.

Drake declared that the deep divisions in his expedition threatened to 'take my wits from me'. He recognised that the class antagonism prevalent because of the Doughty crisis played a large part in these, gentlemen and sailors being clearly at odds with one another. This was a potentially disastrous situation for it was essential to the success of the voyage that the crews aboard the ships be cohesive fighting units. Antagonistic displays of differences in social rank had now become altogether too divisive for this to be the case and Drake was determined to grasp the nettle and put a stop to them. 'I must have it left,' he said. 'I must have the gentleman to hale and draw with the mariner, and the mariner with the gentleman.'[3] This was an extraordinarily daring, even revolutionary, statement in a society where distinctions of rank were always made evident in the belief that in such ways the proper proprieties of the social order would be preserved.

Drake had the greatest respect for these last, but as a seasoned commander he knew very well that professional competence was altogether more important to the success, and even the survival, of an expedition such as this. He was not a leveller preaching democracy – the idea would have been all but incomprehensible to him – but rather was insisting that the right to command was not vested in a man simply by virtue of his birth (as Doughty had believed) but by his known ability, his training, and his professional rather than his social standing. Drake was wholly in sympathy with the idea that 'gentlemen are very necessary for government's sake in the voyage' and added that was why he had brought gentlemen with him. Ordinary sailors, he believed, were naturally unruly without their superiors but were equally necessary to any expedition. He then added that those who were unwilling to accept the idea that professional distinction mattered quite as much as class were welcome to sail home on the *Marigold*. Let such men beware, however. 'If I find them in my way I will surely sink them, therefore you shall have time to consider hereof until tomorrow.' The option of quitting the expedition under such circumstances was taken up by no one. All the men agreed to sail on with Drake and under the terms he had imposed.

Drake was now unquestionably in sole command and was determined to make the fact absolutely clear. To prove his point he suddenly turned to the captains and masters of his ships and relieved every one of them of their duties. It was a shocking and arbitrary gesture. What allegedly gave Drake the power to do it – and the power over life and death that he had exercised in dealing with Doughty – only gradually emerged as the stunned congregation continued listening to his sermon. It was now that Drake decided to spin the story about the visit Walsingham had supposedly made to him, and his subsequent interview with the Queen. To the ordinary sailors it was a compelling insight into their General's status. Those who had paid attention to Doughty's gossip had believed that Drake was merely Hatton's man or the creature of the men who ran the Navy. Such speculation was, Drake made clear, contemptible, the foolishness of 'a company of idle heads that have nothing else to talk of'. Drake's acquaintance with such grandees as Essex and Walsingham led straight to the Queen herself. If he was anybody's man, he was hers.

It was the Queen who was the driving force behind the expedition, she who desired 'some revenge' on Philip of Spain, she who had recognised that Drake was the man for the job. He waved a bill for a thousand crowns before his crew, saying it was proof that Her Majesty had personally invested in the voyage. Significantly, he did not let the men read the document. Instead, he insisted they were all part of an expedition of national importance and the servants of the Queen. Drake's own authority derived directly from her and, before he set sail, Elizabeth had personally 'committed her sword, to use for his safety, with this word: *We do account that he which striketh at thee, striketh at us*'. To plot against Drake was to plot treason. He was the Queen's representative, and order, unity and command flowed from her to him. Division in the ranks, weakness and failure were all unthinkable. Declaring that such things would be a disgrace to the country and a cause for triumphant contempt among their Catholic enemies, Drake rammed his point home for one last time. 'It is only Her Majesty that you serve and this voyage is only her setting forth.' Now, with his men awed, united, and fired with national pride and deep anti-Catholic sentiments, Drake – self-fashioned by whatever means as the public embodiment of the regime he served – could finally order their departure from Port Saint Julian.

It was such pious and patriotic sentiments that ensured Drake's iconic status among Victorian imperialists and the writers and novelists who popularised their ethos of empire.[4] To such men (and they were mostly men) Drake's spirit was a priceless national asset existing beyond the reach of time – the supposed quintessence of all that was English. 'Of such captains as Franky Drake, Heaven never makes but one at a time; and if we lose him, goodbye to England's luck, I say,' declares a character in Charles Kingsley's *Westward Ho!*, a novel about Drake and his followers first published in 1855 and so coinciding with the Crimean War, which is the real point at issue. The brutal young hero of the book is intended to personify the muscular, manly virtues and their attendant excesses which supposedly characterised Drake and his men and which, with Drake himself as their focus, would hopefully inspire similar qualities in young Victorians eager to ride into the valley of death and protect the nation – not from wicked Spanish Catholics (whose evils Kingsley depicts with savage relish) but from the equally corrupt and dangerous Russians who were currently threatening the Empire.

Here was a portrayal of a type of Britishness inspired by Drake that stood against anarchy and all its foreign works. It was the firm hope and conviction of Kingsley and his followers that 'the English race is probably the finest, and that it gives not the slightest sign whatsoever of exhaustion; that it seems to be on the whole a young race, and to have very great capabilities in it which have not yet been developed, and above all, the most marvellous capability of adapting itself to every sort of climate and every form of life'. The British could hardly fail. God and Darwin, acting in curious alliance, had seen to it that the English ruled the world because, as the English, they were best fitted to do so. History gave them a manifest destiny and Drake, patriotic and Protestant, became the ideal figure from the past to inspire a new generation in proving the fact, and in leading foreigners a little way towards that 'renovation of the blood, which commerce, and its companion, colonisation, are certain to bring'. Empire was a moral and improving force, and Drake, leading his pirate ships round the desolate coasts of South America, became an embodiment of 'that type of English virtue, at once manful and Godly, practical and enthusiastic, prudent and self-sacrificing, which . . . was exhibited by the worthies whom Elizabeth . . . gathered around her in the ever glorious wars of her great reign'.

The apogee of such ways of thinking came in the 1870s and the ensuing decades when Drake was once again on hand to inspire the nation, and its young men especially. By this time the Empire was enormous, consisting of about 400 million people scattered across India and much of Asia, the Americas and Australasia. In the words of an enthusiast, the Empire consisted of 'one continent, a hundred peninsulas, five hundred promontories, a thousand lakes, two thousand rivers, ten thousand islands'. Improving means of communication – railways, steamships and telegraphs – helped to bind it all together and allowed British merchants to boast that 'this country is more than ever the entrepot for the world'. The Foreign and India Offices, the Admiralty, and the War Office administered the vast, and vastly complex, mechanism with all its subtle problems, strengths, weaknesses and contradictions, while the so-called 'New Imperialism' of the age offered for mass consumption a crude and often jingoistic version of the responsibility for taking up 'the white man's burden'. The English were to rule as benignly as possible over 'new-caught sullen peoples, half-devil and half-child'. White male adolescents in particular needed to be introduced to such notions and be inspired by them. Into the breach stepped the author G. A. Henty with titles such as *Under Drake's Flag*.

Henty's books were specifically aimed, in his own words, to 'inculcate patriotism' among a future officer class. This they tried to do through a heady mixture of hero-worship, Christian militarism and sheer gung-ho adventure. Henty's Empire is a soldier's Empire. Intended to be given as prizes or presents by adults to schoolboys, novels such as *Under Drake's Flag* disparage intellect (Ned Hearne, Henty's archetypal hero, is the despair of his schoolmaster father) and revel in the sort of action expected from would-be imperialists. Ned speaks for them all when, separated from Drake at Port Saint Julian, he tells his companions:

> I propose that we try and cross the continent. It is not so very wide here, and we are nearly in a line with Lima. The Admiral means to go on there, and expects a rich booty. He may be months before he gets round the Horn, and if we could manage to be there when he arrives we should be rescued. The first thing to do will be to get our living somehow, the second to get farther inland, the third to make friends with the first band of natives we meet.[5]

The last proves less easy than hoped, and the blacks only accept what is shown as the boys' inherent English superiority and natural gift for rule after Ned and his companions have been tied to a post and resolved that 'if we must die, let us behave like Englishmen and Christians'. When they become prisoners of the Spanish they determine that 'should it become necessary to keep up their character as Spaniards by pretending to be true Catholics, they would disclose the truth'. All of this comes to pass, but the boys escape from the Inquisition in true Henty fashion when 'each produced a pistol from his breast, the one levelling his at the head of the Grand Inquisitor, while the other faced the foremost of those advancing towards them'. Finally reunited with Drake, the boys are gratified by his apparent approval of their sterling imperialist virtues. Drake is seen as the guarantor of the imperial ideal.

Novels such as *Under Drake's Flag* still have an undeniable pace about them but their dangers (especially given their phenomenal popularity) were evident to some contemporaries at least who claimed that Henty and his kind had made the British 'the most conceited people on the earth by their encouraging a boy to believe that he, personally, is equal to two or more Frenchmen, about four

Germans, an indefinite number of Russians, and any quantity you care to mention of the remaining scum of the earth'. Two generations or more were nonetheless moulded by Henty's imperialism and it is easy to see why. As the eminent historian A. J. P. Taylor declared, Henty's books are 'tales of adventure such as have been told since the beginning of time'. It is perhaps tempting to think of such enthusiasms as belonging to boyhoods long outgrown, but such is not the case. Despite their anti-Semitism, overt racism and glorification of violence, Henty's novels have achieved a cult following among the Christian Right in the United States. There, especially among the more than one million 'home-schoolers' – those whose parents have taken them out of the state educational system from religious considerations, distrust of academic fads or simple fear after recent spates of shootings – Henty has achieved great popularity once again. Novels such as *Under Drake's Flag* have very considerable sales and influence because it is believed they represent 'true' history rather than history rewritten according to the criteria of political correctness. Drake the Victorian hero marches on.

The Elizabethan Drake had other concerns. After Doughty's execution the three ships remaining to his expedition – his own *Pelican*, the *Elizabeth* and the *Marigold* – left Port Saint Julian on 17 August for the Strait of Magellan and what Drake himself knew would prove to be one of the most daunting stretches of the expedition.[6] Many of the crew still felt that an atmosphere of moral pollution hung over them because of the Doughty incident and believed that they should have 'a general communion and some necessary doctrine tending to love and Christian duty'. Fletcher willingly officiated, the exercise ending 'with prayer to God for Her most excellent Majesty, her honourable Council, and the Church and the commonweal of England, with singing of Psalms and giving thanks for God's great and singular graces bestowed upon us from time to time'. Protestantism could indeed be a cohesive force, one that made for social discipline and control even under the most difficult of circumstances.

It is possible that during these days Drake also held the ceremony in which he renamed his ship. *The World Encompassed*, slightly modifying Fletcher's original account by changing the date of the occasion, states that this happened just as the fleet was about to enter the Strait. Drake apparently ordered his vessels to strike their topsails in homage to the Queen, and then 'in remembrance of his honourable friend . . . Sir Christopher Hatton, he changed the name of the ship, which himself went in, from the *Pelican* to be called the *Golden Hind*'. Something of the sort may well have happened (a golden hind was part of Hatton's coat-of-arms) but it seems that the name was not widely used at the time nor even generally accepted among Drake's own crew. It was only during the last decade of the sixteenth century that the name began to gain wide currency.*

When Drake finally arrived off the Strait he found the wind against him. He was obliged to anchor about a league and a half outside the entrance and wait there until conditions changed and favourable winds and currents could carry him through. By 24 August he had been able to continue his voyage and had found three islands. These were named St Bartholomew, whose feast day it was, St George in honour of the nation's patron saint, and Elizabeth Island for the Queen. It is far from certain that Drake took possession of this last for the Crown as *The World Encompassed* states, since none of the strictly contemporary sources mention the fact and the men who actually sailed with Drake seem to have been far more interested in the abundant supply of penguins they found there. Fletcher could not decide if these birds more resembled a duck or a goose, but he was intrigued by the fact that they could not fly and put up a strong resistance when the men tried to capture and kill them. Despite the struggle put up by the birds, Drake's crew managed to kill several thousand of them in a day and found them to be very good and wholesome.

Not everything however was 'so necessarily and plentifully serving the use of man'. Drake and his men found the Strait of Magellan to be a terrible and terrifying place. Notorious winds blew through the bleak landscape, sometimes urging the ships on but more often hurling them to port or starboard in the narrow channel, sometimes throwing them back the way they had come while, at

---

* Hereon, the *Pelican* is referred to as the *Golden Hind*.

their worst, 'these winds would come together, and meet as it were in one body, whose forces being become one, did so violently fall into the sea, whirling, or as the Spaniard saith, with a *tornado*, that they would pierce into the very bowels of the sea, and make it swell upwards on every side'. The weather was also bitterly cold. Frozen mountain peaks edged the horizon and 'from these hills distilled so sharp a breath, that it seemed to enter into the bowels of nature, with a great discomfort of the lives of our men'. The trees below these hills and mountains were so bowed under the weight of snow and ice that their branches met together and, acting as a protective cover, allowed medicinal herbs to flourish beneath them 'as it were in our summer'. The place was a strange combination of the malevolent and the benign.

A little way distant, the countryside provided food for 'comely and harmless' hunter-gatherers, naked people with vividly painted and decorated bodies, 'the men making red circles about their eyes and red strokes upon their foreheads for the most part, and the women wear chains of white shells upon their arms, and some about their necks, whereof they seem to be very proud'. Fletcher was intrigued by the makeshift homes in which these people temporarily lived and compared them to the arbours in English gardens. It seemed that these natives owned almost nothing beyond the bare necessities their way of life called for, their knives being made of finely sharpened mussel shells while 'their water pails, drinking cups, and boxes, are made of the barks of trees sowed together with threads of the guts of some beasts, like lute strings'. Their boats too, beautifully designed vessels in which the men transported their families, were likewise made of bark and earned Fletcher's particular admiration. 'In all our travels in any nation,' he declared, 'we found not the like boats at any time for form and fine proportion, in the sight and use whereof princes might seem to be delighted.'

For all the difficulties they encountered in passing the Strait of Magellan, a measure of good luck and Drake's expert seamanship ensured that the crews made the passage in record time. Their luck, however, did not hold. A first suggestion of this occurred on 4 September when Drake dropped anchor and was baffled at being unable to find the outlet to the Pacific. A search in a southerly direction proved fruitless, but a party sailing north eventually found what they were looking for and, on 6 September the expedition sailed out into the vast expanses of Drake's longed-for Pacific Ocean. As we have seen, the geography of this region was barely known – the area had not been fully explored – and maps were consequently inaccurate. Ortelius' chart suggested an expedition should take a north-westerly course but, doing so, Drake's men found only open sea. Fletcher was quick to suggest that the errors in the charts were deliberate misinformation maliciously circulated by the Spanish to lead good Protestants such as he and his colleagues astray.

The real perils they now faced however had nothing to do with man at all. Having travelled for several days on a fair wind and made perhaps some seventy leagues, Drake and his crew ran into a storm so furious that no sail could be carried. For several more days the little ships were driven west-south-west and then back again towards the Strait. Fletcher exaggerated when he said that they were thrown about for 'the space of 56 days', but the horror and fear, deepened in superstitious minds by a lunar eclipse, could seem to some of the crew at least like an expression of the wrath of God, a divine judgement perhaps on what had taken place at Port Saint Julian. For some, Doughty's ghost still haunted the expedition. Fletcher was certainly minded to think so, and he was on the night watch when, as he claimed, he heard the fearful cries of the drowning sailors as 'the bark *Marigold*, wherein Edward Bright, one of the accusers of Thomas Doughty, was Captain, with 28 souls' sank beneath the merciless waves 'or rather mountains of the sea'. This was a ghastly, morale-damaging loss.

By 7 October, Drake's ship and the *Elizabeth*, carried by the mountainous billows, found themselves tossed into a rocky harbour near the mouth of the Magellan Strait. The storm was still raging and they could not remain safely there – as Fletcher reported 'our cables broke, our anchors came home' – and Drake decided that he and Winter should lie outside their anchorage, hauling into the wind. Throughout the evening the two ships remained more or less in each others' sight, but when darkness fell they were separated and the *Elizabeth* was driven towards the shore while Drake was tossed far west-south-west into the boiling ocean. It was agonising times for both Captains since their ships were now alone in perilous and barely charted seas. Winter himself anchored for two days off the mouth of the Strait, lighting fires at night in the hope that Drake would see them. Disappointed, he then sought a safer anchorage just inside the Strait itself, waiting there for three weeks while he 'looked still for Master Drake, and for a change of wind'. In these things he was again to be disappointed, as he was in his plan of sailing to the Moluccas or Pacific Spice Islands as he and Drake had discussed. Winter's own men refused to consider so challenging a possibility and Winter, by his own account, reluctantly ordered them to head for England. There, he was at length fairly well received and his story (in a form deliberately distorted by the government who wanted to cover the whole matter in veils of misinformation) was circulated.

It took little over a week for the newly returned Winter's news to reach the ears of the recently appointed Spanish Ambassador, Bernadino de Mendoza.[7] An able and energetic man, the scion of a leading Spanish family and an army veteran of some distinction, Mendoza rapidly established an efficient secret service in England to supply him with information. He even had a Catholic member of the Privy Council in his pay. Much court gossip (some of it misinformation deliberately leaked) came to him in such ways and was passed on to Madrid. Among such items was news of Winter's return and, rather more importantly, information about Drake's voyage to date and his astonishing feat of passing the Strait of Magellan in particular. From now on Drake's name – variously misspelled – was to cross with increasing frequency before King Philip as he sat at his desk in the Escorial weighing up the dangers his vast empire was subject to. Slowly, as his knowledge of Drake's stature increased, Philip would begin to fashion him into a man of seemingly demonic power. Even now he was learning that the Englishman's courage and skill meant that the Pacific was no longer a safe Spanish lake. The passage through the Magellan Strait had ensured that, for where Drake had been, other heretics and pirates would surely follow.

The English too, proud and delighted at his success, praised Drake's 'excellent discovery . . . in his passage through the Straights of

Magellan, which being then so rawly known, he could not have passed unless he had been a man of great practice and rare resolution'. This was no less than just, but the expedition had so far proved disappointing in terms of finding useful anchorages, while its dangers had been without any substantial reward. Now however, as Drake and his crew prepared their northwards voyage through the Pacific, annoying the Spanish and the King of Spain in particular became a principal aim. Raiding expeditions and piracy were to go hand in hand with reconnaissance. By 28 October the crew was in the region of the Strait of Magellan once more and, two days later, went ashore to revictual on seal and penguin meat. They then took a zigzagging course in search of the Chilean coastline, finally reaching the island of La Mocha on 25 November.[8] The island was situated off La Imperial, the great gold-mining centre of Chile, and it seemed possible that fabulous wealth might yet fall into the hands of the expedition. La Mocha itself seemed to promise abundance, and after almost a month at sea Drake's crew were delighted to trade with apparent friendship for the plump sheep, hens and maize which the native Indians offered. Fresh water was also urgently needed and it was agreed between the parties that they would go ashore the following day to collect it.

But the situation was not as straightforward as it seemed. The natives were people who had fled from the mainland to escape 'the bloody cruelty of the Spaniards' who had subdued them to slavery in their gold mines. They were determined to protect the peace and safety they enjoyed on La Mocha 'with the continual shedding of the blood and the eating of the flesh of the Spaniards when or howsoever they can come by them'. The Spaniards were the only Europeans they knew, and when some of Drake's men foolishly, and against his orders used the word 'aqua' for the water they so earnestly desired, the Indians naturally thought the Englishmen were their enemies and prepared an ambush for them.

The banks of the creek where the two parties had agreed to reconnoitre was thickly covered with high reeds which easily hid the 'bloody soldiers' as they waited to attack. As the English made their way towards them they could see a little reception party waiting at the agreed landing place and two of Drake's men went ashore. Their boat was seized at once, the men themselves were made captive, and the armed soldiers hidden in the reeds suddenly emerged, together with a volley of arrows, and fell on their prey. 'Not any one person escaped without some grievous wound,' Fletcher recorded, and Drake himself was 'shot in the face, under his right eye and close by his nose, the arrow piercing a marvellous way in under *basis cerebri*, with no small risk of his life; besides that, he was grievously wounded in the head.' By dint of cutting their mooring rope the anguished party was eventually able to drift away. The arrows nonetheless continued to rain down on them 'as thick as gnats in the sun' until the men finally reached the safety of their ship. Two hundred armed natives, brandishing weapons tipped with pure silver that glinted in the light, made it perfectly obvious that any hope of rescuing the two captured Englishmen was vain and Drake, refusing to make a bad situation worse by firing on the Indians with the great shot stored on his ship, ordered his shattered crew to sail north until they found a new anchorage, probably at Quintero.

There were no vessels in the harbour save for a canoe in which some Indians sat fishing. One of them, a man named Felipe, could speak Spanish, as could da Silva and some of Drake's men. It emerged from their conversation that although this port was empty of Spanish ships there was a potential prize anchored in the little harbour of Valparaiso. Would Felipe guide them there for a price? He would indeed and, sailing by night, Drake entered the harbour at Valparaiso and managed to convince the unsuspecting crew aboard *La Capitana* that he and his men were their fellow countrymen. As eighteen of Drake's crew then rowed over to the unsuspecting vessel, its tiny crew and their black slaves opened a cask of wine and greeted their guests with a drum roll. Once the English were aboard *La Capitana* the Spaniards were quickly made aware of their terrible mistake. All – save one who jumped overboard and swam ashore – were made Drake's prisoners as he himself came aboard, eager to see what wealth the vessel contained. There was wine, timber and perhaps 200,000 pesos in gold packed in four iron-bound, leather-covered chests. At last Drake was in his element and his men were able to steal what they considered to be their just deserts. Not content with what the captured ship contained however, two boatloads of Englishmen were dispatched to the deserted town where they raided the warehouses for victuals and then desecrated a little chapel, stealing what they gleefully thought of as the superstitious paraphernalia it was decorated with. This was indeed a raid to lift Protestant spirits, a promise of things to come. These riches would fall the more easily into Drake's hands now since, with a professionalism appropriate to a great pirate, he also managed to seize the rutter that belonged to *La Capitana*'s pilot and master, Juan Griego, who, along with his stolen ship, was pressed into Drake's service. Drake himself then sailed out of Valparaiso and returned to Quintero, where the useful Felipe was allowed to get on with his fishing.

Sailing north once again, Drake and his two ships made landfall at Tongoy Bay on 11 December but, finding little of any use to them there, sailed further along the coast to La Herradura where they rounded up some pigs and found a small quantity of drinking water. As they did so a shot rang out. A look-out in the crow's-nest of one of Drake's ships gave warning that a posse of at least fifty armed horsemen had ridden out from the nearby town; the English at once hurried away, but one of them, Richard Minivy, was killed as the men scrambled for their boat. *The World Encompassed* made this small episode into an emblem of the whole Anglo-Spanish conflict. Minivy is shown as the archetypal English hero, 'over-bold and careless of his own safety', more than willing to take on impossible odds and, if necessary, die in the process. Having rushed to a brave, and glorious, if wholly futile, death, what happened next was an epitome of all the papist evils associated with the Spanish Empire. Minivy's 'dead body being drawn by the Indians from the rock to the shore, was there manfully by the Spaniards beheaded, the right hand cut off, the heart plucked out; all of which they carried away in our sight, and for the rest of the carcass they caused the Indians to shoot it full of arrows ... and so left it to be devoured of the beasts and fowls'. These details probably owe more to righteous indignation than scrupulous reportage, but their propagandist purpose is clear. Such 'extreme and barbarous cruelty' showed how the Spaniards in their tyranny lived 'in continual dread of foreign invasion by strangers, or secret cutting of their throats by those whom they kept under them in so shameful slavery, I mean the innocent and harmless Indians'. The great-hearted English pirates, by contrast, knew perfectly well what honours were due to a hero: and they returned to the shore when it was safe to do so in order to bury the hapless Minivy's headless corpse.

By 22 December, Drake had arrived at barren Bahía Salada where he proposed to refit his ships. Determined to be fully prepared both for piracy and shore raids, he ordered the assembly of one of the prefabricated pinnaces he had brought with him. The hull of this little vessel was ready for caulking within a fortnight, after which sails were made for it and a small bronze gun was mounted in the bow. A crew of fifteen men and his captured Spanish pilot then accompanied Drake as he sailed south in search of water and the *Elizabeth* and the *Marigold* which, it was hoped, might have reached this agreed point of rendezvous. They had not. After a day's sailing, contrary winds and hostile Indians forced Drake to return and, once arrived back, he determined to careen his ship.

This was always a hazardous activity but an absolutely necessary one since the wooden hulls had to be stripped of the marine growths – the weeds, shells and other detritus – that fouled their underwater surfaces and so greatly reduced their speed and manoeuvrability.[9] These last were highly desirable qualities for vessels engaged in the sort of activities Drake was now proposing but, in addition, careening a hull also allowed the men to see and repair whatever damage had been inflicted by the worms that were so prevalent in tropical waters. In order to achieve all this, a ship such as the *Golden Hind* was left afloat but placed on its beam ends by dint of shifting its ballast and then hauling it down with tackle rigged to the masts. This naturally put enormous and dangerous stress on the hull, which could easily be damaged even to the extent that the seams would open and the ship fill with water and sink. Under these circumstances, it was clearly undesirable that careening should occur too often and various preventive measures were taken to limit the effects wrought by the shells, worms, and other creatures that attached themselves to a ship's bottom. The Spanish believed that some English ships were given a coating of ground glass below their waterlines, but in fact layers of goat hair, pitch, tar or tallow were altogether more common. A thin cover of planking was then nailed over this through which the worms could eat their way before supposedly choking themselves to death on the hair and tar that lay smeared beneath.

The shifting of the ballast involved in careening the *Golden Hind* meant that the crew were now able to get at the guns stored beneath it. The storage of these munitions amongst the ballast stones was a serious matter since their great weight at the bottom of the ship had, up to now, lowered the vessel's centre of gravity. Just how considerable that weight was can be imagined by the reports of Drake's armaments later sent to Spain in the accounts given by his freed Spanish captives. Keen to assess the threat Drake posed, they provided Philip with the alarming fact that the *Golden Hind* carried seven pieces of cast-iron artillery at each side on the lower deck, and two large cast-iron pieces at the poop near the helm. In addition to these, on the upper deck Drake carried six heavy pieces, of which two were bronze. This combination of bronze and cast-iron cannon is an interesting indication of the important tactical advantage that English ships such as Drake's enjoyed.

For all their superiority as instruments of death, bronze cannon were extremely expensive and tended, by and large, to be the prerogative of princes. The English, however, unlike many of their continental rivals, were perfecting the production of cast-iron cannon which, at a fifth of the price of their bronze cousins, made them altogether more readily available to men like Drake, who could thus sail hostile seas comfortable in the fact that their firepower was at least the equal of any enemy they might encounter. Such a tactical advantage ensured that English ships could readily match the aggressive ambitions of their Captains and guaranteed that such vessels, while they were not adequate for reliably provisioning far-flung colonies, were wholly suited to piracy and the theft of goods and treasure of enemies who had set themselves up as colonial powers on a grand scale. It is such basic and practical facts as these that gave the lie to Elizabethan dreams of empire but helped to ensure the astonishing feats achieved by the Queen's sea-dogs.[10]

And, just in case such superior firepower should prove insufficient, horrified Spanish captives noted that Drake also carried an abundance of other armaments: 'fire-bombs and darts with a certain kind of artifice for setting fire to the sails of ships; chain balls for breaking topmasts and other deadly work ... and many arquebuses, corselets, pocket pistols, trappings, pikes and a great quantity of many different kinds of arms'. To move such munitions up to the ports as he now did was a clear indication that Drake was sailing waters where he could expect both danger and rich prizes, the latter of which could be stowed where the guns had once been hidden and would, it was hoped, be of at least a comparable weight. When all this work was finally complete, Drake's ship was one of the most heavily armed and lethally efficient European vessels in the whole of the Pacific, and one adequately prepared for the piracy and shore raiding that were now his principal aims.

Drake left Bahía Salada on Monday, 19 January 1579, pointing his two ships north again, 'and with the launch sailing ahead to look for the port of Copiapo which they failed to see and therefore passed by without obtaining water or anything'. By this time, the newly assembled pinnace had begun to leak and it was clearly necessary for it to be recaulked. The need for fresh drinking water was also becoming urgent and, after his men had repaired the pinnace and obtained some fish from the local Indians in exchange for knives and other things, the crew sailed on in search of water guided by a native they had taken from his fishing boat. Arriving at Puerto de Tarapacá about a hundred miles to the north, Drake landed a party of his men and 'lighted on a Spaniard who lay asleep, and had lying by him 13 bars of silver, weighing in all about 400 Spanish ducats'. These were naturally stolen. With the heavy-handed irony sometimes displayed by the editors of *The World Encompassed*, the chronicle tells how 'we would not (could we have chosen) have awakened him from his nap: but seeing we, against our wills, did him that injury, we freed him of his charge, which otherwise perhaps would have kept him waking, and so left him to take out (if it pleased him) the other part of his sleep in more security'. Later, they came across another Spaniard who, helped by an Indian boy, was driving a pack of some eight llamas burdened with eight hundredweight of refined silver in the pairs of leather bags hung over their backs. Unable to endure to see 'such a gentleman turned mere carrier', as *The World Encompassed* puts it, they offered him their services and made sure that his treasure was taken down to the beach where their pinnace was waiting for it. So far the pickings had been easy, and Drake now sailed on to Aricia where he confidently expected more.[11]

Aricia was an attractive and prosperous little place, which 'seemed to us to stand in the most fruitful soil that we saw all along these coasts, both for that it is situated in the mouth of a most pleasant and fertile valley, abounding with all good things, as also in that it hath continual trade of shipping, as well from Lima as from all of other parts of Peru'. This last implied the possible presence of silver from the mines, and one of the two ships Drake found in the port contained over forty bars of bullion 'of the bigness and fashion of a brickbat, and in weight each of them about 20 pounds'. This treasure was promptly stolen, as was the wine aboard the second vessel which was then burned. With their spirits perhaps heightened by the stolen wine and the music they played while they drank it, the men aboard Drake's flagship pointed their guns at Aricia and went across to the town with the intention of hunting out more booty. A posse of some sixty armed men made the leader think better of the plan and, having sent ashore some of his captives, Drake made for Puerto de Chule where he believed a ship containing 500 bars of Spanish gold destined for Lima lay at anchor.

Progress up the coast was slow and so Drake dispatched his pinnace, but when the men arrived at the port they found the treasure ship was empty, advance warning of Drake's appearance having been received from the captives he had so recently freed. The locals were delighted to foil Drake in this way, and his aggrieved men were obliged to compensate for their disappointment by stealing the empty treasure ship and towing it out of the harbour. Four vessels and a pinnace were nonetheless too many for the General's purposes and so the three captured vessels were stripped of their valuables and allowed to drift away. Then, with the crew of the *Golden Hind* now numbering about seventy men, Drake sailed on up the coast, captured one of three ships to which he gave chase, and took some of its officers prisoner. The information cajoled out of them was valuable in the extreme. It seemed that a great ship loaded with silver was even now bound for Panama, while two other vessels, also heavily laden with silver, were expected in nearby Callao, the port for the city of Lima.

Lima, the capital of the Spaniards' immensely rich Peruvian silver empire, roused the editors of *The World Encompassed* to a paroxysm of anti-Catholic hatred.[12] Not only was this the place where the Inquisition held Drake's erstwhile colleague and fellow pirate John Oxenham a prisoner, Lima was believed to be nothing less than a South American Sodom where the influence of the Pope and all 'his devilish illusions and damnable deceivings' spread like an unchecked cancer to corrupt everything it touched. In such a place as this, God-fearing, Bible-reading Protestantism gave the only scintilla of spiritual hope amid almost universal corruption. Virtuous English eyes were inevitably drawn to its tiny and pitiful glow in order to bear witness to the fact that, despite the papists trying 'with tooth and nail to deface the glory of God, and to shut up in darkness the light of the gospel', God would not allow His truth to be so utterly occluded. There were a few people in Lima – a mere dozen of them – who had bravely defied Catholic enormities and professed the true doctrine. Their fate was as ghastly as might have been expected. Six were bound to one stake and burned, the rest remained in prison to suffer the same fate within a few days.

Knowledge of such horrors was perhaps salutary but Drake, believing that the active enforcement of Protestant virtue was also the means of enforcing discipline and unity among his crew, had by this time taken on the role of their pastor as well as their commander. Attendance at his prayer meetings aboard the *Golden Hind* was obligatory, and the Spaniards he captured looked on with curiosity and baffled ignorance at the form these occasions took. Drake would appear on the poop deck. There, a table was placed for him along with a box with an embroidered cushion on top of it. Drake would then send for a copy of what was either Foxe's *Book of Martyrs* or the Bible in English and, when this had been placed in front of him, he would strike the table twice with the palm of his hand. Nine of his crew then appeared, each of them carrying a copy of the Psalms. 'Then the said Francis Drake crossed his hands and, kneeling on the cushion and small box, lifted his eyes to heaven and remained in that attitude for about a quarter of an hour.' After that, Drake read the Psalms in English for about an hour until his musicians 'brought four viols, and made lamentations and sang together, with the accompaniment of the stringed instruments'. Finally, with these solemn devotions complete, Drake would order a boy (perhaps his nephew John) to come and dance in the English fashion, a delightful rounding off of the ritual which the Catholics probably thought was an integral part of the heretical service.

Meanwhile, devotions notwithstanding, the business of piracy had to go on. One of the three men Drake had captured in his last attack on Spanish ships was a Portuguese pilot. Drake now ordered him to guide them to Callao where it was believed they could have their Protestant revenge on papist enormities. The man did as he was told but, on sailing between the mainland and the island off the port, Drake's vessel struck a shoal and appeared to have run aground. Believing that the Portuguese had done this maliciously, Drake threatened to cut off his head. There were no further incidents after such a warning but, as the *Golden Hind* was entering Callao, another vessel came alongside and anchored close by her. This meant a fight.

Drake ordered his Spanish prisoners to ask where the vessel had come from and learned that it had sailed from Panama. He then commanded his captives to reply that he himself was master of a Spanish galleon out of Chile. As we have seen, Drake had by this time learned that John Oxenham and his colleagues were being held prisoner in Lima and it was clearly part of his purpose to secure their release. Putting half a dozen men in his ship's boat and a further twenty or thirty in his pinnace, Drake and his crew made their way as silently as they could towards the Spanish vessels anchored in the port and cut their cables. It was Drake's hope that the wind would carry these ships out to sea where he would then be able to seize them and hold them as a ransom against the release of Oxenham and his companions.

Brave and imaginative though the plan was it failed because the wind fell and the enemy ships remained motionless. It was also disappointing that they contained no bullion and, determined to get something from their enterprise, Drake attacked the ship newly arrived from Panama. For all that one Englishman was killed, the raiding party were unable to take the vessel and an angry Drake retreated to the *Golden Hind* from where he fired a cannon shot at his intended prey. This went through both sides of the ship without killing anyone, but the frightened men aboard abandoned her and made for the shore. The English then proceeded to seize the deserted vessel, undeterred by the intervention of some customs officials who came out in a boat to investigate what was going on. Nonetheless, as far as the English were concerned, the raid on Callao had proved disappointing, despite the capture of the Spanish vessel and, the following morning, they let the tide carry them out of the port.

Two or three Spanish vessels and a launch put out of Callao in pursuit. Drake, thinking he might have to fight, summoned to the *Golden Hind* all the men he had placed on the captured vessel, leaving aboard her only some of his prisoners, including the pilot he had captured in Valparaiso, Juan Griego. This was a mistake, for the information Griego subsequently gave the Spaniards greatly added to their knowledge of the danger they were in. They had already taken precautions against this, ineffective though they proved to be. Drake had no sooner begun his raid on Callao than Spanish dispatch riders were sent off to the Viceroy in Lima. Don Francisco de Toledo received them at one in the morning and, within an hour, he had set out on the road to Callao at the head of 200 poorly armed men who had been summoned to the public square by the frenetic pealing of church bells. He made what speed he could but the enemy, who he now knew to be an English pirate, was already far out to sea by the time he arrived. The Don nonetheless resolved to chase but Drake had the advantage of both wind and time. Besides, the Spanish vessels were not in a fit state to follow for they were unballasted, carried no food, and were insufficiently armed. Many of the men aboard them were, besides, badly seasick. 'Finally, at the end of much discussion, it was resolved to return in order to obtain reinforcements so as to sally forth again, better equipped to attack the enemy.' For the moment it seemed that Drake could raid with impunity.

In the meantime, the recently freed Juan Griego provided the Spanish with a great deal of detailed and alarming information about 'Francisco Draquez, a medium-sized man, robust and a great mariner and cosmographer'. Griego told them everything he knew about the English expedition's aims and achievements to date – information which confirmed their worst fears. The interrogation of John Oxenham had already given the Spanish authorities a good idea of what Drake might achieve were he to sail into their South American waters, but Oxenham had given it as his opinion that Elizabeth would never allow Drake to navigate those waters. Now, all too plainly, he was there. Something had to be done. Three days after Drake's appearance off Callao an earnest meeting between the Viceroy and the Royal Audienca of Peru was held and various emergency measures to restrain the activities of 'Captain Francisco Draquez' were resolved upon.

It was evident to the worried Spaniards that the presence of Drake off their coasts might well 'render it impossible to carry on trade between this kingdom, the isthmus and Spain, or to transport thither the King's silver and that of private individuals, without incurring great risks and expense'. This would be fatal to the Spanish war effort. The officials feared, too, for the damage Drake might do to ports further down the coast. So great was the emergency felt to be that money would have to be taken from the royal revenues before Philip's explicit permission for this could be obtained. This was duly done, and a bark readied and ordered to visit all the ports along the coast to tell officials what was happening and give orders to appoint watchmen and guards. Any Spanish vessels the bark met with on its way were to be ordered to travel with great vigilance and a realisation of their own insecurity, while every effort was also to be made to seek the 'Lutheran' pirates until they were found. It was all to no avail. By the time the Spaniards were ready, Drake had a head start of fifteen days and, as the Spanish pursued him, they learned with mounting horror of the damage he had caused and which they were powerless to stop.

By 24 February, Drake had arrived at Paita. There he seized a merchantman, which was promptly deserted by all its crew save its master, the pilot, and some black slaves who confirmed the nearby presence of the great galleon loaded with silver which Drake had been told about some weeks earlier. About twenty miles north of Paita, Drake fell on yet another Spanish merchant ship but, finding it contained nothing of real interest to him, took prisoner only one of the black slaves he found aboard. Arriving at Los Quijimes on 28 February, he found a Spanish ship out of Guayaquil belonging to one Benito Diaz Bravo riding innocently at anchor. The hapless vessel was boarded at once and the pirates laid their hands on 15,000 pesos in gold, along with a huge golden crucifix and some enormous emeralds. Drake then stripped the captured ship of its sails, which he wrapped round its anchor and cast into the sea. This prevented the ship sailing ahead to warn of his presence. Drake was in an ecstasy of excitement for he guessed very well that soon he would be able to capture the great silver galleon he knew was in the vicinity. He boasted to his most recent captives 'like a shameless robber fears not God or man' that the prize would not escape him.

Nor did it. The official name of the vessel Drake was after was the *Nuestra Señora de la Concepción*, but it seems that ordinary sailors at least knew her more colloquially as the *Cacafuego* or 'Shitfire'.[13] It was spotted from the crow's-nest of the *Golden Hind* around noon on Sunday, 1 March by John Drake, who thereby won for himself the coveted gold chain his uncle had promised to the man who first sighted it. John Drake later said that, in order to capture the prize, Drake pretended not to be following it and, to prevent his own ship from sailing too fast and thereby giving the game away, he hung cables and mattresses over the side of the *Golden Hind* which went dragging along as a consequence. The canny commander also lowered his sails and hid his lethal little pinnace from view. By nine o'clock that night he had crossed the course of the Spanish ship and immediately came alongside. The vessel's owner and pilot, San Juan de Anton, gave a salute which was not returned. Anton was at once suspicious but refused to be cowed and, according to his own testimony, as the English ship neared his own, one of Drake's Spanish speakers called out that their crew was English and that they demanded he strike his sails. The plucky Anton, whose vessel was unarmed, replied: 'What – England demands that I strike sail?

Come and do it yourself.' This was a clear act of defiance and, on hearing it, 'they blew a whistle on the English ship and the trumpet responded'.

Drake prepared to seize the all too vulnerable prize in the time-honoured way. As about sixty arquebusiers shot off a volley, he ordered his bow chasers to fire chain-ball shot at the enemy. This destroyed Anton's mizzen mast and sent it tumbling into the sea, along with its sail and lateen yard. As arrows continued to fly at the Spaniards, Drake fired a second shot from one of his larger guns while again ordering Anton to strike sail. As he did so, some forty English archers climbed from the quickly launched pinnace and swarmed up the Spanish rigging. They found the wounded Anton alone on deck, defiant and silent. He was at once made a prisoner and carried to the *Golden Hind* where Drake apparently embraced him, saying, 'Have patience, for such is the usage of war.' He then ordered the wretched man to be locked up in the poop cabin with twelve men to guard him. It took Drake and his men six days fully to rifle the unarmed *Nuestra Señora de la Concepción* and load the booty aboard their own ship. This fact alone suggests the quantity of treasure seized was prodigious. All of the witnesses were more or less agreed on this. Anton confessed that he had gold, silver bars and silver coins aboard to the value of 362,000 pesos. He was also carrying some 40,000 pesos of gold and silver which had not been registered with the Spanish authorities. Da Silva claimed that there were 1,300 silver bars aboard, along with fourteen chests crammed with gold and silver coins.

Drake's pinnace had to make five journeys to transport so vast a treasure but it is inconceivable that his men, their eyes bright with the certainty of reward as they grunted under their burden, realised how important a moment of their country's history they were participating in. It took one of the most luminous minds of the past century to point this out. 'The booty brought back by Drake,' wrote J. M. Keynes in *A Treatise on Money*, 'may fairly be considered an origin of British Foreign Investment.' He then explained why. 'Elizabeth paid off out of the proceeds the whole of her foreign debt and invested a part of the balance (about £42,000) in the Levant Company; largely out of the profits of the Levant Company there was formed the East India Company, the profits of which during the seventeenth and eighteenth centuries were the main foundations of England's foreign connections; and so on.' Keynes scrupulously avoided using the word 'empire' and the passage as a whole is a perhaps pardonable exaggeration from a scholar who quipped that he would prefer to be vaguely right than precisely wrong. Nonetheless, published in the first year of the Great Depression of the 1930s, the reference suggests once again how Drake, as so often, emerged into national consciousness as an inspiring figure in a time of crisis.

Drake's sudden, unprecedented affluence seems to have made him unusually generous. He presented Anton with a musket, a gilded corselet and a silver bowl engraved with the words 'Francisqus Draques'. He also gave him such useful supplies as iron and tar, along with little gifts for his men. In addition, Drake provided Anton with a letter of safe conduct addressed to John Winter and others of Drake's officers requiring them to do the Spaniard no harm nor rob him over again. This may or may not have been sincerely meant, but it certainly gave the altogether false impression that other fierce and rather less merciful English pirates were cruising the area and that no Spaniard was safe. Drake then reinforced the threat by saying that he had a licence from the Queen of England to rob the Spanish and to recover the money Hawkins had been so vilely cheated of in his dealings off San Juan de Ulúa. He added that he also knew about the execution of various of his colleagues in Panama and the sorry state of John Oxenham languishing in the Peruvian jails of the Inquisition. Realising perfectly well that whatever he said would soon be reported to the Spanish Viceroy, Drake told Anton that if any harm came to Oxenham and his fellows then he would personally see to it that more than 2,000 Spaniards would suffer. They would be 'hanged in the presence of the Viceroy so that he shall know it and the heads will be sent him'.

Drake made sure that Anton fully understood that the English pirates had legitimate cause for grievance, and that such threats as these were one necessary tactic in Drake's campaign. The other was to spread as much misinformation as he could. Everybody wondered what he would do next and, above all, what route he would choose for the homeward journey that was surely imminent. Realising this, and laying out a large and expensive Portuguese map before Anton (Drake said it had cost him more than 800 cuzados), he discussed the various ways he might take before releasing the man in the certain knowledge that he would pass on whatever he said to the Spanish authorities. There were several possibilities for the homeward journey. Some were merely the fictions of geographers' ignorance, while others were altogether more feasible, even though they demanded the utmost navigational skill. In discussing these permutations, Drake's purpose was clearly to confuse the Spaniards; once he was satisfied that he had done so, he kept his own counsel and locked the map of the world with its tempting and necessary vistas safely away.

6

The Circumnavigation of the Globe

Four: The Voyage Home and Drake's Knighthood

March 1579–April 1581

Now Drake's overwhelming concern was to get his booty safely back to England. The charred draft of his instructions makes plain how he proposed to do this. He was 'to return by the same way homewards as he went out'. There is a certain neat, desk-bound common sense about this but circumstances made such a plan wholly out of the question. The sheer success of the expedition's recent raiding and piracy meant that large stretches of the Pacific coast of South America were likely to be in a state of high alert and bristling with hostility. Nor was this all. Drake knew from his own experience that returning by way of the Strait of Magellan would be courting disaster in storms that could drive his fabulously freighted ship towards a pitiless maze of rocks. Sitting in his tiny cabin, his beautifully ornamented maps spread out before him to display the lineaments of a barely charted world, he recognised that another route would have to be found.

It is possible that he toyed with the idea of sailing to the Strait of Anian – the supposed western exit of the fabled Northwest Passage

– which cartographers such as Ortelius and Mercator believed divided America from Asia around latitude 40 or 50 degrees north and then led across the top of America itself towards the Atlantic.[1] It is rather more certain, however, that he had already given serious consideration to heading west across the vast wastes of the Pacific and returning to England via the Moluccas, the fabulous Spice Islands. He had mentioned such a plan to Winter, and an extraordinary piece of luck would soon favour this idea. What is clear from all this uncertainty is that very practical matters of seamanship and strategy only now dictated that what had once been intended as a voyage of reconnaissance and piracy became that circumnavigation of the globe which was one of the supreme achievements of the Elizabethan age – and one that would ensure Drake's own enduring place in the nation's consciousness.

His most immediate problem was the securing of an adequate supply of fresh drinking water. On 6 March, having released Anton and his most recently captured pilots, Drake sailed for the island of Cano. It took him over a week to get there, but the place seemed to be a useful anchorage where he could once again set about careening his ships while sending out his pinnace to watch for enemies and potential prizes. He was not long disappointed of the last for, on the afternoon of 20 March, a merchant vessel out of Panama belonging to one Rodrigo Tello hoved into view. A few arquebus shots and a wounded passenger were sufficient to convince Tello that surrender was his only option. His captured ship was brought to the island harbour where its modest cargo of sarsaparilla, lard, honey, and maize was unloaded and placed on the shore while the treasure in the *Golden Hind* was transferred to the captured ship in order to lighten Drake's vessel in preparation for the business of caulking her down to the waterline.

While these necessary tasks were proceeding, Drake closely questioned his new captives and found that they were a prize altogether more valuable than the little cargo they were transporting. Alonso Sánchez Colchero and Martin de Aguirre carried with them charts and sailing directions which accurately depicted the north-west coast of America as far as 43 degrees along, with invaluable information about the route to the Spice Islands.[2] Without these it is entirely possible that Drake would never have been able to get his cargo safely home. It was clearly essential that he win these men over to his side by whatever means he could, but he was not minded to exercise his charm. They would be browbeaten, bullied and bribed. Drake ordered that they were to be kept under guard in the pinnace and only taken off it when he was celebrating divine service aboard his own ship. Then, with evident distaste, they were allowed to tell their rosaries away from the rest of the crew. Kept under guard even during their devotions, the men were further humiliated when one of the English sailors got hold of a crucifix, stamped on it, splintered it and threw the pieces into the sea in order to express his disgust at popish trash and Catholic superstition.

Having released his other recently captured prisoners with only a few scraps for their supply, Drake summoned Colchero to an interview. He told the frightened man that his crew had informed him he was a pilot on the 'China route', in other words the passage across the Pacific to the Philippines and the Moluccas, and let Colchero know that he wished the man to conduct him there. The cringing Spaniard said he did not know the way, that he was poor, that he had a wife and children, that he was not a pilot at all but only a sailor. Drake looked at him contemptuously and told him 'not to plague him by speaking such nonsense'. Colchero would do what he was told, whether he would or no, on pain of hanging. The desperate man, obliged to acts of treachery by Drake's altogether more formidable willpower, begged to be allowed to write letters to the Viceroy of New Spain and his own wife to explain the situation he was in. Drake, realising it was to his advantage to concede, permitted the man pen and paper on condition that the Spanish speakers aboard the *Golden Hind* could translate what he wrote to make sure that he said nothing objectionable. The slightest suggestion of that and Colchero would be hanged from the yardarm. Drake then ordered his men to weigh anchor. He now knew that the westerly route to the Spice Islands began at Acapulco and he pointed his ships in that direction.

While they were off Realejo, Drake turned to Colchero once

again and set about trying to master him. Drake was a wealthy man. There was a great deal of silver and gold aboard his ship. Colchero would be welcome to a little of this if only he would renounce his faith and become a 'Lutheran'. Drake added that he would 'confer great mercies upon him'. The man's resistance weakened and he was finally bought for fifty golden pesos. This was an encouraging sign, and Drake now resolved to use him in his proposed sacking of Realejo and the subsequent destruction of the Spanish trading vessel he knew was being built there. Colchero was the man to guide him into the harbour for his map had shown the place was guarded by a dangerous sandbar. Despite his newly pocketed pesos, Colchero refused. He claimed he had never been into the port and did not know how to handle its difficulties. Drake turned the full force of his contempt on him. He put a rope about Colchero's neck and strung him up until he fainted, whereupon he let him down only to string him up again until the man nearly passed out for a second time. Colchero was then lowered once more and imprisoned in an iron cage in the hold.

Furious at being cheated of his way, Drake sailed on along the Central American coast until, on 4 April, he encountered yet another Spanish ship sailing in a southerly direction. The Spanish steersman shouted that Drake was to get out of his way and not come alongside. The English made no answer, 'pretending to be asleep'. Meanwhile, Colchero was quickly released from his prison and brought up on deck so that, when the Spaniards shouted questions as to who Drake was and where he had come from, an authentically Iberian accent could tell them that they had sailed from Peru and were captained by a well-known sailor on that route. This lie having been broadcast, Drake ordered the attack. It was sudden and decisive. Drake crossed his victim's poop and demanded that those aboard strike sail, reinforcing his commands by firing seven or eight arquebus shots. The Spaniards were able to put up very little resistance, and the English swarmed aboard but, for the moment, did no personal harm to anyone beyond seizing the swords and keys of the passengers.

Among these last was a Spanish nobleman called Don Francisco de Zárate.[3] Courteous to the point of fawning, intelligent and observant, Zárate noted all that was going on around him. He was taken aboard the *Golden Hind* where he found Drake pacing the deck. With exaggerated Spanish courtesy he fell to his knees and kissed his captor's hands. Drake was clearly won over by this, being wholly unused to such behaviour from great men. He took Zárate to his cabin, bade him be seated, and began to interview him. 'I am a friend of those who tell me the truth, but with those who do not I get out of humour,' he began. 'Therefore, you must tell me (for this is the best road to my favour), how much silver and gold does your ship carry?' Zárate told him it carried none. Drake repeated his question, and Zárate said that his vessel only contained some small silver plates and cups that he himself used.

Drake changed the topic of conversation. Did Zárate know the Viceroy of New Spain? Zárate said he did. Were any of the man's relatives or property aboard the captured ship? 'No, sir.' Perhaps this was just as well, since Drake now threatened his captive by suggesting the revenge that he, as an English gentleman whose honour had been slighted by Spain, would wreak on the Viceroy. Zárate made no reply and Drake, standing up, bade Zárate go with him to observe the punishment now being meted out to the newly reimprisoned Colchero. Zárate looked at the aged and cowed pilot as Drake told him to sit down, 'For it is here that you will have to remain.' Zárate resigned himself to the indignity, but Drake told him that he did not intend to humiliate him immediately but wanted to know whether he knew who Colchero was. Zárate said he had never seen him before, and Drake told him the man's name before releasing the pilot and escorting both his captives back up on deck. A long but unrecorded conversation followed until it was time to dine.

Zárate was clearly impressed by the order, discipline and conspicuous luxury with which this pirate was surrounded. Drake bade Zárate sit next to him and, offering him food from his own plate, told him not to grieve since his life and property were safe and he would soon be released. Some nine or ten of Drake's gentlemen – including Doughty's cowed brother John – shared the table with them and were clearly in awe of their Captain. None of them dared to sit down before they were asked to do so and, a gesture of deference so important to the Elizabethans, none of them dared to put his hat on until repeatedly urged to do so by Drake. The dining arrangements were not only formal but sumptuous. Drake was clearly determined to impress this newly acquired aristocrat, who noted that the food was served on silver dishes with gold borders and gilded garlands. The coats-of-arms engraved on them were, Drake untruthfully suggested, his own. He would appear a gentleman at all costs. As the men ate, Drake's musicians played on their viols while the easily fetid air of a small and crowded cabin was sweetened by the perfumed waters which, Drake said, had been given to him by the Queen of England. In such ways as these, in borrowed, and to some degree factitious, splendour, Drake the pirate and would-be godly magistrate appeared as the centre of order, hierarchy and justice. It was a scene to impress even a hidalgo familiar with the starched and corseted formality of Spanish etiquette.

But it was not only such moments as this that won Zárate's admiration. He saw very clearly that Drake preserved an admirable discipline among his crew. The ordinary seamen were young, fit and well-trained. Their arquebuses were kept scrupulously clean and, while Drake treated them with obvious affection which was returned with respect, Zárate was quick to note that he punished the least fault. It was all very impressive, and Zárate paid informed tribute to Drake as a commander, and as a navigator who had mastered the supreme skill of determining latitude from the measurement of the altitude of a heavenly body by means of his astrolabe. So skilled a pirate could readily conquer the seas off Central America, but what particularly impressed Zárate was the fact that the illustrations in Drake's journal-rutter depicted everything so naturally and faithfully that 'no one who guides himself according to these paintings can possibly go astray'. Such illustrations were as dangerous as they were wonderful, and Zárate recognised that Drake was making a record that was of national importance to the enemy.

Sunday being a suitable occasion for display, Drake ordered that the *Golden Hind* be dressed over-all while he himself appeared in his finest clothes. It was with such gentlemanly show as this that Drake went about his piracy, examining everything aboard the newly captured vessel, taking various little possessions of Zárate's own and saying they were for his wife. Reluctant, however, to appear as a common thief, Drake presented Zárate with a small brazier of silver. Drake discovered that his prisoner's ship was laded with linen, oriental silks and exquisite white Chinese porcelain. These last were rare, exotic and extraordinarily valuable items, and Drake managed to secure no less than four chests full of them before telling Zárate that he could depart the next morning and escorting him back to his ship where he distributed a handful of coins among the Spanish crew. Such rare generosity was not sufficient to persuade the men to tell him where he could obtain precious drinking water, however, and so he took more decisive action. 'He caused Juan Pascual to be put by force in his sloop saying that he would hang him if he replied a word.' With that Drake took his leave of Zárate and headed in the direction of Guatulco, content in the thought that his bunk would now be warmed by 'a proper Negro wench' called Maria who was an item of booty stolen from the Spaniards.

Drake arrived at Guatulco on 13 April.[4] Compared to his recent gentlemanly piracies, his raid on this barely defended little back-water was conducted with all the savagery that militant anti-Catholicism inspired in both him and his men. In the later part of the morning, some two dozen of his crew were dispatched to the port where they wholly surprised the 300 Indians and a handful of Spaniards resident there. The local mayor tried to muster a force to repel the attackers but his men fled as soon as the English fired a few shots. The leading citizens were at once taken prisoner and the house of the local bigwig, Gomez Rengifo, was raided of 7,000 pesos and a valuable gold chain while, in order to make clear the zealous purity of their Protestant beliefs, the man who led the assault tore a crucifix from the wall and smashed it down on a table, telling its horrified owner that it was just a pagan idol. Having seized what they wanted from Rengifo, the English then moved on to the local church where they laid their rapacious hands on the chalices and the monstrance, along with richly embroidered vestments and altar cloths which they were determined to use as towels. The sacrilege was completed by scattering the Communion wafers and trampling them underfoot while systematically vandalising the images of the saints with which the church was decorated.

The local friar had already been taken aboard Drake's ship and now, as the rest of the raiding party returned, they found the anxious man telling his rosary which they promptly tore out of his hands and destroyed. But the 'Lutheran' violence was still far from over. It was Holy Week and good Catholics were supposed to be fasting. When mealtime came round Drake's captives were offered meat which they guiltily accepted, only the priest refraining. It was then time for prayers. The captive citizens of Guatulco would now be shown more of what good Protestantism entailed. Drake's table, box, and embroidered cushion were brought out on the deck, along with his copy of Foxe's *Book of Martyrs*. He read from this for some time, telling the Spaniards that it was to him what the Bible was to them. The accounts of savage punishments and the lurid woodcuts with which Foxe's volume was decorated clearly lifted Drake's spirits and roused his anti-Catholic virulence. 'He spoke much evil of the Supreme Pontiff and his power over kings, and then turned to his congregation and asked: "How can it be tolerated that a prince or monarch is to kiss the foot of the Pope? This is a swindle, and Saint Peter did not do thus".'

Rengifo was clearly intrigued by the book and Drake asked him why he took such an interest in it. The Spaniard replied that he wondered if the volume was some sort of breviary or a guide to devotion in the Catholic manner. Drake, who was probably a friend of Foxe's, was speechless with indignation but, after a while, said that the book was a very good one and, opening it, proceeded to show his captive various of its illustrations. There was, for example, a picture of the burning of Thomas Hutton which showed the devout, bearded man, dressed in a penitential shift and tied to a stake, praying as hideous flames leaped around his body. Thus, Drake told Rengifo, did the Spanish treat virtuous English Protestants in Castile. Thus was martyrdom placed near the core of Protestant faith and Protestant politics. But there was more. Another woodcut showed a plump and worldly pontiff seated on his throne, the triple crown balanced on his head and holding the keys of St Peter in one hand while he stretched out the other in benediction over a grovelling Holy Roman Emperor. A figure in the foreground of the crowd was shown turning away in disgust at this image of papal worldliness, but the greater part of the clerics gathered behind the Pope – variously tonsured, mitred or wearing their cardinals' hats – are clearly satisfied with the whole proceeding. Thus, for devout Protestants, the worldliness, the cruelty and political chicanery of the Catholic Church.

According to Rengifo's own testimony, Drake proceeded to give him a lecture which epitomised his public motives for sailing to the Pacific and attacking Spanish Catholics. The lecture was clearly intended for the ears of the Spanish authorities to whom indeed it was duly reported. Drake told Rengifo that he was well aware that the Spanish considered him to be a devil 'who robs by day and prays at night', but he made it clear that he was doing this at the behest of the Queen of England who had ordered him to come to these parts. He was only doing his duty as a good and loyal Protestant. Nothing would prevent him continuing with his work and, to further justify his actions, he returned to a well-worn theme: 'I am not going to stop until I have collected the two millions that my cousin John Hawkins lost, for certain, at Saint Juan de Ulúa.' The old, rancorous incident, endlessly repeated by Drake, suggested at once his own slighted family honour and the entirely reasonable desire of a nation to take revenge on a perfidious foe. As a piece of self-promotion it was masterly. It implied that the Spaniards themselves were responsible for the miseries Drake was inflicting on them and they should recognise the fact.

There was one last surprise in store. The following morning Drake despatched a party to the shore to barrel up supplies of all-important drinking water from the places that the now bound Juan Pascual would show them. The mission was accomplished and Drake eventually freed his prisoners. He then, suddenly, ordered da Silva to be placed on the Spaniards' ship with a number of other sailors. The Portuguese pilot had been extremely useful to Drake through the last many months, had learned sufficient English for them to hold conversations and create the basis of a seeming friendship and, it appears, had been persuaded to take more than a passing interest in the Protestant devotions held aboard Drake's ship. To abandon da Silva now and hand him over to the mercies of the Spanish was certainly to condemn him to the rigours of the

Inquisition but Drake, it seems, was unconcerned about this. He gave the elderly man to understand that he had changed his mind about the route he would take for home and was now seriously considering navigating the mythical Strait of Anian. Only if he did not find this would he sail for the Spice Islands. Here was one way of protecting himself, his plans and his crew by spreading misinformation. Another was to talk about the Moluccas route so vociferously that the Spaniards would begin to think that he protested too much (as indeed they did) and clearly intended to return via the Strait of Magellan. Many of the Spaniards also thought that Drake's immediate destination was Acapulco. In fact, all of these guesses were wrong, which was precisely what Drake intended. The journey home would be his greatest challenge, and to clothe it in mystery and confusion were his best means of protection.

Drake not only managed to confuse the Spaniards. Chroniclers of the famous voyage continue to dispute precisely what Drake did next. The contemporary accounts are contradictory, some saying that he sailed west to latitude 48 degrees, but this does not agree with either Hakluyt's published account or with *The World Encompassed*. A deliberate campaign of misinformation by the English government after Drake's return may well have been responsible for this, and the confusion spread to the printed maps that subsequently detailed the voyage. Efforts to use such information to prove conclusively that Drake landed in the general region of San Francisco are unsound. So, it will appear, is the archaeological evidence. In an issue clouded by historical uncertainty – and perhaps a measure of special pleading – the most that can be safely said is that he probably used Colchero's navigational materials to navigate the coast of Lower California, searching for a safe anchorage where he could rest, revictual and repair his ship in preparation for the long journey to the Spice Islands.[5] The stories told in *The World Encompassed* of his being crowned by awed Californian natives, his declaring the whole region of 'Nova Albion' subject to the Queen of England, and the notion that he intended to found a colony there and erected a brass plate proclaiming his deeds, probably add more fantasy than fact to an already obscure situation. As such, the tales are interesting because they say so much about attitudes to newly discovered lands and peoples at the time *The World Encompassed* was being put together.[6]

What is perhaps most evident is a sense of bemused racial superiority stemming from the Englishmen's confidence in their technological and social achievements, along with their belief that true religion had been vouchsafed to them alone. The Indians are portrayed as comparatively simple people, armed with bows and arrows and making things out of feathers. Being true human beings they have an ordered social life of sorts: a language and a hierarchy with a king at its apex. They nonetheless apparently recognised themselves as being inferior and there are repeated references to the idea that they wanted to worship the English as gods. Peaceable and admiring though they seemed, Drake and his men were nonetheless resolved not to trust them. 'Our experience of former infidels . . . made us careful to provide against an alteration of their affections or breach of peace if it should happen'. Here indeed are people conceived, in Kipling's much later and notorious phrase, as being 'half-devil and half-child'. Much of the description of Drake's supposed activities in California is what would become the familiar cant of imperialism, and sounds themes that continued to be played right up to the time of Henty's novels and beyond.

These fantasies about foreign races are particularly strained when it comes to matters of colonisation. The two decades from the mid-1570s saw the Elizabethans under the leadership of such men as Grenville, Gilbert and Raleigh making strenuous if unsuccessful efforts to found colonies in the Americas, and *The World Encompassed* strives to place Drake firmly within this tradition. By the time the book was being written, Drake himself was personally acquainted with the acute logistical and military difficulties such enterprises had faced on the eastern American seaboard, and the description of what he supposedly achieved on the other side of the continent is clearly designed to wish these problems away. Not only is Drake shown taking the initiative in matters of colonisation, the natives are revealed as people whose deepest longing is to be taken over by an imperial English power. It is all a little too good to be true.

Conveying complex ideas without a shared vocabulary was

obviously difficult, but *The World Encompassed* suggests that gesture alone was quite sufficient to convince Drake that the native ruler and his advisors wished him to 'become their king and patron: making signs that they would resign unto him their right entitled in the whole land, and become his vassals in themselves and their posterities'. Indeed, so delightful did the prospect appear to the Indians that they set about joyfully singing a song and crowning Drake 'because they were not only visited of the gods (for so they still judged us to be), but the great and chief god was now become their god, their king and patron, and themselves were become the only happy and blessed people in the world'. Drake, unsurprisingly, was happy enough to play along with such ideas, hoping, we are assured, that the true Protestant God had contrived this episode in imperial fantasy for the honour and profit of the English nation. We are told that he 'willingly took the sceptre, crown, and dignity of the said country into his hand'.

All of this is conceived, of course, as a great act of patriotism by which Elizabeth (whose favour Drake was desperately trying to regain) could enjoy the riches of the land as her own and rule 'so tractable and loving a people' while, at the same time, becoming 'a mother and nurse of the Church of Christ' who would bring ignorant savages into 'the right knowledge and obedience of the true and ever-living God'. Here is the imperial dream of England in a nutshell, and Drake is shown naming the new colony 'Albion' in order that it might 'have some affinity ... with our own country, which was sometime so called'. The spinning of a phoney tradition seems to give its blessing to the intentions of the would-be imperialists while, to make sure their claim, Drake is shown erecting:

a plate of brass, fast nailed to a great and firm post; whereon is engraven Her Grace's name, and the day and year of our arrival there, and of the free giving up of the province and kingdom, both by the king and people, into Her Majesty's hands: together with Her Highness' picture and arms, in a piece of sixpence current English money, showing itself by a hole made of purpose through the plate; underneath was likewise engraven the name of our general, etc.[7]

In other words, the colony was English and trespassers would be prosecuted. To reinforce this idea, *The World Encompassed* is careful to point out that the new colony of 'Albion' is safely distant from any Spanish territories, while a plate answering to the description given above was found near San Francisco and placed in the Bancroft Library of the University of California. Recent scientific tests have suggested that the plate was made sometime between the eighteenth and twentieth centuries, most probably in the late nineteenth or early twentieth century. It is, in other words, a fake – the final wish-fulfilment fantasy in this whole episode of Drake the self-fashioned imperialist.

Empires and submissive natives notwithstanding, Drake almost certainly knew from his Portuguese sources that leaving the American coast in April would involve him reaching the West Pacific at the beginning of the hurricane season. Time spent avoiding this possibility could be well used for preparation, and it was with his ships careened and reprovisioned that Drake finally made his uneventful crossing of the Pacific in about seventy days. Late in September his crew sighted what was probably one of the Palau Islands. The native people were intensely curious about the new arrivals and made from the shore in their skilfully constructed and gaudily decorated outrigger canoes. As they came nearer, so it was possible for the English to observe them more closely and note their artificially elongated earlobes, their habit of letting their fingernails grow very long, and the fact that their teeth were wholly discoloured by their persistent chewing of betel leaf.

At first sight it seemed that these people wanted to trade in a fair and peaceful manner, but Drake's crew gradually suspected a plot: that they were being drawn nearer and nearer to the shore so that the natives 'might (if possible) make the easier prey both of the ship and us'. It soon became apparent too that the natives' desire to trade was itself a front. Theft rather than business seemed to be their real concern 'for if they received anything once into their hands, they would neither give recompense nor restitution of it, but thought whatever they could finger to be their own'. Such observations from pirates aboard a vessel freighted with stolen booty are rich in unconscious irony, but tempers soon became frayed and the islanders started hurling the stones they had concealed in their canoes. For all that Drake himself was, in the words of *The World Encompassed*, far from 'meaning to requite their malice by like injury', he considered their behaviour an affront and gave orders that one of his cannon be fired at the canoes.

The World Encompassed does not mention the fact that some twenty of the islanders were killed, saying merely that gunpowder had 'the desired effect' and so frightened the natives that they leaped from their canoes and hid beneath them until they believed they were safe. Such a fright did not prevent other parties of men rowing out to Drake's ship, however, and apparently offering to trade on reasonable terms. Nonetheless, 'under that pretence they cunningly fell a-filching of what they could, and one of them pulled a dagger and knives from one of our men's girdles, and being required to restore it again, he rather used what means he could to catch at more'. Despite these difficulties it was essential that Drake take on water and he remained anchored off the island for a couple of days until, having got what he wanted, he sailed away from a place his crewmen robustly called 'the Island of Thieves'.

Drake now sailed as far west as Mindanao before turning south to the Spice Islands which he sighted early in November. He was almost certainly making for Tidore (a well-established Portuguese base) when he had the good fortune to be diverted.[8] The *Golden Hind* had been observed by the watchmen of the Sultan of Ternate who sent out two of his 'caracoas' – large and formidable open boats rowed by upwards of a hundred oarsmen and often armed with small cannon in the bow and stern – to find out what Drake was doing. When the emissaries of the Sultan discovered that Drake and his men 'were neither Portuguese nor Spanish but English Lutherans ... they returned to tell the King and he soon sent to invite them to come ashore at once, offering them port room and everything necessary'. This was an offer too good to refuse. The Sultan of Ternate was a shrewd and warlike native chief who controlled the bulk of the clove trade and thus of a cargo which the merchant adventurers back in London could sell for a substantial profit. The Portuguese had tried to monopolise this market, doing so by siding with now one and now another of the local chiefs, thereby exasperating the Sultan who was eager to find other Europeans with whom he could do business.

The story of Drake's dealings with the Sultan of Ternate became increasingly elaborate as time went on. The wealth to be won in the Spice Islands would become of great importance to English merchants building up their great sea-borne empire, and it seemed desirable to hint that this development had an excellent and heroic pedigree. Drake's dealings on Ternate could be made to fit the bill. In the earliest account of the matter, John Drake simply stated that the galleys of the Sultan came out to escort the *Golden Hind* to a well-protected harbour where the English were given victuals and spice- and cloves in exchange for linen and other things. Apparently Drake himself then spun the rather curious story (probably based on his intuition that male chauvinism, rather than the truth, would be more acceptable to a Muslim potentate) that he was the representative of the King of England who was, in his turn, a brother of the King of Spain. The Sultan, suitably impressed, was said then to have offered Drake the freedom of the island and invited him ashore but, in what was in fact an atmosphere of mutual suspicion, Drake declined to go and sent some of his men instead.

It seems that Drake did indeed manage to secure a cargo of some six tons of cloves, but Spanish sources suggest that his means of getting hold of them were not wholly straightforward. The Sultan's principal source of revenue was the ten per cent duty he charged on the export of all locally grown spices, a right that he enforced with considerable rigour and which Drake apparently chose to hold in contempt. The Sultan in his turn demanded Drake's head and Drake himself, 'expert in fraud' though he was, resolved on flight before thinking better of this and bribing his way into the good will of the 'astute tyrant' who then offered him an interview. The upshot of this meeting and those that followed it was that the Sultan 'should be a friend and confederate of the Queen of the English nation, and that factories should be founded there very soon'. All of this is quite possible, even if stories that the Sultan handed over himself and his fiefdom to the English are clearly wishful thinking. Drake certainly showed an interest in establishing a trading post in the Spice Islands soon after his return home. In later years the East India Company would make much of the alleged verbal agreement between Drake and the Sultan, and the influence and allure of Drake's dealings in the Spice Islands played their part in England's subsequent founding of a vast, and vastly rich, empire in the East. This is an example once again of Drake being wished into the role of a founding father of the British Empire.

In reality, Drake spent less than a week in Ternate before setting off to find somewhere altogether safer where he could careen his ship and prepare for his long voyage home. He stayed for about a month in an anchorage on the coast of what he later named Crab Island because there were found 'many crabs on land who breed without ever entering the sea'. The island was densely wooded and 'among these trees, night by night, did show themselves an infinite swarm of firey-seeming-worms flying in the air, whose bodies (no bigger than an ordinary fly) did make a show, and give such light as did every twig on every tree have been a lighted candle, or as if that place had been the starry sphere'. For all this bounty, water had to be fetched from a nearby island, but such essential supplies could only be taken aboard ship when the expedition's blacksmith had repaired some iron-hooped casks on his little portable forge, which now had to be fired with charcoal since the supply of coal the expedition had brought along was exhausted.

There were also other practical and altogether more brutal matters to attend to. Maria, the black woman Drake had taken on board many months earlier, was now heavily pregnant. There were some doubts about the paternity, but a brief clause in one account of the voyage gives a wretched indication of what may well have been going on when it states that the woman was 'gotten with child between the captain and his men pirates'. A woman close to giving birth would have been a difficult responsibility on the long homeward voyage, while the embarrassment that would inevitably arise once the *Golden Hind* reached port would clearly be considerable. Drake was prepared to face neither problem and decided to solve both with a glib heartlessness that he hoped would hush the matter up. The poor pregnant woman, with two other black male slaves, was marooned on Crab Island with no more provisions than 'rice and seeds and fire to populate the place'. It was a disgraceful incident and, deservedly, Drake's sins found him out. The great historian William Camden, writing his semi-official account of the nation's doings, publicly berated him for behaving 'most inhumanely' in the matter.

There followed a month of somewhat aimless and difficult tacking as Drake sought a passage into the Indian Ocean. Contrary winds made matters worse for they obliged him to alter his course southwards, and to 'beat up and down with extraordinary care and circumspection', since the sea they were now sailing was a difficult and dangerous maze of rocky islands and treacherous shoals. Many considered this part of the circumnavigation altogether worse than their experiences in the Strait of Magellan, but it was only on 9 January when the crew 'supposed that we had at last attained a free passage, the lands turning evidently in our sight about to Westward, and the wind being enlarged' that disaster suddenly struck. During the first night watch, 'even in a moment', the *Golden Hind* was tossed upon a shoal with no apparent hope of ever getting free.[9]

What had briefly seemed benevolent winds drove the port side fully against the reef, forcing it ever more firmly on to the treacherous rocks. It seemed that the crew could look forward to nothing but 'the ghastly appearance of instant death' and that the only thing they could do was commend themselves to God. 'To this purpose we presently fell prostrate, and with joined prayers sent up to the throne of grace, humbly besought Almighty God to extend His mercy unto us.' But mere passive fatalism was not enough – not yet, at least. The men were bound to do what they could to save themselves, and Drake knew that it was his duty to lead, to set the great example and inspire them with that combination of iron courage and deeply practised seamanship which was his to command. He had to fashion himself before them all as the great commander he truly was, and this was one of the supremely testing moments of the whole circumnavigation.

In the darkness and amid the howling waves, Drake invigorated and comforted his men by speaking earnestly of the joys that surely awaited them in heaven, even as he ordered them to take such practical measures as they could. Drake did indeed lead by example, plying the ship's pumps himself with all the physical vigour at his disposal. On this occasion the often inefficient Elizabethan engines worked well and, freeing the ship of water, showed that the timbers were as sound as they could be under such dreadful conditions. If this alone could not save them at least the ship was not in imminent danger of being smashed to matchwood, and this fact 'we acknowledged to be the immediate providence of God alone insomuch as no strength of wood and iron could have possibly borne so hard and violent a shock as our ship did . . . except the extraordinary hand of God had supported the same'. Heroism – Drake's Protestant heroism – and the mercy of the Almighty towards the righteous here combine in a way that suggest the very deepest concerns of sixteenth-century seamen.

It was still necessary for Drake to keep encouraging and inspiring his men by his own actions and, realising that a greater degree of safety could be achieved if only they could get an anchor hold, 'in his own person he . . . undertook the charge of sounding' the seabed. This sensible measure proved altogether desperate, for the water around them was so deep that no anchorage could be found. This fact most of the men were fortunately unaware of since Drake, cunning even in desperation, wisely chose to lie about the difficulty and encouraged them with 'cheerful speeches' instead. The prospects before them were indeed terrible. The *Golden Hind* was jammed so fast that the vessel could not be moved. The men faced the bleak option of either staying aboard and facing certain starvation since there were victuals for only a few days, or trying to make a desperate passage against contrary winds to distant dry land. Those few who could be put aboard the pinnace would, if they were lucky enough to survive at all, face a life of 'perpetual misery' on a strange and inhospitable coast among wild animals or 'the barbarous people of the heathen'.

Meanwhile, the ghastly night wore itself out in prayer and 'other godly exercises' until dawn rose and 'we again renewed our travail to see if we could now possibly find any anchor hold which we had formerly sought in vain'. The effort was as useless as before, and it seemed that the only thing that could save them now was a miracle.

The exhausted and terrified men, realising that all human effort was futile, surrendered themselves to the mercy of God and the ministrations of Francis Fletcher who, in order that their faith might be the better strengthened, and the comfortable apprehension of God's mercy in Christ be more clearly felt, preached a sermon. The content of this roused Drake to a paroxysm of anger which he thought it wiser not to express for the time being, instead ordering his crew to throw the cargo overboard in the hope of lightening the vessel sufficiently to let it float free. *The World Encompassed* suggests that everything as it first came to hand went overboard. This did not include the looted treasure, but among the goods jettisoned were three tons of the valuable cloves obtained in Ternate, two cannon and a quantity of precious meal and beans. The scrupulous Protestantism of *The World Encompassed* makes clear that it was not this serious sacrifice that saved the ship and its crew, but God and God alone. As the tide turned, so the wind changed direction. These were clear acts of divine mercy which at last freed the keel from the rocks and 'made us glad men'.

Thus was true faith apparently rewarded but, it appeared, not all deserved such benevolence. It seems that, at the height of the storm, when the agonised crew were exhausted and terrified, the sermon Fletcher preached to them made plain how the fearful predicament they were in was a just judgement of the Almighty's on the heinous guilt they all bore for the judicial murder of Thomas Doughty. The black waves, the furious winds, the fatigue and near despair were nothing more than the crew deserved as they waited for an imminent and dreadful death. This was the theology of a desperately frightened man, and events had proved Fletcher utterly wrong. The *Golden Hind*, its Captain, crew and treasure, had all been saved by what many chose to believe was the providence of a just and loving God. Fletcher had failed to trust this. He had failed to understand the works of divine mercy and substituted for them the vengeance of a wrathful deity. Far worse, he had reopened an old wound and rubbed salt into it. He had threatened to undermine the morale of the crew with his pessimism and, worst of all, had challenged Drake's alleged authority and moral responsibility in an area where Drake himself knew all too well that he was particularly vulnerable.

Such matters could not go unpunished. Drake was determined to have his revenge and silence the feeble cleric once and for all. In executing Doughty *pour encourager les autres* Drake had claimed to be acting with an authority that, in truth, he held at best tenuously, if at all. His gamble had nonetheless paid off. He had got his way and masterfully held his crew together. Now, faced with the necessity of repeating the exercise and made confident by his anger and his previous success, Drake proposed to show Fletcher and the rest that he possessed powers spiritual as well as temporal with which he could excommunicate the dangerous priest. He had Fletcher nailed fast to one of the hatches and, calling all the crew together, locked him in irons as he himself sat cross-legged on a sea chest. Then, without any semblance of a trial or even of an enquiry, he pronounced sentence: 'Francis Fletcher, I do here excommunicate thee out of the church of God and from all the benefits and graces thereof and I denounce thee to the devil and all his angels.'

This was an exercise in absolute and arbitrary authority which no one, it seemed, dared challenge. It could readily be believed, by superstitious minds at least, that the forces of darkness might be conjured up to swallow those who threatened Drake's authority. But the sentence of excommunication – this apparent consigning of Fletcher to damnation – was not all. To claim to be able to cast a soul into perdition was a dreadful but insufficient punishment. The body too must be threatened and humiliated. Looking across at his powerless victim, Drake charged Fletcher upon pain of death not once to come before the mast for, if he did, he swore he should be hanged. The guilty man would have to remain below deck. Finally, to complete his revenge and silence Fletcher utterly, there was the very potent instrument of ridicule. The disgraced cleric was, once more upon pain of death, ordered to wear a label round his arm for the rest of the voyage. The words on the label were simple and to the point: 'Francis Fletcher the falsest knave that liveth.' Drake had, on the basis of his own say-so, appointed himself a figure of absolute legal and spiritual authority, and it was in this assurance that he sailed on in search of much-needed victuals to replace those that had been thrown overboard during the recent crisis.

On 8 February, the *Golden Hind* reached Baratina.[10] Fruit, vegetables, spices and grains were all available from the 'comely' and 'civil' natives in exchange for linen cloth which they made into girdles and rolls for their heads. Java, the next port of call, was a sophisticated and intriguing place where Drake stopped for a fortnight and possibly longer. The governing rajahs in particular, naked to their waists but wearing exquisitely coloured silk sarongs, were often invited aboard the *Golden Hind*, while parties of Englishmen paid visits to the local villages and probably participated in the delightful communal meals that were held in buildings specially erected for the purpose. Sociability was indeed a characteristic of the Javanese and brought with it its attendant problems. 'The French pox is here very common to all, and they help themselves, sitting naked from ten to two in the sun, whereby the venomous humour is drawn out.'

The Javanese were also shrewd business people and made sure that Drake paid handsomely for the provisions he needed. Half a dozen tons of rice and supplies of plantains, coconuts, sugar cane, chicken, cassava and beef could only be obtained in return for the very finest pirated fabrics aboard Drake's ship. It cost him in the region of £4,000 to revictual but, thus supplied, he set sail on 26 March, heading west-south-west for the Cape of Good Hope. This was a long, placid journey of some two and a half months. No good anchorages were found when they finally spied land, but the torrential rains at least allowed them to refresh their supplies of water before sailing for Sierra Leone and the Guinea coast which they reached on 22 July. Here Drake could get provisions for his famished men that would see them through the final leg of their journey.

While Drake was on the last stretch of his momentous expedition, another ship was making its way to Cadiz. Among the things it carried was a packet of letters.[11] These letters included two despatches from the Viceroy of Peru, two further letters from the President of the Court of Panama, and the first reports from the Viceroy of New Spain concerning Drake's entry into Guatulco. The missives were already nearly a year old, but their scrupulously factual contents laid bare to the Spanish authorities the depredations that Drake and his men had made to Spanish property around the coasts and seas of Central and South America. They thereby proved that the seemingly limitless transatlantic resources of the King of Spain could no longer be enjoyed without interference.

A precis of this unwelcome information was duly made by the President of the Council of the Indies and found its way on to Philip's crowded desk. The President himself pressed for urgent action. What had happened was greatly to be lamented, and serious deliberation should be given to a matter which was of such present and future importance. The President thought that the real remedy would be to catch Drake before he got home but, if this failed, then perhaps His Majesty should consider demanding that the heretic English Queen order the restitution of what Francis Drake had seized, something it was hoped she could hardly deny once the situation had been made clear to her. The harassed King, all too familiar with the overexcited suggestions of his advisors, penned a short and scrupulous note in the margin of the memorandum. 'It would be very well to take all suitable steps in this matter and to write to Don Bernadino to speak to the Queen; not now, but after the Englishman has returned thither.'

Don Bernadino de Mendoza, having been apprised of the situation, set about energetically watching for Drake's return and gathering every shred of evidence against him that he could. Copies of his colleague's memoranda had been sent to him and the personal interest of the King ensured the Don's keenest attention. It is perhaps ironic that the greater part of the detailed information concerning Drake's return to England comes not from his enthusiastic fellow countrymen but from the hostile and gimlet-eyed attention paid to his doings by a man who passionately hated all that he stood for. Spanish agents were despatched to the West Country ports where Drake was expected to land. They informed Mendoza that those members of the Privy Council who had a financial interest in the circumnavigation had ordered the local Justices of the Peace to see to it that Drake would be able to land his bullion without difficulty and stow it in a place of safety. Such altogether sensible precautions made Mendoza wary and he was rightfully fearful that, with the highest in the land abetting Drake's efforts, the Spanish authorities had little chance of reclaiming what was rightfully theirs.

It was probably on Monday, 26 September 1580, that Drake finally dropped anchor in Plymouth.[12] It was a moment of triumph and apprehension combined. The success of the mighty undertaking was now evident but Drake could not know for certain about the state of the homeland he was returning to. England was surrounded by Catholic enemies who would seize the throne at once if anything happened to Elizabeth. Her death would mean Drake's own, and a local fisherman was pressed to say if the Queen still lived. She did indeed, but Plymouth was in the grip of a plague epidemic and Drake was unable to go ashore; he had though, as Mendoza's agents noted, the satisfaction of greeting his wife who was rowed out to see him on his ship. These personal matters having been attended to, Drake then despatched the expedition's trumpeter, John Brewer, to London to inform the Queen of her most loyal servant's safe return. Drake then waited for her reply.

This, when it came, was disconcerting in the extreme. Her Majesty was deeply embarrassed by what Drake had done and informed him that the Spanish Ambassador was already asking for restitution. At first glance, it seemed that Mendoza had the law on his side, for an agreement had recently been signed whereby the English and Spanish authorities agreed to the reciprocal return of stolen property. An agreement was one thing, however, implementing it was another. Batteries of well-fed lawyers were on hand to obfuscate, prevaricate, raise technicalities, and generally ensure that, whatever the position might be on paper, the hard fact of the matter was that possession was nine-tenths of the law. Elizabeth herself was perfectly well aware of this. Her first reply to Drake had been intended for Mendoza rather than for Drake himself, and private letters soon followed telling him that he need not be unduly concerned. This was assurance enough, and Drake set about the altogether pleasurable task of unloading his priceless cargo which, the Spanish agents noted, was locked in a tower near Saltash and guarded by forty men who were to answer to the new Lord Mayor of Plymouth. This task complete, Drake himself could prepare for London, taking with him, as the Queen had requested, some samples of his booty. Several heavily laden packhorses made their dogged way to London and the royal presence at Richmond.

Richmond was the favourite of Elizabeth's many palaces: a vast fantastication of towers, pinnacles and domes, all surmounted by gold and silver weathervanes so constructed that they sang like harps when the wind blew through them. Inside were an uncountable number of rooms where beautiful, slender columns rose to an efflorescence of delicate fan vaulting that was, in its turn, vividly coloured by the light that filtered through massive stained-glass windows. Here the Queen waited to receive her pirate. Perhaps she was dressed, as she so often was, in her customary white and black, the severity of the colours offset by the diaphanous mystery of her veils and the prodigious extravagance of the ropes of pearls she so greatly loved. Her reddish-gold hair framed a fair, pale, freckled face, which would have been painted with egg white, alum and borax that had been moistened with the freshest water. Elizabeth's hands were her finest feature and she was proud of her long and beautifully tapering fingers which sometimes she would cover with gloves, sometimes adorn with rings from her immense collection of jewellery, or artfully display by clasping one of her ostrich feather fans with their richly decorated handles. Her eyes were fine – deep grey and piercingly intelligent – and it was these she turned on Drake as he entered her presence, knelt before her, and displayed his booty.

They were closeted together for six hours or more, enraptured by the gold, the silver, and by emeralds as long as the Queen's own fingers. There was much for Drake to say and he was invariably eloquent in a direct and forceful way when speaking in his own praise. There were stories of storms and encounters with primitive tribesmen, of fights with Spanish ships off barely navigated coasts, of meetings with silken Orientals and, above all, the constant suggestion of the sheer heroic scale of what had been achieved. Drake's seamanship had put him in the forefront of Western European oceanic enterprise. He was not the first man to circumnavigate the globe but he was the first to return and bring with him not just his ship and its fabulous cargo but the greater part of its crew as well. As a technical achievement the circumnavigation was remarkable. The magnificent chart Drake had made, and the detailed journal-rutter he had kept, bore witness to what he had done and were, much to Mendoza's horror, presented to the Queen as information of such great national importance that she ordered all their details to be kept secret under pain of death. The record of achievement was long. The Strait of Magellan had been navigated and the vastness of the Pacific, the world's greatest ocean, had finally been penetrated by an English ship. Drake's wish, expressed years before on a mountain top in Panama, had finally been realised. The western coast of the Americas was now a little more certainly known than before and trading with the Spice Islands was now a distinct possibility. Above all, Drake's circumnavigation of the globe had made abundantly clear that the English had become a maritime nation to reckon with in every ocean of the world.

The English could annoy the King of Spain wherever they would, and this was a source of comfort to the Queen who, though resolutely opposed to outright war, was all too aware of the growing power of her still unofficial enemy.[13] It was painfully evident that the position in the Netherlands was deteriorating since the new Spanish commander, the Duke of Parma, had begun to win back large parts of the south and north-east of the region. But such military successes as these, deeply disturbing though they appeared, were far from being the only cause for English concern. Death in the royal house of Portugal left Philip the closest legitimate male heir to their vast empire, to their fighting galleons and the great natural harbour of Lisbon. It seemed that two empires might be ruled by one crown, thereby allowing Philip to become quite simply and dreadfully, 'the greatest king in the world'. The Netherlands would easily fall to such a man, and once they had succumbed, England might yet be in his grasp. Some suggestion of what Philip had in mind was made clear during the very month of Drake's return. Lisbon had fallen to the Spanish King and now, in his efforts to frighten the heretic Queen, Philip authorised the despatch of some 800 Spanish and Italian volunteers to Smerwick in Ireland. Catholicism, it seemed, was knocking at the back door of Elizabeth's realm, and it was only by dint of massacring all but twenty-three of the invaders that the initiative was rebuffed. English politicians, and strategists such as Drake himself, now began to focus plans for the future around the figure of Dom Antonio, Prior of Crato and the illegitimate cousin of the late Portuguese King, who they chose to think of as the rightful heir to the throne.

Meanwhile there was the question of what to do with Drake's fabulous haul of booty. There were problems. Elizabeth had to gamble that Philip would not make the matter a cause for open war and, rather more pressingly, deflect the worries of English merchants trading with Spain. For all the tension between the two countries, Spain was still England's chief trading partner and English merchants might at any one time have upwards of a hundred ships, 2,500 sailors, and considerable property around the Iberian peninsula. All of these could easily be seized in retaliation for Drake's actions. A deftly disingenuous letter was drafted in which the Queen explained that Drake had set out on a voyage of discovery and that if he had plundered the Spaniards then that was hardly something for which the merchants could be blamed or for which the King could reasonably punish them. Such bluff and brinkmanship were necessary skills, but so too was a devious exercise of common sense. The Privy Council had earlier come to the decision that the treasures should be itemised and sent for safekeeping to the Tower of London. Leicester, Hatton and Walsingham, who were all investors in the enterprise but who had not been present at the meeting, realised that this was foolishness. They argued that the Spaniards had no very clear idea of how much had been stolen from them and that there was no point whatsoever in giving them the means by which they might come to know. Vagueness would make their claims for restitution difficult to establish and Elizabeth, seeing the wisdom of their advice, rescinded her earlier order and commanded that it should be bruited abroad that Drake had returned home with only the smallest pickings and that his depredations were no great matter. Drake, and a representative of the Queen, were then ordered to return to Devon, Drake himself having received the Queen's permission to take an extra £10,000 of loot for himself in addition to whatever sums he had already secreted away.

There were, meanwhile, two troubling problems to deal with,

problems which had to be handled with all the adroit and pitiless guile that was Elizabeth's to command. The headless ghost of Thomas Doughty stalked these busy days, paler than the stolen silver but potentially as ominous. His trial had been a travesty and his execution an outrage and his brother, trying to ensure that this was not forgotten, attempted to prosecute Drake on a charge of murder in the Earl Marshal's court. This was a serious matter. It turned worse when Drake went to the Queen's Bench, submitting that the Earl Marshal's court could not exercise jurisdiction in the case and the Lord Chief Justice ruled against him. The matter was quietly dropped only when Elizabeth refused to fill the post of Lord High Constable, one of the judges whose duty was to preside over trials concerning offences committed outside the realm. A bitter John Doughty, denied justice, began talking wildly in his cups and was finally indicted for conspiring with a Spanish spy to have Drake murdered. He was imprisoned without a hearing and subsequently had his petition to be tried and released rejected. It is clear from this that all of those involved realised the Doughty affair was a dangerous and disgraceful matter, which could easily do harm to the success of the expedition and even to the Queen's reputation. In a country that did not yet enjoy the benefits of *habeas corpus* John Doughty stood no chance at all, and there is no evidence to suggest that he was ever released. Drake's expedition had brought back booty calculated by some at nearly 23,500 pounds troy weight of silver and over a hundred pounds of gold, in addition to numerous valuable and bejewelled trinkets. This was the equivalent of a normal parliamentary subsidy and, in the pitiless world of real politics, manifest injustice meted out to a powerless man seemed a small price to pay for such advantages.

There was also the question of Mendoza. The Ambassador and his spies were still watching, with barely concealed hatred, every move made by the Queen, her pirate, and their fellow accessories after the fact. It was necessary to make life as difficult as possible for Mendoza too, and so the furiously protesting Ambassador became the butt of Elizabeth's most skilfully humiliating diplomacy. She sent a couple of her secretaries – men of little standing – to tell the representative of Spain that he had no right whatsoever to complain about her reception of Drake. He had told her about the voyage and she was satisfied in her own mind that he had done no damage to the subjects of the King of Spain nor to his personal possessions. As a final rebuff, she added that she would not receive Mendoza in his official capacity until he, in his turn, could adequately explain his master's recent actions in Ireland. Mendoza was placed in an impossible position. The harassed man gathered such information as he could and fulminated to no purpose, while Drake had forty-nine members of his crew sign a largely worthless declaration stating that they had sunk no Spanish ships and had not killed or even maimed any Spanish subjects. The little silver and gold they had taken was far less than it was said to be – a trifle. This exasperating document was circulated while politicians altogether more adroit than Drake saw to it that the whole matter of restitution became lost in a maze of legal niceties. In such ways as these Elizabeth got what she wanted. She held on to the greater part of the stolen wealth while, at the same time, avoiding open conflict with the King of Spain. Drake had proved himself a most useful man.

Drake was now as famous as he was rich, both the people's darling and that of his sovereign. The greater part of the nation happily 'applauded his wonderful long adventures and rich prize'. To be sure, they knew little enough in detail about either, but precise knowledge was perhaps less important than the enormous sense of national pride and relief that focused on a man whose deeds fulfilled the dreams of the popular imagination. Drake was the glamorous and self-made hero, the millionaire, the giant-slayer, and the good Protestant whose success against the forces of Antichrist were a sure and certain witness to 'the power and justice of the Lord of Hosts'.

Drake revelled in it all and displayed his wealth with the prodigality of a parvenu. A full-length portrait from this time shows him dressed in vivid gold-trimmed scarlet silk, his determined face as square and chubby as the hand that seems to press down, rather than merely rest, on the globe beside him. Here are wealth, power and the conspicuous prestige of a self-made man accepted by his society. As his motto reminds us: thus great things spring from small. Only the morally scrupulous were critical, and only a few members of the hereditary elite disparaged his vulgarity. Lord Sussex, speaking for both, told Drake that it was no great achievement to become rich by attacking an unarmed merchant ship such as the *Nuestra Señora de la Concepción*. Drake angrily protested, but the Earl of Arundel silenced him by saying he was shameless and impudent. The circles of the very highest in the land were not to be as easily invaded as a Spanish ship, and a few such men shared the uncommon view that Drake was nothing more than 'the master thief of the unknown world'. He might indeed try to buy friends like a gangster with a wad of banknotes, but there were those who would not succumb. Burleigh, always opposed to the expedition, declined a gift of ten bars of gold, telling Drake that he would not be a receiver of stolen goods. This was hurtful, no doubt, but it hardly seemed to matter greatly. On New Year's Day, 1581, Elizabeth appeared at court wearing a crown of emeralds and a diamond cross presented to her by Drake and worth, as Mendoza sourly guessed, something in the region of 50,000 ducats. There were even whispers of a knighthood.

Such favours were not lightly given. So public an act as knighting a pirate could only cause the deepest offence to Spain, and the timing and circumstances had to be right for so calculated an insult.[14] By April 1581, they were. The desperate rebels in the Netherlands declared Philip their Spanish master deposed, and nominated Francis Hercules, the Catholic Duke of Alencon and the brother and heir presumptive to the French King, their 'prince and lord'. French support for the Protestant Dutch seemed guaranteed and Elizabeth, as the leading Protestant figure in northern Europe, felt obliged to move closer to the repulsive little Duke, the man she called her 'Frog' and who she had for some years now kept dangling on a string with promises of marriage. She had little or no intention of honouring these. The entire nation, from her highest councillors down to the shrillest Puritan preacher, loathed the proposed alliance as she well knew, but Elizabeth realised, as many of them did not, that a feigned dalliance would at least buy her time while the European states were kept wondering how the balance of power across the continent might finally settle. Elizabeth would pretend to let her Frog woo her for a while and so allow high politics to be conducted as high farce.

She decided that Drake – the nation's hero and the man whose hatred of Spain was notorious – could play a small but significant part in her delicate and desperate diplomatic manoeuvring. By knighting her pirate and terrorist in full view of the delighted French delegates who came to press their master's suit, Elizabeth could show how serious she was in supporting both them and the rebellious Dutch against the might of Spain. Not only this: by giving Drake a title she would so hugely please the nation at large that their delight might in part deflect their anger at her pretended courtship of a Catholic grandee. Drake's fame made him a useful item in a propaganda war, and if that gave him the assured place among the gentry he so desperately wanted then, it could be argued, this was nothing less than he deserved.

The French delegates arrived and two months of junketing ensued. A vastly expensive temporary dining hall was erected in the grounds of Whitehall. There were bear baitings, glittering tilt yard pageants, and sumptuous dinners thrown by Elizabeth herself, Leicester, Burleigh and Drake. On the Queen's orders the *Golden Hind* was taken to Deptford and placed in a dock there as a visible expression of Drake's achievements. Elizabeth then graciously accepted an invitation to banquet aboard the ship. £10,000 of looted Spanish silver was coined to defray the expense of what was to be the greatest of feasts since the days of Henry VIII. Drake's flagship was scrubbed, painted, varnished and dressed over-all. Large crowds gathered. The Queen arrived with her Frog's representative, the Marquis de Marchaumont. A gilded sword was produced and the Queen said, jokingly, that she had come to cut off Drake's head before commanding him to kneel and, handing the weapon to Marchaumont, bidding him dub Drake a knight.

With the ceremony over Drake himself rose to his feet as not only the great circumnavigator of the world, but also the man who had now crossed the rubicon of privilege which divided the gentry from the rest. In gratitude, he presented the Queen with a diamond-studded frog to honour her matrimonial plans. It was a seemingly glorious occasion, for all that the bridge which connected the ship to the shore collapsed and threw some hundred people in the muddy water. Drake, now Sir Francis, was also now more than ever before the nation's hero. His fame 'became admirable in all places, the people swarming daily in the streets to behold him'. Woe betide those who criticised him or dared 'mislike' him. 'Books, pictures and ballads were published in his praise' while his 'opinion and judgement concerning marine matters stood current'.

It seemed for centuries that the acclamations would never die down. The knighting of Sir Francis Drake (usually misconceived as having been carried out by the Queen herself) is part of the iconography of English history, a moment that has become a deeply potent symbol of national identity and one to be especially treasured in times of crisis. This was duly recognised nearly four hundred years later when the sword used to dub Drake was brought out once again to honour another great circumnavigator – Sir Francis Chichester. On 7 July 1967, *Gypsy Moth IV* berthed at Greenwich where Queen Elizabeth II, contrary to usual precedent, conferred the honour in public before a large crowd and the many millions more who watched the scene on television. The pageantry, the sense of occasion, the very deliberate feeling of continuity with a past and glorious age, consciously played on deep emotions. This was timely, for Chichester and his little ship had returned in triumph to an England whose imperial superpower status had, over the past two decades, evaporated with unprecedented speed. In country after country across Africa, Asia and the Caribbean, the Union flag had been lowered for the last time. The figure of Drake was, as so often, available to suggest what once had been, or was thought to have been. But all this was – and only could have been – a moment of reflected glory. Still the flags were coming down, and the sterling crisis that broke a few months later and necessitated an immediate British military withdrawal East of Suez made clear that the world power, which allegedly derived in part at least from the treasure once looted by Sir Francis Drake, was now finally and comprehensively spent. Drake and his reputation were entering a post-imperial world.

7

The Great Caribbean Raid

1585–1586

Sir Francis Drake needed a house suitable to his new wealth and status. Buckland Abbey seemed ideal.[1] Situated conveniently close to Plymouth and in the countryside of his childhood, Buckland Abbey took Drake back to his roots and showed very clearly how far he had transcended them. The property was impressive if not conspicuously beautiful. The Abbey had been seized from the Catholic authorities at the time of the Reformation (it was wholly appropriate that Drake should own such a building) and retained many signs of its ecclesiastical origins. The Abbey Church had been converted into the main house, and the installation of two wooden floors inside the nave created a three-storey dwelling that had an oak-panelled and richly plastered great hall newly constructed in the tower. In addition to this there were extensive outbuildings, orchards and an impressive tithe barn. Much of the conversion work had been carried out by the Grenville family who, at the time of Drake's expression of interest in the property, held it from the Crown in such a way that letters patent were required in order that it should be sold. These were duly obtained and a complex series of negotiations was entered into whereby the fully furnished house passed first to Drake's agents for the then considerable sum of £3,400. Drake himself finally received his letters patent on 7 June 1583, confirming that the new knight was indeed the rightful owner of a property with royal connections. Sir Francis Drake – seaman, circumnavigator and pirate – was now officially a part of the landed gentry. *Sic parvis magna* as his motto proclaimed: 'thus great things spring from small beginnings'.

A coat-of-arms and a motto were matters of great importance to an Elizabethan gentleman for they were the outward and visible sign of his status.[2] They were something that Drake had long hankered after and seem, indeed, to have been a persistent fantasy of his. Precisely what the coat-of-arms and motto on the silver salvers aboard the *Golden Hind* might have been is unclear but they were certainly not those which eventually became Drake's own. It is just possible that the salvers were engraved with the device of Sir Bernard Drake of Ashe, which Drake spuriously laid claim to – this to the intense annoyance of Sir Bernard himself, who is said to have accosted Drake in a public place and boxed his ears for his impudence. The story goes on to tell how the Queen, hearing of this unfortunate incident, vowed that Drake should have 'a new coat of everlasting honour'.

The coat-of-arms eventually granted by the College of Heralds on 20 June 1581 was rich in that visual symbolism which the Elizabethans so greatly loved and with which they could so skilfully suggest the ideals of the world in which they lived. The helmet above Drake's shield was adorned with a globe, on the top of which was a ship under sail. The ship was trained about with golden hawsers held by a hand appearing out of the clouds, and the whole was completed by a red dragon and the words *auxillio divino*. The device suggests that the circumnavigation to which it so clearly alludes was to be understood as God's blessing on a Protestant hero's enterprise. The images on the shield itself cleverly and wittily reinforce this idea. The silver 'fesse wavy' set on a black background prompts thoughts of the oceans and their perils, while the two silver Stars of Bethlehem, above and below, symbolise at one and the same time the star that shone over Christ's birthplace and the heavenly bodies by which Drake so brilliantly navigated the globe. Science, faith and Protestant nationalism are all combined, but this it seems was not enough.

The parvenu wanted a past and chivied the College of Heralds until he got one. Drake would have it known to the world that he was indeed entitled to use Sir Bernard Drake's crest, albeit in modified form. What was for Drake an all-important addendum was at last granted. This suggested that the self-made man was a gentleman 'born and descended of worthy ancestors such as have long time borne arms as tokens and demonstrations of their race and progeny' which Drake 'by just descent and prerogative of birth . . . may for the arms of his surname and family bear'. There is a strong suggestion of bullying and the factitious about this. The meetings between the heralds and Drake cannot have been easy, and the addendum (unusual in itself) has every appearance of a compromise agreed to by men Drake had overruled. It is particularly significant that the document does not have the long-suffering Sir Bernard Drake's signature on it. It seems too that the original globe and the ship did not meet with Drake's whole-hearted approval either. They pointed all too obviously to what he had done to deserve them and he often chose, instead, to use a version of Sir Bernard's eagle displayed. The whole rather shoddy tale suggests how even a figure of known heroic achievements was abashed and made envious by the aura of traditional authority surrounding ancient families, and one of the most telling actions of Drake the self-fashioned man was to pretend that he derived his status from the past rather than from what he himself had accomplished.

Other items were also necessary for the newly ancestral gentleman. Among the loveliest objects of Elizabethan conspicuous consumption are the portrait miniatures painted by Nicholas Hilliard. Hilliard and Drake were probably related, and it is highly likely that Drake stood godfather when Hilliard's son was baptised Francis on Christmas Eve, 1580. Hilliard's miniature shows the seadog as the affluent Elizabethan gentleman in a carapace of silk, wearing a heavy gold chain, his round head with its shrewdly observing eyes and rather large ears rising from a ruff of fantastically dentilated lace.

It was suitable that such a man should become a Member of Parliament, and Drake attended the session at Westminster which began on 16 January 1581, but it is not clear what seat he represented nor that he did very much to justify his presence. Before the close of the next session in 1584–85 however, Drake had remarried.[3] His first wife Mary, a shadowy woman who had spent so little of her wedded life with her famous husband, had died at the start of 1583 and was buried at St Andrew's Church in Plymouth on 25 January. It is unlikely that Drake's grief was particularly profound, but altogether certain that his new wife, Elizabeth Sydenham, was a considerable catch. She was young, intelligent and attractive. She was also rich. She was the only child of a Somerset magnate, George Sydenham and his wife Elizabeth and, in an era of arranged marriages, both parties no doubt felt that this was a satisfactory West Country alliance. It was cemented early in February, 1585.

Once again, Drake's private life is almost entirely invisible to us – the public man predominates – but it was perhaps his courtship that, among other things, inspired Drake to a more active participation in the second parliament he attended.[4] Certainly, he was concerned to appear as a godly magistrate with strong West Country sympathies and interests. He served on a committee considering the contentious 'Bill for the better and more reverent observing of the Sabbath Day' which proposed prohibiting such popular activities as bear-baiting, hawking, hunting and morris dancing. This was a sign of the times. The increasingly loud and articulate voice of evangelical Protestantism was now seeking to create a godly society by regulating the activities of its poorer neighbours especially, doing so by enforcing rigid codes of sexual morality, sobriety, piety and regular hard work. The popular customs which seemed to threaten the controlling instruments of the local church and the local pulpit were being increasingly disparaged by those who shuddered at the consequences of pro-faning the Lord's Day with traditions that were potentially anarchic, possibly heathen, and certainly associated with the old world of Roman Catholicism. As a Protestant apparatchik who had enforced the strictest standards of devotion on board his ships (very largely as a means of social control), Drake may well have been in sympathy with such initiatives, but the Queen was not. She had a personal enjoyment of such traditional festivals as the May Day revels. More than this, as a politician she was deeply suspicious of the influence the godly were clamouring for and she was determined to muffle if not silence it. An enthusiastic Commons pushed their Bill forward. It went through the Lords and was eventually presented to

Elizabeth who quite simply refused to sign it. The sabbatarian cause was temporarily set back.

Drake also sat on the committee 'for the confirmation of letters patents made unto Mr Walter Raleigh' which were the legal origin of one of the most important, if ill-fated, developments in Elizabethan maritime enterprise, and one in which Drake himself was to be closely involved. As the most vaultingly ambitious of the gentlemen of the West, Raleigh, rapidly rising in the Queen's favour, was the heir to many of their schemes for colonisation. Those cherished, and tragically followed, by Sir Humphrey Gilbert were particularly important to him. Savage experiences in Ireland had convinced Gilbert of the possibilities and potential importance of colonisation, but neither of his efforts to found colonies in North America was a success, the second indeed leading to his death. Raleigh, on the other hand, set about his attempts in a way altogether more ambitious and sophisticated. Realising the importance of interesting the Queen in the matter, he sent a reconnaissance expedition to Roanoke where he intended to found both a colony and a base for armed raids on Spanish shipping in the Caribbean. Simultaneously, intellectuals began to show an increasing interest in the possibilities of colonies, John Dee inventing the phrase 'British Empire' in his attempt to show that his fellow countrymen had a just claim to North America because of the alleged conquests made there by King Arthur and Prince Madoc. Colonisation was also enthusiastically urged by Richard Hakluyt, whose *Discourse of Western Planting* was intended as 'a brief collection of certain reasons to induce Her Majesty and the state to take in hand the western voyage and the planting there'.

Elizabeth, ever pragmatic, refused to be swayed by arguments that made too great a demand on her purse but was happy enough to make contributions to initiatives led by private individuals such as Raleigh in the familiar hope of profiting from them. The idea that the state should take the initiative in colonisation was, as Elizabeth knew, something wholly beyond its means, and this reluctance to commit the country to the enterprise was one of the major reasons for its repeated failure. She nonetheless lent Raleigh's expedition her ship the *Tiger* which, with four other vessels, left Plymouth in April

1585 carrying about 600 men. Sir Richard Grenville was in overall command and the tough, experienced Ralph Lane was responsible for the many soldiers that were carried. Drake had been part of the parliamentary committee that helped get official approval for the venture and, as we shall see, he was later to play a crucial role in saving it from disaster.

Drake was now the local grandee that the citizens of Plymouth wanted as their own and, in the autumn of 1581, they named him as their new Lord Mayor. His term of office does not seem to have been marked by conspicuous efforts to improve the lot of the citizens (it was nearly a decade later that Drake involved himself in such things and then to his own considerable profit) and it seems he was more interested in making investments that would work for him. Just after his term of office, Drake spent the considerable sum of £1,500 on buying forty pieces of property in the city from William Hawkins, along with an interest in the town mills. Paying what was quite possibly an inflated price, it is clear that he was determined to make his presence felt as a local grandee and, in addition to the houses and commercial properties he bought in Plymouth itself, he became master of several local manors. All of this suggests considerable activity on Drake's part, but the huge profits to be won from piracy and the sea still had the greatest hold on his interest. The house, the coat-of-arms, the portrait and the attendances at Whitehall were all minor embellishments when compared to the oceans, vast and perilous, from which this man had created himself.

No sooner had Drake returned from the circumnavigation than he was involved in numerous projects designed for legitimate profit, for plunder, and for demonstrating English maritime strength as the political situation with Spain moved ever closer to open hostility. Walsingham suggested setting up a company to explore and prospect for gold and silver in countries not lawfully possessed by any other Christian prince, the idea being that the treasure and the profits should be administered by an English equivalent of the Spanish Casa de Contratacion, which would not only greatly enrich the Queen but also provide Drake with a handsome ten per cent return. There were further high-level discussions between

Walsingham, Leicester, Hawkins, Frobisher, Winter and Drake, which proposed sending Drake himself with a fleet of ten ships to the Moluccas. There he would meet up with Henry Knollys, who would have navigated the Strait of Magellan and raided Spanish ports along the Pacific coast. Neither of these plans came to anything, partly as a result of the Queen's interference.

The Portuguese Pretender, Dom Antonio, had now arrived in England in a state of apparent poverty but with the welcome news that the island of Terceira in the Azores was still loyal to him.[5] It was clear to Elizabeth and her advisors that a base there could be used for wreaking havoc on the Spanish fleets, and plans went ahead for the occupation of the island by a force to be led by Drake. He was to harbour off the island and wait for the *flota*, but if he missed it he was to sail on to the West Indies and create mayhem there. Dom Antonio's presence also raised the possibility of the English inveigling their way into the Oriental trading posts of the Portuguese, and another plan involved Drake's sailing from Terceira to Calicut where he was 'to establish the trade of spice in Her Majesty's right as a party with the King of Portugal'. This plan proceeded far enough for Drake himself to send a ship to reconnoitre Terceira, but mutual difficulties and recriminations between those involved led once more to the collapse of the enterprise. This development was ensured by the fact that Mendoza made it perfectly clear that the King of Spain would regard Elizabeth's open support for the Portuguese Pretender as a declaration of war. As a result, she commanded that all the ships, their ordnance, men and victuals be discharged. An embittered Dom Antonio, believing that he had been cheated, eventually departed for France where he persuaded Philipo Strozzi to lead a French force to the Azores, where it was humiliatingly defeated by the great Spanish naval commander, the Marquis of Santa Cruz.

So much initiative on the part of Drake and his colleagues was not allowed to go wholly to waste. Leicester in particular saw that there was a possibility of a trading voyage to the East Indies via the Cape of Good Hope to be salvaged from it, and leading courtiers, along with a small number of London merchants and Drake himself, put up the money to finance this. Martin Frobisher was originally chosen as the commander of the force but was eventually – and unfortunately – replaced by Edward Fenton, who sailed with a number of the men who had been on Drake's circumnavigation, including John Hawkins's nephew William and Drake's page the young John Drake, who had helped him prepare his sea charts and rutter. Fenton, a soldier rather than an experienced sailor was, besides, vain, moody and irresolute. Such disadvantages were not helped by his chief pilot, Thomas Hood, whose skills were not normally those expected of such a man. 'I give not a fart for all their cosmography,' he loudly declared, 'for I can tell more than all the cosmographers in the world.' Not surprisingly, the expedition was a disaster and soon disintegrated. Hearing that a powerful Spanish fleet was on its way to the Strait of Magellan, John Drake sailed south, but his ship was wrecked in the River Plate and he and his companions were captured by the Indians. They were held in slavery for a year before John Drake himself and a few friends made their heroic way to Buenos Aires where they were recognised, captured and sent to Lima for questioning by the Inquisition. John Drake eventually repented of having been a 'Lutheran', and the Spanish powers, in their mercy, sentenced him to remain on Spanish soil for the rest of his life. Fenton himself, meanwhile, had sailed to San Vincente where a fight with some Spanish ships led to the death of a number of Englishmen. Some of the disillusioned survivors determined to leave Fenton to his own devices and returned to England, while Fenton himself sailed about inconclusively and quarrelled so badly with young Hawkins that, when he himself returned humiliated to England, he entered port with Hawkins in irons.

None of this was remotely encouraging, particularly in view of the deteriorating international situation. The King of Spain was enjoying a period of considerable success.[6] Diplomacy and large quantities of money brought the French Catholic forces to his side, and the Duke of Parma had made spectacular and threatening progress in the Low Countries, capturing not only Dunkirk and Nieuwpoort, but also Bruges and Ghent. The death of Elizabeth's 'Frog' in June 1584, and the assassination of the Dutch hero William of Orange the following month, appeared to compound the Spanish successes and encouraged Parma to lay siege to Antwerp with its huge commercial resources. England appeared to be increasingly under threat, and many of Elizabeth's leading councillors – Leicester and Walsingham in particular – recognising that war with Spain was becoming inevitable, urged ever more forcefully that the Queen agree to a pre-emptive strike. Elizabeth, as was her habit, prevaricated. Open aggression was the last thing she wanted, for all that the personal threat to her was increasingly evident. In 1584, for example, Philip had agreed to support Mendoza's involvement in an assassination plot devised by Francis Throckmorton which would put Mary, Queen of Scots, on the vacant English throne and attempt to marry her off to some suitably Catholic prince. The plot was exposed before it came to anything and Mendoza was ordered to leave the country. The seriousness of the situation was becoming increasingly evident, however, and tentative negotiations were opened with envoys from the Netherlands with a view to forging a formal Protestant alliance.

Elizabeth's sea-dogs in the meantime were nurturing other projects. In July 1584, William Hawkins put forward a plan to bring English privateers together under Dom Antonio's flag in the hope that they would be joined by the Dutch and the Huguenots. In addition to this combination (unlikely as it was ever to materialise), it was expected that the Portuguese colonists would revolt and that the Iberian Atlantic fishing fleet would be destroyed. In such ways, it was hoped, the vast material resources of the Spanish Empire would be significantly paralysed. What Hawkins was suggesting in urging such measures was something new: a co-ordinated and officially licensed privateering war against Spain rather than unofficial acts of random piracy. What he was calling for, in other words, was state-sponsored terrorism. In his memorandum, Hawkins drew attention to a voyage proposed by Drake which, he suggested, might best be made lawful by sailing under the licence he was asking for. Clearly, Drake was still active, and another document makes clear that he was assembling a major expedition, supposedly for the Moluccas. Forty thousand pounds was to be raised to equip eleven ships, four barks and twenty pinnaces, the Queen in the usual way to bear half this expense, while such leading magnates as Drake himself, the Hawkinses, Leicester, Hatton and Walter Raleigh were to make up the rest. The fact that 500 of the men on the expedition would be soldiers indicates that this was intended as an aggressive rather than just a mercantile expedition, and its real targets were probably Peru and Panama.

The Queen, however, as so often, changed her mind about Drake's project yet again and withdrew her support, but the expedition was kept in being even while she continued her diplomatic war. In April 1585, as a gesture of support to the Dutch, Elizabeth suspended all English trade with Antwerp and the Spanish Netherlands in general. Philip responded by embargoing the unusually large number of English ships currently anchored in Iberian ports. They had been invited there under safe conduct to sell grain to make up the deficiencies of the recent Spanish harvest but, when the courageous crew of the *Primrose* managed to escape and carry back with them to England the Corregidor of Biscay, his captured papers proved that the English ships had been embargoed as part of Philip's campaign against the Protestant Queen. Tempers in England were now running very high indeed. English merchants trading with Spain demanded the right of reprisal, while they and many others were frightened that the embargoed ships would be used to invade England itself. Hostilities were coming ever closer.

A small English force was ordered to Newfoundland to attack the Iberian fishing fleet there, and returned with a great many ships and some 600 captive mariners. For all that Spain eventually agreed to release the impounded English ships, Elizabeth issued letters of marque to those of her subjects who had suffered from the trade embargo. The letters allowed such people legally to plunder any vessel they found sailing under the Spanish flag. Because of this increased involvement of the merchant interest, formidable new ships and resources of capital suddenly became available for the struggle at sea. As Antwerp fell and a treaty with the Dutch rebels was signed by which the English promised to provide over 6,000 regular troops for the rebel forces, so Sir Francis Drake was once again given permission to purchase stores and press sailors for a voyage 'into foreign parts'. War was now all but inevitable and Drake was to lead its most important naval offensive.

The preparations were watched with mounting excitement by a nation in the grip of war. Crowds flocked to Woolwich to see the ships London had provided sail 'with great jollity' down to Plymouth, where they would join with the rest of Drake's forces.[7] These forces were impressive both in terms of their size and the standing of the senior personnel involved. Twenty-one ships, four pinnaces and ten companies of soldiers had been assembled to create a force numbering upwards of 2,300 men. Drake himself sailed on the Queen's ship, the 600-ton *Elizabeth Bonaventure*, one of a new breed of fast, highly manoeuvrable and heavily armed 'race-built' galleons constructed from the early 1570s onwards by John Hawkins, now the Treasurer of the Navy. These vessels were, as we shall see, developments of vital importance to national security, and Drake was fully to appreciate their qualities. In addition to an excellent ship, Drake had as his flag-captain one Thomas Fenner, a professional seaman widely experienced in privateering activity who, as long ago as 1564, had made a voyage to Guinea. Drake would take the man into his trust, as he would also another great Elizabethan sea-dog, Martin Frobisher. Frobisher – volatile, black-haired and passionately brave, the man whose portrait hangs in the studious quiet of the Bodleian Library and shows him carrying a gun – sailed as Drake's Vice-Admiral on the redoubtable *Primrose*.

The Lieutenant-General of the land forces and commander of the *Tiger* was the fiercely professional soldier Christopher Carleill, a stepson of Walsingham's. He was the man who had first been chosen to command Fenton's unfortunate expedition, and had had both naval and military experience under the Dutch. He had, besides, served in Ireland, where he was involved in frequent disputes with the Lord Deputy who accused him of piracy – insinuations which led to Carleill's being recalled just in time to join Drake's expedition. Serving under Carleill was his chief of staff, Captain Anthony Powell, two aides-de-camp and ten other Captains who included a William Cecil (possibly Burleigh's grandson) and Walter Bigges, who left an invaluable account of the expedition. The men these officers commanded were drilled by Carleill into a highly professional fighting force and were heavily armed with muskets, bows and arrows, pikes, and a fearsome array of other weaponry with which they could inflict savage damage while remaining protected by 'morions' – hat-shaped helmets – and either light brigadines reinforced with metal rings or corselets of plate metal. They were an impressive force to frighten an enemy and, when ill-disciplined, to frighten their commanders too.

In addition to these men, Drake ensured that members of his own family and long trusted colleagues sailed with him. The ship he had himself contributed to the expedition was put under the command of Thomas Drake, his youngest brother. Tom Moone, a long-time follower, was put in charge of the *Francis*, while among the veterans of the circumnavigation were Captain George Fortesque in the *Bark Bonner*, Captain John Martin in the *Bark Benjamin*, the skilful navigator and engineer Edward Careless who was in charge of the *Hope*, and Richard Hawkins who was enjoying his first command as the Captain of the little *Duck*. There were also the obligatory gentlemen. These included Sir William Winter's son Edward, who commanded the Queen's other ship, the *Aid*, and Francis Knollys, the Queen's cousin and Leicester's brother-in-law who, probably because of these connections, was made Rear-Admiral in the *Galleon Leicester*.

One other great courtier was also proposing to sail on the expedition and came very close to doing so. Sir Philip Sidney, the aristocratic genius, poet and romantic hero of the English Protestant cause, had begun to convince himself that a land war with Spain in the Netherlands was unlikely to defeat a power that he saw as violating every natural and divine law.[8] Sidney believed that Spain and Philip II were the embodiments of tyranny and cruelty, and he sided firmly with those many devout Protestants who believed Spanish Catholicism was a monstrous and hypocritical evil, 'lively images of the dark Prince, that sole author of dis-creation and disorder who ever ruins his ends with over building'. Sidney was resolved to hasten that process of self-destruction. His ambitious and agile mind, naively enthusiastic rather than politically shrewd, believed that it was possible to form a pan-European alliance against Spain of which Dutch and German Protestants would form a natural part, and to which even France and Italy would subscribe. These new crusaders would invade and hold some well-chosen haven in Peru, Mexico, or both. They would attack the devil not in his heartlands but where he was most vulnerable: in his overseas possessions.

Sidney had a developed interest in New World affairs and, according to his devoted biographer and friend Fulke Greville, Drake's expedition of 1585 was entirely of Sidney's 'own projecting, wherein he fashioned the whole body with purpose to become head of it himself'. It was to be a combined land and sea operation, and to ensure its success Sidney chose as officers 'the ablest Governors of those martial times'. Greville, by this of course meant Drake, and suggested that the relationship between the two men would be one of equal commanders once the expedition had set sail. Such an idea can only have been anathema to Drake himself. The circumnavigation had revealed the perils of joint command, and Philip Sidney – grandson of the Duke of Northumberland, a courtier and intellectual – would have been as great a threat to Drake's autonomy as would Dom Antonio who, like Sidney, was threatening to sail with Drake and was put up with him at Buckland Abbey. Something needed to be done and Drake, probably aware that Sidney was involving himself without the Queen's permission, wrote to Elizabeth. She at once sent orders that Sidney was to return to London and stated that Drake was only to sail when the young man was well on his way. Drake's sleight of hand achieved its purpose and a disappointed Sidney returned to the capital with Dom Antonio.

Even with this potential source of conflict removed there would be problems enough: problems with logistics, problems with discipline, problems with disease, and problems with Drake himself. Assembling and provisioning so large a force was no easy matter, particularly given the familiar inefficiencies of Elizabethan chains of supply. Even when the expedition finally set sail on 14 September, the ships weighed anchor without adequate supplies of water or victuals. All of this suggests that the departure was made in haste, and Carleill explained the reason for this. The fleet set sail, he wrote, 'because the wind being fair upon our coming from Plymouth we were loath to lose the same for any small matters . . . and withal were not the most assured of Her Majesty's perseverance to let us go forward'. In other words, the mighty force was launched in a hurry because, while Drake knew that the wind was favourable, he feared that the Queen might not long remain so too. Elizabeth's tendency to prevaricate was infamous and it was well to prevent her from exercising it. There was too much about which she could have second thoughts.

Her only surviving instruction to Drake was the authority to make a demonstration on the Spanish coast in order to secure the release of the embargoed English merchant ships and their crews. Even in this area she was not willing to accept overall responsibility, saying of Drake with glib and practised shrewdness that 'the gentleman careth not if I should disavow him'. The expedition was not, in other words, an open declaration of war. Its secret purposes nonetheless made clear that it virtually was such. A great deal was riding on undisclosed intentions: in addition to dealing with the problem of the embargoed English ships, it was clearly expected that Drake would capture the Spanish treasure fleets and thereby win for the Crown the financial resources to help Elizabeth provide for the greatly expensive army she was now preparing for the assistance of the Dutch rebels. Walsingham in particular was fully aware of the gravity of this task, believing that the very survival of Northern European Protestantism was dependent on it, and he wrote urgently explaining how he believed 'in very truth' that on Drake's success 'dependeth the life and death of the cause'. It would be piracy and coercive intimidation that would save Protestantism, and plunder that would secure its victory. But there was more.

With an untold wealth of Spanish treasure stolen from the *flota* and sent safely back to England, Drake himself was to sail on to the West Indies to destroy the three great centres of Spanish trans-atlantic commerce: Santo Domingo, Cartagena and Panama, while also, if possible, seizing Havana and thereby blockading Mexico and rendering unavailable to Spain the rendezvous of her homeward-sailing treasure ships. For all that these purposes were supposedly secret, the Spaniards were perfectly capable of seeing what was intended. As one high official wrote to Philip, the generally accepted and most reasonable explanation of Drake's activity was that, in agreement with the Queen of England, fleets had been raised in her ports for the purpose of raiding the coasts of Philip's realms and seizing his ships. Drake had, the correspondent continued, given assurances that he could win a victory and carry off a great sum of money. Forewarned, however, was not necessarily to prove forearmed.

Nor were the English initially any more lucky. Despite Drake's hugely ambitious intentions, contrary winds made sure that his ships took at least a week to clear the English coast. This caused him anxiety, for the conditions made it perfectly possible that a message might yet be received from the Queen cancelling the entire expedition. So concerned was Drake about this that, after dinner on 17 September, he took Carleill and Frobisher aside and told them that he was minded 'to put [in] either with France or Ireland, upon any forced occasion rather than with England, thereby to be the better assured from any stay which Her Majesty . . . might happen to lay upon him'. The little private conversation was perhaps understandable in the circumstances, but Drake's 'earnest protestation' of the trust which 'he did and daily had to repose in' Carleill and Frobisher suggests other and more profound difficulties that he faced as leader of the expedition.

The vital matter of establishing a clear chain of command and principles of discipline was particularly troubling to him. Open negotiation did not come easily to Drake, and advisory committees troubled him. Too many views threatened to blunt the edge of resolution and Drake was by temperament most content when he ruled by the force of his personality, supported in his decisions by a small band of hand-picked favourites whom he valued both for their loyalty and their seasoned and proven professional expertise. Frobisher and Carleill were such men, and it was entirely proper that in a huge and potentially unruly expedition Drake should have been closest to his Vice-Admiral and the man who commanded his soldiers. He did not at this time know Carleill particularly well, but the man's reputation was vouched for and Drake felt, besides, an immediate rapport between them. This feeling was warmly returned, Carleill writing of Drake that he never 'had to deal with a man of greater reason or more careful circumspection'. It was with Carleill's secret help that the expedition moved on with the sailing orders by which the whole venture was to be governed. This was a circumspect way of proceeding which, putting trust in experienced men, inevitably rubbed raw the egos of those who were sailing in positions of responsibility because of their birth rather than their achievements. Time would eventually bring these matters to a head.

In the meantime, as the expedition made its way to the north-west coast of Spain, prizes had to be sought and captured. A vessel carrying a cargo of dried fish usefully supplemented Drake's inadequate stores after its crew had been set adrift in an open boat. Rounding Cape Finisterre, Drake pressed the newest of seven French ships into his fleet before, on 27 September, arriving at Bayonna at the mouth of the Vigo River. The alarmed locals quickly mustered in great numbers, lighting warning fires and waving their flags as drummers rattled out the alarm. Undaunted by such a display, Carleill landed with 700 men and prepared to parlay with the emissaries who were sent out to ask him what he would have. Carleill told them that he was come to get those Englishmen who were held in prison there, free imprisoned English merchants and their impounded goods, and then revictual. The Spaniards told him that their King had already ordered the release of the merchants and their property, but added that they were prepared to sell the invaders grapes, apples, oranges and suchlike.[9]

While they were waiting for these, the English diverted themselves by breaking into and burning a chapel from which they stole such few papist treasures as it contained. Drake himself came ashore where, having satisfied himself that the captured English merchants were indeed free, he continued to negotiate for all-important supplies until a ferocious storm broke and sent him and his men scurrying back to their ships. When the storm eventually died down there followed several days of alternate raiding and negotiation. Spotting some cargo boats leaving Vigo, Drake ordered his closest followers – Carleill, Thomas Drake, Moone and young Richard Hawkins – to follow them. The men successfully captured the prize, but their only reward was some vestments and a silver cross from the local cathedral, along with a quantity of wine, sugar and the 'usual pillage'. A raid on Vigo itself resulted in a haul of about 6,000 ducats and the execution of one English soldier who was unfortunate enough to get caught. The ill-disciplined ferocity of the looting English soldiers was nonetheless a cause for grave concern and clearly shocked Drake, not out of any residual sympathy for their victims – that he was wholly without – but because it made all too worryingly obvious that such naked and unrestrained violence from so many men posed a potential threat to the security and well-being of the entire expedition. This issue would become a persistent problem.

The local Governor agreed to allow Drake time in which to revictual, and his ships stayed in Vigo for another week while these necessary duties were carried out. For so huge an expedition assembled at so vast an expense, such proceedings were far from glorious, despite Carleill's boast that their purpose in trespassing on the very heartland of the Spanish Empire was 'to make our proceedings known to the King of Spain that he may find and see more apparently that we nothing fear any intelligence he hath gotten by the spials he hath either in England or elsewhere'. Such words proved to be bravado of the most pathetic sort. While the English were busy dividing up dried fish and oranges, the Spanish treasure fleet from Panama sailed safely into its home port loaded with one of the most fabulous cargoes it had ever been the delight of the officials at the Casa da Contratacion to unload and itemise. The Spanish spies whose abilities Carleill so disparaged were, of course, perfectly well aware that Drake and his expedition were sailing around Finisterre, and it was no doubt in order to secure the infinitely greater prize borne by the *flota* that they allowed them to get away with their petty depredations for so long. When the facts eventually emerged they were, naturally enough, greatly embarrassing to Drake who blustered about having missed capturing the *flota* by a mere twelve hours, the reason for this being 'best known to God' Who could rather conveniently be blamed for the foul weather by which the English ships had been hampered.

The response in the Escorial was altogether more triumphant and decisive. Philip's mind was suddenly and resolutely focused on the English problem.[10] Enough was enough. The heretic Queen's increasingly aggressive actions played an important part in this. Her encouragement of Dom Antonio, her punitive action against the

Iberian fishing fleet, her letters of marque, and her readying of soldiers to help the rebels in the Netherlands were hardly matters that could be longer ignored. More than this, the election in May 1585 of Pope Sixtus V, burning as he was with Counter-Reformation zeal, brought to the international scene a new force to be reckoned with. The Spanish Ambassador to the papacy was repeatedly told that 'some outstanding enterprise' was absolutely necessary for the good of the faith. For a while Philip protested that he was doing quite enough by fighting the heretics in the Low Countries. The bellicose Pope would not agree. He wanted to demonstrate the might of Catholicism and was determined that the defeat of England should bear witness to it. He put pressure on his own Ambassador to Spain (a courtier of the Grand Duke of Tuscany's) who urged the King to war. Philip was informed that the papacy and Tuscany alike would contribute to the cost.

Now, with the huge resources provided by the recent safe arrival of the threatened *flota* and indignant that English pirates should be rampaging across the soil of the Spanish mainland, the King determined on action against the Protestant axis of evil. On 24 October 1585, he dictated letters to Rome and to Florence in which he accepted the Pope and the Grand Duke's invitation to conquer England. His fierce, seasoned and victorious army in the Low Countries would be his means of achieving this and the triumphant Prince of Parma was invited to draw up the plans. Catholic diplomats across Europe concurred in telling their masters that Drake's actions in Galicia were nothing less than Elizabeth's declaration of hostilities. The Catholic world had a common enemy, embodied in a fundamentalist heretic who thought nothing of launching his forces against the once inviolable European centre of world trade. The diplomatic mask had finally been stripped off and, as the grave and cautious Burleigh declared, England was now about 'to sustain a greater war than ever in any memory of man it hath done'.

Blithely unaware of the dire consequences of his recent actions, Drake pointed his fleet in the direction of the Canary Islands, a council he had reluctantly convened having decided that Palma should be their next destination.[11] On 27 October, as he was passing Tenerife, information provided by a passing French pirate left him in no doubt of the terrible truth of his failure to encounter the Spanish treasure fleet. He now knew that he had utterly failed to achieve one of his expedition's primary objectives, and when news of this spread through the ranks as it was bound to do, the men (soon to be disillusioned further by their failure to take the well-defended city of Palma) might prove dangerously restive. This simply could not be allowed to happen. Their behaviour off Vigo had shown how riotous they could be and, in consultation with Carleill once again, Drake drew up instructions for their discipline. Soldiers quitting their company without leave or pillaging before permission had been given to do so would be punished by death. None was to break open or break into anywhere unless ordered to do so by his Captain who, in turn, was to obtain permission for such actions from an officer of the highest rank. None of the pinnaces were to be left unattended or used to carry unlicensed booty, while those attempting to steal for their own gain would forfeit their part in the expedition's spoils and be deemed persons 'not worthy of credit'. Since this was an expedition sailing under the auspices of the Queen, anything of value belonged to her and proper account would have to be made of it. Gold, silver, jewels, or any other things of moment were to be handed over to appointed officers who were to keep it in chests that could only be opened with the use of four or five different keys.

It was with such discipline as this hurriedly put in place that Drake's expedition eventually reached Santiago in the Cape Verde Islands. Here, a night raiding party of 600 men landed as the islanders themselves fled, taking such valuables with them as they could. The lack of surprise rendered Carleill's disciplined efforts at landing his men unnecessary and the town fell without resistance. The resulting prizes consisted of ordnance and gunpowder, a large and useful supply of victuals, and one new caravel which was added to the fleet while the other seven accompanying it were stripped and set adrift. The raid was in truth modest enough, but Drake himself was clearly still exercised by problems of discipline within his forces. He now made plain that he considered it necessary that every man be bound to his superior by swearing an oath of fealty. The wording of these oaths was probably devised by Drake in consultation with Carleill and Frobisher, but when the plan was announced on 19 November and the oaths themselves were read out by the expedition's chaplain, trouble erupted. Knollys had not been consulted in the matter and the insult to his dignity rankled. Was he not a son of the Treasurer of the Household and the brother-in-law of Leicester whose large ship he captained? Had he not an Oxford education, received a lawyer's training at Gray's Inn and been twice elected to Parliament? That his opinion should not have been sought on the matter of the oaths was intolerable.

His anger was, given the social conventions of the time, understandable. Gentlemen sailed on expeditions such as this partly because they were considered the natural leaders of society, those to whom deference was proper. Discipline and cohesion among officers who had risen through the ranks on account of their abilities – 'tarpaulins' as they would come to be called – could easily become strained, and it was generally believed that fractiousness could be avoided through the mediation of a social superior. Drake, as we have seen, paid tribute to this notion during the Doughty crisis. Now, however, difficult circumstances, Drake's vast experience and his titanic ego tested the convention to its limit and beyond. Faced with such circumstances, Knollys responded with what dignity he could. He was perfectly prepared to swear the oath of allegiance to the Queen, he said, but he asked for time in which to consider the other oaths. He copied them out and then left the meeting in high dudgeon, a mood that was not improved by a rather silly row started by the expedition's chaplain. Still smarting from the way he had been treated, Knollys complained to Drake about the chaplain's behaviour and Drake responded by losing his temper and telling Knollys to his face that he and his closest companions were seditious and dangerous men. Egocentricity and pecking-order politics were the bane of many Elizabethan expeditions, but it is clear from the extremity of Drake's behaviour that conflicts of authority with his social superiors exposed a deep-seated insecurity for which he invariably overcompensated by asserting the full power of his will. Certainly, even now, he would not let the matter drop, and in his increasing anger he sought to isolate Knollys by removing several of the man's closest colleagues from his command.

A more public example of the sort of fierce legality Drake was determined to impose on his fractious expedition was required and, on 25 November, 'was one Thomas Ogle, steward in the *Bark Talbot*, hanged in the west end of Saint Jacomo for buggery committed in his steward's room with two boys'. Apparently a full jury of twelve men was convened and Ogle, having confessed to what the law described as 'detestable' and 'abominable' offences, died very penitently. Now, with his authority apparently secured by a public execution, Drake marched his men inland and burned Santo Domingo to the ground before returning to Santiago to do the same and then setting off for the West Indies. Perhaps Drake believed that he had restored law, order and purpose to his expedition, but he was soon made aware of the fact that he had to deal with an invisible and altogether more insidious enemy – disease. The fever hospital in Santiago was situated next to the church and the score or so of patients who lay dying there passed their contagion on to Drake's men. Very soon a hundred of them aboard the *Elizabeth Bonaventure* were seized 'with extreme hot burning and continual agues, whereof very few escaped with life, and yet for the most part not without great decay of their wits and strength for a long time after'. A desperate Drake ordered bleeding of the victims as the only remedy he knew, but the progressive loss of two or three hundred men was a catastrophe that would play a decisive part in his later changes of plan.

On 18 December the disease-ridden fleet reached Dominica from where, having traded with the natives for a modest supply of victuals, it headed north, stopping at the island of St Christopher where it was hoped that the sickest of the men might recover. In fact, twenty of them died there, and it was with a seriously depleted force that Drake sailed on to the bay of another Santo Domingo which he reached on New Year's Day, 1586, guided there by a pilot whose small vessel he had seized.[12] The city had once been the pride of the Spanish Empire in the New World, its seat of power and its centre of wealth. Now it was in sad decline. Trading ships no longer came there and the population, halved from the thousand inhabitants of its glory days, was diminishing year on year. It was nonetheless believed by the Spaniards themselves that Santo Domingo was impregnable, its natural defences being such that it was universally considered that the only possible landing place was under the guns of the castle. The Spaniards who watched the approach of Drake's sails assumed they were entirely safe. Indeed, so blasé were they that there was not even a picket on duty at Hayna, the point at which Drake and Carleill chose to land.

No Spanish signal fires blazed through the darkness and no warning was sent to the threatened city as a force of somewhere between 800 and 1,400 English pikemen and musketeers landed unopposed in an extraordinarily professional night operation. They made their way under the leadership of Carleill and Powell towards the rear of the city as Drake, 'having seen us all landed in safety, returned to his fleet, bequeathing us to God, and the good conduct of Master Carleill and our Lieutenant General'. While the soldiers made their way unopposed towards the city, dawn rose to reveal to the now incredulous inhabitants the full panoply of Drake's fleet as it sailed up and down before the city. So contemptuous were the English of the ineffective fire of the Spanish artillery that they did not even bother to respond to it. Instead, as noon approached, they manoeuvred into a more menacing position while the two columns of English soldiers, with music playing and standards flying, marched towards the doomed city. In the words of a contemporary English ballad celebrating the feat:

> Courage, courage, our captains cry,
> Good soldiers now let's fight like men:
> Then all at once ran valiantly,
> Their shot discharged, with weapons then,
> They lay one load on either side:
> Though five to one yet durst not bide.[13]

A pandemonium of fear engulfed the inhabitants who fled to what cover they could find. Their paltry 150 soldiers fired a single salvo, which killed a single English soldier, before they were scattered by

14. The fight at San Juan de Ulúa.

15. The natives steal Drake's sailing cap.

16. The taking of the *Cacafuego*.

17. Drake in Ternate.

18. A Victorian version of the knighting of Sir Francis Drake.

19. Engraving showing the plan of the attack on Santo Domingo, 1585.

20. Drake the circumnavigator.

21. Drake's despatch
from Cadiz, 1587.

22. Sir Martin Frobisher.

23. Sir John Hawkins.

24. Drake's burial at sea.

25. The taking of
Don Pedro.

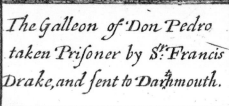

*The Galleon of Don Pedro
taken Prisoner by Sr Francis
Drake, and sent to Dartmouth.*

26. A modern version of the
Golden Hind passing under
Tower Bridge.

Carleill's men who came on in rapid and solid array, their advance made more terrible by the cannon fire that now rained down on the city from Drake's ships. The ancient pride of Spain collapsed in terror and ignominious defeat as the banner of St George was unfurled over the city towers and Drake's men shot off their ordnance for joy at having won the town. As the humiliated Spanish soldiers fled in disgrace, the English declared that they had been given Santo Domingo as a New Year's gift.

An orgy of burning, looting and slaughter ensued. Santo Domingo was subjected to what the verse chronicler Juan de Castellanos and his prose plagiarist, Fray Pedro Simon, called 'the bestial fury of the heretics'. As a conscientious historian and priest (if not a great poet) Castellanos made much of this. He and Fray Simon show Drake's men doing everything they could to offend Catholic sensibilities. Papist superstition was turned against its adherents. It was said that Drake fortified the buildings he seized by placing on their outer walls images of Christ, 'His most holy Mother' and other saints, in order that the Catholics might not fire at them. He was counting on the idea that the Spaniards would hold it the lesser evil that he should destroy the city than that they should show irreverence to their holy images. Then, after robbing the laymen, Drake and his forces laid their sacrilegious hands on the goods of the church, carrying off all the bells and everything else they could find. And still the sadistic ingenuity continued. 'Not content with this, they bitterly offended our Catholic piety by their insults to the most reverend images of Our Lord and the Holy Virgin, cutting off arms and legs, using them as seats or burning them to cook their food, all of which it was said was done by the order of Francis Drake.'

Castellanos and Fray Simon fashion an image of Drake as the incarnation of Protestant evil, telling not only how the 'Lutheran ministers' of 'the heretical pirate' constantly preached their creed but how 'the Protestant' himself 'would send from time to time to some of the fugitives, with whom he conversed in jovial and conceited tones, jeering at the fear of our people who had allowed his fatigued and harassed soldiers to take possession of the town without resistance, and attacking our Christian religion to justify his heresies and robberies'. The Spanish, by contrast, are shown as supine and decadent. The young men of Santo Domingo are exposed as spineless fops untested in war and so concerned with boasting about how they would meet Drake and cut down his men and sink his vessels that their speeches exhausted their energies. 'Had the inhabitants taken heart . . . they would easily have repulsed that scum of the earth.' But they were unable to do so. They could not stand against such a man as Drake. He is seen as an 'astute tyrant', but Castellanos also felt bound to do justice to the sheer personal force, the terrifying charisma of the enemy. Drake is pictured standing triumphant and vigorous amid the wreckage he has caused and thereby acquires an ironic nobility:

> Hes hombre rojo de gracioso gesto,
> Menos en estatura que mediano;
> Mas en sus proporciones bien compuesto
> Y en platica, medido cortesano.
> Respuestas vivas, un ingenio presto
> En todas cuantas cosas pone mano,
> En negocios mayormente de guerra
> Muy pocas veces o ninguna yerra.[14]

He is a ruddy man of graceful gesture, of less than average stature but elegantly proportioned and of courtly gesture in his speech. Of lively retort and quick wit in all he sets his hand to, and in trade – especially of the warring kind – he hardly errs at all.

Rubicund, gracious, quick-witted and able, Drake is at once heretic and hero, the man who carries all before him and subdues the enfeebled pride of Spain.

So much, it seemed, for the Spaniards' vainglorious motto attached to the royal escutcheon hanging in the city's principal building: *non sufficit orbis* or 'the world is not enough'. When the humiliated city officials gathered beneath it in the hope of negotiating some sort of truce they were too embarrassed even to translate the words for the victorious Drake, whose men observed that their Protestant Queen would now oblige the Spanish King 'to lay aside that proud and unreasonable reaching vein of his'. And then to business. How much, Drake was asked, would it take to make him go away? A million ducats, he replied. Garcia Fernandez de Torrequemada, King Philip's factor for Hispaniola, looked at him with all the contempt a defeated man could muster and replied that he would take his departure. Drake 'might continue to burn the city as he had begun', since in Torrequemada's opinion, the city could not pay over ten or twelve thousand ducats.

The haggling went on for several hours, Drake getting ever more heated with 'heretical animosity' as he was obliged to come down first to 100,000 ducats and from that to 40,000. Torrequemada asked for time in which to calculate the maximum he thought could be paid. He was given this and returned within an hour saying that he needed to see the houses the English had already burned since nothing could be asked for these. Drake complained that this was mere shilly-shallying but, after a further two hours, the Spaniard got his way and one of his colleagues was sent to assess the damage. On his return, Torrequemada decided that the city could pay 20,150 ducats at the most. The situation was now getting very tense and, when it seemed that the negotiations would fail, Drake agreed to 25,000 ducats – 'although,' Torrequemada added, 'for my part I gave him no assurance except that I would return with an answer, yes or no, within three days.' Inevitably Torrequemada had to submit and the inhabitants of the ravaged city eventually found the agreed sum by dint of having the Bishop contribute such plate as he had saved from the Cathedral while the women dropped their pearls, gold, jewels, silver chains and earrings on the sadly trembling scales. Beyond this, Santo Domingo had nothing to offer save for some victuals, some hides and some clothes.

It was a pathetic haul, made worse by ill-disciplined savagery. 'At our coming to the town's end we burned an abbey in which lay an old friar dead,' wrote the journalist aboard the *Leicester*, 'who was killed by some of the soldiers which were disorderly.' This was nothing less than the truth. For all that the Spanish authorities noted that Drake was feared and obeyed by his men and punished them resolutely, discipline was still a major problem. There were 'many quarrels betwixt captain and captain'. All of this had to be adjudicated and punished, and, in the words of the *Leicester*

215

journalist again, 'the captains leading staves did walk about the shoulders of the poor soldiers'. Indeed, so bad did matters become, that some thirty or forty soldiers were stuck in the prison cells beneath the Cathedral. 'How lamentable a matter this is I refer it to the judgement of others,' the writer opined. But by far the most serious confrontation was that between Drake and the disaffected Knollys, still feeling aggrieved by Drake's behaviour towards him, who wrote the leader a long and rather highfalutin letter protesting his own good intentions and lamenting his treatment. There were further inconclusive meetings between the two men but it seemed that their differences were irreconcilable. Finally, on 26 January, some sort of conference or council was held at which it was decided that Knollys should 'prepare to go aboard the *Bark Hawkins*, that he should have that day and the next to carry his things aboard her', and that he should be accompanied by his closest colleagues with a view to them all being sent back to England. Knollys was apparently quite content with this decision, but to relieve a man with important connections at court of his command was a serious matter, suggesting the severity of the strains within the expedition and the depth of the social divisions.

Such difficulties and disappointments notwithstanding, the propaganda value of Drake's sacking of Santo Domingo was enormous. By early April, news of what he had done was known in Spain, where it was said that he had 'carried off and done damage to the tune of over two millions'. Nor was this all. 'He killed or ill-treated all priests and monks he could get hold of, and is fortifying himself in San Domingo.' The authorities in Madrid were appalled. 'I keenly regret that the Queen of England makes war on us so boldly and dishonestly,' declared Cardinal Granvelle, 'and that we cannot get our own back.' Fear and rumour gave Drake a power far beyond that which he really possessed. Castellanos tells how it was said that his expedition consisted of more than 20,000 men and that his ships carried supplies of bricks and building materials for forts. It was rumoured that a second fleet had proceeded by the Straits of Magellan and was preparing to attack from the Pacific side in order to gain possession of the entire Spanish realm in America. It was also said that the slaves in Santo Domingo had risen and helped the English to kill the Spaniards and had, in their turn, been killed by the English unless they should rise against them. Full-scale conquest was imminent. Even the Indians should be carefully watched since they knew too much about Spanish weaknesses and hated their masters. None of them could be trusted and they had become good horsemen and excellent shots, unlike the Spaniards who had degenerated into vice. The Indians were, indeed, a particular worry and Pedro Sarmiento, one of the great figures of Spanish South American imperialism, declared that they were at heart idolaters, loathed the doctrines and discipline of the Catholic Church, and that the English – worse even than they – would allow them free rein and encourage them to obliterate every trace of the true faith throughout the continent.

How could all this be accounted for? Why had God allowed Drake, the English heretic, to ravish the pride, the wealth and power of Spain? What part was this 'Lutheran' fury playing in the divine plan? Padre Castellanos took upon himself the examination of his nation's conscience. Devout, humane and intelligent man that he was, he soon found a satisfactory answer. Drake was God's way of punishing the Spaniards for the genocide they had inflicted on the local peoples – the '1,600,000 full-grown men, to say nothing of the swarms of women and children' – they had exterminated in their lust for wealth and worldly power. 'Without temerity,' Castellanos wrote, 'we may say that God allowed this judgement to fall upon the inhabitants as a just punishment for their atrocious cruelty to the natives.' As priests, both Castellanos and Fray Simon sincerely believed that 'the might of man is in vain against the divine scourge' – against Drake. Such a conclusion was more than the Spanish authorities could tolerate. Castellanos's huge chronicle of Spanish events in South America was sent to Madrid and the first of its three parts was published in 1589 as *Elegias de Varones Illustres de Indias*, but the last part and the 'Discurso del Capitan Francisco Draque' in particular fell foul of the censors. The image of Drake the Protestant pirate and terrorist as the embodiment of the wrath of God was too heinous for general consumption. It was best to suppress it. The chronicle was circulated only in manuscript and had to wait for publication until 1921, nearly forty years after Fray Simon's prose version had been obscurely printed in Bogota.

Thus the power of Drake's image, an image celebrated in his homeland by the ballad writer Thomas Greepe in his *True and Perfect News of the Worthy and Valiant Exploits, Performed and Done by that Valiant Knight Sir Francis Drake*. We have already seen that Greepe's verses can lay no claim to poetic sophistication, and that is just the point. The ballad writer was in some respects the tabloid journalist of his day. His appeal was popular, his audience the ordinary, widely scattered and often illiterate people of a country with no very sophisticated means of spreading news. Ballads filled the void. This was recognised when, in August 1586, and in the interests of national security, ballads were required to be submitted to the censor and licensed. Greepe's work thus expressed how the authorities wished Drake and his exploits to be seen. There was no mention of the fact that his men were decimated by fever, that discipline was at breaking point, and that the booty was disappointing. Drake is portrayed as a new Gideon smiting the enemies of the Lord, a contemporary Protestant super-hero:

> His rare attempts performed and done,
> With honour, fame and victory;
> The like before whoever won,
> That you can call to memory.
> Therefore I pray for England's sake:
> The Lord preserve the noble Drake.[15]

His victories are indeed God and the Queen's. Therefore:

> Triumph O England and rejoice
> And praise thy God uncessantly.[16]

In such ways as these a hero was fashioned for a time of crisis. Drake was being willed close to the core of national consciousness.

Meanwhile, across the Caribbean, worried local governors took what precautions against Drake's activities they could. Realising that this would be the likely outcome of his sacking of Santo Domingo, Drake headed straight for Cartagena, hoping to catch his next victim largely unprepared. He arrived there on 9 February.[17] The citizens, forewarned of his approach, made hurried preparations to protect their naturally well-defended city while the elderly Governor, Don Pedro Fernandez de Busto, ordered that women, children and treasure be moved into the hinterland. Military reinforcements were summoned, weaponry and munitions were brought out, cleaned and mounted. Barricades were erected across street openings, a chain was thrown across the inner harbour, and an incomplete barricade with a trench was constructed across the Caleta, or spit of land, which extended westwards from the main harbour entrance.

During these preparations, news came of the fall of Santo Domingo and of the heretic English pirate's strength. These reports so dented morale that the Governor was obliged to harangue the citizens and soldiers at open meetings even while further frightened and inadequate measures were taken for the defence of the city itself. Spirits lifted slightly when a boat from Spain arrived with news that raised false hopes of an approaching royal armada, but this information had barely been digested when Drake himself appeared on the horizon. The Spaniards hurriedly deployed their inexperienced forces – 'not soldiers, but merchants and artisans unaccustomed to war' – but their ordnance did little damage as Drake sailed into the lagoon without any effective resistance being offered. As night fell, Carleill prepared to lead a large contingent of men along the Caleta. When they had disembarked Drake gave them a pep-talk in which he told them that they must take Cartagena or die rather than return defeated. To reinforce this he told them that no man would be readmitted to an English ship if he returned without being able to tell of victory. Cowards would be hanged.

The Spaniards were not expecting a night landing and those of their soldiers who had not already slipped away bungled the plan that had been prepared for an ambush. Carleill meanwhile, hampered by the lack of a competent guide and the poisoned stakes that had been planted on his route, made his difficult way along the shoreline shrouded in protective darkness. Only the little spots of his men's lighted matches betrayed their whereabouts, but the Spanish guns that were ineffectively aimed at them lit up the night sky, so allowing Carleill's men to discover the breach in the Spaniards' hastily built barricade. The English pikemen advanced yelling while the Spaniards, under the command of Captain Alonso Bravo, readied themselves as best they could behind piles of wine butts, calling on St James for help and spurring themselves on with cries of, 'They are heretics and few!' All of this availed them little. The ensign of Bravo's company was slain by Carleill himself and a disconsolate Spanish voice was heard crying out, 'Retire, gentlemen, for we are lost!' As they did so, the English broke through the pathetic defences and followed their fleeing enemy into the doomed city. By daybreak, Carleill's men were in possession of the market square and were loudly cheering St George. It was an English victory, a Protestant victory. In the words of Fray Simon, 'Providence had chosen the heretic Drake to scourge his children who, living on these coasts in wealth and power, slept soundly, neglecting the commonest precautions.' He added that, 'They were destined to awake beneath the buffets of their Father, recognising their sinfulness and amending their lives.'

While Carleill was distinguishing himself along the Caleta, an altogether less successful diversionary attack was being launched against the chained entrance to the inner harbour. It was led by Frobisher who was driven off and returned to the fleet with the dead and dying in his pinnaces. Drake was furious. Although it is only the Spanish sources that report the matter, it seems that Drake in his anger may have determined to set an example: he led the attacking band back into the range of the guns on the fort, only to encounter the same shattering fire and lose four or five men along with the mast from his pinnace. If this indeed happened, then it is possible that Drake arrived in time to witness the destruction of the two royal galleys, moored in the harbour and unable to move because of the shallowness of the water and mutiny among their crews. Such misfortunes were compounded when a barrel of gunpowder accidentally exploded on one of the galleys and the slaves, newly unchained, immediately escaped, after which both vessels were burned by order of their commander. Despite all this, the fort proved difficult to capture, but Drake eventually took about 200 of his men to the Caleta and continued to bombard the fort, thereby preventing its defenders from offering any resistance to Carleill and his victorious men.

With the city fallen, Drake took up residence with Alonso Bravo, the commander of the defeated forces on the Caleta. Despite the difficult circumstances, a semblance of friendship grew up between the two men and Bravo, like other Spanish observers, no doubt came to see the side of Drake that he habitually presented to defeated foreign dignitaries: 'sharp, restless, well-spoken, inclined to liberality and to ambition, vainglorious, boastful'. He was also, as Bravo was to find out, intensely grasping. The old man's wife died while Drake was staying with him and Bravo was allowed to fetch her body back for burial in the Cathedral. Drake himself attended the service, a dignified and grand occasion. However, when it came to settling Bravo's ransom, Drake harshly demanded 5,000 ducats, saying that he really wanted 6,000 but was prepared to offset the difference in consideration of the hospitality he had received.

Ransom, plunder and extortion were, of course, the whole point of the exercise, and the judge who prepared the report on Drake's activities in Cartagena provided a vivid picture of the Englishman's way of proceeding. The Governor of Cartagena, the Bishop, and certain of the leading citizens had gathered together and considered that it would be best to ransom the city before it should be damaged any further. Thus resolved, they decided to approach Drake in person. They arrived to find him in a furious temper. 'It happened that Francis Drake had in his possession certain of Your Majesty's royal despatches which were found in the Governor's house.' Drake had had one of his Spanish speakers translate these for him and found that the despatches were 'warnings of the coming of the English; and because in them it read "Francis Drake, corsair" he was much offended, as though he were not a corsair'. Clearly, Drake saw the incident as a cue for an outburst of righteous indignation, and because he had 'a good deal to say on this point, the Bishop replied to him with much spirit and courage in words becoming to Your Majesty's service'.

The 25,000 ducats the Spaniards offered for the city were none-theless wholly unacceptable to Drake who had demanded half a million. It was by now becoming clear that financially at least the expedition was a disaster, and Drake proceeded to try and salvage it as best he could by his usual methods. After each unsatisfactory meeting with the Cartagenian authorities he burned and looted another part of the city. The citizens themselves were gambling on the imminent arrival of the supposed Spanish Armada, but Drake let them know he was contemptuous of what such a fleet might achieve and continued to line his own pockets as well as filling the coffers of the Queen. The judge's report is badly damaged at this point but it suggests that, in addition to extorting 5,000 ducats from Bravo, Drake obtained a good deal more money from private individuals who paid him to redeem Negroes who had fled from them to the English, and for wines and oils and other merchandise which they had left buried and hidden elsewhere. It was only when Drake's cannon – whether or not accidentally, as he claimed – destroyed the newly built and as yet unfinished Cathedral that the citizens capitulated and agreed to a payment of 107,000 ducats. Drake insisted that the greater part of this be paid in bullion, which had to be 'borrowed' from the Crown's store of silver ingots.

This was hardly a princely sum and Drake had, besides, other pressing problems to contend with. Morale among his now bitterly fractious men was at a low point. Some of them even told Bravo that they were aggrieved because Drake had once promised them wealth beyond their dreams and now 'they saw that their part would be small'. These resentments were not eased when Drake insisted that each of his men who had Spanish coins was to explain not only how and where he got them, but was to hand them over at an official rate of exchange. But even Drake could only exert his will so far. When he ordered that all of the gold and silver be taken to a central depository there was so much general mistrust about fair dealing that the order, it seems, was not carried out. Instead, there was hostile muttering against Drake and his leadership. 'All the gentlemen said he would not again find any to go out with him from England.' In these circumstances ill-discipline remained a serious problem and even a soured Frobisher asked Drake why the Spanish called 'such a shameless rascal "Your Excellency" when he was a low fellow who had been given command of the fleet because he knew this coast'.

Perhaps it was best to go home. Drake reluctantly called a meeting of his disillusioned officers to decide what they should do.

It appeared that the sea captains were willing to face any challenge the Spanish might pose, but the land captains were disillusioned and disappointed. They were also clearly nervous of how Drake would respond to their views since they expressed these in the most circumspect and humble way. It was clear to them, however, that deaths, injuries and low morale meant that they could do very little more. Their advice was that it seemed 'better to hold sure as we may the honour already gotten, and with the same return towards our gracious sovereign and country'. To prove that theirs was not a merely selfish concern, they agreed that the ransom money from Cartagena owing to them should be distributed among 'the poor men who hath travailed with us in the voyage, meaning as well the Sailor as the Soldier, wishing with all our hearts it was such or as much as might seem a sufficient reward for their painful endeavours'. It was clear that more ambitious plans would have to be shelved. There was no point in hoping that the expedition could go on to Nombre de Dios, raise a great force of *cimmarones*, and ransom the city for a million ducats before crossing over to Panama and securing a million more.

Ambitious dreams had collapsed, but even as this dismal truth was becoming evident, fever continued to decimate Drake's men and he could now probably call on no more than 700 able-bodied individuals, roughly a third of his original force. He was not easily to be put off, however. It seemed to him that, at the very least, his best course was to set sail for Cuba. This he did on 31 March but, since he had put all his captured ordnance on a leaky boat seized from the enemy, it was necessary to return to Cartagena two days later, unload the cannon and distribute them through the rest of the fleet. He remained off the sacked city for another fortnight, gathering what supplies he could for the next stage of his voyage while the defeated Spaniards looked on, certain that the disillusioned and even disintegrating English expedition would not attack Havana because they had 'many disputes with one another and they agreed on nothing'. In this at least they were correct.

Invidious and depressing though his situation was, news of Drake's depredations at Santo Domingo and Cartagena stiffened the King of

Spain's resolve. Early in 1586 he had written to the Marquis of Santa Cruz asking what men and ships would be needed to protect his home coasts from future attacks by Drake and his kind.[18] The Marquis dutifully composed a memorandum but added that, in his view, attack was by far the best means of defence. England should be invaded, her heretic Queen toppled and the activities of her pirates thereby brought to a stop. Flushed from his recent success against the forces of Dom Antonio, the Marquis presented himself as the ideal leader of such a campaign, hoping that he would 'emerge just as victorious from it as in the other things that I have done for you'. Such enthusiasm recommended itself to the King, who saw that Santa Cruz's plan – the origin of the Spanish Armada – was as audacious as it was innovative.

The Spanish authorities were fully aware of previous attempts to invade England (historical research had formed part of their earlier attempts to devise an invasion strategy) and Santa Cruz clearly saw himself as a second William the Conqueror. He proposed that he should assemble a task force at Lisbon from where it would sail and, in a single amphibious operation, land at a vulnerable point along the English coast and crush the detested enemy with all the speed, power and surprise it could muster. With a thoroughness characteristic of Philip's imperial bureaucrats, Santa Cruz costed his proposal with extraordinary but probably factitious accuracy. The King would be obliged to spend 1,526, 425, 798 *maravedies*. For this enormous sum (about a million pounds in modern money) he would be able to gather 150 ships which would carry 55,000 troops and their equipment. So impressive a fleet would be made up not only of twenty-five of the royal Spanish galleons together with those newly come to the Crown from Portugal, but merchant vessels from around the Mediterranean, the Bay of Biscay and the Baltic. But this was far from being all. The Marquis calculated that a further 400 support vessels would be required. The whole purpose of this unprecedented tonnage was defensive. Sailing in the most strictly disciplined formation, its function was to bring Santa Cruz's army safely to an English beachhead where 200 landing craft – among which were forty galleys and six galleasses – would disembark the men along with their field and siege artillery from behind the protective curtain of the main Spanish fleet. Santa Cruz's 55,000 seasoned troops would then advance on their chosen target, supported by four huge batteries of cannon on specially constructed wagons drawn by pack animals. Three thousand pioneers would ensure that this massive force could wreak what havoc it would.

This fantastic plan received the royal assent on 2 April 1586. The Marquis of Santa Cruz was ordered to Lisbon to prepare the fleet that would crush Drake or, as the King called it, 'the navy for the defence of my realm, and for the destruction and punishment of the pirates who threaten its coasts'. At the same time, Juan Martinez de Recalde was ordered to set about gathering together and embargoing the scattered merchantmen that were required to augment the tonnage assembled by Santa Cruz, while the experienced administrative abilities of the Duke of Medina Sidonia were given over to raising troops and supply vessels. An empire — vast, humiliated, hurt, angry and resolved — was finally inspired to decisive action by Drake's piracies and was gathering the entire might of the world's most terrible war machine to throw against half an island.

Drake himself in the meantime, his vicious and vindictive force decimated by disease, riven with conflict, and bitter in its disappointment of expected gain, made once again for the coast of Cuba. Now, in addition to its other problems, the fleet's supplies of drinking water were running ominously low. Little if any water could be found when they put in at Cape San Antonio. Contrary winds kept them from filling their barrels at Matanzas, and by the time they returned to San Antonio they were obliged to take desperate measures. Pits had to be dug in the hope of salvaging what rainwater they could. Slaves were employed in this work, and so too was Drake himself. The gloriously resilient figure Castellanos had celebrated showed himself once again. Enormously strong, ever prepared to set an example, the Spaniards watched in amazement as Drake waded fully clothed and shod into the sea, the waves lapping about his armpits while he carried demijohns of all-important water to his ships.

He also had to think about strategy. He called a meeting of his officers and told them that he would not attack Havana unless victory would be easy and certain. It was clear that this was not to be, when the English ships came near the port. They were driven back by gunfire and, after a few days lingering in the Guacurano River, the expedition headed for the coast of Florida. Drake was, as always, determined to raise morale through action, and he now resolved to attack San Augustín, which fell to him with ease since its Governor had only an unfinished log fort from which to defend the place. On Drake's appearance, he withdrew under the cover of night. The townspeople had already been evacuated and some of their possessions had been looted by the local Indians, so that it was a simple matter for Drake's men to march in, burn the town, strip it of valuables and add a small deserted ship to their own fleet.

While Drake was occupying himself in San Augustín, three of his black slaves deserted and later told the Spanish authorities that the English pirate had had every intention of taking them and their fellows to the colony Raleigh had founded further up the coast at Roanoke.[19] It is clear from such statements as this – as well as from Drake's attack on San Augustín – that he was determined to weaken, if not break, the Spanish hold on Florida and give as much support as he could to the English colonists there. In this last respect at least he achieved the opposite of what he intended. The Roanoke colony had been through a very difficult time indeed. Relationships with the local Indian peoples were extremely tense, partly because of the English chief officer Ralph Lane's extremely aggressive behaviour. In addition, supplies of food were dangerously low. Indeed, the position was growing desperate and Drake's arrival led to a full-scale rethinking of the entire operation. On 9 June, the watch aboard Drake's ships saw the signal fires the Florida colonists had lit and a boat was sent out. Drake himself was then taken to Port Ferdinando, which was not deep enough for his larger ships to anchor in. Obviously, the colony was not sited in a strategically desirable position, and what Lane wanted in addition to food (of which Drake himself had very little) were men, boats and arms with which he could safely reconnoitre the coast.

Drake provided him with the 70-ton *Francis*, half a dozen boats, two experienced sailing-masters, crews, armaments, tools, clothing and such modest supplies of food as he could afford to share. These gifts were accepted and had almost been transferred into Lane's keeping when a great hurricane blew up. Its ferocity was devastating. Ships broke free of their anchors and boats and pinnaces were destroyed, while the *Francis* disappeared altogether. There was also loss of life, and a feeling of gloom and hopelessness descended. It seemed that the only sensible thing to do was to abandon the settlement altogether and return to England. Retreating in hurried disorder, Lane's men tossed books, maps and even pearls into the sea and, without waiting for the return of three absent colleagues, set sail for home. It is possible that, in order to make room for Lane and his men, the substantial number of Negro slaves and South American Indians Drake had brought with him were abandoned on the North Carolina coast. Nothing is known about their fate.

This was an ignominious end to an undertaking that had achieved only a fragment of its enormous intentions. Drake's battered expedition arrived home late in July, 1586. Spanish spies watched its arrival and informed Mendoza, who was now resident in Paris, that such booty as Drake had seized was being unloaded. Even this was a bitter and depressing experience for the little over a thousand men who returned alive. They knew that there was insufficient money to cover their promised wages, and Drake was obliged to despatch messengers to Burleigh to plead for funds. These were slow to materialise. Far from enjoying the expected fabulous haul of stolen wealth, the investors found that they had made a loss of something in the region of twenty-five per cent. The Privy Council eventually sent commissioners to give the men half pay. Understandably upset about this, they protested, and the Councillors responded by sending a committee to investigate. This eventually decided that the full sum of £6,000 first requested by Drake should indeed be distributed, but if any of the men continued to show themselves obstinate then they were to be put in prison. Drake himself, in the meantime, put in a claim for expenses of £60,400, a vast amount that was eventually reduced to £57,000. As the Privy Council recorded with conspicuous understatement, Drake's expedition, for all the high hopes with which it set sail, had not achieved 'so good success as was hoped for'. Meanwhile, the Spanish war machine was daily augmenting its power.

8

Cadiz

1587

Everything, including folly, seemed to hasten the approach of war. In the late spring and early summer of 1586 Mary, Queen of Scots, fatally entangled herself in the snares set by Walsingham for her destruction. She wrote a letter to Mendoza in Paris saying that she was still in favour of the old plan of having Elizabeth murdered and then ascending her throne by the force of Spanish arms. The letter was intercepted before being sent on, and Walsingham so contrived matters that Mary was introduced to Anthony Babington, one of her hot-headed admirers, who had earlier plotted to murder the entire Privy Council and now was ready to undertake the assassination of Elizabeth herself.[1] Mary's written acquiescence in his plans for regime change was sufficient to warrant her death, but what justice and the security of her state demanded, Elizabeth was profoundly unwilling to concede. The months that followed the revelation of the Babington plot were perhaps the most personally anguished of her reign. Leicester, her favourite, was away leading her troops in the Netherlands where his mismanagement and vainglorious incompetence were devouring vast sums of money the Queen could hardly afford. At home, her closest advisors, including Walsingham and the staunch and trusted Burleigh, were putting enormous pressure on her to execute the Scottish Queen. Elizabeth, in her agony, characteristically prevaricated and sought every means to avoid an action deeply repugnant to her. In the intervals of worry she beguiled her time with a new favourite, the youthful Earl of Essex, but it was a woman close to nervous collapse who was finally persuaded to sign the death warrant and who had then to face the international consequences of what she had done.

Mary was executed on 18 February 1587. Spanish ambassadors across Europe at once set about vilifying the 'English Jezebel' who had agreed to the murder of an anointed queen who was related to most of the principal royal houses of Europe. The diplomatic campaign prepared the Catholic powers for the 'Enterprise of England' and Philip's fulfilment of his role as the one man who could bring a heretic nation to heel. Matters would have been made easier for him, strategically at least, had anyone been able to find Mary Stuart's will in which she supposedly conceded the throne of Scotland to him. Archives in Rome, Paris and Simancas were turned upside down in the effort to find what had probably never existed but, if Mary's will was a phantom, it was becoming increasingly clear to the English that Philip's preparations for war were not. Throughout the months of the Babington plot crisis, John Hawkins had sailed with eighteen ships off the Iberian coast. The rumours of Spanish naval preparations were confirmed by the prisoners Hawkins took and it was now an acknowledged fact that Spain was preparing to invade England.

But the Spanish plans had developed from the enormous if comparatively simple campaign first urged by Santa Cruz. Philip had also asked another of his strategists, the Duke of Parma, to offer his ideas.[2] These, arriving after a long delay, were to prove as influential as they were ultimately disastrous. Parma, of course, was a military man and he thought in military terms. He was also far less original a thinker than Santa Cruz. He sent a twenty-eight page document to Philip which was duly placed on the King's groaning desk late in April 1586. What Parma proposed was a surprise landing of 30,000 of his own troops who were to be ferried across from Flanders on a flotilla of sea-barges, disembark on the coast between Margate and Dover, and then march on London. Parma argued plausibly that this plan had every chance of success 'given the number of troops we have to hand here, and the ease with which we can concentrate and embark them in barges, and considering that we can ascertain, at any moment, the forces which Elizabeth has and can be expected to have'. Even the notorious difficulties of the Channel could be waved aside. 'The crossing only takes ten to twelve hours without a following wind (and eight hours with one).' Clearly, an armada was not uppermost in Parma's mind. Ships were a minor consideration but, since Drake's activities had forced the King to mobilise a fleet to protect his Atlantic seaboard, they might have their uses. They could either sail up the Channel to reinforce the troops who would have already landed in Kent and, in so doing, keep the passage between Flanders and England clear or, 'if your fleet is large, well-provided, well-armed and well-manned', it could create a diversion in the hope of drawing the English away from the straits of Dover.

Such reasoning had its appeal and Philip, undecided for the moment, turned the plan over to Santa Cruz's assistant who, in turn, sent the papers to Bernadino de Escalante, major-domo to the Archbishop of Seville and a trained geographer and priest who had been much preoccupied with plans for the 'Enterprise of England' during the last two decades. Having considered various possibilities presented to him and drawn a map and a wildly inaccurate little picture of the Tower of London based on memories of a fourteen-month stay he had made in the city three decades earlier, Escalante set to work. Confident that 'through Jesus Christ crucified every-thing is possible', he began wedding Parma's proposals to those of Santa Cruz. What he came up with was a two-pronged approach. A great force of 120 ships and 32, 000 soldiers should be assembled in Lisbon and sent on a diversionary expedition to Waterford or Milford Haven. While the English were dealing with this, the reinforced Spanish army in Flanders should tie down the English forces there before crossing the Channel and surprising London. It seemed that the King of Spain could enjoy the best of both plans and, when Escalante's thoughts had been given a few further modi-fications by Santa Cruz's assistant, they were passed on to Philip with the advice that so complex an operation should not be launched until August or September 1587.

Philip, an armchair strategist convinced that he had a real familiarity with all matters English, was determined to stamp his own mark on this hybrid plan. He believed that his advisors had so far done very well, but how much better it would be if the great diversionary armada sent to Ireland suddenly left for the Channel after some two months of engaging with the English. It would have by that time established a bridgehead and drawn the English away from the real focus of attack. Now it could be used to keep the Channel safe for Parma's men who then – and only then – would land near Margate in preparation for their march on London. This was a seemingly small but utterly fatal change. It did not occur to the King that it would be at best immensely difficult for two vast and independent forces to meet up with pinpoint accuracy across the 700 miles of sea that separated them. It did not occur to him either that Parma's forces might have no navy to protect them as they disembarked under the watchful eyes of hostile Dutch and English warships. The new master plan, now deeply and disastrously flawed, was sent by mail to the commanders who were to execute it. There was to be no more discussion about strategy. The Spanish King, his advisors and people, were all eager for war, victory, and a Catholic triumph over the heretic Queen and 'Francisco Draque' who had dared to ravage their coasts.

Drake himself during this time had been busy looking for backers in England and the Netherlands for a voyage to assist 'the King of Portugal, Dom Antonio, or on some other service'. Elizabeth herself had sent him to the Low Countries, where he arrived on 3 November 1586. He was charged with two duties. First he was to deliver money and reinforcements to Leicester's army, and he was also to ask the leaders of the Dutch for help in furthering Dom Antonio's efforts to regain his throne. Drake suggested that the Netherlanders' aid was necessary for this strategically important move, but the Dutch could see no obvious advantage to themselves in such a long-term plan and, after the shortest of intervals, told Drake that they were not prepared to assist him though individual towns could offer ships, men and supplies if they wished to. The response, although expected, was disappointing, but Drake continued readying a fleet, taking Dom Antonio himself to see the seven ships he had prepared and telling the Pretender that he would return him to his throne or die in the attempt.

It was becoming increasingly clear, however, that Drake's little force would have to be rapidly augmented and used for matters of altogether more immediate import. Philip's preparations for war were a topic of increasingly deep concern, and urgent action was of the essence if he was to be effectively checked. As usual, the sea-war was to be waged by a joint-stock company – a combination of private enterprise and state-sponsored terrorism. On 18 March 1587, Drake signed an agreement with nineteen leading merchant adventurers, promising that half of 'whatsoever commodity in goods, money, treasure, merchandises, or other benefit whatsoever shall happen to be taken by all or any of the foresaid ships or their company, either by sea or land, that the same shall be equally divided according to their proportions'. The other half of the pillage was to go to the Queen who contributed four warships. These were the *Elizabeth Bonaventure* which was again to serve as Drake's flagship, along with the *Golden Lion*, the *Rainbow* and the *Dreadnought*, lethally efficient ships of the 'race class' type perfected by Hawkins. The little *Spy* and the *Cygnet* were sent along with them, while Drake himself contributed three or four of his own ships, and the Lord Admiral, John Hawkins, and probably William Winter, each contributed a single vessel. The royal flotilla set sail from Dover on 27 March, and eventually reconnoitred with the ten ships provided by the London merchants in Plymouth. Drake's fleet now consisted of sixteen ships and seven pinnaces.

As always, there was trouble even before the expedition weighed anchor. Local sailors were fractious to the point of refusing to sail with Drake. Quite what the problem was is unclear (memories of the treatment they and their fellows had received after the Caribbean raid might have had something to do with it), but Drake took prompt action. As he told Walsingham: 'I have written to the Justices for the sending of some of those that are run away into our counties, to send them to the gaol, and there to be punished by the discretion of the Judges which are now in the circuit with us.' He added that he had also communicated with the Lord Admiral on the matter, 'For if there should be no punishment in so great a matter in this so dangerous a time it may do much hurt to Her Majesty's service.'[3]

The letter has a stylistic elegance uncharacteristic of Drake's correspondence and it was almost certainly composed for him by a secretary. What is particularly interesting about this is the light the letter throws on the way Drake himself interpreted the forthcoming expedition. If he was issued with written orders these have not survived, but it is clear that it was generally understood he had been charged with attacking those ports where the Spanish fleet was being assembled and inflicting ruinous damage on the vessels while, at the same time, ensuring that Spanish supplies were intercepted. Every effort was also to be made to see that the vast enemy fleet did not join up together in one body and Drake was, besides, to capture such treasure ships as had the misfortune to cross his path. Drake clearly understood this ambitious programme in deeply Protestant terms. He was self-consciously acting for the Lord's chosen people. 'I thank God,' he told Walsingham, 'I find no man but as all members of one body to stand for our gracious Queen and country against Antichrist and his members.' Protestantism and patriotism combined in a crusading ideal against the axis of Catholic evil, forming the explicit ideology that drove the expedition. Drake, the self-fashioned embodiment of this, was determined to emerge as the Protestant and patriotic hero. 'The wind commands me away,' his secretary wrote for him. 'Our ship is under sail. God grant we may so live in His fear as the enemy may have cause to say that God doth fight for Her Majesty as well abroad as at home, and give her long and happy life, and ever victory against God's enemies and Her Majesty's.'

It was well indeed that the winds were favourable for, back in London, the Queen's all too familiar prevarication had once again seized her. This was far from surprising and, under the circumstances, far from reprehensible either. She was still deeply strained from ordering the execution of Mary, Queen of Scots a month before, and was barely on speaking terms with her leading counsellors. Just as dangerously, she was being misadvised by her Ambassador in Paris who, unbeknown to her, was a double agent. Sir Edward Strafford had every qualification for his post, save money. He was distantly related to the Queen, his mother had been one of her ladies-in-waiting, and his brother-in-law, Lord Howard of Effingham, was England's Admiral and a member of the Privy Council. None of this meant a full purse. Strafford was frequently obliged to beg Elizabeth for money which was not forthcoming, and his debts eventually became so pressing that he found his guilty way to the door of Don Bernadino de Mendoza which was opened to him as he declared himself ready to help the Spaniards in any way he could short of plotting the Queen's death. Welcome ducats were now available and Mendoza was supplied with accurate and important confidential details about events in England, even as Strafford sent a stream of misinformation about Spain's allegedly pacific intentions back to his Queen.

Certain of these letters had now arrived in London and convinced Elizabeth that she had been wrong to send Drake out to attack Spain's ports. She would continue to make every effort to avoid conflict and, misled by those in whom she should have been able to place her trust, she sent a memorandum to Drake ordering him to 'forbear to enter forcibly into any of the said King's ports or havens, or to offer violence to any of his towns or shipping within harbour, or to do any act of hostility upon the land'. Nonetheless, if amphibious operations were going too far, piracy was not. It was Her Majesty's pleasure that Drake was 'to get into your possession (avoiding as much as may lie in you the effusion of Christian blood) such shipping of the said King's or his subjects as you shall find at seas'. The memorandum made it perfectly clear that Elizabeth had her eye principally on the treasure ships which Drake was to capture and despatch to England 'without breaking bulk'. But the missive was never received. Mendoza's manipulations were defeated by the contrary wind that made sure a young scion of the Hawkins family never rendezvoused with Drake who was now free to carry out his original purpose.

By 5 April, Drake's fleet was off Finisterre where 'we were encountered with a violent storm during the space of five days, by which means our fleet was put asunder, and a great leak sprang upon the *Dreadnought*'. The storm was weathered, the fleet regrouped, and the leak was repaired. Urgency and quick-witted competence were the order of the day. Throughout, Drake was at his most ruthless and brilliantly improvisatory best. By 16 April his men were off Lisbon – a well-protected port and difficult of entry – where his second-in-command, William Borough, fell on a small craft and seized papers which told how a large merchant fleet was lying unprotected in the Bay of Cadiz. Suddenly the Spanish warships rocking in the security of Lisbon could wait. To sail at once for Cadiz and destroy the supply ships and the greater part of the Spaniards' facilities for equipping and victualling their warships would ensure that the galleons in Lisbon could continue to rock in impotent glory.

Drake issued orders that his men should sail immediately to Cadiz. Here was the sort of inspiration that was the mark of his genius, and lesser men were scorched by it. This was not the way things were done. Improvisation was improper. Convention required the sort of consultation with his leading officers that Drake loathed and to some degree feared. He totally overruled a complaining Borough, who grumpily declared as they set sail for Cadiz 'that there might have been conference had with such of the fleet as knew the place'. Indeed, Borough was insistent on this. As the fleet was making for the port he tried once again to urge a consultation. Drake would have none of it. The fate of his country and his own reputation were dependent on ruthlessness and surprise rather than the careful compromises and considerations of a committee. 'He would not stay,' Borough opined, 'but bare away straight, and I followed him next.' This was leadership.[4]

As Cadiz came into view, it became obvious that its wide mouth was protected by forts and artillery, while inside rode a squadron of nine galleons. Confident in the protection these supposedly offered, some five dozen vessels, many of them merchant ships without crews or sails to move them, lay at anchor. Busy, sweating men, preoccupied with the tasks in hand, shifted great barrels of wine, oil, biscuit, dried fruit and wheat. Here were the provisions for an armada – and a sitting target. Surprise was still the essence of success, and Drake's ships, innocent on his orders of any identifying flag, moved nearer and nearer to their prey. When they were finally spotted around five in the afternoon it was casually imagined that they were the vessels of Juan Martinez de Recalde returning, as expected, from the Bay of Biscay. Drake sailed on as orders were given to load the cannon. A couple of little boats commanded by Don Pedro de Acuña came out to rendezvous. Their greeting was answered by terrifying and unexpected fire from the *Elizabeth Bonaventure* which then, with Drake aboard, drove the helpless little vessels back into Cadiz. The attack was about to begin. Don Pedro de Acuña, surprised and desperate, ordered his galleys to turn and present their armed sterns to the oncoming enemy. Hastily their crews loaded and fired, but the English cannon had the longer range and sailed remorselessly onwards as the galleys were driven off.

The pillaging was fierce and easy. A huge 1000-ton Genoese merchantman was quickly captured, along with a galleon out of Biscay. Then or later, as Drake's men took to their boats and pinnaces and darted among the helpless enemy ships, so five loaded Indiamen were seized, stripped and burned. Even a galleon belonging to the Marquis of Santa Cruz fell victim to the aggressive little boats that surrounded it. Nightfall came and the chaos continued. Such of the victims as could move at all cut their anchor ropes and fled as best they could to the inner harbour. Others took shelter under the guns of the fort. The constant barrage fired from there did little more than light up the sky and fitfully illuminate the pandemonium. All the great galleys could achieve was the capture of five English sailors aboard a little stray pinnace.

Morning light brought with it the Duke of Medina Sidonia and several thousand of his troops. The ruined ships and ravaged cargoes were beyond his power to save but Cadiz itself might yet be protected from the triumphant fury of Drake and his men. The inner harbour had at all costs to be guarded and 6,000 soldiers hurriedly threw up new shore batteries to engage with the enemy. Undaunted by such preparations, Drake ordered his men to advance on the inner harbour. There were treacherous shoals there, and one of his ships ran aground. Drake quickly transferred his men to his boats and pinnaces, but now the great bronze cannon of the Spaniards were in place. The Spaniards held the forts, they held the bridge, and the sack of Cadiz itself was no longer a possibility. Drake ordered his crew to turn back and returned to his flagship even as the pedantic but loyal Borough (who had been told nothing of this latest manoeuvre), quitting his *Golden Lion,* sailed his pinnace into the harbour searching for his General. As he did so, Medina Sidonia turned his cannon on the *Golden Lion*, holed its hull, and shot off the leg of the master-gunner. The wind had fallen, the ship was becalmed and, in Borough's absence, the master knew that desperate action had to be taken. The men were hurried into the boats and, putting ropes about the *Golden Lion* itself, rowed with every muscle straining as they hauled their stricken vessel to the outer harbour. There Borough went aboard his ship again, fighting with the utmost valour, and later claiming that 'the spite of the enemy was ever chiefly against the *Lion*'. His own spite, however, was reserved for Drake. This was not how things were done.

Others thought differently. The ruination of the Spaniards was surely the work of the Lord. The English victory was obvious, glorious, decisive. Everybody knew that the 'great provision of shipping and victuals' in Cadiz was, as Robert Leng who sailed on the expedition wrote, 'prepared against England'.[5] It could easily be seen as the devil's store. 'But the almighty God,' Leng continued, 'knowing and seeing his wicked intent to punish, molest, and trouble his little flock, the children of Israel, hath raised up a faithful Moses for the defence of His chosen, and will not suffer His people utterly to fall into the hands of their enemies.' Drake was God's chosen leader of His chosen people, and Drake knew (or thought he knew) how to capitalise on this extraordinary exaltation of his fame. The one man who was more than any other responsible for popularising the notion of the English being the people of God was the author of *The Book of Martyrs*, and Drake had his secretary draft a letter to Foxe which was to be sent 'haste and post haste'. The letter purported to be Drake's own account of the attack on Cadiz. It was also a careful piece of devout Protestantism in which the recent success and the continuing danger are both seen as matters ultimately controlled by the Lord of Hosts. Drake signed the letter and added a postscript in his own hand. 'Our enemies are many,' he wrote, 'but our Protector commandeth the whole world: let us all pray continually, and our Lord Jesus will help in good time mercifully.' The letter conveys very precisely the image of himself as a devout Protestant hero that Drake desired to fashion. As he hoped, the letter achieved wide circulation for, in addition to handwritten copies being made, it was printed at the end of the pamphlet containing Thomas Greepe's account of Drake's exploits in the Caribbean. Taken together, these two works were a most effective means of enhancing Drake's reputation and image.

Meanwhile, foreign accounts of his exploits circulated rapidly around Europe but were less concerned with hagiography than with strategy. A reasonably accurate French version of events was soon compiled, and a similar if shortened version of this was sent to Venice by the Venetian Ambassador in Madrid. The Ambassador was fully aware of the enormous propaganda advantage Drake had won. Spain was pulsating with bitter gossip. Elizabeth's pirate had obviously pulled off a remarkable feat and remarks were now current to the effect that 'this woman has shown the world how they can strike at the Spaniard in Flanders, in the Indies, and in his own house; and that these injuries inflicted by Drake will raise many considerations in the minds of other Princes, and also of the King's own subjects.'[6] When the Venetian Ambassador's report reached home, the citizens of the Serene Republic were delighted. John Wroth wrote to Burleigh, telling him how 'the setting out of Sir Francis Drake to the sea is marvellously approved in these parts, and affirmed to be the only means of hindering the prosperous success of the Spaniard's attempts'. An embittered Philip, agonisingly aware that the English and their state-sponsored terrorists had struck a devastating blow at the very heart of his empire, felt himself obliged to play matters down. Writing to Mendoza of the Cadiz raid, he declared that 'the damage . . . was not great, but the daring of the attempt was so'.

In reality, of course, Philip was deeply concerned. What would Drake do next? The strategic possibilities were obvious to the Venetian Ambassador. 'The King and his council fear lest, as Drake is master of the sea, and as they cannot at once send out a fleet strong enough to fight him, or even to keep him in check, he will have easy facility for working havoc on the coast, for preventing the junction of the squadrons of Seville and Biscay with that which is lying at Lisbon; and for harassing the galleys that are coming from Italy.' As if that were not enough, 'He will also be able to keep an eye on the movement in Portugal, and can go to the Azores to await the Peruvian fleet.'

The pirate himself was perfectly well aware of these advantages. He had sailed out of Cadiz pursued by nothing more than a few ineffective fire ships and some of Acuna's galleys which were only a minimal danger to him. While in Cadiz, he had learned of the whereabouts of the squadron from Biscay mentioned by the Venetian Ambassador but, failing to capture it before it harboured at Lisbon, he held a meeting of his closest advisors and decided to launch an attack on Sagres. William Borough, now a deeply aggrieved man, had once again not been consulted and refused to agree to the plan.[7] An amphibious landing to seize at most three or four cannon was, he thought, pointless in itself and highly dangerous. Spanish galleys were sharking around ready to pick off Drake's men when they were at their most vulnerable, which they would indeed be if they made such a landing. A letter was called for, and in it Borough spelled out the problems he foresaw with a clarity and force seasoned by long experience. 'To land men requireth a land wind or calm weather and smooth water, that the ships may be brought to anchor near the shore,' he wrote. This posed problems enough, but even if the men were to land safely it was uncertain when they would return, and, 'If in the meantime the wind should chop off into the sea upon the sudden, what then?' The whole plan was absurd. 'Do you think it meet that the ships should remain at anchor, and put all in hazard to be lost and cast away?'

The proposed action was, besides, in direct contravention of what had been agreed back in England. The instructions of the Queen and the Privy Council had been clear: Drake was to cruise off Cape St Vincent and to do his utmost to prevent the as yet still scattered squadrons of the Spanish fleet from meeting up at Lisbon. It was no part of his task to go off on a frolic of his own and sail 'wither you will, and to attempt and do what you list'. But these measured and reasonable objections were not Borough's only reason for complaint. He had not been consulted in the matter. He was not merely Drake's second-in-command, but 'the Vice-Admiral of the Sea unto the Lord Admiral', and he considered Drake's behaviour an affront to his own rank. That Borough only came to learn of the proposal to sack Sagres when he heard a group of men discussing the plan as they stood in a group outside of Drake's cabin was a mortifying insult. It was Drake's arrogance, his autocratic sweeping aside of other men's opinions regardless of the experience on which they were based that rankled most deeply and seemed most dangerous. Drake quite simply would not listen, would not consult. 'I have found you always so wedded to your own opinion and will that you rather disliked, and showed as that it were offensive unto you, that any should give you advice in anything.' This was indeed the man, and the headlong certitude of genius was deeply offensive to Borough. Drake would allow nothing – absolutely nothing – 'to be effectually propounded and debated'. At last we are given a glimpse of how Drake conducted his councils. He either bamboozled his officers with cheerful bonhomie before sending them away 'as wise as we came, without any consultation or council holden', or 'showed briefly your purpose what you would do as matter resolved in yourself'. Borough hinted that Drake might take a few chosen spirits into his confidence and confer with them (a distasteful proceeding which Knollys had objected to) but the upshot of his autocratic ways was disaffection and, in Borough's opinion, sheer reckless stupidity.

Such straight talking, seasoned as it so evidently was with common sense, experience and legitimate grievance, made Drake incandescently angry and threw him back on the very devices that all too often angered his senior officers. For two days he shut himself away with his Captain, Thomas Fenner, and his chaplain, Philip Nichols. He would indeed take advice, but only from those whose supine acquiescence he could rely on. The conclave of three men concocted a reply to Borough's letter, and summoned the man himself to Drake's flagship to hear what had been decided. Drake, still burning with indignation, rounded on his second-in-command and accused him of treating him like an incompetent boy. Nichols and Fenner spelt out the accusations in detail. The first said that Borough had charged Drake with 'negligence, which is a great fault to be in a governor, and therefore I had greatly offended; the other said I did not only advise him, but rather instruct him and teach him as a tutor what he ought to do, which was likewise an offence'. Under no circumstances whatsoever would Drake tolerate having his professionalism impugned nor would he be lectured. The punishment for those who dared such things was condign. Borough was relieved of his command and ordered back to the *Golden Lion* as a prisoner in his own cabin.

A letter of apology was ignored, but Borough's advice about the Sagres landing, for the moment, was not. Drake sailed to Lagos on the Algarve coast. This was a mistake. As he sailed his fleet into the harbour and landed a thousand men, the Spaniards allowed the English soldiers to march some five miles from their ships until they were under the walls of the heavily fortified citadel. Only then did they attack, inflicting considerable carnage on Drake's forces so that he was obliged to order them back to their ships and sail ignominiously away. It seemed as if Borough, now sitting mute in his cabin, had been right about the dangers of amphibious landings, and it was possibly the fury that this caused which determined Drake to prove him wrong. He sailed back to Sagres.[8] Here he bombarded the castle for two hours until its commander surrendered. The next day, as Drake and his senior officers returned to their ships, he left his men to loot the town. The Spaniards described what ensued as the English 'committed their usual feasts and drunkenness, their diabolical rampages and obscenities'. It was an orgy of pillage. 'They stole everything they found and then set the place on fire, having first committed a thousand excesses and diabolical desecrations on the images of the saints, like wicked heretics.' Thus the behaviour of God's chosen people.

Drake had proved Borough wrong and now, somewhat mollified, he could give his time and energy to altogether more significant considerations of national security. He had been charged with intercepting Spanish supply ships and, for a fortnight or so, he cruised off Cape St Vincent with this purpose in mind. It was less exciting work than sacking a city, less rewarding than capturing a treasure ship, but nonetheless a task of overwhelming importance. Drake knew this perfectly well and had already written to Burleigh saying that success in such an activity would 'tend to the advancement of God's glory, the safety of Her Highness's royal person, the quiet of her country, and the annoyance of the enemy'. Success indeed was his. Quite how many vessels he captured is unclear but he was in no mood to be modest about his achievements. He wrote to Walsingham that, 'It hath pleased God that we have taken forts, ships, barks, caravels, and divers other vessels more and a hundred, most laden, some with oars for galleys, planks and timber for ships and pinnaces, hoops and pipe-staves for casks, with many other provisions for this great army.'

It all seemed modest enough, but the effect on the Spaniards would be devastating. Smashing barrels was a very serious matter indeed at a time when the huge supplies of food gathered to fill them were difficult to obtain and would, without these necessary containers, be left to rot in expensive uselessness or be sold off cheap or even given away. It is not only an army that marches on its stomach, and the fact that Drake's actions seriously hampered Philip from provisioning his fleet was a matter of the utmost strategic importance. Drake had not defeated the Spanish Armada but he had made it impossible for it to sail in 1587 and had thus won for Elizabeth and England that most vital of commodities – time. But time of itself would not pay for the defence of the realm or even for Drake's expedition. He had been ordered to use his skills as a pirate, and early in May he sent back two captured prizes as an earnest of his intent.

He faced serious problems all the same. Disease was now beginning to lay his men low and morale had begun to flag when news was obtained of a rich prize cruising the waters off the Azores. So serious had matters become aboard the ships that even the fit among Drake's crew were reluctant to sail out in pursuit of the galleon. The sudden descent of a violent storm further depressed and exhausted their spirits, and ships began to peel away from the fleet. Among these was the *Golden Lion* with the imprisoned Borough still aboard. Nearly fifty of the men on the ship were sick when the man who had replaced Borough was presented with a petition begging that the *Lion* make for home. The man had no idea what he should do and simply made his craven way to the *Elizabeth Bonaventure*. Borough meanwhile, loyal and professional to the last, urged the men to stay with the expedition, but they would not listen and returned to Dover. Here, even as Borough was penning his justification of his conduct, punishment was immediate and unquestioning. The men were mutineers and were thrown into jail pending a fuller enquiry. Meanwhile, off the Azores, a furious and contemptuous Drake convened a court martial. Its mood is clear from Borough's later description of how Drake 'panelled a jury, and upon their verdict (by his law and himself the judge) pronounced sentence of death against me, the Master of the ship, the boatswain and other, and made full account that at his return home the same judgement should have been executed upon us, but if he had gotten us at sea he would have performed it there'.

Such a display of temper did nothing to alleviate the sickness now sweeping through Drake's men. Supplies were running as low as morale, and, as always, Drake saw that resolute action was the only answer. He wrote to Walsingham saying that he hoped, 'God will bless us with some little comfortable dew from Heaven, some crowns or some reasonable booty for our soldiers and mariners.' Money was the surest medicine and the glitter of gold and silver would guarantee that 'all will take good heart again, although they were half dead'. Drake did not have to wait long before he was proved right. By 8 June he had reached San Miguel where the nightwatch spotted the sails of a Portuguese galleon belonging to Spain. The remaining nine ships of the fleet sailed directly for it as dawn rose. The Portuguese Captain demanded that Drake identify himself and received a terrifying reply. English flags and battle pennants suddenly unfurled from the masts of the English ships which then surrounded their prey and fired at it from every side. As Drake and his men prepared to board, the Captain surrendered the *Sao Phelipe*, the Spanish King's own vessel, along with its fabulous cargo: cloth, carpets, silks, dyes, china, lacquer, hugely valuable spices. There was even a small casket stuffed with gorgeously bejewelled knick-knacks which, after Drake and his decimated crew had finally returned to Plymouth, he took in person to London and presented to the Queen. This haul amounted to an enormous propaganda coup.

The capture of the *Sao Phelipe* was not, however, just a glorious reward. It was a justification of the new breed of ships Hawkins had been building since the early 1570s.[9] These marked a great technological advance on their Iberian rivals. For all their variety, Portuguese and Spanish galleons, built to carry large quantities of men, provisions and armaments, were neither fast and easily manoeuvrable, nor heavily gunned in relation to their tonnage. The new ships sailed by Drake and his colleagues were the reverse of this. Hawkins's experiences at San Juan de Ulúa had long ago convinced him of the limitations of vessels like the *Jesus of Lubeck* with their lofty castles fore and aft. He had set about rebuilding such old vessels or commissioning new ones with, as shipwrights declared, 'the head of a cod and the tail of a mackerel'. These ships had more efficient rigging and sail plans, longer and more heavily loaded gun-decks, and were much faster and more manoeuvrable in the home waters they were principally designed for.

Contemporaries were fully aware of their superiority to Iberian vessels and wrote enthusiastically of 'our swiftness in outsailing them, our little draft of water in comparison to theirs, our stout bearing up of our sides in all huge winds, when theirs must stoop to their great disadvantage many ways'. The English superiority in firepower was also praised, since their ships' relative ease of handling allowed them to turn twice as fast as their rivals 'so discharging our broadside of ordnance double for their single'. The gunfire unleashed against the *Sao Phelipe* reinforces this idea. After the debacle at San Juan de Ulúa moves had been made to standardise the sizes of English armaments, while technical developments had again created important advantages. English naval guns were mounted on box-shaped carriages which were economical on space and easily and quickly handled and reloaded. The Elizabethan warship was now a fast and dangerous floating platform for cannon, an instrument perfectly adapted to its aggressive and predatory purposes – to Drake's purposes especially.

Eulogy enveloped him on his return. Pedlars hawked greasy copies of Greepe's ballad and Drake's letter to Foxe along the lanes and across village greens of the country. Other more learned hands penned prose pamphlets. Henry Haslop, for example, published his account of Drake's exploits as *News Out of the Coast of Spain*, claiming that it was 'written by a gentleman of his company . . . as the very truth'. Heavy-handed though the work is, it is an interesting example of how Drake's contemporaries set about fashioning him as a hero. Both the Biblical and the Classical worlds are ransacked, with a display typical of Renaissance scholarship, to provide parallels to Drake's achievements and make him a shining example of Protestant fortitude and a national icon. The letter to Foxe, Haslop claimed, 'shows his devotion and confirms his religion', vital matters for the somewhat Puritan Haslop who saw England as so darkened with sin that its people might easily turn away from this model of rectitude and earn divine retribution. This might fall on them at any time. 'Our unthankfulness doth threaten punishment, and there is no way to withstand the wrath of the just God,' Haslop warned. He also believed there was a duty to praise the country's heroes for the moral well-being of the nation as a whole. 'The heathen set us down a rule, that is to dispose our lives for our country, to ascribe our honours to God, to begin in His fear, to continue in His truth, and to end to His praise: so hath this memorable man Sir Francis Drake done: he hath studied to withstand his country's enemies, laboured to enrich us by their impoverishment, and made us strong by their weakening.'

But the chorus of praise was not universal. There was still the matter of Borough to be dealt with, and Drake tried to silence him by adding accusations of cowardice and desertion along with suggestions of mutiny to the charges already levelled against him. Drake was not even above countenancing some viciously underhand moves to get his way. Two of his men, Captains Platt and Spindelow, were sent to see the sailors from the *Golden Lion* imprisoned in the Marshalsea. Here, with 'threatenings and persuasions' they convinced the 'simple' crewmen to swear to the truth of a pack of lies. The men later confessed what they had done and the case against Borough fractured and collapsed, even as the aggrieved man himself reminded the court set up to try him that Drake was said to have deserted John Hawkins off Saint Juan de Ulúa and executed Doughty in a manner legally dubious at best. There were skeletons to rattle and it was best they were silenced. Borough was cleared of the charges against him.

But while the people celebrated Drake as their hero, the Queen and the Privy Council took steps to distance themselves from his most recent exploits. They were not yet ready to take on the might of Spain and there was a possibility that they could yet appease

Philip. The order countermanding Drake's amphibious operations
– the order he had never received – proved extremely useful in this.
Burleigh, writing a wholly disingenuous letter to Andreas de Loo,
Spain's de facto representative for England, tried to exonerate the
Queen from all blame for what Drake had done by saying that her
part in the matter was 'unwitting, yea unwilling', and that she was
still 'greatly offended with him'.[10] As for the capture of the *Sao
Phelipe*, Elizabeth had no idea of what its value was but, considering
the depredations committed by the Spaniards on English shipping,
its capture could hardly make up for the losses the English had
sustained or inhibit the Queen's subjects 'to seek their helps by
reprisals'. These were the words of a contented man, for it was only
now that Elizabeth had agreed to visit Burleigh at his great palace of
Theobalds as an indication that she was once again friends with the
man who, more than any other, had urged on her the execution of
Mary, Queen of Scots. Elizabeth was, deep in her heart, devoted to
this the greatest of her advisors, and her visit of reconciliation had
been made more sweet by the fact that it was at Theobalds she
learned of Drake's return from his raid on Cadiz and the fact that
her share of the booty from the *Sao Phelipe* and elsewhere was worth
about £40,000, well over half an annual parliamentary subsidy.
Burleigh and Elizabeth could afford to lie, even if they had to
pretend to disparage the man who had enabled them to do so.
Burleigh himself later wrote that Drake was in disgrace for the
outrages he had committed but no one believed him, least of all in
Spain.

There 'the loss of the carrack, which Sir Francis Drake did take,
breed[s] marvellous grief', grief so profound that the Spaniards
could only attribute Drake's success to black magic, saying that he
'worketh by a familiar'. Fear and fury even stalked the Escorial.
Philip ordered the immediate construction of forts along the Spanish
and Caribbean coasts. He raised 20,000 more troops. He trembled at
the expense, and trembled for the safety of the *flota* whose cargo
would hopefully cover it. It seemed that there was only one more
sensible thing he could do in response to Drake's campaign. Sick and
worried as he was, Philip reluctantly ordered his great maimed
Armada to postpone its sailing. This was humiliating to him and the

Spanish people alike. The citizens of Madrid were known to be muttering bitterly about Drake's success and their King's response to it. Hearing of this, a harassed Philip turned to those about him and said, 'So now they have lost respect for me even in Madrid, and say that all the harm that Drake has done and is still doing arises from my slothfulness.'[11] The insult was unbearable.

9

The Defeat of the Spanish Armada

1588

As Philip set about reassembling his Armada – slowly, with great difficulty, and at huge and ever-mounting expense – so he came to see the campaign his ships would lead as a panacea for many of the troubles threatening his empire. He would be able to crush the English presence in the Netherlands, guarantee the safety of his Iberian coastline, and hope that his galleons could cross and recross the Atlantic unmolested. Drake was his principal enemy in these last two concerns and, just as Drake's actions had long since convinced the King and his advisors that the threat the English posed could only be effectively deterred if Spanish forces 'put their house to the torch', so Drake's raid on Cadiz now gave the King's plans an added urgency and caused him constantly and fatally to tinker with them.[1]

The raid on Cadiz and its aftermath had been a heavy but not a fatal blow. Ships could be rebuilt and casks and barrels replaced, but the expense in money and time was nonetheless considerable. Matters were made worse by Philip's urgent need to fortify his home shores, and then to refit the battered ships of the Marquis of Santa Cruz when they returned to Lisbon after a fruitless quest to find and destroy Drake and his fleet. These were grave matters, but altogether more serious were the changes in strategy Drake's actions now obliged Philip to take. The King was sick in body and traumatised by the insult to his pride. Periods of inactivity alternated with compulsive letter-writing to his principal commanders. Perhaps, he suggested, it would be best to launch a three-pronged attack. They could make a diversionary raid on Scotland and send the Armada to capture Southampton or the Isle of Wight, while Parma was readying his troops in the Netherlands for the great assault. Establishing a bridgehead in Ireland seemed increasingly out of the question. There was no longer time for that.

Parma was distinctly uneasy. The fact that he was to ship huge numbers of men across the Channel was one of the worst kept secrets in Europe. There was no hope of surprise. Worse, expenses were mounting alarmingly and Parma frankly told his master that, 'If you find yourself without adequate resources to undertake such a great enterprise as this . . . I incline to the view that it would be better to defer or drop it.' Philip refused to listen to such opinions for long. He himself would oversee all aspects of the matter in his usual way, and a firm letter was sent to the Duke telling him to get on with his job with all speed and no quibbling. There was no discussion of the huge logistical problems the King's prevarications and sudden certainties caused, no assessment of the enormous difficulties posed by his final decision that a mighty fleet and a vast army should reconnoitre off the shallow coast of the Low Countries, fringed as it was with dangerous sand banks and fast and hostile ships. The 'Enterprise of England' must proceed.

Drake had a clear insight into the tactical advantages the short-comings of the Spanish plans gave him and his fellow countrymen, even if their own preparations were almost equally hampered by logistical problems, disagreements and royal prevarication.[2] Land defences were woefully inadequate. Maps were sketchy, mobilisation haphazard, armaments paltry, and training almost non-existent. It was only late in the day that the Privy Council even got round to issuing orders for a reserve army to defend London, and this was to be made up of men seconded from the vulnerable Home Counties. Other men were ordered to defend the Queen's person. They were eventually sent to Tilbury, where a little fort was being quickly thrown up to serve as the military headquarters of the Earl of Leicester who had recently been recalled from his disastrous command in the Netherlands. There was no integrated system of coastal defences – no integrated land defences at all – and all that the nation at large could rely on were the beacons built on the high points along the coast, their iron baskets filled with tar-soaked brushwood, which would burn in angry warning to Drake and his men when the greatest fleet in Europe made its imperious and terrible progress towards its prey.

It was obvious that England's only defence was its fleet, and obvious to Drake at least that the fleet should once again be used to destroy the enemy as close to its home port as possible. It was obvious to Drake, too, that he was the man to lead such a force since he was the only officer in nearly fifty years who had experience of commanding sizeable squadrons – the twenty-five ships and pinnaces he had led on his chaotic expedition to the West Indies in 1585 and the smaller number he had sent to Cadiz. Drake spent anxious, difficult weeks in London with the political grandees. Adequate preparation and adequate information were both necessary if the all-important element of surprising the Spanish was to succeed. 'The advantage of time and place in all martial actions,' he informed the politicians, 'is half the victory.' He nonetheless extricated himself from a too-hasty plan to weigh anchor at once, telling the Privy Council that sailing out to attack the Marquis of Santa Cruz would be to indulge in a dangerous wild-goose chase. He was right for, as we have seen, the weather more effectively damaged the Marquis's fleet than Drake might have done and his time was more valuably spent in the capital. There was much preparation still to complete, a proper plan of defence still to be drawn up and, equally important and equally difficult, a proper chain of command to be agreed.

Meanwhile, most of the English fleet of some thirty new ships was anchored at Plymouth. Others were at Southampton or in the Thames, while seven ships under the command of Frobisher were patrolling the Channel and the Netherlands coast. The royal ships had still to be readied for action. Careening was the order of the day. Drake, his rank in the enterprise still undecided, was to take a flotilla of royal ships to Plymouth where seven galleons and twenty-nine armed merchant ships would be his responsibility. His flagship was to be the 400-ton *Revenge*. Readying the fleet was slow but, by the start of 1588, Drake's vessels were assembled in Plymouth where they were to be refitted by William Hawkins. During February, Hawkins could report back to his brother that work was going forward and that his men were even then careening the *Revenge*. Preparations were nonetheless far from being efficient or straight-forward. Drake received orders to provision his fleet for two months but not the money to do this. The people of Plymouth, in the meantime, were required to dig deep into purses already made light by the interruption of trade, while Elizabeth seized what oppor-tunities she could to save money, lives and her country by postponing the war. News of the illness of the Marquis of Santa Cruz, Spain's great Admiral, was not a possibility she could let pass by.

To Philip, of course, the Marquis's illness was yet another crisis to overcome in order that the heretic enemy should be defeated and herded into the Catholic fold.[3] The wretched Santa Cruz had been bombarded by a series of angry letters from the Escorial. He must hurry. Delay was intolerable. 'So much time has been lost already,' Philip opined, 'that every further hour of delay causes me more grief than you can imagine.' The grief it caused Santa Cruz was beside the point. He made his excuses in vain, and Philip's impatience rendered his professionalism useless. The sharp eyes of the Venetian Ambas-sador saw that Philip was by nature obstinate and convinced that his real mastery of European affairs allowed him an overview of the situation denied to others, problems reinforced by the King's unshakable belief that God would do for him what he could not do for himself. What Philip was in fact left to do was find the vast amount of money necessary for his enterprise. He was paying out 30,000 ducats a day. The sale of his late wife's jewellery might go a little way towards covering this, but his real state of mind was revealed when he wrote to one of his councillors saying, 'Finding money is so important that all of us must concentrate only on that and on nothing else, because whatever victories we may win, I do not know what will come of them (unless God performs a miracle) without money.'

As he wrote, Santa Cruz's illness was entering its final stage and preparations for war were collapsing along with his health. The port of Lisbon was in a shambolic state and, as Santa Cruz died, lamented by few and mourned by fewer, Philip turned over command to one of his greatest aristocrats, the Duke of Medina Sidonia. The Duke, if he had never fought a battle at sea, at least had a reasonable record on land, an altogether more distinguished one as an administrator and, above all, a social position that would apparently brook little questioning of his orders. The loyal Medina Sidonia reluctantly took up his unwanted command, knowing in his heart of hearts that the enterprise was almost certainly a folly. His letter to the King expressing his doubts was, however, intercepted by two of Philip's advisors who told him that he was not to 'depress us with fears for the fate of the Armada, because in such a cause God will make sure it succeeds'.

Drake was expressing a similar confidence in the Lord of Hosts. He and his secretary drafted a long and carefully worded letter to the Privy Council in which he argued that a properly prepared and successful pre-emptive strike against Spain would prove His concern. The people would see it as God's victory (their usual response to Drake's achievements) and the effect on national morale would be exactly what any skilled strategist desired. Confidence, national consciousness and faith would convince the nation of its invincibility and 'they will be persuaded in conscience that the Lord of all Strengths will put into Her Majesty and her people courage and boldness not to fear any invasion in her own country, but to seek God's enemies and Her Majesty's where they may be found'. The members of the Privy Council in particular should know, and rest confident in the fact, that for all the men Spain could muster, 'the Lord is on our side, whereby we may assure ourselves our numbers are greater than theirs'.

The Lord was nonetheless more likely to help those who helped themselves, and clear strategic thinking was vital.[4] It was evident to Drake at least that Parma's great army in the Netherlands could only embark safely if they had the Spanish Armada to support them. The weakness in his plans that Philip would not see – the enormous difficulty posed by the rendezvous of his two great forces – was the advantage that Drake was determined to seize. Drake's letter outlining his strategic thought shows that, on paper at least and with a secretary to help him, he could manage that tone of fawning self-effacement that was so unnatural to him and so necessary when dealing with people in the highest circles. He was perfectly well aware that his plan concerned the very survival of England itself, but his usual tone of hectoring and dogmatic intuition – the tone that had so grated on Borough and others – was here replaced by something completely different. 'I am most humbly to beseech my most gracious Sovereign and your good Lordships to hear my poor opinion, with favour, and so to judge of it according to your great wisdoms.' He was aware of the strategic advantages to be gained from a successful proof of the idea that attack is the best means of defence, and he carefully outlined how this might be achieved. The Spanish Armada was the 'groundwork . . . whereby the Prince of Parma may have the better entrance' into the country. Disabling this force would not only raise English spirits enormously, it would depress the Spaniards and, more importantly still, give Parma's ambitions 'such a check' as to render him an altogether less fearful enemy. All Drake needed, he said, was fifty ships. Allow him to take these to the coasts of the King of Spain and 'we shall do more good upon their own coast than a great many more will do here at home'. Speed was of the essence. 'The sooner we are gone, the better we shall be able to impeach them.'

Clear strategic thinking had nonetheless to be supported by adequate information and adequate preparation, and Drake showed that he was well aware of this. He knew better than anyone else that the strength of the English ships lay in their armaments and manoeuvrability, and pointed out as patiently and forcefully as possible that more powder and shot were urgently required if these qualities were to be successfully exploited. 'Good my lords I beseech you to consider deeply of this, for it importeth but the loss of all.' This problem of munition supply was central and would remain so. Drake also knew (it was a relatively minor matter but one that could be exploited to great effect among the often divided councils in Whitehall) that the Spaniards were equipping their ships with English flags, a form of camouflage that might just bamboozle their enemy. One of Drake's spies had told him about this and he presented it as a gross insult, saying that it proceeded from 'the haughtiness and pride of the Spaniard' and was something 'not to be tolerated by any true natural English heart'.[5]

The resonant phrase did not convince everybody. Hawkins still favoured patrolling the Spanish coast and gathering more information, especially since this would ensure that the greater part of the English fleet stayed at home to protect the nation. Most agreed with him. The difference in thinking – the difference between caution and the wholehearted embracing of the high risk – is a measure of Drake's originality. That he eventually began to get his way was a tribute to the power of his conviction. Hawkins, Frobisher and others gradually became convinced by his plan, and Drake was eventually ordered to leave half his fleet in Plymouth and take the rest to attack the Spanish fleet in Lisbon. Aware that such a compromise measure boded ill, Drake wrote over Walsingham's head to the Queen explaining that he needed more ships than he had been allowed and that he needed to be fully confident of the loyalty of his men. He wrote reassuringly that, 'I have not in my lifetime known better men, and possessed with gallanter minds than Your Majesty's people are for the most part,' but he was aware of the difficulties that had been posed by Borough and was concerned lest a repetition of such incidents would imperil the plan he now had in mind. It was also necessary – as it nearly always was – to insist that his fleet be properly provisioned. 'An Englishman, being far from his country, and seeing a present want of victual to ensue, and perceiving no benefit to be looked for, but only blows, will hardly be brought to stay.' Men with no prospect of booty in sight would certainly not fight on an empty stomach, and 'here may the whole service and honour be lost for the sparing of a few crowns'.

In tactical terms at least, Drake was beginning to get his way, but serious doubts preoccupied those in high places. It was not considered that Drake was a man suitable by birth (and possibly by temperament) to command such an expedition as he was proposing and it was decided that the Lord Admiral, Howard of Effingham, should have overall responsibility. Drake was ordered to accept the Vice-Admiral's flag at Howard's hands and, for all he considered himself to be the Queen's Vice-Admiral by right, an elaborate display was mounted when Howard himself arrived off Plymouth. Drake, who up to that time had been flying the Admiral's flag, now lowered it in submission to Howard who, in his turn, lowered the

Vice-Admiral's flag from his own mast and, amid the tumultuous cheering of the crews, sent it in a pinnace to the *Revenge* to make clear to all what the chain of command was from henceforth to be.

Howard himself was a man of tact, maturity and considerable professionalism. Throughout, he suavely managed what could have been a difficult situation and, after attending Communion with Drake, wrote perhaps with some relief to Walsingham that: 'I must not omit to tell you how lovingly and kindly Sir Francis Drake beareth himself.' Drake was clearly determined to show himself loyal both 'to Her Majesty's service and unto me'. Would Walsingham please write privately to Drake thanking him for this. In such ways was a titanic ego to be handled, and it was now a matter of finalising their immediate plans. Drake argued vehemently in support of his own. Still there were disagreements about these, and it was only over the course of time that Howard was persuaded that the Vice-Admiral was right. With becoming tact he wrote yet again to Walsingham saying, 'I confess my error at that time but I did and will yield ever unto them of greater experience.' The tarpaulin had convinced the aristocrat, but it was now too late to get his way. The English tried to leave Plymouth no less than three times, but on each occasion storms and contrary winds drove them back and then, around 29 July, they heard that Medina Sidonia had been sighted off the Lizard.

The Duke had made immense efforts to get so far. The shipyards of Lisbon had been forced to work efficiently. He had done much to rationalise the ill-assorted collection of cannon that his 130 great ships (he had an additional 300 auxiliary vessels) would carry.[6] In addition, he had almost doubled the number of troops available to him to 18,973. It seemed that everything human effort could do had been done when, on 30 May 1588, the Armada's standard was unfurled to reveal the Royal Arms of Spain blazoned between images of the Virgin and the Crucifixion, all of which were placed over the blood-red diagonals that signified a crusade. Converting the English heretics from their erroneous ways would now be an easy matter 'because God our Lord, Whose cause and most holy faith we defend, will go ahead, and with such a Captain we have nothing to fear'. Medina Sidonia himself tried to give every appearance of believing this but he was, in truth, a deeply troubled man whose problems were to multiply cruelly. His passage from Lisbon was bedevilled by storms which scattered parts of his fleet and damaged ships. Repairs had to be made. Putrid provisions had to be jettisoned and adequate replacements found. All of this caused delay and produced an anxiety bordering on despair. But towering over these worries was the dreadful fact that he had as yet received no word from Parma with whose forces he was supposed to rendezvous if the Enterprise of England were to have any chance of success. These were grim thoughts as dawn rose on Saturday 30 July, its pale and drizzly light punctuated by the fierce, defiant little flames of the brushwood beacons which, flaring one after the other, warned Drake and the nation at large of the Armada's imperious, slow approach.

Was Drake, as the famous story tells, really playing bowls when the news reached Plymouth?[7] It is quite possible that he was, but there is no exactly contemporary evidence of the fact. The earliest printed reference to the incident comes from a political pamphlet published in 1624 in which the Spanish Cortez or parliament is imagined reminiscing about the events of 1588. The Duke of Braganza refers to his country's navy sailing into the Channel and surprising the English 'while their commanders were at bowls upon the Hoe of Plymouth'. If this is not entirely an invention it may rely on folk memory. A version of the tale retold in 1736 suggests that Drake wanted to play the match out, but his famous and variously phrased comment that there was time to finish the game and beat the Spaniards too is almost certainly even later. What is perhaps most interesting – even most endearing about the story – is not its truth but the fact that it has stuck in the memory, stuck as a vivid example of that supposed Englishness which Drake has been so often made to embody, in this case the quality of grace and self-control under stress. The influence of such things is incalculable.

The fact nonetheless remained that, once the Spaniards had been spied, extremely strenuous exertions had to be made to get as many of the ships in the English fleet away from Plymouth harbour as possible, and this despite contrary winds and difficult currents. 'Warping out' was the only option. This entailed each of the ships sending off one of its boats to drop the main anchor as far as was possible in front of it and then drawing the main ship forward on the extended cable by muscle power alone. It was a process which the crews – already hungry, anxious and fatigued – had to repeat many times. Heroic efforts and straining arms eventually resulted in some fifty-four ships being warped out of Plymouth and then undergoing the dangerous night manoeuvre by which they were sailed across the front of the enemy to gain the weather-gauge or advantage of the wind. A small decoy squadron was, in the meantime, left to tack close to the shore so as to confuse the Spaniards about English intentions. By two o'clock the following morning, the English fleet had indeed gained the weather-gauge and, as dawn rose, the Spanish galleons were seen ranged into a tight and terrifying crescent before them. There was something in the region of two miles between the horns of this fearful battle array. For the first time, Drake, Howard and the rest could clearly see the sheer terrifying magnificence of the Armada – the greatest war-machine on earth. It was awe-inspiring, chilling, wholly unfamiliar and bent on their destruction. Amazement and deep concern spread through the English ships. 'We never thought,' one man wrote, 'that they could ever have found, gathered and adjoined so great a force of puissant ships together and so well appointed them with their cannon, culverin, and other great pieces of brass ordnance.'

Howard, with his ships ranged one behind the other or 'line-ahead', issued a 'defiance' as the ancient etiquette of battle required when war between two combatants had not been officially declared.[8] A little 80-ton English bark, aptly named the *Disdain*, filled her sails and moved forward in the wind until, entering between the horns of the dreadful crescent, it fired a single token shot into the mighty enemy before coming about and beating back to the safety of the home fleet. Battle could now commence and a wary and inconsequential encounter followed. As Howard sailed on, keeping line-ahead (something wholly contrary to all the Spaniards' rules of engagement) so Drake in the *Revenge* led his ships in a similar formation to the right horn of the Spanish crescent and the ships commanded by Juan Martinez de Recalde in the *San Juan de Portugal*. This soon became the focus of the action. The English fired more than 300 rounds, damaging the *San Juan*'s rigging and sending a ball through the foremast from one side to the other. But the English would not be drawn into a heavy engagement. The Armada was too daunting, too unfamiliar, and after some two or three hours their fleet withdrew to a safe distance, Drake commenting that, 'We had them in chase, and so coming up unto them there passed some cannon shot between some of our fleet and some of them.' Respect for the heavy Spanish cannon on the English side and Spanish amazement at the manoeuvrability and battle formation of the English ships had led to a stand-off and an enhanced mutual respect.

Now bad luck and disaster played their part. The Spaniards were moving up the Channel when a sudden and terrible explosion tore the *San Salvador*, one of their most heavily armed galleons, to pieces. Two of its decks, its sterncastle and wrecked steering-gear blew about in lethal and gigantic splinters. Half its men were killed, burned, or drowned as they tried to escape. Medina Sidonia halted, turned back to help, extinguished the fire before it reached the main magazine, and took off some of the dreadfully wounded men along with the paymaster's treasure. Later the *San Salvador* was approached by John Hawkins who hoped for a prize but found 'the stink in the ship so unsavoury and the sight within board so ugly' that he left and had the stricken vessel towed to Weymouth.

While this disaster was visited on the Spaniards, Howard ordered Drake and the other Captains to trail the Armada and wait for the rest of the English ships to come out of Plymouth and catch up with them. Drake was specifically ordered to lead the pursuit, the lantern on the stern of the *Revenge* indicating the course the fleet should follow as darkness fell. The command was sensible but Drake (who at bottom considered himself to be the Queen's Vice-Admiral rather than Howard's second-in-command) did not follow it. He knew that one of the vessels that had come to the aid of the *San Salvador* was the mighty *Nuestra Señora del Rosario* commanded by Don Pedro de Valdes. His vessel had collided with some of those of his compatriots out of Biscay as he had come about and, in the process, he had damaged his bowsprit. The *Rosario*'s steering was now badly affected and the vessel collided for a second time, an accident which brought down the *Rosario*'s foresail and yard, along with much of its foremast rigging. The unsecured foremast broke and its entire length fell against the mainmast. The *Rosario* was now effectively immobilised, and a request for help was sent to Medina Sidonia. He at first agreed to come to Don Pedro's aid but then was persuaded out of it. A helpless *Rosario* was now a target for any English Captain who approached. Around nine in the evening the *Margaret and John*, one of the ships provided by the City of London, came up to skirmish. For all the damage inflicted on the *Rosario*, this was an unequal fight and the *Margaret and John* backed off. Drake extinguished the lantern on the stern of the *Revenge* (if, indeed, he had ever lit it) and, in defiance of his orders, sailed off in the dark, later declaring that by dawn he was, much to his professed surprise, confronted by the wounded ship.

If anyone knew how to take a Spanish prize it was Drake. The nimble *Revenge* sailed in close to the *Rosario* and, with barely a struggle, Don Pedro came aboard under a flag of truce. His position was hopeless, for all that he commanded the fourth largest and one of the best gunned vessels in all the Armada. Against a fast ship like the *Revenge*, captained by a man like Drake who dared to sail in close and defy him, the pomp and size of Don Pedro's galleon and its ponderous, mighty guns were useless. After a few moments left alone he shamefacedly surrendered his ship and its contents. This was privateering at its most efficient, but it was also more. Once aboard the *Rosario*, Drake could examine with a professional eye those mighty guns which had seemed so fearsome when the great crescent of the enemy first formed up in the dawn light the day before.

What would have been immediately obvious to Drake as he looked at the Spanish armaments was how closely crowded together were the *Rosario*'s forty-six cannon.[9] These guns were kept loaded at all times so that only a single man standing beside each of them with his lighted linstock was needed for the ship to discharge a mighty salvo. This gave the clue to the Spaniards' battleship tactics: the easy discharge of a single broadside was intended to be sufficient to cripple an enemy's ships before an enormous quantity of soldiers, having fired with portable munitions, boarded their victims to overpower them with artillery, pikes and hand-to-hand fighting.

That this was the Spaniards' preferred technique was made perfectly clear by Philip himself when he wrote to Medina Sidonia saying, 'The aim of our men must be to bring the enemy to close quarters and grapple with him.' For this were the galleons designed, and any other tactic would have proved extremely difficult, particularly the repeated firing of the guns. The sheer bulk of the carriages on which these were mounted, their consequent crowding and the lack of space between them, ensured that it was extremely difficult for the guns to be reloaded once the ships were closely engaged. It was not a major expectation that they should have to be reloaded, and the fact that the half-dozen or so men who assisted the chief gunner and his two officers were soldiers who, after the tasks allotted them had been performed, were required to go elsewhere on the vessel and prepare for boarding only reinforced the fact.

This was a discovery of vital importance, for it would have suggested to Drake how the very different configuration of the English ships could be exploited to immense advantage. That the Spanish galleons were ponderous and difficult to manoeuvre had been adequately displayed by the catastrophic collisions which had brought the *Rosario* to its present humiliating position. English ships, by contrast, were agile. They had been designed as predators and their armaments were of a piece with this. Their cannon were mounted on lighter and altogether smaller carriages which meant that there was sufficient space around them for the crews who manned them to haul them in manually after firing and then reload them with relative ease. A continuous bombardment could therefore be kept up during an engagement, while the ships' superior manoeuvrability meant this engagement could be conducted at close quarters of their commanders' choosing. In other words, the English ships were as sleek as sharks and just as dangerous. Professional discipline only added to their lethal efficiency. English gun crews were teams dedicated to their task. They were not expected to double as soldiers but to fire and fire again when they had their hapless enemy at their advantage.

On the proper exploitation of such knowledge might the fate of the nation depend. Drake knew this. In an account of the Armada struggle, written within a year of the English victory and under

Drake's close supervision, it was clearly spelled out that the gunners on the English fleet, sharing a common discipline, language and sense of national identity – and so bound together by ties altogether stronger than those that loosely knit the polyglot crews of the Spanish Empire – 'made good use of the most reliable quality of their most excellent and speedy ships, not crowded out with useless soldiers, but with decks clear for the use of artillery, so that they could safely play it any hour to harm the enemy, at any moment when it suited them best to do so'.

Such knowledge as he had now gained was priceless, but there were also more tangible rewards for Drake the fighting sailor and for Drake the pirate. He knew that the English ships were grievously under-supplied with the powder and shot on which their success depended. The great haul of these found on the *Rosario* proved extremely useful. More than this, there were 50,000 ducats aboard along with important prisoners to ransom. Eventually, a little over half of this wealth reached the Queen's exchequer and, while some was distributed among Drake's senior officers, it is not difficult to imagine where the rest might have gone. The whole incident is the measure of the man. Drake had flagrantly disobeyed orders and followed his own headstrong genius in what could have been a catastrophic gamble. It was not. He had won for the English a sure insight into a mighty enemy's mortal weakness. He had captured a vital supply of munitions when these were desperately needed. He had also captured a sizeable haul of gold which would go some way at least to help pay the crippling costs of saving the nation.

It was just the sort of behaviour to make Drake the bitter enemy of his peers. Although for the moment he kept his lips sealed, the ever jealous and hot-headed Frobisher began to nurture the festering hatred for Drake that was already evident during the great Caribbean raid and which would soon rancorously explode in venom and spite. To Frobisher, Drake the Protestant national hero of popular acclaim was no such thing. Drake's seizing of the *Rosario* was a matter of the merest spineless greed: 'like a coward, he kept by her all night, because he would have the spoil'. It is far from certain that Drake knew that there was indeed gold aboard the ship, but it was the successful piracy and Drake's pocketing of the profits that raised Frobisher to a pitch of apoplectic jealousy. 'He figured to cozen us of our shares of 25,000 ducats, but we will have our shares, or I will make him spend the best blood in his belly,' he later declared.

Drake's disobeying orders, and the absence of his guiding stern lantern in particular, meant that the English fleet was scattered during the night.[10] Howard reported that the nearest of his ships 'might scarce be seen . . . and very many out of sight, which with a good sail recovered not his Lordship the next day before it was very late in the evening'. Meanwhile, Medina Sidonia, rearranging his battle formation, had gained a twenty-four-hour advantage, but as he sent yet another message to Parma – this time telling him that he was approaching the Channel and asking for pilots to guide him towards their agreed rendezvous – he did not realise the advantage in tactical information now being built up by the English. Drake himself caught up with Howard late on Monday evening, but the wind fell that night and the following morning shifted to give the Armada the weather-gauge. The Spaniards moved in to attack, determined, as they were trained, to grapple with the English. The encounter lasted for two hours but the English refused to be drawn close and fired at the galleons repeatedly. In the meantime there was another encounter off Portland Bill. Frobisher in particular was involved in a fierce skirmish but, much to Medina Sidonia's anger, was saved by a sudden change in the direction of the wind.

Howard took advantage of this to launch a major attack and ordered his men 'to go within musket-shot of the enemy before they should discharge any one piece of ordnance'. This was the English tactic and 'the Spaniards were forced to give way and flock together like sheep', their ships fleeing and colliding in such a way that it was, as one Spaniard noted, 'a disgrace to mention it'. Medina Sidonia's own flagship was attacked but could only fire some eighty rounds for the 500 with which the English assailed him. They so smothered him in smoke that for more than an hour his compatriots could not see him. Medina Sidonia eventually emerged from the combat and, while sending yet another urgent message to Parma, rearranged his battle formation. The English in the meantime were becoming increasingly aware that, despite Drake's efforts, their supplies of powder and shot were running perilously low. So far, for all their nimbleness and speed of fire, they had inflicted all too little damage. As Medina Sidonia, increasingly anxious about his rendezvous with Parma, began to wonder if he should wait in the relative safety of Spithead, the English, led by Drake, sought another engagement.

The ungainly *Gran Grifón* was spied trailing behind the enemy fleet off the entrance to the Solent. It is virtually certain that it was Drake's *Revenge* that sailed swiftly across her beam, fired a close-range broadside, came equally swiftly about and then fired another, after which further devastating gunfire raked the *Gran Grifón*'s stern. The Spanish ship was struck forty times and many of the soldiers on board were killed, while the greatest of its guns barely responded at all. This was an exceptionally brave demonstration of English mobility and firepower, and showed what might be achieved in a really close encounter. The soldiers aboard the *Grifon* were eager to board a ship that had sailed so close to them. Other Spanish ships gathered round, and by the time Medina Sidonia had sent in yet more vessels to help save the damaged *Grifon* the two sides had shot off some 5000 rounds before the English withdrew, the *Revenge* having received a direct hit to its mainmast. Drake had shown what could be achieved but, at the same time, he had illustrated that while individual Spanish ships could be attacked in this way, the Armada as a whole still appeared invincible.

Drake himself was almost certainly obliged to withdraw in order to repair the damage done to the *Revenge*, for all that Howard named him, along with Hawkins, Frobisher and himself, as a commander of one of the four squadrons into which the English fleet was now divided in order to prevent the Spanish from entering the Solent. In Drake's absence it was Hawkins and Frobisher who took the brunt of the following day's battle, but an English attack launched further down the line obliged Medina Sidonia to fire a gun from his flagship to call all his galleons together so that they could resume their voyage along the coast. This move infuriated some of the Spaniard's senior officers because it took away any chance of forcing an entry into the Solent and thus 'the best anchorage in the whole Channel'. Here, the Spanish might have waited in relative safety for news from the Duke of Parma. Would the Duke, Medina Sidonia wrote to him again, be so good as to send him some forty or fifty swift ships from Dunkirk with which to face the nimble English? No answer came.

The following day saw both fleets becalmed but, when a westerly wind arose on 6 August, the Spanish fleet sailed on and came in view of the French coast. They sighted Boulogne but still had no news from Parma. They sailed on and eventually Medina Sidonia 'determined to enter before Calais, seven leagues from Dunkirk, where Parma could come and join him'. At five in the evening he ordered his Armada to drop anchor in Calais, a mere twenty-five miles from the Army of Flanders. The damage he had sustained so far was relatively slight and it might yet be possible to fulfil his master's orders and topple the heretic Queen. If only he could hear from Parma. 'I have constantly written to Your Excellency,' Medina declared yet again and in near despair, 'and not only have I received no reply to my letters, but no acknowledgement of their receipt.' At last a reply did indeed come, despite all the difficulties with weather, bad roads and fighting that had held up their earlier correspondence. It contained what was for the Spaniards the grimmest news. The Duke of Parma 'had not embarked a barrel of beer, still less a soldier', and he would not be ready to join Medina Sidonia for another six days. Meanwhile the English fleet, reinforced now to some 140 ships from Seymour's squadron that had lain off the Downs, was anchored in battle order a mile to his rear while, between the Armada and Parma's army lay the treacherous banks of Flanders, denuded by the Protestant Dutch of every buoy and marker that might have allowed the Spanish Admiral to find a way through.

A position that seemed desperate to the Spanish appeared equally so to the English. If they were not fully aware of Parma's state of unpreparedness they knew perfectly well that their very survival depended on his never meeting up with Medina Sidonia and on the complete destruction of the Armada. A great and historic council was held aboard Howard's *Ark Royal*.[11] It was decided that a fire-ship attack should be launched against the enemy that night, when spring tides and a westerly breeze would carry the lethal incendiaries to the core of the enemy fleet and cause untold destruction – destruction made worse by the pandemonium that would inevitably spread among the great vessels which, it was hoped, would collide and knock against each other to increase the damage further. Eight little English ships were chosen, and packed not just with combustible material but with loaded guns which would explode of their own accord as soon as the fire touched them.

Medina Sidonia was prepared for this most dreadful of attacks but, for all that two of the fire-ships were towed away by heroic Spanish soldiers, panic proved stronger than discipline. As the flaming and exploding English ships drifted in, the frightened Spaniards cut their anchor cables. The pride of the vast Armada was reduced to a bobbing chaos. Terrified Captains headed as best they could for the open water, and dawn rose to show a mere five galleons facing the English fleet. Of these, the *San Lorenzo* presented the greatest threat and had to be taken out. In the two hours this took, the Spanish ships began regrouping in their familiar crescent formation which they desperately tried to preserve in the terrible nine-hour battle that now waged between Gravelines and Ostend. But it seemed that everything was against them.

Wind, weather, and a rough sea pitted the forces of nature against the galleons, but it was the English, led by Drake in the *Revenge* which had fired the first shot in the Battle of Gravelines, who inflicted the greatest damage. The English moved in very close as they now knew that they could, their trained gunners firing round after round after round of their precious surviving munitions. Mighty galleons were riddled with shot like sieves, while their great guns, when they could be fired in retaliation, began to pull apart the shattered timbers of their vessels. As they tried to flee, many Spanish ships ran aground in the treacherous, shallow waters and their men were picked off by the Dutch, who thus contributed their part to the maiming of the pride of Spain. 'God hath given us so good a day,' Drake wrote to Walsingham, even though his own *Revenge* had sustained several hits, being 'pierced with shot above forty times'.

These shots included two to Drake's own cabin where one of his captives from the *Rosario* had his toes blasted off. It seemed better for the *Revenge* to withdraw and let the other ships continue the fight if Drake's vessel and its valuable prisoners were to be saved. This was at best a prudential action – the response of a dyed-in-the-wool pirate rather than an unswerving patriot – and Frobisher loudly declared that Drake was either 'a cowardly knave or a traitor' for behaving in this way.[12] As his compatriots continued to risk their lives by destroying or capturing eight ships of the Spanish Armada in the ways that Drake had done so much to show were possible, Drake himself stood out with his very real limitations revealed, the limitations not just of the man but of a navy led for the most part by men schooled as he was in oceanic plundering and to whom a full purse was an important mark of a successful campaign. It was this conflict between the public good and private gain that, in the next few months would, more than anything else, bring the defeat and disgrace that were soon to envelop Drake's career more lingeringly than any sea fog.

10

The Lisbon Expedition

1589

Exhaustion and bitterness crept through the victorious English fleet. Frobisher was loud in Drake's denunciation, calling him a braggart, a cowardly knave and a traitor in front of Howard and the newly knighted Sir John Hawkins. Drake himself was sufficiently wary of his rival's threat to run him through the guts to see that Frobisher's outbursts were put in writing and witnessed. He was also careful to protect his reputation with the Queen and those in authority, writing a carefully drafted letter to Walsingham in which he expounded on Howard's 'honourable using' of him, thereby suggesting that there were no divisions or animosities at the highest level of command. The rancour nonetheless remained, greatly aggravated by the £4,000 Drake had gained from the *Rosario* incident. This was a princely sum, and one to be envied by Frobisher especially, as he set about the long and difficult process of trying to get himself reimbursed from the hard-pressed government for all the considerable expenses he had laid out in his country's defence.

The cost of the campaign, indeed, plagued everybody.[1] An angry John Hawkins was obliged to badger Burleigh for money to pay off the crews, but Burleigh was at his wit's end as he scraped about to find the cash. The crews themselves were then ravaged by disease as they waited morosely for their wages. It grieved Howard's heart 'to see them that hath served so valiantly to die so miserably'. He did what he could, ordering the crew of the *Elizabeth Jonas*, for example, to ditch her stinking ballast and light fires of wet broom in the hope of putting the infection to flight. More than 200 of the ship's company of 500 had already died, but when others were, with great difficulty, recruited or pressed to replace them, the disease broke out worse than before and there was a real fear that 'the like infection will grow throughout the most part of our fleet'. By late August it was evident that 'many of our ships are so weakly manned that they have not mariners to weigh their anchors'.

The ships on which these sick and dying men had served were themselves in an exhausted condition. The ever-practical Hawkins realised that they all needed 'a thorough new trimming, refreshing, and new furnishing with provisions, grounding, and fresh men'. But the necessary financial and human resources were almost impossible to obtain. News came on 25 August that the battered Armada was now to the west of the Orkneys and toiling homewards through the ferocious storms that would seriously deplete its numbers. That the forces of nature were playing an altogether more decisive part in the defeat of the enemy than ever the English ships had done was yet another form of discontent for disillusioned officers, dealing as best they could with the squalid and depressing problems that came with demobilisation. There was, besides, hovering over all this, the very real worry as to what Parma's army of invasion might yet do. The prospect certainly concerned Drake. 'The Prince of Parma,' he wrote, 'I take him to be as a bear robbed of her whelps; and no doubt but, being so great a soldier as he is, that he will personally, if he may, undertake some great matter.' Drake was particularly worried that Parma might land on the Kent or Essex coast, and these fears were not allayed until late in August when it became clear that Parma was not going to ship his army over to England on the high spring tides but, instead, was moving it to lay siege to Bergen-op-Zoom.

For all that the threat posed by Parma appeared to have diminished for a while, this was hardly the time for a harassed Walsingham to write to Howard asking him to consult in secret with Drake about 'the desire Her Majesty had for the intercepting of the King [of Spain]'s treasure from the Indies'. The plan might have made sense to hard-pressed officials in Whitehall. It might have seemed, indeed, the one desperate way in which they could solve the nightmare of the financial crisis they were in. It was easy enough for them to argue that the Armada was a spent force and that, by capturing the treasure fleet, attempts to rebuild it would have to be postponed for valuable months. What these landsmen refused to recognise was the sheer practical difficulty of what they were suggesting. The year was growing late, the privateering season was almost at its close and, as Howard sarcastically remarked, an expedition to the Azores was a rather more considerable undertaking than a trip across the Channel. Besides, there were not half a dozen royal warships fit for such a venture and, in his exasperation, Howard resolved to send Drake to London 'although he be not very well, to inform you rightly of all'.

Drake's was a thankless task. He had to explain to a worried Queen and her worried Privy Councillors that their desperate hopes and plans were impractical. They believed that their financial salvation lay in seizing the *flota* as it passed the Azores, but they had to be made to understand that there were not 'any ships here in the fleet anyways able to go such a voyage before they have been aground, which cannot be done in any place but at Chatham, and now that this spring [tide] is so far passed it will be fourteen days before they can be grounded'. It would take at least another fortnight to complete the necessary caulking, careening, inspecting of ropes, the replacement of worn tackle and the erection, where necessary, of new mainmasts. All of this would have been a tall order at the best of times, and it meant now that it would be at least the middle of October before the ships reached their desired destination. By then it would almost certainly be too late to achieve anything.

As Drake put his depressing case, so it was listened to by Burleigh, Walsingham, Howard (who arrived a little after Drake), Seymour, and the doyen of English soldiers, Sir John Norris, a man famous for his service with the Elizabethan army in the Netherlands and Ireland. These were not men easily to give up in despair and, as they pooled their intelligence, their worries and their ideas, so a new plan began to emerge. If it was impossible to seize the Spanish treasure ships, it might yet be possible irreparably to damage those Armada vessels which, despite war and weather, had managed to limp back to Lisbon. Crippling Spain's rebuilding of its maritime power now moved to the centre of concern, and speed was of the essence.

Something had to be done in the early spring of 1589. Any delay would be hugely to Spain's advantage, and Philip had already gained the time in which he could build up his coastal and harbour defences, especially around Lisbon which, as Drake himself knew, was a port exceptionally difficult of entry to an enemy. But what was now being proposed could not be done by ships and sailors alone. An army was essential. An amphibious operation was the only solution. It was here that Sir John Norris would play a vital part, and thinking in Whitehall began to revolve around the idea of Drake and Norris sharing command in a campaign whose principal objectives would be, in order of priority: burning the Spanish ships in Lisbon, taking Lisbon itself, and then sailing on to storm the Azores, which would be held and used as an English base from which to exercise a stranglehold on Spain's Atlantic trade. There is little evidence to suggest that Drake was the father of this ambitious scheme, but it was clear to all concerned that he and Norris were the men ideally suited both to preparing and leading it.[2]

It was also obvious that the cost of the campaign would be exceptionally great and equally clear that this cost could not be borne by the government alone. Preparations for the Armada had cost Elizabeth a quarter of a million pounds, she had paid out a further £400,000 to support the Protestant struggle in the Netherlands, and more sums had gone to help the Huguenots in France in their conflicts with the Catholic League. All of this had more than doubled the annual government expenditure. The royal savings had been reduced to a pitiful sum, taxation had spiralled, and the government had gone to the City and even abroad for loans. It is hardly surprising that, for all the strategic advantages so clearly to be gained from destroying the remains of the Armada, the idea of seizing Spanish treasure remained a high priority. Drake was the uncontested choice for such a job but, over and above this, his charisma and reputation were such that he could make an invaluable contribution to the alternative means now being sought to raise the huge sums that Elizabeth and her councillors required for their new plan.

Drake was the man who had seized the *Cacafuego*, rifled the *Sao Phelipe*, and even profited from the raid on Cadiz. If anyone could persuade the gentry of the West Country to join as stockholders in a vast new enterprise, he could. His involvement would attract officers and ship owners who, for all they might be reluctant to meet their mounting tax bills, would nonetheless willingly hazard part of their fortunes in an enterprise tending at one and the same time to national prestige and who knew what personal profit. But Drake's influence reached out to other areas too. He had for some time now carefully cultivated his friendship with the Portuguese Pretender Dom Antonio. What if the raid on Lisbon were sufficiently successful to inspire the Portuguese to rise against their Spanish overlords and place Dom Antonio on the throne? Huge commercial advantages would accrue to England since gratitude and obligation would oblige the Portuguese to open up their erstwhile trading empire to the merchants of London. Men of vision in the Guildhall and the Exchange could see the possibilities of 'a continual trade for us to the East Indies'. Drake, already familiar with operating partnerships with such men, might readily persuade them to extend to the new enterprise part at least of their capital and credit.

His partnership with Norris could only make the prospects more inviting. Norris had wide-ranging contacts among gentry families ardent for military honour and the financial rewards that might accompany this. He was, moreover, well-known for his military involvement in the Netherlands, and there was perhaps no Englishman alive better placed to persuade the Dutch to levy men and munitions. From being the man charged by the Lord Admiral with the unenviable task of proving to the Privy Council that its original hopes were beyond realisation, Drake was, along with Norris, rapidly becoming the person who could smash the residual Spanish threat at sea, wrench the Atlantic trade from Spain's mighty grasp, and open up for the benefit of his fellow countrymen the immense opportunities once enjoyed by a soon to be liberated and grateful Portugal. It was a dazzling responsibility.

The preparations for such an exercise required Drake to spend a great deal of his time in London. A house in the capital became desirable and, on 6 November 1588, Drake purchased the lease on a prestigious building in Dowgate Street, close to the Thames and many of the prosperous halls of the City Livery Companies.[3] The house itself was called the Herbar and had recently been renovated by Sir Thomas Pulliam, serving him as a profitable investment. The house, along with its garden, cellars and outbuildings, cost Drake over £26 a year. His residence in London also allows us a brief glimpse of his social life at this time. It is clear that he brought his wife with him and that Don Pedro de Valdes – the prisoner he had captured aboard the *Rosario* and who was housed with Drake's 'very good cousin' Richard Drake – was a widely popular ornament of his society. Many of the senior Armada officers and other people of 'higher and lower degree' visited the Don, who was quite clearly an intelligent man with a gift for languages since, during his enforced stay in England, he helped compile the first Spanish-English dictionary. Certainly, he was close to Drake's wife who spent a considerable amount of her spare time with him. The Queen too was aware of de Valdes's presence, and she and Drake spotted him one day when they were walking in St James's Park, the Queen turning to Drake and saying: 'God give thee joy of this prisoner.' Elizabeth clearly hoped that her pirate would ransom him at a considerable profit, but she was also determined to give prudent encouragement to the altogether greater naval plans that Drake was nurturing.

This was no time for prevarication, as Elizabeth fully realised. An exhilarated Norris was sent to the Netherlands to raise troops, arms and transports. Elizabeth promised £20,000 in money and 'six of her second sort of ships' along with munitions, victuals and the instruments of land war that Norris would require. Drake pressed his advantage. The Queen was in a giving vein. He asked for a commission under the Great Seal 'for the defence of this realm'. He also asked for the authority to obtain shipping, grain, transport, the appropriate licences for any of the gentry who would volunteer to go with him and (the fruit of long experience) the Queen's promise that she would bear the entire cost of the expedition if she saw fit to countermand it. Her advisors meanwhile, worried that the expedition might yet fall through – not because of royal prevarication but through the financial difficulties encountered by Drake and Norris – were pleased when a treasurer was appointed and given £3,000 to cover immediate expenses, the remainder of the royal contribution being payable when Drake and Norris had raised all of the £40,000 they had undertaken to find in the City. In such ways as these, it was hoped to ready six royal warships and twenty armed merchantmen for Drake to command, along with 12,000 soldiers, 1,000 pioneers, cannon, victuals and transports for Norris. Everything would be ready by 1 February 1589.

It was not, of course. This was partly due to problems with the Dutch: problems which were very largely of English making. Parma's mighty army had failed to take Bergen-op-Zoom and it now seemed entirely possible that the Netherlanders could provide the troops and armaments that would be so essential to the success of the expedition.[4] Norris presented his proposals to them but had to wait six or seven weeks for an answer. He had arrived in the Low Countries with an additional 1,500 men to reinforce the English troops already there, but rumour strongly suggested that the Dutch would refuse to pay for these and Norris's anxious thoughts turned to the 5,000 foot and 1,000 horse that Elizabeth had already supplied to her so-called allies. Now that the threat from Parma had receded, would it not be possible to bring these men home? Elizabeth agreed to this and asked the Dutch to hand over to her commanding officer in the Low Countries thirteen bands of foot and six of horse. By the middle of December it seemed that the Dutch were willing to agree and to provide, in addition, ten fully supplied warships on the condition that a body of English soldiers was allowed to remain in Bergen and Ostend. It all seemed eminently satisfactory but speed was still of the essence since, not only might Parma renew his offensive with the spring, but increasing hostility between Huguenots and Catholics in France meant that the men taken from the Low Countries might soon be needed for matters other than those which Drake and Norris had in hand.

What might have just been possible was spoilt by diplomatic maladroitness. Tactless instructions sent by the Queen to her representative in Holland infuriated the Dutch, for Elizabeth was now demanding that more than the agreed number of soldiers be withdrawn from Bergen and that all her forces in Ostend should leave there too. Such demands were in total contradiction to the terms that had been agreed and, not surprisingly, the Dutch were 'marvellously nettled'. They refused to compromise, and Elizabeth promptly did everything she could to meet the terms of her original agreement. It took a month for these new orders to arrive, however – important time uselessly squandered – and, even when he received them, the peeved and foolish English commander in the Netherlands behaved with such a blatant disregard for the niceties of international relations that the waning enthusiasm of the Netherlanders for the entire project reached a new low. Only six of their promised ten bands of foot soldiers were embarked and they made minimal efforts to ready either their warships or transports. This reluctance of the Dutch spread to the officers commanding the English troops still garrisoned in the country who were prepared only slowly and reluctantly to release the men under their command. Once these were free to join Drake and Norris, freezing harbours and contrary winds kept the men cooped up on the Dutch coast until early March. In the end, only half the promised companies of infantry ever appeared. The companies of horse, in the meantime, were found to be wholly exhausted and unsuited to the forthcoming engagement. The warships promised by the Dutch never materialised, and only half the quantity of arms they had agreed to supply ever found their way to England.

It was all very depressing, but the reluctance of the Dutch was not the only difficulty that had to be faced. The over-enthusiasm of the English also raised considerable problems. The proposed expedition was enormously popular in England and men flocked to Drake and Norris's standard. They had initially budgeted to victual 10,000 men for four months at a total cost of a little over £28,000. This seemed reasonable, but numbers soon grew out of all proportion. 'Since our first assembly of the determined number of men for this service,' the two leaders informed the Privy Council, 'the army hath been almost doubly increased, especially of late . . . by the repair of many gentlemen and divers companies of voluntary soldiers offering to be employed in this action.' It seemed foolish to turn such men away, and Drake and Norris almost certainly had a use for them that they were not willing to divulge. Nonetheless, when a planned 10,000 soldiers rose to 19,000 (numbers enlarged yet again by the presence of over 4,000 sailors) it became painfully obvious that the men could not be easily fed.

By 1 April, alarming quantities of the assembled victuals had already been consumed and only another six weeks' worth remained. And now contrary winds ensured that not one man in this vast amphibious force could set sail. Drake and Norris had already spent over a third more than they had budgeted for. They had no cash. They had no credit. The only thing to do was turn to the Queen and insist that she honour her agreement to feed the men all the time the winds were against them and, as Norris reminded her, a large, unoccupied and hungry army was a very dangerous thing. The men had been levied on the Queen's commission and so she was responsible for paying their wages. If the men were not paid 'the country will be utterly spoiled, robberies and outrages committed in every place, the arms and furniture lost, besides the dishonour of the matter'.

The situation was made worse for the Queen by the unexpected expenses in which Drake's management of the preparations had already involved her. Elizabeth had promptly and honourably paid a large part of the agreed first tranche of the £20,000 she had promised. The remainder was supposed to be payable when the private adventurers Drake had persuaded to help fund the expedition had raised their full sum of £40,000. Drake was barely a fortnight into his preparations, however, when he wrote to the Queen demanding that she immediately send him the full £17,000 still outstanding to cover the cost of victuals. He had indeed promises of money from the City, but very little of this had actually been remitted and it was hoped that the example now urged on the Queen would 'induce the adventurers to bring in their adventures with greater readiness and expedition'. Burleigh saw the sense in this even if Elizabeth did not, and the money was eventually handed over. Tempers on all sides were now becoming badly frayed and the irascible Norris wrote to Burleigh loudly complaining that, 'We have never received any favourable answer of any matter that was moved by us, were it never so just or reasonable, but contrarily threatenings and chidings.'

If things were looking bad, they were about to get worse. Returning spring brought renewed hostilities in the Netherlands where Parma was enjoying unexpected success, while turmoil in

France resulted in Elizabeth being asked to find money for a loan of a further £27,000. The Scots, too, were pressing for a subsidy to help reduce rebellious Catholics there and, as Drake and Norris's expedition continued to be held back by contrary winds, what was for the Queen at least a wholly unlooked-for problem was suddenly inflicted on the whole increasingly disastrous enterprise. A little before dawn on Saturday, 5 April, Elizabeth's young favourite, the Earl of Essex, arrived in Plymouth after a hard, thirty-six-hour ride from London.[5]

Volatile, handsome, magnetic, self-willed and unrestrainable, Essex was determined to throw in his lot with Drake and Norris to increase his fame and, just as importantly, repair his debt-ridden fortunes. Elizabeth had not authorised his being there, but it is highly probable that his presence was not unexpected by either Drake or Norris. To a young man of twenty-three such as this, Drake – rich in experience, years and pocket – surely appeared an extraordinarily charismatic figure: the portly, ageing but domineering sea-dog who stares out from a portrait painted in the manner of Marcus Gheeraerts around this time. To throw his lot in with Drake might be to redeem it. Here, besides, was an escape from his role as a pampered darling. Drake, for his part, was fully aware of the advantages this glamorous young man brought with him. As a popular hero and great aristocrat, Essex had immense social prestige, and Drake knew, besides, that the young man was intensely loyal to him. But what attracted Drake terrified the Queen. Essex's stepfather Leicester had shown all too painfully by his conduct in the Netherlands how a great aristocrat might behave once he was away from Elizabeth's immediate control. However precise and forceful royal instructions might be, such men could bend them, wilfully misinterpret them, or even defy them. Elizabeth had done her best to tame Essex's headstrong nature but she knew that there was 'no rule with him'. Sir Francis Knollys was despatched to bring Essex back to court. The Earl of Huntingdon was sent on a similar mission. Eventually, Essex, now aboard the *Swiftsure*, was forced into Falmouth by contrary winds. This was not disagreeable to him since there he could hope to 'avoid the importunity of messengers that were daily sent for his return'. He had, besides, 'some other causes more secret to himself'.

This perhaps hints at some private understanding between the young earl and the old sea-dog, and implies that Essex probably knew that Drake had no intention of following the Queen's instructions to the letter. Her priorities – the priorities of the state and its security – were not the same as those of Drake and his closest followers. They nurtured dreams altogether more tempting and grandiose than the destruction of the remains of the Armada which they now knew had limped home not to Lisbon but to Santander. Contrary to the Queen's explicit instructions that a raid on Lisbon was to be only a very minor consideration, Lisbon loomed large in Drake's thoughts. For all that destroying the remains of the Armada would help preserve England in safety and ensure that the Azores might be had too, there was little prospect of immediate reward in such an action compared to what might be gained from placing Dom Antonio on the Portuguese throne, expelling the Spaniards from the country as the Portuguese people rose up in his support, and thereby having access to what would be the Pretender's vast trading empire.

Nor were soaring ambition and dishonest divergences from the Queen's wishes the only problems. The way in which the expedition had been financed guaranteed that Elizabeth, who was only one, albeit the largest, of its shareholders, could not assert absolute control over it. Drake himself had invested £2,000 in the project and his merchant colleagues in the City of London were as anxious as he to see a healthy return on their money. Capturing Lisbon, and with it English influence over the newly revived Portuguese Empire, would ensure this, and everything points to such a plan being Drake's principal concern. It was no doubt the lure of entering and holding Lisbon that had made Drake and Norris reluctant to trim the size of their army and they had, besides, Dom Antonio's promise not only that his people would indeed rise in Drake's support, but that Portugal would pay for the English army of liberation ten days after it had landed and keep it in its service thereafter. It was these conflicting desires – the practical if relatively unglamorous plans of Elizabeth for national security, and the wild dreams of wealth and personal advantage nurtured by Drake and those closest to him – that would account for the expedition's eventual ignominious failure. It is clear that the Queen was the altogether shrewder strategist but, once the expedition had set sail, it was obvious too that her wishes would not be obeyed. The execution of national policy had fallen into the hands of a pirate.

It seemed at first that this might not be altogether a bad thing. The expedition could profit by taking advantage of unexpected opportunities. By 6 April, Drake and his colleagues had learned that 200 ships 'of divers nations' had recently arrived off Coruna – a port relished by English sailors as 'the Groyne' – and that these were laden with a store of munitions, masts, cables and other provisions intended for Spain. It was hoped that seizing these would at one and the same time greatly inconvenience Philip's refurbishment of his Armada and provide the English with much-needed quantities of victuals. It was with the immediate prospect of plundering these that Drake and Norris's expedition finally sailed from Plymouth on 18 April 1589. Drake himself sailed aboard the *Revenge* once again and gave orders that the flotilla should be divided into five squadrons of sixteen to eighteen ships each. The expedition duly arrived off Coruna on 24 April, only to be immediately disappointed.[6] The 200 ships were nowhere to be seen, and only one Armada galleon and some half dozen other vessels were found riding there. These were destroyed and the English now resolved on sacking the lower of the two towns into which Coruna was divided. Nine thousand soldiers were eventually disembarked and, for all the defence put up by the fortress in the upper part of the town, the lower town of Coruna fell with minimal losses and provided a plentiful store of provisions.

That should have been sufficient. The expedition should have sailed away to get on with its more serious business. Instead, Drake's forces lingered around Coruna for another fortnight, attempting to storm the well fortified upper town but failing totally to do so, partly because they had not been provided with adequate siege guns and partly because the English ships positioned themselves so badly that the Spanish galleys were able to sail in and out and provide the defenders with adequate supplies. Even vigorous attempts to attack the Spanish defences proved incompetent. Mines were ineptly used and, when the Spanish towers fell, they fell on the English troops.

More men were buried by cascades of rocks and an ignominious retreat became absolutely necessary. The men were discouraged by this early reverse which had, of course, alerted the Spanish authorities to their presence. Norris managed to defeat the 7,000 enemy troops that were sent to relieve Coruna, but very little else was achieved beyond the capture of 150 brass cannon and a shipload of Spanish pikes and muskets along with large quantities of potent Spanish wine. This last produced the inevitable results. The troops got furiously drunk and not only their savagery towards the citizens of Coruna but also their own later illness was blamed on drink.

On 9 May, with nothing of substance achieved, the siege of Coruna was abandoned, the men were re-embarked, and the whole disintegrating expedition set sail for Lisbon as Drake and his colleagues had always intended. Two weeks had been hopelessly wasted, and the entire Iberian peninsula was aware of the threat posed to it. Any element of surprise was now utterly out of the question. Excuses for such a failure and such a flagrant breach of the agreed aims of the expedition had to be found and these were quickly forthcoming. Why had Drake and Norris not sailed for Santander? They offered two reasons. They said first that they had consulted the other senior officers – a proper procedure Drake was always averse to – and had learned from them that the westerly wind made it unwise for them to take a very large fleet through the dangers of the Bay of Biscay. Such technical matters as seamanship were made to sound plausible, but they fitted ill with Drake's normal ways of going about things, and it may reasonably be supposed that the fact that he had little if any intention of going to Santander surely contributed to the decision.

The sailors offered one excuse and the soldiers supplemented it with a second. The fact that Norris and his men had failed to take Coruna was an embarrassment and it was clearly best to convince the Privy Council that they had learned from their mistakes. 'We find by experience it is very hard to distress any shipping that is guarded by the ordnance of a town except we were able to take the town.' They had failed to take Coruna, Norris added, because the Queen had not provided the necessary siege pieces. This was quite possibly intentional on her part since her overriding aim was the destruction of shipping rather than of towns, but Norris's comments neatly and nastily shifted the blame and it was now obvious that the failure at Coruna would be repeated 'in every place where we come, to the extreme hindrance of the service' unless the Queen did something about it. 'We write to my Lords that it will please their Lordships to move Her Majesty that we may be supplied with artillery, powder, and other provisions.' The Queen's explicit instructions having been disobeyed, it was now being suggested that she was at least partly responsible for the consequence.

This was just the sort of ill-disciplined chaos that Elizabeth greatly feared. She had taken what precautions she could to limit the damage which she foresaw. She ordered Anthony Ashley, one of the Clerks of the Privy Council, 'To go with the commanders on the expedition, to observe their action, use his influence and counsel with them, and to report by letter the progress of affairs.' Neither Drake nor Norris were men to be daunted by a civil servant and they had little difficulty in subduing Ashley to their joint will. They had argued that Spanish shipping could only be destroyed if the forts that protected it were seized first. It was a small matter to convince Ashley that such strategic considerations ruled out an attack on Santander, and the overawed scribe wrote back to his mistress saying: 'Santander by report is as strong as the higher town of the Groyne, whereunto the cannon must of necessity be brought if we shall prevail according to the generals' instruction.' Elizabeth was powerless to defend her interests against such manipulation as this, especially when Drake and Norris had convinced themselves that the 200 heavily provisioned ships they had hoped to seize in Coruna were now almost certainly moored in Lisbon.

To Lisbon they would go. There they would find booty, and there they would put Dom Antonio on his rightful throne. Honour, glory and the wealth of the East Indies would all soon be theirs. In comparison to such dreams as these, unfounded though they were, the altogether more practical and urgent business of smashing the remains of the Armada and blockading the silver fleets was a paltry thing indeed. It would be very helpful, Norris wrote to Burleigh, if the Queen were to send 'a supply of thirty companies out of the Low Countries' to help them achieve their aim. The absurdity of such a suggestion shows how far the cancers of fantasy and greed were eating away at serious strategic thought. But even the fantasies kept shifting. By the time the expedition set sail on 8 May, Drake had heard that a rich Indiaman was harboured in Peniche, a town some fifty miles north of Lisbon. The rumour was, of course, irresistibly attractive to him, and plans were quickly reformulated to take account of it. By the time they arrived at Peniche the ship had sailed away, but it was resolved that Peniche itself should be the base from which they would attack Lisbon.

Essex had his longed-for moment of glory when he led the English troops ashore to attack the 5,000 Spaniards defending Peniche.[7] The garrison fell after a two-day struggle, but if the English had won themselves a bridgehead they had destroyed conclusively any hope of surprising the enemy. Nor was this their only tactical blunder. Even now it might just have been possible for them to fall on Lisbon and capture it, had the entire expedition sailed for Cascaes on the mouth of the Tagus, only sixteen miles down river from Lisbon itself. Communications would have been relatively easy if the troops had been landed there and taken out the forts that protected the passage to Lisbon while Drake's ships made their way up the river. Their passage might have been a swift one and Cardinal Archduke Albert who was defending the sprawling city with a mere 7,000 largely disaffected Portuguese troops might have been obliged to surrender. Such a plan was not followed. Instead, it was agreed that Norris would march his men overland to Lisbon while Drake would sail round to Cascaes and reconnoitre with Norris once his soldiers reached the capital.

What was the thinking behind this foolish decision, which ensured that the two parts of an amphibious expedition would divide and make communication between themselves at best extremely difficult? It was as if the English were determined to repeat the blunder King Philip had made, the blunder which had helped ensure the defeat of the Spanish Armada. It is virtually certain that their recent experiences at Coruna had convinced the English command how difficult it was to take a well-defended port, and there was good reason for them to think that everything would have been done to make Lisbon impregnable. It was felt best not to risk both the army and the navy simultaneously or, above all, too soon. The only hope of seizing the city lay in its citizens rising up against their Spanish overlords and welcoming the English in as their liberators, as Dom Antonio had said they would. If the Portuguese did not feel their pulses quicken as an army of liberation marched towards them, then that army would have to disengage itself as quickly as it could and make for its still secure and unengaged ships which would rapidly carry it away to the Azores. These would then be captured as a prelude to establishing a stranglehold over the fabulous wealth of the Spaniards' Atlantic shipping. It was probably with these ideas in mind that Norris marched his troops off for Lisbon on 18 May. Drake, standing on the brow of a hill, watched them depart and shouted good luck to each of the officers as they passed by. When the parade was over, Drake himself sailed for Cascaes and the mouth of the Tagus.

Norris's overland march was a ghastly business. Even in May the heat was sweltering, many of his troops were sick, and all became progressively more and more exhausted. Nobody had thought to provide them with a baggage train, provisions were in short supply, and Dom Antonio himself had forbidden them to live off the land. The barely 6,000 men fit for duty were pitifully under-supplied for an attack and were, indeed, attacked themselves. The position grew desperate. Essex distinguished himself by allowing the most cruelly afflicted of the men to ride in his carriages but, as the rest limped and sweated their way along the dusty roads, their fatigue made them easy victims to bands of Spanish soldiers. 'Vive el rey Dom Antonio!' the soldiers, easily mistaken for Portuguese, called out. Perhaps this was an encouraging sign that the people really would rise up and, with a flicker of hope, the English let their enemies pass them by unopposed. This only made it easier for the Spaniards to wheel about, turn on the English, fall on them, and cut a dozen throats before being repulsed. So much for the spontaneous rising of the Portuguese people. The Spaniards had taken steps to suppress that before it became a possibility by making sure in the most savage way that the citizens of Lisbon 'had time to consider the danger they ran if they revolted and to see sentence executed on some who favoured Dom Antonio'.

As Norris and his men approached the outskirts of Lisbon only a few beggars – losers under any regime – cheered for Dom Antonio. The streets of the city were deserted. People would not rise up until their would-be liberators took the town, and the city itself could not be taken unless they themselves encouraged it. The position was desperate, and the Spaniards did everything they could to keep it so. The Cardinal Archduke was not foolish enough to risk a battle, but he was wily enough to lure the exhausted English into the maze of Lisbon's suburbs where he could fire on his hapless enemy. For all that Norris eventually managed to drive the Spaniards back into the fortified heart of Lisbon, there was very little else he could do. The Spaniards were now able to fire on him at will from behind the safety of their ramparts, and the few friars who shuffled their way to Dom Antonio's side after his repeated requests for support hardly suggested that an insurrection was about to occur. Adequate supplies of food and powder kept the Spaniards plump and powerful while the English – sick, hungry and running low on gunpowder – could only squabble with Dom Antonio until they finally saw fit to retreat to Drake and his ships moored off Cascaes. As they marched humiliated away, their path was littered by those of their number who had not the strength to go on.

Drake was still anchored off Cascaes. There were those who thought that if he had sailed boldly up the Tagus then 'we would have entered the town'. But Drake did not navigate the sixteen miles that lay between his ships and the army. He was later to make his excuses, saying that it would have been too dangerous for him to sail past the defensive forts along the bank without the support of Norris's troops. He could argue that the Queen herself had forbidden him to take risks and would only condone operations in Portugal if they were launched 'without any great hazard'. More convincingly, he could excuse his behaviour by the failure of communication which had been caused by the decision he and Norris made to divide their forces at Peniche. News was slow to reach him and when he did finally hear from the army, it was in full-scale retreat. Without certain knowledge of the situation in Lisbon, it would have been the merest foolishness on his part to take two-thirds of his fleet up the river on the first fair wind, for all that he said he was willing to do so. Now, instead of the glories and the riches he and Norris had imagined, they lingered for a few days off Cascaes, forlorn and disillusioned, in the hope that supplies might come from England and allies arise in Lisbon. Neither happened. But something had to be done and, on 3 June, a council was held at which it was decided that the English expeditionary force, depleted and demoralised as it was, would sail off for the Azores.

It is difficult to avoid the suspicion that, over the last few days, this had become Drake's principal purpose. This was why he had not taken his ships up the Tagus. It was obvious that the Portuguese had not risen up to welcome him and equally obvious that, under these circumstances, he could not afford to risk a single one of his ships to the enemy galleons and guns waiting to attack him. He would not even do so when he heard of the plight of the army. He did not dare to. The success of the expedition and the salvation of his own reputation now lay in a successful attack on the Azores. But, as Drake was all too clearly aware, that attack itself was a project of the utmost risk. His flat defiance of the Queen's orders had left the Spanish galleons in Santander unmolested. It would have been so easy to destroy the sea power of Spain as it rode in that unvisited port 'all unrigged and the ordnance on the shore and some twenty men a ship only to keep them'. Drake might have 'done such a service as never subject had done'. Greed and dreams of glory and a head-strong, arrogant trust in his own genius had, however, blinded him to the obvious and to his duty. Now he was victim of his own vaingloriousness, for some at least of the fifty or more galleons in Santander might yet be readied to escort the treasure fleet and defend the Azores. Drake had failed to smash the enemy who might yet smash him and, knowing this, he had lingered off Cascaes in order that he might yet have a full fleet with which to encounter the Spanish who, but for him, might have been unable to sail at all.

The capture of some five dozen hulks that had sailed in from the Baltic with masts, spars and cables for the Spanish warships might temporarily have convinced Drake that the enemy was still maimed, but events were to demonstrate that, however wounded, Spain could still fight, still threaten, and still damage him. Even as a message arrived from the Queen ordering the immediate return of the exasperating Essex, it became known that she would send Drake and Norris no more assistance. Whatever they were going to do they would have to do with the forces they had. A small company had been left to guard Peniche, but when ships were despatched to bring these men and vessels back to the main convoy it was found that their commander had gone home and that the Spaniards had taken those cannon he had left behind and used them to kill the troops that guarded them. Now the galleys sheltering in Lisbon were about to attack the English ships that rode scattered and stationary across the windless bay. The most separated of these were easily picked off and it was only a sudden breeze – in the view of some of the men a breeze sent by divine intervention – that allowed the English to sail away to relative safety.

For some, that safety was to be found in sailing to England. For others, there was yet the hope of sacking Vigo. This they did successfully, but their victory brought them nothing. The citizens had fled with their treasures and, as Vigo was put to the torch, the only comfort the English could find was in the wine that had been left behind. Two thousand troops had been needed for this petty triumph, but it was obvious that they were now all too feeble to achieve much more. It was resolved that the fittest of them should be put on twenty ships which Drake would sail off with in the hope of seizing the Indies fleet. He parted from Norris who was now to return to England, but the fierce southerly gale that suddenly rose up scattered Drake's vessels and their only option was to follow the badly leaking *Revenge* in which the disgraced Drake himself was limping for home. He had achieved nothing and left much undone. The Spanish navy could still be refitted, while the exhausted English ships were as unfit for service as the greater part of the men who had sailed on them.

The eulogy that greeted the returning fleet was as thin as the paper on which it was printed and equally ephemeral. It was easy enough to say that Drake and Norris had 'won a town by escalade, battered and assaulted another, overthrown a mighty prince's power in the field, landed our army in three several places of his kingdom, marched seven days in the heart of his country, lain three nights in the suburbs of his principal city, beaten his forces into the gates thereof, and possessed two of his frontier forts'.[8] Such achievements profited nothing. Drake, the great Protestant hero, was only as good as his last victory and he had now returned in ignominious failure. It could no longer be assumed that God was on his side, and his colleagues and superiors were quick to show that neither were they. The national humiliation ran very deep, for it was obvious now to any tavern strategist that, by failing to annihilate the Armada while it rocked in pitiful vulnerability in Santander, Drake above all men was responsible for the cruel but inescapable fact that the golden chance of national security had evaporated and that the English no longer had – as they so easily might have – the unchallenged command of the seas. Drake, who had done so much to bring this so close, had wilfully lost the endgame, and the man who had once been compared to every hero in antiquity and scripture was greeted with a mounting chorus of contempt, even as those men of his who were fit enough to do so purloined what they could from the ships in which they returned.

Elizabeth in her cold fury was minded to think of Drake's breaking of her commands as treasonable. By 27 July, the Privy Council was in session, and Drake and Norris were summoned before it. They were jointly charged with never intending to go to Santander and so destroying the remains of the Armada, with the fact that they had failed to sail there even when they had had an opportunity to do so after the attack on Coruna and, finally, that they had landed in Portugal without trying to ascertain whether Dom Antonio's claims that the people would rise up had any substance to them. Both men denied that they had had no intention of going to Santander and blamed their failure on contrary winds and what they alleged would have been their going to a place where they could not have landed their troops. As for ascertaining the state of public opinion in Lisbon, they had no 'means to try what party Dom Antonio had but only by landing their forces' which was precisely what they had done.

The Privy Council then turned to Drake alone. Why had he not sailed directly from Peniche to Lisbon and destroyed the enemy shipping there when, as they were reliably informed, the wind would have permitted him to do so? Drake tried to bluff his way out of this accusation. He needed to know, he said, what state the English army was in before attempting such an enterprise and, while landing certain Portuguese to ascertain this, he made efforts to discover from the local inhabitants how strong their support of Dom Antonio really was. He had been prudent, he suggested but, at a council of his senior officers, he had discovered that the weakness of his men was 'so extreme as they were not able to handle the tackle of their ships' and that it was considered by all too dangerous to go on. He had, nonetheless, been 'desirous to have performed as much as in him lay' and he had given orders that two-thirds of his best ships should be readied to sail into Lisbon if a favourable wind arose. This last only happened when Norris himself returned to Cascaes with his army. It was a lame and disingenuous performance, but the Privy Council did not see fit to push matters further. It was clear to everybody that Drake, who had fashioned himself as the image of the Protestant national hero, and a man of power and violence, had betrayed the Queen who was the source of his values, doing so by exalting his own image and genius at the expense of what they were supposed to serve. He left the meeting and returned to his London house a hero no more.

11

Defeat and Death

1596

Drake was now out of favour and there were those who were determined to put him out of mind. For a man in his position, published accounts of his exploits were of the greatest importance in keeping his name before the public eye, to preserving his self-respect, and even to reingratiating himself with those in authority. This proved to be surprisingly difficult. We have already seen that a ten-page narrative of his circumnavigation – 'The Famous Voyage' – was only inserted into Richard Hakluyt's monumental *Principal Navigations, Voyages and Discoveries of the English Nation* at the last moment. In a country where censorship was relatively swift and efficient, there were ready means by which the accomplishments of a disgraced hero could be suppressed, especially when his activities touched on matters of state security and the reputation of the Queen. The greatest exploit of the greatest English navigator of the age only just made it into the official history but, when Raphael Holinshed was revising his *Chronicles* for a new edition, the book was called in and extensive material on Drake was cut out. Drake did what he could to see that an Italian narrative of the defeat of the Spanish Armada gave him full recognition for his place as Vice-Admiral when it was finally published and translated, but he could reasonably complain that his reputation, in print at least, was not all that it might have been.

There was only one thing to do. He would set the record straight himself and present the published account to the Queen in the hope that his actions would speak for themselves and win him back his place in her favour.[1] As Drake wrote in his dedicatory letter to Elizabeth, he 'thought it necessary myself' to make clear the background and details of all the 'attempts made and successes had, during the whole course of my employment in these services against the Spaniard'. Revising materials largely prepared for him by Philip Nichols, who had actually sailed with Drake on many of his later voyages, Drake himself disingenuously claimed that he was writing his account for the public good. He was not in his own (or Nichols's) words 'setting sail for maintaining my reputation in men's judgement, but only as sitting at helm, if occasion shall be, for conducting the like action hereafter'. The work, in other words, was intended as a *vade mecum*, a practical guide for annoying the King of Spain. But a man who works on an exculpatory narrative to curry favour with those who have withdrawn it is hardly likely to be either straightforward about his motives or entirely honest about the facts. We have seen that both *Sir Francis Drake Revived* and *The World Encompassed* contain a measure of self-glorifying fantasy. We have also seen that neither work was published until long after Drake's death, when the image he so carefully fashioned of himself became accepted as the truth and thus a substantial part of the Drake myth: the story of the little boy whose devoutly Protestant family was driven away from its home by wicked Catholics, who found his life's work while acting heroically against Spain, who missed capturing a fabulous treasure at Nombre de Dios through the merest bad luck, and who was treated as the chief of the gods by primitive tribesmen on the west coast of America, people whose greatest ambition was to be absorbed into the as yet non-existent British Empire.

But fashioning such often spurious images of himself was not Drake's only interest at this time. For all he was growing old and was beginning to suffer the pains of old age – soon after his less than glorious appearance before the Privy Council he so badly pulled his muscles while extinguishing the coals burning in one of his London fireplaces that he was 'very unable to stand without much grief' – there was much else for him to do, especially when he returned to Plymouth.[2] He sat as MP for the city in the 1593 session of Parliament which was much concerned with raising money for a fleet to defend the country against Spain. A terse note records the speech Drake made in which he 'described the King of Spain's strength and his cruelty . . . and wished that frank aid to be yielded to withstand him, and he agreed to the three subsidies'. Drake sat on the committee that discussed the matter, his interest kindled by the fact that the Queen was talking about sending him out with 'a great navy' to fight the Spaniards who had been busy trying to bribe disaffected Scots over to their side.

Drake was also appointed a member of the committee set up to oversee the fund that Burleigh's son, Sir Robert Cecil, suggested should be provided for the relief of poor, sick and wounded servicemen. This generous move was not met with the spirit that had suggested it, many Members of Parliament fearing that it would merely encourage idlers and vagabonds. The plan went ahead all the same, and knights such as Drake were required to contribute twenty shillings each. The very real fear that the country was being infiltrated by Catholic priests also came to the attention of the House, and although Drake spoke on 'the Bill exhibited against the recusants', it is not known exactly what he said, though it was hardly likely to have been temperate. He had already declared his own zealous Protestantism by swearing the oath of allegiance to the Queen in Exeter Castle late in the previous year.

There were also other, more important matters concerning Plymouth that he needed to attend to. The Spanish fleet Drake had failed to destroy in Santander was now repaired and ready to sail again. The Privy Council wrote to him, concerned that the enemy would land in the West Country and ordering him to confer with the local dignitaries to find out the best ways in which the galleons could be destroyed should they venture into Plymouth. The townsfolk, not unnaturally, panicked at the thought of imminent invasion and, while they did so, Drake replied to London asking that a new defensive fort be built. The old castle was strengthened, re-roofed, given a new strong gateway, and provided with four iron cannon and seven brass ones. This was a necessary but expensive business and means had to be found to pay for it. It was decided that this should be done by levying a tax on the pilchard industry. The fishermen, cunning and ungenerous when it came to matters of their own small purses, evaded payment by secretly landing their catches in secluded bays. It proved impossible to suppress this blatant tax evasion and, in the end, Drake himself and various other wealthy local men were required to meet the charge.

Drake was also involved in various other local projects at this time. Supplying Plymouth with adequate drinking water had for long been a problem and, in 1589, the local council eventually resolved to deal with the matter by paying Drake £200 to construct a canal that they had had designed for them. He struck a good deal, for not only did he have his fee for undertaking the work but he was allowed to build six new grist mills along the canal to add to those which he already owned, and to have the use of these new ones for the next sixty-seven years. The fee the council paid him covered the cost both of digging the canal and building the mills which, when they were fully operational, brought Drake something in the region of a further £200 a year. Drake could get things done, but money was always more important to him than the public good and, rich man though he was, when he was asked to ensure that the defences of Plymouth harbour were adequate, he moaned about the expense and was asked to submit a bill.

Drake and Hawkins were also ordered to oversee the refitting of ships for the English Navy in Plymouth. Hawkins himself was extremely active at this time, for he not only had his official duties at the Admiralty to fulfil but a head buzzing with plans. The years after the Spanish Armada were the golden age of Elizabethan privateering.[3] The privateering war against Spain which Drake had done so much to encourage was now an established fact. Hawkins had six galleons sailing out by way of reprisal, and numerous others followed his example. The failure of Drake's Lisbon expedition had made it clear to all that this was a far more satisfactory way of annoying the King of Spain than mounting grand and disorderly expeditions to harass him in his heartlands. That all English ships might and would attack Spanish vessels whenever they encountered them was an accepted practice and the rewards were spectacular. The position was particularly satisfactory to the Queen, who could now enormously increase her tax revenues by enterprises launched at the risk and expense of her subjects. In the meantime, her deepest purposes in her foreign policy were, as they had always been, the long and necessarily expensive efforts she made to secure her country from attack by Catholic powers on the other side of the Channel. The money she gained from the successes of the privateers was used to support the Protestant cause in France and the Netherlands.

There were also further advantages to win from this great expansion of maritime activity. The country's economic status was extremely volatile. Depression and poverty were rampant, and men thrown out of work by the collapse of England's trade with the Iberian peninsula could throw their prodigious energies into privateering and win in this way a measure of prosperity when more legitimate means were denied them. Aristocrats, professional sailors, merchant-ship owners and ordinary men were widely attracted to the possibilities that privateering opened up to them, seasoned as such activities were by the dignifying claims of Protestant piety and patriotism. Mendoza was kept informed of this and wrote lamenting to his master how the English were 'building ships without cessation, and they are thus making themselves masters of the seas'. He went on to tell how they were not only 'sending a multitude of vessels to Barbary with arms and munitions, but have now begun to trade with the Levant, whither they take tin and other prohibited goods to the Turks, besides fitting out ships daily to plunder on the route to the Indies'. English ships, trading across the globe, their holds heavy with the treasures of Brazil, Africa, the East and West Indies and North America, led to a great increase in shipbuilding, nautical expertise, legitimate wealth and an annual income of between £100,000 and £200,000 from other less creditable maritime activities.

Drake was now in an excellent position to see the results of this last form of enterprise since, perhaps inspired by the cynical idea that poachers turned gamekeepers are ever the most zealous officials, the Privy Council named him 'Commissioner for the Causes and Reprisal'. In other words, it was his task to help settle the often furious disputes that broke out between the victors and victims of privateering and to inventory and assess the value of the booty obtained so that the Queen had her due in tax from it. There was much work to do and, on occasions, the goods involved were of fabulous value. It was hardly to be expected that a man who had spent his lifetime as a pirate would be over-scrupulous when temptation was virtually thrust into his hands. When a fabulously freighted Venetian argosy arrived in Plymouth, Drake did not see fit to inform the Vice-Admiral of Devon about the matter and, for all that he set about making an inventory of the captured treasure, bags of pepper, a barrel of mace and 'divers jewels' remained unaccounted for. Letters were exchanged between Plymouth and London, and although a large part of the haul was eventually reclaimed, some of the pepper was put in new bags and was not handed over to the authorities. On another occasion, Hawkins and Frobisher captured a great quantity of cochineal, but Drake was put in the difficult position of ordering them to hand it back to its owner. This they did, only to seize it once again and return to Plymouth as Drake was given peremptory orders to see that the cargo was given back to its rightful owner a second time.

The most fabulous of all the captured vessels to reach the West Country was the Portuguese carrack, the *Madre de Dios*. The vessel had fallen victim to John Borough and that remarkable character, the privateering Earl of Cumberland. The sailors who captured the ship began their looting even before it reached port. The treasure aboard was phenomenal. There were 537 tons of spices, and the value of the pepper alone was estimated at £120,000. There were, besides, jewels, pearls, amber and musk, a cross mounted with a huge diamond and a fabulous pendant intended for the King of Spain. News of the haul drifted across the West Country like the fragrance of the captured spices, and hordes of the greedy descended to buy from the sailors their looted treasures for a fraction of their real value. Authorities were sent down to try and impose control, and bags of seed pearls, amulets of gold and such items as 'a fork and spoon of crystal with rubies' were seized. Cecil intended that the latter should be given as a present to the Queen, but he was horrified by what he saw. 'Fouler ways, desperate ways, nor more obstinate people, did I never meet with.' Eventually, Sir Walter Raleigh, briefly released from the Tower, was despatched to impose order and £150,000 of booty was finally accounted for.

It was a haul to inflame the passions of a man like Drake, who must surely have recalled his own capture of the *Cacafuego* and the *Sao Phelipe*. Perhaps such things might be done again. He and Hawkins were irresistibly tempted, and Hawkins had other plans in mind as well. It was obvious how successful rampant privateering could be, but both men still felt the lure of grand strategy. Hawkins had for a long time nurtured a plan designed to break Spain's Atlantic sea power by which a dozen of the Queen's ships would patrol constantly between Spain and the Azores. Each fleet would be replaced every four months and, since Hawkins suggested he could find private adventurers to pay for the wages and victuals, the plan recommended itself by its cheapness as well as by the possibility it offered of strangling Spanish trade and perhaps compelling Philip to sue for peace. Nothing came of the proposal, and Hawkins's attempts to use the Queen's ships to intercept the *flota* in 1586 also achieved very little. When he tried again in the summer of 1590 in combination with Frobisher he was again unsuccessful, and it was becoming increasingly clear that it was going to be very difficult, if not impossible, to block the Spaniards' supplies of silver.

Philip himself was beginning to entrust much of his New World wealth to newly built, fast and well-armed frigates while, in England, interest in co-ordinated plans of action waned as the privateers grew rich. What the Spaniards principally dreaded however was a concerted raid on their Caribbean colonies. Both the Earl of Cumberland and Sir Walter Raleigh had planned such expeditions for 1592 and, the following year, Drake regained sufficient of the royal confidence to receive a warrant for a joint command with Hawkins to lead a similar expedition made up of three of the Queen's ships and twenty merchantmen. This plan fell into abeyance as English forces were sent successfully to rout the Spaniards in France (a venture which cost Frobisher his life) but in 1594, with the Spanish threat now diminished, the plan to send Drake and Hawkins to Panama was revived.

Here once again was the persistent and never-realised dream of sailing to the heart of the Spanish colonial empire and seizing it with violent hands, thereby reducing the Catholic giant to a wan and lifeless invalid incapable of evil and obliged instead to watch its rival grow strong, rich and dominant among the Western European Atlantic kingdoms.[4] It was a dream to fire Drake's ageing powers, a dream to rival that which, when he was a young man, had sent him to plunder the silver supposedly hoarded at Nombre de Dios. It was a dream to place beside that which had sent him to explore the possibilities of a British presence in the wastes of Patagonia and then caused him to sail round the world. It was a dream of violence, greed and Protestant triumph, like those which had sent him to Santo Domingo, Cartagena, Cadiz and Lisbon – the sort of dream whose visions of shining mountains of bullion could all too easily blind a man to practical reality, common sense and the more mundane needs of his country. It was nonetheless the sort of dream that could so fire Drake's genius that others would be swept up by his seemingly inexhaustible energy, and a dream which, if only it could be realised, would surely redeem his reputation, salve his bruised and tremendous ego, and win for him once again that favoured place in his sovereign's gaze which he had once enjoyed. Drake, growing old though he was, would surely emerge newly self-fashioned as the Protestant national hero – rich, victorious and wholly admirable.

Drake invested £10,000 in making his dream a reality, possibly selling the remainder of the lease on his London house to raise the capital. Private investors supplied more money and some twenty-one well-armed and substantial merchantmen, but it was the Queen who was once again the principal contributor to this joint-stock venture. Elizabeth provided £30,000 in cash and six of her best ships led by the new *Defiance*, a vessel of some 550 tons which was to serve as Drake's flagship. For all this, parsimony was the order of the day. The lavish and dangerous squandering of resources that had characterised the disastrous Lisbon expedition was to be avoided if at all possible. No salaries were to be paid; instead, men who sailed were promised a share of the plunder. This was not a tempting offer. The closing stages of Drake's expeditions had too often been bedevilled by difficulties over pay. As a result, few now volunteered and it became necessary to send out the dreadful pressgangs to find men who against their wills would serve as soldiers, sailors, carpenters, gunners, smiths 'and other artificers and seafaring men as shall be sufficient to furnish all the ships'.

Such hasty, rough proceeding produced its own problems. The quality of the soldiers in particular was very far from being adequate, a large number of the 1,000 or so who eventually sailed being new to military service – a problem made worse by the insufficient training they were given. Nor was this the only difficulty. Some 2,500 men were eventually obtained for the expedition and they needed to be fed. The Lisbon debacle had shown how difficult and potentially dangerous a matter this was, and it is clear that both Drake and Hawkins were determined to keep the costs strictly under control and even to skimp in order to 'free them from incurring any great loss, whatsoever befell of the journey'. Drake in particular was uncharacteristically careful, and although it seems that he was responsible for victualling a little over half of the men, he spent merely £13,000 on the task compared to Hawkins's £19,000. This ill-considered meanness was to have severe repercussions, but it was far from the only problem that beset the expedition even before it set sail.

The efficient Spanish espionage system in the country was busy, and its information was supplemented by what could be learned from Don Pedro de Valdes, Drake's fierce-faced if suave prisoner from the *Rosario*. Released after five years of relatively amiable captivity for the modest sum of £3,550, de Valdes believed that Drake's plan was to capture Puerto Rico and from there harass Havana and San Juan de Ulúa. De Valdes kept his ear close to the ground for he knew that such plans might change and, a little while before he left the country, he believed that the expedition was now intended for Curacao, which would allow it to raid the notorious treasure route between Nombre de Dios and Cartagena as well as attacking treasure-laden Spanish galleons sailing down to the area from New Spain. That the real focus of Drake and Hawkins's interest was Panama was also known to the Spaniards, and orders went out from the Escorial telling the authorities in Santo Domingo, Havana, and Panama itself to ready and repair their defences. This, slowly but decisively, they did, but other Spanish activities were of altogether greater and more immediate concern.

A Spanish hit-and-run raid on the Cornish coast was an uncomfortable pinprick reminder of the dangers the country still faced, but altogether more serious was the intelligence that now reached London and told how Spain was mobilising an Armada stronger than that of 1588. Philip was still determined and, in his determination, revived old plans. Part of his force was to invade Ireland as a diversionary tactic. The rest was to sail against England in 1596. The news was of the utmost seriousness, and Elizabeth responded with her customary realism. A significant part of her Navy had been given over to Drake and Hawkins, whose long-drawn-out preparations seemed as incompetent as their professed aim of capturing Panama now seemed fantastic compared to the threat posed so suddenly to England itself. The hope of raiding Panama, she wrote 'may haply fail for nothing can be made so sure'. Indeed, the apparent dilatoriness of her commanders underlined the fact. 'Your own delays hath made your journey now so notorious (yea in particular to the Spaniard) as they have sufficient warning to provide for your descent.' The joint-stock venture Elizabeth had agreed to, and generously helped to fund, had suddenly and necessarily to become a vitally important element in the defence of the realm.

The old, disastrous problem had reared its head again.[5] On the one hand were the immediate strategic needs of the country and, on the other, the expectations of the private investors who wanted a handsome reward for the money and shipping they had already committed. The initial wildly ambitious plan that all parties had agreed to was now to be complicated and potentially undermined by an absolutely necessary reassessment of its initial purpose. Orders were sent down from London. Drake and Hawkins were now told that they were to sail first for the enemy coast to wreak what damage they could. After that they were to try and capture the *flota*, and only then sail to the West Indies if – and only if – they had already destroyed such Spanish ships as might be making for Ireland. In any case, the entire expedition was to be back in its home port by May ready to play its part in repelling the new Armada.

The immediate reaction to this order was anger and dismay. Drake and Hawkins wrote to the Queen pointing out with barely restrained impatience that the whole fleet would have to be entirely reorganised if it were to serve purposes for which it had not originally been intended, and making clear that she would have to pay for this. As for giving their promise that they would return by May, that they quite simply could not do. The situation was exasperating beyond belief, and Drake and Hawkins summoned up what aid they could to urge the Queen to change her mind even while they were readying themselves to fight her enemy. Essex, an old ally from the Lisbon days and still a favourite of Elizabeth's, was a supporter of theirs who had used his considerable influence to persuade a number of leading soldiers to join the expedition, and was now written to in the warmest terms. Would he please 'stand strongly for us that the whole charge may be borne by the Queen, else look we for nothing but the like discontentment or worse than that of the Portugal voyage'. A harassed Elizabeth, left with so little room for manoeuvre, conceded that operations on the Spanish coast and in the Atlantic might be waived, but under no circumstances whatsoever were Drake and Hawkins to delay their return beyond the middle of May.

The impasse was solved by a chance event that was to prove itself a disaster. News suddenly came in that a Spanish galleon of fabulous wealth had limped in, rudderless and mastless, at Puerto Rico where it might easily be captured. The money the Queen so desperately needed was lying helpless and waiting for her. Drake and Hawkins wrote begging that they be allowed to sail to Puerto Rico with all speed and enormously enrich themselves and the other investors with easy pickings before sailing on to Panama. This purpose was now reduced to the status of a suitable target for a hit-and-run exercise rather than the linchpin of a grand strategy. It was all overwhelmingly tempting and strategically ridiculous. To send out such a force as had now been assembled to cause a brief annoyance to the King of Spain in Panama made little sense while, to make known and divert such a fool's errand by going to Puerto Rico first was the height of absurdity. But greed and need were adding force to the momentum already built up by the expensive preparations Drake and Hawkins had made for their voyage and, on 28 August, a little over a fortnight before the Spaniards in the

Caribbean received orders to save their treasure ship at all costs, they set sail.

The Victorian and later historians, following in the footsteps of the pioneer Drake biographer Sir Julian Corbett, made much of their hero's being the founding father of the English naval tradition. Corbett, who had a deep and almost visceral response to the power of the Victorian Navy, presented an image of Drake as a statesman and strategist, faulted to be sure and warped by the execution of Doughty, but still a great leader and an upstanding Protestant gentleman. The Lisbon expedition and, even more, Drake's last voyage, show this to have been at best an overstatement and an oversimplification. What is so interesting about Corbett's image of Drake, however, are the circumstances that gave rise to it. His biography which he called *Drake and the Tudor Navy: with a History of the Rise of England as a Maritime Power* appeared in 1898.[6]

This was a decade when something close to panic gripped the nation with the prospect of the huge increase in German rearmament. The strength of the German navy was particularly feared. Popular journalists such as W.T. Stead of the *Pall Mall Gazette* thundered that 'our naval supremacy has almost ceased to exist' and demanded a rapid programme of rebuilding. 'Not only our imperial position but the bread of twenty millions out of thirty millions of our population depends entirely upon our dominance of the sea.' If that were lost, or even weakened then 'our existence is at stake'. Here was 'a cry of patriotic anxiety rising in the country to which no Ministry could close its ears'. A spate of novels imagined the effects of a German invasion, while Corbett's book turned to history for a reinvigorating image of national salvation. There was an enormous market for accounts of national heroes and world travellers whether contemporary or from the past. Much sentiment gathered round them and even Joseph Conrad, that most subtle analyst of imperialism, could write in *The Heart of Darkness* of those 'great knights-errant of the sea' like Drake who, with pristine integrity had set out to explore and colonise. 'Hunters for gold or pursuers of fame, they had all gone out on that stream, bearing the word, and often the torch, messengers of the might within the land, bearers of a spark of the sacred fire'. It was to this world that Corbett's biography appealed. Drake was for him the founding father of a navy which was a world force for moderation, peace with dignity and civilised values, and a national guarantee of independence from those with unlimited and unrestrained ambitions.

Such an image of Drake is hard to recognise today. It is to some degree true that his circumnavigation of the world in particular 'inflamed the whole country with a desire to adventure unto the seas', but that desire was motivated essentially by piracy and a drive to terrorise the enemy rather than the founding of a tradition of self-proclaimed noble imperialism. The Elizabethan Navy was in the hands of men who, like Drake, were schooled in oceanic plunder and worked with merchant adventurers who sought profit from their involvement. This was not a state navy. Nor could the state afford such a thing on a significant scale. A distinct, professional fighting force at sea quite simply did not exist as yet, and Drake's last voyage was to expose all too rawly the shortcomings of the system within which it operated and, above all, the dangerous room it gave for men of titanic ego to get their way in the absence of traditions of serving first and foremost the nation's well-being.

Something of this last difficulty was all too painfully obvious to the men who were now sailing with Drake and Hawkins, and there were those who were gravely worried by their different personalities. The two men had grown up in the same house, shared the same early ambitions, and sailed on the same early expeditions. Hawkins, at sixty-three, was ten years older than Drake, but the Drake who had dined off silver plates to the music of viols during his circumnavigation of the globe owed much to the Hawkins with whom he had sailed on slaving expeditions to Africa and who he had left (some said treacherously deserted) after the debacle at San Juan del Ulúa. It was the Spaniards' treachery there that – Drake made sure people knew – had fired his enmity for Spain, an enmity he shared with Hawkins and had exploited with the utmost skill as he began the swift and very public process by which he fashioned himself into the defining image of the Protestant national hero. Drake had much in common with Hawkins and owed him a great deal, but they were, in truth, men of a very different stamp.

The years Drake spent so conspicuously in the public eye – flamboyant, extrovert, self-publicising and self-enriching years that had helped galvanise the enthusiasms of a tiny nation in its war with a mighty empire – had been largely spent by the careful Hawkins in altogether different ways.[7] If the disaster at San Juan del Ulúa had been used by Drake for the wholly uninhibited and very public advancement of his own career, the incident had propelled Hawkins into the altogether more secluded back rooms of the Admiralty where he had spent much of his time thinking and planning. Intellectual, rigorous and orderly, his finely educated mind worked its way to the heart of a problem and solved it methodically. It was Hawkins who saw that the country's best defence against the Spaniards lay in naval combats that should be made largely to pay for themselves. He it was who saw that cutting off the Spaniards' supplies of treasure could be the principal means of immobilising their war-machine, and who knew not only that an efficient and relatively uncorrupt management of every aspect of the Navy was essential to this (a reform which he succeeded in carrying through), but that the new, fast and lethally armed ships he had helped design and which had proved their worth against the Armada were likewise essential to the nation's survival.

All of this was the work of a man, at once visionary but careful, whose subordinates held him in affection and respect. Such men knew that Hawkins was by temperament the polar opposite of Drake who, for all that they recognised 'his very name was a great terror to the enemy' knew that he was also 'self-willed and peremptory', and too often an overbearing bully. At his best Drake was an improviser of genius and at his worst a man so headstrong that he would listen to no man's opinion save his own. Thomas Maynard, one of the soldiers serving on the expedition, defined the difference between the two when he wrote of: 'a man old and wary entering into matters with so laden a foot that the other's meat would be eaten before his spit could come to the fire'. They were, he added, 'Men of so different natures and dispositions that what the one desireth the other would commonly oppose against.'

This was obvious six days out from port. The fractious

relationship between the two men kindled into a bad argument when Drake asked Hawkins to relieve him of some of his poorly victualled men. Hawkins sharply blamed Drake for bringing too many men with him and refused to offer any help 'unless he were entreated'. Bitter words ensued, their force widening the rift between them and, on Hawkins's part at least, deepening the regret he was beginning to feel for involving himself to the tune of £10,000 in an expedition whose confused strategies surely distressed his analytical mind. Matters could only get worse. The victualling problems that afflicted Drake's squadron were real, oppressive and dangerous. For all that Drake himself tried, in his usual manner, to ensure discipline and cohesion by commanding that divine service should be held twice a day, morale was clearly under threat. In Drake's view there was only one thing to be done. He had always seen vigorous action as the means of stirring up his men's spirits and the promise of money as a way of ensuring their loyalty.

A week after his first row with Hawkins, a second council was called at which Drake proposed that they attack either the Madeiras or Gran Canaria. Spoils and 'good refreshing' victuals would surely be available to them there. They would almost certainly have the advantage of surprise, and initial success would breed more success in the weeks to come. Hawkins, his mood now frosty and rigorous, tartly condemned the idea as a folly. 'First there could be no need considering our small time out; secondly not possible to carry it without hazarding all; and thirdly not good to lose time, which would never be recovered.' If Drake were really in dire need of provisions and water then Hawkins would let him have some of his own. The logic, the common sense, the rigidity of a man who had a plan and would stick by it were all, when reinforced by the simple and sensible offer to make the expedition's victuals go round more fairly, insupportable to Drake. Cool reasoning was always the way to heat his temper, and it is clear that he was so apoplectically angry at being denied his way that a threatened Hawkins too began to lose his self-control. In the vivid words of one of those watching the incident: 'now the fire which lay hid in their stomachs began to break forth'.[8]

Drake furiously declared that if he did not get what he wanted then he would go off on his own way with his own men. Hawkins would have to go to the Indies without him. The old man was perhaps too weak, or too shrewd, to allow such a disaster to happen. The fury that had destroyed Doughty and humiliated Knollys, Borough and others was now directed at him. Those present urged him to give way and, realising that he could not resist and that dividing the fleet was the worse of two evils, he agreed to sail with Drake and attack Gran Canaria. It was risky, it was time-wasting and, as Hawkins believed, ultimately unnecessary. But there was nothing he could do. As dawn broke on 26 September, the fleet arrived off Las Palmas.

Drake had got his way but now spoiled any advantage it might have given him. It was late in the season and, for all that the local authorities were aware of the English presence, they were not expecting an attack and were not prepared for it. The advantage could just have been Drake's. He let it slip. He wasted precious time reconnoitring the bay and placing buoys that would guide the assault force in when it was launched. This took all morning and gave the Spaniards time to shake off their surprise and man their defences. These were not particularly strong, and bureaucratic disagreements had prevented them from going ahead with recent plans to improve them, but by the time that fifteen of the English ships were approaching through surf altogether too furious to allow them to land safely, the troops in Las Palmas were ready with cannon and musket fire. An hour or two earlier and they would have been able to do little, but now it was the English who lost the initiative and wondered whether they really ought to risk the whole future of the expedition on such an exercise as this. Four of their men had already been shot by the time they decided to abandon the attempt and retreated to the west end of the island for water. Here some poorly armed shepherds managed to overcome some of them and take them prisoner.

The humiliation gave Hawkins the bitter satisfaction of knowing that he had been right. Time had been wasted, men lost, morale damaged, the whole expedition put in jeopardy – and now not even any provisions could be found beyond some water. But if Hawkins had been proved right he had himself, all unwittingly, exposed the expedition to far greater danger than had Drake. He had carelessly talked about its plans 'in the hearing of the basest mariners', some of whom had been captured while they were getting water. Now, as Hawkins and Drake sailed hastily and ignominiously away, so newly arrived Spanish reinforcements rounded up the men they had left behind and forced out of them all the information they needed. Warnings were sent to Puerto Rico and Spain. Eight Spanish galleons were readied for pursuit.

The only thing for the English to do was to sail on to the West Indies where, as they approached Guadeloupe, the straggling little *Francis* was captured by one of the frigates commanded by Don Pedro Tello de Guzman, who had now received his orders to sail out and salvage the battered Spanish galleon that was the English expedition's purposed prize. The English plans were rapidly revealed to Don Pedro, and when a second English bark that had witnessed the whole incident caught up with its main fleet, Drake and Hawkins realised that any hopes of surprise they had were dead. Struggle rather than any easy theft was now inevitable.

It was a rare example of tactful consideration on Drake's part that led to the next disaster. He was all for urging attack as their best means of defence, but Hawkins was against this. He argued, with reason, that the English fleet was not ready and Drake conceded the point to the now sickly old man 'being loath to breed his further disquiet'. The English spent the next ten days getting their guns up from below deck and mounting them. As Drake was to realise all too bitterly later on, this was time disastrously wasted. While the English were very slowly readying themselves for a fight, the Spaniards (who by now had a good idea of the size of the English expedition) were able to hurry off to Puerto Rico and warn the island of the approaching peril. The presence of the battered treasure ship was a great help in this: its Captain was an able and energetic man who brought with him not only a fabulous cargo, which it was clear must be protected, but the means to do more. He had sailed with men, artillery, and an adequate supply of munitions which was soon increased by supplies brought from Havana. The arrival of Pedro Tello de Guzman provided a further 300 men who were despatched to the main strategic points, while the empty treasure ship and a large merchant vessel were placed in the mouth of the harbour in front of their ships, to be sunk as the English approached.

This they now did in the clear morning light, making for a piece of the northern shore that was not strongly defended. Even here they hesitated, as Hawkins himself lay dying. The interval gave the Spaniards time to move up four large guns and take expert aim. One shot crashed through the cabin of the *Defiance* where Drake and his officers were eating. Two of them – Sir Nicholas Clifford and Brute Brown – were mortally wounded, while Drake's stool 'was struck from under him as he was drinking a cup of beer'. As Brown's life ebbed away on the deck of the smashed cabin, Drake looked at him and said, 'I could grieve for thee, but now is no time for me to let down my spirits.' Others were less resilient. In his cabin aboard the *Garland*, and as the terrible cannon fire continued to rain down, Hawkins's life was slipping away, his disease hastened by a broken heart. His hopes and life's work were in ruins, guilt and despair gnawed at him, and he begged a friend to see that the Queen would accept £2,000 from his estate to atone in some degree for the disastrous expedition which he had urged and that would now have to be led by the overbearing Drake.[9]

Drake was now the sole commander of a disintegrating expedition.[10] What was he to do? He moved his ships to a place of greater safety and called a council of war. It was decided that they would take the town by first entering the harbour and burning the ships anchored there. In the dead of night some twenty-five or thirty well-armed pinnaces and small boats sailed under the guns of the castle and engaged desperately with the enemy. Such courage was to no avail. Four of the frigates were indeed set alight but three of the crews managed to extinguish the flames, and the only ship where the conflagration really got hold served merely to illuminate the scene for the gunners in the fort, who bombarded the English boats so ruthlessly that, after an hour's struggle, they were forced to withdraw. The losses were relatively heavy, perhaps forty men on each side being killed, although the triumphant Spaniards later boasted that they had slain 200 English soldiers. The survivors were by now sharply disillusioned. The Spaniards were able to take further measures for their own defence, and Drake agreed with his Captains that a second attempt on the harbour would threaten the whole enterprise. It was necessary to stop morale from collapsing further and, in a gesture wholly typical of him, Drake airily boasted to his men that, 'I will bring thee to twenty places far more wealthy and easier to be gotten.'

This was untrue. Intelligence of Drake's activities moved swiftly round the Caribbean to Santo Domingo, Cartagena, Rio de la Hacha and, finally, to Panama which had once been their goal. Four days were spent on necessary repairs and in building additional pinnaces before Drake made for Rio de la Hacha, the little pearl-fishing settlement he had visited as long ago as 1568 and which, since it was small, he took easily and then ruthlessly plundered for such treasures as it contained. He rested his men for a week while negotiations for a ransom were conducted, the amount to be paid in pearls. These, when they arrived, were of far less value than the sum requested and Drake angrily rejected the offer, only to be told by the Governor that he had strung out the negotiations so long in order to delay the English while word of Drake's presence was spread. A furious Drake destroyed the town, the pearl fisheries, and some nearby villages. He then left. Three weeks had already been squandered in vindictive uselessness, and two more days were added to this when Drake moved against the little settlement at Santa Marta. This he sacked and then sailed away, but he knew now that it was impossible to fall on Cartagena since the Spaniards were fully aware of his presence and would doubtless have taken defensive measures against it. In desperation he resolved to make for the Isthmus of Panama.

He arrived first at Nombre de Dios. The town fell to him with little difficulty. The old man was now revisiting the scenes of the earliest expeditions he had commanded, the places where with the unsapped energy of youthful ambition, he had marched through the equatorial forests with an army of black warriors. Here, where the treasure trail wound its dreadful way, he and his white-shirted companions had pressed their ears to the ground in the hope of hearing the distant clatter of mule hooves as uncountable quantities of silver made their way to the coffers of the King of Spain. Here, with the vigour of a young man's invention, he had sailed his pinnaces down the Chagres River to sack, plunder, enrich himself and maim the might of the Catholic enemy. Here, too, he had once climbed a hill and seen at a glance the two greatest oceans of the world and begged God that he might one day be able to sail an English ship in the barely known Pacific. All that he had done and more – much more. He had learned to command men by daring more than they would, and by inspiring them, bullying them and never letting them glimpse a scintilla of doubt or weakness in his pitiless will. Here, he had begun to fashion himself through courage and calculation as the great Protestant and national hero which he had indeed become. He would allow nothing, not even the truth, to get in the way of that. There had been embarrassing defeats at Nombre de Dios but, back in Buckland Abbey, a pile of yellowing papers presented that defeat as something glorious, something of enduring if wholly imagined heroism, in which his men had gathered round their wounded Captain as they stared upon ingots of silver glittering in the candlelight that illuminated the treasury. If he had done all of this once, he could do it again. Drake summoned a council of war.

It was decided that one of his army officers, Thomas Baskerville, should lead a force of somewhere between 600 and 900 men across the mule track to Panama. He was to capture the city and then Drake was to bring up the rest of his forces in boats along the Chagres. Baskerville set out on his terrible march. It was the winter season and ill-shod and hungry men slipped and slogged their desperate way along the muddy and difficult road for two gruelling days until they reached the Capira pass. There the Spaniards were waiting for them. One of their more able officers, Alonso de Sotomayor, had discussed the defensive position with the Italian engineer who was responsible for fortifying the Spanish presence in the West Indies. This had been a thankless task made difficult by prevarication, rows over money and bureaucratic inertia. Nothing had been done to defend the Capira pass, but de Sotomayor saw at once its strategic importance and reinforced the place with more than a hundred soldiers and a hastily erected barrier of tree trunks. Baskerville waited for the dawn light before launching his attack.

The bloody struggle lasted for three hours, during which the Spanish soldiers welcomed reinforcements and obliged the English to retreat with heavy losses. All they could do now was return back along the dreadful road to Nombre de Dios exhausted, defeated, and numb with despair.

The mood was contagious and desperate. Drake was about to take his boats up the Chagres as agreed, but the return of Baskerville's men showed him that there was no point. The old resolution momentarily failed in him. Grief seized his heart. The once familiar landscape of his triumphs now appeared as a waste-land through which, it seemed, he could only wander in ignorance and aimlessness. 'He never thought any place could be so changed, as were from a delicious and pleasant arbour into a waste and desert wilderness.' And yet the old force was not quite spent. Men were to be led, the Queen was to be served, treasure was to be had for the asking, and the Protestant Lord would not desert him. Drake looked once again at the alien shore and found the words to express his resolve. 'It matters not, man, God hath many things in store for us, and I know many means to do Her Majesty good service and to make us rich, for we must have gold before we see England.'[11] This was the old Drake, the indomitable Drake, Drake whose nature it was to stretch his energy and genius to their limits and snatch triumph from defeat. He was refashioning himself in his old image to inspire both himself and his men alike. But the courage was a carapace and the words a lie. Defeat was written across his joyless face.

He gave orders to go on to Escudo Island for rest and refitting of the ships. But this was clutching at straws. Drake could no longer pit his titanic ego against the forces of despair. His reserves were wasted and now he was ill. As his fleet put out to sea with him for one last time, a ghastly and bloody dysentery sapped his remaining physical strength. He took to his cabin and lay in frail anguish on his bed as the *Defiance* made for Porto Bello. His officers visited him, and one of them chivied him about debts and his possessions even as Drake found just sufficient strength to dictate and sign a codicil to his will naming his brother Thomas as his heir and executor. Then, commending his soul to Christ and his body to the earth, Drake asked for his corpse to be entombed at the discretion of his executor. Drake tried to reconcile his brother to the wretched aide who had sought to bully him on his deathbed and, when the two men had shaken hands, Drake had himself dressed in his armour and took to his bed once again. Some time around 4.00 a.m. on 28 January 1596, he died. Baskerville had his body placed in a lead coffin and sailed the *Defiance* into the harbour at Porto Bello where, about a league out from the shore, Drake's coffin was let down into the sea, 'the trumpets in doleful manner echoing out this lamentation for so great a loss, and all the cannons in the fleet were discharged according to the custom of all sea funeral obsequies'.[12]

Epilogue

As the funeral music died away the silence was filled with acrimonious voices. What should the fleet do now? Where should it go? Two of the greatest Elizabethan sea-dogs had been lost – first Hawkins and then Drake – misfortunes which, added to the riven atmosphere of indecision and the abject failure of the voyage to achieve anything of note, showed that this was the low point in the sea war with Spain. The council of remaining Captains, aware of the ignominy and blame that would be heaped on them back home, met in a mood so tense and guarded that careful notes were made of their every comment, every suggestion. It was surely necessary for them to make some gesture of defiance towards an enemy that had so wholly outmanoeuvred them and exposed them to the perils attendant on their own headstrong way of going about things, Drake's especially. Never had his ego, his willpower and his defiance been more evident than on this last voyage. Never had his luck and genius so completely failed him.

Drake died with all that had made him great drained from his spirit, and his disillusion and hopelessness proved contagious to those he left behind. The fleet lingered off Porto Bello for a few days in the wan hope of extracting a ransom from the Spanish. But what could they do after that? They talked – talked at great length – each hour and each man's opinion corroding that impulse to decisive action which had always been Drake's response to a setback. Perhaps they should go on to Santa Marta, always assuming that was not too difficult. From there they could sail to Jamaica and revictual, and then – it was the last, desperate reach of shared fantasy – they could perhaps make a raid on Honduras. The contingency plan showed the true tendency of their spirits. If their dreams failed, the Captains decided, they would return to England. This was what happened, but even their journey home was a wretched matter. Scattered after an inconclusive encounter with a small Spanish fleet, each of the Captains made his excuse to chart his own way back. By the time the ships reached port, discipline had so collapsed that the little booty taken on the voyage had been stolen by the men. Drake's lifelong aim of strangling the Spaniards' treasure supply had dwindled to the miserable reality of mutinous petty theft.

The Spaniards, by contrast, were exultant. When the news of Drake's death was heard, Seville was illuminated. Philip II was said to have shown more pleasure at hearing of his great enemy's loss than he had at any time since the massacre of Saint Bartholomew's Day. This was a Catholic triumph, and the poet Lope de Vega was to write an epic poem, *La Dragontea*, which suggested that with Drake's defeat the true Church was finally vindicated.

Such jubilation was misplaced for, even in death, Drake had been able to inflict long-term damage on the Spanish even if he himself was unaware of it.[1] So terrible was Drake's name that the mere knowledge of his presence in the Caribbean had caused the Spaniards to assemble a formidable navy to sail in pursuit of him. It failed in this task, but its numbers had been made up from ships intended to escort the *flota* which was obliged to remain defenceless in Cadiz and so become an easy prey for the joint English and Dutch fleet that swooped down on it in July, 1596. As a result of this, communications between Spain and its American treasure store were so badly damaged that, the following year, the Spanish Crown was obliged to declare itself bankrupt. It was as though Drake's ghost had had its revenge and brought to a final crisis that persistent, exhausting attrition seen earlier in his own raid on Cadiz and the part he had played in the defeat of the Spanish Armada. Partly as a result of these events Spain, for all its power, saw its influence and commercial advantage gradually but irreparably contract as its resources of men, money and ships dwindled. Imperial Spain was exhausting itself in the effort to stem its terminal decline and, as a consequence, the development of North America especially fell largely to Protestant and English-speaking powers.

The international situation was changing and events in England helped in this. With the death of Elizabeth and the accession of the peace-loving James I, it appeared that the sea war with declining Spain was no longer worth fighting and a treaty was signed between the two powers in 1604. Memories of Drake, meanwhile, began passing into national legend and were shaped to fit the aspirations of the burgeoning British Empire. Drake was seen (often rather too simply) as one of its founders and it was believed that he would remain one of its protectors: a perpetually vitalising spirit. Early in December 1895, Sir Henry Newbolt completed a poem in which he imagined Drake's ghost rising from its coffin in the waters off Porto Bello and addressing his Victorian fellow countrymen. They were not to worry about their destiny. For all the build-up of foreign powers around them (Newbolt was referring principally to the Germans and the ambitions of the Kaiser), the English had a great tradition of achievement at sea on which they could draw – a tradition personified by Drake himself whose ghost now gave his orders, as was appropriate for a naval officer, in a voice that was loud and clear:

> Take my drum to England, hang et by the shore,
>   Strike et when your powder's runnin' low;
> If the Dons sight Devon, I'll quit the port o' Heaven,
>   An' drum them up the Channel as we drummed them
>   long ago.

This once famous poem and the ethos it speaks for have also passed into history but, even in a post-Imperial age, the figure of Drake continues to exercise an extraordinary power. It has never quite been possible to let him go. Even as recently as 2002, plans were afoot to locate his body in the Caribbean depths and perhaps even raise it and bring it back to England. The fascination of Drake remains and will doubtless continue to play its part in a world increasingly riven by the problems of aggressive national identity, state-sponsored terrorism and religious hatred – the forces among which, four centuries ago, Drake himself began to fashion his abiding image.

Notes

Prologue

1. For details of the 1567 voyage see 'The Troublesome Voyage' in Hackluyt, *Principal Voyages*, X, pp. 64–74 and Wright, *Caribbean Voyages, 1527–1568*, pp. 115–62.
2. For Philip II and the governance of the Spanish Empire see Parker, *Grand Strategy, passim.*
3. Technical matters concerning storms at sea are illuminatingly discussed in Scammell, 'European Seamanship in the Great Age of Discovery', *Mariner's Mirror*, 68 (1982), pp. 357–74.

1: On the Margins

1. Drake's parentage and boyhood are discussed in Kelsey, *The Queen's Pirate*, pp. 1–13 and 401–17.
2. European discovery of the Atlantic trade routes is discussed in Fernandez-Armesto, *Civilisations*, pp. 481–91.
3. Discussions of the daily lives of Elizabethan sailors can be found in Dyer, 'The Elizabethan Sailorman', *Mariner's Mirror*, x (1924), *passim* and Lloyd, *The British Seaman*, pp. 25–45.
4. Elizabethan navigation is comprehensively discussed in Waters, *The Art of Navigation, passim.*
5. For the Elizabethans in Africa see Hair, 'Protestants as Pirates, Slavers and Proto-Missionaries: Sierra Leone, 1568–1582', *Journal of Ecclesiastical History*, 21 (1970), *passim.*
6. The Caribbean trade is fully discussed in Andrews, *The Spanish*

Caribbean: Trade and Plunder, 1530–1630, passim.

7. Lovell's expedition is documented in Wright, *English Voyages to the Caribbean, 1527–1568*, pp. 95–112.
8. See Kelsey, *The Queen's Pirate*, pp. 21ff.
9. See Hair, *loc. cit.*
10. *ibid.*
11. Spanish notions of imperial identity are discussed in Parker, *Grand Strategy*, pp. 11–45 and Pagden, *Lords of All the World*, pp. 37–46.

2: The Caribbean Pirate

1. Drake's first marriage is discussed in Kelsey, *The Queen's Pirate*, p. 44.
2. The forms of Elizabethan anti-Spanish and anti-Catholic sentiment are discussed in Maltby, *The Black Legend, passim.*
3. For Philip II and the Ridolfi plot see Parker, *Grand Strategy*, pp. 160–63.
4. See Fuller, *The Holy State*, pp. 132–141.
5. For these two early expeditions see Kelsey, *The Queen's Pirate*, pp. 45ff.
6. The principal contemporary source for the expedition is Nichols, *Sir Francis Drake Revived*, 1628, reprinted in Hampden, ed., *Francis Drake: Privateer*, pp. 53–104.
7. *ibid*, pp. 58–62.
8. *ibid*, p. 49 for a reproduction of the frontispiece.
9. *ibid*, pp. 66ff.
10. *ibid*, pp. 81-100.
11. *ibid*, p. 85.
12. *ibid*, pp. 96–102.
13. *ibid*, p. 89.
14. *ibid*, p. 104.

3: The Circumnavigation of the Globe, One: Preparations

1. For the matter of John Drake's will see Kelsey, *The Queen's Pirate*, pp. 64–66 and 415–17.
2. The Irish campaign in which Drake took part is discussed in 'Reduction of Rathlin in 1575', *Notes and Queries*, Third Series,

5 (January 1864), *passim*.

3. For Thomas Doughty's early career see above and Kelsey, *The Queen's Pirate*, pp. 74ff.

4. The principal contemporary and near-contemporary documents for the circumnavigation are gathered in Vaux, *The World Encompassed by Sir Francis Drake, passim*; hereafter cited as Vaux. For Drake's defence of his reputation see John Cooke's narrative in Vaux, pp. 215ff.

5. The background to the planning of the circumnavigation is discussed in Andrews's, 'The Aims of Drake's Expedition of 1577–1580', *American Historical Review*, 73 (1968), pp. 724–41; 'Beyond the Equinoctial: England and South America in the Sixteenth Century', *Journal of Imperial and Commonwealth History*, 10 (1981), pp. 4–24; 'On the Way to Peru: Elizabethan Ambitions in America South of Capricorn', *Terrae Incognitae*, 14 (1982), pp. 61–75.

6. For political responses to the international situation see Wernham, 'Elizabethan War Aims and Strategy', *Elizabethan Government and Society, passim* and Parker, *Grand Strategy*, pp. 164–67.

7. The text reconstructed by Taylor is reprinted in Andrews, 'The Aims of Drake's Expedition of 1577–1580', p.734.

8. See Kelsey, *The Queen's Pirate*, p. 81f.

9. For the prerogatives of gentleman status see Coward, *Social Change and Continuity*, pp. 3–4, 41–2 and 104–5.

10. For the *Pelican-Golden Hind* see Kelsey, *The Queen's Pirate*, pp. 82–84.

4: The Circumnavigation of the Globe, Two: The Voyage Out

1. For the first stage of the circumnavigation see Vaux, pp. 7ff.

2. See *ibid* pp. 13ff.

3. See Fletcher's narrative, *ibid*, pp. 13ff.

4. Da Silva's account of the circumnavigation is given in *ibid*, pp. 254–268.

5. The incident is recounted in *ibid*, pp. 191ff.

6. See Samuel Johnson's *Life of Sir Francis Drake, passim*.

7. Fletcher's account is given in Vaux, pp. 27–31.

8. See John Cooke's narrative in *ibid*, pp. 27–31.
9. For the Argentine *pampero* see Wagner, *Drake's Voyage Around the World*, pp. 53ff.
10. For Doughty and Chester see Vaux, pp. 196ff.
11. For the Patagonians see *ibid*, pp. 58ff.

5: The Circumnavigation of the Globe, Three: The Middle Passage

1. For the events at Port Saint Julian see Vaux, pp. 56ff.
2. The Doughty trial is recorded in *ibid*, pp. 165–174 and 201ff.
3. *ibid*, p. 231.
4. For the literature of Victorian imperialism see Bratlinger, *Rule of Darkness*, Eby, *The Road to Armageddon* and MacKenzie, *Propaganda and Empire*, *passim*.
5. Henty, *Under Drake's Flag*, p. 72.
6. For Drake's rounding the Strait of Magellan see Vaux, pp. 279ff.
7. For Mendoza see Kelsey, *The Queen's Pirate*, pp. 207ff.
8. See Vaux, pp. 238ff.
9. Careening is discussed in Scammell, 'European Seamanship in the Great Age of Discovery', *loc. cit.*, pp. 360ff.
10. Developments in Elizabethan shipping are discussed in Roger, 'Guns and Sails in the First Phase of English Colonisation', *passim*.
11. These events are discussed in Vaux, pp. 107ff and 240ff.
12. See *ibid*, pp. 108ff.
13. See Nutall, *New Light on Drake*, pp. 155–79 and Wagner, *Drake's Voyage Around the World*, p. 361.

6: The Circumnavigation of the Globe, Four: The Voyage Home

1. For Drake's options at this point in the circumnavigation see Andrews, *Trade, Plunder and Settlement*, pp. 155ff.
2. For Colchero see Kelsey, *The Queen's Pirate*, pp. 164ff.
3. For Zárate see Nutall, *New Light on Drake*, p. 108ff.
4. See Vaux, p. 113f.
5. Kelsey admirably outlines the conflicting theories in *The Queen's Pirate*, pp. 174ff.
6. See Vaux, pp. 115ff.
7. *ibid*, p. 132.

8. Events in Ternate are given in Vaux, pp. 137ff.
9. *ibid*, pp. 150ff.
10. *ibid*, pp. 158ff.
11. Nutall, *New Light on Drake*, pp. 211ff.
12. For Drake's return to Plymouth see Kelsey, *The Queen's Pirate*, pp. 204ff.
13. For the international situation see Parker, *The Grand Strategy*, pp. 164ff.
14. See Paul Johnson, *Elizabeth I*, pp. 257ff.

7: The Great Caribbean Raid, 1585–1586

1. For Buckland Abbey see Kelsey, *The Queen's Pirate*, pp. 219–22.
2. *ibid*, pp. 222-25.
3. *ibid*, p. 238.
4. For these evangelical initiatives see Hutton, *The Rise and Fall of Merry England*, pp. 123-32.
5. For Dom Antonio see Parker, *The Grand Strategy*, p. 167.
6. For the international situation see *ibid*, pp. 168ff.
7. Contemporary materials for the Caribbean raid are gathered in Keeler (ed), *Sir Francis Drake's West Indian Voyage*, *passim*; hereafter cited as Keeler.
8. For Sideney see Howell, 'The Sidney Circle and the Protestant Cause in Elizabethan Foreign Policy', *Renaissance and Modern Studies*, 19 (1975), *passim*.
9. See Keeler, pp. 78–89.
10. Philip's response to Drake's activities is explored in Martin and Parker, *The Spanish Armada*, pp. 79ff and 89–91.
11. See Keeler, pp. 126ff.
12. *ibid*, especially pp. 238–47.
13. Greepe, *True and Perfect News*, Biii.
14. The lines from Castellanos are quoted in Wright, *Further English Voyages*, p. xi. For Castellanos generally see Jameson, 'Some New Spanish Documents Dealing with Drake', *English Historical Review*, xlix (1934), pp. 14–23 and Jenner, 'A Spanish Account of Drake's Voyages', *ibid*, xvi (1901), pp. 46–62.
15. Greepe, *True and Perfect News*, Cii.
16. *ibid*, Aiiii.

17. See Keeler, especially pp. 160-79 and 247-62.
18. For Philip's response see Martin and Parker, *The Spanish Armada*, pp. 90ff.
19. For Drake and the Roanoke colony see Quinn, *The Roanoke Voyages*, I, pp. 244-55.

8: Cadiz, 1587

1. For the Babington plot see Paul Johnson, *Elizabeth I*, pp. 283-6.
2. For these developments in Philip's strategy see Martin and Parker, *The Spanish Armada*, pp. 93ff.
3. Drake's letters and other documents concerning the Cadiz raid are gathered in Corbett, *The Spanish War*, pp. 97ff; hereafter cited as Corbett. For a modern account of the Cadiz raid see Martin and Parker, *The Spanish Armada*, pp. 40–1, 108–11 and 114–17.
4. Borough's affidavit justifying his actions is given in Corbett, pp. 168ff.
5. Leng's account is reprinted in Hopper (ed), *Sir Francis Drake's Memorable Service*, pp. 11–23; hereafter cited as Hopper.
6. For these accounts see *ibid*, pp. 35ff.
7. See Corbett, pp. 123–30.
8. *ibid*.
9. These developments are discussed in Martin and Parker, *The Spanish Armada*, pp. 34ff and Padfield, *Maritime Supremacy*, pp. 24–6.
10. See Hopper, p. 44.
11. Martin and Parker, *The Spanish Armada*, p. 111.

9: The Defeat of the Spanish Armada, 1588

1. Philip's revisions to plans for the Armada are discussed in Martin and Parker, *The Spanish Armada*, chapters 6 and 8, *passim*. I am indebted to this excellent study.
2. English preparations for the Armada are discussed in Kelsey, *The Queen's Pirate*, pp. 308ff.
3. See Martin and Parker, *The Spanish Armada*, pp. 119ff.
4. See Kelsey, *The Queen's Pirate*, pp. 311ff.
5. Quoted in *ibid*, p. 314.

6. For the sailing of the Armada see Martin and Parker, *The Spanish Armada*, pp. 139ff.

7. The sources for the game of bowls are discussed in Bracken, *History of Plymouth*, pp. 92ff.

8. The opening of the struggle is described in Martin and Parker, *The Spanish Armada*, pp. 146ff.

9. The strategic value of Drake's capture of the *Rosario* is admirably discussed in *ibid*, pp. 152ff.

10. See *ibid*, pp. 153ff.

11. See *ibid*, pp. 173ff.

12. For Frobisher's response to Drake's behaviour see McDermott, *Martin Frobisher*, pp. 364ff.

10: The Lisbon Expedition, 1589

1. The English aftermath of the Armada is described in Martin and Parker, *The Spanish Armada*, pp. 263ff and Wernham, *After the Armada*, pp. 5ff.

2. Drake, Norris and the background to the Lisbon fiasco is admirably documented in Wernham, 'Queen Elizabeth and the Portugal Expedition of 1589', *English Historical Review*, lxvi (1951), 1–26 and 194–218. These groundbreaking articles were subsequently reworked into the opening chapters of Wernham's *After the Armada*. For Drake and Norris's early involvement in the plan see *ibid*, pp. 17ff.

3. For Drake's life in London at this time see Kelsey, *The Queen's Pirate*, pp. 345ff.

4. For the Dutch involvement see Wernham, *After the Armada*, Chapter 2, *passim*.

5. For Essex see *ibid*, pp. 100ff.

6. The situation at Coruna is described in Wernham, 'Queen Elizabeth and the Portugal Expedition of 1589', *loc. cit.*, pp. 204ff.

7. The raid on Lisbon itself is discussed in *ibid*, pp. 205ff.

8. Anthony Wingfield quoted in *ibid*, p. 214.

11: Defeat and Death, 1596

1. The background to the preparation of *The World Encompassed*

is discussed in Quinn 'Early Accounts of the Famous Voyage' in Thrower, (ed)., *Sir Francis Drake and the Famous Voyage*, pp. 33–48.

2. For Drake's activities during this period see Kelsey, *The Queen's Pirate*, pp. 370ff.

3. See Andrews, *Trade, Plunder and Settlement*, Chapter 11, *passim*.

4. The contemporary materials are gathered in Andrews, (ed) *The Last Voyage of Drake and Hawkins*.

5. See p.277 especially.

6. For Corbett see Schurman, *The Education of a Navy* and *Julian S. Corbett, 1854–1922: Historian of British Maritime Policy from Drake to Jellicoe*.

7. For Hawkins's career see Williamson, *Hawkins of Plymouth*, *passim*.

8. See Kelsey, *The Queen's Pirate*, pp. 379ff.

9. See Williams, *The Sea Dogs*, p. 216.

10. See Kelsey, *The Queen's Pirate*, pp. 385ff.

11. Quoted in *ibid*, p. 388.

12. *ibid*, p. 391.

Epilogue

1. For these effects see Parry, *The Spanish Seaborne Empire*, pp. 256ff.

Bibliography

Andrews, Kenneth R., 'The Aims of Drake's Expedition of 1577–1580', *American Historical Review*, 73 (February 1968), 724–41.

—— 'Beyond the Equinoctial: England and South America in the Sixteenth Century', *Journal of Imperial and Commonwealth History* 10 (1981), 4–24.

—— *Drake's Voyages: A Reassessment of their Place in Elizabethan Maritime Expansion*, Weidenfeld and Nicholson, 1967.

—— *Elizabethan Privateering: English Privateering During the Spanish War, 1585–1603*, Cambridge University Press, 1964.

—— 'The Elizabethan Seaman', *Mariner's Mirror*, lxviii (1982), 245–62.

—— 'On the Way to Peru: Elizabethan Ambitions in America South of Capricorn', *Terrae Incognitae*, 14 (1982), 61–75.

—— 'Sailors and the Sea', in Nichol, A. ed., *Shakespeare in his Own Age*, Cambridge University Press, 1964, 21–36.

—— *The Spanish Caribbean: Trade and Plunder, 1530–1630*, Yale University Press, 1978.

—— *Trade, Plunder and Settlement: Maritime Enterprise and the Genesis of the British Empire, 1480–1630*, Cambridge University Press, 1984.

——ed. *The Last Voyage of Drake and Hawkins*, Hakluyt Society, 1972.

Aubert, Vilhelm and Oddvar Arner, 'On the Social Structure of the Ship', *Acta Sociologica* 3 (1958), 200–219.

322

Blake, John W., *European Beginnings in West Africa, 1454–1578* (1937), rev. ed., *West Africa: Quest for God and Gold, 1454–1578*, 1977.

Bracken, C. W., *A History of Plymouth and her Neighbours*, Plymouth, 1931.

Bratlinger, Patrick, *Rule of Darkness: British Literature and Imperialism, 1830–1914*, Ithaca, 1988.

Brooks, Eric St John, *Sir Christopher Hatton: Queen Elizabeth's Favourite*, Jonathan Cape, 1946.

Canny, Nicholas P., *The Elizabethan Conquest of Ireland: A Pattern Established 1565-76*, Harvester Press, 1976.

—— ed. *The Origins of Empire: British Overseas Enterprise to the Close of the Seventeenth Century*, The Oxford History of the British Empire, vol. I, Oxford University Press, 1998.

Clulee, Nicholas H., *John Dee's Natural Philosophy: Between Science and Religion*, Routledge, 1988.

Corbett, Julian S., *Drake and the Tudor Navy*, 2 vols., 2nd edn., 1899.

—— *The Successors of Drake*, 1900.

—— ed. *Papers Relating to the Navy during the Spanish War, 1585–1587*, Navy Records Society, 1898.

Coward, Barry, *Social Change and Continuity in Early Modern England, 1550–1750*, Longmans, 1988.

Cumming, Alex A., *Sir Francis Drake and the Golden Hinde*, Jerrold and Sons, 1987.

Dyer, Florence E., 'The Elizabethan Sailorman', *Mariner's Mirror*, x (1924), 133–46.

Eby, Cecil D., *The Road to Armageddon: The Martial Spirit in English Popular Literature, 1870–1914*, Durham, 1987.

Fernandez-Armesto, Felipe, *Civilisations*, Macmillan, 2000.

Fuller, Thomas, *The Holy State and the Profane State*, 1642.

Greenblatt, Stephen, *Renaissance Self-Fashioning from More to Shakespeare*, University of Chicago Press, 1980.

Greepe, Thomas, *The True and Perfect News of the Worthy and Valiant Exploits, Performed and Done by that Valiant Knight Sir Francis Drake 1587*; facsimilie ed., by David Watkin Walters, Hartford, 1955.

Gwynn, David, 'John Dee's *Art of Navigation*', *The Book Collector*, 34 (1985), 3 –22.

Hair, P.E.H., 'Protestants as Pirates, Slavers, and Proto-Missionaries: Sierra Leone 1568–1582', *Journal of Ecclesiastical History*, xxi, no. 3 (July, 1970), 203–224.

Hakluyt, R. ed., *The Principal Navigations, Voyages, Traffics and Discoveries of the English Nation*, 12 vols, Glasgow, 1903–05.

Hampden, John, *Francis Drake, Privateer: Contemporary Narratives and Documents,* Eyre and Methuen, 1972.

Haslop, H., *News out of the Coast of Spain*, 1587.

Hayes-McCoy, G. A., 'The Completion of the Tudor Conquest and the Advance of the Counter-Reformation, 1571–1603', in T. W. Moody, F. X. Martin and F. J. Byrne eds., *Early Modern Ireland, A New History of Ireland* vol. 3, Clarendon Press, 1991.

Henty, G. A., *Under Drake's Flag*, 1891.

Hopper, C., ed., *Sir Francis Drake's Memorable Service . . . By Robert Leng*, Camden Miscellany, v, 1863.

Howell, Jr., Roger, 'The Sidney Circle and the Protestant Cause in Elizabethan Foreign Policy', *Renaissance and Modern Studies*, 19 (1975), 31–46.

Hutton, Ronald, *The Rise and Fall of Merry England: The Ritual Year 1400–1700*, Oxford University Press, 1984.

Jameson, A. K., 'Some New Spanish Documents dealing with Drake', *English Historical Review*, xlix (1934), 14–31.

Jenner, G., 'A Spanish Account of Drake's Voyages', *English Historical Review*, xvi (1901), 46–66.

Johnson, Paul, *Elizabeth I: A Study in Power and Intellect*, Weidenfeld and Nicolson, 1974.

Johnson, Samuel, *The Life of Mr Richard Savage, the fourth edition, to which are added the Lives of Sir Francis Drake and Admiral Blake*, London, 1749.

Keeler, Mary Freared., *Sir Francis Drake's West Indian Voyage*, Hakluyt Society, series 2, vol. 148, 1981.

Kelsey, Harry, *Sir Francis Drake: The Queen's Pirate*, Yale University Press, 1998.

Keynes, J. M., *A Treatise on Money*, Macmillan, 1930.

Lloyd, Christopher, *The British Seaman, 1200–1860: A Social Survey*, Paladin, 1970.

MacCaffrey, W.T, *Queen Elizabeth and the Making of Policy,*

1572–1588, Princeton University Press, 1981.

MacKenzie, John M., *Propaganda and Empire: The Manipulation of British Public Opinion, 1880–1960*, Manchester University Press, 1984.

Maltby, W. S., *The Black Legend in England: The Development of Anti-Spanish Sentiment, 1558–1660*, xxx, 1968.

Martin, Colin and Geoffrey Parker, *The Spanish Armada*, rev. Ed. Manchester, Mandolin, 1999.

McDermott, James, *Martin Frobisher: Elizabethan Privateer*, Yale University Press, 2001.

Naish, F. C. Prideaux, 'The Mystery of the Tonnage and Dimensions of the Pelican-Golden Hind', *Mariner's Mirror*, xxxiv (January 1948), 42–45.

Nuttall, Zelia, ed., *New Light on Drake: A Collection of Documents Relating to his Voyage of Circumnavigation, 1577–1580*, Hakluyt Society, series 2, vol. 34, 1914.

Padfield, Peter, *Maritime Supremacy and the Opening of the Western Mind: Naval Campaigns that Shaped the Modern World, 1588–1782*, John Murray, 1999.

Pagden, Anthony, *Lords of All the World: Ideologies of Empire in Spain, Britain and France, c. 1500–c. 1800*, Yale University Press, 1995.

Parker, Geoffrey, *The Grand Strategy of Philip II*, Yale University Press, 1998.

Parry, J. H., *The Age of Reconnaisance: Discovery, Exploration and Settlement 1450–1650*, University of California Press, 1963.

—— *The Discovery of the Sea*, University of California Press, 1974.

—— *The Spanish Seaborne Empire*, University of California Press, 1966.

Penzer, N.M. ed., *The World Encompassed and Analagous Contemporary Documents Concerning Sir Francis Drake's Circumnavigation of the World*, Nico Israel, 1971.

Quinn, David B., *Drake's Circumnavigation of the Globe: A Review*, Fifteenth Harte Lecture, delivered in the University of Exeter on 14 November, 1980, University of Exeter, 1981.

—— 'Early Accounts of the Famous Voyage' in *Sir Francis Drake and the Famous Voyage 1577–1580*, ed., Norman J. W. Thrower,

33–48, University of California Press, 1984.

—— *The Roanoke Voyages, 1584–1590: Documents to Illustrate the English Voyages to North America under the Patent Granted to Walter Raleigh in 1584*, 2 vols, Hakluyt Society, London, 1955.

—— *Sir Francis Drake as Seen by his Contemporaries*, John Carter Brown Library, 1996.

Read, C., *Mr Secretary Walsingham and the Policy of Queen Elizabeth*, 3 vols, Oxford, Clarendon Press, 1925.

'Reduction of Rathlin in 1575', *Notes and Queries*, Third Series, 5 (5 January 1864), 89–92. [anon article]

Roger, N.A.M., 'Guns and Sails in the First Phase of English Colonisation', in *The Oxford History of the British Empire*, vol. I, Nicholas Canny, ed., *The Origins of Empire: British Overseas Enterprise to the Close of the Seventeenth Century*, pp. 79–98.

Scammell, G.V., 'European Seamanship in the Great Age of Discovery', *Mariner's Mirror*, lxviii (1982), 357–76.

—— 'Manning the English Merchant Service in the Sixteenth Century', *Mariner's Mirror*, lvi (1970), 131–54.

Schurman, D. M., *The Education of a Navy: The Development of British Naval Strategic Thought, 1867–1914*, University of Chicago Press, 1965.

—— *Julian S. Corbett, 1854–1922: Historian of British Maritime Policy from Drake to Jellicoe,* London, Royal Historical Society, 1981.

Taylor, E.G.R., 'Master John Dee, Drake and the Straights of Anian', *Mariner's Mirror*, xv (1929), 125–30.

—— *Tudor Geography, 1485–1583*, Methuen, 1930.

Temple, Richard C., 'An Appreciation of Drake's Achievement' in N.M. Penzer ed., *The World Encompassed and Analogous Contemporary Documents Concerning Sir Francis Drake's Circumnavigation of the World*, Nico Israel, 1971.

Thrower, Norman J. W., *Sir Francis Drake and the Famous Voyage, 1577–1580*, University of California Press, 1984.

Vaux, W. S. W., ed., *The World Encompassed by Sir Francis Drake, Being his Next Voyage to that to Nombre de Dios, Collated with an Unpublished Manuscript of Francis Fletcher, Chaplain to the Expedition*, Hackluyt Society, series I, vol. 16, 1854.

Wagner, Henry R., *Sir Francis Drake's Voyage Around the World: Its Aims and Achievements*, John Howell, 1926.

Waters, David W., *The Art of Navigation in England in Tudor and Early Stuart Times*, 2nd ed., National Maritime Museum, 1958.

Wernham, R. B., *After the Armada: Elizabethan England and the Struggle for Western Europe, 1588-1595*, Oxford University Press, 1984.

—— 'Elizabethan War Aims and Strategy' in Bindoff, S.T., J. Hurstfield and C.H. Williams, eds., *Elizabethan Government and Society*, OUP, 1961, 340–68.

—— 'Queen Elizabeth and the Portugal Expedition of 1589', *English Historical Review*, lxvi (1951), 1–26 and 194–218.

—— *The Return of the Armadas: The Last Years of the Elizabethan War Against Spain, 1595–1603*, Oxford University Press, 1994.

Williams, Neville, *The Sea Dogs: Privateers, Plunder and Piracy in the Elizabethan Age*, Weidenfeld and Nicholson, 1975.

Williamson, James A., *Hawkins of Plymouth: A New History of Sir John Hawkins and of the Other Members of his Family Prominent in Tudor England*, 2nd ed. Adam and Charles Black, 1969.

Wright, Irene A., ed., *Spanish Documents Concerning English Voyages to the Caribbean, 1527–1568*, Hakluyt Society, series 2, vol. dxii, 1929.

—— *Further English Voyages to Spanish America*, Hakluyt Society, series 2, vol. 99, 1951.

Index

Nature Lessons

Lynette Brasfield

St. Martin's Press ⚓ New York

www.stmartins.com

ISBN 0-312-31034-X

First Edition: May 2003

10 9 8 7 6 5 4 3 2 1

To my sister Sally

Nature Lessons

Chagrin Falls, Ohio
October 1995

A cool breeze carried the smell of fall's first fires into our half-packed living room, setting motes tumbling in a late-afternoon shaft of sunlight. Elbows on my knees and chin on my fists, I sat on a cardboard box and stared at my mother's unopened letter, which I'd propped against my stone warthog's back right leg. A South African stamp had been stuck upside down on one corner of the envelope.

I knew my mother's letter would bring news of enemies: her letters always did.

Beneath me, the box began to crumple, inch by slow inch. Like my life, I thought. Perhaps I'd slip gradually off the edge and dissolve into a puddle of unhappiness on the hardwood floor. In time, I'd evaporate upward, leaving only my clothes behind. When my ex-fiancé Simon arrived on Monday to pick up the last of his things, he'd find my empty Levis, red sweater, and scuffed tennis shoes huddled within a Stonehenge of packing crates and wardrobe boxes.

I'd have disappeared into another dimension.

In Africa, where I'd been born, people believed such things could happen. When I was a child, our family's Zulu maid, Prudence, had told many stories of magic and metamorphosis: of shape-shifting snakes, and dwarfish zombies called *tokoloshes,* and mysterious middle-of-the-night vanishings. She had faith in a world within our world—one teeming with ancestral spirits who debated the wisdom of intervening in family squabbles, played tricks on humans to alleviate the boredom of eternity, and appeared in dreams once in a while to offer advice to their earthbound progeny.

I listened, now, but heard only my neighbor scraping leaves from his gutter and a cardinal whistling in a tree. Were ancestors patriotic? Had they ridden the trade winds home when, five years before, I'd sworn the Oath of Allegiance and become an American citizen? Or left in a huff when I said *barbecue* instead of *braai* and watched baseball, not cricket?

A magenta leaf parachuted into the room, skidded across the floor, and came to rest next to the envelope.

I bent forward to pick up the letter, remembering what Prudence had told me: without descendants, ancestors could no longer inhabit the spirit world. Forty, unmarried, and childless in Chagrin Falls, I was endangering their continued existence. I had no brothers or sisters to make up for my inattention to procreation as I careened through short-term relationships: Gareth the violinist in New York, Ned the editor in Houston, Danny the carpet-cleaning entrepreneur in St. Louis, and Tran the computer programmer in Seattle. Not to mention the fiancés who'd book-ended the eighties—Terry the accountant and Eduardo the chef. And now Simon the cardiac surgeon, my third fiancé, who'd lasted nearly a year, and had been gone a month.

The Three Fiancés. It sounded like a bad movie. Or a singing trio.

Layers of transparent tape—topped with a red geranium of wax—sealed the envelope. I stood and headed to the study, where a clock, supine on the floor, told the ceiling it was three thirty. A beret-wearing skeleton named Mortimer slouched next to the gold first-place trophy I'd won for my podiatrist-promoting *Do Bunions Make You Cry?* ad campaign. On the desk, Simon's plaster-of-paris viperfish grinned at my clay hyena.

Our combined household had looked more like a fish-and-fauna store than a traditional home. Which had pleased us both. We were globally compatible.

I tilted the French shutters and gazed outside. From the same vantage point, five weeks before, on a late-September Saturday, I'd watched Simon greet his ex-wife Cilla as she dropped off Tess, their four-year-old daughter. Simon was a large, rumpled, good-looking man with hazel eyes, dark hair, and eyebrows like caterpillars. Cilla was tall and pale and once again slender, though she'd had a baby less than a month earlier. She wafted rather than walked. I was in a thin phase, but irrevocably short, freckled, and sandy-haired.

He'd touched Cilla's blue-black hair briefly—fondly—and she smiled up at him. Tess stood between them, dressed in a denim pinafore as triangular as a paper doll's. Father, mother, daughter. If people were furniture, I thought, they'd be sold as a set.

Cilla drove away in her Mercedes. Simon and Tess approached the house. I opened the front door and walked onto the porch to greet them.

Tess stopped. "Don't like you," she said.

"Come now, Tess," Simon said. "Manners." He'd kissed my cheek. "You look great in those jeans."

Tess tugged at Simon's sweater. "Dad? Now that Mommy doesn't have a boyfriend anymore, can't you come home?"

Cilla had left her divorce-causing father-of-her-new-baby jazz musician? I stepped back, knocking over a planter. "Want to see my warthog, Tess?"

"Don't like pigs," she said, disappearing into the house.

"Warthogs have four tusks," I told the closed door. "In the wild, they shuffle around on their knees foraging for food."

Simon enfolded me in his arms. "Tess'll come around, Kate," he said. "It's only been what? Ten months or so?" His body tensed. After a moment he repeated, "Ten months," but this time in the sad, valedictory tone people use when they mean, *Well, it's been great, but all good things must come to an end.* Or so it seemed to me.

I pressed my cheek against Simon's rough sweater. He smelled of ironed shirts. I worried that he and Cilla might reconcile now that she was unattached. But a week later, I'd been the one to break up with him.

I slammed the shutters closed and rooted in the desk drawers. Finding a pair of scissors, I cut open my mother's letter. Bagheera, my black cat, wandered into the study, hopped sideways at the sight of the skeleton, recovered, meowed, and bumped his head against my leg. His tail antenna-straight, he led me into the kitchen.

I glanced at the trash can: letters were lost in the mail every day. Why not this one?

After tossing the envelope on the counter, I dispensed chicken kibbles into Bagheera's bowl. He crunched his dinner, his name tag clinking against the china rim. Why didn't companies sell mouse-flavored cat food? I pictured an ad: *Try Mice. They're Nice!* A bug crawled along the sink, I washed him down the drain, wondering why it seemed more humane to drown than squash an insect, why I thought of a bug as a "he," not a "she," and whether, with a magnifying glass, you could tell the sex of an insect.

Finally I picked up the letter and carried it to the family room, where I knelt to light the gas fire. When the flames bloomed blue and orange, I sat on the couch and began reading.

Durban, South Africa
Dear Kate,

Last week, I was taken from my flat and incarcerated in hospital. They say I have cancer (which is absurd—no one in our family has ever had cancer). This is your Oom Piet's doing, of course. He is afraid I will expose him as a murderer. It's sad that you have an uncle who is a murderer, but there it is. We can't choose our relatives.

Since you left I have told you to stay in America, thinking you were safer there, but now you will need to come and rescue me, I'm afraid. There is a nurse here, Miriam, who has agreed to mail this letter. She will draw a map on the other side of this page. DO NOT ALERT THE HOSPITAL AHEAD OF TIME THAT YOU ARE COMING! OR OOM PIET!

I hope you haven't cut your lovely curls, poppet. Your head is the wrong shape for short hair.

> *Love,*
> *Mother*

I visualized my mother scribbling the letter as she sat in her favorite armchair, her glasses glinting in the lamplight, her thick legs—tucked to the side—encased in stockings, beneath which unshaven hair would've curled into small Catherine-wheel whorls. I pictured a cigarette seesawing on the rim of a sailor-hat ashtray. Smoke-tusks curving from her nose. The smell of overcooked vegetables—cabbage and boiled onions—drifting from the kitchen.

You will need to come and rescue me? In previous letters—I'd received less than half a dozen in eighteen years—she'd *insisted* I not return to South Africa. I'd been glad to comply. Especially as she appeared to be coping well on her own. Had kept the same job for years. In 1990, on the same day Nelson Mandela was released from Pollsmoor Prison, she'd retired and had seemed content.

My uncle, who must be in his late seventies by now, was always the villain of her stories, though we hadn't seen him for decades.

I crumpled the letter and threw it in the flames. Ashy fragments floated up the chimney.

Bagheera jumped on my lap. I stroked his soft fur, and he stretched along my thighs, resting his warm chin on my knee. Outside, color leached from the sky. My young neighbor, Troy, raced across his lawn, trailing a recalcitrant red kite along grass still fragrant from the previous night's rain. Moments later I heard his mother summon him inside. The cadence of her voice hurled me through time and space and a tumult of emotions so that all at once I missed my long-ago mom, the one who'd rocked me to sleep when I was ten and terrified that an *umamlambo*—a shape-shifting snake with the power to render you insane with one glance of its round flat eyes—had transformed itself into my bedside lamp.

I couldn't call her. She hadn't owned a phone since 1967, when she claimed our conversations were being taped and kept in the basement of the Parliament Buildings in Pretoria.

And the letter had said she was in the hospital. Which hospital?

The fire snapped. I gaped at the flames. I'd burned the map along with the letter.

It was a sign from my ancestors. It was karma. Fate. Kismet. I would do nothing.

Bagheera purred on my lap like a living blanket. After a minute or two, I reached for my address book on the side table. I'd call the caretaker of her apartment building, Mevrou Bakker. We'd never spoken, but I had her phone number. It was after eleven on Saturday night in Durban, but that might work in my favor. She was almost certain to be home. I dialed. After a few rings—double purrs, instead of the single tone I was used to in the States—someone picked up.

"*Ja?* Mevrou Bakker." The woman's voice was high-pitched.

"This is Kate, Violet Jensen's daughter. The woman in three-sixty-one?" I wound the telephone wire python-like around my finger then released it, leaving red welts in my flesh.

After a silence, she replied. "Mevrou Jensen's daughter? Now how do I know for sure? Why would you call now, hey?"

"I'm worried about her." I gave her my mother's maiden name. My address and age. Even told her about my favorite toy as a child—a purple hippopotamus.

She breathed into the phone. "Violet warned me to be careful about calls like this." In the background, a radio chattered in Afrikaans. "If you're her daughter, why haven't you visited her, hey? Then I'd know who you are for sure, *jy weet?*"

"I live in America."

"There are planes."

A total stranger was making me feel guilty. "Please check on my mother." I flicked the lamp switch off and on.

"She's not here. She hasn't been here for days." She hung up.

Again and again I called, listening to the rings, picturing the sound rippling, Doppler-like, in the humid Durban air. October was early summer in South Africa: I remembered the itchy feel of the heat on my skin; the way rain fizzed and steamed on our window ledge and sweat dripped off the tip of my mother's nose when she ironed.

I spoke to directory assistance and wrote down the numbers of local hospitals. I talked to late-night receptionists and clerks and lost myself in a maze of voice mails. On the pad in front of me, I drew wild faces with staring eyes and checkmark eyebrows and lips the shape of an upside-down V.

No one by the name of Violet Jensen had been admitted to any of the hospitals.

When I called the police, they said they'd do their best, but they were short-staffed—Zulu and Xhosa factions were clashing outside Ixopo. Street crime was on the upswing; a French tourist had been murdered.

I poured Bagheera off my lap, stood, and stared out the window at the darkening sky. Later in the week, I was due to pitch an ad campaign for an antacid product, ReFute. If Bellish & Associates won the business, I'd likely be promoted from senior copywriter to creative director.

And on Tuesday, the last day of October, I was moving to an apartment in Shaker Heights. I hadn't wanted to stay in Chagrin Falls after Simon and I broke up. Though I loved the town—its hundred-year-old homes, Memorial Day parade, and riverside park—it wasn't a good fit for a woman who regretted not having married: the place was explosive with nuclear families.

In the dim, firelit family room, I reached into my pocket for Simon's handkerchief and held it to my nose, breathing in its fresh-laundry smell. I'd loved the way he carried a handkerchief. It reminded me of my dad, who'd used his to wipe chocolate from my mouth or tears from my eyes. Once, when we were at a cricket match in Johannesburg, my father had knotted each corner and put the square of cloth on his head to protect his bald patch. I'd draped it over his face when he died. His nose had made a small hill in the fabric.

Was that when my mother's troubles started? When my father had his heart attack? Or had she been ill before then?

Years ago I'd stopped thinking about the whens and whys and hows of my childhood, believing my past irrelevant to the person I'd become. Why revisit it now?

Outside, the sky had turned ebony. The Milky Way glimmered with the ephemeral light of today's and yesterday's stars, and, on the horizon, a pale three-quarter moon kept its shadowy secrets. An owl hooted in the darkness.

I opened the front door to the crisp-apple smell of a fall night and sat on the steps, listening.

Johannesburg, South Africa
July 1966

When my father died, on my eleventh birthday, July 10, 1966, my mother said the government was responsible, and that was the first time I heard about The Plot to Split Us Apart.

Dad had been helping me blow out my candles.

The cake was chocolate sponge topped with scalloped icing and blue sprinkles. It sat on a doily on a china plate. I'd helped Prudence mix the batter and put the pan in the oven.

We were sitting on three sides of the dark oak table in the dining room. I faced the bay window. The winter sun cast straggly shadows across the lawn and rockery, one of my favorite places. Among the stones I liked to corral snails, grow daisies, and stage long-running plays in which my Barbie dolls fought off dinosaurs beneath the ferns or picnicked with large, friendly bears among lilac and white alyssum. Ken kept house. In summer I read books in a hideaway between the oleander bushes near my mother's rose garden. While I explored the Indian jungle with Mowgli, or Equatorial Africa with Rider Haggard's heroes, the breeze carried a ferment of smells and sounds into my lair—the fragrance of roses, the warble of yellow-breasted *bokmakieries,* and the low hum of conversation between my mother and our gardener, Winston, as they discussed pruning and watering and the curse of mildew. Winston was a tall Xhosa man with a broad chest and ropy arms. I liked him because he helped me plant seeds and make mud swimming pools for my dolls. He explained interesting things about *shongo-lolos*—shiny black centipedes—and spiders and worms. Most days, he wore old pinstriped suit-pants tied around his waist with a piece of string. He was smart: he'd spent several years at Fort Hare University studying botany. His bare chest shone as if polished with floor wax, and he smelled of Lifebuoy soap.

Late afternoons, gray clouds would belly across the sky like a herd of rhino and I'd run for shelter before the stampede turned to rain.

Next to my cake stood a jug of milk and three glasses.

Behind my dad at the head of the table hung a framed photograph of my Welsh grandparents. They pointed to the longest sign in the world, which read LLANFAIRPWLLGWYNGYLLGOGERY-CHWYRNDROBWLLLLANTYSILIOGOGOGOCH. It means, "St. Mary's Church in the hollow of the white hazel near a rapid whirlpool and the church of St. Tysilio of the red cave." Dad could say it in Welsh without spitting, which he said was quite an achievement. My grandfather—a doctor—and grandmother had died in a bombing raid in London during World War II, leaving my father an orphan at fourteen. He'd become a janitor in a medical office and educated himself by reading magazines in the waiting room, from *Ladies' Home Journal* to *Reader's Digest*. He knew interesting, odd things. Like, if you throw boiled spaghetti at the wall and the noodle sticks to the paint, it's ready to eat. And earthworms are hermaphrodites. At first I thought he meant earthworms could be their own brothers or sisters. For a while I wished I were an earthworm, since it didn't seem like our family was going to get any bigger.

Dad sold detergent to large stores such as Greenacres and Belfast. My mother said he wasn't a traveling salesman—he was in retail.

When he lit the candles on the cake, the flames waved like flags. He sat back and ran his fingers through his curly sandy hair, which resembled mine except for his bald island. Mom fussed with the napkins. She was slim, dressed in a navy-blue shift with pearls, her chestnut hair framing high cheekbones and a wide mouth.

Dad had played golf earlier in the day. He walked eighteen holes and he looked pale and tired. "The wax is dripping into the icing," he said. "Time to blow, Katie." He scooped up a dollop of chocolate and licked his finger.

"Oh, Taffy, for goodness sake, wait!" Mom said. She called him Taffy except when they argued. Then she called him David Llewellyn Jones. They'd been fighting since the previous Sunday, when the police had arrested Winston. We'd seen the Black Maria leaving our house as we returned from the zoo. I was sent to spend the night at my friend Isabella's while my parents went to the police station. But they couldn't get Winston back. When I asked the next day why the police took him away, Dad frowned and then said it was a problem with his passbook, which natives—black people—had to carry at all times to prove they were living where the Nationalist government said they must live.

The problem was, Winston didn't have a passbook. He refused to carry one. Mom had insisted on hiring him last year anyway. Dad hadn't wanted to. That was why Dad was so angry with my mom the day after the arrest. He'd often said it didn't pay to defy the government—not this one—no matter how much you hated apartheid.

Mom turned her head toward the kitchen door. I dug my finger into the icing, too. My dad winked. Mom raised her voice and called. "Prudence! Plates, please."

Prudence was a short Zulu woman with big eyes and coppery skin. She reminded me of an owl. Often she stared out the window, lost in thought, as though something fascinating were happening outside. She said her ancestors possessed her now and again: it was important to listen to what they had to say. Recently, they'd suggested she start her own business in Soweto, selling beer at a shebeen.

"Mom, let's take a picture," I said.

She tapped her fingers on the table. "I don't know where the camera is."

"You had it at the zoo, Vi," my father said.

"Prudence!" Mom called again. "Oh, just blow, Katie, the candles are making a mess of the cake."

I filled every inch of my lungs. Prudence arrived with the forks and plates on a tray and waited. My mother patted me on the back, which I wasn't expecting. The air burst out. All eleven candles continued to flutter.

"Help me, Dad," I said, giggling.

He leaned forward and blew hard. All but two candles stopped burning. Then, with a look of surprise, my father placed his hand on the left side of his chest as if he were about to sing our national anthem, "Die Stem." He took a couple of shallow breaths and toppled sideways off the chair. I thought he was pretending to be one of the Three Stooges. But he'd crashed to the floor quite hard. I peered at him over the edge of the table. "Dad?"

"David Llewellyn Jones," my mother said. "Stop fooling around."

He made rasping sounds. Mom stood, walked around the table, and knelt at his side. She looked puzzled. I jumped off my chair and crouched next to her. Dad was lying flat on the floor, arms splayed. I could smell his hair cream. The radio was playing Fats Domino. His body shuddered. He couldn't be having a heart attack because he was only thirty-nine. Only old men had heart attacks.

Mom patted his cheek and shook his shoulders as though she'd finally lost all patience with him. "Taffy! What are you doing? Get up. Get up."

She pressed her lips on his mouth, blowing breath into him, then hit his chest with her fist. He stopped making noises. His eyes were open but they were blank and shiny like blue marbles. I wanted him to blink. I waved my hand in front of his face.

Prudence came around the table and stared. "What's wrong with the *baas*?"

"I don't know," I said, feeling guilty. "He blew my candles too hard."

She dropped the tray, screaming, *"Hy's dood! Die baas is dood!"*

One of the plates wheeled along the hardwood floor and headed out the door as if it had gotten a terrible fright. Others shattered into sharp edges, and forks and spoons bounced and skittered between the table legs. That's when I started to cry, as if broken plates were the problem.

My mother held Dad's wrist, pinching it between her fingers. Then she dropped his arm, rocked on her knees, and clasped her hands under her chin. "The government's assassinated him." She rose to her feet, clinging to the edge of the table. She sounded angry.

I was scared. I wiped my eyes with the tablecloth and peered around, expecting to see a man with a gun. A few years before we'd heard on the radio that the American president, John F. Kennedy, had been assassinated by Lee Harvey Oswald, who was then shot by Jack Ruby. I crept to the window and peeked outside. No one was around except the boy next door, who flew his balsa wood plane into the fence.

Prudence crawled on the floor, wailing, picking up pieces of smashed china. I rushed over to my dad and thumped his chest, the way Mom had done. By now, tears were dripping down my cheeks.

My mother stood, frowning. "I'll call the ambulance." She picked up the cake, the jug, and the glasses, placed them on the dresser, then swept the white cloth off the table and draped it over Dad's body. She ran to the phone in the hallway, leaving me with my father wrapped in our best linen.

I pulled the tablecloth down around his neck. If he were alive, I didn't want him to suffocate beneath the heavy fabric. I took the handkerchief from his pocket and laid it carefully over his face. The cloth didn't move.

Winston had told me a man's breath becomes his ghost when

he dies. I looked around, thinking a white flapping thing might fly out the window.

Two candles still burned, the wax puddling on the cake. I stood and blew them out. The smoke burned the inside of my nose.

The ambulance arrived. Men with dangling stethoscopes carried Dad out on a stretcher. Mom followed them inside the van. The doors banged shut. *Mossies* flew from the telephone wires at the sound of the siren. Across the street, Isabella's mother came running to her gate.

Prudence took me to her *kya,* her little room behind the house. The legs of her iron bed stood on bricks to prevent *tokoloshes* from climbing up in the middle of the night. She made tea on her stove and put three spoons of sugar in each mug. We sat on her blanket and she held me in her arms, crooning a lullaby. It was a mixture of Zulu and Afrikaans words: *Thula thula, thula baba . . .* I put my head against her chest and listened to her heartbeat.

I knew I should think only about my father, but after a while my mind began to wander. On her bedside table, I saw a pile of books: *Kirstenbosch Gardens: A Photographic Tour. South African Railways and Airways: Infrastructure and Related Information. The War of the Worlds* by H. G. Wells. Old copies of *The Star* newspaper.

"Have you read *The Time Machine*?" I asked, wishing it were possible to go back, say, three hours, and blow out the candles myself.

Prudence's chest shook with laughter. Her breath wheezed as if her lungs were bellows. "Me? I can't read, Katie, *kindjie.* Those books are Winston's. When he saw the police had come to arrest him, he asked me to look after them."

I realized it was exactly a week since Winston had been arrested. Last Sunday. I'd probably never see *him* again, either. At dinner, the day after he'd been taken away, while we ate cottage pie, Mom said he'd disappeared into the system. Her voice trembled. She said she'd lost the only person who understood roses.

Dad ignored her.

Mom had ripped a dinner roll into shreds. "Any minute now the police will say he's dead—they'll claim he beat himself up and committed suicide by jumping out of a window at John Vorster Square." John Vorster Square was the police headquarters in the city. But like the other prisoners, he would've been pushed, she said. "Damn Nationalists persecute people who've done nothing wrong."

Then the next morning at breakfast, over bacon and eggs, she asked Dad whether he agreed the new showerhead looked awfully like a microphone. When she switched it off, it had made a funny noise, not a *normal* gurgle. Did he suppose the government was after us, too, now?

"You're being absurd, Violet," he said, "We're white. They won't touch us." Then he picked up his briefcase and left.

"Good-bye," my mother said to the empty doorway. She'd eaten three slices of toast and marmalade without stopping, and afterward she had gone outside to the rose garden.

"When will they let Winston out?" I asked Prudence.

"The *polisie* can keep people in prison for ninety days." She tucked my hair behind my ears. It sprang forward.

"So he will come home after that?"

"Unless they keep him another ninety days. And then another ninety days."

"Why? Just because of his pass"? I sat up. "Do you think he will die in prison?"

"He did something they cannot forgive."

"What?"

She shook her head. "When it's raining, young girls must hide or they might be struck by lightning and changed into stars."

Prudence often said things that at first didn't make much sense, and then you'd realize suddenly, in the bath or on your way to school, what she meant. This time I knew she thought I was too young to understand about Winston. I considered asking more questions, but then I remembered my dad.

"I don't want Dad to be dead," I said. Could he be playing one of his tricks, like the time he made it appear as though the top of his thumb had been sliced off? Perhaps when the ambulance arrived at the hospital, the doctors would unwrap him and he'd wink at the nurses the way he winked at waitresses and say, "Only pulling your leg!" But I knew that wouldn't happen. I leaned my head against Prudence's chest again. Her apron smelled like chocolate icing. I could feel tears rising.

She rocked me. "Daddy's your ancestor now. You mustn't worry. The *baas* is in the sky with *Unkulunkulu,* watching over you."

When my mother arrived home, she tucked me into bed with my purple hippo. My dad had given me the hippo on my seventh birthday. I was far too old for a stuffed toy, but I loved him.

Mom sat on the edge of the bed and rubbed my arm till it began to burn. I shifted away.

"He's gone, poppet," she said. "They said it was cardiac arrest, but I know better."

"Are you going to call Aunt Iris?" I asked. Aunt Iris was her sister. She was married to my uncle, Oom Piet.

My mother's face crumpled like plastic near a lit match. "It's because of your uncle and his connections with the government that your father is dead. I don't understand how Iris could have married that man!"

My uncle was Afrikaans. We were English-speaking South Africans, which meant we were descended from British, not Dutch settlers. English-speakers were usually businesspeople. Afrikaners, it seemed, were mostly farmers or civil servants or railway workers, or served as National Party Members of Parliament—MPs. Nationalists had passed the apartheid laws. But there were plenty

Afrikaners who were more liberal than the English, and plenty English who were more racist than Afrikaners, Dad always said.

Oom Piet belonged to the *Broederbond,* which was a secret Afrikaner organization similar to the Masons, except members believed whites were the superior race and blacks were born without the ability to run countries. God meant natives—who were also known as nonwhites or non-Europeans or Bantu—to serve whites, the Dutch Reformed Church said.

I gazed up at Mom. Her nostrils seemed huge.

"What's the government got to do with Dad dying? He isn't black, like Free Mandela," I said. Because of the graffiti I saw on walls in the city, I thought Mandela's first name was Free. He was one of the black men who had been imprisoned the year before for being communist and planning revolution.

Mom began weeping. I sat up and hugged her. After a while Prudence came in to check on us, and led my mother to her bedroom. I heard the door open and close.

For a long time I lay awake, listening to the wind keening and my mother crying in her room. When it was quiet, I crept into her bed and put my hand on her sleeping body, feeling it move with each breath.

Chagrin Falls, Ohio
1995

The word *hippopotamus* is Greek in origin and means "river horse"—but viewing the hippos in their enclosure at the Cleveland Zoo, I decided they were closer to a frog/hog hybrid, given the peering amphibious eyes on the tops of their heads and their round, slick bellies. The air smelled of droppings, which the animals disperse by flicking their tails very fast. In Africa, a legend claims that hippos were allowed by the creator of the world to live in water by day, but only if they consented to fertilize the shore at night. They are assiduous at maintaining their end of the bargain, the animal keeper told me. No pun intended, he said.

It was Sunday afternoon, the day after I'd received my mother's letter. My expedition to the zoo was an attempt to reconnect with my ancestral spirits, whose advice—apparently inaudible in the suburbs—I thought I might more easily hear amidst grunting and barking and trumpeting animals from Africa.

That morning, I'd called hospitals within twenty miles of Durban, as well as a few in Johannesburg and Cape Town. Mevrou Bakker, the caretaker of the flats, either hadn't answered her phone or had slammed it down at the sound of my voice. I'd left a couple of messages, one in broken Afrikaans. *"Ek is haar dogter,"* I said. I wasn't sure if I'd claimed to be my mother's daughter or her doctor. I'd learned Afrikaans in school, but as an English-speaking South African rarely spoke the language.

Not that my mother believed in doctors, anyway. They were in league with the government.

I gripped the railing. The corner of a brass plaque dug into my palm. *Though crocodiles occasionally kill baby hippo*, the plaque said, *adults are relatively safe from attack.*

As a child, I'd thought animals lucky to live in a world where the rules were clear. Some creatures were predators, some prey, and some both. But whether you were zebra, warthog, or cheetah—or hippopotamus—you knew your role in herd and family, who your enemies were, and how to defend yourself. You were born with the right instincts.

One of the hippos lifted his body from the water, so that his skin shone purplish-wet in the afternoon sun. He opened his salmon mouth, displaying ridged palate and tusky teeth. Then he nodded his head up and down. Twice.

Was it a sign? I released the cold steel bars I'd been grasping. I was the crazy one, not my mother, taking instructions from a hippo.

The final game of the World Series—the Indians against the Braves—was scheduled to begin in a couple of hours. I crossed my arms against the cold, wandered away from the enclosure, pushed through the zoo turnstile, and caught the bus home to Bagheera and baseball.

While brainstorming slogans for Lawnlands Funeral Home and Cemetery at the agency on Monday, I realized how much I wanted the creative director position, how much I needed to feel vested in something, even if it was only a long-term advertising strategy. I'd had about as many jobs as boyfriends. After ending my engagement to Terry, my first fiancé, I'd left San Diego and traveled around the States, treating the country like a large theme park. For eleven years, I rolled into different cities and coasted through jobs—catalogue writer, toy salesperson, secretary, journalist, public relations assistant, video store assistant manager, and advertising copywriter—and a slew of men, including Gareth, Ned, Danny, and Tran.

But when I turned thirty-five, I realized the rides were getting shorter and shorter and bumpier and bumpier. I felt queasy. Emotion sickness, I decided. Time to settle down. I landed a job at Bellish & Associates' Los Angeles office and met Eduardo, my second fiancé. A year later, single again, I'd relocated to Cleveland, where I'd had four lonely but peaceful years before Simon.

Now I fooled around with tag lines: flippancy often led to more profound thought. *Dirt Cheap!* I typed. *Pass it Along to Someone Who's Passing On.* I found clip art of coffins and created three pairs. *Try Our Boxed Sets!* Then I remembered my mother's possible cancer. Guiltily, I clicked on the ReFute Antacid new-business presentation. Unable to concentrate, I glanced around my office. Should I water my plants? The ficus in the corner was about to expire. To avoid rejection in any form, I decided in the future to replace potted plants every six months, *before* their leaves turned flaccid or brown or blotchy.

Though, of course, it was I who had split up with Simon.

For days after talking to Cilla in the driveway, he'd seemed preoccupied—watched the baseball playoffs, but never knew the score. Read the first chapter of his novel several times, as though the words presented a puzzle he couldn't solve.

One night he handed me a glass of wine, sat on the couch, and rested his size-thirteen feet on the coffee table. He pressed the power button on the remote. Flipped through channels. Switched the television off. Arranged the remote on top of a pile of magazines, aligning the oblong precisely with the corner. Rubbed his eyebrow. Laced his fingers together and stared at them. Took his feet off the coffee table. Then he reached for his beer, took a gulp, and turned to me. "Kate? I had a blood test earlier this week," he said. "I got the result today."

He'd contracted AIDS? In the time it required for him to swallow and place his glass on the coffee table, I'd reviewed every recent article I'd read on the illness, estimated his possible lifespan, worried I might be infected, pictured myself weeping at his graveside, wondered how he might have gotten the disease—while performing surgery?—thought about the new medication that was helping people live longer, felt glad he had good medical insurance, pondered whether he could possibly be bisexual, remembered the previous night's lovemaking, decided bisexuality was unlikely, couldn't imagine he took drugs, and concluded I loved him so much, nothing mattered except we remain together.

"Cilla's baby—Jerome?—I'm his father," Simon said.

My brain felt like a packed auditorium in which someone had yelled "Fire!"—my thoughts were dashing about trying to find an exit and bumping into each other. Jerome was Simon's son? His ex-wife Cilla had had the baby in late August. I calculated: we'd already been dating when Jerome was conceived. The conflagration in my head spread to my chest.

The night the divorce was final, Simon said, they'd consumed a couple of bottles of wine while discussing how to structure visitations with Tess. Somehow they'd ended up in bed. He apologized again and again. I watched his lips move, but heard only a few words: *Stupid . . . sorry . . . it's you I love . . . really stupid . . . meant nothing.* When I didn't respond, he picked up his beer and turned the glass around and around. Bubbles swam through amber to the surface, forming craters in the white foam.

"Cilla suggest reconciling?" I asked eventually.

He hesitated, then nodded. "She doesn't really want to get back together, I don't think. It's because of Jerome. And Tess, of course."

I said I had to be alone for a while—that if he didn't leave, I would.

After I heard the garage door wheeze shut, I climbed into bed and curled up in a ball. The cul de sac was silent. This somnolent Cleveland suburb didn't suit me, after all. Why did I think I'd fit in? That I was capable of settling into marriage and family life?

I got out of bed, sat on the rocking chair, and rocked viciously. How dare Simon expect me to forgive him? The baby even had one of my favorite names. I leapt from the chair on its forward swing and walked around the house, turning photographs of us facedown. I kicked Simon's coelacanth replica, breaking off a fin and cutting my toe. I found the superglue, but couldn't reattach the fin. Fin. Finished. It seemed the worst of omens.

By five in the morning, I knew I could forgive Jerome's conception—but not his reality. If Simon and I stayed together, his mind would always be elsewhere, with his kids. Every time we disagreed, he'd wonder if he'd done the right thing marrying me. Or I'd think he was wondering whether he'd done the right thing. Whenever Tess saw me she'd say, "Don't like you." Jerome's *first words* would be, "Don't like you." In time, my insecurity would make me moody and distant and flippant. Eventually, Simon would sit me down on the couch. "I find I don't like you either," he'd say.

And so the next day I told him I wanted us to live apart, at least for a while. Maybe forever. I couldn't deal with uncertainty.

But Bernie—who also worked at the agency—had thought I should give Simon another chance.

"Divorcing people do dumb things," she'd said. "I know it's tough, with a baby involved. But Simon won't go back to Cilla. Didn't you tell me she hated his fish models and made him keep his skeletons in the closet?"

We giggled. "In the *basement*," I'd said. "And he only has one skeleton. That I know of."

Now the office intercom blared. I swiveled on my office chair. Maybe I should ask for custody of Mortimer when Simon came to pick up the last of his things in—I looked at my watch—eight hours and seventeen minutes.

I glanced at the phone on my desk. Should I return to South Africa? But what about the new business meeting on Thursday? I closed the ReFute document and walked to Bernie's office. Two years before, I'd hired her as my assistant, and six months ago, she'd been promoted to senior copywriter—my level. We were good friends, though competitive at work.

"I don't know what to do," I said, leaning against her doorjamb.

"Tell the client the focus groups liked it," she said without lifting her head. "That usually makes them happy."

I flopped in a chair. "I mean, shall I go back home?" On Sunday, I'd called her at home and told her the gist of the letter. "My mother might be *imagining* she has cancer."

Bernie pressed the DO NOT DISTURB button on her phone. "She's a hypochondriac, too?"

"Not like . . . no." A medical Zelig, Bernie often became convinced she was ill with whatever disease was currently in the news. Her health obsessions were a boost to charity. When she thought she had melanoma, we walked seventy-five miles to raise money for the American Cancer Association. After her fingers tingled three days in a row, we organized free stroke screenings at a local drugstore. "The odd thing is that she's missing," I said. "She never leaves her flat. How's your hammertoe?" Bernie had been working on the podiatrist account.

"Better. Knock on wood." She grinned, waving away an account coordinator who was advancing with a sheaf of papers in his hand. "Oh, Kate. You've gotten odd letters before, didn't you say? And everything's turned out fine."

I fiddled with a cast of a foot she was using as a paperweight. The previous night, I told her, I'd dreamed that Prudence was standing next to a pile of stones, beckoning. "Long ago, when Zulu people traveled, they stacked stones in a heap—called an *isivivane*—to pay respects to the local spirits. So I thought maybe the dream was a sign I must go on a journey," I said. "And then I went to the zoo, and . . ." I stopped, thinking how superstitious I sounded. And superstition was similar to paranoia: a tendency to come to irrational conclusions based on random sets of events. "Never mind."

Our boss, Paul Mhlenge, walked past the open door and lifted a hand in greeting. We returned his wave. Paul always brought to mind Joshua, a black friend I'd had when I was fourteen; they shared the same high cheekbones and broad forehead. When we first met, I was afraid Paul wouldn't like me because I was a white South African. Once a black man in a shoe store had refused to serve me when he found out I was from Durban. I'd slunk out, accepting guilt by reason of nationality.

But Paul and I enjoyed each other's company, claiming kinship as fellow African-Americans. Though he wasn't as African-American as I was: his parents were from Kenya, but he'd been born in Santa Fe.

Bernie put down her pen. "Go, Kate. I can stand in for you at the pitch." She came around the desk and hugged me. "Dave and I will take care of Bagheera. Paul will understand. I'll present your ReFute ideas on Thursday, and we'll get the account. The client will be a kind, charming man who'll fall madly in love with you when you return." She rubbed my back. "You need the break, what with Simon and all."

After work, I walked along the banks of the Chagrin River, the wind cool on my cheeks. Mauve clouds bruised the sky. I loved Ohio: the certainty of four seasons made life seem so manageable, so *defined,* somehow, compared to Durban's year-round mugginess.

A family of mallards arrowed across the river. Chagrin Falls was an ideal place to live if you had children and liked ducks. Or liked children and had ducks, for that matter. Neither of which applied to me. Just as well I was moving to Shaker Heights. I headed out of the park.

Along Washington Street, I passed a travel agency. Hanging in the window was a poster of giraffes in Kruger Park. They were bending to drink at a water hole, legs wide apart, knees at an angle, necks arching to the surface. I stopped. When I was young, my mother used to read me Rudyard Kipling's *Just So Stories:* how the leopard got its spots, how the rhinoceros ended up with a wrinkly skin, why the elephant has a trunk instead of a nose. Sometimes she'd invent her own stories. My favorite had been the one about a giraffe who used his neck as an accordion. He played *boeremusiek* at weddings, earned lots of money, and flew to New York, where he fell in love with the Chrysler Building.

Once, a long time ago, I had loved my mother.

Was she lying in a hospital bed convinced doctors were pumping carcinogens through her IV?

I kicked a bottle cap along the sidewalk and watched it somersault into the gutter.

Back home, I carried the last of Simon's odds and ends from the bedroom to the study. As I reached the bottom of the stairs, I heard his Volvo crunch to a stop on the gravel. I peered out the window, then—not wanting to seem to be waiting—I turned, trotted to the kitchen, and began piling dishcloths into an open box. Simon knocked, waited, then pushed the front door open. I reached for packing tape, listening to him walk across the family room. He approached the kitchen and stopped in the doorway. His chin was shadowy with early-evening beard. I'd loved to cup his jaw in my palm first thing in the mornings, feel his bristles prick my skin. Had I been checking to make sure he was real?

"Nearly done with the packing," I said. The tape screeched as I pulled it from the dispenser and aimed it at the box. It stuck to my fingers. I ripped it off and tried again.

"Sad to see the place like this," he said.

I struggled to bring two flaps together, suppressing the urge to get up, grip his shoulders, and shake him. *Why did you do it?* I wanted to say. *You spoiled everything.*

He stepped into the kitchen and reached out as if to take my hand. I gave him the tape.

When the flaps were joined, he batted the side of the box with his palms. It sprang into a square. We both stared at his handiwork. I pressed an air bubble in the tape. He stood, watching my fingers smooth the wrinkle.

I looked up. "How's Tess? And the baby?"

"Jerome? Kate, honey." He held out his arms. I wanted to step into that circle of warmth, nest against him, listen to his heartbeat.

I got to my feet, fetched the broom from the far corner, and swept polystyrene peanuts into a dustpan. "Yes. How's Jerome?"

Simon dropped his arms and leaned against the door frame. The shoelaces on his left sneaker were coming undone. Strands of his hair stuck up like small TV antennae. I stopped sweeping.

"We took him to the zoo," he said. "He smiled when he saw an aardvark. He liked the warthog too."

The zoo? They went to the zoo? I rested the broom in the corner. "Jerome's a sensible baby," I said, surprised that words could escape my throat, which felt as twisted as a strand of DNA.

"Much more sensible than his father," Simon said. "Who is a complete idiot. Kate. I miss you. I am so very sorry."

His father. I couldn't form words, bereft by the image of the family at the zoo—Simon, Cilla, Jerome, and Tess: the sun shining on their dark hair and pale cheeks as they laughed to see the aardvark root for insects, while, in a different part of the park, a sandy-haired, freckled woman talked to hippos.

I picked up the broom again and pushed a ball of used tape toward a pile of trash. Bagheera wandered in and swatted it with his paw.

Simon opened his mouth as if to say something, but instead blinked a couple of times, turned, and left the room. I leaned against the counter and stared at the toaster until everything around it went out of focus. I heard him banging around, opening the door, and loading his car. He made several trips.

The refrigerator, unconcerned, made ice.

Simon returned to the kitchen with Mortimer under his arm. The skeleton's beret had slipped over one eye socket, giving him a debonair expression. "Call if you change your mind," Simon said. "I haven't stopped loving you, you know."

My throat had closed up. I nodded.

"I'll be going then?" he said.

I pushed the broom slowly along the tile. Should I suggest we talk in a few days? Should I tell him about my mother? A tap dripped into the sink.

"Okay," Simon said. "I understand. Take care." He walked from the kitchen.

I stared at the line of dust I'd created. When I heard the front door shut, I dropped the broom, ran to the family room window, and watched him reverse down the drive. He reached the street and stopped. For a minute, the Volvo remained motionless. Its headlights picked out a ghost-kite entangled in an oak tree. In the gusting wind, its white streamers beat against the branches.

As I made up my mind to run toward Simon—wave my arms, tell him not to go, I loved him—he backed out, turned the car, and accelerated down the street. A pile of leaves whirled into a yellow dervish, danced in the glow of the streetlight, and disintegrated onto the verge.

Johannesburg
1966

People laden with casseroles and condolences and roses and scented white lilies knocked at our door in the week after Dad's death, but Mom turned them away. "Please leave us alone," she said, and, seeing her stern face, they did, stranding clouds of perfume in our entrance hall. I watched from the window as they shook their heads and walked down the stucco path to their Fords and Zephyrs and Fiats.

"Grief does funny things to people," I overheard one woman say. "And of course Violet has always been quite eccentric."

Every morning when I woke, for a few minutes I wouldn't know why I felt so sad, and then I'd remember. I'd get up and do things, one after the other, until it was easier to breathe. Sometimes I sat between the oleander bushes with my books, wondering whether I'd see Dad in Heaven one day, and, if so, how old he would be. If I died when I was seventy-five, would he still be thirty-nine? Would he push me around in a wheelchair? What did people *do* in Heaven? Would Dad be able to play golf with my late grandfather? *What if God got Dad's name mixed up with someone else's and he ended up in Hell?* It bothered me because Jones was such a common name.

On the whole, I preferred Prudence's theory: that he had become a spirit-world-inhabiting ancestor who would advise me on important matters from time to time.

"Speak through my hippo, Dad," I whispered one night when the wind's moan scared me.

Mom made the priest swear he wouldn't tell anyone the day or time of the funeral service. She said privacy was necessary for her to cope with her grief.

Prudence fluttered her hands up and down. "The *baas*'s spirit will be restless if we don't give him a good send-off," she said. The backs of her hands were brown but her palms were pale, as though hard work had worn away the color.

"Stop flapping," Mom said. "I know what I'm doing. Go make tea."

Mom refused to call Aunt Iris or Oom Piet. "Obviously they're aware of what's happened," she said, "because Oom Piet caused all our problems." But I wasn't sure they did know Dad had died. This time of year they usually went on vacation to the Wild Coast.

My uncle and aunt and cousins Koos and Andre lived on a cattle farm halfway between Johannesburg and Pretoria. Whenever we visited them, I'd nearly choke on the smell of cow dung. But there was a stream on the border of the farm and it was fun to fish with Andre, or race sticks on the current, though if Koos were around, we usually ended up fighting. They'd put me in the old pigsty, saying I was a British prisoner-of-war.

Oom Piet kept a *sjambok*—a whip made of elephant hide— leaning in a corner of his study. He said he would use it on the servants if they stole. I never actually saw him beat them. He'd carry the whip around, though, and run his thumb along the surface while he talked to the maid and the farm bossboy. I thought of Oom Piet as the Snake. Like Aunt Iris, he didn't have much of a chin. He was tall and stretched out, with a flat head which swayed when he talked. He hugged like a python, too, and always wanted me to sit on his lap. He said he loved God, country, family, and rugby, in that order.

Aunt Iris glided behind Oom Piet like a gray shadow, always ready to do whatever he asked: bring him his rum and coke, play his favorite melodies on the piano, and she'd wear her blue poplin dress—the one with the ruffles—to church. She had a temper, though; she'd snap if you did something to upset her, like take a syrupy *koeksuster* off the plate before the adults had made their choices. Her mouth would gape wide, showing her incisors, when she bit into her dessert. She was the Shark.

Mom and Aunt Iris arranged flowers and baked fruitcakes. They sat on the *stoep,* drank hot tea, and discussed perennials, annuals, and flowering shrubs.

But six months before, we'd pretty much stopped seeing them, because my father and Oom Piet had argued about the Boer War, which had taken place at the turn of the century. Oom Piet said the British had been as bad as the Nazis, putting innocent Afrikaans families in concentration camps where typhoid and other diseases had flourished because of poor sanitary conditions. My dad said it wasn't true, they were POW camps, that was all. Anyway, Oom Piet should be ashamed to be a *Broederbonder.* Their voices got louder and louder. Dad called me from the garden, where I was petting a stray piglet and listening through the open window. He said we wouldn't be coming back to the farm if he had anything to do with the matter.

One Sunday about a month before Dad died, Mom went by herself to see Aunt Iris but came back angry and said as far as she was concerned she didn't have a sister anymore. She wouldn't explain why.

"We only visited them because they were family," she said. "But that's not a good enough reason any longer."

Somehow my aunt and uncle *did* find out about Dad's death, or knew already, if my mother was right, and halfway through the service, while we were singing "The Lord Is My Shepherd," they arrived at the church. Hardly anyone was there: only me and my mom and Prudence and a man and a woman with a baby who seemed surprised to see a coffin but stayed anyway. I think they were late for a christening. My mother kept sending them furious looks.

We didn't hear the church doors open because we were facing forward singing about pastures green, but I felt a breeze and the altar cloth fluttered. The priest lifted his eyes from the psalm book. I glanced behind us, and so did my mother. There they were, dressed in black, my aunt and uncle.

"How dare you come here!" my mother said. "After what you've done!"

Prudence continued singing; she had a beautiful voice which seemed to circle in the air like a bird. But everyone else stopped, including the priest.

My mother pushed past me and exited the pew, turning into the aisle. She was wearing an emerald linen shift and pearls. She looked like a film star. "Go!" she said. "You murdered him!"

Oom Piet and Aunt Iris advanced. "Please, Aggie," my aunt said. "We're here to mourn with you." Mom's full name was Agatha Violet; Aunt Iris was the only one who called her Aggie, though.

Mom put her hands on her hips. I joined her in the aisle. "She said go!" I said, almost enjoying myself despite the fact it was my father's funeral. I felt I had my mother's permission to be as rude as I liked.

Prudence stopped singing.

Aunt Iris looked at me. "Katie, dearie, you don't understand."

"Leave us alone," I said.

My mother started walking down the aisle, shooing my aunt and uncle away as if they were farm animals who'd wandered inside by accident. "Outside!" she said. "Outside!"

"Aggie! We want to take care of you!" my aunt said.

"I hold you responsible for Taffy's death," Mom said. She pushed and shoved and batted at them until they gave up and left through the big oaken doors. Then she stayed still for a while, her back to us. Her dress moved as her rib cage heaved up and down.

She turned and strode to her seat. The sun shone through the stained glass windows, patterning her face mauve and blue and yellow. Her cheeks were wet. I touched her hand but she shook it off. She glared at the priest. "Well? Continue."

Prudence bowed her head.

When we left the church, the father of the out-of-place family came up and said it had been a lovely service.

After the funeral, my mother sat in her favorite blue-and-white floral armchair. Every flower had a little yellow center. Once I'd colored in some of the petals with blue ballpoint pen and nobody noticed. So I colored in more and created a face: if you approached it from one angle, it smiled; from another, it frowned. It scared Prudence. She thought the image was the spirit of her aunt Selala, who had puffed up and died from a bee sting the week before.

My shiny patent leather shoes were pinching my toes. I sat on the couch opposite Mom. It was scary to think of Dad burning into ashes like a big log of wood. "How did Oom Piet kill Dad?" I asked. Though it was hard to believe he'd murder anyone, my uncle did once poison *kaffir* dogs from the kraal because he was angry they kept toppling his dustbins. I'd come across Andre, furious with his pa, trying to feed water to the dying dogs. They were twitching and making grunting, retching sounds. To this day, I felt ashamed I'd run away instead of helping—I was scared I'd throw up—and for some reason my shame made me even madder at my uncle.

Mom pointed to the lamp on the table. The bulb was encircled by canvas painted with a picture of a forest fire, so when the light was on, flames appeared to flicker through the branches. "It may be bugged," she whispered. "We won't speak of your father's death again."

"Bugged?"

"By the Nats."

"Gnats?" I said.

"Fitted with a recording device. By the Nationalists."

The Nationalists had been in control of the government since 1948. I'd heard Dad say that people of British descent, as we were, talked Progressive—the political party that wanted to get rid of apartheid right away—but voted United Party, the party that wanted gradual change. At the same time, they hoped to heck the Nationalists stayed in power, because the economy needed cheap black labor. English-speakers wouldn't admit it, he said, but many of them wanted their way of life to stay exactly the same. It was easy to blame the Afrikaners for apartheid.

Mom wasn't making a lot of sense saying the Nats were bugging our lamp, but parents often didn't. They told you to read books, then said you needed to play outside more; when you played outside, they complained when you got dirty and told you to come inside and read.

When I asked Prudence if she thought my father had been assassinated, she said it was possible, but she didn't think so, though it was true the prime minister, Dr. Verwoerd, was a bad man, and the government did terrible things to people, things I was too young and too white to understand.

There was no one else to consult. By now it was the July holidays—our winter break—and my best friend Belinda was visiting her grandparents in Ceres. Mom's parents were long buried in a dusty cemetery outside Benoni. They died in a train crash. They'd worked on the railways, which my mother didn't want anyone to know, because it wasn't just the wrong side of the tracks where she grew up, she said, it *was* the tracks. Her grandparents had been Irish. They came to South Africa in the late eighteen hundreds and failed at farming. Potatoes were different here, they said.

Because Mom had been poor, she'd studied etiquette books and learned how to act rich. That's why we had a silver bell to summon Prudence, though we never used it.

Mom said we'd be safe as long as we stayed close to the house. She needed time to think about what to do next. I slept with Dad's golf clubs on my bed.

We went to the SPCA and brought home a big clunky rottweiler called Cadwallader. He was supposed to frighten Enemies but he only frightened me. I crept past him in the kitchen while he slobbered over his bones. He threw himself against the concrete fence at night. Parts crumbled to the ground.

After the service, Aunt Iris and Oom Piet called again and again. "Leave us alone, you sods," my mother would say into the phone, "or I'll write to the newspapers about you. Scandal means nothing to me. *Sods!*" Finally she pulled the plug out of the wall. "He'd lock me up if he could, poppet. But I'm not going to let him, you see?"

"What scandal?" I asked.

"There isn't one," she said.

My mother wrote in her red notebook for hours and smoked Westminsters. She consumed at least eight cups of Earl Grey a day. Teabags, she believed, were lower class, and you had to warm the teapot with boiling water before putting in tea leaves, then fill it to below the spout. Prudence baked *melktert* and cakes to cheer us up. She taught me how to make fudge. When it boiled, the mixture plopped into craters.

Mom and I ate and ate and ate. What else was there to do? Whenever I asked questions, she put her fingers to her lips and said, "Shhh."

After a few weeks I got bored. One day I walked two miles to Zoo Lake, where I tried to catch fingerlings with a piece of thread and a safety pin. Kids messed around in boats with their fathers. No one came anywhere near me. It was hard to believe we had Enemies.

One afternoon toward the end of July while I was doing a jigsaw puzzle on the dining room table, a man with a bristly nose came to the door. He resembled a wildebeest. He said his name was Dr. Swart. Aunt Iris had asked him to check on my mom. Mom made him tea, fed him oatmeal crunchies, and spoke quite charmingly, dabbing the corners of her eyes with a lace-edged handkerchief whenever he mentioned Dad.

When he left, carrying a bag of peaches from our tree, she laughed. "They're trying to say I'm crazy, poppet. Sending psychiatrists here to trip me up. I'm too smart to fall for their tricks."

"Why would they say you're crazy?" I asked.

"In Russia, they do that all the time. They send people to Siberia. To the gulags, you see?"

"But this isn't Russia," I said.

"I didn't say it was. Finish your jigsaw puzzle."

I gave up.

At dinnertime, sitting at the kitchen table, she said we would move to Durban as soon as she got things organized. We wouldn't tell anyone we were going.

Prudence's plum *konfyt* was bubbling on the combustion stove, so the air smelled sugary. She'd put the roast chicken and vegetables on the table and had gone out to her *kya* to listen to the radio. She preferred ration meat and *putu,* a kind of sludgy white porridge, even though my mother wanted her to eat our food.

Durban was a beach city in the province of Natal where people went on holiday because it was hot all year round. The move didn't sound like a bad idea. I was tired of worrying about my uncle. Belinda was a good friend, but I wasn't sure my mother would let me return to school in Johannesburg. And I kept looking at spaces where Dad had been, like the end of the dining-room table and the driver's seat in the car and his favorite armchair, and feeling sad. It might be easier to go somewhere he'd never been.

Mom cut into the chicken and fat bubbled from the skin. "Rents are cheaper at the coast, too."

Dad hadn't left much money and we didn't own the house on

Lees Avenue. It turned out he hadn't made commission for months; his company wasn't doing well. The last batch of their leading detergent, Spotless—*Now You See Them, Now You Don't!*—contained too much bleach. Patterned fabrics became white as milk. Housewives were furious when they found out it wasn't their maids' faults, after they'd gone to all the trouble of sacking them. Dad hadn't told us, and my mother never read the business pages of *The Star*.

My mother hacked off the drumsticks, then placed meat on my plate along with peas and carrots and potatoes and stuffing. I made a volcano out of the mashed potatoes and spooned gravy into the crater. "What about Prudence?"

"Prudence has her own plans." Mom sat down.

A lava flow of gravy flooded my vegetables. "What's she going to do?"

"Start a shebeen in Soweto."

I ate my brussels sprouts so fast I nearly choked and tears came to my eyes. "Is it because of the laws she can't come with us?" I knew black people were restricted to certain places because of the Group Areas Act. They could go to jail if they didn't obey. There was also the Mixed Marriages Act, which said whites and non-whites couldn't marry, and the Immorality Act, which said you couldn't even kiss someone of the opposite sex who was a different color. Police used telescopes to look into people's bedrooms. They were really stupid laws. *Criminal laws,* my mother said.

"She *could* come to Durban. She was born in the area, in Umhlanga Rocks. She's here in Johannesburg illegally, actually. She doesn't *want* to leave."

Not only didn't I have brothers and sisters, I was running out of adults. I shoveled down my stuffing.

She picked up her knife and fork. "I'm not going anywhere, of course," she said. "As long as you always do as I say. If you don't, Oom Piet will split us apart, you see?" All at once she sniffed her chicken like a hyena at a kill. She stood, opened the trash can, and shook her plate so her food fell in. Then she grabbed my plate and slid the chicken and stuffing off with the edge of a knife, leaving the peas and potatoes behind.

"What are you doing?" I said, astonished.

"Food smells funny. I *thought* I saw Iris in the grocery store the other day, following me around, fiddling with things in my cart while I picked out apples. She put drugs, or maybe poison in the box of stuffing, that's what she did." She returned to the table with my plate minus the meat. "Just eat your vegetables."

"But what would she put in the food? Why?"

"Oh, poppet. LSD, drugs to give us hallucinations, make us sick. I wish I could explain everything, but I can't." Mom lit a cigarette.

"Aunt Iris might follow us to Durban."

Mom gazed at me with opaque eyes. Dad once told me camels have an extra eyelid to protect their eyes from drifting sand. Sometimes I thought she'd grown one too. These days it dropped down whenever she spoke of our relatives. "She won't know we're there." She rose and went to her room.

I helped Prudence wash the dishes. She said she couldn't write to me in Durban because she couldn't write, but she'd think about me lots. I asked about Winston and she shook her head and said many black people disappeared into prisons and were never seen again so I should forget about him. She said not to say his name in front of the madam because it would start her talking about the government. And the Nationalists were everywhere, so it was better to complain out of doors.

Prudence baked scones. When they were ready, we ate them with hot plum *konfyt* and cream.

In the middle of the night, I woke up with a stomachache. I ran into the bathroom and held onto the toilet seat like a life preserver while I threw up. I squinted at the vomit-soup floating below, remembering how bits of stuffing had floated in the gravy along with my peas. Had our food been poisoned? I vomited again, deciding I wouldn't eat another thing until we got to Durban.

En Route to Africa
October 1995

After Simon left with Mortimer under his arm, after I'd watched his Volvo disappear around the corner, I bubble-wrapped the last of my wild animals—soapstone zebra, teak baboon, and ceramic chameleon—and sorted through my papers, tossing items into crates one after the other, as if boxing my possessions quickly would prevent memories of Simon stowing away and traveling with me to my new apartment. I stopped for a moment when I found, in my don't-know-how-to-categorize-this file, an old photograph of my mother and me at Amanzimtoti Beach. We stared from the snapshot, our similar green eyes wide, as if astonished to find ourselves in this room at this time. In our fists we held identical ice cream cones.

I tucked the photo in my wallet, placed it in my purse pocket where I kept one of Simon's handkerchiefs, and dialed the police in South Africa.

No news.

I called directory assistance once more, this time trying to track down Oom Piet. But there were three hundred Du Plessises—fifty of whom were Piets—in the Johannesburg/Pretoria/Witwatersrand area. Anyway, I didn't believe he had anything to do with her disappearance, not after his nearly thirty-year absence from our lives. Maybe one of the doctors looked like my uncle, and in a medicated haze my mother assumed he was Oom Piet.

What if she *were* dying? I grabbed Bagheera, who happened to be passing by, and crushed him to my chest. The guilt, the guilt. Hello, *Heart of Darkness.*

I placed my cat four-paws-square on the floor and picked up the phone. I was able to get a seat on a direct flight from New York to Durban the following afternoon—Tuesday, October 31, Halloween—a little sooner than I'd expected, but the only option if I wanted to travel within the next week. I'd have enough time in the morning to supervise the movers.

Bernie came to pick up Bagheera. She said she would focus on the ReFute presentation tomorrow, now that she'd finished writing the podiatrist ads.

"How's your hammertoe?" I asked.

"Still pounding," she said, hugging me. "Take care, okay?"

High above the Atlantic Ocean the following evening, I peered through the plane window at the glimmering constellations, which, I knew, would look very different viewed from the southern hemisphere: either upside down or finally right way up, depending on your perspective. American stargazers would visualize a hunter with a dagger in the night sky and call him Orion, while in the same celestial cluster, children in Cape Town might see three zebra and a lion. And the moon would seem lit from the other side.

A flight attendant dressed as a witch handed out blankets and pillows. I'd forgotten it was Halloween. I looked at my watch. Six o'clock Ohio time. In Chagrin Falls, small ghouls and vampires would be trolling the neighborhood for candy. Simon liked to dress as Bigfoot and lope from house to house.

Halloween was a great tradition, I'd decided when I arrived in the States—after all, if presidents and saints had their own days, why shouldn't devils and ghosts? And ancestors? Simon agreed.

He told me about a Japanese ethnic group who believed animals were the spirits of dead people. According to the myth, hunters were doing their prey a favor by killing them, because then the spirits could return to Heaven. They enjoyed a short stay on Earth, but didn't want to stick around forever.

Sounded like the men in my life.

I tucked the pillow between my cheek and the bulkhead. My longest-lasting relationship—nearly two years—had been with Terry, my first fiancé. We met in 1976 at the Hiking & Biking Company in Johannesburg, where I worked as an assistant catalogue copywriter, and he as the accounting manager. Terry—who, at thirty, was nine years older than I—was a compact, well-proportioned man: muscles, nerves, and bones neatly arranged, mind as rational as a theorem. He was my first lover, and enjoyed teaching me techniques from a manual he propped against his gooseneck lamp. We spent entire weekends in bed. After we broke up and I slept with other men, I realized why he needed the manual.

In the beginning, Terry loved the way my mind flitted from word to word and subject to subject, how, within moments, pedal could lead to peddle and then to petal. He said most women bored him, but I amused him.

After the chaos of my childhood, I was magnetized by his unswervingly pragmatic approach to life.

"Of course I love you," he'd say, when I questioned him. "Would I be with you if I didn't?"

"Will you always love me?" I asked once, running my finger through his chest hairs.

"I have no idea," he said. "One can't predict the future."

I liked that he didn't try to claim what might not be possible. It seemed to me I could trust him.

Then, astonishingly, he asked me to marry him. It was early 1977. Soweto, the black township near Johannesburg, had exploded in riots six months before. Thousands of schoolchildren rebelled against the government's edict that lessons must be taught in Afrikaans, which to blacks was the language of oppression. Teenagers massed in the streets. The police and army moved in, shooting hundreds and hundreds of high-schoolers. Or so we learned via word of mouth—the government didn't admit to the extent of the massacre. The media was censored. Signs of revolution were everywhere: strikes, bombs, street demonstrations. We heard rumors of a Kill-A-White day. People crowded the SPCA looking for large dogs—rottweilers, Dobermans, Alsatians.

"There're three possible outcomes to this unrest," Terry said the night he proposed.

We were lying in bed, his arms encircling me. I felt like a boat in harbor. "You're the lee of my life," I said into his chest. He smelled of soap and sex. I moved my hand toward his groin.

He kissed my forehead. "We need to leave the country. This is how I see it: either there'll be a temporarily effective crackdown, resulting in further atrocities and only delaying black rule. Or there'll be a bloodbath during which twenty-eight million deservedly hostile black people annihilate four million whites."

I caressed his inner thigh. I didn't want to think about what was going on outside the room or what might happen in the future. I wanted to lead a normal life, at least for a while. Later I'd worry about other people.

He released me, rolled from the bed, and pulled on his socks. He always put his socks on first. He started at that end of his body and worked his way up. "Or—which I think is unlikely—we'll begin negotiations toward shared power, initiating a long period of change during which the economy will suffer, educational standards will decline, and crime will increase." He pulled on his Jockeys.

"What if we stay and fight the system?" I asked. "Become heroes of the revolution and turn things upside down? Once we're settled, I mean." We'd been planning to move in together.

"Kate. You're not making sense."

"Not heroes, then. Just—protest at rallies. Carry signs. Write to the paper."

"Do you really want to be thrown in prison and never heard from again?" He tugged on a T-shirt. "Statistically, our chances of achieving any measurable difference are tiny."

I snapped on my bra. Of course he was right.

"We could move to the States and marry there. A friend has offered me a job in San Diego," he said. "We'll be happier there."

Dizzied by the word *marry,* I sat on the bed. I forgot whether I was dressing or undressing. I undid my bra, thought for a moment, then hooked the straps together again and reached for my blouse. "That sounds logical."

My mother said I was wrong if I thought I could escape the government by crossing the Atlantic, and deluded to think Terry would marry me.

The flight attendant offered orange juice. I shook my head. Most of the passengers were asleep, lulled by the mumble of the plane's engines. On the movie screen, actors mouthed words. The woman next to me whistled softly through her teeth.

After living with Terry for nearly a year in San Diego—with no mention of a wedding date—I realized he'd begun to find me exasperatingly whimsical. No longer did he wrap me in his arms for hours, like a strange and precious object he'd found and couldn't bear to let go. His gaze would slip away from mine. He suppressed sighs. "No," he responded once when we were playing bridge, "I *don't* think the King of Hearts looks like Orson Welles. Concentrate, Kate. This isn't fun and games."

I was tiring of his logic. Tidiness and order and stability had lost their charm. I stopped alphabetizing our books. He re-alphabetized them.

We hardly talked. Our conversations were like beginners' tennis: lots of missed connections. I told him about my job at the Menu Venue, where I composed interesting names for mundane meals—

like, *Meatloaf, and Say Hello to Mash.* He said he doubted whether creativity whetted anyone's appetite.

I wondered if he stayed because he felt responsible for me. It made sense. He'd been brought up to be accountable, to lie in beds he'd made. But I didn't consider breaking up with him, not then. I refused to let my mother be proven right.

One day, I received a letter from her.

Dear Poppet,

I imagine by now you've discovered your fiancé is being un-faithful. I wanted to warn you, though, not to come back here. Oom Piet is up to his old tricks. DO NOT RETURN!

I showed Terry, explaining how she believed my uncle responsible for all our problems, including a rat that once died under our refrigerator and stank for weeks until we found its rotting body. Before, I'd told Terry only that my mother and I were estranged, that she and I just didn't get along.

He frowned. "That's bizarre. You're exaggerating, right?"

I shrugged and polished the faucets, leaving blotches of Silvo, which I knew would annoy him. Why had I bothered to try to explain my mother? No one could possibly understand what life with her had been like. Better not to tell people: I didn't want anyone's pity.

Then I began noticing how frequently he made trips to the store and dry cleaners. *Was* he seeing someone? Sneaking out to call a girlfriend?

But I refused to be suspicious. I didn't want to be like my mother.

One day Terry said he'd gotten crabs—pubic lice—from the health club. I laughed. I told him not to bring them home, we had enough pets. I asked if they walked sideways.

He rolled his eyes and went on another business trip.

Then, in the summer of 1979, he informed me one breakfast-time that he'd contracted a nonspecific urinary infection, so we wouldn't be able to make love for a while.

Was it the nonspecific part that bothered him? He so liked to be sure of his facts.

I stirred my cereal with my spoon, drowning a few wayward cornflakes. I looked up. Terry wore wide-wale corduroys and pointy tan shoes. I hated those corduroys. And the shoes.

"You're having an affair," I said.

He was washing the dishes in soapy water before putting them in the dishwasher. He lifted a plate, rinsed it under a stream of water, let it drip, and polished the china to a high shine. "Don't be absurd."

"You work late. You always have to go on trips to L.A. You bring home flowers, but you don't smile when you give them to me."

"Kate, you're reading too much into insignificant things."

"I'm not."

He placed the plate in the dishwasher. "Maybe you're the paranoid one, not your mother. What next, your uncle's making me do it?"

I threw my cereal in the sink. I couldn't win: if my mother was paranoid, so might I be; if she weren't paranoid, I had an overactive imagination.

After that, I didn't push the fidelity issue. But ennui consumed me. My dresses mysteriously slipped off hangers to the closet floor in the middle of the night; piles of bills and letters and other household jetsam gathered on the dresser and kitchen counter and desk; the oven grew fickle, so our dinners were either overdone or underdone. Our relationship staggered along like a wounded animal, finally collapsing in a heap the night a woman called asking to speak to Terry Scott—the Terry she'd met at a recent party. There were three Terry Scotts in the book. Was this his number?

"Did he wash his glass before accepting a drink?" I asked. He had.

That evening, I told him to leave. "Did you ever love me?" I asked.

"Of course," he said. "I wouldn't have asked you to come to America, otherwise. But you're so damn flippant and guarded all the time. I could never have a normal conversation with you."

Was he right? Was I guarded? I thought I'd been quite open. People didn't tell other people *everything*. Did they?

Leaning against the window now, feeling the plane engines thrum against my temple, I realized I hadn't thought about Terry for a long time. I tended to shut the years behind me, one by one, like doors, and ignore the hammering demons. It might not be what therapists meant by closure, but it worked for me.

We were within seven hours of Durban. I felt suspended between past and future: simultaneously, inchoately, both child and adult Kate. I pulled the Amanzimtoti Beach photograph from my wallet and stared at the two of us: mother and daughter. What did my mother look like now that she was in her early seventies?

As we flew deep into the African night, thirty-five-thousand feet above the Congo and the Serengeti and Zambia, my reflection turned spectral in the window. I imagined spirits and restless ancestors flying alongside the plane, surfing on the jet stream like dolphins of the dark. The night sky shimmered: was *umpundulu*, the lightning bird, spitting fire? Flapping his wings to make thunder?

The moon shone on the clouds below so it seemed we skimmed across snow. I pulled down the shade, shutting out the night, lifted the blanket to my chin, and closed my eyes, wondering what—or who—had possessed me to return.

"You want a Zola?" A large black cabdriver wearing a shirt decorated with yellow bananas grabbed my bag as I emerged from the airport terminal.

Though my flight had landed early in the morning—six o'clock—already it was hot and sticky. I longed for an air-conditioned room. "The Oliphant Hotel, please," I said. "What's a Zola?"

"A fast cab. In honor of Zola Budd." He half-bowed as he opened the car door. I slid in the back seat, remembering the barefoot runner who'd tangled legs with American Mary Decker Slaney—or vice versa—in the 1984 Olympics. Zola Budd had competed as a British citizen because South Africa had been banned from the Olympic Games at the time.

The radio blared choral music as we drove toward Durban, or *eThegwini,* as the Zulu called the city. My cotton blouse grew damp against the vinyl seat. From my window, the sun-splattered, yacht-dotted Indian Ocean, coastal banana trees, and undulating sugar-cane fields looked much the same as they had two decades earlier. The stench of molasses and dead fish permeated the air as we passed the docks, which were lined with tugboats, tankers, and ships flying Liberian flags. Anchors dribbled rust down their steel sides. Seagulls swooped to perch on coils of rope. In the seventies, a worker had been buried in sugar in one of the huge silos. *Good night, sweet prince*, I thought, remembering the line from *Hamlet*.

Within half an hour we were on the beachfront, which had changed considerably. The paddling pools had been reconfigured, and the aquarium repainted and renamed Sea World. And now black and brown people sat on hotel balconies eating breakfast with whites, waited in line for the same buses, and, festooned with buckets and spades and surfboards, headed to the same beaches.

I felt as though I were watching an old movie, familiar but long forgotten, colorized to reveal new shadings and depth and vibrancy. Though happy to see the changes, I experienced an odd sense of dislocation.

Once in my hotel room, I checked my messages back home. Bagheera was fine, and preparation for the ReFute pitch on Thursday was going well, Bernie said. I was worried about the presentation. I felt toward my ads the way parents do: I was proud of them and wanted them to succeed. And now they were going to graduate without me.

Nothing from Simon. Why would there be?

I showered, dressed in a pair of white cotton pants and short-sleeved teal T-shirt, and headed down to the lobby. When I emerged onto the street, a rickshaw driver wearing a multicolored tunic and foot-high tiara made of feathers and painted tusks gestured toward his two-wheeled cart.

I shook my head and walked along Upper Marine Parade. If I continued in that direction, I'd pass the Sunken Gardens, where, one hot afternoon nearly thirty years earlier, I'd watched a man watching my mother, and wondered if he might be a government agent as she'd claimed. In the Sunken Gardens, too, I'd betrayed my black friend, Joshua, an event I'd done my best—along with many others—to forget. Now wasn't the time to evoke such memories, or I might catch the next plane back to the States. I stopped, turned right, and headed west toward my mother's flat.

The farther from the beachfront I walked, the dirtier the streets became. Beggars of every color held out their hands—a scene as racially mixed and politically correct as photos in an American corporate brochure. A man bumped into me and I clutched my bag. The concierge had warned me not to carry valuables.

When I turned onto Grosvenor Street, I nearly tripped over a black busker sitting on the sidewalk. Two stumps protruded from his torso. He'd wrapped his truncated limbs in a fraying pair of pinstriped pants similar to the ones our gardener Winston used to wear. On the sidewalk in front of him was a cloth cap containing a few fifty-cent and rand coins. He picked at a guitar made from half a rusty oilcan strung with wire.

I opened my bag, reached for my wallet, and held out several South African rand notes. The man smelled rancid, as though he'd been cooked too long in the sun.

"Do you remember when people used to throw coins from the flats?" I asked. Black teenagers, dressed in rags, had played home-made instruments on the sidewalk; police tended to leave the makeshift bands alone as long as they didn't loiter too long. Flat-dwellers stood on balconies to listen, and if they liked the music, they disappeared inside, twisted coins in pieces of paper, and flung them into the street.

The beggar's eyes were filmed and rheumy. "*Ja.* Money storms. *Reen van die hemel!*" He fingered a scar on his forehead and smiled. "Ping!" he said.

I gave him money. I'd changed dollars into rand when I registered. Each note was illustrated with a different wild animal—rhino, elephant, water buffalo.

He laughed, spraying phlegm. "*Dankie, dankie, missus. Wat is jou naam?*"

"Kate," I said.

"*Goeiemore,* Kate." Then he loped away, using his two stumps and the palms of his hands to move along, his improvised guitar tucked under his arm. As I replaced my wallet in my purse, I realized I'd given him a lion—fifty rand, about twelve U.S. dollars—not a rhino, as I'd intended, which would have been ten rand, or two dollars. He'd disappeared around the corner. I shrugged and continued walking.

A couple of white teenagers leaned against a boarded-up bottle store—liquor store—watching a low-rider car veer along the street. The driver leaned out and banged the metal door with his palm. *"Lekker lekker,"* he yelled, making smacking sounds in my direction. I picked up my pace, strode three blocks, and stopped, glancing up at Kingfisher Court. The building seemed to move, but it was an illusion caused by shifting clouds.

My mother might be inside. Or she might not. Neither option sounded good.

I crossed the street, entered the building, and caught the elevator to the third floor. When I reached number three-sixty-one, I halted and stared at the door. A new veneer hadn't concealed the dent next to the peephole. The damage had endured. I rang the bell.

No one answered, though I pressed my finger hard on the buzzer for at least two minutes. "Mom. It's Kate!" I yelled. "Mom? It really is me."

Silence, except for a radio playing rap music.

I banged on the door. "No one sent me. Are you all right?" I rapped until my knuckles burned.

The door of the adjacent flat opened, and a man popped his head out, like a weaverbird from its nest. "I haven't seen her for a while. You need to talk to the caretaker. Flat one-oh-three."

I took the stairs to the first floor and rang the bell.

A plump woman answered the door. She wore a sleeveless pink-and-orange dress made of Crimplene, a stretchy dimpled fabric. She looked like a human sunset. Fat swung from her upper arms, the way my mother's used to. I felt breathless, thrown back in time. The smell of mielie-pap porridge drifted from the inside of her flat. A large sunflower clock and a tapestry—oos, wes, tuis is bes—hung on her wall.

"Ja?" she said. *"Kan ek jou help?"*

"*Goeiemore,*" I said. "Mevrou Bakker?" My Afrikaans deserted me. "Um . . . ek . . . I . . . about Mrs. Jensen in three-sixty-one? I'm her daughter. I tried to call you—we spoke once. From America."

She crossed her arms on the shelf of her cerise stomach. "Her daughter, huh?" She took me in and her lips thinned as if my appearance offended her. Didn't I look prodigal enough?

Mevrou Bakker frowned. "The woman in that flat, she warns me to be careful of strange people asking about her."

"So she's here!" I said in relief, though the muscles in my legs tightened as if preparing for my escape.

"The flat is empty now." The caretaker slammed her door. A puff of wind lifted my hair.

I rang the bell again.

She opened the door. "And I don't know where she's gone, so no use asking me. *Totsiens.*" She shut the door.

Once more I rang the bell, pressing until my finger hurt.

Again, she opened the door. "*Asseblief,* please, go away. We've had enough trouble here."

"What kind of trouble?" I asked. "Is she sick? Was there an ambulance?"

"Go, please."

This time, after she slammed the door, I heard the key turn in the lock.

Durban
1966

On September 6, 1966, the day after Prime Minister Verwoerd—leader of the National Party—was assassinated, my mother and I left Johannesburg for Durban. Dr. Verwoerd had been stabbed to death by a parliamentary messenger named Dimitri Tsafendas. Tsafendas was insane, the police said. He claimed he was being eaten from the inside out by a giant carrot-loving tapeworm that instructed him to murder the prime minister. Mom said we should feel sorry for Tsafendas if he were crazy, though in her opinion, his tapeworm had a point.

We drove along the N1 in Mom's old powder-blue Fiat 500. My dad used to say the Fiat went so slowly Mom could be arrested for loitering. She'd sold his Ford, planning to use the cash, along with money left in the bank account, to pay the rent until she found a job as a legal secretary. She'd worked as a typist before they married.

I felt like I was going on holiday. Mom sang as she drove: *Fly me to the moon/Let me play among the stars/Let me see what spring is like/On Jupiter and Mars.* She loved Frank Sinatra and Nat King Cole.

The sun shone high in the sky and wispy clouds blurred into blue. It was the beginning of the Michaelmas holidays, the start of spring. I'd missed an entire term: Mom had arranged for me to study at home until we left, telling the principal I had chicken pox.

She'd been so convincing I'd woken up itchy some mornings. Now I'd have one term of Standard Four at my new school before the year ended, then, in January, I'd be in Standard Five. After that, high school.

The road unfurled through Heidelberg, Harrismith, Van Reenen's Pass, Ladysmith, and Estcourt, then over Mooi River and into Pietermaritzburg, the capital of Natal province. I traced our progress on the map with my finger and imagined myself an explorer. I'd recently learned about the Voortrekkers who had forged their way into the interior in covered wagons during the seventeen hundreds, and though we were English-speaking, not Afrikaans, and heading in the opposite direction, I imagined myself a pioneer.

About thirty miles south of Pietermaritzburg, we stopped for tea and scones at the Rob Roy hotel overlooking the Valley of a Thousand Hills. We sat on the verandah. The jasmine smelled so strong I thought its scent was visible, but it was steam rising from our teapot. Hills rippled into the horizon, threaded with paths dotted with tiny black figures carrying babies on their backs and spiky bundles of firewood on their heads.

"That's why natives make such a racket inside the house, you know," an old woman sitting at the next table said to her friend, inclining her head toward the view. "Because they're used to shouting from hilltop to hilltop."

"Some people have no idea what they're talking about," my mother said loudly.

The two old women gave her a peculiar look and then turned away.

My mother shook her head. "Honestly!"

The scones arrived, brought by an Indian man in a white tuxedo-like outfit whose breath smelled of strange spices when he leaned forward to place the tray on the white linen tablecloth.

"Thank you," my mother said. She took an enormous bite of her scone. A blob of cream stuck to the tip of her nose. She pursed and patted her lips then picked up the silver teapot. She smiled, but all I could see was the splodge. Terrified I'd begin giggling and not be able to stop, I looked away. To distract myself I stared at my crazy-mirror reflection in the silver teapot and made faces until Mom said I'd better not because the wind might change.

"Remember? That's why warthogs have scrunched-up snouts," she said.

A man walked past and tripped over the rug because he was gaping at my mother instead of looking where he was going. She was plumper than before, but still pretty.

It occurred to me that I was happy. I had her all to myself. We would be more than mother and daughter—we would be close friends and advise each other on handbags and scarves. When I was a little older, people might ask if she were my sister.

When we arrived in Durban the humidity slapped us in the face like a steaming hot cloth. We drove down West Street, toward the beachfront, past fishy-smelling Durban Aquarium, and turned left onto Upper Marine Parade. As Mom had promised, to our right, opposite the beach, were paddling pools and kiosks selling ice cream and candy-floss, and an arena where teenagers shrieked in Dodgem cars, and the Cuban Hat restaurant with an outsize yellow plaster sombrero on its roof. Tall Zulu men crowned with huge headdresses pranced like horses between the harnesses of rickshaws.

The farther we drove along the beachfront, the shorter and grubbier the buildings grew, and when we neared the end of the line, my mother turned left and we drove deeper and deeper into the shadows away from the sea. Blocks of flats were named Flamingo Heights, Cormorant Place, and Hoopoe View. But there were no trees, only buildings. And no birds, except for a couple of anxious seagulls.

The car continued through a red light. "Hey!" I said, turning to my mother, who was pumping the brakes. I gripped the dashboard. Luckily, no one was in the intersection except for a boy on a bicycle who pedaled fast and made it out of our way. The Fiat rolled to a stop outside a tall building called Starling Flats. Mom put her head down on the steering wheel and sobbed. Her back heaved.

"The car died too?" I asked.

She nodded.

I patted her shoulder, feeling a sudden rush of protective love.

She pointed to a TO LET sign in a window. "You think this will be all right?" She blew her nose. "We can't afford much, you know. Otherwise we'd live in Durban North, in a house."

"Yes, this seems like a nice place," I said. Starling Flats was the ugliest building I'd ever seen. The exterior was grimy, the windows scummy from the thick ocean air. Next door was a scabby park— or maybe it was a vacant lot—littered with crushed beer cans and cigarette *stompies.*

Mom talked to the caretaker and paid one month's rent. During the first few days, we had no furniture and slept on the floor in sleeping bags. Mom went to get groceries and I explored. At least we were near the beach. If you rode the lift to the rooftop, where shirts and pants and sheets flapped on clotheslines, you could see red-bottomed ships hovering on the rim of the ocean waiting to load goods in the harbor, as well as yachts and sailboats and waves speckled with surfers. The air was rich with the smell of seaweed. If you took the lift to ground level, walked six blocks, and made a right past the corner store where maids sat on the low concrete wall, chatting and gesticulating and drinking *maas*—a kind of sour milk—you ended up on North Beach where white women basted to brown.

Bits and pieces of our former life arrived in the moving van: the blue-and-white floral chairs and coffee table with bandy, clawed legs, which I imagined might run out the door, fed up with the lack of space. Our flat consisted of a living room/dining room separated from the bedroom by a concertina divider. The beds had to be pushed together to leave room for our chest of drawers. I chose the bed next to the window and used the windowsill as a shelf where I put my hippo, a photo of my father, my favorite books, and a bead doll Prudence had given me. In the kitchenette, the stove and refrigerator looked as though they were trying to elbow each other out of the way.

Our Formica table was now the dining room table.

Mom placed her Belleek vase on a side table next to the lamp, together with an ashtray shaped like a sailor's hat, which I'd found in a gift shop the first day we arrived. On the side it said, WELCOME TO DURBAN. YOU WON'T WANT TO LEAVE!

Shortly before school started, my mother and I caught the bus into the city center, climbed off at Smith Street near City Hall, and walked up Grey Street, where Indian merchants sold bolts of startling pink and orange fabric, and women with red dots painted on their foreheads glided in saris from shop to shop. We climbed up mysterious stairways and discovered halls where tulle and silks and satins spooled out on endless tables. Squeezing between waterfalls of color, we fingered the fabric and breathed in the smell of new cloth. I spun wire racks of Simplicity patterns, seeking dress designs my mother could sew on her Singer. The air when we emerged into the streets was redolent with masala and cumin and coriander and we stopped to eat vegetable samosas fried in hot oil.

All at once I had to pee. I said, "I'm going to the loo," but realized my mother hadn't heard me. She was searching among odd buttons at a vendor's stall. I noticed a sign saying NONWHITES outside the door of the restroom. But I was desperate. I'd be quick. Mom hated apartheid so I didn't think she'd care. Once, at Zoo Lake, she'd taken a marker pen from her bag and scribbled over the EUROPEANS ONLY sign on one of the benches.

I went in, opened the swing door to a stall, and nearly gagged on the urine smell. I pulled down my panties, squatting above the rim, thighs straining. I heard clattering heels.

"Poppet?" My mother yanked the door open. "This is not our toilet! Out, out! Who told you to come in here?" She seemed frantic, so I hauled up my panties and followed her out, a trickle of warm pee dribbling down my thigh. People stared at me.

"Nobody told me," I said.

She yanked me all the way to the bus stop, her packages bumping against my side. "The police," she said, "the police might see you."

"But—"

"Quiet."

We waited for the bus in silence. Mynah birds squawked in the tree overhanging the shelter, which was covered with droppings. Birds had it easy.

My mother's breath hissed through her teeth. Why was she so angry?

When we climbed on the bus, the driver asked where we were going. My mother said, "Battery Beach, but maybe you know already," and gave him twenty-cents fare. He looked puzzled.

I sat down. "How would he know?"

"They're clever."

"Who? The government?"

She put her finger to her lips.

At home, she made tea, warming the pot first as usual. Then she sat down on her favorite chair in the corner, opened her pack of Westminsters, and smoked one after the other. Once or twice she missed the ashtray and flakes of ash fluttered to the floor.

"I'm sorry," I said eventually, wondering if she would ever get around to cooking dinner. "I didn't know it was wrong. I mean, I did, but I didn't think it mattered, just once, if you had to go."

"But now we have to be extra careful not to attract attention." She leaned forward and her eyes glittered behind her glasses. "I've had an idea. We're going to change our name from Jones to Jensen."

"Jensen?" I was momentarily distracted. I would have preferred Le Roux, or Du Maurier, or something much more romantic. *Fiona La Fevre* sounded good. Jensen sounded like an English butler from the P. G. Wodehouse stories my father used to read.

She sucked on her cigarette and exhaled. Because she smoked so much it was beginning to seem as if her breath were blue. Putting her Westminster on the rim of the ashtray, where it teetered, she said, "Never tell anyone—anyone!—about our old name, or we'll be discovered, and you'll be taken away from me." She stabbed the life out of her cigarette and hoisted herself to her feet. "Time for dinner."

I followed her to the kitchen, watching her bottom wobble. Since Dad had died, she'd been eating toast and marmalade and puddings and potatoes. That's why we'd gone shopping for fabric—she needed new dresses. Even the skin on her face had begun to droop, like melting white wax.

She stirred ground beef and onions and eggs and bread crumbs together into little cakes she called *frikkadels,* which she fried in fat drippings and served with soggy sheets of cabbage and stringy Hubbard squash. I missed Prudence's juicy lamb chops and jacket potatoes served with a dot of butter.

"What I'm going to do is this: I'm going to start keeping notes," Mom said. "It's all very complicated. Piet's uncle's cousin twice removed—that would be Sarel Du Plessis—is employed by the Bureau of State Security, BOSS. The people who spy for the government. The whole Du Plessis clan is involved. You see?"

I didn't. "Why are they after us?"

She flipped the *frikkadels.* "To frighten me. For reasons you're too young to understand."

"How did they kill Dad? You didn't say."

She lowered her voice. "You never know who's listening." She pointed her spatula toward the electrical outlet. "Maybe they put something in his beer at the golf club."

"But he didn't have anything to drink at the golf course. He rushed home because it was my birthday."

She dumped the *frikkadels* on a plate. "But, but, but. Who told you that?"

"He did."

"Poppet. You need to trust me, please."

After dinner, she unscrewed all the covers of the electrical outlets and shone the torchlight into them. I didn't say anything.

I went into the bedroom and lay down on my bed, wishing I could talk to Prudence. "Hippodad, things will be more normal when school starts, don't you think?" I said.

It sounded as though he said *yes*, but of course I knew it was only the kettle beginning to whistle.

On the first day of the new term, I dressed in my school uniform and stood in front of the mirror my mother had propped against the door. My uniform was a white dress with a maroon Peter Pan collar. At my waist was a cloth belt with a see-through plastic button. A Panama hat, encircled with a maroon-and-cream-striped ribbon decorated by the school crest, was wedged onto my thick curls and threatened to bounce off at any moment. An elastic band, tucked under my chin, kept the hat under control. Both my mom and I wore eyeglasses with blue plastic frames. She'd started wearing her spectacles more and more.

"You look nice," she said.

The sun pooled through the window. If I stepped a few paces back, I appeared thinner, and wavier, as if I were underwater. I assumed the wavy part was the mirror's fault. My mother, who stood beside me, wore a lime-colored dress. She'd started wearing a two-way stretch as a foundation garment, but still the fabric strained over her stomach. The room smelled of lilac hairspray.

We were quite similar in appearance. I wasn't sure how I felt about that anymore. We'd both rounded out: Mrs. Tweedledum and her daughter.

"You look nice too," I said.

My school was in Durban North, the rich part of town across the Umgeni River, miles from where we lived. Mom refused to let me go to the local one with other poor kids. We might have Enemies everywhere, but I expect she felt the ones in Durban North would at least be higher class.

After her second cup of tea, she left the flat. She couldn't come with me because she was starting work as a legal secretary with Brink & Boudeman on Smith Street. The buildings in the city center were tall and gray, like filing cabinets. I pictured the floors opening out, like drawers filled with tiny people.

I made toast and marmalade, longing for my father, who cooked the best scrambled eggs in the world. He followed a recipe he'd clipped from *Good Housekeeping* when he was a night janitor in Wales. I could almost taste the cheddar cheese he sprinkled on top.

Through the window, I could see the rear of a block of flats veined with pipes and zigzagged with fire escapes. The surface resembled a gigantic Snakes-and-Ladders game. From my bedroom on Lees Avenue in Johannesburg, I'd had a view of a mulberry tree. On warm Highveld afternoons, bees had buzzed around the fruit.

Before I left to catch the municipal bus—I had to catch two to get to Durban North—I said good-bye to Hippodad.

The class stared at me when I walked in. Their eyes swiveled toward me, then away, like a single multi-eyed space monster. I smiled and my top lip caught on my teeth but I managed to force my mouth closed.

After a couple of days, I began to recognize some of the kids, like Piet Vermeer and Sarie Viljoen, who were easier to remember because they both had strong Afrikaans accents. Usually Afrikaners went to different schools than English-speaking kids—not because they had to, as was the case with natives, but because of the language difference.

At Little Break a girl with pigtails came up to me.

"Where are you from?" she said.

"Johannesburg," I said.

"Why did you come here so late in the school year?"

My mom had said not to talk about Dad's death. Besides, I wanted to be like everyone else. I felt muddled. "My dad was transferred here," I said. "And we'll be moving to Durban North as soon as we find a house."

"Oh. My name is Elsie. You can sit with us, if you like." She offered me grapes.

"Thanks a bunch," I said. She didn't get the joke.

A week later, playing field hockey, I tried to hit the ball into the goal and instead broke Cheryl Brown's nose. Her blood glued the grass blades together. Kids said I was jealous of Cheryl because she was pretty and popular. Elsie was her best friend, and said I wasn't welcome in their group anymore. Mark Poulos called me Big Bottom.

At dinner, I couldn't help crying a bit when I told my mother what had happened. She slapped fried fish fingers on my plate. They slid in the grease toward the edge of the plate. "So this girl ran right into your stick? What a terrible thing to do to you!"

Dad always said she took things too seriously. Earlier in the year she'd written an angry letter to his boss when he wasn't promoted. It was all in capital letters and had seventeen exclamation marks. I saw her writing it and asked him what had happened when his boss read it. He said he'd intercepted the envelope. *Better not to upset your mother if you can help it,* he'd said. *It doesn't take much to set her off.*

I poked my fish with my fork. "It was my fault. I should have been more careful."

She held the frying pan like a weapon. "Who is this child?"

"Mom, it's okay. Never mind."

She went into the kitchen, returning with a loaf of bread and butter. "You watch out for those kids."

I chewed my chips, trying to think of a different subject. "How was work?"

"Tiring. But they seem to appreciate how fast I type. Ninety words a minute, you know."

I pictured her fingers moving up and down fast, like hummingbird wings.

She smiled and sliced the bread. "Not bad, huh?"

After dinner I listened to the seven o'clock news on the radio. The government was bulldozing District Six in the Cape, resettling thousands of Coloureds—people of mixed race—in different towns. The newscaster said it was for the best, because it had been a slum—a "black spot"—with rats and garbage everywhere. Why didn't they ask people if they *wanted* to leave instead of loading them onto lorries and just taking them to another place? Prudence had said the police sometimes got families muddled up and parents couldn't find their kids.

My mother was asleep in her chair, her mouth open, snoring faintly.

Did she think we'd be dumped in a different city and maybe separated if Oom Piet learned our whereabouts?

"Jensen," I whispered to myself. "My name is Kate *Jensen.*"

Because Mom left early in the morning, I packed my own lunch, inventing interesting sandwich combinations like Marmite and sugar, or marmalade and mayonnaise. Now and again I bought a Crunchie bar from the downstairs vending machine. Or a cream doughnut at the tuck shop.

I was doing well in tests. After a few weeks, the most wonderful thing happened. I found a friend: Hettie Williams. Hettie was the most popular girl in our class. She was already twelve and wore a bra. Her hair was shiny black with red tints. The minute she left the school grounds, she hiked up her skirt, rolling it up beneath her belt, showing as much of her thighs as Twiggy, though Hettie's legs weren't as thin. Hettie made sure I was sitting near her in class. She kept meaning to tell her parents she needed glasses, she said. The blackboard was fuzzy so she had to check my work to make sure she'd written things down right. I thought she could see fine, but I didn't say anything.

"Kate," she said one day, "look. Patrick's head is bigger than the world globe." She leaned toward the blond kid sitting in front of us, Patrick Osch. "Excuse me," she said. "Could you move? Your left ear is blocking out America." It wasn't *that* funny, but we couldn't stop giggling.

In sewing class we were supposed to be learning how to mend socks and I said, "Darn!" in a pretend-surprised way, which set us off again.

The next day, when I threw a Super Ball on the ground and forgot to get out of the way and broke my glasses, she helped me pick up the bits and pieces and stood with me at the bus stop so I wouldn't climb on a black bus by mistake and end up in Umlazi. "Want to come home with me?" she asked. Her eyes had violet spokes, like bicycle wheels. "We could do our homework together."

"I can't come today," I said. "We don't have a phone and I'm not allowed to call my mom at work, so I can't tell her where I am. But maybe tomorrow?"

"Bring your makeup. We'll experiment."

I managed to grope my way home. I found my spare glasses. After dinner, when my mother was ironing, I told her what had happened. Brown curls of hair clung to her forehead, which glistened with sweat. She asked me who had done it and wouldn't believe me when I told her I'd thrown the ball myself. When I mentioned Hettie's name, a funny expression crossed her face. She put down the iron and it hissed. "What does this girl's father do for a living?"

"Why do you care? If he's a dustman, say, does it matter?" I made myself a banana and anchovy-paste sandwich.

"No," she said, "but I'd like to know all the same."

"Well, I don't know."

"He works for the government, doesn't he? Hettie's an Afrikaans name." She yanked the plug out of the wall. "You want your uncle to find out where we are?"

My skin prickled. Hettie was being cast as an Enemy. "Hettie's short for Henrietta. Her last name is Williams."

"Williams. Really? Williams . . . I'll make a note. Poppet, I tell you what, I'm too tired to cook." She walked into the living room and pulled her wallet out of her bag. "Why don't you run down to the store and get meat pies and Chelsea buns?"

I was glad the subject had changed. I took the money, nearly knocking over her favorite Belleek vase, caught the lift to the lobby, and trotted six blocks to the store. A wrinkled white man smelling of beer lurched out of an alleyway. Lots of hoboes lived near us. They preferred the warm weather in Durban. So did cockroaches.

After nine o'clock, while Mom slept, I took an old lipstick and powder compact from her drawer and put it in my school case. I stayed up and finished my homework, making up a story about my father, the boat we owned, and a forty-pound fish we'd caught in the Umgeni River. It was supposed to be a true story about a day with a parent. I wrote about my father because I didn't think people would believe a day with my mother.

In class the next week, my teacher, Mrs. Schorn, said the essay about my father and the forty-pound fish was the best in the whole class and showed imagination—maybe too much, because she doubted if there were any forty-pound fish in the Umgeni River, certainly none easily caught by an eleven-year-old with a small fishing rod and worm.

"It's beautifully written, Kate," she said. "That's why I wanted you to read it aloud. But in the future, remember there's a difference between fact and fiction."

I should have simply nodded and gone to my desk. Instead, I made things worse. "I meant a fourteen-pound fish," I said. It was amazing how, when you told one lie, another seemed to follow. My father was always strict about telling the truth. I hoped he wasn't looking down from Heaven at that particular instant. Or floating around the room, if he were a spirit.

"Fourteen pounds?" Her lips turned down. "What kind was it, exactly?"

Suddenly I couldn't think of the name of one fish in the entire world, besides a whale, and there were no whales in the Umgeni, that much I knew. I tried to picture Durban Aquarium, but all I could see was the blue water slopping against the glass. My cousin Andre and I used to fish in the stream at the bottom of Oom Piet's farm, but I couldn't remember what we'd caught. Not much. A fingerling or two.

"Kate?"

"Salmon," I said, finally.

Some of the kids laughed. Mark Poulos held up his hand. "Ma'am, there aren't any salmon in the Umgeni," he said. "And salmon don't grow so big."

"I must be mixed up with another fish," I said. The class laughed. I felt the heat rising to my cheeks, overtaking my whole body, as though I were a crayfish somebody had dropped in boiling water. The school was on the top of a small hill and from the window I could see playing fields and tiled roofs and beyond the houses the ocean, scalloped with waves. I wished I could dive in and cool off and swim all the way to Japan and become a geisha girl.

"Quiet, everyone." Mrs. Schorn patted me on the shoulder. "Wonderful descriptions, anyway. Perhaps we can talk at Little Break."

I collapsed into my seat, mortified. Hettie leaned toward me. She cupped her hand over my ear and said, "Guess you're *off the hook,*" and started to giggle.

Maybe because I'd been on the verge of tears, I exploded into laughter instead. I couldn't stop, though Hettie managed to control herself. I snorted and the snot in my nose bubbled out. The other kids stared and giggled. Except for Patrick Osch. He looked sorry for me. I didn't want to be pitied by fat-headed Patrick.

Little Break was right after English. Mrs. Schorn was my favorite teacher, which made things worse. She was dressed in a fashionable granny-print dress with lace along the bodice, and she smelled of incense. "Kate, I know you've had a difficult time adjusting," she said, holding my hands in her soft palms. "I understand your father left your mother while you were living in Saudi Arabia? That must have been difficult for you."

Saudi Arabia? I pictured my father's spirit riding a camel. "Oh.

Yes." I fiddled with the button on my belt. Why had my mother made up such a story? I supposed to stop them from digging into our past and asking what school I'd previously attended.

"Poor little thing," she said, squeezing my hand.

I wished she weren't being sympathetic, because it made me want to cry. It felt as though an enormous yawp might burst from me, so loud that birds for miles around would be frightened and fly away.

"But there's no excuse for misbehaving, and especially not for lying." She gave me her handkerchief. It had a little bouquet of flowers embroidered in the corner and smelled of lilac. "Here." Then she patted me. "Go enjoy your break."

Hettie was waiting on the playground. One of the boys yelled, "The whopper told a whopper!" but Hettie put her arm around my shoulder and steered me away.

"Don't worry about them," she said. "So maybe you and your dad didn't catch a big fish. Who cares?"

After school, we ran down the steep driveway, picking up speed as we approached the bottom of the hill, then slowing down. We walked past hibiscus hedges and scented flower beds and clematis-draped walls to her house at the end of a cul-de-sac. It was a single-story brick house with a big garden. A lilo floated on the surface of her pool, which was built in the shape of a comma. She had two kittens, Oliver (because he always wanted more) and Gulliver (because he liked to roam), and an Alsatian dog called Voetsak.

"But *voetsak* means 'go away,' " I said. *Voetsak!* was about as close as a word came to being a swearword without being one.

"My dad thinks it's funny," she said. "He says it'll serve someone right if they come onto our property and yell at the dog. He'll head toward them instead of running away. But I call him Voetie."

"So what does your father do?" I asked. We perched on stools in her kitchen, which was nearly the size of our entire flat. Hettie's mom was at a Parent-Teacher Association meeting. Her maid Beauty baked cheese scones and we drank Coke. The air smelled of butter. I blew through my straw and the fizz dampened my nose.

"He's a private investigator," she said. "I'll show you his study. He collects magnifying glasses and murder weapons."

A private investigator wasn't quite the government, but I could imagine what my mother would say if I told her. I would never be allowed to talk to Hettie again. I sighed and wiped my nose with the back of my hand. It seemed like lying was going to have to become a way of life.

"What's your dad like?" Hettie said. "Does he really fish?"

"No." I decided to tell her the truth. "You know what, I don't have a dad. He died in July. My mom and I live in a flat on the beachfront. I don't know if we'll ever move. We're quite poor right now."

She munched on her food and narrowed her eyes. "Your dad is dead? That's sad. But you said—"

"I miss him lots. So—" I tried to think about something else and reached for another scone. I didn't want to be always crying in front of her or she would think I was no fun.

Hettie put down her scone and wiped the crumbs off the table with a napkin into her palm, then shook them onto her plate. She folded her napkin, leaned forward, and grasped my hands. "Listen, Kate, I'm sorry about your dad. But if you want to be friends with me, you have to tell me the truth about everything. Okay? What this means is you lied to me and I don't like being lied to, okay?"

"It's not like I usually lie." I panicked and spilled my Coke. Beauty reached to wipe it up.

"Okay," Hettie said. "So don't."

"I won't. Knock knock."

"Who's there?"

"Isabelle."

"Isabelle who?"

"Isabelle necessary on a bicycle?'

She giggled. I shifted on my stool in relief and nearly fell off, which made her giggle more, so I teetered on purpose a little longer. "You're funny," she said. "Come. I'll show you my dad's stuff."

The study smelled of pipe tobacco and leather. There were glass cases on the walls with old guns called blunderbusses, pearl-handled daggers, and *assegais*—spears—as well as shields made of animal skins and a *sjambok* like Oom Piet's. A bookcase was filled with books on the Boer War. On his desk was an ashtray in the shape of a skull.

My mother would have fainted.

"So what happened to your dad?" Hettie asked, sitting in her father's leather chair, swinging her feet. "How did he die?"

I told her about his heart attack.

She felt sorry for me, so she let me flip through her dad's fingerprint collection. She swore he had Jack the Ripper's thumbprint. I didn't think *that* was true.

We played hopscotch in her driveway and listened to Beatles singles and I pretended to swoon over Paul, though actually I preferred John.

Then we worked on her arithmetic homework.

When my mother asked for the second time what Hettie's father did for a living, I said he was an undertaker. I said he hardly went anywhere besides the morgue, and her mother stayed home and helped with grieving families.

Mom, who was sitting in her usual chair with her legs tucked to the side, broke matches into small pieces and tossed them into her ashtray. "You're playing with fire, poppet."

"Hettie's family doesn't know Oom Piet," I said.

She stopped fiddling with bits of wood. "They told you that? You've spoken to them about your uncle?" Her hand covered her mouth. Her fingertips left a smudge of ash on her upper lip. "Oh, poppet, what have you done?"

I picked up my school case, intending to go to the bedroom

until she forgot about Hettie—at least for today. I decided never to mention Hettie's name again. "I didn't—"

"Don't lie, please." Looking stern, she untucked her legs and put her feet on the floor. "Tell Hettie you won't obey her orders." She wobbled upright.

"She isn't order—"

"That uncle of yours," she said, "he has no conscience! No conscience! And now this Hettie girl . . ." She put her face close to mine. "You told her, didn't you?"

"No, I—"

My mother straightened and backed away from me. "If Oom Piet finds us, it will be your fault. When I'm locked up, being brainwashed," her voice rose to a squeak, "I'll be very sad to think it was my own daughter who betrayed me." She lumbered to the kitchen.

After a minute, I followed her. "Mom. Hettie isn't—"

"Oh, dear, poppet. How can you be expected to understand?" Her cheeks were wet. The chopping board was covered with cut-up onion, bread crumbs, and chicken noodle soup mix. She wiped her nose with a dishcloth. Her eyes were red.

I stared at the sliced onions, unsure whether she was crying or not. "I won't tell anyone about Oom Piet, okay?"

She tipped the mixture into an enamel bowl and sniffed loudly. "Go away, please. I'm cooking dinner."

After Hettie and I became friends, kids mostly stopped calling me names out loud, though occasionally I'd hear giggles and whispers of "Big Bottom" and "Fat Arse." I hated myself for being unable to stop eating doughnuts and chocolate and meat pies and Chelsea buns, as if an *abathakathi*, a Zulu witch, had cast a spell on me and sent a *tokoloshe* to make me hungry all the time. *Tokoloshes* were small evil beings that acted as witches' familiars, visiting victims at night. Once I slept with a cup of cooking oil and the saltshaker next to my bed because I remembered Prudence saying *tokoloshes* were scared away by oil and salt. But after three nights, it still hadn't worked, and so I made popcorn instead.

Then Mom baked a lemon meringue pie for dessert because I'd done well in my English test. I refused a second slice.

"What's wrong with my pie?" she asked, sniffing the meringue. "It tastes funny?"

"It's very good," I said, sighing, and ate another slice.

Some kids didn't like me because I knew so much—like how to spell coelacanth, and who discovered gold on the Witwatersrand (his name was George Harrison, same as the Beatle), and the fact that Soweto was short for South Western Townships. But Hettie liked me *because* I was smart. She felt she was stupid and sometimes she cried when her dad got upset about her bad marks. Every day I looked forward to seeing her at school.

Hettie was like a sister and friend and mother and cousin and aunt and uncle all rolled into one. I didn't care what anyone said about her using me, I knew she liked my company too. She couldn't have only pretended to laugh when I said funny things. We sat together at break and played jacks. And she stopped sneaking glances at my exercise books in class. I went to her house after school nearly every day, helping her to understand fractions, even improper ones.

My mother didn't know how often I went to Hettie's place because I was back by the time she got home.

At the end of the year, I earned first place in class. Everyone cheered at the award ceremony or anyway it sounded like everyone. Lots of the mothers patted me on the head afterward. Mine wasn't there. She said it might be dangerous to be seen. My report card noted I'd be promoted to Standard Five in January. *Kate is a delight to teach,* it said.

I hung my medal around Hippodad's neck.

On the second to last day of school, Hettie yanked me into the girls' restroom. "You're going to have to help me more next year," she said. "My dad got home last night from his business trip and saw my report. He's mad with me. Look." She lifted her skirt and pulled down her panties. I noticed how pretty they were: pink with white lace. But then I saw her bottom was striped with purple-and-green bruises.

"He says it's the only way I'll learn," she said. "In between smacks I have to say, 'I will do better.'"

I hugged her and said I'd make sure she got an A in the future. She cried so much I thought she would melt. "I'll tell the teachers about him," I said.

She pulled away from me. "Are you crazy? He'd most likely *kill* me then. Family matters aren't supposed to be discussed outside the home, you know. Maybe I shouldn't have told you."

"I won't say anything," I promised.

The next day, I put a dead mouse in one of her father's desk drawers. I'd found the corpse in the alleyway near our flat and kept it in Tupperware to hold in the stench. It was nice and ripe. A fly, legs up, was rotting in one of its eyes. I grabbed her dad's *sjambok*. I was going to throw it in the compost heap. But then I thought Hettie might be blamed, so I left it leaning against the wall.

On our first Christmas Day without my father, Mom said it was best not to think about him, and that she didn't plan to mention his name again, at least not indoors, where she might be overheard.

Through my hippo, I reassured Dad I would keep in contact and update him about my activities on Sunday mornings in case he'd been astral traveling during the week.

Mom roasted a chicken for lunch but didn't stuff the bird for fear of Aunt Iris's tricks. It was the middle of summer—over ninety-five degrees, and humid. The fat dripped from the chicken's pimply skin and perspiration dripped from ours. Mom boiled a Christmas pudding. It steamed on the serving dish and we steamed in our chairs. She gave me a pair of plastic binoculars from OK

Bazaars, saying they might come in handy. I gave her an ornamental poodle that turned different colors depending on the weather. She said pink was her favorite shade, which was just as well because it was always hot in Durban.

On Boxing Day, we rode the train along the south coast to the seaside village of Amanzimtoti, traveling beyond the industrial area and sulfurous refineries, past Umlazi township, past tropical vegetation lining the railway tracks, and across rain-swollen rivers unfurling their brown tongues into the Indian Ocean.

At the station, holidaymakers leapt from the train onto the platform and we just made it out the door before the train hissed and moved on. As we walked toward the exit, I kept an eye out for abandoned bags, thinking about the bomb that had exploded in Johannesburg Station during an evening rush hour about two-and-a-half years earlier, just after my tenth birthday. I'd read the article in the *Rand Daily Mail* over and over again. GIRL IN FLAMES SAT ON THE FLOOR AND WEPT, the headline said. A man had placed a suitcase, actually a petrol bomb, next to a twelve-year-old girl, her mother, and her grandmother, who were sitting in a glass-enclosed area near the top of an escalator. Then he ran away. Six minutes before, a "cultured African voice" had called in a warning to local newspapers. But the bomb exploded, setting people alight and driving glass into their flesh. An old woman died, and the little girl and many others were disfigured for life. So was a baby.

Later the police arrested John Frederick Harris, a white man who said he did it because he hated apartheid.

My parents talked about the bomb after dinner one night.

"Violence is never the answer," my father said, sipping his Scotch. "These people need to be patient."

Prudence stopped clearing the table and glared at the back of his head.

"What if they have no other way to fight this awful system?" My mother was knitting a yellow scarf. She knitted many scarves, but never wore them. She said she found it therapeutic: scarves had a beginning, middle, and end. You knew where you were with scarves. She clacked her needles.

Prudence clattered the dishes and stomped to the kitchen.

"There are better ways," Dad said. "Negotiation, for example." He picked up his book and went to read in the bedroom.

"But who are black people supposed to negotiate with?" Mom said into the air.

It wasn't long after the bomb that Mom hired Winston. When Dad objected because Winston didn't have the right papers, she told him she was following Mahatma Gandhi's advice regarding passive resistance to unfair government laws and Dad should approve of her methods. He slammed his fist on the kitchen counter, flung his golf bag over his shoulder, and left for the golf course.

Was that when their arguments had started? Up till then they hadn't had many fights, not that I could remember, anyway. I thought they loved each other. Once, after I was supposed to be asleep, I crept along the corridor and crouched on the floor outside the living room because I wanted to listen to Mark Saxon and *No Place to Hide* on the radio. Mark Saxon was saving the world from a monster whose bite turned people's faces into featureless blobs. Through the crack between the door and the wall, I saw my parents kissing each other like people in films, their bodies pressed against each other, her hand on the back of his head. I crept along the corridor to my bedroom, feeling a little disgusted, but also happy. I couldn't get to sleep, though, because I suddenly pictured my mom and dad pulling apart from the kiss and having faces as blank and noseless as white soccer balls.

Now I was glad to reach the end of the station platform. After the bomb, I'd had nightmares about people on fire, screaming, their eyes pulped into bloody jelly from glass shards.

"This way," Mom said, pointing to a tarmac road winding past a caravan park and tall hotels. Bright striped beach towels hung over balcony railings, flapping in the wind like flags.

When we got to the beach, we placed our blanket on the sand

next to the lagoon, which was lined on one side by banana trees. The smell of seaweed drifted on the breeze. Concession stands sold Walls Ice Cream and red toffee apples and candy-floss. My mother wore a navy-blue swimming costume with a little pleated skirt covering the tops of her thighs. Mine was similar, but it didn't have a skirt. It wasn't likely any of the kids from my school in Durban North would see me. Otherwise I wouldn't have worn my costume for fear they'd tease me. I swam in the ocean until my fingertips crinkled. Without my glasses, I could barely make out the beach, let alone my mother, but our blanket was red, and that helped me find our picnic spot, though I nearly joined a family from East London by mistake.

While we ate our egg sandwiches and beetroot salad, barefoot black women knelt before us, flourishing shell necklaces and beads and woven baskets. My mother examined the goods, turning the baskets over and over, then shook her head. "No, thank you," she said, as if they weren't quite up to her standards. We had no money to spend, of course. The women turned their palms upward and eased to their feet, their knees glistening with sand, and searched for better customers. Vendors calling, "Cokes-and-Fanta-and-biltong-and-popcorn!" gave up on us. Biltong was too salty for me anyway. I couldn't understand why anyone would want to gnaw dried meat.

After lunch, I squatted next to rock pools, searching for anemones I thought I might cook for dinner, but found only sea slugs. I followed a crab until it disappeared into a crevice in the rocks, then I ran sideways along the beach until I found my mother.

"How about a Fairy Cone?" she said. A tan suited her. It made her eyes look even greener through her glasses.

At the ice cream stand, I asked a woman with hair curled on top of her head like an ocean wave to take a picture of us with my mother's old Brownie camera. Mom took it everywhere with her but hardly ever took photos.

On the beach, after I'd licked the last lick, I leaned my back against my mother's bent legs, which protected me from the cool wind. I watched the sun slip down the sky until the clouds turned ivory and pale pink, like the inside of a conch-shell.

"The sky was that color the night I first saw your father," Mom said. They'd met during the Second World War: he was in the Royal Navy, and his ship had docked in Cape Town. She'd worked for the war office. "He was very handsome."

I loved to hear the story. They'd been in the cable car swaying up the side of Table Mountain when he asked her to marry him. She said yes, and the next day he bought her a tiny emerald pendant he said matched her eyes.

"Those were the good days," she said. "Long before Oom Piet took it upon himself to wreck so many people's lives."

I held myself still. I was afraid she would spoil things. But she didn't. "I loved Dad very much," she said.

We were quiet on the train home. She gazed out the window. I nearly fell asleep with the motion. It sounded as if the wheels were saying, "Hello—good-bye. Hello—good-bye. Hello—good-bye."

After Christmas, until around May, my mother seemed mostly to have shaken the fears that had gripped her. It was strange the way they came and went. For months she didn't mention Oom Piet or the government. I thought perhaps she'd decided to forget about him the way she'd forgotten about Dad. She didn't even display her wedding photograph. I still spoke to Hippodad, though of course I realized I wasn't going to hear my father's voice ever again. But sleeping with my hippo kept sadness from settling on me like a fog. He was my last link to my life in Johannesburg.

Mom and I were like roommates. In the morning, we rushed to catch our buses, gulping hot tea and gobbling toast and marmalade as we dressed. We met at dinner, listened to Mark Saxon and *Death Touched My Shoulder* on the radio, and went to bed at the same time. She cooked. We shared the laundry, which had to be done in the bathtub. We squeezed sheets and towels and dresses through wringers until the buttons on my school uniform were chipped and scratched. I ironed my uniform each morning. The fabric was getting thinner and thinner. I wasn't. Layers of fat were slowly covering up the old me, the way drifting sand buries ancient cities.

I didn't have to do all the chores. Zulu men employed by the building owners took out garbage and cleaned toilets. They wore white tunics and shorts with red trim and were known as flat boys, which made it sound as if they could slip in underneath the doors—as if *they'd* been through the wringer.

Mom seemed content at work, though she kept to herself because, she said, there were a lot of peculiar people at the office.

I missed my father and Prudence. My mother said she didn't know where Prudence lived. She hadn't left a forwarding address. It hurt that Prudence could stop caring about me so easily. She must believe as my mother did, that the past was the past. And so I decided I would forget about *her*.

When the radio news announcer talked about the number of recent arrests due to Pass Law violations one afternoon, I thought about Winston. Once I'd asked him why he didn't carry a passbook.

He was sitting on his haunches, weeding. He shook soil from dangling roots. "There are those who think I am dead. I wish to keep it so."

I'd squatted and wrenched a weed from the ground. "So you don't have a wife and children back home in the Transkei?" Then I half-turned and buried the plant, because I realized it was a geranium.

Winston yanked out more weeds without saying anything. I thought he hadn't heard me. I tried again. "So you don't have chi—"

He tossed weeds in the wheelbarrow. "I worked in the mines. My child—a boy, Nkosi—was ill. The shift-boss did not tell me of the message for a few days because he needed workers and did not want me leaving for home. But then, you see, it was too late. Nkosi died."

I hadn't known what to say, whether asking more questions would make him sadder, so I weeded quietly for a while, then brought him water with ice. I wished afterward I'd asked Nkosi's age and where Nkosi's mother lived.

Without thinking, when Mom got home from work the night I'd listened to the news about the pass arrests, I asked if she thought Winston was still in prison. She hurried me out of the flat, took me to the park, sat me on a bench, and demanded to know who had mentioned his name. "The government's had its way with him," she said, "and we don't want the same to happen to us. You be careful, poppet. Are you still seeing that Hettie character?"

"Oh. No," I said, hating myself for lying yet again.

For two days after that conversation, Mom stayed in bed and cried.

In May I won a national essay competition run by the Wool Board. I'd entered a short story about Ali Baa-baa and the Forty Sheep, who were on the lam from prison. One character was called Mutton Jeff. I won a trampoline, but they agreed to give me the money instead, because the trampoline was about the size of our bedroom. I bought my mother a record player and put the balance in the bank. The *Tribune* came to the school and took my photograph. My mother cut the story out of the paper and taped it on the wall.

"You look so different, with that pudgy face," she said. "No one will recognize you. And they haven't given our address, so we should be safe."

Then, in early June, Mom started talking about the government in earnest, saying their agents were making her life difficult at work. Noises were being piped through the desk legs into her head. The sounds made it difficult to concentrate, and she was making lots of mistakes, which you couldn't do as a legal secretary. She was typing documents for a case involving a black woman who had been beaten by her white boss and it was important to get the facts right. I suggested maybe plumbers or electricians or renovators were working in the office below.

She squinted at me in a peculiar way and asked if Hettie had ordered me to say that. My heart jumped the way it had one day when I'd started crossing the road without looking and had suddenly seen a bus bearing down on me.

"Where did you get the word 'renovators,' then?" Mom said. "It's not a word you would know."

But I did.

"Oom Piet will be here soon," she said. "I know it."

By then I'd made friends with a girl called Sandy, who lived with her divorced mom in a two-bedroom flat three floors above us. Sandy owned a piano. I could hear the music at night, the plinkety sound competing with the news on our radio and the buses and the mewling of the baby next door.

"I want to be a prodigy," Sandy had told me. "So I don't have much time to play outside."

Although she was often practicing, it was nice to have a friend who lived close by, someone I didn't feel I had to impress the way I had to impress Hettie. I worried Hettie would stop liking me, because she was so much prettier, and I wasn't good at flirting with boys, and she kept wanting to talk about them. She had a crush on Mark Poulos. I told her I had a crush on Desmond Baxter. He had white-blond hair and blue eyes. After a while, I found I *did* have a crush on him. He ignored me, and I ignored him. But that meant nothing. Boys hid their feelings, Hettie said.

Over weekends sometimes, Sandy and I would go to the paddling pools and slip down slides and wriggle our toes in the warm water, at least until we realized babies and small children peed in it. We fed seagulls stale bread and watched fathers throwing beach balls to their daughters and talked about what our dads had been like. Her father had fought terrorists on the Caprivi Strip and now lived in Pretoria.

Once we went to the Snake Park. It stank. The attendant put a mouse in a cage and a python swallowed it. We saw the shape of the mouse, still alive, squirming down the snake's neck. I told Sandy I had to leave. The python had reminded me of Oom Piet.

A few times, while our mothers were at work, we dropped water on people's heads from Sandy's window. I suggested we call the game "brainwashing." Then we made a mistake. We soaked the caretaker, and we were caught. The caretaker came to our door and told Mom I was a bad child and ought to be disciplined. My mother slammed the door in her face.

"It's not *your* fault," Mom said to me. "Sandy is a bad influence on you."

"But I suggested it."

She shook her head. Her jowls wobbled. "No, poppet. You're a good girl. You wouldn't misbehave like that. You were *told* to do that. Oom Piet's starting his funny business again."

"I was not told to do it." I clenched my fists. When I did something good, it was because I was her smart daughter. When I did something bad, it was because other people had forced me to. I suppose I should have been happy I wasn't blamed, but it made me uncomfortable. I *wanted* her to punish me.

She pulled out a pen and notebook and started writing. "Did you know Sandy's mother's maiden name is Du Plessis?" She wiped ash off the arm of the chair with the flat of her hand. The paint on the wall around her had yellowed from cigarette smoke. Du Plessis was Oom Piet's surname. "You're not to play with her anymore."

My heart felt like an elevator that had broken its cable. It plummeted down my spinal cord and smashed into the bottom of my stomach. "But it *was* my fault. And Mom, there are thousands of people in South Africa with the name Du Plessis. It's like Jones in Wales!"

She gazed at me. "Don't. Say. Jones. Our name is Jensen."

"Sandy is my friend."

"Your friend?" She laughed. "No. No, she's not. I hear the child called this silly game 'brainwashing.' Her mother made her say that, you see? But the fact is, brainwashing is a serious matter. It happens before you're even aware of it." She leaned forward, her glasses glinting. "You'll never have real friends, poppet. Those who get close to you will always have their own reasons. Now, please, you tell Sandy you can't play with her."

I ignored her. But my mother made a point of staring at Sandy's mother every time they rode the lift together. Mom didn't say anything. Only stared. Once she followed her to her door, then turned back at the last minute.

The following Saturday I put on my swimming costume and knocked on Sandy's door. "Let's go to the paddling pools," I said.

She peeked through the small kitchen window facing out onto the corridor. "Your mom slapped my mom and said she was your uncle's whore cousin. I'm not allowed to play with you or speak to you anymore. Your mother's *crazy*, did you know that?"

The window slammed shut.

My face burned.

I went downstairs to yell at my mother. She'd just woken up and was in a terrible state. She said Oom Piet was about to strike. She made me close the curtains because the sunlight was giving her a headache. Even after I turned the radio off, she kept saying there were noises. I sat on the bed and stared at her. I'd heard about hippies taking drugs and having hallucinations. Was she being fed LSD?

Because I was afraid to leave her alone, I did my chores. I cleaned the kitchen, wondering what the truth was about Oom Piet and whether my mother would stay this way forever. As long as I had Hettie, I could manage.

At about ten o'clock that Sunday, while I was sitting on a swing in the park reading a book, I saw my mother ambling from the flats. Was she going to the Sunken Gardens, where she liked to sit on a bench near the rosebushes? I watched. A man emerged from the corner café. He had metallic silver hair and a nose like a fish eagle. He stood and smoked a cigarette until my mother walked past. Then he threw it to the pavement and mashed it under his shoe. He kept a steady pace behind her. She glanced over her shoulder once, and he halted, pretending to wait for a traffic light to change.

Curious, I stood up and began following them. They turned down a street. I ran to Marine Parade and looked right and left. They were nowhere in sight. Then I jogged to the Sunken Gardens and peered over the edge of the balustrade. My mother was wandering among the roses. She stopped every now and again, leaning her head toward the blossoms as though to inhale each individual scent, touching the flowers like a blind person. The silver-haired man was sitting on the edge of the fishpond. He trailed his fingers along the surface as though he were trying to attract the attention of the goldfish, but most of the time he kept his eyes on my mother. After about ten minutes, she picked a rose and climbed the steps toward street level. He stood. I ducked.

When I lifted my head, they'd both disappeared.

Were we being spied on? Had my uncle sent the beaky-nosed man to follow my mother?

I couldn't sleep that night.

On Monday, I propped my hippo on the windowsill in our bedroom while I packed my books in my school case. "Hippodad," I said, "one day I'm going to marry a handsome rich man and never have to do any chores ever again." I thought my mother was in the kitchen having breakfast. She had four pieces of toast and marmalade and three cups of tea every day before work.

Then I saw her standing in the doorway, reaching to get her handbag from the top of the dresser. She laughed. "You'll never be married. Never have kids. Your uncle's going to spread rumors about you, the way he did about me. No one will want to touch you."

She left the room. The front door slammed.

"I don't believe her," I said to Hippodad. "Cheers. I'm off to school." My dad always said "cheers" instead of good-bye.

. . .

At Big Break, Hettie and I cut our fingers and became blood sisters. My finger wouldn't stop bleeding so I ran cold water over it in the sink. The pain made me feel good.

That night, Mom lay on her bed staring at the ceiling. She didn't say a word. Neither did I. I was beginning to think Sandy was right. My mother was crazy. Though my Oom Piet's political views were extreme, and wrong, I saw no reason why he would want to hurt us, his family. Even Dad—who hadn't liked Oom Piet one bit—agreed my uncle was very protective of his relatives. And Oom Piet was a homebody, Aunt Iris liked to say. He loved his cattle farm and didn't want to be bothered going anywhere, not even Johannesburg or Pretoria, unless he was invited to weddings or funerals. I couldn't imagine him taking the trouble to drive to Durban. Mostly I remembered him draped on his recliner watching rugby, drinking rum-and-coke, and ordering Aunt Iris to cook him *'n lekker potje,* or stew, for dinner. Some weekend mornings he was *babelas,* which meant he'd had too much to drink the night before, and yelled at his dogs for barking.

On Tuesday, Mom insisted on knowing why I was catching the six A.M. bus. I made the mistake of telling her I was going to help someone with her homework before school.

"Hettie, I suppose. That girl is using you, you know," she said. "She's a manipulative child. I've warned you."

I blundered around the room, looking for my glasses. "I have to go," I said when I found them.

"Oh, poppet," she said. "You'll see she's not to be trusted. You must stop playing with her, please."

What if my mother followed me to school and said terrible things to Hettie's mother? Once I'd thought I'd seen her head bobbing above the hedge lining Hettie's driveway. Was she spying on me? Or was I hallucinating? Being fed drugs too? I picked up my school case and fled.

All day Hettie tried to make me promise to let her copy my paper during the coming mid-year arithmetic test, which I didn't want to do. But what if she dropped me? I imagined the other kids circling like hyenas in the playground.

After school, Hettie waited with me at the bus stop and explained how I could iron my hair and look like Jean Shrimpton.

The weather had remained humid, though winter was supposed to have arrived. The sweat left wet rings beneath my arms despite the deodorant I'd begun using. It felt as though a film of grease covered my skin. My thighs rubbed together on the way home from the bus stop. When I got to Starling Flats, the lift was broken. I hauled myself up the stairs and opened our door.

Mom was home, sitting in her favorite armchair. Her lower arm moved up and down like a railroad signal, a cigarette between her fingers. I thought I might suffocate from the smoke. She'd drawn the curtains, so it was gloomy and hot inside the room. The ashtray was overflowing with *stompies*. I could smell rotten vegetables, probably the potatoes in the kitchen I was supposed to have thrown in the Dumpster. They'd started growing small trees.

She looked up. "Poppet. The bus turned onto the wrong street. The driver was trying to kidnap me," she said. "I jumped out while it was still moving."

Things were getting curiouser. Alice in Wonderland had no idea. I closed the door. My eyes adjusted to the dimness. "Why aren't you at work?" Mom's knee was bruised and oozing blood. "The driver probably made a mistake. Maybe he was new to the route."

"So they *have* brainwashed you. They're turning you against me. You don't believe a word I say." Her voice was flatter than the top of Table Mountain.

Putting down my school case, I looked around. The blue ceramic lamp lay on its side on the floor. Wires tentacled from electrical outlets. The wastepaper basket had been emptied in the middle of the room, pages torn out of my *Just So Stories*. I could see the crumpled picture of an elephant. One of the sofa cushions had been ripped apart. Stuffing spewed from its center.

I moved toward the couch. The radio was on, but all I could hear was static. A line of flies sat on one arm of the broken ceiling fan, as if waiting for a ride. One buzzed into the air and landed on my arm. I flicked it off. A lorry rumbled on the road outside.

A cloud of smoke mushroomed from my mother's mouth. "My boss was putting drugs in my tea, to confuse me, you see? So I walked into his office and upended my cup in his coleus plant. I told him I knew what he was up to. That I knew he was in cahoots with Oom Piet. I shouldn't have let on. I've made them angry now, poppet." She spoke in a monotone. "Of course they fired me when they knew I knew. Very soon now, Oom Piet will come to take me away." She waved her cigarette toward the mess. "I was trying to find the bug."

I sat. The cushion sank beneath me. My foot nudged a piece of cloth. I bent over and picked it up, feeling its smooth texture between my fingers. It was purple. Hippo. My hippo! My Hippodad! He had been disemboweled. He'd become a rag. I got off the chair and knelt on the floor, scooping the stuffing together, trying to bundle it into the cloth. The smell of Cobra floor polish reminded me of the day my father had died. I knew I shouldn't cry. The hippo was only a toy. I screwed up my face.

My bead doll, the one Prudence had given me, lay headless under the coffee table.

Mom held a napkin to her knee with her left hand and smoked with her right. "They're clever at hiding their little recorders."

I got to my feet, feeling dizzy. A few scraps of foam rubber floated to the floor. Bars of sun slatted the wall. My mother tapped her finger on her cigarette. Ash fell. I watched the flakes fall to the floor. I blinked tears from my eyes and walked toward her, catching a whiff of her sweet-talcum-and-smoke smell. I stopped. "Oom Piet isn't after us. He isn't a government spy," I said. My voice sounded high and strange.

The baby next door wailed.

"I'm sorry, but he is." My mother said. "Poor poppet."

"What did you do to my hippo?"

She tapped her cigarette on the edge of the ashtray. "People are listening every second. They're probably listening now."

"You're seeing and hearing things that don't exist," I yelled.

She peered at me. "You're on their side now, are you, poppet?"

I took a step toward her. "There isn't a *they.*"

Slowly she twisted the end of her cigarette in the ashtray, watching her fingers at work, then nodded. She gazed up at me, looking amused. "I've seen you talk to that stuffed animal." She gestured to the remains of Hippodad. "So either you're speaking to a piece of cloth, or you're communicating with your uncle. Which is it?"

I swept my hand across the bookcase, knocking the Belleek vase, my mother's favorite wedding gift, off the end table and onto the rug. China bounced and skittered across the floor.

She frowned at the broken vase. "The poppet I know wouldn't do something like that. Was it Hettie who gave you instructions, poppet? Was it Hettie?"

My head felt tight, as if it might explode. "*Nobody made me do it.* Why do you say that all the time?"

"You used to be such a good girl. But you're so easily influenced."

I opened the record player, picked up the needle, and ripped it across the Nat King Cole record sitting on the turntable, the one I'd bought with my Ali Baa-baa money. Then I yanked the stylus so it broke. "You're right," I said, keeping my voice calm. "I'm a perfect child, but every now and again the government tells me to do bad things."

My mother just said, dreamily now, "Poor poppet! What they've done to you, it's terrible, terrible."

That's when we heard the knock on the door. We both turned and stared as though the door had suddenly come alive. A piece of the vase teetering on the edge of the bookcase fell to the floor.

The banging grew louder. My mother cupped her palms over her ears.

The door opened. Oom Piet stepped into the room and stared at us, swaying slightly, his tongue licking the corners of his thin wet mouth.

Durban
1995

After my conversation—if you could call it that—with Mevrou Bakker, I headed to Durban General, the hospital where, the hotel concierge had said, an elderly white lady suffering from cancer would usually be treated. Perhaps there'd been a clerical error, and she'd been admitted after all? I walked toward the gabled building, which perched at the top of a slope next to an old stone Anglican church and cemetery. Flamingo lilies and hibiscus bushes flanked the path. The smell of hot wet soil rose from the flower beds. Should I be checking gravestones instead? It struck me how much easier my life would be if my mother were dead. A familiar mixture of guilt and unhappiness and anger giddied me. I stopped, dug in my purse for my wallet, pulled out the Amanzimtoti photo, and stared at her blurry face.

On the lawn, two Indian mynahs conversed. When church bells pealed, the birds flew away. I followed their flight until they merged with the sky. Then, as if I'd been given a sign, I climbed the steps toward the entrance. I imagined my mother tethered to blinking machines, tied down Gulliver-like, with Lilliputian nurses scurrying around her large, pinioned body.

My first fiancé Terry told me once I was too damn metaphorical. I said talking to him was like mailing a letter and never being sure it arrived. He'd thrown up his hands.

Simon, though, loved metaphors and metaphysics. Once we'd

spent an entire summer afternoon debating whether a house was the space inside the walls or the walls around the space. In the end, we concluded the air inside was the important part, because it recast itself every time you moved, or rearranged the furniture, and so it was more yours than the walls. Then we'd headed for our bedroom and changed its configuration a few times.

Durban General had no record of a Violet Jensen being admitted. I asked to tour the wards. Now and again I halted in midstride, thinking she might be one of the old women swaddled in sheets, their faces pale and turned to the ceiling. The matron hurried me past AIDS wards; I caught glimpses of emaciated men and women and children, their arms thin as storks' legs.

"It doesn't seem as though she's here," the matron said, after we'd visited the private rooms. Tall and black, she was a stately emperor penguin of a woman. "You've talked to your mother's doctor and health insurance, I assume, to see if there've been any claims?"

"Yes. Nothing." Assurance Ltd. made good profits from my mother. I paid the premiums: she never consulted doctors.

We stood in the lobby near the emergency room. A man on a stretcher was wheeled past in a rush of nurses. I thought of my father. I put my hand against the wall to steady myself.

"You okay?" The matron patted my shoulder. "She's probably fine. Maybe she went in for tests, and they were negative, and she decided to go on a nice trip to Margate."

Shade brindled the dust beneath the flamboyant tree, which demarcated the border between the police station and an office park. Next to the steps, a group of men squatted around a game board bearing pebbles and bottle caps as counters. A flag, limp from the heat, drooped on a flagpole.

I walked up the steps, announced my presence to the man behind the counter, and sat on a bench to wait my turn. The walls were marked with yellow Sellotape stains. Nelson Mandela had probably once been featured on a WANTED poster close to where his framed presidential photograph now hung.

Eventually I was called into an office crammed with stainless steel cabinets. A dish of African violets wilted on a small table next to a ziggurat of manila files, and a lone fly circled a coffee cup. The woman behind the desk rested her head sideways on her left fist as though her neck, unpropped, would be incapable of supporting any weight.

"A sergeant visited her flat yesterday," she said. "There was no one there. The caretaker stated the resident had informed her she would be gone for a while. On holiday." She gazed at me. "So it seems like the case is closed."

"My mother never travels."

"Lady," she said, shutting the file. "You live in the United States now, right?"

"Yes."

"When did you last see your mother?"

"A while ago." Guilt rose to my skin like sweat.

"How often do you talk to her?"

"She doesn't have a phone," I said.

"You write? When did you last write?"

"That's irrelevant."

The policewoman smiled, fingering a single hair on her chin. "Long time, hey? So you don't know what she's been up to recently."

"But I do know she's missing."

The woman's head bobbed as she leaned forward. "We've got a lot more to worry about here than old women going away without telling daughters who live thousands of miles away. Street kids living in gutters in Umlazi. People dying of AIDS by the hundreds every day." She folded her arms, pleased with her litany. "This isn't America. We've got problems you can't begin to imagine." Tapping the file, she rose to her feet. "We'll let you know if there are any further developments."

"How dare you lecture me?" I said, a little late. "I don't—I'm not—I used to be—"

The policewoman opened a drawer. "Why don't you check with the CIA, lady?"

I turned and left the building. The sun had turned the sky a punitive white. I put on my sunglasses. A bus stopped, revved its engines, and spat smoke. I sat on a bench. I couldn't stay in my hotel room for maybe weeks waiting for news. A silver plane zipped across the sky. Should I go home?

A small boy too young to be alone trundled a wire toy truck along the road, and a thin dog urinated against a tree. I wasn't accomplishing anything sitting here. Might as well try Mevrou Bakker again. I hailed a cab and slid in behind the driver. Ladysmith Black Mambazo blared from patched speakers on the back shelf of the car, where a bobble-headed lion nodded. The driver kept time on his steering wheel. We passed mosques and street markets and Indian shops selling spices and silks and saris, turned onto West Street, and headed toward Marine Parade, where the bright colors of the aquarium and Funworld gleamed in the sun. A seal barked, and I felt frightened for a moment, I wasn't sure why.

After dropping me off, the cab sped away, trailing jazz in its wake.

Mevrou Bakker's door was open. She was bending over her laundry basket. The creases of her pale knees were visible between her dress and suntan knee-highs. I walked in, shut the door behind me, and sat on her sofa. The cushions sank so that my knees felt higher than my head. Her parrot glared at me. "Go away," it said. "Go. Away."

"I'm not leaving until you tell me what happened to my mother," I said, half to the parrot, and half to Mevrou Bakker. A cageful of yellow budgies stopped twittering. I considered taking one hostage.

Mevrou Bakker turned and looked at me, lifting her upper lip. "You get out of my house, hear?"

"Go away," the parrot said.

I burst into tears. I hadn't intended to cry. In fact, I'd been congratulating myself on my composure. It was the parrot's fault. I hauled myself out of the sofa, walked into Mevrou Bakker's bathroom, unraveled the pink toilet paper, folded it into squares, and blew my nose.

She stood in the doorway with her hands on her hips. "You've got a cheek, young lady." She stared at me. "Jus' *sommer* walking into my house like this. Acting like you own it."

I sniffed and blew my nose again. She frowned.

But she didn't comment when I followed her to the living room and sat down again. She lowered herself into a chair and continued folding her laundry. An Alpine range of big-cupped bras began to form on top of the basket. She frowned. "There's something funny going on and I don't want to be a part of it."

"Look," I said. I rooted in my bag, found my wallet, and pulled out the snapshot of my mom and me at Amanzimtoti Beach.

Mevrou Bakker took the photograph with the tips of her fingers. She reached across the table and picked up her glasses and squinted. "This girl is a plump little thing."

"She's eleven. I'm forty."

"No need to be rude."

The budgies twittered.

"Pretty birds," I said. They clustered in a corner of the cage.

Mevrou Bakker squinted at me over the tops of her tortoiseshell frames. "I don't know." She bent over and folded towels, stacking them in the basket. "You can't be too careful in this world. At first she talked a lot about her daughter. Then she said maybe you were now her enemy." She shook out a large T-shirt. "I was scared when you called. And some strange things she said came true. It's like she had a sixth sense, you know? She'd say, 'Loreen, I'm telling you, the tenant in number one-fifty-three is odd.' And then I found out he baked *dagga* cakes, you know, pot, and sold them to teenagers. Or she'd say, 'Don't trust the woman in six-twenty-seven. She won't pay rent.' And she didn't, it turned out. It was hard to know what to believe."

"I understand perfectly," I said.

She shaped the T-shirt into squares. "Your mom and me got to be friends, in a way, in the last few months. It was like she needed someone to confide in, *jy weet?* And she liked gin rummy. So we started to play on Sunday afternoons." She crooked her finger, and I leaned toward her. "About two weeks ago, her brother-in-law—Piet, his name was, I think—came to visit. Afterward she was in a state. She told me he wanted to keep her quiet about something that happened in the sixties. But she said she wasn't going to."

I leaned against the couch cushions. Why, after a nearly three-decade absence, would my uncle visit my mother?

"Your mother said with this Truth and Reconciliation Commission being convened, the time had come for people to know what he'd done. *Ja.* She was going to make this Piet pay for his crimes." Drops of perspiration formed a wet moustache on Mevrou Bakker's upper lip. "He was a *Broederbonder.*"

"The *Broederbond*'s still around?"

"Well, actually, it's not the *Broederbond* anymore. It's the *Afrikanerbond.* And they're not like they were. They say they'll work with the new government, see, to help make things better. With Mr. Mandela. But there are splinter groups, extremists, who are still angry, still believe in a separate white state. The newspapers call them the Third Force. *Ja.* Oh *ja,*" She smoothed towels with the flat of her hand. "The Third Force sets people one against the other. Blacks against blacks, especially, you know? They want the country to be in chaos and then they'll have whites take over again by military force. *Ja.* So there's the Third Force, and then there's other former *Broederbonders* who did bad things to black people who want to pretend now that they didn't. Everything is very muddled here now, *jy weet?*"

So my mother thought Oom Piet belonged to a racist group called the Third Force—and that they were now after her? "She didn't have cancer, though, right?" I stood and walked across the room, stopping at the parrot cage.

"Hello?" the bird said. "Good-bye."

"Cancer? No. I don't think so," Mevrou Bakker said.

I turned, surprised to feel as relieved as I did. "So when did she disappear, exactly?"

Mevrou Bakker reached for a vast negligee. "Your mom was frightened after your uncle came. She said she had business to attend to, then she was going to change her name and go live in another city before he returned. She wouldn't say which one. She said not to tell anyone she was going permanently, not even the police." She stared at me. "And not to believe anyone who said they were here because they were worried about her."

Perhaps my mother had taken a trip to Cape Town, where she'd once suggested we go to escape Oom Piet. I imagined her peering out of a cable car going up Table Mountain. *Who's operating this thing?* she might say. *Something funny's going on. This is the wrong mountain!*

"You saw the man who visited her?" I asked.

Mevrou Bakker examined a stain on a pink blouse and tossed it to the side. "I saw a tall man, thin as a telephone wire, but I don't know who he was." The radio was playing accordion music. Every time a melody ended, the parrot tipped its neck to the side as if surprised. "I'm not the kind who interferes in other people's lives."

"No."

She rose, headed for the mantel, and grabbed a box of birdseed. After opening the door of her parrot's cage, she poured food into his container. "*Daar's hy,* Benjamin!" Then she turned to me. "Anyway, she paid me advance rent for a month and then I didn't see her, not even going to the café to get her cigarettes. Two nights after she and I spoke, I heard loud knocking—it echoed down the stairwell. It went on and on. By the time I got upstairs, no one. Place was empty." She shut the cage door. "The first time the police came I said I knew nothing. Second time I told them she'd gone on holiday. I thought she escaped like she wanted to. *Ek weet nie.* I don't know."

"Holi-day. Holi-day," Benjamin said.

"Did she say she'd call you?"

"No. She wasn't going to. Didn't believe in phones. Most of the time I think she carried out her plan and then sometimes I worry a bit. I checked her closet and saw the dresses she wears every day, *jy weet?* She doesn't have many. I don't know what she can be wearing. Then you came." She replaced the box of birdseed on the mantel. "This is a peaceful building. I can't have disturbances here. I'll lose my job."

"Can I go into her flat and look around?"

She hesitated, then tipped her head like the parrot. "*Ja.* I suppose so." She grabbed a circle of keys from a hook on the wall.

Durban
1967

When my mother saw Oom Piet in the doorway, she hoisted herself from her chair and sailed across the room like a great ocean liner. I followed her to the door and stood just behind her. My uncle had lost more hair and his head looked flatter than ever.

"Violet!" he said. "I'm here to help."

Mom planted her palms on his chest and shoved. "Go away."

My uncle staggered backward. "Please! Don't fight us, Violet. We care about you."

"Go away," Mom said, crossing her arms.

He rambled on about how much he'd worried. He said he wanted to take care of us. Aunt Iris had been frantic. Two beds were made up at the farmhouse.

My mother gazed at him. After every one of his sentences, she said, "Go away."

He stared over her shoulder at me and his black eyes were wet and shiny as though he were about to cry. "Kate, *hoe gaan dit? How are you?"* The sound of Sandy's piano filtered down the stairwell.

I scowled, feeling confused. My mother had been right: he'd come to take her away. *Had* her boss been in league with my uncle? *Were* we being spied on?

"Kate, *meisie.* We're here to help. Your ma is not well. She has not been well for a while."

Mom gripped my elbow. "Poppet, this is an evil person! You have to trust me."

I stared at my uncle. I thought about Mom's strange behavior and the bugs. The odd stories she told about her boss. The bus driver kidnapping her. The way she sniffed food. What she'd done to my hippo!

"We've been so worried," Oom Piet said, blinking. "You could stay on the farm with us, *skattie*, while your mom goes somewhere to get better."

Mom breathed through her nose. I glanced at her. What if I chased my uncle away, and she went even crazier and killed one of my friends? How embarrassing! Well, worse than embarrassing, of course.

"Poppet. He's going to take me somewhere terrible!" Mom tightened her grip on me. "I *told* you he was coming. I was right, wasn't I?"

I loosened her hand from my elbow, thinking about the beaky-nosed man who had followed Mom. What if Oom Piet *were* working with the government to harm us? I'd spoken to Prudence and Winston, and read the *Sunday Tribune* and listened to the news often enough to know the government had been accused of terrible things: locking people away without trials, murdering and torturing them. Whites, too, like Denis Goldberg, who'd been imprisoned with Mandela.

England, Australia, and France said they might refuse to play rugby and cricket against the Springbok teams unless things changed. Sanctions had been proposed.

Oom Piet leaned forward and took my hand, his palm slimy with sweat. "My, you've grown, Katie. Nice and plump, like a ripe berry."

I snatched my hand back.

Mom glared at my uncle. "Why don't you *voetsak*? We're fine. Katie, you tell him we're fine."

A mixture of smells wafted around the room: cabbage, curry,

fried fish. A cockroach crawled along the floor. They had become quite bold recently. I'd once seen a white one peek out from underneath the stove. My mom said it was an albino. On the farm, there were pigs and horses and cats.

My brain felt like a hot air balloon—untethered and drifting, unable to find a place to land. I was still feeling shaky from seeing my hippo ripped apart. I didn't feel like I could make any good decisions. I sat on the couch.

"Katie," my mother said. "Tell him we're happy here."

"You're family," my uncle said. "My responsibility, now that your father is gone."

Prudence had told me that in some African cultures, a widow married her late husband's brother, because it was now his duty to take care of her. Was that what Oom Piet had in mind? I didn't think Aunt Iris would appreciate it.

"Andre says he can't wait to see you," my uncle said.

Would Koos make me eat caterpillars again?

"Kate, please," my mom said. "Don't go with him." She sounded very sad.

Oom Piet touched the corners of his mouth with his tongue.

My mind thunked back to earth. "Oom Piet," I said, standing up and moving next to my mom so we blocked the doorway completely and made a solid wall of flesh, "my mother is probably the best mother there is. She makes wonderful school lunches and is thinking of joining the PTA. I'm coming first in every test. My picture was in the paper because I won a national essay competition."

"Congratulations, *skattie*."

"So you see, everything is fine here. And if you try to make us go, I'll tell lies about you to the police. I'll tell them you . . . you . . ." I thought of Hettie's dad. "That you hit me with your *sjambok*. I'll even hit myself with a *sjambok* so I have proof!"

Oom Piet leaned toward me. His breath smelled like the dead

mouse I'd put in Mr. Williams's study. "Listen now, you're too young to understand—"

"I'm not going. Neither is my mother." I put my hands on my hips. "We understand exactly why you're here. And we want you to go. Now."

He drew himself up. "Your mother needs medical help, *kuiken*. And this place—! It's a mess."

I glanced behind me. Stuffing and broken china littered the floor. Electrical cords sprouted from the wall. "It was me," I said. "I was having a tantrum. I'm nearly a teenager. Please leave us alone."

Then I gave him another push in the chest, shut and locked the door, and pulled the chain across. "There," I said to my mother, dusting my hands. "That's that then."

Oom Piet banged on the door for a long time. Mom and I held each other. She felt like a giant pillow, except I could feel her heart beating.

Eventually he said, through the door, "Okay. For now, okay." We heard his *velskoens* slither away along the passage.

My mom kissed me on the forehead. "You're a trouper, Katie. But he will come back, you know."

I shook my head. "I think I scared him away."

My mother blew her nose on her handkerchief. "First we'll have tea and tidy up. Then we'll sew your hippo together again. I thought they'd got to you, but they haven't, I see." She shook her fist at the fan. "We'll show you!"

I felt a little sick, unsure whether I'd done the right thing.

After putting on the kettle, she fetched old stockings from her drawer, put them inside the purple rag, and sewed my hippo's stomach together. He was much the same as before, except lumpier than he'd been in Johannesburg. But then so was I, and so was my mother.

"How the Hippo Got His Hump," she said. She hardly ever said anything funny anymore.

My heart lifted. "I used to pretend he was Dad. That's why I talked to him."

"Ah," she said, smiling.

I used Sellotape to fix my *Just So Stories* and helped glue the Belleek vase. It looked like a jigsaw puzzle, but my mom said it had character. I lifted Nat King Cole off the turntable. "I'll save to buy you another one."

"Not to worry, Katie." Mom turned to a music station on the radio and we did a jig to "Baubles, Bangles, and Beads" by the Kirby Stone Four. She said she loved the Kirby Stone Four about as much as Frank Sinatra. She seemed dizzy and spoke really fast, from excitement, I suppose.

After checking both ways in the street to make sure Oom Piet wasn't around, we walked to the store to buy a new lock for the door, a new lamp, and fish and chips for dinner.

Now that Oom Piet had come and gone, I hoped things would return to the way they'd been during the first half of the year. But the next morning at breakfast, Mom said we should move to Cape Town and change our name again. We argued over the Cocoa Pops. I couldn't bear the thought of being teased again and having to find new friends. Leaving Hettie was unthinkable. She was the only person I trusted. Also, we were about to take our mid-year exams and I expected to do well and get lots of praise from the teachers. "Mom, I don't think Oom Piet will come back," I said. "And if he does, I'll threaten him again. I want to stay here." I really believed I'd scared him off. I felt like Shaka, king of the Zulu, all-powerful.

"Because of Hettie, I expect. I told you. You can't trust Hettie. And the govern—"

"Please be quiet, Mom. I'm not going to Cape Town. Ever," I said.

A couple of fat flies with iridescent wings sat on her toast, rubbing their forelegs together. She was lucky they didn't buzz into her mouth, it was so wide open.

The same day, Wednesday, Mrs. Anderson taught a nature lesson she called *Suits, Spines, and Spikes.* It was about the different ways animals fend off predators and survive in the veldt.

"Cheetahs can reach forty-five miles per hour in three seconds and run at a speed of sixty-three miles per hour for twenty seconds. So their prey has to be swift *and* smart to escape." She walked toward the slide projector. "Creatures camouflage themselves too. Impala have blond coloring which allows them to blend in with the veldt if they stay still. And some animals wear protective suits of armor. Others shut down when they sense danger."

She showed us slides of the African pancake tortoise, which has a flattened shell, allowing it to crawl into crevices and under overhanging rocks when threatened. We also looked at pictures of porcupines and anteaters. The textbook said: *When menaced by predators, scaly anteaters roll themselves into a ball and present an impenetrable surface of tough bony plates to their attackers.* Scaly anteaters curled up quite often, the teacher said, even when they really had nothing to fear.

It was safer that way.

After school, Hettie and I ran around her garden chasing Voetie, pretending to be cheetahs, then jumped off tree branches, flapping our wings like hawks.

When I got home, our bags were packed. Mom said we would catch the evening train to Cape Town. She'd call the movers when we arrived there, have them pack up the flat and send the furniture by van.

I leaned back against the wall and kicked the skirting board with the heel of my brown school shoe. "Tell me why the government would do all this stuff—spying and everything."

She puffed blue clouds. "They want to lock me away so I won't say anything about Oom Piet being a murderer."

"Why don't you go to the police? Why can't you tell them what happened? Why can't you tell *me*?"

"They're part of The Plot to Split Us Apart. And if I tell you the details, they'll lock you away too. Separately."

At that moment, imagining myself behind bars with smelly rats scrabbling in the corner of my cell, I nearly agreed to leave. But then I thought of Hettie again. "I told you, I'm not going," I said, my heart banging in my chest.

Mom stared as if I were an Enemy, then sat down and pulled out her big red notebook and started writing.

Our bags rested against the door. I unpacked mine, crawled onto my bed, and opened *The Secret Seven*. Mom took out a deck of cards and played Patience, ignoring me. I read and reread the first chapter. I thought about telling her what I'd learned at school, but I didn't want to set her off again. She might decide my teacher was sending messages in my lessons.

I wasn't sure what she was thinking, whether she'd simply given up her plans. I read my book, but glanced up every now and again. We ate dinner in silence. Later in the evening, I said, "So we aren't going to Cape Town, right?"

She looked up from her notebook, a kind of diary. I'd read parts of it once: it contained family trees linking all sorts of people, even Mr. Lahore, the Indian man who sold fruit and vegetables from his truck on Friday afternoons. She hid it beneath her mattress while she was sleeping and carried it with her at other times. Once in a while she ripped out pages and stuffed them in envelopes.

Her eyes gleamed. She put down her pen. "I can't pick you up and carry you, can I? But if Oom Piet comes and takes you away, well, it'll be your own fault, then, poppet, won't it?"

"Maybe I'll want to go with him next time," I said.

Over the weekend, I studied. My mother didn't say a word. She lumbered around the flat with a resigned expression. Sometimes she took out the classified section of the paper and circled jobs. We had enough left in the account for a few more months' rent, she said.

On Sunday afternoon, I walked down to the beach. The weather had turned cooler—it was about seventy degrees Fahrenheit. Durbanites wore jerseys and cardigans, while families from the Transvaal put on their swimming costumes and waded into the surf. It was the time of year when kids were told the story about the little boy who put a jellyfish on his head and said, *"Look, ma, my new hat!"* and the jellyfish stung him and he died. Mom had told me it was a cautionary tale, which meant it wasn't true. But it didn't mean the parents telling the story were *lying,* exactly. It was a fable. A warning.

How could you ever know what was true and what wasn't?

The last time we'd been to the beach with Dad, in Scottsborough, he'd sculpted an ocean liner, the *Queen Elizabeth.* Now I lay on my back on my towel, listening to the mewing of seagulls and the *shoosh* of the waves. Was my father somewhere in the sky entertaining the spirits of dead children, building ghostly sand castles? When I was younger, maybe I would've believed that's what clouds were. But by now I was pretty sure Heaven was a fable, too—a story people told to comfort other people—and ancestors were figments of Prudence's imagination.

Hettie was pleased to see me first thing Monday morning. "I think I finally understand fractions," she said. "You're so smart. And I don't care what anyone says about you being a *doos,* I'll always be your friend." She pointed to my chest. "You need to tell your mom to buy you a bra."

I looked down. The fabric was nearly transparent. When I stretched, I realized, you could see two swollen pink islands. My nipples! No wonder the boys had been staring. Especially Patrick

Osch. I draped my arm over my chest for the rest of the day.

We took our English, Afrikaans, and Nature exams.

After school, I helped Hettie study, then caught the bus to the city center, and the one to the beachfront. When I arrived home, my mother was in her chair staring at our new lamp. It was navy, and matched our blue-and-white flowered sofa and armchair. The shade was conical, like the hats Chinese people wore in my geography book. The wireless wasn't playing. I glanced around. "Where's the radio?"

"If we're going to stay, we have to do a clean sweep of this place. Get rid of the bugs, you see." She started unscrewing the lightbulb.

I decided to ignore her. "Mom, I need a bra."

She shook the bulb close to her ear. "A bra? Why?"

I pointed. "You can see right through."

"Hettie told you that, I suppose. Why's she interested in your breasts? Have you undressed in front of her? Did she tell you to?"

My face flamed. I turned, pushing open the squeaky divider between the living room and our bedroom, thinking I would take my books to the park to study. Our arithmetic exam was the next day. I skirted my mother's bed and opened the closet door, searching for my baby-doll dress. It had a gathered bodice, which would hide my embarrassing bumps, and no belt, so it would be cool. Maybe Hettie had an old bra I could borrow. I pulled the dress off the hanger and tossed it on my eiderdown.

My mother's shoes squeaked on the parquet floor. I took off my shoes and socks. Usually she stayed in the other room when I changed. "Go away," I said. I kicked my shoes under the bed, turned my back, undid my belt and my buttons, lifted my school uniform above my head, and quickly pulled on the baby-doll dress. The stitching across the bodice scratched my skin.

I heard my mother's stockinged thighs swish together, and then stop swishing. I smelled her tobacco and sweet-talcum odor as she leaned toward me, her breath loud.

She put her face close to mine and whispered, "Now I know why I can never find the recorder." She placed her hand on my arm. It clung like a strange tentacled sea creature, damp and white and slimy. "Poor poppet. What they've done to you!"

Did she think the bug was hidden on me? Tucked behind my ear like a hearing aid? I pulled away. "I'm going to the park."

My mother blocked me. She tugged at my dress. "Take this off."

"What?" I recoiled from her touch and tried to get around her. "Leave me alone."

She bent, took the hem of my dress in her hands, and with a sudden movement yanked it upward, wrapping the fabric around my head, pushing me onto my back on the bed. I flailed, struggling to get up, and a book from the windowsill fell on my chest, its corners cutting into my flesh. Her sharp fingernails hooked into the loose elastic of my panties and pulled them to my knees. She wrenched my thighs apart and stuck her finger up me. She pushed and pushed and wriggled it around so it felt like there was a snake inside me. My insides felt scratched. I couldn't breathe. I snapped my thighs together, screaming, kicking at her head. I heard her glasses skitter to the floor.

"It has to be done," she said.

I managed to pull my dress from my face. I rolled off the bed, fell onto the floor, and crawled on my hands and knees to get away from her. She stood on the edge of my dress and thumped my shoulders so I fell again. My panties tangled around my ankles. I felt her fingers try to spread my bottom.

"They'll do anything, poppet!" she said. "You don't know what they're like, this government. Nobody believes me!"

I used the ledge of the windowsill to pull myself to my feet, grabbed my dictionary, and hit her across the face. She began to cry. She sat down on the bed, and put her hand on her cheek, and I saw a flash of red blood on her fingers. The blow hadn't cut her skin. It was my blood. I yanked my panties up, then ran into the living room and opened the front door and raced down the stairs and through the lobby and out the building and onto the street and ran and ran and ran and ran and ran and ran and ran.

Durban
1995

Mevrou Bakker turned the key in the lock.

"Wait," I said. "I need a moment." I backed up against the corridor wall, the brick cold through my blouse. What if my mother hadn't answered the door when we knocked, but was nevertheless inside, sitting in her blue-and-white-flowered chair?

My insides felt as though they'd grown sharp edges. I placed my palm flat on my stomach.

"Are you feeling sick?" Mevrou Bakker said. "I don't think the Third Force is inside the flat, you know."

I nodded. "No. Sorry."

She pushed the door open and I peered in. The walls were now eggshell. My mother's armchair had been reupholstered in a dull yellow fabric. Was that the vague outline of her body I could see on the dented cushions? An ashtray on the side table bristled with filters, and a teacup containing a quarter-inch of tan sludge lay on its side next to a sugar bowl, which was protected by a little net weighed down with orange beads.

I might have been entering a holograph of my childhood, turned ochre with the years. I touched the arm of the chair, releasing a puff of ash, and wiped my fingertips on the tray-cloth.

On the bookcase was a framed photograph of my parents on their wedding day. I picked it up. My mother hadn't displayed the photo after we left Johannesburg. I wondered why. She looked beautiful: slim and aristocratic, her hand dainty on her brocaded wedding gown. My father—handsome in a tuxedo, his sandy hair slicked into place—helped her into the car.

Simon had reminded me of my father, not physically, but in the way he sometimes hugged or kissed me suddenly when I was in midsentence. Had he been that way with Cilla? Was he that way with her now? I looked at my watch. What time was it at home? Nine in the morning. He'd be at the hospital, maybe in the operating room sewing up someone's chest. I hoped he was concentrating. At the agency, since our breakup, I'd often found my mind drifting as I wrote ads for antacids and beer and spaghetti sauce. Copywriters could daydream, but cardiac surgeons shouldn't. Maybe patients here or there died because their doctors' relationships had just ended. Well, I couldn't feel guilty about that too.

At the door, Mevrou Bakker stared. "You okay?"

I replaced the photo next to the Belleek vase, its glued seams a dark yellow. "Do you mind if I look around?"

She hesitated, glancing at her watch. "An hour or so. Then I go off duty." She shut the door.

I walked over to the bookcase and squatted in front of it, pulling out books I'd loved as a child—*Just So Stories, Winnie the Pooh, The Wind in the Willows.* On the frontispieces, long ago, I'd written: THIS BELONGS TO KATE JENSEN! Barely visible beneath my scratchings was the name Jones. I piled the books on top of the bookcase, thinking I'd take them back to the States. I glanced around the room. Bunny ears spiked the top of her television set, which seemed anachronistic—television had only reached South Africa in 1976; I'd never seen one in our flat. A vase containing dusty yellow silk roses sat on the center of the dining room table. The place smelled sour, like an old closed-up movie theater reeking of smoke and spilled sodas.

In the kitchen, cans of Benedict peas and baked beans and condensed milk lined the shelves. A potato decomposed in the sink; a clock ticked on the wall. I rifled through tax receipts and bills in her concertina files, which she still stored beneath the sink. A recipe notebook lay open on the counter. The chocolate-stained page was headed THE THROW-TOGETHER CAKE. The ingredients were in my handwriting. I paged through the book. A recipe for *frikkadels!* Who in her right mind would cook *frikkadels?* But no notes about my uncle, no escape plans.

In the bathroom I checked my reflection in the mirror to make sure I hadn't also yellowed over the past two decades, then flung open her medicine cabinet so hard a tub of Pond's leapt off the shelf like a suicide.

A tattered lace cloth covered the chest near her bed. I opened every drawer. I dug through nylon panties and bras and slips and sachets of sickly lavender. I yanked the cupboard door open and plucked dresses and blouses off hangers. I knelt and threw her size-ten shoes one by one over my shoulder. They clunked on the parquet floor.

I returned to the kitchen and ripped THE THROW-TOGETHER CAKE page from her recipe book. After folding the page and putting it in my bag, I opened the cupboard above the stove where she kept her cookbooks and shoved the notebook inside, dislodging a thick stack of papers, which dove to the floor. I knelt to pick them up.

Among the papers were four manila envelopes, entitled FAMILY TREES, HETTIE WILLIAMS, PIET AND IRIS DU PLESSIS, and PERSONAL—which, I remembered, contained scribbled notes about Enemies. As a child, I'd found scraps of paper lying around the house, tucked in books or stored with shopping lists. I thought of stowing the envelopes back in the cupboard, but instead I carried them to the table in the living room and sat down.

The envelope marked HETTIE WILLIAMS held papers, crackly now with age, that I'd seen before—describing Hettie's father, his career as a private investigator, and his "connections" to the Bureau of State Security, or BOSS. A piece of paper headed "Observations," annotated with dates, revealed that on several occasions my mother had caught buses to Durban North and followed Hettie and me after school. She'd watched us through the hedge. She saw us kissing with tongues the day Hettie wanted to practice for Mark Poulos.

My skin felt as though a thousand fleas danced on its surface.

I found a list of my classmates—*Up to No Good*—with asterisks next to Hettie Williams and Patrick Osch and Jennifer Barrell and Jackie Winterbottom, who, according to the notes, was the worst of the lot, and had introduced me to my black friend Joshua.

"Ha!" I said. "Not true." Jackie was someone I'd invented. I gazed at the Belleek vase, remembering how good it had felt to push my mother's vase onto the floor—to see it break—to know I'd destroyed something she held dear.

Mevrou Bakker put her head around the door. "Agh, man, what's this mess here now?"

I glanced around. The flat was as much in disarray as the time my mother disemboweled my hippo. "I'll tidy up."

She frowned. "Fifteen minutes."

I opened the FAMILY TREES envelope.

One of the jumbled matrices was headed "Rotten Apples: A Summary." The wavy pencil lines connected people I'd never heard of, and a few I had. Under the names she'd written details: where they worked, addresses and phone numbers, links to other Rotten Apples. She'd crossed out old addresses and added new contact information. Oom Piet was highlighted in yellow: he now lived in Drieplek, south of Johannesburg. The entry was dated the previous week. No question now: it *had* been he who'd visited her. I felt angry—his visit had re-ignited her paranoia, which had seemed to be in remission for years. Why hadn't he left her alone?

To the far left, a branch carried the words *Willem Marais: Postman sent to spy on us, May 15, 1966.* Two months before my eleventh birthday. That note surprised me. I'd always assumed my father's death had triggered my mother's delusions, though I'd never been certain.

The name Lydia Cronje (*David's mistress. Slut died in 1979.*) had been scribbled in thick letters on a separate little sapling next to the main family tree. Other women's names adorned the branches: Jessie. Margaret. Reinette. My father had had affairs? Or my mother just imagined he did? I couldn't know for sure. I hesitated. Did I really want to delve further into my mother's life? I pulled a thick pile of papers from the envelope marked PERSONAL. Her birth certificate. Marriage certificate. Secretarial diploma. Pressed roses. Several buttons. Newspaper clippings: HOW TO EAT ON A SHOESTRING. GETTING RID OF APHIDS. BOMB HORROR: WHO DID IT? I read the article about the bomb: it speculated that the white man who planted the station bomb in Johannesburg in 1964 had worked with a black accomplice, maybe a member of the ANC.

And then I found a letter from John Plotkin, Plotkin & Plotkin, regarding the divorce of David and Violet Jones.

My parents were planning to divorce? I checked the date. July 8, 1966. Two days before my father's death.

Dear David and Violet Jones:

Please review the attached rough draft as a precursor to next week's meeting regarding the dissolution of your marriage.

> *Sincerely,*
> *John Plotkin,*
> *Plotkin & Plotkin*

My mouth tasted as though I'd eaten iron. Surely I would've remembered angrier arguments, longer silences? They had fought terribly the week before his death. But what could have happened to precipitate such a sudden separation? And why did I feel so upset? What difference did it make after all these years?

Close to tears, I scanned the draft. The proposed settlement was only four pages: my parents had owned nothing except the Fiat, the Ford, and furniture. A thousand rand in cash, which was to be split between them. Probably the money that had kept us going every time my mother lost jobs. The last paragraph was entitled "Custody of Child." It said: *Petitioner is vested with sole legal custody of Katherine Sarah Jones, born July 10, 1955. Respondent agrees to have no contact with child except for annual Easter and Christmas visits, if requested.*

Katherine Sarah Jones. The name sounded like someone else's.

Respondent agrees to have no contact with child . . .

My dad had agreed never to see me again?

I wished I hadn't come to South Africa. I wished I'd stayed in the States. I wanted to crawl into a closet and roll up into a ball and never come out.

After a moment, I reread the paragraph. My father was the *petitioner*, the one who'd instigated the proceedings, who wanted custody of me. My mother was the respondent—she hadn't sought the divorce because of his infidelity, or her perception of his infidelity, as I'd assumed from her notes. Dad had sought the divorce. Why? Because my mother had been acting strangely?

A wild idea struck me—*what if my mother had killed my father?* Poisoned him because she was jealous of his mistresses (if they really existed) and angry that he planned to divorce her? Then blamed it on my uncle?

I stacked the envelopes to take with me and tidied up, throwing things into drawers, recoiling at the touch of my mother's ancient pink robe. Except for the cake recipe, there was no evidence of my existence. No photographs. No letters. No old school certificates. Not even the newspaper cutting from the time I won the national essay contest. But when I searched her concertina file once more, I discovered an envelope addressed to me. I pulled out the letter. It was dated 23rd October—five days before the one I'd received in Chagrin Falls the previous Saturday.

Dear Poppet,

Oom Piet's been here. I have proof *he is a murderer. You are old enough now to know the truth of what happened. But I am in danger. He will do anything to keep me quiet. Do not let him know you are still in contact with me! He thinks you are lost in America. Stay there! Treat those around you with caution. He is a member of the Third Force. As always, he will recruit people you know to spy on you.*

IF YOU GET ANOTHER LETTER, IGNORE IT. *It will have been written under duress to lure you here.*

For a while I thought you had *become my enemy. But I don't think you have it in you. Do you remember our picnic down the coast one Christmas holiday? That was such a lovely day, wasn't it? You looked like a plump red lobster when we arrived home. Only baby fat, of course. Although they pumped you up afterwards, with steroids, I imagine. Poor poppet!*

Love,
Mother

P.S. I'm not the crazy one, you know. No matter how hard Oom Piet has tried to make it look that way.

I stood and opened a window, stuck my head out, and breathed deeply. I smelled paint thinners and glanced to my left. A man on a hanging platform smoothed a brush along the exterior of the building. He stopped in mid-motion, stared at me, then glanced away. Down below, on the street, the beggar with amputated legs pointed up to the flats. He was talking to a tall, thin man. The man's face was in shadow. Oom Piet? My mother would have assumed so. The most innocent arrangement of people could suggest a conspiracy.

Returning to the table, I pulled papers from the PIET AND IRIS DU PLESSIS envelope. The heading on the first page said: "How the Murder was Committed."

The door opened. I turned. Mevrou Bakker.

"Thanks for letting me search the flat," I said, stashing the papers in the envelopes and placing them in my bag. I picked up my old books and tucked them in the curve of my arm. "Sorry to have bothered you."

She patted my shoulder. "You seem very upset, *meisie*. She's probably all right, *jy weet?* I'll call you if she comes back, *hoor?*"

After giving her my hotel number, I left the flat and caught the elevator. When I emerged onto the street the air felt thick and moist, like an agglomeration of sweat. I put down my head and walked fast. People streamed from office blocks. Bus after bus disgorged workers; I was caught in a riptide of humanity hurrying home to sundowners and slippers and supper.

"Kate?" Someone touched my arm.

I pivoted. The beggar-amputee gestured toward the building and muttered something. I stared up. Mevrou Bakker was standing at her window, watching me. I felt a tug on my shoulder. An old white man breathed stale brandy into my face, then turned and darted across the street, my bag under his arm. I yelled, but he dissolved into the crowd, which enmeshed me when I tried to follow.

Clutching the books I'd taken from my mother's flat in front of me like a shield, I hurried through the crowded streets back to the Oliphant Hotel.

Now that my bag had been stolen, along with the envelopes containing her scribbled notes, I had no clues as to where my mother might be. And the police hadn't seemed in the least interested in her disappearance. Was I going to have to contact Oom Piet? It seemed likely he *had* visited her, based on Mevrou Bakker's description of the tall thin man she'd seen. Fortunately, or unfortunately, I remembered my uncle's address from the family tree: 3, Third Avenue, Drieplek. Translated into English, Drieplek meant Threeplace, so it had been easy to memorize.

My mother would've held my uncle's agents responsible for the theft. But the concierge had warned me before I left the hotel that pickpocketing was an everyday occurrence in the city.

On the way up to my room, I mentally inventoried the contents of my purse: lipstick, map, tissues, a hairbrush, and my wallet, in which I'd placed only one credit card and two hundred rand in cash. And the Amanzimtoti Beach photograph. The elevator doors opened. I stepped into the corridor, picked up the newspaper lying outside my room, slid the cardkey in the door, tossed the paper on the wicker chair, and stacked the books—*Just So Stories, The Wind in the Willows,* and Gerald Durrell's *My Family and Other*

Animals—on the desk. I poured myself a glass of water and drank slowly. I called the credit-card company. That done, I flopped backward onto the bed and stared at the ceiling.

Whatever truths or delusions the envelopes contained were now gone. I'd never learn "How the Murder Was Committed." I'd been curious to read that note. Though many of her stories were quite detailed, my mother hadn't been able to explain how the government—and, supposedly, Oom Piet—had killed my father. Of course, I didn't believe he'd been murdered: I'd seen the death certificate when I was eleven. Cardiac arrest. When I found the certificate in a drawer, I told Prudence I imagined his heart being marched off in cuff links. She'd flapped her hands and raised her eyebrows. Later, I realized I'd meant to say "handcuffs."

A seagull balanced on my balcony railing. The bird lifted its wings and floated away into the twilight on the salty breeze. From the street below, I could hear vendors hawking baskets and beads. *Sangomas* offered *muti*—medicine—and advice to the ailing.

In Johannesburg, Winston had smoked herbs called Lion's Ear, which he told my mother was more soothing than tobacco.

"Come to my *kya* and try it," he'd said to her. He was standing on our verandah in front of the golden shower creeper. Yellow sun flickered on his green shirt so he appeared to be part of the plant. Winston had a way of blending in with his surroundings.

My mother had smiled, but shook her head and continued snipping azaleas.

Looking back, Winston's behavior had been extraordinarily bold for a black man in a country where too much familiarity across the color line could get you arrested.

I sat up on the bed and rested my chin on my knuckles. Based on what Mevrou Bakker had told me, there were two possibilities. One, after my uncle visited my mother, she'd voluntarily left Durban and was wandering around Cape Town or Port Elizabeth or East London at this very moment. She'd written the letter about cancer to get me to South Africa so I could help her settle into a new home under a new name. Maybe she'd left a clue in her flat as to her whereabouts, and I'd missed it? Or, two, Oom Piet had forcibly taken her to a doctor for a check-up; they'd found cancer and she *was* now in a hospital, probably near where he lived in Johannesburg. That seemed most likely. She believed he'd put her there to keep her quiet about his involvement in my father's death.

Why had Oom Piet turned up at her door concerned about her welfare after all these years? Had Aunt Iris sent him as an envoy, wanting to reconcile now that the sisters were elderly?

I reached for my old books, felt their heft, ran my finger over their fraying spines, and lifted them to my nose, breathing in their musty smell. When I flipped through *Winnie the Pooh,* I found, in the middle of the story about Owl and his Necessary Dorsal Muscles, a yellowed scrap of paper in my mother's handwriting: *Hettie will hurt you, poppet. I tell you this for your own good.* I slammed the book shut and pushed the pile away.

I decided to call Bernie. Evening in South Africa was daytime in Ohio, so I knew she'd be at the office working on the ReFute presentation. She'd cancelled all her meetings so she could focus on it. When she picked up the phone, she said the presentation was going well, but she'd begun to feel nauseated. Did I think she had a stomach ulcer?

We talked for maybe half an hour. I confided more about my mother's paranoia than I'd confided to anyone. Except Eduardo, an ex-fiancé, who was an ex-fiancé for that reason.

"But I still don't get why she would she think the government was after her," Bernie said.

"She was irrational."

"It couldn't have been true? You're sure?"

I felt a tremor of irritation. Why try to explain what she was like? "I guess you had to be there. Bernie, I have to get dinner. I'm starving. I'll call you tomorrow after the presentation. Good luck." I placed the phone back on its cradle and glared at it. The police hadn't pursued white suburban women, spied on them, and recorded their conversations. Not unless the women worked for the Communist Party or the African National Congress, the ANC.

And my mother hadn't been politically active—or only once that I remembered, and then not for long.

The evening sun slanted across the hotel room and lit the gold thread woven through the duvet cover. I recalled a Sunday morning maybe thirty years ago, when we lived in Johannesburg, on Lees Avenue, and I'd perched on the edge of my mother's bed, watching her get dressed for a meeting. I must've been ten—it was the Christmas holidays, 1965, the year before my father died. She draped a black sash over her white dress. I advised her to wear green or red in honor of the season, and she'd smiled.

"It's a uniform. I'm going to demonstrate," she said.

Outside, on a tree branch, a bright yellow weaverbird swung by its claws from its nest. Sunshine flooded the room and lit a spotlight on my mother's mirror.

"Demonstrate what?" I thought she might be having a Tupperware party, like the ones my friends' mothers held. But except for gardening, my mother wasn't good at domestic things.

She laughed. "That black people should have the same rights as we do."

I'd heard my dad's shoes squeak along the linoleum floor in the kitchen; he'd returned from golf. He stood in the doorway, frowning. "Why the sudden interest in politics?" he asked her.

My mother had been coiling her hair into a knot. Her hands were still for a moment. She continued to gaze into the mirror. She cocked her head. Then she tucked a stray hair into her bun. "It's not right, what's happening."

"You didn't used to care."

"I cared. I just didn't do anything about it."

My father stood in the doorway for a while, his arms crossed. I could hear him breathing. Then he'd looked at me, jerked his head toward the bedroom door and said, "Prudence says dinner will be ready in five minutes." I'd trotted off, a little afraid of his temper.

The hotel room was growing dark. I switched on the lamp. Shadows leapt on the walls like ghosts. But my mother hadn't been a female Joe Slovo, heading up a guerrilla force. Her interest in the Black Sash movement had faded quickly. In Durban, she'd never attended their meetings.

I needed to call Oom Piet. I reached for the telephone directory. My hand nudged the folded newspaper, which flopped open. I glanced at the headlines. TRUTH & RECONCILIATION COMMISSION TO START HEARINGS SOON. I read the article: Archbishop Desmond Tutu invited those who had suffered under apartheid to testify for posterity, and those who had perpetrated acts of violence—government agencies and the African National Congress—to tell their side of the story in exchange for possible amnesty.

The previous summer, in Chagrin Falls, Simon and I had watched a documentary on the proposed commission. The narrator had spoken of families split up during the resettlement of "black spots" like Sophiatown; reclassifications of husbands and wives, one as Coloured, one as White, so they had to live apart; of people detained without trial for years. Of unaccountable deaths. How white policemen—after barbecuing *boerewors* late one night and drinking peach brandy—had cut human limbs from black corpses, tossed them onto the fires, flipped them over and over because the fatty parts took a while to burn, then thrown the charred bones to their dogs.

Rigid with horror, I'd barely been able to watch. I'd been familiar with apartheid policies, but shocked to realize quite how brutally they'd been implemented. I went to the bathroom and threw up.

Now I read to the end of the article. It was hard to believe that such truths could lead to reconciliation.

My fingertips were black with newsprint. Feeling like Lady Macbeth, I headed to the bathroom and washed my hands in soapy water.

I returned to the desk and paged through the Gauteng phone book, looking first for Tshabalala, Prudence, but found no entry. I remembered her surname because it had sounded like a song from *The Sound of Music*. She'd intended to move to Soweto after we left for Durban, though she might still be working at the house on Lees Avenue. Often, as one white family succeeded another, servants had stayed on at the home as though they went with it, like the drapes. Though times were different, now.

There were only seventeen Du Plessises in Drieplek, three of whom were Piets. I picked up the receiver and dialed, imagining my uncle in his recliner, watching rugby and sipping rum-and-coke. The second number was his.

"Du Plessis?" he said.

He sounded exactly as I remembered. I hung up. If Oom Piet had had something to do with my mother's disappearance, why alert him I was on my way?

I walked onto the balcony and inhaled the sultry air. Glancing down at the street, I saw the beggar with the oilcan talking to one of the rickshaw drivers beneath a streetlight. I stepped away from the railing. Surely the beggar wasn't following me? I debated whether to go downstairs and challenge him. But what would I say? *Who were you talking to outside Kingfisher Court? Why did you distract me—so that someone could steal my bag with the information about my father's murder? Is Oom Piet paying you to keep an eye on me?*

The moon slipped behind a shell-shaped cloud. I slid the door closed and turned on the air conditioning. At what age had my mother's paranoia begun?

Around forty, I guessed. My present age. Or that's when I first noticed her strange behavior. I looked around the room. Maybe an *umamlambo* was loose—the shape-shifting water snake which, Prudence had claimed, could drive people insane with one glance of its flat round eyes. You never knew when one was around, she'd said. It could change into a kettle, or a stick, or a sunflower.

I decided to go to the restaurant. I'd hardly eaten all day. Lack of food was making me delusional. And if someone were after me, I'd be safer in a crowd.

After booking a flight to Johannesburg—the earliest available left Durban at noon the next day and arrived at 1:10 in the afternoon—I reserved a room at the Johannesburg Sterling, thinking that it might take a while to find Oom Piet. I'd keep the room at the Oliphant, too, in case I was able to return to Durban the same day.

Then I freshened my makeup, ran a comb through my chaotic hair, and caught the lift downstairs.

Durban
1967

My baby-doll dress flapped against my legs as I ran away from my
mother along Marine Parade. The soles of my bare feet burned
and my inner thighs felt sticky with blood. When I stopped, finally,
I found myself near the aquarium, which loomed near the pier.
My breath sounded as loud as the barking seals. It was getting
dark, and there was hardly anyone around, though I could hear
the distant chatter of adults from a hotel verandah across Marine
Parade. I stepped onto the beach and walked on the crunchy sand
until I was up to mid-calf in the ocean. I washed myself clean, and
the cold water swirled around my legs, turning my skin goose-
pimply. Phosphorescence flickered in the arc of the waves. I pooled
water into the cup of my hands and splashed my face, tasting the
salt on my lips.

Looking toward the horizon where ships sparkled, I thought I
might continue walking until I drowned and became an ancestor.
Except, of course, I didn't have children, so I couldn't be one.

And I didn't really want to die.

I waded out of the water and sat on the damp sand, stared at
the ocean and dreamed of living in a country far from my mother.
I knew it was impossible while I was a child. But, one day, someone
handsome and kind would marry me and we'd own a house with
three bedrooms—one for us, and one each for the kids, a boy and
a girl. We'd build a small zoo in the backyard, where we might

keep a warthog family and a pygmy hippopotamus. My husband would bring home bunches of flowers and hold me tight and tell me he adored me. The girl-child would wear pretty clothes. Her friends would come and play at our house, because her mother— me—would bake the most delicious cakes and be friendly and tell funny stories that made everyone laugh. Her friends would say *I wish my mother were like yours.*

The wind felt cold on my wet cheeks. I remembered a night long ago on Lees Avenue, after my kitten Smokey had been hit by a truck and killed. I'd been sitting in the rockery in the dark crying. I think my mother was at a Black Sash meeting and Dad was on a trip selling detergent.

Winston emerged from the shadows and sat beside me. Cicadas chirped in the bushes. The air tasted dusty, as though grit from the mine dumps had blown into the suburbs.

"Mustn't cry," he said, drawing in the sand with a stick.

"I'll never be happy again," I said, following the motion of his hand. Of course, I knew nothing then of real unhappiness.

He was quiet for a while, then pointed to the cloud-smudged moon. "Some Xhosa believe the ocean at the edge of the world holds fresh moons. They're there, you see, though it is hard to imagine sometimes."

"Tomorrow's another day, you mean?"

He'd nodded.

Now I looked toward the ocean and pictured round white moons bobbing like rubber balls in the water, waiting their turn to bounce into the sky.

The waves glittered to shore. I wiped my face dry with the hem of my dress, stood, and walked home.

My mother was asleep. Seeing her made my whole body tremble. I lay on my bed and stared at the ceiling. People thumped around the flat upstairs. Tiny pieces of plaster fluttered down. I would have to tell someone about her, ask for help. She would surely feel happier if she got better. Still, I didn't want to call Oom Piet— one way or another it seemed to me he had caused all the trouble. Something he had done must have caused my mother's condition, otherwise why would she talk about him so much? Perhaps I should confide in Mrs. Schorn. Although she wasn't my class teacher anymore, she was kind, often stopping in the corridor to ask how I was. She seemed to have forgotten my lie about the fourteen-pound salmon in the Umgeni River.

In the morning, I told my mother I would cut off her fingers if she touched me again. I brandished a vegetable knife and ostentatiously put it in my pocket. On the bus, I took it out and realized it was a potato peeler.

At school, Hettie begged to see my answers on the arithmetic test. "My father'll hit me if I fail," she said. "Please, Katie! In case I suddenly can't remember what a common denominator is."

I agreed partly because I could still picture the stripes on her bottom from the *sjambok*. Also, I was scared if I didn't do as she asked, she might not like me anymore and right now she was the only person who did.

Mrs. Schorn was the moderator. She patted me on the shoulder as I walked into the room. "Going to make us all proud, Kate?"

I nodded. I couldn't speak. She probably thought I was nervous. When she squeezed my shoulder, I wanted to cry.

In the exam room, the desks were lined up close to one another. I chose one at the back and Hettie sat at the one next to me. She flashed her palm—she'd written notes on her skin.

The problems were easy. It felt like there was nothing in the world but me and my pen and paper. I loved the feeling of being transported to a place where it was only you and your brain, and your body didn't matter at all, nor did other people. Then I heard the triple-cough signal from Hettie. I was tempted to ignore it, but pictured her father with his hand raised.

I slid my paper to the edge of the desk, gazing out the window as though I were thinking. I *was* thinking, but not about the sums. I was thinking how upset my dad would have been if he'd known I was cheating. I almost forgot I had problems to finish. It was drizzling. The ocean was gray and flat and hard-looking, like cement. I bit the end of my pencil. The lead tasted bitter on my tongue. Pieces of pencil started to break off.

Then I heard Mrs. Schorn's voice. "You girls are cheating!"

"No!" I spat splinters.

"Kate. I thought better of you," she said. "Come with me, the two of you."

I couldn't confide in her now about my mother. She'd think I was lying, this time to get out of my punishment. So I was rude instead. When she asked in her soft voice why I'd done it, I told her I'd been possessed by evil spirits. She took us to the principal, who said Hettie and I would have to spend two weeks in detention when school started again after the July holidays. And I wouldn't get the academic trophy.

When I arrived home, my mother said she'd been tailed.

"Who are you, Eeyore the donkey?" I asked. I told her I didn't intend to talk to her ever again. We could continue living together, I said, but I didn't want to hear any of her nonsense. She could like it or lump it.

She shook her head. "Poor poppet."

I knew what she was thinking—*they've brainwashed her!*

That night I decided to tell Hettie everything. She was my friend, after all. Maybe her parents would adopt me. I let myself daydream. Her mother would tuck me in bed at night and make vegetable soup when I was sick. I would help Hettie with her work, so her father would have no reason to hit her anymore. He would be so pleased he would change his ways and become kind and begin to love me as if I were his own daughter. In the afternoons, instead of walking to the beach, I would sit in our garden or swim in the pool or plant Barberton daisies the way I used to with Winston.

In the morning it was humid again. The sun poured through the window and saturated my bed so I woke sweaty. My mother snored. Her breath smelled seaweedy. The flat seemed to be getting smaller and smaller. I thought I might choke on the thick air. I grabbed my school uniform.

She'd pinned a note to the collar.

Poppet, to explain my actions, I wanted you to read this entry in my notebook. You need to understand what we are up against.

June 27, 1967. The Williams family is part of the plot. They are related to the Du Plessis family (see chart below). The daughter, Hettie, is being used to corrupt Kate. She is inviting sexual play, asking Kate to touch her vagina and vice versa. She has planted a bug inside her. I can't get to it. The father is involved. He is a private investigator connected to the police. It is time to confront the man. I don't want to play into their hands. But this is too much! I will write a letter detailing what has happened and by the time the authorities get it, the child and I will be safe in Cape Town. It's the best I can do.

I'd once watched my cousin Koos sprinkle salt on a slug. Its soft body bubbled and fizzed. That's how I felt: like my insides were dissolving.

With the note was a family tree, with branches covered in names in her loopy handwriting. I didn't look at it. I folded the paper and put it in my pocket.

All the way to school on the bus, I turned hot and cold, thinking about the time Hettie and I had undressed and compared breast sizes. I opened the window but the air was as warm as my cheeks.

. . .

Hettie and I didn't have a chance to talk much before school started. She was in a quiet mood anyway. She said her dad blamed me for the cheating. He'd asked her if I was the strange little girl from the wrong side of town.

We were going over sections of our test papers in class. I had to sit through square roots and the French Revolution.

At Little Break I told Hettie the things Mom said about bus drivers, how they tried to take her directly to the Parliament Buildings in Pretoria but she always got off in time. Hettie flipped her black hair between her fingers and laughed, as if I were telling one of my jokes. The bell rang.

Chalk dust sifted through the sunbeams. Mrs. Anderson's nail screeched on the board. I survived parts of speech, evaporation, and the life cycle of a butterfly, or caterpillar, depending on which one you thought came first. By the time Big Break arrived, I couldn't wait to tell Hettie the whole story. She was upset because she wanted to kiss Mark under the stands—she'd smuggled in lipstick for the occasion—but she said okay.

Her lunch box had neat compartments with half a dozen grapes, a peanut butter sandwich with the crusts cut off, a small square of cheese, and a row of crackers. I bit into my chocolate bar. A loud Indian mynah squawked.

I told her about Oom Piet, the government, and the drugs.

"But that doesn't make sense." Her round eyes got rounder. "Your mom's not a communist, right? She's not *black*, is she?"

"No." I told her my mom's suspicions about Sandy's mother. "And she thinks your dad's a spy."

We were sitting on a picnic bench, under the shade of an acacia. Three *mossies* were pecking at the ground. Hettie crumbled a piece of her sandwich onto the wooden slats of the table, then gathered up crumbs between her right forefinger and thumb and threw them toward the birds. They fluttered away then settled on the ground and nudged the bread with their beaks. "That's weird."

Two girls were jumping rope on the netball court to the right of us. Their feet banged on the ground. Mark walked past with his friends and winked at Hettie.

I touched her arm. "I don't know what to do."

She scuffed her shoes on the ground and scooted a little way down the bench.

I kept talking. I couldn't stop myself. "One day I got home from school and I saw wires hanging out the wall. I knew the maintenance man had come, but she said to me, 'See, I told you people were listening to us.'"

Hettie stared at me. "Are you lying again?" She closed her lunch box lid and pursed her lips.

"No, it's real. Hettie, you have to help me."

She scowled. "Is this supposed to be a joke? Well, it's not funny." She stood up.

I grabbed her arm and pulled her next to me. I was desperate. I took the piece of paper from my pocket. "See, here's proof!"

She read it. She looked as though she might throw up. "You and your mother are sick," she said. She crumpled the piece of paper and dropped it on the ground. She got up and walked across the quadrangle and sat down next to Susan Wakely and Brenda Jacobs.

When I followed Hettie, she turned away. Susan and Brenda stared at me, nudged each other, and giggled.

"Hettie?" I said.

"Get away from me, Big Bottom," Hettie said. "Fat Arse."

The green lawns slipped away one by one as the bus drove away from Durban North and toward the city. I climbed off at Farewell Square. Instead of catching the connecting bus to the beachfront, I walked to the docks and watched the ships, thinking I might stow away and go to Wales. See if I could find anyone related to me in Bangor, where Dad had been born. But relatives weren't proving to be my favorite people. And my father was dead, dead, dead. I took my hippo from my school case—I'd been carrying him with me since my mother attacked him—and threw him in the oily sea.

Then I went to the Natural Science Museum and wandered among the stuffed animals and displays. I read the inscription beneath the glass case containing a partial dodo skeleton: THE DODO WAS A TRUSTING BIRD, AND AS A RESULT, SAILORS LANDING ON THE ISLAND OF MAURITIUS WERE EASILY ABLE TO HUNT THEM, LEADING TO THE EXTINCTION OF THIS SPECIES.

Dumb dodo.

On the bus home, I remembered our nature lesson, *Suits, Spines, and Spikes.* I took out my textbook and turned to the photographs of tortoises and armadillo lizards and fleeing springbok. I touched the picture of the scaly anteater rolled up into a ball. I examined a photograph of a stick insect you couldn't tell apart from a twig.

And then I smiled. I knew how I'd protect myself in the future. If my mother started talking about The Plot, I'd run from the flat or walk away from her into the other room, even if I ended up going around in circles like the polar bear at the zoo. Or I'd stare at her with blank eyes so she couldn't see what was going on inside me. I'd do the same with the kids at school. And I could hide in plain sight, like a chameleon: I wouldn't say a word in class. I'd study, though, and learn the ways of the human world, and migrate far, far away from Durban as soon as I was old enough to survive on my own.

A man across the aisle stared at me. I tucked my knees into my chest, put my arms around my legs, and presented him with the curve of my back.

At my stop, I got off the bus and practiced bounding like an impala chased by a lion.

Outside our building, I noticed a Zephyr the same color as Oom Piet's. I ran upstairs. He and Aunt Iris were in our flat. A man in a white coat, holding a syringe, was standing over my mother, who sat docilely in her blue armchair, her arm outstretched, palm up.

Durban
1995

The Twee-Oliphant Restaurant, on the mezzanine level, was decorated with a mixture of East Indian and African artifacts: beads, woven baskets, and tasseled Persian rugs. Statues of Indian and African elephants, their trunks entwined, were grouped at the entrance, and soapstone tigers and leopards lounged in lit niches. On the floor lay stacks of dried cobs and gourds brimming with cumin seeds and spices and grains. Simon would've loved the jaw of a Great White shark grinning in a corner, bony mouth wide enough to swallow Mortimer, the skeleton, in one gulp, along with several coelacanths and a school of rabbitfish.

I chose a barstool, thinking I'd appear less conspicuous than sitting at one of the round tables where lovers and friends and tourists chatted in myriad languages: Sotho, Venda, Hindi, Xhosa, Zulu, English, Afrikaans, German, French. Flat woven fans, shaped like aces, waved above the diners. The air smelled faintly of spilled beer and wicker furniture. On the counter, a clump of purple begonias burst from a clay pot. The menu featured photographs of exotic dishes—crocodile spare ribs, ostrich steaks, and fried mopane worms that looked like small greasy phalluses. I grimaced and ordered a pink gin and prawns peri-peri. When my drink arrived, I stirred the ice cubes with a swizzle stick, attempting to free a trapped lemon wedge. I refused to think about anything except food, drink, and sleep until the next morning.

The bartender leaned against a mirrored column, watching me. "Here on holiday?" he asked, holding a glass to the light. "Seen Reverend Dube's grave?" He replaced the tumbler and picked up another. "One of the first places President Mandela visited after the election last year."

"Doo-bay?" I thought of Frank Sinatra's "Strangers in the Night"—*Dooby dooby do . . . dooby da da da . . .*

"The first president of the African National Congress—the old South African Native National Congress?"

"Oh. Dube." I felt ashamed of my frivolous response, and experienced the now familiar sense of disconnection from my own country's past. As white children, we'd lived in a colonial cocoon, read about Farmer Brown's pig and English boarding school adventures, and studied leaders like Paul Kruger and Winston Churchill. Not Reverend Dube, Oliver Tambo, and Nelson Mandela. In primary school, I'd learned about Dick King, South Africa's Paul Revere, who rode hundreds of miles from Durban to Grahamstown to seek reinforcements for British troops holed up at what was now the Old Fort. *His* statue and grave I'd visited.

"Where's Reverend Dube's monument?" I asked.

The bartender checked the cleanliness of a wineglass. "Inanda. But an attractive woman like you shouldn't go alone." He winked.

"Good point. I'll join a tour," I said.

He shrugged and turned to fill a brandy bottle.

The prawns were taking forever. I found myself looking forward to them as company, not just food.

My second fiancé, Eduardo, had loved shellfish—but not the same way Simon did, which was alive and crawling around rock pools. Eduardo was a chef, famous for his amazing bouillabaisse. *Like there's a party going on in my mouth,* I heard a customer once say. Eduardo's father was Spanish, his mother Scottish. We met at a catered event for my clients, where he and I debated whether people actually enjoy rare tuna or simply feel they ought to eat it that way. Eduardo had gleaming olive skin and sensual lips. My whole body seemed to buzz in his presence. He was loud and funny and not at all thrifty. He wore a kilt on New Year's Eve—Hogmanay—and could dance the flamenco.

After he'd proposed on Santa Monica Pier, I decided to be candid about my past: how, sometimes, I found it difficult to show emotion. I didn't want him to leave me for the reasons other men had. One of my many previous boyfriends—Ned—had ended our relationship because he said I shut down like a garage door whenever he thought we were getting close, and he didn't think he would ever find the opener. He wasn't even sure there was an opener.

Before that, Gareth had sat me down at the Delhi Deli and over chicken masala told me that, if I was in the Witness Protection Program, he wanted to let me know what a good job I was doing. He had no idea what my life had been like prior to meeting him. And if I weren't in the Witness Protection Program, he thought we should break up, because he didn't want to stick around and find out I had once been a Mafia hit-woman.

Hurt after Ned and Gareth broke up with me, I made sure to leave Danny and Tran at the first hint of an argument: better to leave than be left, I thought. I wasn't sure why I felt the urge to flee, or curl up into a fetal position and croon quietly to myself the minute I thought I was falling in love. But by the time I met Eduardo, I was beginning to realize I needed to change if I wanted a long-term relationship. And I'd have to risk confiding a little about my mother's condition.

In bed, fingering my diamond ring, I showed Eduardo the photo of my mother and me at the beach. "She's a very suspicious woman," I told him.

"Looks-wise, you take after her," he said, "except you're much thinner." He ran his finger over my hipbone. "Och, señorita, lassie, I love you."

At the time I was a size six. Early in relationships, I was usually at my lowest weight. "I'll never be like her," I said, pulling a picture of my father and me from the bedside drawer. "See? I have my father's nose. And chest, actually."

"I like small breasts," he said, and moved to prove his point.

Over the next few weeks, the story of my childhood emerged in bits and pieces. Eduardo flinched when I told him my mother had once smashed a mirror she thought the government was using as a surveillance camera.

"She's paranoid? Violent?" he asked, ripping the vein from a pale gray shrimp.

"No," I said. "At least not with people." I decided not to mention the incident with Sandy's mother, whom she'd slapped. "She doesn't bounce off the walls. She copes."

After lunch, he went to the Los Padres National Forest to play his bagpipes, which was his habit when stressed, then came home with bunches of sweet-smelling wildflowers.

I thought we were going to be all right. I thought we would marry and have children.

Then one of my mother's letters arrived.

Dear Poppet,

I am surprised to hear you are marrying this Eduardo person. Have you really thought this through? Don't tell him ANY-THING I've told you about Oom Piet. He'll try to get you locked up. He'll say you're crazy. You know by now what the government's like. Or you should, after all these years.

De Klerk says he'll set Mandela free soon. Perhaps things will be better then. But I'm not so sure. Don't come home: it's not safe yet.

Are you still fat? Spanish men like fat women, I understand.

Love,
Mother

I showed Eduardo.

"Is she on medication?" he asked.

"She refuses to see a doctor of any kind. She'd think the pills were to poison her."

He nodded. "Very sad."

That weekend I left a note to tell him I was at the store. *Back soon. Love you madly (so to speak). Kate.* He wasn't amused. We weren't laughing much anymore.

Around the same time, I was afraid I might be laid off. It was 1990: the country was going through a recession. I'd recently started at the Los Angeles office of Bellish & Associates and knew the usual policy was last hired, first fired. Eduardo's forehead wrinkled every time I mentioned my concerns.

Then, after I received a promotion instead of being let go, he said, "See? You shouldn't have been so . . . fearful." He stared at me. "You know, I'll stick by you, whatever."

"There won't be a whatever," I said. Because of my mother, he was afraid I might become paranoid too? I assumed that's what he was implying. Until then, I hadn't thought much about the hereditary aspect. I don't know why. Perhaps because I'd always felt so rational compared to my mother, I never imagined I'd be anything but sane. I talked to my doctor. She said the illness was unlikely to manifest itself at this point if it hadn't already. I asked about future children. Without examining my mother in person, she wouldn't say. But she estimated the chances were less than 5 percent. And there was usually an environmental trigger—you could have the gene but never show signs of mental illness, so I shouldn't be overly concerned.

I told Eduardo.

"Five percent?" he said.

My leg muscles tightened, but I didn't run. Maybe having children *was* too much of a risk.

One day I complained I seemed to get more computer viruses than anyone I knew. I'd lost an entire marketing strategy.

"Well, Kate, it happens," he said, dumping a failed soufflé in the trash.

"I know. I don't mean I'm being targeted," I said.

"I wasn't implying I thought you thought you were being targeted."

But suddenly he wouldn't let me chop celery. He said I was clumsy and might end up fingerless, and he would miss my fingers.

Was he really worried about my lack of coordination? Or, now that he knew there was mental illness in my family, did he think I might be violent? I wished I hadn't confided in him. Soon I began censoring my words, avoiding any conversations that might spark concern about my sanity. I didn't criticize government policies. Didn't worry aloud when his restaurant began failing. Didn't tell him the smoke alarm was going off at odd times. Eventually I became virtually mute. My skin prickled every time he gazed at me, but for all the wrong reasons. Though I still loved him—or the couple we *had* been—I told him it was over.

"I'm not your *enemy*, Kate," he said, sitting on the couch, his bagpipes resting next to him like a large plaid porcupine.

I ran out the door. He called several times afterward, but I refused to see him. My whole childhood I'd guarded my words, not wanting to provoke an unwanted response from my mother. I couldn't spend my adult life the same way.

About a month later, I realized how preoccupied he must have been with his business challenges. I hadn't offered much sympathy. Instead, I'd seen hidden motives in his behavior where none existed.

Was this the start of my mother's illness in me? Paranoia was the most self-involved of mental illnesses: it made you assume you were the focus of everyone's attention.

I went on vacation to the Galapagos, where no one knew me, and communed with the animals.

Shortly afterward, Bellish & Associates offered me a job at their headquarters in Chagrin Falls, Ohio.

Four years later, when we got engaged, Simon talked about having a baby. He wanted a son. I'd told him my mother was eccentric, but not the details. I knew if we decided to have children, I'd have to tell him the whole truth about her, and I was afraid it would scare him away, as it had Eduardo. I joked that pregnancy was a primitive way to reproduce. So much could go wrong in the manufacturing process, especially at my age—one little crimp in the DNA, and who knew what I might deliver? Tess would be enough, as far as kids were concerned, and I'd always wanted a little girl. Furthermore, I thought there was hope for Tess and me; one of her Barbies had resigned her corporate job and become a veterinarian.

Simon laughed, and we—or I—had tabled the discussion.

The prawns arrived, arranged on a platter in an oval like parachutists holding hands in freefall. The bar counter was elbow-to-elbow with people. Deciding I preferred a table, I scanned the room, searching for the maitre d'. A man seated alone stared in my direction—neglect must suit me: I hadn't paid much attention to my appearance since getting off the plane that morning.

The man stood. He was tall, angular. Limbs loosely put together, as though crafted by a puppeteer. Receding blond hair. I blinked. Large head.

"Patrick?" I said. "Patrick Osch?" The last time I'd seen him, we were fifteen, acting in *Hamlet,* produced jointly by the girls' and boys' high schools. Years before that, at Norwood Primary, my friend Hettie and I used to tease him about his head, which seemed too large for his body. Hettie would jab him in the side when he wasn't expecting it, threatening to tip him over. She claimed he'd tumble to the ground if we messed with his equilibrium.

"Kate Jensen?" He approached me. "Good heavens. It *is* you."

My mother would've said Patrick was a spy working for Oom Piet. "Talk about coincidence!" I said, ignoring her ghostly voice. I'd had enough of conspiracy theories for one day.

Patrick hugged me, which startled me a little. As a rule, South Africans weren't as quickly affectionate as Americans, whose warmth I'd grown to appreciate, though I never felt quite comfortable in the arms of virtual strangers. I patted Patrick's back awkwardly, as if he were a giant child in need of comfort. He let go. He looked very *King Solomon's Mines,* very Allan Quatermain, in his khaki shirt, blue jeans, and laced *velskoens.* "Join me?" Patrick gestured to a chair at his table. "I'm on holiday from work. Here to see my parents. They're in their eighties, now, and in one of these retirement places, you know? You?"

"I live in the States now," I said, sitting, happy to see someone I knew. "Visiting . . . relatives. Won't be here long."

"Surprised I haven't bumped into you sooner," he said. "When I'm in Durban I always stay at the Oliphant. It's where all the expats come when they visit. Here or the Malibu Hotel. So I generally end up talking to someone from the past. Fact is that hardly any of my friends still live in South Africa." He sat and picked up an amber drink, probably Scotch. "You aren't staying long? Pity. What can I get you?" He gestured to the waiter, then gazed at me over the rim of his glass. "Kate, the wild-animal lover. I remember one of your stories in Standard Four—what was it, 'A Crooked Lion Goes Straight'?"

I smiled, flattered he remembered a story I'd written when I was eleven.

"These days I work at Hluhluwe Game Reserve. If you were here for a while, I could've taken you on safari," he said.

"Always wanted to meet a game ranger," I said, amazed. I'd always thought Patrick would end up an actuary.

Over dinner, we talked about what we'd been up to in recent years. Between safaris, he'd sired two children and gone through a divorce. "I don't think I'm the marrying kind, after all," he said, mashing his *bobotie*—a mild curry made with ground lamb, fruit, and nuts, and topped with a milky sauce—onto the back of his fork. "Seems unnatural, you know? Though klipspringers mate for life. Do you know them? They're brownish-gray buck with stripy ears."

"I know what you mean," I said, shelling a prawn, conscious of trying to visualize Simon's ears. "I don't think I'll ever marry either. I guess I'm like a trapdoor spider. I emerge briefly to mate then return to my lair."

Patrick laughed. "Works for me."

I focused on my dinner, licking the butter off my fingers and using my fork to chase every last grain of rice. Patrick told me how much he loved working in the game reserve. Rhino were his favorite animals, and Hluhluwe was famous for its white rhino. The name, he said, came not from the animal's color, but the Afrikaans word *weit,* which meant broad-lipped. He loved living here, where he'd been born.

"We're as African as the Xhosa or Sotho," he said. "Sometimes I get angry when it's implied we whites don't have the same right to live here as blacks. My family's been here for two hundred years. How long do we have to stay to claim legitimacy? And if we're not South African, what are we?"

I wasn't sure if there was an answer.

After dinner, Patrick suggested a walk and, unwilling to be alone with my thoughts, I agreed. We strolled down Marine Parade and wandered along a pier. Fishermen perched on the edges, their lines threading into the sea. Leaning against the railing, I breathed in the kelpy fragrance. Moonlight rippled on the broad back of the ocean. On the horizon, a necklace of ships' lights glittered. Was my mother heading to Cape Town on one of them—standing on deck, the wind blowing her chestnut hair off her face, her eyes scanning the crowd for Enemies? I shivered.

Patrick slung his jacket over my shoulders. "Don't want you catching cold." He gazed at me. Waves left a lattice of lace as they shimmered to shore. "Kate. I always had a crush on you, you know."

Maybe because of the gin and the wine, I told him a little about my three fiancés—how my relationships never seemed to work out. "It started with Allan, in high school, remember? I think I'm going to give up on men." A fisherman flexed his rod and his catch plopped onto the pier, a silver flash in the moonlight.

"But it sounds like it's always you who leaves," Patrick said. He cleared his throat. "Kate. Do you, er, do you still think my head is too big?"

I laughed. "No. Is my—"

"Absolutely not," he said, smiling and putting his arm around me. Patrick's body felt bony, unlike Simon's comfortable bulk.

My eyes were wet. I blamed the wind. "Better get back," I said, moving out of his embrace.

Patrick hit his brow melodramatically with the heel of his hand. *"What a falling-off was there* . . . do you remember I played Hamlet's father's ghost in the school production?"

"I do," I said. "I'm sorry to be so boring, Patrick, but I've had such a long day, really. I have to go to bed or I'll fall asleep on my feet like one of your rhino."

He adjusted his jacket around my shoulders and we headed down the pier and through the carnival grounds. The sweet smell of candy-floss—cotton candy—was so strong I imagined if I stuck out my tongue, the air would taste of sugar. *Try your luck,* the carnies sang out from the sideshows. *Try your luck.*

"Whatever happened to Hettie?" I asked as we crossed the road, narrowly avoiding death by errant taxicab.

"Hettie? Took the chicken run—you know, left the country."

"She was afraid to stay?"

Patrick glanced at me. "Just an expression. She had a very good reason to go. As you did, I'm sure. So you didn't hear about her, hey, in America? Why would you, I suppose. Hettie's whole life was splashed over the Sunday papers here, ages ago now. Her mother stabbed her father with a kitchen knife—he'd beaten her with a *sjambok*. At the trial, it came out that Hettie had been abused, too, as a child. Not sexually—but hit, often. Nobody knew."

But *I* had known. I'd seen Hettie's green and purple and yellow bruises: oil slicks on her pale skin. I thrust my hands in my jeans pockets and stared at the pavement in front of me as I walked. My cheeks burned. Why hadn't I told the teachers? Because Hettie would've been furious. We'd promised to keep each other's secrets. Even after we fought, she'd never let anyone know my father was dead—that he wasn't in Saudi Arabia, as my mother claimed. Nor had she said anything about my mother's note, though she had told my classmates I was weird.

How different might our lives have turned out if we'd *not* kept our promises? If the teachers had been alerted? Would they have believed us? I longed to talk to Hettie, though for years I'd loathed her with the intensity people reserve for someone they've once loved.

The hotel was within sight. "Hettie's mother kept quiet all those years because she was afraid her husband would kill them," Patrick said. "The police found a room packed with guns and murder weapons. He collected them, he said."

"We're here," I said, feeling nauseated, grateful to arrive at the hotel entrance. The bellman held the door open. I rushed into the lobby and sat on a couch, my head in my hands.

"You okay?" Patrick sat next to me. "You were friends for a while, I remember. Don't worry. She's all right. She lives in New Zealand now."

I looked up. "Do you have her address? And thanks for dinner. It's been lovely to see you."

"I'll ask around, see if anyone knows it." He wrote his number on an old receipt. "When you get back from Jo'burg, give me a call." He kissed me lightly on the forehead. *"Fare thee well!/The glow-worm shows the matins to be near . . .* something something *. . . adieu, adieu, adieu!"*

Smiling, I said good-bye, then, punch-drunk with the emotions of the day, I wove my way to my hotel room, my sandals clicking on the faux-marble floor. After brushing my teeth, I slipped into a cool silk nightie, slid into bed, and pulled the sheets over my face. For a long time, I thought about Hettie.

And Patrick, who had been Hamlet's father's ghost. And Allan, who had been Hamlet. And klipspringers, who partnered for life.

And Simon. Who had wanted to visit South Africa and stay in a game reserve. I'd said I'd prefer East Africa. We'd discussed spending our honeymoon in the Serengeti.

A breeze blew in the open window. A foghorn sounded. How wonderful it would be to spend a night with Simon in a lodge on the broad flanks of the Umfolozi River—our sun-warmed bodies braided on cool white sheets, a fan twisting slowly above us, the smell of dust and thatch and fragrant amaryllis in the air. A lion roaring in the distant veldt. In the morning, kestrels and malachite sunbirds might spread their wings and whirl into the teal sky. Perhaps a warthog family would surprise us as we ate breakfast on the verandah, and we'd watch as mother, father, and children trotted, tails up, along the rutted dirt road and into the long grass.

Would we bring Tess? Could she learn to love warthogs? I turned onto my side.

Suddenly I imagined Tess holding a purple hippo. Every child should have a purple hippo. Should I buy one for her? I could send it anonymously. Maybe on her fifth birthday. *Hippo Birthday to You . . .*

Jerome had liked the aardvark at the zoo, Simon had said. I didn't think I'd ever seen a large plush aardvark.

The digital clock flashed one o'clock. It was six in the evening Ohio time. Should I call him? Why not? Just to tell him I was in Africa, and that if he'd forgotten anything in the move, and thought the item might be in my boxes, he should call Bernie, because she had the key to my new apartment. Maybe we'd start talking. I'd say, *Let's have lunch when I get back.* And he might say,

That sounds like a good idea. I miss you. And I'd say, *I miss you too.* And then he . . .

I sat up. I adjusted the pillow. I reached for the phone, then drew back my hand. Now wasn't a good time to talk to Simon. But I really *should* let him know I was in Africa.

Why? In case I'd inadvertently packed Darwin's *The Voyage of the Beagle,* and he needed to verify a fact about albatrosses? Or in case I'd stowed *Gray's Anatomy* in one of my crates, and there was an emergency in the middle of the night, and Simon couldn't get to a library, and a patient died because he'd forgotten the routing of an essential artery and had no reference book?

Right. I smiled, leaned toward the phone, punched the buttons, and held the receiver to my ear.

"Hello?" Cilla said.

Durban
1967

Oom Piet sat on the couch, his hands clasped in front of him, staring at Aunt Iris, who knelt at my mom's chair. She stood when I rushed in. Mom was staring into space. The doctor in the white coat squinted at the syringe, holding it up to the light.

"No!" I dropped my school case and launched into a tackle like Tommy Bedford, star of the Springbok rugby team. But even the heft of my body wasn't enough to knock the doctor off his feet. He didn't budge. I stepped back with my elbow up, as if I were about to ram him.

"Katie! Please! This is for everyone's good, *skattie*," my uncle said.

My mother's eyes fixed on me. "Your uncle doesn't want anyone to know it was murder. That's why he's doing this." She curled her fingers around mine. The touch of her flesh revolted me, and I pulled my hand away.

She blinked. "Poppet?"

The doctor lowered the syringe and pointed the needle at her arm.

Mom shrugged, raising her shoulders slowly and then letting them sag. "I can't fight anymore," she said. "I'm so tired, poppet." She turned vaguely to Aunt Iris. "Well, then. You be good to my little girl."

"I will, Aggie," Aunt Iris said. I'd forgotten she called my mom Aggie.

Mom held out her arm, inner elbow toward the doctor as if she were presenting a gift. Her skin was pale, her blue veins visible. I smelled a sharp whiff of alcohol from the cotton swab. The doctor tourniqueted her upper arm, aimed, and sank the needle into the crease of her elbow.

I sat down, aghast.

"It's for the best, Katie," Aunt Iris said.

My mom rasped a laugh, or maybe it was a cough. "At any rate, you can see I was right about them, poppet, wasn't I? The drugs they feed me—it makes me so confused. Sometimes I don't know what's real and what isn't, you see." She rubbed her forehead as if she had a headache. "You'll be all right. It's me they want, really. They'll brainwash you, but they won't hurt you." Then her eyes slipped away and her lids shut.

If I hadn't refused to go to Cape Town, we might have escaped. It was my fault this was happening. My fault Oom Piet had come back.

Mom's head lolled. Oom Piet and Aunt Iris and the doctor stared at me. I wished I could turn myself into a bowling ball, knock the adults' legs down like pins, and roll out the door, down the steps and far away.

The doctor helped my mom to her feet. She leaned against him and they shuffled toward the door.

"Say good-bye to your mom, dearie," Aunt Iris said. "She's going somewhere to get better."

I couldn't speak. The walls were steepling in on me. The door closed.

Oom Piet said they were taking my mother to a rest home, where she could get lots of sleep, talk to doctors, and learn to trust people again. He said the shock of my father's death had caused what he called "restless thinking," which I suppose is why he thought a rest home would help. She had done a great deal of resting, though, since she'd lost her job, and it didn't seem to have made any difference. Quite often she'd lain on her bed examining the ceiling, as though a set of instructions would appear the way they had for Moses.

Aunt Iris packed my clothes. She locked the flat, and my uncle half-dragged me into the lift and through the lobby. Then they bundled me into the car. I felt like a piece of luggage without handles. I still hadn't said anything. I couldn't.

My uncle turned the key in the ignition. "We'll be in Jo'burg by midnight."

"We don't know how long it will be before your mom gets better," Aunt Iris said, craning her neck, her face in profile. Her single shark-eye stared at me. "She'll be fine, though. You mustn't worry. We'll call the school tomorrow and tell them you won't return until next term."

The car started. I gazed through the rear window and for miles and miles watched the road disappear behind us. I wondered if I'd ever see my mother again.

"Everything okay back there?" Aunt Iris said. "On the farm Andre and Koos will share a room and you'll have your own. I even bought a pink bedspread."

A pink bedspread! Was that supposed to make me happy?

I faced forward, frowning. Aunt Iris smiled. "Soon we'll go shopping for pretty clothes. Would you like that?"

Usually I made my own clothes using our Singer sewing machine and Simplicity patterns. They might have been Simplicity for some people, but not for me. It took forever to match seams, and I knew the zippers up the back of my dresses looked like wriggling eels because one side of the fabric usually ended up shorter. Thank goodness for school uniforms. Over weekends, because I lived far from the school, most of my classmates didn't see me so they couldn't tease me about the things I wore. New clothes would be nice. Maybe a miniskirt. What might it be like to wear clothes from a real shop, clothes you could try on first to see how they fit, instead of having to imagine yourself into a sketch on a packet? I felt a stab of guilt. *What was I thinking?*

The car seat smelled of hot plastic—it was covered with blue vinyl. Bending my knees, I tucked my legs inside my dress, hugged my knees, and put my head down on my arms.

"Ag, shame, Piet, I feel so sorry for her," Aunt Iris said in a whisper.

"*Ja*, it's sad. But we have to do this," he said. "Better for everyone. For Violet, for Kate. For us, too, I'll admit. Such a scandal. If word got out . . . it's not good to have something like this known about the family."

That my mother was crazy?

But maybe she wasn't. Look what had happened! Like she'd said, Oom Piet had split us apart. And a man *had* followed her. But she'd been wrong about Hettie. Except it was true that I couldn't trust her. Hettie! I thought perhaps I would send her a blood-smeared postcard from my uncle's farm: *Have been kidnapped— mother was right—uncle is evil. Send help.*

The motion of the car rocked me to sleep. When I woke, I couldn't remember where I was. I sat up and gazed through the windscreen. The Drakensberg mountains rose up ahead, shaped like dragons' teeth. The sun was setting. Blood-red clouds raked the sky. Little black kids ran alongside the car, their ragged shorts flapping against thin legs, hands holding tiny toy bicycles made of wire, their shouts muffled. My aunt rolled down the window and threw out a bag of Smarties.

"It'll take more than Smarties to satisfy that lot," Oom Piet said.

My aunt closed the window, rubbed her eyes, and slid down in her seat. I noticed her hair was chestnut and wavy, like my mom's, and my heart shifted a little in my chest.

The smell of cow dung was as strong as ever when we drove onto the farm. It was two hours to midnight, nearly the next day, July second. I realized I'd soon be twelve. My father had been dead a whole year. I was glad he'd been cremated; otherwise, I'd be picturing his body melting away into the earth, being eaten by maggots, turning into a skeleton. Sometimes I wished I didn't have an imagination. It made life complicated. Maybe my mom had a severe case of imagination.

My aunt heated vegetable *bredie* and buttered thick slices of bread. I'd thought of going on a hunger strike but I wasn't able to resist when she put the plate on the table. The food slipped down my throat.

"How are you feeling, Katie, lovey?" my aunt said.

I slurped the stew.

She put her arm on my shoulder. I reached behind me, picked her arm up, and dropped it.

Koos and Andre stared at me. They were fifteen and thirteen. They had crew cuts. Most teenagers wore their hair much longer. "She hasn't got good manners, has she, Ma?" Koos said. "Maybe we'll have to teach her how to behave."

Aunt Iris cleared away the plates, banging them together. She turned on the tap and sloshed them in the water. "You leave her alone, you hear me? She's been through a lot."

After a hot bath, I put on the pajamas she'd laid out on the bed. They were soft flannel, decorated with hearts. She came in and kissed me on the forehead. I was too tired to resist.

The next morning it was cool when I woke up, so I pulled the bedspread up to my neck. I stared at the ceiling. Where was my mother? Was she in a dank cell, like the dungeons at the castle in Cape Town, where you could still see marks prisoners had scrawled on foot-thick walls using fingertips they'd worn to bloody stumps? Were rats and cockroaches nibbling at her toes? But she wasn't a criminal. She was in an asylum. I pictured men and women in green gowns wailing in corridors and people nodding their heads up and down and claiming to be the king of Spain or Napoleon or Jesus Christ. She was only there because I hadn't agreed to escape with her! *How could I have betrayed my own mother?* I hated Oom Piet. I was beginning to see my mother's point: if you didn't know who the Enemy was, precisely, it made sense to treat everyone with caution.

A gray kitten jumped on my pillow and mewed, then licked my ear. I reached over and cuddled its soft, furry body in my hand.

I knew, suddenly, what was about to happen. Aunt Iris would walk in and tell me it was mine.

After giving the kitten a kiss on its forehead, I put it on the mat on the floor next to my bed. I pulled the sheet and blankets over my head.

The door opened. "Katie? Are you awake? Did you see the kitty we bought for you?"

It was dark under the covers. I smiled. I was one step ahead of them.

On the farm, I practiced camouflage. I wore a leaf-colored dress and read books high up in the oak tree like a plump praying mantis. When Koos and Andre found me, they threw apples. I let the fruit hit and bruise me. It felt good, as if I were being punished for not having protected my mother, for having recoiled when she touched me.

When Aunt Iris noticed the bruises on my arms, she frowned. "Where did you get those?"

"Andre and Koos took me into a cave and tortured me," I said. She frowned. But she didn't do anything, and eventually the marks faded to dirty brown, then disappeared entirely.

I enclosed myself within the walls of my room, imagining myself the giant tortoise at the Mitchell Park zoo in Durban, coming out only for breakfast, lunch, and dinner. I didn't speak except to say things like, "Pass the salt, please." I began to shrink, because I ate carrots and grilled fish and green beans, which tasted wonderful after meat pies and sticky buns and chocolate from the vending machine. Not that I told Aunt Iris how much I was enjoying her food. When she asked if I'd like to go and see a movie or buy granny boots and a granny-print dress, I stared at her with empty eyes.

I knew I was making them unhappy. It pleased me to upset them. Especially when I saw Oom Piet hit one of the farm laborers across the head with the flat of his hand and call him a *fokking kaffir*.

In the middle of the day when the sun was warm, I'd walk down to the stream, roll around in the water pretending to be a crocodile, then bake on the rock like an iguana. It was peaceful, the only sounds an occasional birdcall and the whisper of leaves in the wind. I liked being alone. You knew where you were with you.

After a while, the bad things about living with my mother faded in my mind, like the apple bruises had from my skin. Instead, I felt guilty. *I hadn't even said good-bye.*

Every day in my diary I wrote, *I cried today,* though after the first few days I hadn't. I was building up proof I was miserable in case I needed to show someone how important it was to send me back to my mother. Once I wrote, *Thought about suicide today,* even though I wouldn't have killed myself. And I made up terrible things about Koos. I said he tried to attack me with a *knobkierie*—a big wooden club. I said he had taken the shampoo out of my bottle and replaced it with Nair hair remover, but luckily I had noticed the smell, otherwise I would have gone bald.

Andre offered to teach me new fishing techniques, but I told him I didn't want to spend one moment in his company. He was a member of an Enemy family. But he was nice to me and once or twice we did fish together and he showed me the right way to cast.

One night my uncle came into my room. He waved his head

from side to side, then leaned forward, looking at my chest and pulling the coverlet up to my neck. "You're growing up, aren't you, Kate?" he said. The heel of his hand grazed my nipple. I hit his hand with my fist.

"Sorry!" he said. "Didn't mean anything by it, child." He stood and left the room.

I hated him. I wrote in my diary he had touched my breasts and attempted to kiss me.

Once I was trying to think up dreadful things they might have done. I couldn't remember what I had already written, so I read through the diary again. I realized it sounded like my mother's stories. I ran out of my room with my diary in my hand. Oom Piet had barbecued *boerewors* for dinner an hour before and the coals were still hot. I threw the book in the *braai* and the pages flamed and turned to ash. I sat outside on the gravelly dirt even when it began to rain. I wished I were made of salt; I would dissolve and disappear. I'd live with my ancestors, and—maybe— see my father again.

The next day, I began a new campaign.

Like a small child, I drew pictures on the wall in crayon. I broke Andre's model airplane. I carved my initials in Koos's favorite cricket bat. I smashed Aunt Iris's crystal wine glasses. I said it was an accident, but she knew it wasn't. I could tell she had started to hate me. She banged my plates down in front of me and didn't try to talk to me anymore. I didn't blame her. I'd have hated me too.

Before I went to sleep, or first thing when I woke up, I worried about my mother. They kept telling me she was doing fine. She even wrote once, but all she talked about was the weather. Durban seemed far away. My life there seemed unreal compared to the bright blue of the Highveld sky and the mooing cows.

But in the middle of August, Oom Piet called me into his study.

"We're taking you back to Durban, Katie. The doctors say your mother is better."

Outside, a plum-colored starling swayed on a branch and the smell of gardenias drifted into the room. I had my swimming costume on; I'd been about to walk to the stream. I was going to use an old birdcage to capture a chameleon that sometimes clung to the branch of an acacia tree and watched me swim. I wanted to experiment with different colored rags to see if it would change to blue and red and yellow. Then I would let it go so it could return to its chameleon friends in the wild.

"Right now?" I said. I put the birdcage down. I could hear the servants clattering pots and pans in the kitchen, preparing to cook the Sunday roast. I lifted my head and stared at Oom Piet. "I mean, good! I can't wait to get out of here."

"Well, we know you haven't been happy. You've made that clear." Oom Piet stood and walked over to the world globe mounted on a tall stand. Using his forefinger and thumb, he twirled it around, and I watched the countries blur by. "Aunt Iris wanted you to stay with us. But I told her no. I said the girl belongs with her mother. You're just like your mother, you know?"

"No. I don't know." I was feeling the strangest feeling: resentment toward Oom Piet, because he hadn't listened to Aunt Iris. Then guilty. And sad. I should be happy to see my mother again. It's what I'd said I wanted. I looked at the mirror behind his desk and rearranged my face into its usual hostile expression.

"You'll be living in a different flat, not far from where you lived before, near the paddling pools. You can practice your swimming there. You're getting quite good." He stopped the globe. "And you must call us if you need help, hey?" He bent his head toward me. "If she starts any funny business, I'll be back."

The kitten trotted into the room and ran up to me and rubbed against my leg. She'd become quite friendly even though I ignored her when my aunt and uncle were around. One day I would have my own cat. He'd be black, and I'd call him Bagheera after the panther in *Jungle Book*.

"Scat!" Oom Piet said, tucking his foot under her tummy and tossing her toward the door. The kitten fled, mewing.

I drew myself up. "I'll never call you."

I turned and left the room, the birdcage bumping against my leg.

The trip from Oom Piet's farm back to my mother in Durban took eight hours in his Zephyr. My uncle stopped outside the entrance to a block of flats called Kingfisher Court.

"This is your new building," Aunt Iris said. "It's a little bigger than Starling Flats."

From the outside, the building didn't appear much different from the one we'd lived in before, except for the dirty mosaic trim across the edges of the balconies. I tightened my grip on my suitcase. My legs felt weak from sitting in the car for so long. We rode the lift and Oom Piet knocked on number three sixty-one, but there was no reply, so he opened the door. My mother was sitting in her chair. She looked up when we walked in. She wore a green dress with a green belt; otherwise, you wouldn't have known where her waist was. Her heavy curls had gone. Her hair had been cut short and her glasses were goggle-thick. She resembled a caterpillar.

The furniture was the same. I noticed how grubby the floral pattern on the blue upholstery had become; threads hung from the corners. The throw cushions were flat and stained. Behind her, the hem of the curtains flapped short of the windowsill. The air smelled moldy.

She didn't get up when she saw me, simply said, "Katie. You're back." I put down my suitcase and gave her the best hug I could, considering she was hunkered down in the chair.

My aunt and uncle brought in a vase of red and white carnations, a telephone, and a week's worth of groceries. They told my mother my father's old company would be sending us a monthly check for one hundred rand now that they knew where we lived. It was from a corporate insurance policy Dad had taken out.

"How are you, Aggie?" Aunt Iris asked. My mother stared through her as if she didn't occupy any space.

"You take care now, Kate," my uncle said. He gave me a piece of paper with their phone number.

"Go away," I said. Oom Piet and Aunt Iris shook their heads and walked out, and I slammed the door to stop myself from running after them. Oom Piet might be evil, but I liked his farm. And I was dreading school.

I ripped up the phone number and let the pieces flutter from my fingers into an ashtray. I cleared my throat. My mother watched me. "Mom? How was it? Are you okay?"

Her eyes slid over me.

I sat opposite her. "The rest home was . . . um . . . restful?" Was she sedated? What had they done to her?

"I slept a lot. Don't remember much." She fingered her box of cigarettes, but didn't open the lid. She pointed at the bags of groceries. "Throw those in the Dumpster downstairs."

"But there are good things to eat in there." I pictured the apples, berries, Post Toasties, milk, orange juice, and cheddar cheese and crackers inside the sacks. "Oh . . . because you think it's poisoned?"

She looked at me blankly. "Why would you say such a thing? No. I'm not going to be patronized by those two, you see? I don't accept charity. And neither should you. Take the flowers, too."

The vase banged against the side of the Dumpster. I pinched my nose with my fingers and stared at the carnations decorating the rotting oozy peels and plastic bottles and dirty nappies. Maybe Mom thought I was an Enemy, and she wasn't going to reveal to me her suspicions about the food. Funnily enough, that cheered me up. I knew how to be an Enemy. I'd had lots of practice on the farm. It was when you tried to be friends that you were vulnerable.

When I returned upstairs, my mother was cooking. I stood at the kitchen door for a while. I could see strands of gray in her cropped hair. I felt a rush of sadness. I couldn't help myself. I said, "I do love you, Mom."

"No need to get sentimental," she said, digging the spatula beneath the *frikkadels*, flipping the greasy meat patties over. She wiped her hand on a dishcloth. "Dinner will be ready in ten minutes."

My bed was once again next to the window, overlooking a barren quadrangle scattered with detritus left by homeless men who liked Durban's mild winter climate. In the mornings, as I headed toward the bus stop, I'd see flattened cartons of Bantu beer, broken bottles of purple methylated spirits, and old newspapers the hoboes used as blankets.

On the farm, I'd lain on my stomach near the stream for hours, watching dung beetles roll tiny balls along the ground with their back legs. But the bugs inside our flat were disgusting. One night I woke to the feathery feel of beetle feet on my face. In the morning I made a doorstop from one of my failed sewing attempts, which prevented the larger cockroaches from sneaking under the door. But smaller roaches ruled at night. I couldn't bear to stamp on them and see their gray intestines dribble out onto the yellow linoleum. I developed a habit of sleeping with my left elbow crooked over my face, which also kept out the flashing neon sign from the Chicken A-Go-Go take-away across the street.

Hettie approached me before school on the first day of the term. Her ponytail bounced as she walked, and she pointed her toes with each step, as though she were a ballerina in a Royal Command performance. I clenched my fists behind my back and stared straight ahead.

"Meet me behind the tuck shop at Little Break," she said. I was surprised she even spoke to me, but I agreed, a pilot flame of hope flickering inside me.

During class, the other kids rolled their eyes in my direction like lizards about to flick out their tongues and zap a fly.

It was cool in the shade behind the sweet shop. I leaned against the brick. While I waited, I blew a bubble with my gum until it burst. Hettie arrived.

She touched my shoulder. For a moment I thought she might ask me to her house and I might say yes. "Did your father hit you? Are you okay?" I asked.

"Shut up about my dad. Don't you dare tell those lies to anyone." She kicked a candy wrapper, then scuffed dirt over it till only the end was visible. "I don't want to be friends anymore, not the way we were. You're kind of disgusting. But I've told the other kids to leave you alone."

I stood up straight and pushed more dirt over the wrapper with my shoe until it was completely buried. I chewed my gum so hard I thought my teeth might crack. "I don't need you to take care of me, Hettie."

"Poor thing," she said. She patted me on the arm.

I slammed her into the wall and her head banged against the brick. "Don't you feel sorry for me!"

She yanked my hair and pushed me, then beat at me with her fists. My glasses fell off and I couldn't see anything but the white blur of her uniform. I tried to grab her wrists but she wrestled me to the ground. She sat on my back and started punching me. I flailed, my nose filling with dirt, but I couldn't dislodge her. I managed to grasp her arm, then lifted my head and bit her. She screamed and got up, kicking me in the ribs. Other kids arrived, dust mushrooming around their shoes.

The prefects dragged me to the office. The principal said, "Kate, only animals bite."

My mouth tasted of dust and blood. "I know," I said.

The principal gave me two weeks' detention on top of the detention I was already serving for cheating during the midyear exams. I told my mother I was staying late at the library after school to study. Patrick Osch was in detention too. He had put a frog in Susan Wakely's desk because she called him Lollipop Boy. I heard a rumor he fancied me.

But I was in love with Desmond Baxter. Not that Desmond cared.

My mother circled jobs-offered ads in the paper or slept. I made sure not to talk about anything much besides food and weather. I fought with kids: I was bigger than most of them, at least sideways. I kept my elbows spiked outwards. I snapped at anyone who criticized me. I purposely bumped into people on the stairs. I linked arms with Jennifer Barrell, a girl with bad breath, and Mavis Plett, whose face was as spotty as a currant bun, and we walked straight, and people got out of our way.

And I taunted the teachers, talking or making rude gestures when they turned to write on the chalkboard. They shook their heads at me, disappointed. On the bus home, sometimes, I wanted to cry. I laid my deeds in front of my mother like a cat bringing home dead mice. The school eventually sent a letter telling her about my bad behavior, but she seemed not to care.

Mostly she kept silent, playing Patience, listening to the radio, occasionally cooking, though she often sent me to the store for meat pies. Now and again she'd tell me the same thing twice, and she often forgot things, like where her keys were, or that she'd already turned on the oven.

She found a job typing invoices at a bathroom-fixture company. Sometimes she brought work home and I did my homework to the tick-tick-tick of her typewriter. She didn't say anything about "them," though occasionally I'd see her sniffing our food. But the expression on her face was puzzled rather than angry.

. . .

At the end of the year, I won first prize in class. Even though I'd become what Mrs. Schorn called a "discipline nightmare," they couldn't deny me the prize. I'd done better than anyone else in the final exams. Some things couldn't be taken from you; some things were absolutes: if you studied, you got smarter, and even people who didn't like you had to respect you.

Hettie poked me in the ribs on the playground. "It's because they feel sorry for you that you got first prize."

"Get lost," I said. I *knew* she was wrong. I rarely felt that sure about anything.

My mother was in a good mood that evening. Her employer had given her a raise. She enveloped me in her damp arms. I squirmed, remembering the time she'd searched me for bugs. Mostly I kept the memory wrapped up—mummified, the way a spider traps and trusses wandering flies in the sticky strands of its web.

After pinning my certificate to the wall with a thumbtack, I lay on my bed, arms crossed behind my head. My mother hadn't said anything *really* peculiar since August—nearly five months. I breathed in till my lungs hurt. Might she be normal again? Nearly normal would be good enough.

I took a long bath and threw in bath crystals. I put on the blouse with the yellow daisies Aunt Iris had bought me—not that I'd worn it on the farm; it would have given her too much pleasure.

My mother and I strolled along the boardwalk. She smiled at a black woman carrying a startled-looking baby in her arms. I said nothing, afraid I'd taint the magic. The evening was cool, for Durban, and the air tasted of salt. We arrived at the Veld & Vlei restaurant, which offered a view of the paddling pools and the Indian Ocean. A quarter moon curved in the sky. Waves rushed to the sand and then the water retreated as if it had thought better of coming ashore.

At the restaurant, my mom ordered sherry, steak mayonnaise, and chips. She seemed to be enjoying herself.

When she finished her second sherry she said, "Your dad would have been so proud of you."

I glowed.

She ordered another sherry. "You'll be in high school soon," she said, sipping. "Excited?" The *c* in *excited* sounded more liked the *sh* in *eggshells*. "Which of your friends is going to Sutherland Girls' High?"

I'd made it a policy not to mention friends, but I was giddy with the relative normalcy of the moment. "Jennifer Barrell and Mavis Plett." To my relief, Hettie was going to the coed school.

The food arrived. She ordered another sherry. We were quiet while we ate our dinner. I had a hamburger and French fries and onion rings. My taste buds rejoiced.

After her last mouthful, my mother leaned against the plush red seatback, which resembled a pincushion. "Coffee," she said dreamily to the waiter, her eyes half-closed. "And a brandy."

"I'm so glad we're together again, Mom," I said. I reached across the table and squeezed her hand. Freckles had begun to spread across her skin, and her wedding ring had almost disappeared into the flesh on her fingers. "See? The government couldn't keep us apart after all!"

She opened her eyes wide. "What?"

The restaurant was hot. I fanned myself with the dessert menu as I glanced toward the door. "Should we go now?"

"Oh, poppet," she said suddenly, as if a retaining wall in her mind had crumbled. "I couldn't have stayed in the rest home a moment longer! I couldn't have!"

"I know, Mom." I fanned myself faster. *Why had I mentioned the government?*

"Do you know what they did to me there?" The waiter brought her brandy, and she plucked the glass directly from the tray and gulped the drink.

Across the aisle, a mom and dad and two kids ate banana splits, licking the cream off their lips. "How about a banana split, Mom?" I gestured to the waiter and pointed to the desserts in the glass cooler. "Can I have one of those?" I turned back to her. "So, Christmas is in a few weeks. What do you want? I'll buy you something really nice. I've been saving my pocket money."

She took a tissue out of her bag and wiped tears from her cheeks. "The windows were high up, poppet. They were barred, you know. And the doors were locked. How your Oom Piet could have done such a thing to me! Sod. How Iris could have let him . . ." She shook her head. "Locked away like a rat in a cage. It stank there too, you see?"

The waiter brought my dessert. "Did you see the book I got as a prize?" I said. The banana smelled disgusting.

"And the food. Dreadful. Slimy porridge for breakfast and lunch. Dry bread and gristle for dinner." A tear ran from beneath her spectacles. "And the noise, the noise! People cackling. Pacing."

"Maybe when I'm older I can work here," I said wildly.

"Dizzy. I feel dizzy. It's because of what they did to me." She knocked over her glass. The amber liquid rolled toward the edge of the table and dripped onto the floor. She made loud crooning noises. *Oh-woo. Oh-woo.* People's forks froze in the air. The cashier covered her mouth with her hand. "I feel dizzy. It's the side-effects." She dropped her knife and fork. The fork clattered to the ground. "One day, poppet, they put me on a table. They tied me down . . ." Snot ballooned from her nose.

I stood and put my hands under her arms, trying to lift her up and out of the booth. "Come, Mom. It's okay. Let's go home now."

"And they shocked me, poppet, you see?" she said. "With electricity. Because Oom Piet told them to."

I was horrified. I stood and rummaged in her purse for money to pay for our food. The manager came over. "It's okay, girlie," he said. "You take your mom home. She's had a little too much to drink."

"When they shock you, it hurts," my mother said, blinking.

I grasped her hands and pulled. "Let's go home. I'll make tea. I'll warm the teapot with boiling water first, okay?"

She pushed herself out of the booth. She leaned against me. Our flat was seven blocks from the restaurant. The streetlights flickered, every other one dark, and our feet caught on the ragged pavement. She lurched like a crippled tanker. I tugged on her arm to keep her straight. After I steered her into the lift, she lolled her head against the wall. I pushed her out when we got to our floor, found the key in her bag, opened the door and put her in a kitchen chair as though she were a large doll.

I made tea and added three spoons of sugar. When I held the mug to her lips, she drank, her lips curling over the rim, sucking the sweet liquid. Then I took off her glasses and dabbed beneath her eyes.

"Come, Mom," I said, putting my arm around her. I got her to bed. She fell heavily on her side. I couldn't get her bulk between the sheets, so I pulled my bed apart and put my sheets and blanket on top of her.

She lifted her head suddenly and said in a clear voice, "Oom Piet killed the person I loved most in the whole world. He really did, poppet. Really."

I don't know why, but at that moment I believed she was telling the truth. My hatred for Oom Piet hardened like lead. If it weren't for him, my father would be alive, and my mother wouldn't be the way she was.

Then she sat up and hugged herself. "You promise you won't let him do that to me ever again, poppet? Promise, poppet?"

I nodded. "I promise, Mom, okay? Now lie down, all right? You'll feel better in the morning." My voice sounded like I was being strangled.

"Good poppet." She lay down, and I smoothed the bedclothes over her until she stopped trembling.

When she began snoring, I sat down and wrote a letter to my uncle. I pressed my pencil hard into the paper. *Dear Oom Piet,* I wrote, *If you <u>ever</u> lock my mother up again and do terrible things to her, I will tell the police you took off your pants and tried to get into bed with me. With best wishes, Kate.* I put a stamp on the envelope, planning to mail it the next day.

"The waiter was told to drug our food last night," my mother announced the next morning. "That's what made me behave so oddly." A cigarette dangled between her ochre fingers; she tapped ash into the remains of her Rice Krispies. Among the puffed rice, gray flotsam darkened and sank. Her breath smelled of stale alcohol.

A fly rubbed its forelegs together on the rim of a marmalade jar. "No." The chair screeched as I pushed it back. "You got drunk."

"Poppet! Who told you to say that?" She wrung her hands. "No one in our family *ever* gets drunk."

Several days later, she resigned her bathroom-fixture-invoice-typing job, because her boss kept making loud noises to frighten her, and appearing from behind when she wasn't expecting him. He'd hung paintings on the wall with confusing designs—pop art, he called it: swirls of black and white, disappearing into a vortex. The morning tea tasted strange. But he never realized she was onto him, she said, smiling. She'd left before he could fire her.

Fortunately, Dad's insurance checks arrived every month. Also, my mother sold her jewelry—the emerald pendant my father had given her was the last to go—and so we were able to pay the rent until she found another job at an import/export firm.

During my entire first year at high school—1968—she didn't

talk much about her fears, or ask about my life, which was fine with me. Instead, after work, she filled in cryptic crosswords or wrote in her red spiral-bound notebook. Now and again she'd rip out pages and stuff them into large manila envelopes. Often, on Sundays, she walked to the Sunken Gardens, her head held high, gazing stonily at anyone who looked too long in her direction. From the window I'd see her stop, cross her arms, and stare at beggars until they slunk away.

In the mornings, she slept late, sweating in the sun pooling through the window onto our beds. Sometimes before I left to catch the bus, I'd watch her eyelids tremble and wonder what it must be like to *be* her, to think the way she thought. Her brain must sound like a cageful of wild, demented birds.

I'd fill the kettle and set the tea tray, then close the door quietly behind me.

Aunt Iris called a couple of times, but I replaced the phone on the hook without speaking. Then one day Mom disconnected it, saying the government was taping our conversations and storing the tapes in Pretoria. Not many families had phones, so I didn't care. I decided my mother was a natural disaster I'd have to live with, the way farmers lived with drought, Californians lived with earthquakes, and New Zealanders lived with volcanoes.

Toward the end of the year, Jennifer Barrell asked if I'd like to spend a long weekend with her and her family at Hluhluwe, a game reserve up the coast near St. Lucia. After reading the "Hi Jean!" column in my *Miss Tween* magazine, Jennifer no longer had bad breath. I was excited at the thought of seeing rhino and hippo and elephant in the wild.

The trip was scheduled for December 16, the Day of the Covenant, a religious holiday. According to certain Afrikaners, in 1838, God helped them slaughter thousands of Zulu warriors, turning a river near the battlefield red with blood and confirming the Boers' right to the land. The older I got, the stranger God's behavior seemed. Why would He sanction such slaughter? And why would

He think Afrikaners were any better than the Zulu? In the Bible, it said something about man being created in God's image. I thought it was the other way around—God was created in man's image. Everyone had a version of Him to suit his or her own purposes. I wasn't too sure there was such a thing as a God. On the other hand, I couldn't see or understand atoms, either, and they existed.

By the time Jennifer invited me to Hluhluwe, my mom had lost the job at the import/export company and found one as a clerk at a shipping firm. She'd come home and flop in her armchair, smoking cigarette after cigarette. After dinner, I asked permission to go on the trip.

She coughed. "Jennifer who?"

"Barrell."

"Barrell." She lit a cigarette. "Is she the one who told you to shave your legs?"

"No," I lied.

"Only sluts shave their legs."

"We'll be staying in a real hotel." The tenant upstairs thumped across his living room. "I'll be sharing a room with Jennifer, so it won't cost us anything. Please, Mom."

Mom slid her finger beneath her glasses and rubbed her eye. "The same *bed* as Jennifer? So she can do whatever she pleases to you while you sleep?"

I held onto the armrest as if I might otherwise slip off the cushion and collapse into a fleshy heap on the floor. I opened my mouth to say *I hate you* but no words emerged.

"Oh, poppet." She reached for the ashtray, knocking it off the side table. A gray cloud puffed around her hand. "What they're doing to you . . ."

I left the room.

On the weekend of December 16 I went to the zoo instead. As usual, the polar bear paced four steps right, four steps left. Then he reverse-walked all the way around his pool, which smelled of chlorine.

Less than a week later, my mother found *Lady Chatterley's Lover* among my schoolbooks. The novel was banned because of the sex scenes the woman has with her groundskeeper. I'd borrowed it from Jennifer, who'd found the novel in her father's bookcase. Though I covered it in brown paper, I should've known it wasn't safe from my mother.

I told her Jackie Winterbottom—a person I made up at that moment—lent it to me.

She shook her head, her face bright pink, ripping pages from the book. "Jackie Winterbottom isn't the problem in this instance," she said. "Though she's not a nice girl either."

Using capital letters, she wrote a letter to the school saying Jennifer Barrell was corrupting me sexually. The principal said she had no desire to hear the details and put us in detention for a month.

"What on earth did you tell your mother?" Jennifer said. It was the last time she spoke to me.

When my mother wasn't obsessed with her fears, she followed a normal routine—commuting by bus to work, reading the paper at night, or listening to BBC programs on the radio. Once she took up pewter carving, creating fantastical small sculptures she claimed were vases. During those periods I tried not to say anything which might spark her paranoia.

Saturday or Sunday afternoons, or on holidays, she liked to go to Mitchell Park and wander among the flowers, and sometimes I'd go with her. On my fourteenth birthday, we stopped in front of the crocodile enclosure, determined to stay until we saw it move. After half an hour, the zookeeper came by and told us the crocodile had been taken to the veterinarian for a checkup. We'd been gazing at a log. My mother laughed. "I could've sworn it was the crocodile," she said. "Shows how the mind can trick you."

Afterward, we ate cream scones at the outdoor restaurant. A monkey stared at us—he was after our food, we thought—but when we wandered to the exit, he continued to trail behind.

"Why's he following us?" my mother said, walking faster.

"Maybe he works for Oom Piet," I said. Then I kicked a stone, regretting my flippancy, waiting for her to launch into a story about my uncle's evil deeds.

But she smiled. "Oh, poppet, that's funny." She gave me a friendly push in the arm, and I nearly tripped. We giggled until our stomachs hurt.

"People must think we're from the loony bin," my mother said.

Several blocks from Kingfisher Court, I found a huge empty sewage pipe abandoned among a tangle of straggly sunflowers growing on an empty lot. The land beyond stretched toward Umgeni Road, where large lorries rumbled on their way to and from factories. The beach didn't attract me any longer—it was a place where I'd had childish dreams of being part of a family again or imagined foolish things like being able to talk to my father's spirit. I was past such thinking now. And, whereas I'd loved to watch the boys with straw-blond hair ride their surfboards on the turn of the wave, now something about the way they looked at me in my swimming costume made me wriggle.

After school, I'd take a snack and a book and curl up in the pipe, my back against the warm concrete, the pungent smell of flowering weeds in my nose. Nobody disturbed me until one afternoon a black kid discovered my hideout. He was about my age, short, with broad flat cheekbones and droopy eyes.

He peered into the pipe. "Can I sit?"

"No," I said.

"Why not?"

"Because." I turned to my book.

"Is it a whites-only pipe?" he said.

I considered. Meeting a black kid my age for the first time was a funny feeling. They lived far away, in the townships—Umlazi and Inanda and Kwa Mashu—or in rural areas, and weren't allowed on our buses or beaches or park benches. But his race wasn't why I was hoping he'd go away. I liked my refuge. I needed a private place, especially since I had to share a bedroom with my mother. At night I could smell the talcum powder caked in her armpits.

"It's not that," I said, indicating he should sit. "What are you doing here?"

"I want to see where white people live. I will live here one day. My mother works at the café. My name is Joshua."

After a couple of weeks, I brought Joshua books to read—*Swiss Family Robinson, Gulliver's Travels,* and Herman Charles Bosman's short stories. We became friends, though I didn't think of Joshua as my boyfriend. For one thing, I knew about the Immorality Act. People could be imprisoned for life for loving someone of a different color. I didn't want to go to jail.

Besides, I had a crush on Allan de Villiers, a boy who caught the same bus to school. I thought Allan was cute, though he was considered rough because he picked fights. He resembled an upside-down cello—muscular chest, narrow hips, long legs. His blond hair flopped over his indigo eyes. His left front tooth was slightly chipped.

Though I didn't plan to tell my mother about Joshua, it gave me pleasure to defy her in any way I could. She was constantly telling me how dangerous it was to mix with people of other races—the opposite of the way she'd been in Johannesburg, where she'd been friendly with Prudence, now and again lending her a blouse or jersey to wear, something white people didn't normally do. Once she'd given Winston one of my dad's ties.

With Joshua, I was simply Kate. That's another reason I grew so fond of him. Also an outsider, he had no expectations of me, not at first, anyway. He didn't care that my clothes were old-fashioned and cheap. His were also either too big or too small.

We talked about books, pop stars, and what the future might be like in South Africa. "Do you think you'd kill me if blacks fight whites?" I asked once.

He thought for a while, poking a stinkbug with a stick. "Not meaning to. But if you were somewhere I was bombing and I did not know . . ." He shrugged.

One day, Joshua found me crying. My mother had come home early and followed me into the bedroom. *You still aren't menstruating. You'll never have children. Let me see between your legs. What have they done to you? Why won't you let me look? Are you deformed down there? What's wrong? Tell me.*

I'd escaped and run to the pipe.

"My mother says crazy things sometimes," I told Joshua. "Once in a while it upsets me."

He patted my shoulder. "My aunt is *sangoma*. She would say evil spirits possess your mother. I will bring *muti* to cure her."

I pictured the consequences if my mother caught me slipping strange herbs into her tea. "Thanks. It's okay, though."

Most of the time, though, it wasn't so difficult living with her, not once I knew how to handle her moods. Usually I just ignored her. Sometimes, late at night, when I couldn't leave the flat, she'd talk in a monotone about Oom Piet and the government, following me around as I moved from room to room. Eventually I'd clamber onto my bed, press myself into the corner of the room, hold the spine of my book out so she couldn't see my face and I couldn't see hers, and I'd disappear into my story.

Poor poppet, she'd say. *You're going to have a lonely, lonely life.* Poor poppet.

Johannesburg
1995

I sat in a hard plastic chair at Durban Airport waiting for my flight to Johannesburg and wondering, after hearing Cilla's voice on the phone the previous night, whether she and Simon had moved back in together. Couples seemed to be everywhere, all very much in love. I wished they would go away.

An old janitor, bent almost double, mopped the same area again and again. Above me, a neon light buzzed. I chewed on a ham sandwich—an early lunch—and drank coffee from a polystyrene cup. Sandwiches in South Africa were served with one piece of meat and maybe a slice of tomato, which made the buttered bread soggy. American sandwiches were symphonies by comparison.

Children played hide-and-seek behind pillars. Across from me, a large old lady in a mauve dress smoked cigarette after cigarette: I peered through the haze. She wasn't my mother.

What would it be like to see Oom Piet again after all these years? And my mother, if she were with him?

I recapped the events—as related by Mevrou Bakker—that had occurred prior to my mother's disappearance: Oom Piet arrives unexpectedly at her flat and then leaves; my mother pays her rent, tells Mevrou Bakker she's going to another city, and instructs the caretaker that if there's any fuss she should tell the police her tenant is away on holiday.

It made sense my mother would leave Durban to escape my

uncle—just as when I was eleven, she'd wanted us to flee to Cape Town. I looked at my ticket. Maybe I was heading in the wrong direction. Maybe I didn't need to visit Oom Piet after all.

But why had she summoned me here in her letter? Had she mentioned cancer because she knew I'd be forced, out of guilt if not love, to respond by coming to South Africa? Had she wanted to tell me in person about Oom Piet's visit and her fears of resumed persecution?

The constant flicker and *bzzt bzzt* of the broken neon light irritated me. I wriggled in my seat. And then it occurred to me: my uncle might've placed my mother in a mental home. A nerve in my leg started jumping. I had to press my hand flat on my thigh to bring it under control. Why would Oom Piet do such a thing now, after all these years? She was an elderly woman. She'd coped well enough for decades. Why would he—in his late seventies— want to be bothered with an old crazy sister-in-law? Whose craziness harmed no one?

The flight was called. I stood and waited in line behind the big mauve lady. Aunt Iris might have told Oom Piet to visit my mother, see how she was doing in her old age. If he had visited her. I had no real confirmation of that; only my mother's claim in the letter and Mevrou Bakker's sighting of a tall, thin old man.

My jaw felt taut, as if it had been wired shut. I remembered my mother sobbing night after night about her stay in the "rest home." Each exhalation had been a breathy wail. *Like a mad dog,* she'd sob, *they tied me down like a mad dog, poppet. And then they shocked the soul right out of me.* On my back on my bed I'd stare into the grainy darkness and curl my hands into fists, unsure whom I most wanted to punch.

The line began to move. I crumpled the empty coffee cup in my hand and tossed it in a trash can. Once on the plane, I threw my bag into the overhead bin. A mental home. Was it possible? I didn't think so. It wasn't easy to commit someone against her will, surely. Especially my mother, who was quite capable of hiding her delusions for periods of time if she thought she was fooling the Enemy. No. She had probably gone to Cape Town, or was hiding out in some obscure city, Modderfontein or Odendaalsrus or Eshowe.

Still, I felt claustrophobic: during the flight, I had to resist the urge to get up and open a window.

As we approached Johannesburg airport, I looked down at Soweto's millions of boxy homes. Prudence might live in one—though these days she could own a home wherever she wanted.

Once in the terminal, I prevented myself from running into International Departures and catching a flight out of South Africa—to Peru, Poland, Patagonia, anywhere far from my uncle—and instead headed toward the exit.

Emerging onto the street, I scanned rows of taxis. Most were old Volkswagen buses, or Kombis. I chose the least beaten-up, climbed aboard, and gave the driver Oom Piet's address.

I sat next to a woman wearing a colorful sarong and turquoise blouse marked with semicircles of perspiration. She smelled strongly of sweat and onions, as though she'd recently emerged from a kitchen. Some men wore loose-fitting Mandela-style collarless shirts and relaxed pants, others, shorts and T-shirts. One old white man with gnarled knees and elbows wore a safari suit—matching khaki shorts and slack-belted jacket together with long socks—a look popular among Afrikaners in the seventies. Louis Armstrong blared from the bus radio, his trumpet loud enough to crumble walls. I rolled down the window with a handle that threatened to fall off in my palm. The dry Highveld air caught at my throat. But a storm was approaching; heavy clouds bellied down on the Johannesburg skyline.

Over the next forty-five minutes, the passengers disembarked one after the other—several black businessmen onto Diagonal Street, Johannesburg's Wall Street, and a few women into a colorful shantytown. We passed the Top Star drive-in, built on top of a mine-dump, where my father had taken me to see Hayley Mills in *The Parent Trap* thirty-three years before. The most fun had been intermission, when we walked to the café to buy Cokes and thick, greasy, salty chips. As we navigated the hills and valleys of tarmac on which cars perched, coils of wire tethering them to speakers, we could see the lights of Brixton Tower and the city of Johannesburg.

The Kombi stopped in a run-down neighborhood. On clotheslines, shirts flapped their sleeves as though working up the energy to fly away.

The driver twisted around. "This where you want to be?"

"I suppose." I climbed out and paid him, and the minibus grumbled away, gears grinding. Sparrows flew from the telephone wires into the gray sky, scattering like flung stones. A dog barked, and thunder growled in reply. I put my hand on the gate.

Oom Piet's small house was painted dun and capped with a thatched roof, very different from the sprawling two-story homestead where I had spent my July holidays so many years ago. On the farm, stray chickens had pecked at the dust in the driveway, and an occasional pig snuffled among the hydrangeas until Grace, the cook, told it to *voetsak*. The lawn had been green and lush. When the wind blew from the north, the smell of cow dung made me pinch my nostrils shut with my fingers. But there'd also been hibiscus days, when I'd inhaled the scented air and turned giddy circles at the bottom of the garden where no one could see me.

I pushed the gate open and walked up the dirt driveway. Grass grew patchily on either side, as if the yard had contracted mange. A disemboweled Zephyr—the same car that had ferried me to and from the farm when I was twelve?—languished in front of the garage. The car's once-white rooftop was freckled with age, body faded to pink. Pieces of engine were heaped on the grass, and the back seat, stuffing exposed, rested beneath an oak tree. If the car were restored to its former condition, I imagined I might catch a glimpse of my young self staring out the window.

As I walked closer, I saw Oom Piet's legs protruding from beneath the car. I stopped. A long arm reached out and felt for a wrench. I watched long fingers curl around the tool and take it beneath the shell of the car.

"Hello?" I said, shrugging my bag firmly on my shoulder.

The legs moved. "*Wag'n bietjie.* I'll be right with you. Nearly done here."

I waited, feeling my skin prickle into goose bumps. A dragonfly trailed its legs along the surface of the birdbath and helicoptered away.

The figure emerged. He drew himself to his feet.

When I was twelve, Oom Piet's head had seemed far away, small, and flat. This man was only about five foot ten and had spiky brown hair. He was much younger. "*Ja?*" he said.

I composed myself. "Koos?" My voice emerged on a much higher note than I'd intended. I sounded like an owl.

"Andre. You are?"

"Kate. Your cousin." Had it been Andre who had answered the phone when I called from Durban?

He wiped his greasy hands on a cloth, examining me. "Well, now. I heard you lived in America. No one knew where exactly." The wondering way he said "America" made the place sound like a distant planet: Jupiter, Pluto, America.

I gripped my purse as if he were about to tear it from me. "I came back because my mother's missing. Otherwise I'd still be there." I felt angry, yet I had no reason to be aggressive toward Andre—Koos had been the bully. But Andre was also Oom Piet's son. Though, of course, I was my mother's daughter, and didn't want to be held responsible for that. Still, I couldn't seem to contain the hostility I'd felt for so many years toward the Du Plessises.

Andre leaned against the Zephyr, still slowly wiping his hands.

He laughed, same as before, like a dying car battery: a-HA, a-HA, a-HA. "So you didn't come all this way to say sorry for breaking my favorite model airplane, hey?"

I'd forgotten. He'd spent days painting the wood with Spitfire markings, and I'd thrown the plane against a wall, damaging a wing. There'd been no provocation for my behavior. But he'd been easygoing, slow to react, and somehow that had made him an enticing target. I blushed. "So do you know where my mother is? I heard your father visited her recently. That makes me think he's responsible for her disappearance."

"No pleasantries, hey? No 'How are you, Andre, after all these years?' " He tossed the rag onto the roof of the car. "Man, Kate, why do you hate Pa? He only tried to help your ma. And you. You're looking good, hey? Skinny."

A small tornado of dust spiraled upward from the driveway. The clouds were closing in on the last scrap of blue. A drop of rain wet my cheek. I wiped it away. "It's just—why did he go to see her? She was coping fine. And where is he, anyway? Is this his house or yours?"

"His. We don't know where your mother is right now. My pa's gone looking for her. That's why I'm here instead of at work. He wanted me to look after his dogs while he was away." Andre leaned against the car chassis. He licked his lips, the way his father had when he was annoyed. "Pa sent money every month when you were growing up. Did you know that?"

I remembered the check we'd received each month. "That was from a trust fund set up by my father's company." The writing had always been in capital letters. No imprinted address. And we'd received payments only after Oom Piet found us in Durban.

The earth shook. The leaves on the lemon tree trembled, but Andre appeared oblivious. "Ja. That's what Pa told her, otherwise he knew she wouldn't take the money." A muscle in his cheek jerked. "Lot of thanks he got for his kindness." He indicated the disassembled Zephyr. "Let me get this stuff into the garage, then we'll go inside and talk." For a moment he didn't move, simply stared. "I've often wondered what happened to you. You were so full of it that summer. Still are, hey?" He smiled. "But I always quite liked you. Remember how we used to race twigs down the stream after storms?"

I'd loved twig races. "I'm not here to reminisce," I said, automatically, still processing the fact that my uncle had sent us money. Without it, we'd have been forced to go to the welfare offices. Had he done it just to salve his conscience?

He looked amused. "The old Kate. Sweet as pie."

While Andre carried the radiator and battery into the garage, I sat on the car seat under the tree, pulling at a rip in the vinyl, tearing the stuffing to bits between my fingers and releasing it so it floated away on the breeze like fluff from a dandelion. Raindrops beat small explosions in the dust. The air smelled of wet, hot tarmac. A cat disappeared into the crawlspace beneath the house.

I rose and walked beneath the shelter of the garage, bumping my leg on an old birdcage. Rust streaked my jeans. "What happened to the farm?"

Andre dragged the car seat along the concrete floor past a Ford truck. "Pa got in trouble. Invested in Argentinian cattle and they didn't do well. We sold the farm in the late seventies. Afterward he had all sorts of jobs. Tried sales, encyclopedias door-to-door. Hated it. All his knowledge was from life, not books. He didn't think it was necessary to know so many things." He shoved the car seat against the wall and wiped his hands on his shorts. "Then he sold garden tools at OK Bazaars. Now he consults with the government on farm labor practices. It makes him proud. His reputation is important to him." Rain pummeled the corrugated roof. He gave me his jacket. "Put this over your head."

Hard to visualize my uncle—whose *church* believed blacks were inferior to whites—working side by side with Mandela's people. I took the jacket, hooded it over me, and ran to the house.

Andre came up behind me, reaching around to open the door. We walked into the living room, furnished with a recliner and two maroon-striped sofas. In the alcove, I recognized my aunt's piano. On the mantelpiece perched a grouping of photographs—one of twelve-year-old me on a rock, soaking in the sun. My skin gleamed with baby oil. "Aunt Iris kept this?"

"Ma worried about you all those years," Andre said. "Pa said you'd be all right. He said you were a survivor."

One of the pictures showed Andre holding a fishing rod. I remembered how he'd presented me with one of his fattest silkworms on my twelfth birthday. I'd put the worm in his bed and, not knowing, he'd squashed it to death. Another photo showed Aunt Iris beaming over a roast turkey on a platter.

"Where's your ma?" I asked.

He picked up her photograph and touched the glass with his fingertip. "She passed away two-and-a-half weeks ago."

"I'm sorry." I was disconcerted to hear of Aunt Iris's death. I'd either ignored or been rude to her, and it was too late, now, to apologize. "What happened?"

"A stroke."

"Sudden? I'm sorry."

Andre nodded, put down the photograph, and gestured toward the kitchen.

I entered and sat at the table. "And Koos? Where is he these days?"

He filled the kettle. "Koos died in Soweto during the riots in the seventies. He was in the Army Reserve, you know. Had served his compulsory time, but they called on reservists to stop the uprising. Broke Pa's heart."

I wondered what my older cousin had been like as a man. Had he made his grown-up victims eat insects and thrown them in a pigsty? "That must have made your dad hate blacks even more."

"Pa doesn't like the cheeky ones. They need to know their place, he says, then he's fine with them."

"Lucky them."

Andre lit the gas ring and put the kettle on the stove. "He did lots of good things for the families who worked on our farm. Paid for schooling, vaccinations. Sent half a dozen kids to university, even, when the farm was doing well. Sometimes black blokes will turn up at the door to this day and thank him, you know."

The ground trembled again. I held onto the seat of my chair. "What was that?"

"Old mine tunnels shifting. You've forgotten the way that happens in Jo'burg? And the sinkholes that open up once in a while and swallow whole houses?"

The kettle crescendoed. I jumped. Andre smiled and poured boiling water on the teabags and swished the water around the teapot.

Rain splattered the windows. "So you don't know where my mother is?"

Andre poured the tea into my mug first, then his. He sat at the table. "Not anymore. She escaped from the hospital. Yesterday."

"Escaped?" Had she bolted out the hospital door, still attached to a drip, thinking the doctors had been instructed by Oom Piet to poison her?

"Walked out."

I added milk and stirred my tea, watching the white swirls dissolve in the liquid. "So—confirm for me. She does have cancer," I said. "She was being treated in the hospital—what hospital, by the way?—and decided to leave without telling anyone." I placed the teaspoon on a napkin and looked up. "That's what happened?"

Andre twined his fingers around his mug. "Not cancer. When they gave her a physical, they found a lump in her breast. They did an ultrasound—it was a benign cyst. There are signs of emphysema, though—"

"They gave her a physical *after* she was admitted?" I stood, my chair screeching on the tiled floor. "Your father had her committed!" I hit my fist on the table so that my mug jumped and fell on its side, and a brown delta of tea spread across the plastic tablecloth. "What's your father's *problem?*"

Andre glared at me. "She's mental, man. That's why she's in a mental home."

"She's seventy-two years old, Andre!" I leaned forward and gripped the table edge, visualizing my mother shaking her fist at barred windows or batting at electrodes attached to her head.

"Listen, Kate." Andre rose to his feet, still clutching his mug. "Pa went to tell her Ma had passed away. They were sisters, after all. Your ma didn't listen, just yelled at him, said she was going to get him locked away this time, he shouldn't have come back, the days when she was scared of him were long over. She called him a murderer and a child abuser. She said she had *proof* and now that Mandela was president, the time had come to expose him. Now what kind of behavior is that, hey?"

Child abuser? Had my mother intercepted the blackmail letter I'd written? I straightened. "So he has her *committed?* Because she yells nonsense at him?"

"My pa wasn't going to take her crap, have his name splashed across the paper, jeopardizing his reputation. He works for the government now, you know?" Andre leaned against the sink. "Plus she needs treatment. So he took her to this Horizon Home. It's a nice place. So she could be cared for, hey?" He shook his head. "You don't understand. We're trying to get her the help she needs. My pa's in the Valley of a Thousand Hills right now, talking to the police. She can't have gone far."

I crossed my arms. "She's harmless. Your father—"

"Harmless?" He banged his mug on the aluminum draining board. "Kate. Your mother disrupted lives. The things she said about my ma made her so sad, hey? And now she was going to ruin Pa with her stories. You know what?" He wagged his finger at me. "If you had let my pa help her years ago, if you hadn't demanded to be sent home after the July holidays, and damaged things, and accused my parents of being monsters, they would've taken care of you for as long as it took for your mom to heal. You stopped her from being treated! And you made my ma cry so many times!" He shoved his mug so that it skidded along the aluminum and splashed into the sink. "*You're* the problem, Kate. Not my pa. You."

I couldn't breathe. I had to get out of that kitchen. I turned and strode out through the living room, pushed open the front door, and stumbled down the steps, along the driveway, and onto the street. The rain had turned to drizzle: droplets filigreed the hairs on my arms. My wet sandals slipped on my feet. Pieces of gravel caught between my toes. When I reached a bus shelter about two hundred yards from the house, I sat on a slatted bench, rested my forearms on my thighs, and clasped my hands in front of me. Strands of wet hair clung like seaweed to my skin. Every now and again a large truck rumbled past, splattering mud.

My mother was in a mental home.

Or, at least, had escaped from one.

A bus stopped and the doors wheezed open. "Where to?" the driver called.

I shook my head. "I don't know." The bus harrumphed and roared off, trailing exhaust.

An ant crawled over my toes, up and down the fleshy hills and valleys, then disappeared into the mud. I remembered the day my uncle and aunt had come to take my mother away. She'd seemed strangely resigned, holding out her inner arm to be injected. Maybe she'd realized she couldn't cope, that it would be better for me to go and live with my cousins. Perhaps she knew she needed help.

I covered my face with my hands. *Had* I prevented her from receiving the right care all these years?

Traffic rumbled past. I breathed in diesel fumes. Why was I so upset she'd been placed in an institution? Because my memories were so vivid of her distress when she returned from the rest home? Because I'd *promised* to make sure she'd never be committed again? After all, she wasn't mad in the way most people think of madness—she didn't attack people with knives, or foam at the mouth, or rock back and forth for hours. Her paranoia wasn't the type that manifests itself in violence and endless ravings. Out-and-out insanity would have been more comprehensible, in a way. But her craziness was evanescent—just when you thought she was completely and irrevocably nuts, she'd act quite normally. She'd constructed her own moral universe, one that made sense to her, and she'd grown comfortable with it. I used to think sometimes she enjoyed her madness. It entertained her.

Locking her away was like hitting a puppy for barking.

Or was I upset for selfish reasons? Because I didn't want to feel tainted, the daughter of a certifiably insane woman?

I took my hands from my face. Whatever the answer, sitting here being splashed by large trucks wasn't helping anyone. The rain continued to sift down, but the sun shone, too, glittering off puddles. A monkey's wedding, my father had called such weather. Neither one thing, nor the other.

After a while, I rose and walked back to Oom Piet's house.

When Andre opened the door, I said, "I'm sorry I rushed off."

He patted my arm. "Agh, Kate, you've had it tough, man. I shouldn't have yelled, either. Don't worry about it, hey?"

"Andre?" I said.

"*Ja?*"

"Also I wanted to say . . . I'm sorry about the Spitfire. And the silkworm."

He took my hand and drew me inside the house. "Come in. Let's finish our tea, okay?"

I stepped into the entrance hall. Oom Piet's old *sjambok* rested against the wall. "If you don't mind—can you just give me the number for the place she was in?" I said. "I need to see her."

Andre nodded. "I understand. You can call from here, if you

like." He indicated the phone. "The number's on the notepad."

I made an appointment for noon the next day to meet with Dr. Naidoo, the head psychiatrist at Horizon Home in the Valley of a Thousand Hills. When I told him I was Violet Jensen's daughter, the doctor at first said that no one of that name had ever been admitted. Did I mean Agatha Violet Jones?

"Why did your pa admit her as Jones, not Jensen?" I asked Andre after I replaced the phone on the hook.

Andre cocked his head and smiled quizzically. "Because it's her legal name. Not for any devious reason, hey, Kate?"

I nodded and called a taxi. It did explain why the police hadn't tracked her down when I'd asked them to search hospital files.

Then Andre rang his pa, arranging for the two of us to meet at one the next day, after I'd talked to Dr. Naidoo. "Pa's looking forward to seeing you. He says you'll like Horizon Home." Andre grinned and pointed out the window. "Here's your cab now."

As the taxi accelerated down the street, I glanced back at Oom Piet's house. *My pa wasn't going to take her crap, have his name splashed across the paper, jeopardizing his reputation . . . plus she needs treatment,* Andre had said. *Plus* she needed treatment? So my uncle's reputation came first. And what was Oom Piet afraid of, if he'd done nothing wrong? I felt angry all over again.

Andre waved from the verandah, licking his lips, his tongue moving slowly from side to side. From a distance he looked just like his pa.

Durban
1970

One Friday night toward the end of 1970, the year I turned fifteen, my mother found out about my black friend Joshua. She said Oom Piet had sent him to make trouble so I'd be thrown in jail. Joshua and I nearly did end up at the police station, but not because of my uncle.

In early September that year, Allan de Villiers, the boy I fancied, was cast as Hamlet in the school play, a joint production of Norwood Boys' and Sutherland Girls' High in Durban North. I'd tried out for Ophelia, certain I could perform the mad scenes with authority. Instead I landed the role of Gertrude. Hamlet's *mother*. When I arrived home, I flicked my Panama hat across the room with a quick wrist motion, as though it were a boomerang, and without picking it up stalked to the bedroom, where I listened to Rod Stewart instead of studying my lines.

"Who sabotaged you?" my mother asked at dinner, pressing shepherd's pie onto her fork.

"Maybe I just wasn't good enough," I said, wishing I hadn't confided—during one of her relatively normal periods—how much I wanted to be Ophelia. Savagely, I cut a slice of cucumber into four parts. For months before the audition, hoping to become ethereal, I'd eaten mostly boiled eggs and tomato soup. After I shucked twenty pounds, my mother decided I was being poisoned. She bought only canned food—pickled fish, baked beans, Benedict peas, and bully beef in shivery aspic, which ironically made it easier to diet. My school uniforms grew loose around the waist. I moved the button on my belt. I wasn't skinny, but I wasn't fat, either.

My mother clanged her utensils on her plate. "Someone made sure you didn't get the role you wanted." With a fingernail she picked at her teeth. "Do you want me to write to the principal?"

I chased a slippery cucumber seed around my plate. "I'm not pretty like Judy Westridge, Mom, okay?" Judy—Ophelia—had long, straight, blond hair. "That's all. *Don't write.*"

She lit a cigarette. "Prettiness isn't the point in school plays. You know the words, don't you?" The dropped match flamed out in the remains of her mashed potato. "Though it's true you've got no flesh on your bones anymore. I'm surprised they didn't cast you as Yorick."

I looked her up and down. "Better Yorick than Falstaff."

She frowned. "Who told you to say that, poppet? That's very rude."

Swallowing the last bite of a green pepper, I left the table, washed my plate in the kitchen, grabbed my Shakespeare from the counter, and headed out to the pier, where I sat under a light near the fishermen and read. Rotting bait smelled like perfume compared to the smoky, cabbagy funk of our flat.

Into the salty wind I muttered my lines: *Good Hamlet, cast thy nighted color off/And let thine eye look like a friend on Denmark.* I flipped the pages, counting the number of scenes I shared with Allan. Four. Only four.

Now that I was thinner, kids looked at me in puzzlement, as if they knew me from somewhere but couldn't quite place who I was. At rehearsals, Patrick Osch, who'd been cast as Hamlet's father's ghost, suggested we practice our lines at his house while his parents were at work. He said he'd read about an acting method where you had to imagine yourself into the character's whole life

from birth, and he thought it would help if we understood what
the relationship had been like between Hamlet's parents before
things started to fall apart.

"Pity me not, but lend serious hearing/To what I should unfold,"
he said. He'd grown tall and better-looking—his body was catching up with his head—but he still wasn't popular. He was smart
and wore glasses. *"To be or not to be?"*

"Not to be," I said. "There's someone else."

Allan had smiled at me the previous day. After practicing Act
V, Scene II, in which I drank from a poisoned chalice and died,
he'd punched me lightly in the left biceps and said, "Good job,
Gertie." I had to stop myself skipping from the stage like a ten-
year-old.

Like me, Allan lived on the beachfront and caught the Marine
Parade bus to school every day. Most of the kids who stayed in
the blocks of flats behind the high-rise luxury hotels were poor
and belonged to "broken families": I visualized arms and legs
strewn around our bedrooms and living rooms, heads preserved
in jars. Our parents had managed to enroll us in richer Durban
North schools by swearing an affidavit they'd soon be moving.
Usually, the authorities didn't follow up once you were in, unless
you misbehaved. But Allan had been caught smoking *dagga*—mar-
ijuana—in the school bathroom. Then he'd cursed at a teacher.
Another transgression and he'd be expelled. I overheard him tell
his friend on the bus that he might have to go and work on the
docks with his father. He said he liked English and acting, but
every other subject was a waste of time. His voice was deep and
made my insides vibrate.

I began wandering down to the Sunken Gardens, where the
beachfront-bus-kids—Allan, Jeff Fisher, Mark Viljoen, Suzie Saun-
ders, and Denise Mallows—hung out most weekend nights. After
dusk, the Gardens teemed with braying frogs and eddying midges
and wild cats whose eyes gleamed among the leaves of tropical
plants lining the ponds. Tangled creepers spread like a green tar-

paulin over the inclines and covered part of an old outdoor amphitheater. I sat on the grass and watched as the boys transformed themselves into jugglers on the deserted stage, mimicking acts they'd seen at Boswell Wilkie's circus, and the girls flicked up their T-shirts, pretending to be Salome doing the dance of the seven veils. Once I caught a glimpse of a security guard among the bushes. But he didn't chase us away. I thought he probably enjoyed watching, especially the Salome dance.

When Allan saw me in the shadows, he'd smile and say, "Hi, Mom. Come to keep an eye on me?" I'd nod, thrilled to be acknowledged.

I had a plan: camouflage. Over time, I'd blend in and before Allan knew it, I'd be part of his crowd. At home, I practiced swearing, which didn't come easily. I had to work at integrating curse words into my sentences. "*Bloody* hot, this water," I'd mutter to myself in the bathtub, gazing at my new breasts peeking above the surface like floating pink land mines, "*Bloody* hot, *bloody* hot."

Hugging my pillow before I went to sleep, I listened to "Sunshine of Your Love" and pictured Allan kissing me. I wanted him to say, *I love you—let's elope to Tahiti as soon as we finish high school.* Tahiti was about as far as I could get from my mother, I decided. Without her, I'd be able to live a normal life. That's all I wanted: to be like everyone else.

Having similar clothes would help. I'd started working at the Chicken-A-Go-Go and hoped soon to own bellbottoms and platform shoes. "*Damn* homemade dresses look like *shit*," I mouthed in the dark, shaking my fist at our closet.

Joshua helped me rehearse my lines. The sewage pipe had been demolished and the land readied for another block of flats. We'd found a new meeting place in the thick bushes lining Battery Beach, where we could talk unseen and unheard by anyone except bottle-toting homeless men who stumbled through the foliage once in a while.

I read him the first act to practice my delivery of the iambic pentameter. Joshua cheered in Scene IV, when the ghost enters.

"It's a tragedy," I said. "You're not supposed to cheer."

"But Hamlet's ancestors are taking care of him. That's good," he said. "They'll tell him what to do."

I put down the book. "What if your ancestors are wrong?"

"You said Hamlet's father came back to make sure Hamlet did the right thing."

"Yes, but what if—just say—the ghost made a mistake? And Hamlet does something brave based on what his ancestor told him, but then he finds out his bravery was based on a lie and he's caused a terrible thing to happen?"

Joshua sifted sand through his fingers. "But Hamlet is still brave."

"You think so?"

"Yes. He dies anyway, in the end."

"I know. It's sad."

"Everyone dies in the end. Otherwise how would we get ancestors? And the evil uncle is punished."

"Evil uncles should always be punished," I said.

My breakthrough with the beachfront-bus-kids came in October, after the school play finished its run. In the Sunken Gardens, the kids were still in the mood to act. Suzie and Jeff had had bit parts in *Hamlet*, and now, like Allan, they wanted to move to Los Angeles and become movie stars.

"I think I'll be a scriptwriter," I told them one night, showing them a skit I'd written about Neil Legweak crashing onto the moon. *I come in pieces for all mankind*, he said, crawling out of his smashed lunar module.

Allan laughed. He said maybe I should develop a script and the beachfront-bus-kids would become a famous company of actors.

The following Friday night, I carried with me a short play I'd written, called *Ham Omelet*, in which the hero's father eggs him on to commit murder most fowl.

To my delight, Allan arrived first in the Sunken Gardens. I stood and waved my piece of paper as if he was a bus I was flagging down. "Allan!" I loved to say his name. "Allan, I wrote you the lead role in my script—Ham. In fact, you hog the stage."

He grinned and gestured toward the crimson bougainvillea. "Let's talk, just the two of us, hey?" We crept into the space between the leaves and the wall, where kids went when they had private matters to discuss. The stink of fertilizer rose from the damp soil.

"Smell that?" I said. "So, you see, the play starts off: *There's something rotten in the state of the park.*"

"You're funny. I like that." He kissed me. My glasses shifted on my nose. His tongue felt like an eel that had swum into my mouth and was struggling to get out. His teeth kept crashing into mine. I worried his chipped tooth might break and I'd swallow it by accident. I hoped I was doing the right thing with my tongue. I thought I might go into cardiac arrest like my dad, because my heart was thumping so hard.

Afterward, when the other kids arrived, he told them we weren't in the mood to talk, and he took me to another part of the park, where we lay on the cool sweet-smelling grass, listened to the Beatles on Lourenco Marques' radio, and played connect-the-stars in the night sky.

I could hardly hear him. He was saying something about Laurence Olivier. My corporeal self might have answered, but the essential me had moved onto a different plane. Every day the next week we kissed on the bus and in the evenings we went to the Sunken Gardens or the beach, where we talked about Woodstock and America and Hollywood.

I had never been happier. I had also never felt as fragile: love had turned me to crystal, and I might shatter any moment.

"Where do you go all the time?" my mother asked.

"I get on a spaceship and fly to Mars," I said, locking myself in the bathroom.

She rapped on the door. "What are you doing in there?"

"Being raped by a tribe of pygmies." I painted lashes Twiggy-like beneath my eyes.

She said I'd been brainwashed, and I said, yes, I thought I had been, and I was rather enjoying it, and then I left for the Sunken Gardens.

I loved to lie in Allan's arms, listening to his heartbeat and feeling his hand stroking my hair. Sometimes, before I went to sleep at night, I found myself crying. The emotion had to get out somehow or I would've spontaneously combusted like one of the characters in *Bleak House,* a book we'd had to read for school. I thrust my face into my pillow so my mother wouldn't hear.

One night, when an especially large sob escaped, Mom patted me on the shoulder. "Being a teenager's tough, Kate, I know," she said.

That made me cry even more. I realized she—or the trapped person inside her—cared about me after all.

I'd been going out with Allan for two weeks when Joshua asked if he could come to the Sunken Gardens. We were playing gin rummy in our hideout. I stared at my cards, unable to tell hearts from diamonds. I didn't want him to meet Allan and the beachfront-bus-kids. They'd think me weird to have a black friend.

"What if you're discovered in a white area after curfew? I don't want you getting arrested," I said, hating myself for my duplicity.

He shrugged. "Lots of things are happening in prisons now. All the leaders are in jail. Like Mandela. So—it wouldn't be so bad."

We sat cross-legged opposite each other on the sand. What if he *were* arrested? I reached over and touched his knee. "I don't want you to go to jail. Not without me."

I hated apartheid but wasn't quite sure what to do about it right now, and neither was Joshua, though he was considering rioting. Eventually, he hoped to be president—after Nelson Mandela—and I would be his speechwriter. I'd suggested getting educated first and then meeting after we had our degrees to discuss next steps. Maybe it was only an attempt to salve my conscience, putting things off like that.

Joshua leaned forward and kissed my forehead.

I jerked back. "Don't!"

He took his hand from my shoulder and sat on his haunches, frowning.

"I mean—you surprised me. And—you know." I glanced at the dark bushes, afraid the police might be watching. I'd read in the paper how they spied on interracial couples.

Joshua nodded. "I understand."

"It's not—it's not because you're black." But in a way it was. I reached for his hand. "I'm sorry."

Joshua ignored my touch, gathered up the cards, and stood.

"Come to the Sunken Gardens on Friday. We're usually there about ten," I said.

He bowed from the waist. "*Yebo,* madam."

"Joshua. No."

But he was gone.

Allan said he didn't understand how I could be friendly with a nonwhite. "They're not even allowed on the same benches, man, Kate," he said. "They aren't like us. And they smell."

"Joshua's different." I twisted a grass stalk between my fingers. Had I just said Joshua was like us and other black people weren't? That he didn't smell, and others did? I was too miserable to correct myself.

Mark and Denise said they didn't want *kaffirs* in the park, but Jeff Fisher, who used to live on a farm near Ixopo and played first-team rugby, told them to shut up. He said he'd had Zulu friends on the farm and they were nice *okes.*

Joshua scrambled down the incline and sat next to me.

My worlds were colliding, and I didn't like it. It occurred to me I'd been practicing my own form of separate development. Social apartheid. My shame made me angry. "This is Joshua," I said crossly, ripping another grass stalk from the ground. "He lives in Umlazi."

Mark held his nose and moved away, though Joshua gave off only the scent of lemony Sunlight soap. I glowered at Mark.

Allan stared at Joshua and Joshua stared at Allan. Then they both looked away. Had Joshua thought of us as boyfriend and girlfriend? Surely not. I considered getting up and saying, *Well, I have to get home. See you all tomorrow,* then running up the stairs and out of the Sunken Gardens. Maybe out of the country. Maybe now was a good time to go to Hollywood.

"So when's the revolution coming?" Suzie asked.

Joshua shook his head.

"He's not here to answer questions," I said, partly to protect him and partly to prevent him from saying something—like, "soon"—that would turn the crowd against him, and by extension me. Out of habit, I patted his hand.

Allan stared.

After a moment, I lifted my hand from Joshua's. Allan shifted away from me. If I moved toward Allan, it would seem as though I was moving away from Joshua. I picked up the grass stalks I'd wrenched from the earth and knotted them together until they were broken and twisted.

Suzie and Denise got up, wandered across to the amphitheater, and sat on the edge of the stage. They whispered, giggled, nodded at the same time, and stood up. "We're going home now," Denise said. "I don't think our parents would want us to stay here." Suzie stared at Joshua over her shoulder as they left, then flicked her head forward before she and Denise flounced up the stairs.

None of the boys said anything for a while. Then Mark stood. "I'm bored."

Jeff Fisher flung pebbles at a frog jumping along the side of the fishpond. "Let's hold frog races." He turned and held out his hand. "Kate, give me your bag so I can scoop them up."

I hesitated. I had a cheap plastic bag I'd bought at OK Bazaars, stuffed with my swimming costume and towel in case we took a midnight dip. I shrugged, emptied my bag, and gave it to him.

When the boys were out of earshot, crouching down to catch frogs in their cupped hands or thumping the pond water to scare them off the lily pads, I said, staring straight ahead, "Joshua, listen. I want to be friends but it's better when it's only the two of us. Do you know what I mean?"

Frogs were scattering across the grass and along the path. Mark kept putting small ones in the bag, but they hopped out.

Joshua stood. "I will go."

If he went, I knew I might never see him again. I looked up at him. "I'm sorry. I didn't mean—" What didn't I mean? I hated this country.

"Get him, get him!" Mark yelled.

I glanced toward the fishpond. Jeff was chasing a large frog. He leapt in the air and jumped on it with both feet, squashing its body onto the pavement. I stood and waved my hands and screamed at him to stop. Allan and Mark whooped and also began chasing and stamping on frogs. I ran toward them, yelling, and slammed into Allan shoulder-first, knocking him off the path. "What the hell are you *doing?*"

He staggered. "Hey, you should be on the bloody rugby team, man."

I forgot about the frogs for a moment. I'd started putting on weight, and now I was terribly afraid Allan had noticed and would stop loving me. I crossed my arms against my stomach. Joshua arrived at my side. I wished he'd stayed where he was. "Just stop it, Allan, okay?"

Jeff laughed and kicked a frog corpse off the path. "Why the fuss? Is someone coming?" Green skin and intestines stuck to the sole of his shoe. He scraped the slimy mess off on a stone and pointed. "Here toad-ay, gone tomorrow. What do you think, Kate? I'm funny, hey?"

"Shut up, man," Allan said.

A crippled frog dragged its smashed leg along the grass. I crouched down, horrified. I didn't know whether I should kill it or let it be. Were frogs cold-blooded? Did that mean they didn't feel pain? Was it possible for any living thing not to hurt?

Joshua bent over, his palms on his knees. "You want me to finish him off, Kate? Better for him to die." He stamped on its glistening body, and I heard a popping, splitting sound.

"Look at that, the *kaffir* knows how to play leapfrog," Mark said. "Oh, shit."

I looked up. The security guard had emerged through the bushes and was marching toward us, his baton swinging from his belt like a heavy pendulum. "Hey! What are you kids doing, hey?" His bushy eyebrows looked like two rows of exclamation marks. He put his hands on his hips and nodded toward the carnage. "What's going on?"

Half-dead frogs twitched on the path. The air smelled rank and fishy. Cars whooshed by on Upper Marine Parade. "Run!" I mouthed to Joshua. But he ignored me. His arms hung at his sides, hands clenched as though he were ready for a fight. As yet, the guard hadn't noticed Joshua, or perhaps that he was black. The shadows cast by a dim lamp shining through the leaves dappled his skin.

The guard pulled out a notepad and pencil. "I want your names and addresses. Your parents will hear about this." He pointed to Allan. "Okay. You first, lad."

Allan rubbed his forehead. Jeff and Mark stared at my plastic bag. A small frog peered out and flopped away.

I sidled a little way toward Joshua. "Go!" I whispered.

The guard raised his eyebrows at Allan, Mark, and Jeff. "O-kay." He snapped his notebook shut. "I'm going to throw you all in *chookie* if you won't give me your names."

Mark pointed at Joshua. "The black kid—he came down the steps and started jumping on the frogs like a savage, man. We were trying to stop him. Look at his shoes."

Joshua stepped into the light. His shoes were slimy with the frog he'd killed.

"It wasn't—" I began.

"Shut up," Allan whispered, grabbing my hand. "I can't get in trouble, Kate, man. I'll be expelled."

The guard stared at Jeff's shoes, which also showed evidence of frogs, and at Mark's and Allan's.

"We ran over the path to get the black boy, see," Allan said. He nudged me with his elbow.

I opened my mouth. The guard looked at me. "You, girl. Is that true?" He glared at Joshua. "And what are you doing in a white area anyway, hey, boy? Hey? At this time of night, *nogal.*"

Allan put his arm around me.

If I said it was Joshua's fault, my friendship with him would be over. If I said it *wasn't* Joshua's fault, the guard would take our names and Allan would be expelled from school. He'd no longer be my boyfriend. The Durban North kids would hear a garbled version of the story and I'd be weird Kate again.

Allan squeezed my shoulders.

A feral cat slipped from a tree and raced into the bushes. Why didn't Joshua run? For a second I hated him, because he was making things so difficult. But why should he run? He wasn't guilty. Our eyes met.

Joshua crossed his arms, breathed in, and nodded slightly, as if finally acknowledging a reality he'd long resisted.

I bowed my head, ashamed he had seen my hesitation. "It wasn't the black kid."

Allan dropped his arm and stood away from me.

"She's not going to tell the truth," Jeff said. "She's a *kaffir-lover!*"

"I'm not!" I said. What had I denied?

Joshua nodded again. He gazed directly at the guard. *"Yebo,"* he said. "I killed the frogs and you know what? One day I'll kill white people like you, too."

The guard unsheathed his baton and struck Joshua across the face. His cheek burst like a ripe paw-paw. Blood dripped onto his shirt. He fell to his knees. The guard bent, grabbed his wrist, and reached for the handcuffs on his belt.

I launched myself at the guard, pushed him off balance, and held onto his arm.

"Yussus! Get off me!" he yelled.

Allan tried to pull me away, but I kicked him. Cursing, he, Mark, and Jeff turned and ran. Remembering my fight with Hettie, I bit the guard's forearm.

"Blerrie animal!" He hit the top of my head with his other fist.

Joshua staggered upright. I pulled at his hand and we stumbled from the park, up the stairs, across Marine Parade, and into a dark alley between tall hotels. When we reached the back streets, we slowed down, zigzagging along the pavement. Joshua leaned into me, dazed. His skin was sticky with blood, his eyes blank.

It was midnight. No buses ran to Umlazi now. "Come to my flat," I said. "I'll put antiseptic on your cheek." I thought perhaps he could sleep in the kitchen and leave before daybreak. Usually my mother was snoring by now and didn't wake till seven.

We walked into the lobby and caught the lift to my floor. The flat was dark. I opened the door and helped him onto the sofa. Red blood seeped into the blue-and-white flowers. I brought him a glass of water and his eyes cleared a little.

"Wait here. I'll get the Dettol," I said. I found the antiseptic in the bathroom and searched for the cotton wool, ducking my head deep into the space beneath the sink, but I couldn't find any. Instead I grabbed tissues and filled a small bowl with warm water.

When I entered the living room, I found my mother and Joshua frowning at each other. He was standing, swaying. She wore shapeless flannel pajamas. She turned when she heard my steps. "Why is Winston here?" she said, rubbing her eyes.

I placed the bowl of warm water onto the table. "He isn't Winston."

She blinked. "Poppet?"

Joshua grabbed the side of the couch for balance. Dazed, he shook his head.

My mother spoke then. "I see what's going on! This boy's been sent by Oom Piet to entrap you. The same thing he did to me. The police could come at any moment. Get him out, poppet. Make him go." Suddenly frantic, she charged at him. "Go! You get out! You get out!"

Joshua pushed past me and opened the door. I ran after him. As I reached the lift the doors closed.

"Poppet!" my mother called. "Come here at once!"

"Joshua!" I raced down the stairs, emerged from the lobby—panting—and peered down the road. But Joshua had disappeared. Above me, a streetlight flickered on and off, on and off, until the bulb gave out and left me in darkness.

Johannesburg
1995

When I left Andre and Drieplek, it was midafternoon, and the sky had turned jewel blue. Hedges were spangled with raindrops and the road steamed, giving off a tarry odor. First I planned to check into the Johannesburg Sterling and dump my overnight bag. I hadn't been able to get an earlier flight back to Durban, and in any case, except for calling the police and Mevrou Bakker, there wasn't much I could do until the following day. I felt a little less worried about her now that I knew she didn't have cancer and this time *had* chosen to disappear.

I rolled down the cab window and slumped against the seatback, trying to get used to the idea that, as Andre had claimed, Oom Piet was a concerned brother-in-law who'd always done what was best for everyone. That Horizon Home was a tranquil retreat, specially set up for elderly people with mental health problems and Alzheimer's. That his pa had chosen the place with great care. I wasn't convinced.

When the cab reached the M1, the freeway flanking the city, I recognized Hillbrow Tower—its radio antenna spiking a scrap of cloud—and the flask-shaped Carlton Center among the skyscrapers. One of the squat gray buildings in the foreground must have been John Vorster Square, the apartheid-era police headquarters where blacks were detained and tortured. Quite often, according to official reports, they "fell" out of windows to their deaths.

As a white person, did I share responsibility for the atrocities that had taken place? I felt so: I wanted to apologize to someone somewhere. Even though I'd been a child then, and hadn't intentionally oppressed anyone. Even though I didn't believe in collective guilt. The wind through the open window whipped strands of hair across my cheek. Not oppressed anyone, no. But I'd betrayed Joshua in the Sunken Gardens.

Under different circumstances, if apartheid hadn't existed, would he and I have fallen in love? At the time, I'd never thought about him that way. Just as a friend. Had my emotional response to him been determined—however unconsciously—by the society in which I grew up?

I didn't know. I wished I could talk to him, but without knowing his last name, he'd be impossible to find. And he might not have any desire to talk to me.

The cab turned off the freeway. The houses in the northern suburbs—Houghton, Parktown North, Dunkeld—were guarded by dogs or protected by high concrete walls topped with broken glass. I longed for Chagrin Falls, where fences were rare. I missed my cat. My overloaded bookcases. Writing headlines. Catching the bus to work with the same people every day—my "bus people," whose names I didn't know, but whose reliable presence pleased me. My "elevator people." And my "deli people"—the egg-salad sandwich guy; the tuna-on-rye-hold-the-mayo woman. I missed Simon.

The cab stopped at the Sterling Hotel. I looked at my watch. Three in the afternoon. Eight A.M. in Ohio. Was he having breakfast with Cilla?

After tossing my overnight bag on the bed in my hotel room, I called Mevrou Bakker. She had no news. After some confusion about Violet Jensen's relationship to Agatha Violet Jones, the police promised to contact me ahead of Oom Piet if they found my mother.

I longed for a shower, but decided to visit the house on Lees Avenue before it got dark. I was curious to see if my memories matched reality. Prudence might still work there, if she hadn't opened her shebeen in Soweto, or if it hadn't done well. What if Winston had survived prison and returned too? I imagined him a grizzled old man raking the flower beds.

And if my father *had* become an ancestral spirit, perhaps I'd sense him hitting practice balls on the front lawn.

First, I picked up the phone to call Bernie, who would've just begun her day at Bellish & Associates. I visualized her at her desk: after settling in her chair, she was known to sit immobile for long periods of time, only her pen moving. The lights switched off automatically when they didn't sense motion, so she was constantly plunged into darkness. She'd learned to adapt; she waved her left arm up and down until she was illuminated once again. Through her glass walls she'd be able to see account coordinators scurrying from cubicle to cubicle, and Basil, the art director, moseying past on his way to lunch, his waist-length ponytail swinging behind him. Someone would be microwaving popcorn. Someone always was. I longed for a whiff, though less than a week before, I'd muttered at its pervasive smell.

Bernie picked up. "Kate! Found your mom yet?"

"No, but I—No. How's Bagheera?" I asked, not quite ready to talk about my mother and mental hospitals, wanting only to connect with the grand ordinariness of life back home.

"Fine. Though he's taken to drinking out of the toilet and peeing in the tub. The other way round would be great."

I laughed. "Sorry about that. He must be stressed."

"Guess what? Sarah—my friend who works at the hospital?—she saw the skeleton you and Simon owned, sitting in a chair in his office. It's got its elbows bent and the hands are on either side of its face and the jawbone's wide open—like the Munch scream, you know?"

I smiled. Simon liked to rearrange the skeleton to reflect his mood. Sometimes Mortimer was *The Thinker*; other times he sat on the recliner with his metacarpals curled around a beer. Cilla hadn't found Simon's or Mortimer's eccentricities at all funny.

"You should call him," Bernie said.

"Mortimer, maybe." I told her about Cilla answering the phone the previous night.

"Kate, there could be lots of reasons. Maybe she was dropping off the kids and he was in the bathroom and yelled for her to pick it up. Maybe she's house-sitting while he's at a medical conference."

"Right."

"Okay, so maybe they *are* back together. Maybe he thought he might as well give it a try because you've been quite clear you don't want him." She sounded annoyed. I knew she thought I should've given him another chance.

I ripped my airline ticket cover into shreds. "How'd the ReFute presentation go?" I'd nearly forgotten about the pitch. I tossed the fragments into the wastepaper basket.

"I threw up afterwards, in the ladies' room."

Whose idea had it been, anyway, to give a medical account to a confessed hypochondriac? "Didn't you *Have the Guts to Eat Chicken Vindaloo*?" I kidded, remembering one of my headlines.

She was silent. "Actually," she began, then stopped. "I'll fill you in when you're home."

My stomach twisted into a pretzel. *When You Need Gastric Action, Take ReFute.* "We didn't get the account?"

"We did, but . . . the thing is—after you left on Monday? I called the person at K&C Pharmaceutical to find out if they were set up for PowerPoint. And we talked for a while. And I got the impression the ReFute brand manager takes his products seriously. So." She paused. "Um, so Paul and I, we developed diagrams, and so on, showing how heartburn occurs, and why it's important to treat it. Long copy blocks."

During our first brainstorming meeting, Bernie had recommended an educational approach. I'd persuaded Paul that humor would work better. He'd changed his mind? "Super," I said, formally. "I have to run. Thanks for handling everything."

I wandered over to the window. The hotel was in the center of a residential area: turquoise swimming pools glittered on green lawns. Lines of traffic wove northward along the highway.

Had Bernie intentionally made sure her ideas were presented and not mine? Did she hope by doing so to get the promotion to creative director I wanted? She'd been a senior copywriter for only six months; I'd remained at that level for two years.

Of course, if she hadn't adjusted the strategy, we might not have won the account.

I turned, gathered up my purse, and headed downstairs, cursing my suspicious genes.

The wrought-iron gates fronting the driveway of 48 Lees Avenue looked the same as thirty years before. I remembered hanging upside-down, my knees bent over one half of the gate, my hair trailing in the dirt, swinging back and forth until the blood rushing to my head made me dizzy.

Leaning forward, I peered up the long driveway. The brick single-story home was set on a crest above a sweep of lawn. Behind the house there'd been a rockery filled with red-hot pokers and alyssum and hydrangeas and ferns. The drooping foliage of a mulberry tree had curtained the fence not far from my bedroom window. I'd plucked the berries and eaten them, still dusty, till my lips turned purple, and peeled off leaves to feed my silkworms, hoping they'd spin pink silk. Peach and pear trees grew in the garden behind the house. In summer the fruit fell and turned mushy, and heavy-bellied bees floated like blimps in the air, descending to feed on the sugary decay until Winston scooped up the fruit and threw it on the compost heap.

The gate squeaked when I opened it. I stopped, fearing a rottweiler—Cadwallader, my former dog—might leap from behind the house and attack me. But he'd hardly leap—he'd be ancient, a canine Methuselah.

My old hideaway, the oleander bush, had grown thick and tangled. I remembered how songs from the radio used to float on the air on summer afternoons, the words evaporating before they reached me, only the melody remaining.

I made my way slowly across the expanse of lawn where Dad and I had played croquet, imagining I could hear the *thwack* of our mallets hitting the ball, but knowing the sound came from next door where a roofer was fixing the neighbor's tiles. I stopped at the neglected rosebushes, remembering how my mother had pruned the wood in winter and in summer set blossoms swaying with a touch of her fingertips. Once she'd shown me my own personal little rainbow in the spray of water as it arced toward the ground.

Now I touched a dead rose, and dry petals floated to the ground.

Car tires crunched on gravel. I looked to my right. A blue Austin, the color of my mother's old Fiat 500, came up the driveway, spraying small stones. The garage doors opened, the car disappeared inside, and the doors thunked shut. The owner of the house must have arrived home from work. I began walking toward the garage, thinking I'd introduce myself. Scent drifted from a honeysuckle hedge. The soil in the flower beds had been newly turned, and an earth-encrusted rake leaned against the wall.

I stopped and stared at the rake, recalling the day my mother had wanted Winston to accompany her to the opening of the new Rose Garden at the Johannesburg Botanic Gardens. She'd driven her bubble-shaped Fiat out of the garage. Though it was Saturday, Dad was at work. I was sitting on the bank next to the elephant grass waiting for Isabella, who was going to come and play Jungles, a game I'd made up. One girl closed her eyes while the other hid dolls in places around the garden. You timed how long it took her to find them and then reversed roles. The fastest person won. Every now and again dolls spent weeks undiscovered until Winston knocked on the glass doors with a mud-spattered Barbie or Talking Theresa in his big hand.

That day Winston had been smoothing the wet soil in the flower beds lining the driveway. My mother stopped reversing, opened the passenger side door, and gestured to him.

"Get in," she'd said. "You can come see the roses with me."

He shook his head, and the sweat on his forehead glistened in the sunlight. "I must mow the lawn after this."

But she wouldn't listen. "Everyone's allowed in. Europeans and natives. Come on."

I'd noticed Winston hardly ever left the house during the day except to go to church on Sundays. Almost every evening, though, at dusk, I saw him slip out the gate and head down the street.

"Get in," she said again.

Eventually he shrugged, dropped the rake, walked toward the Fiat, bent down, and pushed the passenger seat forward. It was unheard of for blacks to sit in the front with their master or madam.

But my mother ordered him to sit next to her. "Sit, sit, sit," she kept saying, louder and louder.

He straightened. "You do not shout at me, please. And you do not use me to parade your liberal attitudes." He turned and strode to his *kya*.

I remember being surprised at his temerity and also the formality of his speech. But I knew he was smart: he'd read lots of books and had spent several years at Fort Hare University.

My mother stayed in the car for a minute. Then she got out and followed Winston. She didn't emerge from his *kya* for an hour. I thought she'd sack him. But she hadn't.

From then on, they'd talked more frequently, about the government, now, as well as the garden.

The side door of the garage opened and a young black woman dressed in a red suit emerged carrying a large plastic grocery bag from OK Bazaars. She stopped when she noticed me. "Hello?" she called. "What are you doing on my property? You selling something?"

"No," I walked toward her, passing the syringa tree, its twigs beaded with poisonous yellow berries. As a child I used to be afraid to sit under the tree, as if the berries might suddenly jump into my mouth unbidden. They stayed put. "I used to live here, years ago."

She looked at me suspiciously. "And . . . ?"

"I was curious to see how things have changed," I said.

The woman frowned. "Well, for one thing, it's *my* house."

Taken aback by her tone, I said, "I didn't suggest it wasn't."

She blinked, and gave a conciliatory half-smile. "Some people assume I'm the maid. You can imagine. Or maybe you can't."

She appeared around my age. I thought how different our lives must have been, though we'd probably grown up within miles of each other. "I'm sorry. I didn't mean to trespass. It's just that this house holds good memories for me, mostly. Have you lived here long?"

She put the grocery bag on the ground and held out her hand. "Thandi Madlala. Only a few months. My mother used to work here. Now my husband and I have bought the place."

Thandi's palm felt smooth and cool. "I'm Kate Jensen."

"Wander around for a while if you like. I have to get inside. Ice cream," she said, picking up the grocery bag.

"I just wondered . . . you wouldn't by some chance know Prudence Tshabalala? She used to work as our maid. I mean, your mother might have—"

"No. When did you live here?"

"The sixties."

Her expression changed. "You lived here in the sixties?"

I nodded. "We left in sixty-six."

"So you were the daughter?"

"*The* daughter?"

"You had a gardener called Winston?"

"Yes."

She gazed at the grass. "I suppose you were too young . . . How old were you?"

"Eleven. How is it you know Winston's name?"

Thandi looked up. "Winston was a freedom fighter. Once quite high up in the ANC. Everyone who's worked in this house has heard his story. The maid before my mother told her, and my mother told me."

"Winston was a freedom fighter?" I remembered he hadn't carried a pass. "Where is he now? What happened to him?"

She didn't say anything for a minute, just swung the plastic bag by its handles and watched the arc it made. "You don't know."

"I remember he was arrested. It was a week before my eleventh birthday. No one heard from him afterward. A couple of months later my mother and I left for Durban."

"He died in police custody," Thandi said.

From where we stood, I could see the ferns that had served as the equatorial forest for my Barbie dolls and the big flat rock where Winston had sat one evening and shown me the giraffe stars—the same stars my dad called the Southern Cross. "I didn't know he was dead," I said, "I'm sorry." Had my mother known? Had Prudence? Why didn't they tell me?

How could I have been so unaware of all that was happening around me? My world had begun and ended at the oleander bush bordering our yard.

Thandi inclined her head. "Children can't be blamed," she said, as though repeating an aphorism. "I have to go. The ice cream will melt."

"Wait. How did he die?"

"Beaten to death after his arrest. But people learned this much later."

"By the police?"

"That's not how the story goes," she said.

"What story?"

She shrugged, her expression hostile suddenly. "I must make dinner. My husband will be home soon." She turned and strode toward the house.

If Winston hadn't been beaten by the police, then by whom? And what did she mean, children—presumably she was referring to me—couldn't be blamed? How could I possibly have contributed toward Winston's death? I ran after her and touched her shoulder as she stepped onto the verandah. "Can you tell me—"

"Look around and then go, please." Thandi moved her shoulder away from my hand, yanked the sliding door open, walked in, and pushed it closed.

I knocked several times, but she didn't return to the door. For a while I continued to stand and stare into the living room. A *bokmakierie* sang in the golden shower draping the trellised verandah. I knocked again, not quite ready to give up, then sat on a wrought-iron chair, upset at the news of Winston's death, hoping he hadn't been tortured. I leaned forward and plucked a yellow flower from the creeper and began shredding the petals.

My mother had been very fond of Winston. Sometimes, I remembered, she'd watch him through the window as he worked. Once in a while, she'd take him tea—in a china cup, not the aluminum mugs usually provided for maids and gardeners. One Thursday, when I arrived home from school, I saw them emerge laughing from the house. I'd been glad my friends weren't with me, because there was something vaguely embarrassing about a mother who chatted so freely with a black worker.

Had my mother known Winston was an ANC member? She must have. They'd often discussed opposition to apartheid. But what I'd overheard had been generic criticisms of the Pass Laws. And the Immorality Act.

The late afternoon sun flashed off the glass doors. I remembered the Easter Sunday months before my father died and everything changed. Dad had left for the golf course. I was sitting on the couch reading one of his books—*Escape from Colditz*—a Second World War prisoner-of-war story, I think. The radio was tuned to the English program, which was playing classical music. Winston knocked, and when my mom came to the door, he said he wanted an advance on his wages so he could put money in the church collection plate. He wore his white shirt and a leather belt around his pants, patent leather shoes on his feet.

"Wait here," my mother said, still in her pale-pink dressing gown. When she returned, she had one of my father's neckties in her hand, the one with navy blue stripes. She gave him his wages and the tie. "Wear this. My husband hasn't worn it for years. You can have it."

"Thank you," he said. "But I do not need this tie."

"I didn't mean to offend you." She held it out to him again. "At least borrow it. It's Easter, after all. You'll look very handsome."

Winston paused, then nodded and took the tie. She followed him out the door. They walked along the path, stopping near the rosebushes. He knotted the tie, staring at her. Her head cocked, my mother held his gaze for a long time.

Then she reached up and adjusted his knot with great care, straightening his collar, too. She pressed her palms slowly across his shoulders and down his arms as if to smooth his shirt. She kept her hands on his wrists for a moment, then let go. He touched her cheek with his palm. I'd been astonished to see such an intimate gesture, and a little afraid. After a moment, he turned and walked down the driveway. Arms crossed, she'd watched him all the way down the street until he vanished from sight.

Had my mother and Winston been lovers?

My fingers were sticky from the flower I'd shredded. I stood up, sat down. I remembered overhearing Oom Piet and Aunt Iris talking about some scandal involving my mother. I remembered how my mother had reacted when I'd brought Joshua home to our Durban flat. After he ran away, she sat me down at the table and said, over and over again, *Be careful, poppet. This boy has been sent by Oom Piet to cause trouble. Like he did with me. The police will come, he will go to jail, and you'll be disgraced.*

Had Winston been arrested because he'd contravened the Immorality Act? Not, as I'd thought, because he lacked a pass? If so, who had turned him in? My father?

I couldn't sit on that verandah any longer. I stood and ran toward the street, across the lawn where I'd played croquet with my dad, past the flower beds where I'd dug swimming pools for my dolls, and past the oleander bush where I'd hidden on hot summer afternoons so many years ago, watching my mother and Winston as they talked quietly among the scented rosebushes.

By the time I arrived back at the Johannesburg Sterling, it was dusk. The sky had shaded to oyster-shell. Evening birds conversed on telephone wires. The traffic lights changed from red to green to amber and back again. Rush-hour traffic stopped and started: for most people, an ordinary day.

But not for me. I pushed through the revolving doors and headed toward the elevator. Had my mother really had an affair with Winston? Was it possible? If so, when had their relationship begun? The day she wanted him to accompany her to the Rose Garden?

I jabbed the fifth-floor button. My mother and Winston! He *had* been a good-looking man. I pictured them in bed. I shut down the image—not because Winston was black—surely—but because no child likes to picture her mother *in flagrante delicto*. She'd betrayed my father. I remembered my parents' raised voices during the week between Winston's arrest and my father's death. I strode from the elevator. Did the stress contribute toward his heart attack? Then she'd been responsible for Dad's death, in a way. Not the government. Not my uncle.

Could Winston have loved my mother? And she, him?

In my hotel room, exhausted, hot, and sticky, I peeled off my clothes and stepped into the shower. I closed my eyes and let the warm water sluice over my body, then turned so the spray pummeled my shoulders. I visualized my mother telling Winston that she, too, was being persecuted by Prime Minister Verwoerd's government. That BOSS was after her, and the electrical outlets were bugged. They'd probably bonded over their shared disgust with the government.

Had her fears been quite as specific before we left Johannesburg? I couldn't remember. I'd never been able to pinpoint when my mother's paranoia had begun. The day of my father's death had been the first time she'd mentioned a "Nationalist plot" to me, but it was possible she'd discussed her fears with fellow adults. Dad would've brushed her off, told her she was being absurd.

But to Winston, her stories might've sounded plausible. If unusual, coming from a white woman. Maybe he thought her brave to speak out.

What if the government *had* spied on her because of the affair and Winston's affiliation with the ANC?

I switched off the faucets and watched drips fall from the showerhead and explode on the tiles. Impossible that bus drivers, bosses, relatives, Hettie's father, Sandy's mother, and even cashiers had been part of some vendetta.

Prudence might know what had happened. But the previous day I hadn't been able to find her number in the phone book.

I stepped out of the shower, dried myself, wrapped the towel around me, and shook my hair like a wet dog after a bath. Could my father have alerted the police, been indirectly responsible for Winston's death? I sat on the bed. My stomach hurt. On the nightstand, the digital clock busied itself changing red dashes into numerals. Six twelve. I hadn't eaten since the ham sandwich at the airport: I must be hungry. Perhaps I'd order room service. I glanced at the phone perched on top of the Yellow Pages. Which might have lists of shebeens in Soweto, now that they were legal. I yanked the book from underneath the phone so quickly that the receiver jangled and bungee-jumped toward the carpet. I grabbed it and put it back on the cradle. Then I flipped through Bars and Restaurants, and found the entry. *Pru's Place: For the discriminating drinker. Proprietor, Prudence Tshabalala. Tours, parties, celebrations.* I dialed—and Prudence answered. Her voice was scratchy with age, like an old LP record. "You're the Kate I looked after?" she said. "Which one?"

When she asked that, I felt something rip inside me.

By eight o'clock I was in a cab heading toward Soweto. Prudence had said there was usually a gap between the early and late drinkers, and we'd have time to eat dinner and talk then. I gazed at the poverty around me: children in tattered clothes, piles of old car tires, ravaged storefronts. I felt guilty for not paying more attention to my homeland while living in the States. Were countries like relatives? Did you owe them something merely by virtue of your birth, the event in your life over which you had the least control?

Patriotism was—literally—a foreign concept to me: only in America, when I began to feel emotional at the playing of "The Star-Spangled Banner," had I begun to understand what the word meant.

I was looking forward to seeing Prudence, convinced, suddenly, that I'd guessed wrong about Winston, and that my mother had simply been friendly with a black man who happened to be arrested for not carrying a pass. Prudence would set me straight, she'd grill her special lamb chops, and we'd talk about old times, remembering the good things about my parents.

Streetlight reflections slipped across the windshield. I wondered when the township had been electrified. In the sixties and seventies, black schoolchildren had studied by candlelight while their parents had hunched over cooking fires and talked in the glow of gas lamps. On the horizon, Sowetans must have seen Johannesburg city skyscrapers flaunting their brilliance against the night sky and, to the north, the suburbs twinkling like a blanket of stars.

The car tires hummed on the tar as we passed one boxy brown house after another, each placed in the center of a small square of dust. Homesick, I pictured Chagrin Falls, where, soon, snow would sift from the sky, and snowmen would appear like plump ghosts on neighborhood lawns.

A red neon sign flickered in a window: P U'S P ACE. Except for an added room, which served as the shebeen, Prudence's house was identical to others on the street—houses a mathematician might draw, with triangular roofs, oblong chimneys, and two square windows on either side of rectangular front doors. In the yard, two spindly trees leaned toward each other as though in conversation. Straggly flowers lined the path to the front door, and, in a circle of light, two black men hunched over a checkerboard on a concrete table.

After paying the cab driver, I stepped onto the muddy verge, slapping at mosquitoes dive-bombing my bare arms. From the tavern I could hear loud talking and the sound of an accordion. I knocked on the half-open door. When no one responded, I walked inside. WELCOME TO SOWETO'S FINEST SHEBEEN, a banner on the wall proclaimed.

Big-gutted middle-aged white men and smiling women wearing African wax-print blouses sat around a long table, drinking sorghum beer from mugs, eating *putu*—a kind of grits with gravy—and speaking in a foreign language—German, I thought. Four black men played cards in one corner, and two women perched on barstools and talked, their bereted heads close together.

A woman wearing a brown dress ladled a tomato-and-onion mixture onto plates. The brown *doek* on her head had been folded and two corners formed small triangles above her temples. She resembled an owl. An old, rather ruffled owl.

I watched Prudence for a while. She seemed incomprehensibly

ancient to me, as though she'd donned the wrong skin that morning when she woke. She turned, noticed me, placed the bowl on the table, and gestured at a young girl wearing a bright scarf tied around her breasts and a black leather skirt. "Leila, you finish here." Prudence came close and put her hands on her hips. "Katie. Look at you! *Jy's mos* beautiful! Freckled like the *baas* and slim like the madam!"

"Lovely to see you," I said, feeling strange to be her height. I stepped toward her and we hugged.

She gestured to a couch near the cash register. "Come, you sit here for a bit, wait for me. This tour group, they'll go soon. They like to eat this junk, you know?"

Flapping her hands the way I remembered, she moved from person to person, smiling, ordering Leila to bring more trays of food and refill mugs. I watched her, like a petulant child suddenly wanting to ask, *Why didn't you come to Durban with us? Why didn't you make any effort to find out how I was doing?* But she could've asked similar questions. Why hadn't I sought her out during the years I worked in Johannesburg at the Hiking & Biking Company? Maybe both of us had chosen the road less complicated, not wanting to get caught up in the messiness of each other's lives. Or maybe she hadn't given me another thought after leaving Lees Avenue.

Half an hour later, after a bus bore away the German tourists— the last group for another hour, Prudence said—I helped her carry chairs outside to the barbecue pit. She put *boerewors*—farm sausage—on the grill. Next to the fire, a yellow dog snored, paws crossed over his eyes.

"So you've done well, Prudence?" I asked, sipping a glass of Nederburg Riesling.

On the grill, the sausages spurted thin geysers of fat, sparking small conflagrations. In the street, teenagers dressed in Kaiser Chiefs T-shirts kicked a soccer ball, scattering when headlights announced an oncoming car. I balanced my wineglass on the uneven ground next to my lawn chair.

"Before the elections, *yebo*, I made lots of money," Prudence said. She poked the coals, and sparks flew like fireflies. "Now, not so much. Democracy is killing the shebeens. The young people, they like to go into the city, to the old white bars and restaurants, to the Carlton Hotel. It's the tourists who come here to drink. They think they're seeing *authentic township life*. The blacks, the whites, they pass each other on the way. Cecil, my son, though, he prefers Soweto."

"So he lives here now?" I remembered a photograph of him at age five, which she'd kept in her *kya*. His grandmother in Umhlanga Rocks had reared him, as had been common in those days because of the Group Areas Act, which often kept families apart.

"There he sits, over there. He's a dentist. The one with the purple shirt." She pointed to the men drinking and playing cards in the light of the outside lamp. "*Moenie* worry if he ignores you. He doesn't like white people. I told him, then don't talk to them." She wiped the ash off the skewer with a cloth and pricked the *boerewors* on the grill. The sausages hissed. "He was fifteen in seventy-six, when this place was in flames, you remember? A friend of his got hurt. The boy had fallen, and a man in an army truck reversed over his legs. Twice. Crippled now. Cecil became angry. He doesn't like this business of Tutu's, either. He says there's no forgetting and forgiving what was done. Crying and lying, he calls it."

I shifted in my seat, horrified, not knowing what to say, or how to transition into questions about my mother without seeming unfeeling. "That's terrible."

She hung the skewer over a hook on the side of the barbecue, reached for a bottle of sauce, and struggled with the cap. Her arthritic hands were twisted like driftwood. How old was she? When I was ten, all adults had seemed the same age.

I took the bottle from her and opened the cap. "Here. And listen. I'll cook. Sit down."

Without the protest I half-expected, Prudence sat. The dog got up and licked her leg, and she reached down to pat his fur. Then she turned in her chair to look at the shebeen. "I don't like leaving Leila to do all the work." She tapped her foot on the dust and stared into the dark beyond the fire, her expression a mixture of impatience and boredom. Suddenly I realized my visit was something she might feel she owed me in some way—not a significant event, nor particularly interesting.

"So what do *you* think about whites?" I said, more aggressively than I intended. I looked at the sausages, unsure what to do. How did you know when *boerewors* were done? You couldn't tell from the outside.

Prudence yawned. "The madam—your mom—wasn't so bad. We laughed a lot."

I turned the meat, wishing I could remember more clearly what my mother had been like before her paranoia blossomed. Though blossomed seemed the wrong word for mental illness. "She's missing."

Prudence twisted from the waist to look at me. "She's missing? They got her?"

"Who?"

"The men from the Bureau. BOSS," Prudence said. "She said they would one day. *Afrikaners* don't forget and forgive, Katie."

The meat flamed. "I think they're done," I said, piling the meat on a plate, feeling as though I'd never have a rational conversation again. Or perhaps I'd discover that everyone else was rational and I wasn't. "When did my mother start saying she was being targeted?"

Prudence stood and scooped mashed potatoes from a large pot onto three aluminum plates, then speared the meat with the skewer and placed the greasy links on top. "At first the madam was the same as all whites. Thought us blacks should feel lucky to live in a civilized country. '*South African natives have the highest per capita income on the continent,*' " she mimicked. "Then suddenly one day the madam joins the Black Sash. I don't know why. And she didn't say much about BOSS. Just now and again." She raised her voice. "Cecil! Your food."

A short, square-jawed man with powerful legs and arms rose from the card table and began walking toward us.

"Better not to say much when he's around. We don't want trouble," Prudence whispered.

Cecil arrived, swaying slightly. He held a metal tankard in one hand. "Who's this?" he asked her, slurring a little.

"You've been drinking too much *skokiaan*," Prudence said, waving the skewer at him. "Here's your food, go eat in the kitchen. Then put more beers in the fridge for the next group. Go."

He turned to me then. "Who are you? One of my mother's little madams, all grown up?"

"Not a madam," I said, tired suddenly of feeling guilty. "Prudence took care of me a long time ago. When she worked on Lees Avenue."

He peered at me. His breath stank of beer and brandy. "You're the Lees Avenue girl? And you dare to come here? After what your father did to Winston?" He spat on the ground. The yellow dog got to its feet and barked at me.

Had Dad been the one who told the police about Winston? Was that why Cecil was so angry, and Thandi had been so uneasy— because they believed my father responsible for an ANC hero's arrest? "What do you think he did?"

Prudence jabbed her son in the biceps with her skewer, as if it were a cattle prod. "Go now! Where is your respect for your mother and her guests?"

Cecil waved her away. "Why is she here?"

"Go," Prudence said, and poked him in the arm again.

Cursing in Zulu, Cecil grabbed the skewer from her, then his dinner off the table, turned, headed for the house, and kicked the back door open. The dog flopped back into the dust.

I exhaled. "Prudence. Did Winston and my mother have an affair?"

Prudence didn't say anything. She spooned gravy on our dinner. I watched it form a moat around the mound of potatoes.

"I have a right to know—don't you think?" I said.

She watched gravy drip from the ladle. "*Nee-a,* why worry about these things now, Katie?"

"Because I should have worried about them before." I took the plate she offered me. "What happened?"

Prudence pointed to the stars. "See what you call the Milky Way? Many people believe it is the bristly spine of a dog. And others say it is a path a young girl made with sparks from a fire." She continued to frown at the sky, as if the constellations had startled her by changing shape.

Through the kitchen window, I could see Cecil stacking beers, stopping now and again to take a swig from his mug.

I picked up my knife and fork. "Were they in love?"

Prudence sighed, sat, and started eating. She bit on a piece of sausage. After chewing for a while, she plucked gristle from her mouth and threw it to the yellow dog, who pushed it around with his snout. "Love?" she said. "I don't know. Doing what they did, a black man with a white woman, in those days, it was dangerous. Winston liked danger."

My thighs began to tremble, the way they did when I was upset. I steadied my plate. "Winston liked a dare? So he slept with my mother? Is that what you're saying?"

"Some things you can't know for sure. Doesn't matter." She reached out to pat my arm. "*Haai,* Katie, leave it alone."

Perhaps my mother thought she was defying the Nats somehow by sleeping with Winston. "He was a freedom fighter, right? Did she know that?"

Prudence nodded. "*Yebo.* He was with the ANC for a long time.

Then he said the ANC wasn't doing enough, so he joined another group, I don't remember its name. They met at night in Alexandra."

"He killed people?"

"He didn't say." She indicated my plate. "You must finish your food. The tour will be here soon."

I looked at my bowl of mush. I couldn't imagine ever eating again. "What happened after Winston was arrested?"

"Some Tswana believe the night is a black sheet and the stars are holes the sun shines through. Others say the sun is sleeping on the other side of the earth."

"For god's sake, Prudence." I knew she might think it kinder to keep the truth—whatever she believed it was—from me. But I felt frustrated and angry. I noticed Cecil standing in the doorway of the house. He began weaving toward us.

"Better for you not to ask too many questions." Prudence stood. "I remember when you were small. 'Why, why, why, why.' Like a hyena breaking a bone again and again to find the marrow." She turned at the sound of Cecil's approach. "Go back inside!"

"Tell her the truth," Cecil said. He stopped and put his face close to mine. The whites of his eyes were tinged ochre. "Your mother entrapped Winston. Your father called the police. Then he invited himself over to the police station and beat Winston up. He killed him. We know, girl."

"Don't you call me girl," I said. "Boy. I mean, jerk." I stood. My plate fell to the ground. "My father's not a murderer."

He lurched forward with his arms outstretched as though he were about to strangle me. Prudence pushed between us. "Go help Leila," she said, jabbing at him with her bent hands like a small angry boxer. "Go help in the bar. Go. Now. Now!"

Cecil rubbed his eyes with the back of his hand. "Fucking whites," he said. "Fucking whites fucking blacks!" He laughed. "Okay, Ma. I'll go. *You* tell her what happened. Maybe she'll believe it then." He turned and made his way to the shebeen.

Tendrils of smoke curled from the dull coals. The breeze caught a scrap of brown paper and whirled it in circles. "Tell me," I said.

When Prudence spoke, her voice seemed to come from far away. "I'll tell you what I saw and heard, Katie, but I know nothing for sure. The night Winston was arrested, after you went across the road to Isabella's, the *baas* and the madam had a big argument. The madam yells at him, 'You did this to get back at me!'—meaning, I think, that he got the police to arrest Winston. The *baas* denies it, but he's yelling at her too. He rushes off to the police station. The madam follows five minutes afterward. About half an hour later, when they come home, in one car this time, she's crying. I put her to bed with hot water and honey. She says, 'Prudence, the government will watch me always, now. Because of Winston.' The *baas*, that night he threw things all over the place."

I remembered my father's temper. Once he'd knocked a pot of stew off the stove because my mother had burned it. She'd done it on purpose because he got home so late. I wondered now if that night he'd been with Lydia Cronje, the woman mentioned in the divorce papers. Had my mother perhaps slept with Winston in revenge?

Prudence continued talking. "The next day when I wash the *baas*'s clothes, I see blood."

I stood and held my hands to the fire, then put my warm palms against my cheeks.

"I didn't think about it much then," Prudence said. "But later he had a bandage on his hand. The madam and the *baas*, they fought all that week, except on your birthday. 'I'll never forgive you,' she says to him. So that's another reason we think . . ." She sighed. "We didn't hear from Winston, but we thought maybe he was lost in the system. That happened, often. Maybe he would come out of the prison one day. A year later we heard that he had been badly beaten. He was close to death by the time the police took him to John Vorster Square."

"The police wouldn't have let my father beat up their prisoner."

Prudence laughed. "In those days? They would, *yebo*. They would have fun, watching a man hurt his wife's black lover. And the *baas* was a jealous man."

Flying ants beat their pale bodies against the gas lamp, lost their wings, and plummeted to the ground.

"And then a week later the government gets your uncle to kill the *baas*," she said. "Your father."

Stunned, I turned away from the fire and stared at her. "You believed my mother?" The yellow dog yawned.

"*Yebo*. Of course," Prudence said.

The wind had picked up, and the two thin trees whipped back and forth in a frenetic tango. I sat on my chair and clutched my cotton jacket around me. "But that doesn't make sense. Why would the *government* want to kill my father? Wouldn't they be pleased with him for beating up a terrorist?"

She shrugged, wiping her hands on a paper towel. "Maybe the *baas* went too far, and so Winston died, and government couldn't torture him to get information. Or maybe they killed the *baas* to teach the madam a lesson, not to sleep with a black man."

"That's crazy."

Prudence sounded as paranoid as my mother. How could the two of us view the world so differently? But then I thought of Cecil's crippled friend, and the atrocities in the TV documentary.

Prudence hoisted herself to her feet. "*Nee-a*. Not crazy. You whites, you don't accept, even now, how bad things were then. Cecil's right, you just don't want to know."

Was that true? I felt disoriented. Over the course of the past two days, everyone I knew seemed to be mutating into someone else: Oom Piet into a concerned family man, not a villain at all. Winston into a murdered freedom fighter, not an almost mythic gardener who told me interesting things about bugs and berries and begonias and mulching and the moon. My mother into an unfaithful wife. She had loved him, a black man, thereby breaking

the law and becoming a possible target of the Nationalist government's special forces. And my father? Who had he been?

I stood. "I don't believe my father murdered Winston. And I
don't believe anyone intentionally killed my father, either. I just
don't."

Prudence inclined her head. "I understand." She looked toward
the road. "The next tourist bus will come soon. There are no taxis
now. Leila will take you back to your hotel. Leila!" She pointed to
a lime-green Volkswagen parked on the street.

We walked together along the path, not saying anything. The
wind gusted and whipped my hair into a frenzy of curls. Leila
arrived, climbed into the car, and opened the passenger door from
the inside.

Feeling sad, knowing I'd never see Prudence again, I bent to get
in, then straightened. "I always watch out for the lightning," I said
to her. "Remember how you said I should, or I might be turned
into a star?"

Prudence smiled then and embraced me. "You were a good little
girl," she said, "but stubborn. Stay well, Katie."

As Leila drove me away, I twisted to look through the rear
window. Prudence was shuffling slowly back toward the shebeen.
The yellow dog followed her, its tail waving a slow farewell.

Durban
1970

Shadows on our bedroom wall shape-shifted into images of dead frogs as I lay awake and restless the Friday night after the events in the amphitheater. I wondered if I'd ever see Joshua again. My heart clenched. It was my fault if he no longer wanted to be my friend. Turning and turning in a muddle of sheets, I tried to picture where he lived. I'd never gone to Umlazi: I had no idea what his home looked like, nor did I know the way there. Certainly no white buses went into the townships. I knew only that he lived in a numbered house on a numbered road.

My mother trumpeted nasally. Across the street, the neon CHICKEN-A-GO-GO sign flashed.

And Allan? He'd break up with me at school on Monday, I knew he would. I curled my body around my pillow.

The streets were quiet, save for an occasional car and the once-in-a-while banshee wail of ambulances and police cars. I thought I might never sleep again, but eventually I dozed off.

Around seven, I awoke to see my mother hoisting herself from her bed. After splashing in the bath, she returned to the bedroom and pulled on her two-way stretch. I closed my eyes, but I could hear her grunts and the snap of elastic. Next came a shirring sound as she pulled on her frock, as she called it, though the word sounded far too frivolous for her large, shapeless shifts. She thumped into the kitchen. After ten minutes, I smelled toast. On good days, she fried eggs and ate them on buttered bread—on bad days she ate six slices of toast and marmalade. We went through lots of marmalade.

I got up, locked the bathroom door after me, showered, and threw on a pair of bellbottoms and a blue floral blouse.

My mother sat at the kitchen table sucking a pen, frowning in concentration, her red notebook open. When I walked in, she looked up. "What was the name of the boy who was here last night?" she asked.

"I don't remember," I lied.

"Oh, come now, poppet! What's his name, please?" she asked.

"Iago."

She arched her eyebrows. "Poppet!"

"Nathaniel . . . Nkomo."

She wrote the name in flowing script. "I'm being serious now. Oom Piet is using this boy to trap you and me into an admission of guilt so the police can arrest us. I can't explain more."

"*I, said the sparrow, with my bow and arrow, I killed Cock Robin.*" I grabbed a piece of buttered toast and strode to the door.

"Poppet." Her voice rose.

My hand was on the doorknob. I turned.

"You didn't have sex with him last night, did you?" she said. "I could smell something on you, you know."

I opened the door and slammed it behind me.

At the library, I found a map of Umlazi. I rode the bus to the outskirts of the white suburbs, then walked two miles to the township. Tarred roads crumbled into dusty streets. There were no telephone wires, no medians lined with trees—only dirt roads bordered by flat-roofed houses built of clapboard, plastic sheets, and corrugated iron. A posse of skinny chickens trailed along a path as if they'd forgotten where they were going. For a while a dog followed me. A "green mamba"—a bus reserved for blacks—

hurtled past. I sat on a bench, wondering how I was going to find Joshua. People stared at me curiously, but most said nothing. A small black girl sat on the bench next to me and ate licorice, threading long strings into her mouth. She continued to sit, staring ahead, not saying a word, until her mother climbed off a bus. They walked down the road together.

Children wore ragged clothes which didn't quite fit: you could tell, from the old-fashioned style, that the shirts and dresses and shorts had been plucked from charity bins. Mothers carried babies on their backs, slung inside blankets they tied around their waists. On their head they bore large boxes filled with groceries: flour and corn and *putu*.

I wandered down street after street. When I knocked on doors, people opened them a crack and looked at me suspiciously, peering over my shoulder as if they expected to see a policeman. Houses were furnished with crates and old sofas: families cooked outside or heated water on fires. A pall of acrid smoke hung in the air, reminding me of pictures of the Industrial Revolution in my history textbook.

Would I exchange living with my mother for a home in Umlazi with a big family? I wasn't too sure. The gutters reeked of sewage and rot. At every stop I described Joshua: about five foot eight, broad forehead, handsome, I said, but with sticking-out ears. Droopy eyes. Usually wears gray pants and a flowered shirt, which he calls his Hawaiian Elvis shirt.

When they asked me what his last name was, I couldn't tell them.

At sunset, I gave up hope. I was frightened. Knots of teenagers had gathered on corners. A boy threw a stone in my direction. Eventually I found my way back to the flat.

On Sunday, to avoid stories about Joshua's connections to The Plot, I told my mother I wouldn't see him again. I knew I didn't have much choice.

"Wise girl," she said. "It would only mean trouble for both of you."

That was an odd comment. Usually she wasn't concerned about the fate of my friends. I'd given up trying to figure out how her mind worked.

When I emerged from the bedroom at dinnertime, my mother was absorbed in her notebook. Now and again, she'd say, "Aha!" and write a few more words, or draw a line connecting two names. I made a ham sandwich, then sat and watched her as I ate.

Some mothers knitted, some arranged flowers; mine dabbled in delusions. She'd begun to revel in her ability to confound Enemies—resigning before she was fired, taking circuitous routes to foil kidnap-minded bus drivers, throwing out "poisoned" food.

Nobody could disappoint her, because she didn't believe in anyone.

Except me. She believed in me—cared about me, in her own peculiar way. It was the people you loved who wielded power.

Enemies were a piece of cake.

I pushed my sandwich to the side. "Can I have a piece of notepaper?"

She ripped a page out of her book and handed it to me.

Dear Allan, I wrote, *I think you are a jerk. I no longer want to be your girlfriend.*

On Monday, when I gave Allan the note on the bus, he read it, crumpled it up, tossed it on the floor, and kicked it under a seat. "Bitch," he said, and stalked to his seat.

My face throbbed with the agony of keeping my features composed. It was one thing to say Allan was now an enemy, but much harder to treat him like one. I stared out the window. I thought I would get off the bus and just walk and walk and walk, stopping eventually in a small town, where I might start a holiday home for cats. Invent a new identity. Then it struck me that was just what my mother had done, in a way—leaving Johannesburg, changing our surname, and starting afresh because she felt persecuted. So I didn't get off the bus.

Allan ignored me. I could deal with that. But word got around I was a slut who slept with black boys. I was jeered. I shut down, speaking to no one except the teachers, and then only when I was forced to answer them. And I ate. And ate.

The rumors died away after a month or two. Kids lost interest in my problems and ignored me. After finishing my homework, I read novels—nearly one a day, staying up late while my mother twitched and grumbled in her sleep—losing myself in alternative worlds.

I decided to leave home as soon as I completed Standard Eight, two years short of my Senior Certificate. My teachers were horrified. They said if I stayed, I'd get scholarships for university tuition. To stop their nagging, I failed a few tests. The Fs bothered me. But I made sure to pass important exams.

My plan was to find a job and study at night. Turn into a different person: someone confident, sexy, worthy of admiration. No one need know about my past; if people found out, I'd move on.

On Christmas Day 1971 I told my mother I was going. A paper hat sat askew on her head. The table was decorated with a bent piece of plastic holly that had survived from Christmases at the house at 48 Lees Avenue. A large chicken congealed in a bed of grease. I'd given her a new notebook—I thought she'd need it. There'd be lots of blame to apportion for my departure.

"Who put you up to this?" She stopped eating.

I wiped my mouth with the napkin, folded it into neat squares, and put the cloth down. "I've booked a train ticket to Johannesburg. I go in a week." My heart was thumping, but my voice was calm. I'd talked to a woman at the local YWCA, and she said I'd be safe staying at the one in Braamfontein near the city center. The South African economy was good, the papers said, though there was talk of upcoming strikes. I'd saved enough money from working at the Chicken A-Go-Go to last for a month or two, until I found a job.

My mother hadn't been fired for six months. I thought she'd cope. Somehow she always did. And how much responsibility did a child bear toward her mother? I didn't know. I felt guilty but incapable of staying with her any longer. It would be a strange and wonderful irony, I thought, if my leaving her—thereby confirming her predictions that we'd be split apart—freed her from her fears.

"A week? A job? But you were going to go to university!" She skewered a potato, pulping the soft white flesh with her fork. "Come on now. Who suggested this to you, poppet?"

I told her I had to go to Johannesburg, because the jobs were there. I said I didn't plan to contact Oom Piet or anyone else.

"You have no skills." She clattered her knife and fork onto the plate. "They'll chew you up and spit you out."

I stared at my plate and counted the flowers around its circumference.

She didn't move for a while. Then she picked up the plates and took them to the kitchen sink. I watched her through the door. She put them down slowly, stared at them for a moment, then snatched up a dishcloth and blew her nose. She walked from the kitchen to the bedroom. I heard her bed creak. She began to sob the same way she'd sobbed the night after dinner at the Veld & Vlei. *Oh-woo. Oh-woo.*

When I was small I'd worshipped my mother. I used to follow her around the garden, watching as she inspected her flowers— every daisy seemed important. She was prettier than all her friends, the ones who'd appear on Friday afternoons to play bridge. Dana, Hilda, Mary. They'd laugh and talk about husbands and recipes and children's parties while I sat on the floor and played with my toy farm animals. When had they stopped coming around? When had my mother changed? I couldn't remember. It was too long ago. I had been too young. I listened to her sobs, thinking of a line from a Yeats poem we'd been studying: *How can we know the dancer from the dance?* How could I tell my mother from her illness?

I entered the bedroom. She lay on her back, her chest heaving. I sat on the edge of the bed and patted her arm. My heart hurt.

She lifted herself onto an elbow. "They've won, poppet, if you go, don't you see?"

I stared at the floor, followed cracks in the wood with my eyes. "Mom, I'm not a doll manipulated by your enemies. I can't live with you forever. And I have no real friends here."

She sat up. "No. No, you don't have friends. Of course not. How many times must I tell you how vindictive your uncle is?" She pulled a tissue from a box on the floor between our beds and blew her nose. "Let's go back to the table and finish our Christmas dinner. There's cake."

"I'm not hungry."

"The things they've done to you. It's terrible. And oh, I've tried so hard to protect you. So hard."

I peered into her eyes, trying to talk to the person she once was. "Why do you think the government hates us? And why do you always say Oom Piet killed Dad?"

She watched her fingers ripping the tissue into shreds, then balled up the scraps and tossed them in the wastepaper basket. "He thought your father was going to create a scandal that would tarnish the family name."

"What scandal? What *everything?*"

"Oh, poppet. It's not something you could be expected to understand at your age."

I leaned forward. "Say I agree we have enemies. What 'terrible things' have they done to me? What's wrong with me?"

She stared at her hands, turning them over and over—palm up, then down—as if she'd newly discovered their existence. Then she glanced up. "A normal child *would* have friends. A nice boyfriend. But no one likes you." She snorted. "Look at you! They've puffed you up like a balloon all over again. You're not exactly easy on the eye. I had a lovely figure when I was your age. And now you're even failing your schoolwork. I told you it would happen this way. I know what the other kids say about you—that you're a slut. I've heard them, at the bus stop. A child of mine!"

And then she put her fat white hand on my thigh. "Poor poppet."

I recoiled and stood. I said, my voice as flat as the side of a knife, "I know how to take care of myself." I turned away so her words would bounce off me. I pulled clothes out of the closet, jammed dresses, jeans, panties, and bras into an old suitcase. My school uniforms fell off their hangers. I left them huddled on the closet floor.

My mother's shoes clacked on the floor as she walked away. I looked around our room one last time: our beds within a foot of each other, the newspaper clipping on the wall, my Rod Stewart poster. My books lined up on the windowsill. I decided to leave them. Even my *Just So Stories*. They, too, were part of my past. I'd write from time to time, give my mother a post-office-box address so she could reach me in an emergency.

In the bathroom, I grabbed shampoo and soap and toothpaste, and thrust bottles and tubes in a plastic bag. The bead doll that Prudence had given me stood on top of the medicine cabinet. It had become a bobble-head doll after my mother decapitated it while searching for bugs. I hesitated, then reached for it and tossed it among my toiletries.

When I walked into the living room, my mother was writing in her red notebook. My sneakers made a mewing sound on the floor.

She looked up. "It shows I was right, I suppose. There's that. Poor poppet. You'll see. You'll never have a normal life."

"Bye, Mom." I closed the door behind me. For a moment I stood and stared straight ahead. Then I walked down the stairs, through the lobby, and onto the street.

On the train to Johannesburg, I vowed to prove her wrong. The next time I saw her—*if* I saw her again—I'd be with my husband. And children.

"Surprise, surprise," I'd say.

Durban
1995

When I arrived at Durban International Airport after a sleepless night at the Johannesburg Sterling, during which I'd had a convoluted three A.M. conversation with Bernie—who couldn't figure out what I was talking about but cheered me up anyway—I rented a battered old Renault. Cab fare to the Horizon Home in the Valley of a Thousand Hills, which was about thirty miles inland, would've been twice as expensive. I thrust the multicolored bills across the counter: rhino, elephant, water buffalo. Patrick Osch had told me a group of rhino was called a crash. I loved the image, picturing a dusty pileup of gray, single-horned, long-spined animals. I felt lonely, and for a moment considered calling Patrick. But what would I say? *Would you like to spend the day with me? I'm going to visit the mental home my mother escaped from a few days ago. Should be fun.*

Maybe, if—when—I found my mother, and she was settled, I'd visit him in Hluhluwe before I returned to the States, ask him to take me on safari. Why not? I'd never seen a warthog in the wild. Never gone to a game reserve. Maybe I could become a game ranger too.

I threw my bag in the trunk of the car. It was nine o'clock— three hours until my meeting with Dr. Naidoo, the head psychiatrist at the home.

On the way out of town, I stopped at Kingfisher Court. Mevrou

Bakker wasn't in. Banging on my mother's door brought no response. I got back in the Renault and headed for the freeway.

While I drove, I attempted to tamp down my emotions and sort my thoughts into two piles: what I knew, and what I didn't know. I knew that Winston had been a freedom fighter; that he and my mother had had a relationship of some kind; that my father had gone to the police station after Winston's arrest, and come home with blood on his shirt; and that someone had beaten Winston to death.

I didn't know who had been responsible for his murder. I didn't know why my mother believed my uncle killed my father, nor how she thought the murder had been carried out. And I didn't know what Oom Piet's role—if any—had been in any of the events that occurred in July 1966.

Seeing women hoeing the fields on the side of the road, I imagined my mother a female Lear, wandering on a heath somewhere and ranting about ungrateful daughters.

Maybe, once I found her, she'd tell me her version of events, and I'd be able to figure out what really happened.

If I ever did find her.

What if she weren't paranoid after all? But I found that hard to believe.

Two stone gargoyles guarded the entrance to Horizon Home. After I announced my presence to the intercom, the gates swung open electronically. I parked, climbed out of my car, walked along a path to the ivy-covered main building, and rang the bell. The door clicked open. Inside, an antiseptic smell failed to mask the odor of urine. Three armchairs were grouped around a coffee table covered in magazines. The walls were painted institution-pink. Old men and women in wheelchairs had been positioned so they could look out of a large bay window, but most were bent forward from the hips, or sloped to the right or left, their eyes incurious. Some nodded at intervals as if contemplating profound matters, and maybe they were.

Behind the counter stood a handsome Indian man dressed in a brown suit. A name tag pinned to his lapel said, DR. NAIDOO. I rummaged in my purse and held out my driver's license. "Kate Jensen. My mother's Agatha Violet Jones?"

"Welcome," Dr. Naidoo said.

A white-coated man pushing a large stainless-steel cart distracted me. I pointed to the door from which he'd emerged. "Is that where they do the electroshock?"

The doctor looked at me diagnostically. "He's one of the cooks."

I followed Dr. Naidoo down the broad corridor and we entered a sun-striped room containing a large pine desk. A ficus dropped leaves in the corner. A fish tank burbled. The window, which was barred, overlooked the garden, where attendants were pushing wheelchair-bound patients, like mothers with grotesquely aged babies. "This place seems secure," I said. "How did my mother get out?"

Dr. Naidoo indicated I should sit and lowered himself into the chair behind the desk. "We're doing our best to learn how she managed to leave the premises." He spoke in a singsong voice and offered a professional smile. "By the way, we don't give electro-convulsive therapy to the elderly. But it *has* proven effective in some cases of schizophrenia. The procedure's not like it used to be, you know, decades ago."

I sat on the edge of the chair and stared at the fish tank. Several fish—zebra-striped, leopard-spotted, lion-blond—gaped at me, their tails flapping, then sped off.

Schizophrenia? "She's not violent," I said.

"Many schizophrenics aren't. People don't realize that schizophrenia is like cancer," he said sternly. "It comes in many different strains and levels of malignancy. Lots of patients live reasonably productive lives. But family members must understand that it is their duty to make sure the patient gets appropriate treatment even if the patient doesn't want therapy. You wouldn't let a family member suffer from diabetes. You'd give her insulin, wouldn't you?"

I stared at the fish tank.

Dr. Naidoo sipped water. "You live in the States, yes? She's alone here?"

I crossed my arms, feeling defensive. "She seemed okay most of the time. She kept her last job for five years. Since she retired she'd even started playing gin rummy with the caretaker of her block of flats." Which I hadn't known before arriving in Durban, but I wanted to sound like a concerned daughter.

The doctor nodded. "It's not uncommon for some patients' delusions to diminish in frequency and duration over time. We're not sure why. Strong emotion can precipitate recurrences, though." He placed his glass precisely within the wet circle it had formed on his desk. "When your mother was brought here, she had laryngitis—at least, she claimed to have laryngitis. Her throat was a little inflamed. We weren't able to do a complete workup of her mental condition or get her on medication before she left us. So I can't give you an accurate diagnosis."

"Then on what basis could you keep her locked up? With only my uncle's story?"

Dr. Naidoo steepled his fingers. "She'd threatened him with physical harm. Medical records from the state hospital indicated an earlier diagnosis. And the things she told Miriam—the nurse assistant—seemed to confirm paranoid belief. Miriam's new. She believed her, was quite worried about her safety, I think." He gazed at his serried fingertips. "I'm not saying institutionalization is necessarily appropriate. We have wonderful medicines that can often be taken on an outpatient basis. The problem is getting patients to be compliant."

"Can I talk to Miriam?" She'd been the nurse who'd helped my mother get her letter mailed to me in Chagrin Falls.

He hesitated, then picked up the phone and paged her. "Miriam didn't let her out," he said. "That sort of thing doesn't happen here."

While we waited, he told me Miriam and my mother had bonded over their shared political views—Miriam's grandfather had been killed by the police at Sharpeville in 1960 when people were protesting the Pass Laws.

Miriam entered, an elegant young woman of about twenty-five, with high cheekbones and ebony skin glowing in contrast to her white uniform. She stared at a Van Gogh print on the wall above Dr. Naidoo's head and sat when invited to do so, keeping her eyes focused straight ahead.

I glanced at Dr. Naidoo and inclined my head questioningly toward the door.

He nodded, rose, and left the room.

I touched Miriam's arm. "Your grandfather was killed at Sharpeville?"

"What do you care?" She glared at me.

My reference to a mass killing wasn't exactly a tactful icebreaker, I realized. I tried again. "Do you know where my mother is?"

"I don't understand why you didn't come. I sent the letter. She waited and waited. She'd hear the phone ringing down the corridor and she'd say, 'There she is. Kate's calling. She'll be here soon.' Except you weren't."

"I was doing my b—"

"You got her letter?"

"Yes."

"Then why didn't you come immediately? It said she had cancer."

"Which she doesn't, I hear."

Miriam looked at her hands on her lap, and twisted a topaz ring on her finger.

"And it takes a few days for a letter to reach the States," I added, defensively. "Even priority."

Miriam looked up. "I'm sorry. But you see, she wouldn't tell me where she was going. If I knew, your uncle's friends in the Third Force might torture me to find out." She gripped my arm and whispered. "She has evidence your uncle killed Winston Maphosa. He'll have to testify before the Truth and Reconciliation Commission. He'll be brought to justice."

"My *uncle* killed Winston?" I put my hand on my chest. Hearing about a murder shouldn't be cause for celebration, but I couldn't help feeling relief that was close to joy: Oom Piet was the villain again, not my father.

"He beat him to death at the police station." Miriam leaned closer. "You better be careful—your uncle would do anything to stop the truth from getting out. Your mother said it's why he had her committed the first time. This time too. To intimidate her. And why he murdered your father. To keep him quiet. Because your father saw him kill Winston. And Winston was a hero of the revolution."

But what reason would *Oom Piet* have to attack Winston? Why would he have been at the police station? And when had I ever believed my mother's claims? She might have accused Oom Piet because she didn't want to think my father capable of such a crime.

"You said something about evidence?" I asked. I remembered the note among my mother's family trees. "How the Murder Was Committed." Winston's murder. Not my father's. Not that he had been murdered . . .

Miriam nodded. "There's a photograph. She has a photograph. That's all I know." She looked down and smoothed her skirt on her knees. "She said perhaps it was as well you hadn't come, because your uncle will probably say you're crazy too, and lock you up. She hopes you don't end up in beds next to each other again. Living with you wasn't easy."

The receptionist poked her head around the door. "Your uncle's here," she said.

Oom Piet stood beneath a wild fig tree outside the front entrance to Horizon Home. Age had curved my uncle's spine. Shadows of leaves mottled his skin. He raised a hand in greeting.

"After all these years, Kate, you turn up like a bad penny," he said. "Not really a *bad* penny, hey?"

"How are you, Oom?" My heart was trying to escape from my chest.

"You're thinner now, I see." He looked me up and down.

"And you're more wrinkled."

He laughed. "Oh, it's Kate all right."

I composed myself. "Sorry to hear about Aunt Iris."

He blinked. "*Ja. Ja.* Very sudden." He pointed a long finger toward a copse of eucalyptus trees outlined against the teal sky. "Let's walk to the bottom of the grounds—see, where it slopes toward the valley? There's an aviary and a little zoo. Dr. Naidoo says it's good for the patients to have a peaceful place to sit." He nudged me with his elbow and whispered, "Amazing, *nê*, a *coolie* has such a job?"

"No," I said.

As we headed down the shaded path, a lawnmower blatted. The smell of new-cut grass scented the air.

"We must find your mother," Oom Piet said, loping next to me.

"Why is it so important to you?"

"You don't want to find her?" He raised his eyebrows.

"Of course."

"You're not fond of her, hey? Poor crazy woman."

For a moment, I thought he meant me.

A security guard opened the gate to an enclosure containing wire cages with birds and animals—iguanas, rock-rabbits, and small buck. Oom Piet gestured toward a picnic table and benches.

We sat opposite each other. A peacock, his tail an iridescent fan of turquoise and green, strutted along a dusty path.

"I met Andre," I said. "Seems to have turned into a decent guy."

Oom Piet smiled. "He's a bit soft, you know?" He patted the back of my hand. I held it still. He took his fingers away, and my hand skittered to the safety of my lap.

The bench overlooked the broad sweep of the valley. Emerald hills shaded to mauve and turned purple with distance. Maybe they *were* purple. Who knew for sure? "So, Oom, why did you have my mother committed this time?"

My uncle waved toward the building. "Horizon Home is a nice place. Isn't it? Hey? Iris's insurance will pay, you know. She left a bequest, wanted her sister properly looked after. It's not like the last place. But your mommy needed treatment badly when you were a little girl. We had to take her to the state hospital. It's important to take care of family members in trouble."

Two of the birds in a small aviary fluttered against the wire. "I know about Winston and my mother, Oom Piet," I said. "You didn't want a family scandal, did you? Not then, not now."

Oom Piet looked away, gazed at a bank of yellow daisies. "I was the only one who had the courage to try to get help for your mother. She needed treatment. You know that. Better than anybody. Why so hostile to me, then, *skattie?*" He rolled his neck around on his sloping shoulders. "*Ja.* Winston." He pronounced each syllable slowly. "Win-ston. The garden-boy. The terrorist."

"Gardener. Freedom fighter."

His eyebrows rose. "Did you know he helped plan the Johannesburg Station bomb attack?"

I remembered a Zulu-language newspaper open on the kitchen table in the Lees Avenue house. A photograph of a little girl engulfed in flames, her mouth open in a scream. The camera had caught her crawling toward her grandmother, whose flesh had been ripped by flying glass. One of the old woman's legs had been nearly severed at the knee. Prudence had come in and taken the paper away, saying I was too young to see such things.

My mother had hired Winston a month or two after the bomb exploded. He'd had no papers and refused to carry a pass. Thandi and Cecil and Prudence had called him a heroic freedom fighter.

I watched the peacock sashay down the path. "I don't believe you." The ANC, in those days, had refused to target civilians. But Prudence had said Winston belonged to a splinter group because he didn't think the ANC was doing enough to overthrow the government.

Oom Piet nodded, his lips curving in a half-smile. "You think terrorists are *romantic,* do you?"

"How would you know if he were involved in the bomb plot, anyway?" I asked, remembering the newspaper clipping about the bomb I'd found in my mother's envelopes.

"The *Broederbond* knew many things."

I shook my head. "You hated Winston because he was a black man who slept with my mother. To you that was a terrible thing. Against your religion. And the law."

He shrugged. "It says it in the Bible."

"Did the police spy on my mother when we lived in Durban?"

Oom Piet's forehead wrinkled. His Adam's apple jounced. "*Lie-fling,* your mother wasn't a political operative or anything. Just a crazy white woman. The police didn't care about her, not after they got Winston." He squinted at me. "I hope you don't think there was a *plot.*" He touched his tongue to the corner of his mouth. "Everyone tried to keep it from you, your mother's affair. Even she did. Bloody *kaffir* didn't know his place." His bones cracked as he stood.

"Shortly before you visited us in Durban, I followed my mother," I said, standing too. "A man with silver hair was stalking her."

He chortled. "*Nee, nee,* not the government. My friend, Karel.

He lived in Durban. He was a private investigator. I asked him to keep an eye on Violet after I recognized your picture in the *Tribune*—for winning the essay competition?—while we gathered the papers to get her committed. Afterward, I had him check on her from time to time. Once she confronted him on a bus. So maybe she thought *he* was the government."

My Ali Baa-baa essay. So that's how he'd tracked us down. I started walking quickly along the path.

"She's mad, all right. Bonkers," he said, loping beside me. "In the early sixties she told Iris your transistor radio was used to broadcast warnings—and sometimes your toys. She and Iris used to be close. The voices told her not to tell your father about them, though. She should only confide in some people."

I remembered now: once she'd taken my radio to be repaired and never returned it. And I recalled her snatching away my blue Teddy bear, saying it had funny eyes. How old had I been? Eight? I'd fussed, so she'd bought me a bigger brown one. Blue was an unnatural color for a bear, anyway, she'd said.

My mother was mentally ill and had been for a long time. I didn't know if I was upset or relieved to feel certain again. "How did you find out that Winston and my mother were having an affair?" We approached the parking lot.

Oom Piet kept pace. "You want to know everything now, *skattie*, hey? Well, your mom and Iris were drinking lemonade on the *stoep*. I was in the garage fixing up the Zephyr. Your mom was saying she and Winston were going to run away to Mozambique and start a flower farm. A flower farm!" He laughed. "She thought it would be dangerous to take you with them to another country. She was asking Iris what she should do. So I thought about it for a few weeks, then I told my friends in the police to go arrest the man." He swiped at dahlias in the flower bed lining the path, beheading several and scattering petals to the wind. "It's true I didn't know he was a terrorist when I turned him in. Funny, hey? That was a bonus for the police."

We reached my Renault. I unlocked the door. The hot aluminum burned my hand. "What happened at the police station?" I said.

He folded his arms, swaying slightly, and shook his flat head. My uncle, the Snake.

"This was so long ago, hey?" he said. "Well, the police invited me to have first go at him—cheeky *kaffir*—so I hit him with my fists. Then your father arrives, mad as hell, picks up a *bleddy* great baton—"

"*You* killed Winston. You made up the story about Winston being involved in the station bomb to justify what you did." I opened the car door, feeling sick. I thought about the photograph Miriam had mentioned. "My mother has proof it was you who killed him." I hoped for once her story was true.

Oom Piet touched my arm. "Kate, leave well enough alone. It's all in the past, hey? We should be on the same side in this. She's caused you much unhappiness. Let's make sure she gets good care now at this nice place."

I shook him off and slipped in the driver's seat.

He stood away from the car. "It's true I roughed up the *kaffir*. But I tell you what, let's see how you feel about this—it was your father who bashed him in the head. That's most likely what killed him. Or maybe the police, later. I don't know and no one will ever know what exactly caused his death. But does it matter, *skattie*, hey? Winston was a murderer! And he took advantage of your mother's sickness. That angered me, too, though I don't expect you to understand. You see things only one way, like your American friends. Blacks good, whites bad."

I slammed the car door shut. The hedges surrounding the parking lot seemed to vibrate. But it was only an illusion caused by heat waves rising from the asphalt. "If there's evidence it was you who killed Winston, I'll be writing Bishop Tutu," I said.

My uncle's black eyes gleamed like glass. "Your mother talks nonsense. And no one else saw what went on in that room. Except the sergeant, and he's dead, hey? There's no record of the *kaffir's* arrest, even. But in this political climate, now—with this Truth and Reconciliation crap—people *will* pay attention to what your mother says." He leaned forward, blinking, and curled his fingers around the edge of the half-open window. "I can't allow such a thing—my name in the papers, my face on the television, my last years spent fighting this lie. I'll lose my job. Already the *kaffirs* killed my son. They're not going to *fokking* judge me." He swallowed twice. "Are you mental, hey, like your mother, to do such a thing to your relatives, take them to the police for no good reason?"

My palms sweated on the vinyl-covered steering wheel. I imagined the doors of Horizon Home banging shut behind me. I looked at Oom Piet. In the full sunlight, my uncle's skin resembled parchment: I half-expected him to disintegrate, in the way of ancient artifacts when brought into the light. "Leave us alone, Oom Piet," I said. "*Verstaan jy my?* Do you understand? I'll find my mother. I'm responsible for her. Not you." I peeled his fingers off the window, turned the key in the ignition, and put the car in reverse.

At the bottom of the driveway, waiting for the electronic gates to swing open, I glanced in the rearview mirror. My uncle watched me, smoothing his pate with his palm.

I swiped the sweat off my forehead with the back of my hand. What if my father had swung the baton, killing Winston, though unintentionally?

On the car radio, a cricket match was being announced—the Springboks were playing the West Indies. Today it seemed incomprehensible that anyone could care about the distance a red ball traveled. The match was taking place at the Wanderers, the announcer said. I remembered Saturday afternoons, long ago, at the cricket grounds, sitting on a blanket on the grass with my father, who wore a knotted handkerchief to keep the sun off his head and explained why fielding positions had such funny names, like deep square leg and silly mid-on, and what made a wicket sticky.

My mother didn't like cricket, so she always stayed home to tend to her flowers.

When we lived in Durban, she'd often walked to the Sunken Gardens on her days off. Or caught the bus to Jameson Gardens, where she wandered beneath yellow cassia and purple jacaranda and red flamboyant trees, breathing in the perfumed air, ending up among her beloved roses.

I looked at my watch: three o'clock. Usually, about this time, she'd order cream scones in the outdoor restaurant.

At the turnoff, I headed left, toward Jameson Gardens.

Some ancient encoded ability to know one's kin must have enabled me to recognize my mother, because when I found her sitting on a bench in the park overlooking a vista of roses, she looked quite different from the large, middle-aged, chestnut-haired woman I remembered.

When I first arrived, I'd jogged along the path past the aviaries, past the lily pond where geese wandered in squawking groups, and past the enclosure where the crocodile lazed in warm mossy water. I'd stopped at the restaurant, thinking she might be sitting there, her notebook open in front of her.

Now I stood about five paces from her. The park had begun to empty as mothers took their children home for early suppers. I could hear the stuttering of a sprinkler and the trill of a bird. The scent of flowers hung heavy in the air. She stared straight ahead. Her mouth was slightly open, and her chest moved with each breath as though it hurt to inhale. She had lost at least one hundred pounds, probably more. She was dressed in the emerald linen shift she'd worn more than thirty years before on the day of my father's funeral, when she'd refused to wear black. It had hung in her closet unworn as she grew larger and larger. Now it sat oddly on her. I drew closer. Her body appeared concave, as if her spine had curved to fit the bench. Her legs poked from beneath the hem of the dress and varicose veins latticed her calves. The skin of her face, neck, and arms had crumpled into a multitude of wrinkles, like discarded plastic wrap. Her hair was stringy and gray.

I wasn't far from the exit to the park. I swallowed once or twice, thinking it would be easy enough to slip out and go back to the Renault, pack up my things, and return to Chagrin Falls. My mother wasn't sick—or anyway, not dying of cancer, according to Andre. Over the years, she'd coped by herself. My presence might upset her as much as her presence was upsetting me. Mevrou Bakker seemed fond of her—I could pay her to keep an eye on her, contact me if necessary.

A thin old man with a walking stick walked toward the bench on which my mother sat. It wasn't Oom Piet, but it was enough to nudge me forward. The man glanced in my direction and hobbled away.

My mother didn't turn as I approached. I lowered myself gradually next to her as though she were a ghostly ancestor who'd disappear if startled.

After a minute or two, I touched her arm, almost surprised to find her skin warm. "Mom."

She turned. Through her thick glasses, her green eyes were rheumy, the lids bloodshot. Her lips had been shakily drawn in coral. She gasped. "Poppet?" She threw her hands in the air. "Poppet! Look at you! What have they done to you? You look terrible," she said. "Haggard, and tired, and so *old*. And what happened to your lovely hair? Who told you to cut it?"

"Who told me? Oom Piet," I said mulishly. Then I felt the urge to giggle. I tried to stop myself. But I couldn't. I giggled and giggled until the giggles began to sound like sobs. I dug in my purse for a tissue, found Simon's handkerchief, calmed down, and blew my nose.

My mother frowned. "You're acting crazy, poppet."

"It's okay, Mom, I'm okay."

"No, you're not well." She coughed. "I'm not well either, you know."

"Maybe we should go to a doctor then?"

"Doctors. What do they know?"

Her skull shone pale and freckled through her hair. She seemed collapsed, as though her insides had been sucked from her.

"Let's go to the restaurant like we used to and order cream scones," I said.

"Cream scones make you fat. I'd think you'd want to avoid them."

She stood slowly, waving away my offered hand. We made our way to the restaurant and found a table beneath an oak tree in which vervet monkeys played, looping their tails around branches, breaking open peanut shells. A toddler—a little boy—chased a flock of pigeons, who flew up in a pink-and-gray swirl, then landed again to search for food. The waiter brought our order.

"Where have you been staying, Mom?" I asked.

She poured a cup of tea. "At my flat, of course. I went there late at night and got up early in the mornings so your uncle wouldn't know. Or that nosy Mevrou Bakker. When have I ever stayed anywhere else?"

"I went to Horizon Home. Miriam told me about Winston. And the photograph."

My mother lit a match and watched the blue flame blossom. She put it to the end of her cigarette and inhaled. Exhaled. She pursed her lips and blew the match until it expired. The smell of sulfur made my nostrils tingle. She coughed and glanced at me. "Miriam believed every word I said, you know." She waved at the plume of smoke. "Unlike *you*. Do you have children yet? No? Drugs, you see. They've sterilized you."

All the old emotions tumbled in my chest: hatred, anger, revulsion. I took a long gulp of my lemonade.

A sparrow pecked at a crumb on the table. My mother brandished her cigarette like a weapon. The bird flew off in a cloud of smoke. "Your uncle's stolen the proof. My envelopes with my notes and so forth."

"The photo was in the envelopes?"

"No," she said. "I had a much cleverer hiding place."

"It wasn't Oom Piet who took the envelopes from your flat—"

"Poppet. Why do you protect these people? Especially after what Oom Piet did to you on the farm—"

She *had* read my letter. She must have steamed open the envelope, then resealed it and sent it off. My cheeks burned. "*I* took the envelopes."

"Where are they, then?" she asked, her eyebrows raised.

"Someone stole my bag. A thief. You know what crime's like here now—"

She sighed deeply. "Poppet. Don't be silly. The place had been searched. I could tell. My recipe book had been moved."

"But—"

"Poppet. Please."

I gave up. "If you had proof Oom Piet was a murderer, why didn't you show it to me before? And where *did* you keep the photo?"

She waved a teabag in her cup. "I've decided teabags make sense after all," she said. "You'd have been upset if I told you about Winston. Because of your father." The light glinted off her glasses. "And I was afraid the police would lock *me* up if I showed them the photograph." She coughed. "They might have questioned whose child you were. Classified you Coloured and taken you away from me. I wasn't going to play into their hands. Remember, poppet, how I used to say they'd split us apart?"

Involuntarily, I looked at my arms.

"Don't be absurd. You're white." She crooked her finger. "Come closer." She smelled, as always, of stale tobacco and sweet talc. "The photograph of your uncle murdering Winston was in your *Just So Stories.*"

Which was in my possession. The book sat on the desk in my hotel room, between *The Wind in the Willows* and *King Solomon's Mines.* I had the proof—if it existed. I gestured for the waiter to hide my reaction, wanting to make sure I did have the picture before I said anything. "How did you manage to take a photo?"

She stabbed out her cigarette. A speck of ash flew up and clung to her hair. "Remember we'd been to the zoo on the day Winston was arrested? So I had the camera with me. When I arrived at the police station—it was one of those little annexes in a shopping center, you know—the front office was empty. I heard a commotion in the back room. When I opened the door I saw Winston tied to a chair against the opposite wall—" She stopped, took a breath, and coughed twice. "Oom Piet was punching him, hard. The sergeant was leaning against the wall with his arms folded, watching. Your father, he was there too. They didn't see me at first—they were facing Winston."

Winston had taught her over the months to record the strange things happening to her, she said—that's why she kept notes, because antiapartheid groups would need proof so they could bring the white butchers to justice one day. She had the presence of mind to grab the camera from her bag and take a photo of the beating. When the flash went off, my father turned. Oom Piet was still intent on punching Winston. My mother thrust the camera into her bag before my uncle realized what she'd done.

"Did Dad hit Winston with a baton?" I asked.

She frowned. "Who told you that? Did Oom Piet tell you that?"

My response was automatic. "No," I said, then realized my uncle had, in fact, told me. "So Dad didn't?"

She glanced at me, then away. "Why would you believe such a thing?" Putting a finger beneath her glasses and rubbing an eye, she added, "He might have, I suppose, before I arrived. He was furious. But he was mostly angry with me, and mad at your uncle for interfering in our business. You know how the two of them fought. Your father hustled me off right away, yelling at Piet. I won't repeat his language." She lit another Westminster. "I didn't know Winston had died until Iris told me a year later, the time she and your uncle came to take me to that dreadful place. When you were nearly twelve. That man really had poor Iris under his thumb." She blew out a plume of smoke. "I didn't care about anything anymore, when I heard Winston was dead. I didn't care if they killed me then. What was there to live for?"

I gazed at the tree canopy. The leaves blurred into green. "Nothing, no. I see what you mean." I blinked.

"And I was beginning to think you might be better off with them. I have to give you credit, though." My mother smiled. "You wouldn't let Oom Piet brainwash you on the farm. You behaved so badly, they let me go before they were finished with me." She puffed at her cigarette. "Poor poppet. The things they did to you! That corrupt Hettie. Filthy, filthy girl, taking advantage of you, so disgusting what she did—"

I had to leave. I signed the check and grabbed my purse. "I'll take you home now. I'll visit you again tomorrow."

She pursed her lips. "Still avoiding reality, are you, poppet? One day you're going to have to stop and confront the truth about that girl."

I drove her home. She clung to the sides of the passenger seat.

She said she'd be safe in her flat, at least for a while, because it usually took months for Oom Piet to dream up new ways to upset her. And he was an old man now. Had I seen how wrinkled he was? People should take better care of themselves.

The Oliphant Hotel lobby was crowded with businessmen and tourists. Children played tag among tall rubber plants. In one corner, a band played: men thrummed guitars and blew saxophones, accompanied by women on marimbas and bongo drums, and late-afternoon drinkers perched on stools at the bar, watching the cricket match on television. I caught the elevator, walked along the narrow corridor, and opened my door to the fragrance of flowers. On the desk, amaryllis lilies plumed from a crystal vase; a purple card perched among the blooms like a tropical insect. Simon? But he didn't know I was in Africa. And why would he send flowers? I read the note: *Kate—Let's get together for dinner. I'll be in Durban another ten days. Patrick.*

Should I call him? I sat at the desk and looked at the card. Maybe we'd have dinner, fall in love, and I'd spend the rest of my life in a game reserve studying the mating habits of warthog and hippo. I propped the note against the vase and stared at his neat handwriting. More likely he'd be ex-fiancé number four. Or I'd break up with him before we got that far. I shook my head. A bunch of lilies, and I'd imagined a life.

Anyway, I wasn't over Simon.

I remembered what Patrick had said when we'd stood on the pier talking about my past relationships: *But it's always you who leaves.* I reviewed the past twenty years. Terry. Gareth, Ned, Danny,

Tran. Eduardo. Simon. Even Allan. Patrick was right—most of the time, anyway, I'd been the one to end things. Either I ran or shut down—behaved the way I had while living with my mother.

It was as if the moon had disappeared, and the tides, not noticing, continued to ebb and flow.

I replaced the card among the lilies, thinking I'd call Patrick later to thank him. I raided the room bar and drank a vodka tonic. For no particular reason, I washed out the tiny bottle and put it on the shelf above the bathroom sink.

Then I returned to the desk and pulled my *Just So Stories* from the bottom of the stack of books. The wind gusted. The cream curtains bellied through the open window like inquisitive ghosts. I smoothed my index finger over the embossed title and opened the book, releasing a musty smell. Pages had been cut out—black-and-white photographs nestled inside a hollow. I eased out the pictures and flipped through the pile.

The first photograph showed my father and me in front of a bear's cage at the zoo. My father wore an open-neck shirt and long pants, and his hand rested on my shoulder. Behind us, the bear sat on its hindquarters, looking up toward the crown of a tree. My ten-year-old self smiled at the camera. I remembered I'd practiced smiling without showing my teeth, I'm not sure why, exactly. I must have been copying a film star. Smiling without teeth made my nose twitch. When I'd explained the problem to my father, he'd shown me how he could make his ears twitch independently of each other.

Most of the pictures were of animals: a blur that might have been a lion, or a cheetah, and an elephant eating hay. Several shots of cages with no indication of anything inside. I'd taken those photos. I'd tried to capture small creatures on film, like *dassies* and tortoises, but they'd blended into the background.

One photo was of the three of us. We stood in front of the Ford. It had been a last-minute shot, taken in the parking lot before we left the zoo. "Wait, Vi," my father had said. "Give me your camera. We don't have a picture of the whole family." She'd shrugged. Dad asked the parking attendant to take the photo. My father looked straight at the lens. My mother gazed off to the side.

Now I understood why going to the zoo always made me feel sad. That day had been the last time my mom and dad and I had been anywhere as a family.

The next photograph was the "proof."

A black man—Winston—was tied to a chair. His head lolled. A gooseneck lamp threw his profile into shadow on the wall. Oom Piet's one hand rested on Winston's shoulder and the other was balled in a fist, ready to strike. Winston's face was dripping with blood. His eyes were closed. A policeman leaned against a filing cabinet, watching.

And my father stood to the side, a baton in his raised hand. I stared at the photo. My father's mouth was open, as though he were yelling something.

Letting my head drop onto my crossed arms on the desk, I imagined the sound of Winston's cheekbones being crushed, blood splattering on my father's shirt, his anger dissipating suddenly when he realized what he'd done. My mother holding the camera—its flash still fading—shocked further into madness by what she'd seen, burying the knowledge forever, blaming Oom Piet for Winston's death.

I lifted my head. What if my father had raised the baton, but never hit Winston? What if he were threatening Oom Piet to stop him from attacking Winston? I looked at the photograph again, then stared through the window at the Milky Way shimmering along the spine of the sky. I remembered one night, a year or so before my father's heart attack, sitting high up on Prudence's bed swinging my legs to and fro. She sat in her straight-backed chair knitting a jersey for Cecil. Zululand nights were cold, and he was growing fast, she'd heard. Earth-almond tea steamed on her gas ring, giving off a nutty aroma. Moonlight angled through her high window onto the wall, where she'd taped pictures of the Virgin

Mary and her Uncle Chitiba. Her Aunt Selala was still alive—it was pre–bee sting.

Prudence pointed to the window. "Can you find a giraffe in the stars?" she asked.

I'd jumped off her bed and pushed open her door, staring at the night sky for a long time. "No. A tortoise, though."

She laughed. "My son Cecil finds a warrior there."

What you see, she'd said, depends on who you are.

My father. I wanted him to be innocent. I gazed at the photo again and touched his face. Odd, the random memories that came to mind: the squeak of his golf shoes on linoleum, his soapy smell—as if the detergents he sold had permeated his skin—and the thump of his briefcase on the floor when he returned home in the evenings. On Saturdays, he borrowed books from the library, and, though they were difficult reading for me, I'd devoured them: the autobiography of a woman with polio who lived in an iron lung; the story of Douglas Bader, the Royal Air Force pilot who lost both legs in the Second World War and twice escaped German prisoner-of-war camps; P. G. Wodehouse's tales of Jeeves and Bertie Wooster; Damon Runyon's *Guys and Dolls*; Jerome K. Jerome's *Three Men in a Boat*, which was still one of my favorite books. I remembered the pinky sweets he gave me as a reward when I'd been good, and his collection of pennies I wasn't allowed to touch until Rag Day, when university floats glided down Jan Smuts Avenue and the crowds threw coins in appreciation. On Thursdays, Prudence's night off, he and I would commandeer the kitchen, and I'd help him heat sweet corn, or baked beans, or cheese sauce—Welsh rarebit—which we ate on buttered toast.

Your father hustled me off right away, yelling at Piet, my mother had said.

If my father had been guilty, wouldn't he have taken the camera from her and destroyed the picture? Maybe. Maybe not. He would have known it proved nothing.

But I did not, would not believe my father a murderer.

Outside, *sangomas* called out their wares. The wind riffled the torn pages of my *Just So Stories*. I'd never know for certain what had happened at the police station. Who hit whom. How Winston died. Whether or not he'd been involved in the Johannesburg Station bomb plot. Which of my mother's fears had been justified, which pure paranoia.

By comparison to mine, her world had been oddly, terrifyingly simple: people were either Enemies Motivated to Split the Family Apart, or Not Directly Involved In the Plot.

For a long time, I studied the pictures taken at the zoo, then tucked them back in the book. After a moment, I added the one of Winston, which was part of my history, too, no matter how much I'd have liked it not to be.

I opened the desk drawer and wrote a letter on the hotel stationery.

Dear Oom Piet,

I am in possession of a photograph that PROVES you responsible for Winston's death. If you try to lock my mother away, I will . . .

After a moment, I crumpled the paper and started again.

Dear Oom Piet,

I have in my possession a photograph that my mother regards as proof of your responsibility for Winston's death. It is not conclusive. Due to the lack of evidence and the possible unreliability of my mother's eyewitness account, I won't pursue this matter with the Truth and Reconciliation Commission.

However, please DO NOT contact my mother again. I won't leave South Africa till I've made sure she is well taken care of. I'll call you or Andre before I go home.

Her paranoia seems to be triggered by stress and I believe you can help her best by staying away from her. I trust you will do as I request.

If I learn you are harassing her, I will take legal action.

Thank you for the financial assistance you provided when I was a child.

> *Sincerely,*
> *Kate Jensen/Jones*

After signing the letter, I put down my pen, headed to the bathroom, showered, brushed my teeth, and changed into my pajamas. I picked up my *Just So Stories.* The pages of the first story hadn't been mutilated. I slipped between the sheets and read "How the Whale Got His Throat." *He ate the starfish and the garfish, and the crab and the dab, and the plaice and the dace, and the skate and his mate, and the mackereel and the pickereel, and really truly twirly-whirly eel . . .*

I wished I could read the story to Simon, who loved everything that swam and crawled and floated in the ocean. I looked at the phone. Then I shut the book and placed it on the nightstand. After switching off the lamp, I closed my eyes and let the soughing waves of the Indian Ocean soothe me to sleep.

The next morning, before going to my mother's flat, I did some research at the library on Aliwal Street. I found no references to a Winston Maphosa in old newspapers, though a couple of documents mentioned a Winston Mpundu who had been released from prison in 1963, had attended meetings with top-level ANC leaders in early 1964, and then disappeared forever. There weren't many references to the Johannesburg Station bombing. The few articles I found seemed to suggest that the main perpetrator, Frederick John Harris, *had* acted alone. He'd been sentenced to death and hanged. The *Rand Daily Mail* said no one had ever identified the "cultured African voice" which had called in a warning six minutes before the bomb exploded.

You do not shout at me. You do not use me as a tool to parade your liberal attitudes, Winston had said to my mother so many years ago. His speech had always been so formal.

I shoved the rack of old newspapers away from me. I preferred to believe that Winston had not been a violent man, and who was there—other than my uncle—to tell me otherwise?

Had my friend Joshua had become a revolutionary? ANC documents and old newspaper articles had made mention of many Joshuas, but none I could identify positively. If he hadn't been a revolutionary killed by the security police, it was possible he'd been necklaced—burned to death, a blazing tire filled with gasoline hung around his neck—during faction fighting between Zulu and Xhosa. Or he might be comfortably middle-aged, his brow even broader now as his hair receded. At this moment, he could be playing soccer with his kids in the backyard while his wife baked scones for afternoon tea.

At lunchtime, I drove to Kingfisher Court, which, with its new coat of paint, resembled a respectable dowager in beige—old, but dignified. I parked the Renault and stepped onto the sidewalk. Women haggled with an Indian vendor for deals on the Granny Smith apples, oranges, paw paws, and granadillas—passion fruit—piled on his truck.

Before going upstairs, I decided to pay a visit to the place where Joshua and I had met in the sewage pipe. The streets were quiet—it was Saturday. After a few blocks, I heard a clanging sound. I turned. The beggar with the oilcan guitar scuttled toward me. Grinning, he pointed at the blocks of flats, then at the dent in his forehead. "I say to everyone, remember the money-storms."

That's why he'd been pointing at Kingfisher Court the day my purse was stolen. I'd probably given him more money than most tourists; it was a logical enough reason to follow me around. Smiling now, I handed him three rhino, about ten dollars.

"Raining cats and dogs!" the beggar said, kissing the money. *"Dankie!"* He loped away, chuckling.

I crossed two more streets. What did I expect to find? Was I hoping to bump into Joshua? I stopped in front of a tall building standing where the sunflowers had grown wild. It was an unremarkable structure: gray, angular, conventional in every way. No Joshua.

But black and white children were playing on the swings in the park nearby, and that pleased me. I turned and walked in the direction of Kingfisher Court.

The elevator took me to the third floor. I knocked at number three-sixty-one.

My mother opened the door and waved me in. "Sit down, poppet." She offered a cigarette.

I shook my head. "Are you eating enough, Mom?"

"You're old enough to smoke, you know," she said, lighting her Westminster. "I'm not hungry these days. The drugs ruined my system."

I offered to make tea, went to the kitchen, and put the kettle on, swishing boiling water around the teapot before adding tea leaves. I carried the tray into the living room and poured two cups. "Mom, you said Oom Piet—or the government—killed Dad. You've never said how."

"The doctor claimed he had an enlarged heart! What nonsense," she said. "They poisoned him, using a slow-acting drug. I forget the name. I wrote it down somewhere." She glanced at my left hand. "Didn't you send a telegram saying you were getting married?"

Sweat trickled between my breasts. A baby cried, and for a moment I imagined it was the same baby who'd lived next door thirty years before. His name had been Algernon.

"Fiancé number three, was it? I have a feeling that's over too. Am I right?" She smiled sadly. "I don't like to say I told you so. But I did."

"He's a good person, Mom. Not perfect, I know. Nor am I."

"Well, I suppose, if you can't trust anyone, you might as well trust someone," she said. "If you're that desperate for a man. Poor poppet."

I hugged myself and gazed out the window. Across the street, where the CHICKEN A-GO-GO sign had blinked, a pink neon cocktail glass flashed pale in the sun. I considered returning to the hotel, packing my bags, and catching a flight to Chagrin Falls. Then I looked at my mother. The old chair seemed to overwhelm her now. Perspiration ran down the tributaries on her cheeks. "Oom Piet's not going to bother you again, Mom," I said. "He got what he wanted, don't you think?"

She frowned and lit a cigarette. "Koos will take over. I'll write it up in my new notebook."

"No," I said, "Koos—"

"Yes, he will," she interrupted. "Why are you always so contrary, Kate?"

I gazed at her. She sipped her tea, sniffed it, then continued drinking. I decided not to tell her Koos had died during the Soweto Riots—not until I'd spoken to Dr. Naidoo, anyway. She was so used to having Enemies. How would she feel without them?

My mother rubbed her forehead. "I'm very tired, poppet," she said. "Very tired. Perhaps I'll rest a little."

I helped her onto her bed and pulled a light coverlet over her. She shut her eyes with her glasses still on. She'd never liked being without them, as if they provided a buffer against the world. For a while only my mother's breathing and the low rumble of traffic broke the silence.

On the yellow wall was a faint mark where I'd once dislodged plaster while thumbtacking my poster of Rod Stewart next to the newspaper article about winning the essay competition. Hippodad had sat on the windowsill, along with my copy of *Hamlet* and bead doll. The photograph of my parents on their wedding day stood on top of the chest of drawers.

My mother's eyes opened.

"Mom, were you very much in love with Winston?" I said impulsively.

"Love," she rasped. "I don't know. What's love?"

"You believed in it once."

"Winston and I were going to live together in Mozambique," she said.

"Leaving me with Dad?"

"Your father said I was acting strangely." Her eyelids flickered as if she were about to fall asleep again. "And I knew I'd be nothing but trouble for you with the government after me." She took off her glasses and put them on the table next to her bed. They'd left deep imprints on the sides of her nose. She rubbed at the marks with her fingertips. When she turned her eyes to me, they were the same deep green I remembered from Johannesburg, where she had hardly ever worn her spectacles. "And I *have* been trouble. Because of me your life has been difficult. I know that, Kate."

I swallowed to stop a noise bursting out of me, a noise compounded of guilt and sorrow and regret for what might have been, and who we might have been. She held a tissue to her mouth and coughed. Close to tears, I went to the bathroom, filled a glass of water, sipped it myself, brought it to the bedside, and handed it to her.

She drank obediently. "Did they find out about Miriam? Has she been fired?"

"Miriam's still there. She's really fond of you, Mom." I pictured Miriam in the flat, the two of them watching the news on TV and cheering the Commission hearings. I sat down again. "You know what Oom Piet told me?"

"No," she said. "He's the one who records *my* conversations. Not the other way around."

"Aunt Iris left you a bequest. There's your pension. And I'll help too, of course. We could afford to have Miriam live with you."

My mother turned away and let her eyelids droop. "I don't know."

Her hand rested on the coverlet. A delta of veins flowed beneath the pale skin. I remembered the fleshy starfish her fingers had once formed on my arm, how her damp touch had repelled me, and I shivered.

Then I willed myself to see a different mother: a chestnut-haired young woman showing a child how to water roses, pointing out a rainbow curving on the spray. And that's the image I kept in my mind when I said, "Mom, I love you, you know." I reached to take her hand in mine. Her skin felt creased and slippery, like waxed paper.

Her forehead wrinkled. "Who told you to say that? We're not sentimental in our family. Somebody must have told you to say that."

"No one . . . well, it doesn't matter," I said.

Her fingers tightened a little around mine. "No," my mother said. "No, I don't suppose it does."

Later that afternoon, I left Kingfisher Court and drove to the city center, parking near Medwood Gardens, a small oasis of green where mynah birds squawked in the trees. I crossed West Street to Farewell Square—now Luthuli Square—and headed to the Natural Science Museum, which was housed within the brass-domed City Hall. Pigeons pecked at invisible breadcrumbs on the pavement and perched on statues—of Jan Smuts, Sir Harry Escombe, and Queen Victoria—and the Cenotaph, which commemorated the First and Second World Wars. Chattering women sat straight-legged on bright blankets or leaned against concrete plinths, surrounded by masks and carvings and gourds filled with fragrant herbs and *muti*. I picked through the offerings and found a *sangoma* doll for Bernie—hoping its influence would keep her healthy—then climbed the stairs and entered the museum where I'd spent hours as a child.

I wandered through the Insect Arcade, repulsed by the monster cockroaches and glad to know I was safe from the tickle of their legs across my skin. An eight-foot-tall stuffed ostrich, its neck periscoping from a thickly feathered body atop muscular legs, guarded the entrance to the Predators and Prey exhibit. Mounted photographs showed a pancake tortoise creeping under a rock, a stick insect mimicking a twig, and impala fleeing across the veldt.

As a child, I would've gone to a park to practice running and creeping and camouflage.

Now I touched the glass exhibits one by one, then turned, leaving the museum and its stuffed animals behind.

I drove the Renault to the amphitheater and parked near the Sunken Gardens. Frogs brayed and flopped along the sides of the concrete goldfish pond. Frangipani scented the air. A wild cat raced across my path, and I watched it disappear behind a crimson curtain of bougainvillea.

Emerging onto Lower Marine Parade, I crossed the road, removed my sandals, and wandered along North Beach, the sand gritty beneath my bare feet. After a while, I sat on the beach, thinking about my childhood and revisiting long-forgotten memories as if the breakers were bringing them one by one to shore. The night sky shimmered above me. I gazed upward and smiled to find a hippo's yawn sketched in the stars.

A seal barked. I looked around. The aquarium loomed to my left. I was sitting in the same place I'd ended up the night my mother strip-searched me. I clasped my knees to my chest, wishing my younger self were here. I'd put my arm around her and tell her everything would be all right. When she was older, she'd live in a beautiful town near a river: a place of spring daffodils and summer parades and brilliant fall leaves and sifting winter snow. She'd have a cat named Bagheera and even a warthog, though he'd be made of stone.

Near me, a lone seagull nested in a sandy footprint. Seawater slapped against the struts of the pier. I took off my jacket, enjoying the cool breeze on my bare arms, the taste of salt on my lips, and the tingle of spray on my cheeks.

When I returned to the hotel, I'd call Simon and tell him I loved him.

And that I believed he loved me.

On the horizon, the full moon slipped from behind a cloud, and for one brief, impossible moment I imagined I saw a circle of light—perfectly round—float on the gleaming surface of the Indian Ocean, waiting its turn to bounce into the sky.

Acknowledgments

Nature Lessons exists in large part because of the people listed below. I am enormously grateful for their kindness, wisdom, enthusiasm—and patience. My thanks to:

Dear friends and fellow writers Michelle Brockway, Dianne Russell, Lisa Skoog de Lamas, Michael Quadland, and Tim Nason;

Exceptional teachers Les Edgerton, Chris Noel, Nance Van Winckel, Helga Schier, and Douglas Glover;

The amazing Betsy Amster, my agent, and the incomparable Jane Rosenman, my editor, who believed in me and my book from the beginning—how can I ever thank the two of you enough?

Bill Callahan, M.D., for the intelligence and energy and uncompensated time he spends helping the seriously mentally ill and their family members;

Susan Smallwood, whose volunteerism has made a difference in so many people's lives, including mine;

And most of all, love and gratitude to my family: my beloved husband Bill, stepdaughters Lisa LeFevre and Kim Florence, and sons Kyle and Dylan Parry, who have brought me so very much joy and happiness.